BUS

CARGILL

Published by U N I V E R S I T Y P R E S S O F N E W E N G L A N D

WAYNE G. BROEHL, JR.

CARGILL

Going Global

Hanover & London   DARTMOUTH COLLEGE

DARTMOUTH COLLEGE

Published by University Press of New England,

Hanover, NH 03755

© 1998 by Wayne G. Broehl, Jr.

Printed in the United States of America

5 4 3 2 1

CIP data appear at the end of the book

Title page illustration overleaf: September 18, 1972: "Trading in wheat at the Chicago Board of Trade has been hectic as indicated in this August, 1972, file photo. The price of wheat has gone over $.60 a bushel higher than the price last spring mainly because the Soviet Union has had one of the driest growing seasons on record" (UPI/Corbis-Bettmann).

Contents

Acknowledgments

In 1992, my book *Cargill: Trading The World's Grain*, the fifth book written by me in a series of business histories under the auspices of the research program of the Amos Tuck School of Business Administration at Dartmouth College, was published by University Press of New England. That book covered the first three executive officers of the company, William W. Cargill, John H. MacMillan, Sr., and John H. MacMillian, Jr. It was a long sweep, extending from the firm's founding in 1865 by W. W., through the administration of John Sr., and then John Jr., until his sudden death in 1960. Now, in this book, *Cargill: Going Global*, I have carried the history of the firm through the years 1960 to 1978, during the term in office of Cargill's fourth chief executive officer, Erwin E. Kelm.

As with the first book on Cargill, Dartmouth College asked that this study be done under its requirement of full scholarly independence. Cargill had recognized from the start of the first book the wisdom of engaging an outside scholar who would be allowed to view the Company at arm's length, with no editorial constraints by anyone. The same financial relationship existed between myself and the Company with this second volume: Cargill made a grant to Dartmouth College to cover my regular salary, with no direct financial relationship between the Company and me. I continue to owe thanks both to the members of the two families involved in ownership of the Company and to senior management for their perception of and enthusiasm for these basic principles of sound business history.

Five senior members of the family provided major input for both volumes: Whitney MacMillan, James R. Cargill, Cargill MacMillan, Jr., W. Duncan MacMillan, and John Hugh MacMillan, III. Particularly helpful here was the privilege extended to me of attending a number of their "family meetings," which were described in more detail in chapter 19 of the earlier study.

Senior management in the Company continued to play a significant role in my research. I was privileged to spend many hours with Erv Kelm, the central character in this volume. I regret that he did not live to see the actual publication of this book. Whitney McMillan, Kelm's successor as chief executive officer, gave enthusiastic support for the project and graciously devoted many hours of his time to increasing my understanding of the Kelm period. Similarly, M. D. (Pete) McVay, who assumed the post of president at Kelm's retirement, provided key insights on the period. William R. Pearce, vice president of public affairs and later vice chairman, continued as a strong personal colleague and advisor. John F. McGrory, retired general counsel for the Company, made a major contribution to this volume, just as he did in the earlier study. James Moe, current general counsel for Cargill, collaborated with McGrory in helping me to understand many of the legal dimensions applicable to this volume. Ernest Micek, who in 1995 succeeded Whitney McMillan as chairman, president, and chief executive officer, has given his support and backing throughout the writing of this second volume. Robert Lumpkins, vice chairman with Micek, has been particularly helpful to me in his knowledge of and insights about this time period. I also was fortunate in being able to spend a number of days with the late Walter Gage, the retired chairman of Tradax, Cargill's Geneva organization. Brewster Hanson, who was president under Gage, also was most generous with his time and provided a unique view of both Tradax and Cargill. H. Robert Diercks, vice chairman under Kelm, provided the kind of perspective on events that was particularly helpful at key points in this book. Similarly, Walter B. Saunders, a vice chairman at a later period, Heinz Hutter, president of the company in recent years, James Howard, and Gerald Mitchell all gave generously of their time and insights. Jim Springrose and Victor Anderson both were particularly helpful in the chapters of the book relating to transportation and the rate cases affecting these.

Retired Cargill senior management all provided continuing resources for my knowledge of the company. I had conducted in-depth interviews with some 85 of these people for the first book and continued to draw on their knowledge and perceptions for the second. I particularly want to pay tribute to Clifford M. Roberts, Jr., a retired member of senior management and lecturer in a number of instances in my Dartmouth classes, for his personal support and thorough knowledge of the Company. I also have had strong support throughout the writing of both books from James R. Cargill, who read carefully at an early stage much of the manuscript for the first volume and also has helped me significantly with the second.

The members of the Cargill public affairs department have been supportive friends. In particular, Robbin Johnson, vice president and head of Cargill's public affairs efforts, provided the kind of leadership and discriminating analysis that can make a project like this much more effective. He read all of the manuscript, more than just once, and gave me insights about Cargill's public affairs positions that were comprehensive and eloquent. Garland West, Jon Yeager, and Lisa Vickstrom all spent considerable time in helping to prepare this manuscript. Jean Spielman Housh, a former member of the group, gave consulting help at key points. The entire Cargill Information Center, first under the leadership of Julia Peterson and more recently under Peter Sidney, has given me the kind of research and information analysis that all scholars prize so much. Senior reference librarians Margaret Drews and Sidnie Ross and reference librarians Cindy Ackton, Mary Louise Lose, Mary Beth Bacig, and Catherine Hayes all have helped me. Sally Klutz and Peggy Johnson, together with Pat Johnson, gave the kind of technical support so important to a sound book. The Corporate Secretary's office is always a central one in business history; Cargill's group, first under Marlene Kurschner and, later, Jeanne Y. Smith, and with significant backup by Anne Carlson, Cheryl Nikko, and Alli Gunlock, were indispensible to me.

Most central of all departments in my research was the archives department. For most of the research in this volume, Mary Beth Bacig performed the key role of archivist; more recently, Shaleen Kirlin-Culbert followed in that role. Paul Dienhart, as editor of *Cargill News*, has provided special input.

My Dartmouth College support group is a long-standing one. I would like to give particular thanks to Dean Paul Danos and to Tuck's executive officer, Mado Macdonald. The Feldberg Library at Tuck School has played a part in the preparation of these books at almost every juncture; I pay especial tribute to Feldberg's librarian, James Fries, and to Feldberg's reference librarians, Betty Snyder, Karen Sluzenski, Jennifer Holt, and Sara Jack. The Baker Library of Dartmouth College is partner with Tuck on these matters; Robert Jaccuad, Virginia Close, Patricia Carter, Joanne Adams, and Marilyn Curphey all have been involved in research on a multitude of occasions. The number of outside libraries and research institutions becomes too large a list to denote individual names. My list in the acknowledgments of the first volume will be helpful to scholars interested in this field.

Last, I would like to remember with thanks the several secretaries who worked with me in producing this manuscript: Suzanne Sweet, Bonnie Meyer, Angela Durkee, Kristy Legace, and Daphne Ellis. Jean Lawe has been my editor for both volumes.

My academic colleagues have been unstinting in giving me help in all aspects of the research. I particularly wish to thank Mira Wilkins, Morton Rothstein, Ray Goldberg, Thomas McCraw, and John Hennessey. In the introduction to this book I have expressed my long-time debt to the superb academic backing I have received from Alfred D. Chandler, Jr.; both books would not be what they are had Al Chandler not given me at so many points his wise counsel.

Finally my love and profound appreciation go to my wife, Jean, who has been my research assistant for both volumes and whose judgment and perspective I continue to trust above all!

Hanover, New Hampshire   W.G.B., Jr.
August 1997

Introduction

In this volume I continue my historical study of Cargill, Incorporated. As I begin, the Company is in its ninety-fifty year, 1960. A complex and compelling saga of growth, chronicled in the first volume, has already occurred. From a very small beginning on the agricultural frontier just after the Civil War, when W. W. Cargill opened a "flathouse" in Conover, Iowa, Cargill today has become one of the largest corporations in the United States, with annual sales of over $56 billion, and is the largest privately held company in the world.

From these humble beginnings, W. W.'s entrepreneurial skill and sense of place in the burgeoning grain-trading scene built the Cargill Elevator Company into a major Midwestern force by the turn of the century. However, outside investments caused W. W. many problems, and his death brought a financial crisis to the firm. The Company was saved from being pushed by its creditors into bankruptcy through the financial acumen and diplomacy of son-in-law John MacMillan, Sr., who brought the firm back from the brink, and nursed it to health, in the process building a strong work force of loyal and dedicated people.

When his mercurial son, John Jr., took the reins in the early 1930s, John Sr. moved back to an advisory role. John Jr. was innovating, exciting, and difficult; he ran the company with a strong hand, moving it into many endeavors, most but not all quite successful. Shipbuilding was carried on during World War II, but the focus remained always on the grain trade. John Jr. initiated many exciting strategies in the grain markets, occasionally verging on difficult ground that brought the government's scrutiny. Throughout his tenure until his death in 1960 the company had signal success, helped particularly by two other family members of the firm, Austin Cargill and Cargill MacMillan, Sr. The interactions of these interesting management men in bringing the Company to its strong position in 1960 take up many of the pages of the first volume, *Cargill: Trading the World's Grain*. I have described these key people in more detail early in chapter 1 of this book.

The trauma in 1960 was as much a watershed for the Company as was 1909, when W. W. Cargill died. Now, in just a few years, the Company had lost all three of the family members leading the business: Austin Cargill died in 1957, Cargill MacMillan suffered a disabling stroke in early 1960 and John MacMillan, Jr., died at the end of that year.

The person who brought the Company through this transition and led it for the next 17 years was Erwin E. Kelm. This period, spanning the 1960s and most of the 1970s, legitimately became "the Kelm years." In his own special, gruff style, this somewhat introverted man grew to become a superb chief executive officer. In the early 1960s, Kelm and his colleagues nursed the firm through a difficult, rather unprofitable period, the causes of which primarily lay at the feet of the Grain Division. Help was sought from Cargill's lead bank, Chase Manhattan, the advice of this outsider was for this one time taken seriously, and the firm turned around. Kelm had a vision of growth and soon began to upgrade facilities in preparation for what he saw as a major push toward exports that did, indeed, soon come.

It was not just in grain trading that Kelm saw growth potential; new endeavors such as flour and corn milling were initiated at this time. At the end of the decade, Kelm once again faced a downturn in Grain Division earnings, and another "mini crisis" had to be resolved. Forthright cost cutting and more refined long-range planning tools brought the firm through this difficulty, too.

In the early 1970s, an amazing set of events began to unfold. The trigger was a huge sale of grain to the Soviet Union in 1972 (followed in the next half dozen years by several other very large sales to them). These in turn produced many profound effects on the U.S. economy, and Cargill and its competitor grain firms spent six years answering to Congressional committees and dealing with new logistical problems as they moved this massive quantity of grain to Russia. Problems multiplied with rising prices and shortages in transportation equipment. One of several complications was a short-lived U.S. government embargo of soybeans for international sale.

This was to become the period of Watergate, and the hearings on that case provided a model for many more investigative sorties into other arenas. The grain trade was caught up in such hearings, first on transportation bottlenecks and then on its very practices for handling and shipping grain. What became known as the "grain scandal" brought a series of revelations in the Congressional hearings that put the grain companies on the front pages of the country's newspapers. Coming on the heels of this public scrutiny was a critically important set of hearings stemming from a wide-ranging look at multinational corporations by the United States Senate. Cargill, as the largest firm in its industry, became a centerpiece of the testimony on the grain trade, and the saga of the "multinational subcommittee" carried Cargill itself into the foreground of public interest and concern. The Company came through all of these hearings in a position of strength and, by the time all the investigative zeal had subsided, had heightened its image as the leader of the industry.

There were yet more issues to face, for soon after the Internal Revenue Service began to investigate corporations' "unusual payments" in operating abroad. The issue of bribes and favors permeated these reports. The IRS insisted on public disclosure of all of these, and Cargill and several hundred other corporations were required to comply. Finally, Cargill faced its own set of issues in a very difficult tax case with the IRS, complicated by a situation involving the pilfering of a document from the Cargill legal department by a Minneapolis-based courier. All of these cases happened in approximately 6 years, making the early and mid-1970s one of the most tense and argumentative periods that the Company had ever been through. Kelm and his team had begun on a modest level; his 17-year-tenure in office had ended in a calmer period. But the Company had been through a fire storm of public interest, disclosure and litigation that moved it into a new realm of public affairs involvement and of heightened communication and disclosure of its business affairs. In this very private industry of private companies, Cargill had taken many new initiatives toward an interface with the public, and the Company had changed itself measurably in the process.

Now there was to be another transition, with Erv Kelm's retirement. Kelm had not been a family member; he was a professional manager. The firm turned again to a member of one of the families, Whitney MacMillan. He had had long training in a wide range of Company activities and in this sense was as much a professional manager as his predecessor. However, he once again brought family leadership into the firm, where he emphasized ethical management. MacMillan, whose tenure was to extend to 1995, served almost exactly the same span of years in office as Kelm's had. A highly skilled management team had been assembled under Kelm, with M. D. "Pete" McVay as the individual chosen as president under MacMillan's chairmanship. The threads of family influence on the Company, never hidden even during the Kelm period, now came to the fore, with strong leadership not only from MacMillan but from James R. Cargill, Cargill MacMillan, Jr., and W. Duncan MacMillan.

As was shown in my earlier book, the first three chief executive officers were inextricably linked with both family and company. Not only was that study a business history but it was also by its nature business biography. I had crafted it on the seminal work of Alfred D. Chandler, Jr., particularly his own model from his book (with Steven Salisbury), *Pierre S. du Pont and the Making of the Modern Corporation*. Professor Chandler stated succinctly why the analysis of that complex modern corporation had to be a combination of history and biography:

This approach permits a careful review of the relationship of the individual to the enterprise. Such an analysis has become particularly significant in the history of the modern corporation where, as was rarely true before in the history of business, the individual must work closely with many other men in the management of a single enterprise. Such a focus, for example, makes possible a detailed analysis of the inevitable conflict between personal goals and ambitions and the impersonal demands of large-scale business organization.

While Erv Kelm was not a member of the family, his was a strong and compelling personality, so much so that the development of the Cargill organization during his 17 years of leadership could also truly be said to have been closely tied to his personal biography. This link is in evidence throughout the second volume. In elaborating upon it, I have included extensive quotations from both Kelm and from the dozen or so key senior management men around him. These were strong-willed individuals with widely different views of important management issues, and this made for an environment of continual thrust and parry. In particular, I have stressed the relationship between Cargill in Minneapolis (actually, in the suburb of Wayzata) and Tradax in Geneva, Switzerland; the latter was the semiautonomous international arm of the Company. The interplay between Cargill and Tradax continues during the period covered in this second volume, never quite resolved but giving focus and bite to management issues that honed and refined the strategies and, in turn, the ethics of the corporation. Indeed, the widely recognized "Cargill culture" grew apace during this period, in part because of this tension. The excellent first-hand documentation of many of these conflicts gives a sense of reality to this relationship, happening in a fast-paced milieu that called for bell-clear decision making and decisive moves. All this occurred under the umbrella of a highly competitive environment epitomized by this particular industry, perhaps more than almost any other industry. The presence of the "open outcry" commodities market, with its frenzied moment-by-moment bargaining and instant decision making, makes this so.

This emphasis on decision making *is* the central focus in this study, and inasmuch as some considerable part of such decision making is done within a privately held family corporation, there are significant insights here into a widespread but less understood form of corporate ownership. However, the Cargill philosophy of management has lessons for all corporations, for this study gives vivid testimony to the ethos of competition and the blending of tradition with the here-and-now. The central thread for this book is that of corporate values. Cargill has exhibited a strong philosophy of management, and its lessons, hard learned, shed light on the way all business operates.

I stated in my introduction to the first volume that a unique Cargill "corporate culture" was evolving, a tradition marked by independence, competitiveness, professionalism in management, and an underlying ethical commitment. I posited then that those qualities remained strongly in place at the end of John Jr.'s tenure. They remain equally strong at the end of *this* volume, after the 17-year watch of Erv Kelm.

CARGILL

CHAPTER ONE

An Attack
of Angst

On the morning of December 23, 1960, John MacMillan, Jr., died. Suddenly, Cargill, Incorporated, was adrift from its dominant—indeed, dominating—chief executive officer.

This was the 95th year of the Company; there had been just three chief executive officers over this long span. W. W. Cargill had founded the Company in rural Iowa in 1865, at a time when the post–Civil War railroad boom had just begun. He followed the tracklaying west from the Mississippi River, building grain "flathouses" in each little town as the region opened up to the advance of the agricultural frontier. Farming provided the impetus for rapid business expansion (more than occasionally, to be sure, followed by a bust). Fortunes accumulated overnight as the businessmen charted their way through the primitive business environment.

W. W.'s mentality fit this fluid, fast-paced world; within just a few years he had amassed a well-integrated set of warehouses and larger terminals and begun lake shipping from a number of well-located ports on the Great Lakes, taking full advantage of the burgeoning of railroad routes. In the process, W. W. formed many business partnerships; his three brothers joined him, with younger brother Sam indispensable as the head of the Minneapolis and Duluth segments of the expanded enterprise. W. W. himself moved to La Crosse, Wisconsin, administering the southern reaches of the businesses.

These decades in the second half of the nineteenth century were expansionist, almost helter-skelter, and W. W.'s personality suited this ethos very well indeed. Not only did Cargill's grain trading and shipping mushroom, but W. W.'s enthusiasms carried him into a number of other businesses. There was a lumber operation in Pine Bluff, Arkansas, and other timberland purchases in both the United States and Canada. He personally promoted a small railroad endeavor in and around La Crosse. Most draining was a huge, capital-intensive land development project in Valier, Montana, pushed along particularly by W. W.'s son Will.

Suddenly, in 1909, the patriarch of this empire died of a heart attack. While the grain business was sound, the other endeavors greatly had overextended him. In particular, the Montana project became a "black hole," so draining of resources that the entire Cargill operations were threatened by bankruptcy. W. W. Cargill's death had brought a true crisis.

Son Will Cargill was a central figure in the debacle and had to be eased out. Fortunately, W. W.'s son-in-law, John MacMillan, Sr., had the business acumen, the caution and the presence (particularly with the creditors) to bring the organization through the transition. John Sr. assumed the role of the second chief executive officer of Cargill and exhibited an understanding of finance and accounting, combined with a cautious and precise management style that was just what the tottering entity needed. By World War I, the Cargill Elevator Company, now concentrating on its primary functions of grain trading and shipping, was back in the black and moving ahead well. John Sr. proved to be a stellar leader, his human relations skills and his highly ethical values providing a role model that built great loyalty and regard for the Company on the part of its people. A "Cargill culture" began to grow under the umbrella of his management style.

John Sr. had his weaknesses, however. His caution sometimes led to lost opportunities, and his regional view of the business was not an appropriate fit for the evolving national and soon international direction that the industry now was taking. Fortuitously, John Sr.'s caution and hindsight soon was countered by the ebullience, optimism, and "forge-ahead" mentality of his oldest son, John Jr. He was the first college graduate in the Cargill/MacMillan families, from Yale University just before the end of World War I. His college mentors had had a great impact on him, although a certain bullheadedness and dogmatism was more than occasionally evident in John Jr.'s frequent pontifications. From a reserve officers program at Yale he left for Europe and the front, soon becoming the army's youngest major. A general took John Jr. under his wing, and MacMillan had several important lessons about organization structure brought home to him in this experience. (He also had a plethora of exciting social contacts in the rarefied atmosphere of the higher echelons of the American forces.) John Jr.'s contemporary, Austen Cargill, second son of W. W., also went through World War I, as a corporal.

John Sr. had an overweening pride in his brilliant son and when the war was over quickly brought him into the Company. John Jr.'s unswerving belief in himself, coupled with an inability to work well with some of the older employees, made his start a rocky one. But his intellect, honed by his Yale economics training, soon made him a perceptive analyst of the grain trade, and he quickly achieved a senior role within management. This period in the 1920s also was marred by a bitter squabble between the Cargill and MacMillan families, pitting John Jr. and his father against Austen Cargill, who had become the scion of the Cargill family. It involved percentages of ownership in the Company, which in turn led to further issues in regard to management policy and questions about John Jr.'s increasingly autocratic leadership role.

Cargill MacMillan, John Jr.'s younger brother, also joined the Company after his graduation from Yale in the early 1920s. This junior member of the family was quite the opposite of his older brother in many ways; indeed, Cargill resembled his father much more closely. He was a gentle man, an intellectual, who graduated steadily toward the finance and tax concerns of the Company. He assumed the role of watchdog and provided a special quality of being able to look at himself and the rest of the family both objectively and introspectively.

Austen Cargill also came into the Company after the war and gravitated toward the periphery of the organization, focusing his attentions particularly on the branch offices. He became a popular person among Company personnel and proved to be the most outgoing and organizationally sensitive person among the family members who were in management.

John Sr. remained the titular chief executive officer all through the 1920s. But a series of heart attacks in the early 1930s caused him to withdraw from major Company decisions and seemingly focused him inordinately on the past rather than the future. As the Great Depression hit ever more strongly, both at the Company and in the country, a serious bank crisis endured by the Company in 1932 resulted in John Jr. taking the reins of leadership.

At the start, it was not a felicitous fit, for John Jr.'s high temperament sometimes led him to fall into a nervous depression. Nevertheless, by 1936, John Jr. was named president of the Company, and while John Sr. continued to hold the role of chairman until his death in 1944, it was John Jr.'s leadership that dominated from that point.

And dominating he was. He had strong views about organization structure, built upon the army examples he had seen back in the war, and believed in a high degree of centralization of authority and responsibility. He spoke and wrote about the philosophy of organization structure from time to time and practiced what he preached. He demanded obeisance, and during his first decade as head of the Company, he made many unilateral decisions, often quite quickly and decisively, indeed, autocratically. John Jr. had a concept of the grain trade as "an endless belt," and this belief tended to focus on centralization of control. He had an eclectic mind, and this allowed him to combine disparate thoughts into fresh new ideas (he held several patents in his own name). For the terminals of the Company, he developed a new "tent" configuration, featuring an unconventional very large storage area which he called the "big bin."

Fascinated by boats and ships all through his earlier years, he now put many of these enthusiasms to the test of practical reality. Cargill's use of the Erie Canal during this period and the Company's innovative development of new inland waterway equipment were masterminded by John Jr. When World War II came, John Jr. turned toward shipbuilding, with a major ocean-going vessel first down the ways. This was followed by a number of smaller ships that were built, surprisingly, in the back reaches of the Minnesota River at Port Cargill, Minnesota, and snaked down the Mississippi to the oceans for combat service as navy vessels.

John Jr. wanted always to win. He was forever positioning the Company to move to new heights that would give it advantage over the other members of the fast-paced, highly secretive grain trading companies with which he was competing. His competitive urge sometimes got him into trouble, with the most striking example the high-profile attempt by the Company in 1937 to dominate a particular corn futures contract on the Chicago Board of Trade (CBOT) (in effect, an attempt at a "corner"). After the highly publicized incident at the CBOT ran its course, the government brought a case against both the Company and John Jr., and after many battles both the Company and the man lost. Cargill received a substantial black eye from this endeavor, although John Jr. never would admit that he had been wrong.

The Company continued its strong growth after World War II and by this time was vying with Continental Grain to be the largest grain trading company in the world. The establishment of Tradax in Geneva, Switzerland, in the mid-1950s, as a semiautonomous European arm of the Company was a particularly important step. World grain trading was indeed different from domestic trading, and having a separate unit of the Company able to move rapidly in the more hurly-burly European environment allowed Cargill to reap the best of both worlds.

In the late 1950s, John Jr. had brought about another major innovation in the transportation of grain by building an ocean terminal in the mouth of the St. Lawrence River, at Baie Comeau. When this was coupled with a major new move for the Company in ocean shipping, the combination was especially potent. The Baie Comeau ocean terminal opened in 1960, a great tribute to the innovative foresight of John Jr. The Company had had mostly excellent years all through the 1950s, culminating in a record level of earnings in 1959 (some $9.2 million). But suddenly, with John Jr.'s death in December 1960, the Company had lost its dominant leader.

W. W. Cargill's death in 1909 had brought about a profound crisis, and certainly there was a "mini-crisis" when John Sr. had his heart attack and John Jr. had taken over in the face of high tensions in the Bank Holiday days in 1933. What would be the situation here in 1960?[1]

Assessing a New Management Team

In 1944, Cargill MacMillan had exhibited once again his lack of personal ego and his perceptiveness about his colleagues when he wrote his older brother about the existing structure of the family at the top of the Company. First discussing Austen Cargill, who had not been close to the MacMillan family since the 1925 incidents, he told John Jr., "Austen is adding, I think, the ingredient that you and I have been looking for. I think we have found our general manager. He has a great deal of the personality that you and I lack . . . I have a feeling that Austen has finally come to the point of view that he is perfectly willing to defer to our judgment. I don't think he has been able to put this thought into words, but I am sure he feels it, namely, that your extraordinary faculty of synthesis is a rare and valuable one." Cargill MacMillan continued about himself: "I rather have the feeling that this ability to synthesize is a Cargill trait and I am sure that Austen has it to a much greater degree than I. On the other hand, I think I have father's ability of analysis, a MacMillan trait." However, he continued, this balance of skills of the three men was still not all that was demanded: "I think we still have need of a fourth wheel. One thing all three of us have in common is courage. Another thing we all lack is psychological ability. Our immediate friends understand us, but all of us shock what might be termed the general public." Thus perceptively recognized by Cargill MacMillan was the need for balance at the top of the organization *and* the weaknesses of the three family members, John Jr., Cargill MacMillan, and Austen Cargill, in regard to this balance.[2]

Austen Cargill died in 1957. And in 1960, first Cargill MacMillan had a severe stroke that rendered him incapable of performing any significant management tasks from that time forward (he died in 1968), then John Jr. died at the end of the year. All three family members of senior management were gone by the end of 1960.

Through these 95 years the Company had been closely held by the members of these two families. There were next-generation members of the two families already in junior positions in management—Whitney and Cargill MacMillan, Jr. (sons of Cargill MacMillan), Hugh and Duncan MacMillan (sons of John Jr.), and James Cargill (son of Austen Cargill). All five of these younger members of the family were in their 30s. None had yet had general management experience; none had been elected to the Cargill board. Erwin E. Kelm, then Cargill's president, together with H. T. "Terry" Morrison (John Jr.'s vice chairman), Sumner B. "Ted" Young (lawyer for Cargill's executive committee), and Joseph H. Colman (a member of Cargill's outside counsel) helped the five younger family members to sort out their upcoming responsibilities.

The five young men then met separately and privately developed a hierarchy of what they considered to be their collectively generated list of family objectives. They wanted control to be maintained by the families. They expressed continuing belief in retention of earnings and in making the capital grow and the desire for strong fiduciary responsibilities to employees. At the top of their objectives was a goal they defined as "best management to the top." In effect, the younger family members were enunciating their belief that the Company needed to have the best-qualified management team, whether or not its members came from the family.

Of immediate concern to everyone, family and management, was the question of who was to fill the board of directors post vacant because of John Jr.'s death. When Austen Cargill died in 1957, Kelm had become executive vice president of the Company, under Cargill MacMillan as president and John Jr. as chairman. When Cargill MacMillan suffered his stroke, in early 1960, John Jr. wrote to his cousin Will Cargill: "His mental powers were seriously impaired but somehow I do not think that will necessarily be permanent . . . it was very evident that he could not carry on, so the Directors gave him a 12–month leave of absence." John Jr. then continued with perhaps an unintentionally dismissive comment: "However, we simply had to have a President in the meantime so we promoted our Executive Vice President to be President . . . with the understanding that if, as and when, Cargill is able to come back to the business, he will come back as Chairman and I will retire, which I am anxious to do." But Cargill MacMillan did *not* come back, and Erv Kelm remained president at John Jr.'s death.

In the next sentence of this letter, John Jr. waxed eloquent about the "four very able MacMillan sons" and his son-in-law, Hubert Sontheim, who, together with Jim Cargill, were clearly those who John Jr. saw as the next generation in management. Indeed, John Jr. had made patently clear that he wanted some of this group of six young family members to be elected to the board of directors early (with Jim Cargill as his first choice).

As the younger family members prepared to meet with Kelm and Morrison, they constructed a seminal written statement, one that stated in very clear terms the underlying values toward leadership held by this next generation of family. It read in part, "We would like for you to consider the value of age to Board members. If a young man goes on the Board, and he turns out to be a poor choice, the Board is likely to be stuck with him for many years . . . [for] a forty-year old man . . . the next twenty five years. To remove him earlier would be not only embarrassing, but demoralizing to all concerned. . . . Older men generally have more to offer, especially in terms of experience." They concluded, "It is our strongest belief that the Board must be made up of the best men available. . . . Under no circumstances do we want you to consider John's promise . . . to be a command to you." A month later, the board heeded this admonition and elected Young, who as a Cargill lawyer was personal counsel to the board's executive committee, to fill the open seat. This overriding objective of always looking for the best qualified to head management has continued down through the years to the present as an article of faith within the families.[3]

Thus, it was clear right from the start that Cargill's new fourth-generation management team was to be made up exclusively of non-family members.

Implicit also was a dominant belief that such members would have needed to come up through Cargill's organization, rather than being brought in from outside.

Erv Kelm as Chief Executive Officer

The choice to head this new management team manifestly was to be Erv Kelm. He had graduated from the University of Minnesota in 1933 as a marketing major at the depth of the Depression, and it seemed logical that he would accept the first of just two job offers, with Montgomery Ward. But he took the other, at Cargill. He entered the college graduate program under the aegis of Julius Hendel and soon became a barley trader in that grain so difficult to grade and trade. By the end of World War II he was a vice president in charge of the grain division.

Kelm was a premier trader, with all of the trader's instincts—fascination with the pace and love of the chase, hard-driving on the final bargain, speculative and willing to take risks but ever concerned about the bottom line. Just like John Jr., he wanted to win. He was too young to have participated substantially in John Jr.'s famous corn case in the mid-1930s, but by 1944 was centrally involved in another landmark Cargill grain trading battle, with the flamboyant trader Daniel Rice. Kelm was one of those on the other end (with John Jr. and Julius Hendel). Then, in 1953, Cargill traded sharply in oats, both cash and futures, and subsequently was charged by the Commodity Exchange Authority (CEA) with having attempted to manipulate price. The Company as a whole and Kelm as an individual were defendants when the case was finally adjudicated by the CEA in 1954; both the Company and Kelm were barred from trading any oats futures on any contract market for the remaining seven months of the year 1954.[4]

The Seventh Management Conference, held at Stillwater, Minnesota, on April 3, 1961, was the first to use the "Apex" materials of Dr. Benjamin Tregoe. Back row, from left: Harry Starr, Portland; Ed Winter and Sid Burkett, Minneapolis; Don Brandenborg, Dave Wentzell, Bill Pearce, and Whitney MacMillan, Lake office; Addison Douglass, St. Louis. Front row: Bob Bartikoski, Jay Berkley, and Art Klobe, Minneapolis; John Savage, Lake office; Jim Randall, Minneapolis; Jim Cargill, Lake office; Royce Salisbury, Albany (Cargill News, May 1961).

But Kelm was knowledgeable about all of the business by this time, having had not only the tutelage of Hendel but the personal enthusiasm of John Jr. about his management abilities. For example, Kelm was on a trip to the Philippines with John Jr., and the latter seemed particularly taken by a Kelm proposal for innovative new methodology in the Company's copra operation there: "He was quite impressed with the idea that I came up with, in this very strange place, that a little boy from Minnesota had figured this thing out." Kelm became operations director of the whole Company in 1954 and a year later was elected to the board of directors.

It is interesting to speculate on Cargill MacMillan's letter of 1944 elaborating the strengths and weaknesses of the three senior family members—himself, John Jr., and Austen Cargill. From the late 1950s, Kelm clearly was the fourth member of this management team. Was Kelm the "fourth wheel" that MacMillan was seeking? If the role was to be filled by an articulate, personable, wide-ranging individual with honed abilities to meet the general public and overcome the lack of "psychological ability" of the other three, Erv Kelm was hardly the right candidate. One of the most inarticulate men in all of Cargill management, Kelm managed, not by persuasion or personality, but (said many of his colleagues) by "grunts." Yet he had a superb instinct for the right decision and was incisive about the decision-making process. He was far less articulate than John Jr. although cut in a very similar mold in many other ways.

Kelm, like John Jr., had an abiding love of grain trading, had been in the grain side of the business for many, many years, and had fought as a trader along with John Jr. and Hendel. His instincts lay in this trading mentality, and despite the outcome of the ill-fated oats case, he had led many great coups for Cargill in the markets, in the process teaching junior members some of the great lessons of this sophisticated but primitive process. Cargill MacMillan's hopes for a fourth person who would be a publicly oriented leaven for the three family members of the management team probably were not realized. Yet in terms of his breadth of understanding of the Company and his constant willingness to learn and deepen his knowledge, Kelm was a first-rate choice as that fourth member. Now he was alone.

Mindful of the stricture of "best management to the top" posited by the younger family members in early 1961, Kelm's team of senior managers assumed heightened importance. Terry Morrison played a unique role. Just after World War II, John Jr. personally had recruited Morrison from the outside; indeed, he was only the second such outsider to be brought directly into senior management (John Peterson, hired away from the Chase Bank at the time of the banking crisis in 1933, was the first). Morrison had essentially *no* experience in the grain trade at this point; he had been a stockbroker prior to the war and had risen to the rank of colonel in the Air Force during that conflict. (A few years later, in 1949, Morrison was given a reserve promotion to brigadier general, and from that moment on—with his blessing—he was called General Morrison around the Company.) He started with the incongruous title of head of the Mechanical Division but soon took on many other assignments as a personal friend and confidant of John Jr. and Cargill MacMillan. He had strong views about college graduate recruiting, always emphasizing the values of a generalist education; he believed in giving more responsibility to senior management (decentralization of authority) and likely was instrumental in turning John Jr. in this direction after World War II.

Morrison joined with Austen Cargill in emphasizing ethical behavior. In 1953, Morrison was elected to Cargill's board of directors and in 1959 assumed the post of vice chairman, the first time that title had been used for an officer. At the death of John Jr., Morrison became chairman of the Company. While he was able to help Kelm only minimally in operating decisions, his influence with the younger family members—indeed, throughout the senior management cadre—was such that he made a special input to the transition.

Although there seemed to be no triggering event for what followed, Morrison wasted no time in weighing in on the matter of ethics. In the July 1961 *Cargill News*, Morrison addressed the issue "Integrity." There was no compromise on this, he said, for "a businessman is either ethical or he isn't . . . a 'shady deal' isn't really shady at all—it is conceived and executed in darkness without illumination of truth or conscience. There are no shades of gray, no dark fringes." The vigorous competition of the day could persuade businessmen "with the temptation to forswear—perhaps just this once—ethical practice," but an ethical businessman would get out of such business altogether before he crossed the line.

Morrison's ending was a surprising one, probably not representing many of his management colleagues' views: "The profit motive is not the proper basis for honest business ethics, although it should be axiomatic that profits . . . are natural by-products. While one must be true to the free enterprise system, and to its business associates and customers, he must be true to himself . . . then the profits he will reap are much greater than any that can be measured in dollars." The message here was somewhat ambiguous, for it was not clear just how his reading of the profit motive could be reconciled. Nevertheless, Morrison's own unswerving attitudes came through in the editorial clearly. Morrison retired at the end of the calendar year 1962.[5]

Just two months later, *Cargill News* returned again to the subject of ethics in a substantial reprise of a speech made by Nutrena's president, Jim North, who expressed concern about the impressions left on American business by a price-fixing scandal in the electrical equipment industry. On the editorial page, the *News* editor suggested a simple (perhaps simplistic) rule: "Business ethics in a firm do not just happen . . . some people in a firm just formulate policies and all the people in that firm should carry them out."[6]

Kelm did not wait until even the following annual meeting of the board of

From left, Fred Seed, executive vice president (president in 1969); Bob Diercks, executive vice president (vice chairman in 1969); Erv Kelm, president (chairman in 1969) (Cargill staff photograph, 1965).

directors to appoint two new executive vice presidents, his key operating colleagues. One was Fred Seed, who had joined the Company after graduating from the University of Minnesota in 1932 and soon became one of the protégés of Julius Hendel. Seed had assignments both as a grain merchant and in the feed and transportation divisions before becoming the key person in the Vegetable Oil Division. From 1946, he headed that division and at that same time joined Cargill's board as the first member of his generation on that body.

The second was Bob Diercks, who also had graduated from the University of Minnesota, in 1937; Diercks took roles in the grain side of the business, first in the export department, then as branch manager and merchandising manager, and finally as vice president in charge of the Grain Division in 1954. He joined the board in 1959. These two divisions, grain and vegetable oils, were central to the Company's operations.

Nutrena, the important feed operation of Cargill had remained a semiautonomous entity, its people always priding themselves on its independence. Nutrena's head (as president) was James North. Cargo Carriers, Inc., the Company's transportation arm, was also semiautonomous (although not quite in the hands-off model of Nutrena), and it too was headed by a president, Lewis Crosby. North was on Cargill's board; Crosby was not.

The other members of the board of directors were the invalided Cargill MacMillan; Albert Egermayer, the senior vice president for finance; Robert Woodworth, who handled public relations; and (elected in August 1961) Sumner Young. Egermayer had inherited the finance post when John Peterson left Minneapolis to join Tradax in Geneva. Woodworth came to the Company in 1942 in the process of an acquisition by Cargill of an elevator in Minneapolis owned by Continental Grain Company; at that time he became a Cargill employee and later took the public relations portfolio.

The non-director officers of the Company in Kelm's team were Herbert Juneau, vice president of research and product development; W. B. "Barney" Saunders, vice president of the Grain Division and protégé of Erv Kelm; Charles Mooers, son of one of the early members of the Minneapolis office; M. D. "Pete" McVay, vice president for vegetable oil, earlier one of Julius Hendel's trainees; Cargill MacMillan Jr., vice president of administration; Robert Harrigan, vice president and comptroller; and the secretary of the Company, lawyer Donald Levin.

This was a skilled and well-trained group, with much experience in the business. One must be careful not to overstate the dominance of John Jr. in the business in that period of the late 1950s, for this team of senior managers were in many cases strong-willed people, not only willing to take independent decisions but pushing for them. Yet Kelm recounted later his feeling of loneliness at the top. He was by nature a taciturn man and kept his own counsel as he moved to become, in fact, the group's leader. Kelm had taken his cues from John Jr.; now he had to establish his own style. His gruffness and sparse responses would seem to have gotten in his way, but apparently they did not— the management team was strongly behind Kelm. Results, though, would be the ultimate criteria, and the jury was still out on this aspect.

Holding his counsel and moving cautiously on alliances, Kelm continued his wide-ranging study of management materials (he already had found the Harvard Business School case studies fruitful) and began to hone some new budgetary concepts he felt would be necessary. Kelm believed that budgets needed to extend out for more than just the following year and began working on the notion that the Company should have five-year budget projections. In this, he was helped measurably by the work of controller Bob Harrigan; Kelm began to put increasing trust in him (Harrigan and his assistant, Vardin West, were specially complimented by the board in a resolution in their meeting of July 27, 1962, a rare event). Kelm also had long-standing personal affinities with Walter Gage, the head of Tradax, the European arm of Cargill. Gage and Kelm had been close compatriots in the Grain Division earlier; already, Gage had visited Kelm a number of times and had kept close telephone links. This connection now expanded.

Kelm was interviewed by *Cargill News* in the next issue after John Jr.'s death; his emphasis was on expansion, and he linked this to the employees'

Margaret Cargill, daughter of Austen S. Cargill, was sponsor in the launching of the towboat
Austen S. Cargill, *December 8, 1960* (Cargill file photograph, 1960; see also *Cargill News,* January 1961).

own personal and family growth. While growth had to be balanced, and "our main base will continue to be agriculture," Kelm also pointed to some related businesses (his example was salt) that gave a close "link-up" with existing businesses. Kelm seemed uneasy that his own administration at the Company went in tandem with a new administration for the country (a Democratic administration had been elected, with John Kennedy as President). "I hope the administration will not decide to impose additional controls on farm production or on the ability of firms such as Cargill to handle farm products." Kelm strongly opted for the free market.[7]

Fiscal year 1960–1961 (ending May 31) turned out most propitious. Net profit was up to over $5 million, a 19 percent gain from the previous year. The return on net worth, in turn, was nicely higher. Cargo Carriers showed a profit, as did Tradax. The Baie Comeau ocean terminal was beginning to work well (but with start-up problems), and other properties had been added. The Company had handled over 21 million tons of grain products in the process. The motor vessel *Austen S. Cargill*, the Company's giant new Mississippi River craft, was in service by the beginning of 1961. This 6,630-horsepower vessel was the largest towboat ever built for a nonpublic inland waterways company. Austen Cargill's daughter Margaret Ann christened the vessel. Its first work trip involved moving 20 barges of grain, the equivalent of

Forty barges, carrying almost 2 million bushels of grain, near the end of their journey down the Mississippi River near Baton Rouge, Louisiana. The barges, being pushed by the towboat Austen S. Cargill, *contain 57,908 tons of grain, or the equivalent in wheat of 72,000 acres. If the shipment were moved by rail, it would have required 1,182 freight cars* (Cargill News, September 1964).

five 100-car freight trains, from Cairo, Illinois, to Baton Rouge for export (its maximum load was 40 barges).

In February 1961, ground-breaking ceremonies were held for Cargill's new Minneapolis office building; Kelm represented the Company, carrying a jackhammer in his hands. Nutrena's dog food television commercial, "Shaggy Dog—Buy Some!" was selected among the finalists in a national TV commercial contest. A Company attitude survey was conducted in mid-1961 by the Industrial Relations Center at the University of Chicago; *Cargill News* was "gratified to find that on the basis of all employees surveyed Cargill placed 5 percentage points higher in its general level of morale than the average of all other firms surveyed recently by the University of Chicago. This is slightly higher than Cargill stood above the average in 1957." The only item falling below the 50 percent favorable response line was that for pay and benefits.[8]

In sum, the Company had come through the difficult year of John Jr.'s death with reassuring results, with Kelm as its chief executive officer for the last five months.

Farm Policy Uproar and Cargill's Middents Plan

One of the first problems that the administration of John F. Kennedy had to deal with in early 1961 was that of agricultural policy. The President had chosen Orville Freeman as Secretary of Agriculture, and the plans of the administration began to move quickly. A vast excess capacity in agriculture had persisted, complicated by huge amounts of surplus grain held in storage. Most of this was owned by the federal government (specifically, held by the Commodity Credit Corporation) as a result of cumulative price support purchases over the years. The Kennedy-Freeman administration knew this full well. Willard Cochrane, the respected agricultural economist, analyzed the administration's thinking: "It also understood, or thought it understood, some other things. First, that a highly urbanized society will not support large and continuing expenditures on agricultural programs; and, second, that a highly urbanized society will not tolerate government policies which lead directly to rising food prices."[9]

President Kennedy had argued throughout his campaign for higher farm incomes. At the same time, he promised reduced farm program outlays—indeed, the stemming of the huge surpluses themselves. How could all of this be accomplished? The administration's answer was to rigorously constrain the supply side of this equation—the farmer's production itself. In other words, mandatory production controls would be instituted. Farmers liked the first half of this equation, the higher prices, but vehemently and vocally disdained the type of mandated production controls envisioned by Freeman and his colleagues. The Kennedy administration moved forward on this supply-side thesis (widely called "draconian" by its many critics), with the battle to be fought out in new congressional legislation for the 1961 "Farm Bill."

Farm policy itself always had involved large numbers of conflicting claimants. There were small farmers, and there were large farmers; there were corn growers, wheat growers, and many others. There were many different

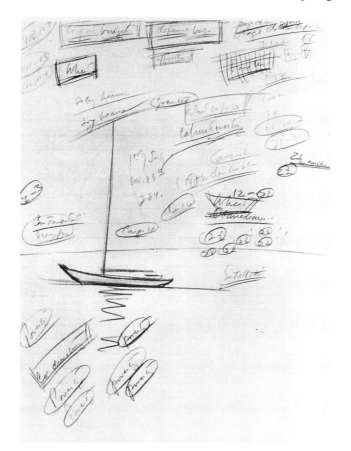

Wheat and soybean export activity engaged in by Cargill and other grain firms were central to discussion of the late President John F. Kennedy with his cabinet at a meeting held October 29, 1963. It was his last cabinet meeting. The name "Cargill" appears near the center of a scratch pad containing doodles by JFK made during the meeting (*Cargill News*, February 1967).

agricultural regions, each with its own special physical conditions and underlying values of those particular farmers. There were multitudes of agribusiness interests, some supplying inputs, others transforming the output as middlemen processors and retail food sellers. The latter, of course, had to face the public, whose food expenditures made up a significant percentage of their family income (although not as large a percentage as in most other countries). This particular interface bred universal preoccupation with prices.

Cargill and its companion grain trading companies long had been particularly attuned to a free-market philosophy. Farm policies since the first days of the Roosevelt administration in the early 1930s had relied on a wide-ranging number of intrusions into the marketplace itself. Price and income supports had been introduced just about every year from the end of World War II. These control mechanisms waxed and waned over time, depending upon circumstances at a given economic point and on the philosophies of the political party in power. In the Democratic Truman administration of the late 1940s and early 1950s, Secretary of Agriculture Charles Brannan had attempted to make significant changes, as had Ezra Taft Benson, the Secretary of Agriculture during the Eisenhower administration. Brannan's approach was for further controls; Benson's was quite the opposite. Neither was able to persuade Congress to make truly significant changes. But now Secretary Freeman was advocating the most stringent control patterns of the postwar period with his proposed mandatory supply constraints.

For Cargill and the other grain trading companies, this was anathema. Their business was built on trading, and it would not be too much of a simplification to say "the more the better." While commodity markets themselves were entirely dedicated to free trade, the origination, transportation, storage, and processing had various levels of constraints within them. But throughout the grain companies there was a thoroughgoing belief in the free market as the best of all clearing mechanisms for the determination of price.

Cargill always had been alert to farm policy changes, and frequently had taken stands on them. With the Freeman plan so explicitly imposing constraints on this process, which the Company felt should be a free one, the Cargill board now decided to take a more proactive role. At its July 26, 1961, meeting, governmental policy was the subject of intensive discussion, and out of this a Company task force, the Public Policy Study Group, was constituted. It was a "blue ribbon" unit, titularly headed by Bob Woodworth, the head of the public relations department, but having as its executive director and manager William Pearce, a young lawyer who had joined Cargill in 1952 and had become assistant vice president and manager of the Company's public relations office in August of 1961 ("a savvy negotiator," said the *Wall Street Journal*). The task force membership included a number of Pearce's colleagues: Gordy Alexander, Mel Middents, John Cole, and Barney Saunders from the Grain Division; Dave Wentzell from feed; Pete McVay from vegetable oil; Cliff Roberts from Cargo Carriers (CCI); Calvin Anderson and John McGrory from the Law Department; and Jim Bowe, a member of the Carl Byoir public relations organization deputed to Cargill.

The task force working papers immediately became useful for public efforts with congressmen, senators, and other influential people in industry and farm groups. Even more important, at least at the start, was the need to inform and bring along a number of key people in the various Cargill operating divisions. Many of these were initial skeptics, wondering why the Company was involving itself in politics and often not too enthusiastic about some of the specific ideas put forth by the task force. One of the lasting heritages of the task force was the internal communication and building of consensus, which, as later events would show, was a strong "plus" for Cargill in the pitched battles in Congress and in agriculture circles in the early 1970s.

When the 1961 Kennedy-Freeman farm program was brought forward, not many weeks after the President's inauguration, the full implications of its supply management approach became clearer. To begin with, there was a particular proposal, billed only as a "procedural" change, which would have transferred to the Executive Branch the responsibility for drafting specific farm programs and granted Congress veto but not amending power. The proposal had as its central feature the use of producer committees as the generating force. This provision of the bill was vehemently opposed and died in committee. A temporary alternative was then passed by Congress and signed by the President (the Agricultural Act of 1961), which extended for one year the important feed grains segment and provided a one-year extension of the previously existing wheat program. These compromises—in effect, the status quo—now set the stage for major skirmishes in the 1962 congressional effort.

It was at this point that certain of the Cargill task force efforts came to be especially important. Mel Middents, from the Grain Division, had long been a student of farm programs and now provided both technical expertise and fresh ideas to the task force. Middents proposed that the payment to the farmer could be separated from the price of commodities in the marketplace. In other words, assuming that the farmers of the country needed a certain income level (the term *parity* had been used for many years), this income level could be obtained by explicitly separate payments rather than by forcing constraints directly on the marketplace itself. The payment was to be directly linked to production of the commodity. Still influenced by output, it was not actually "decoupled," in the way that word has been used in more recent farm legislation discussions.

The Cargill proposal ("nicknamed the Middents Plan," wrote Dan Morgan in his important book, *Merchants of Grain*; the *Wall Street Journal* called it "the Cargill Bill") was defeated in the House and not taken up in the Senate; but with the backing of Sen. Hubert Humphrey and Rep. Albert Quie, both of Minnesota, the essence was adopted in compromise efforts in the Senate/House Conference Committee. For the first time, a separate direct income-support payment would be made in addition to a price-support loan rate that was closer to a market-clearing "free market" price. For example, in what became the program for 1963, corn carried a price-support loan rate of $1.07 per bushel; added to this was the income-support payment of $.18 per bushel, giving a total support of $1.25. Similarly, barley had its loan rate set at $.82 per bushel, to which was added a support payment of $.14 per bushel, giving a total support of $.96. Middents further suggested that the payment in lieu of price support (the $.18) would be a payment in kind (PIK) rather than in cash, that the farmer would be required to use this additional amount of money to buy grain from the government for his own use or to sell, thus lowering the surplus overhang. The PIK approach did not stay in the bill, however—the support payments were to be denominated in cash. (PIK *did* become a feature of governmental policy in later years.)

There were further provisions involving acreage to be diverted (in other words, taken out of that particular grain's production on the farm if the farmer chose to be in the government's program). Lost in the process, from Secretary Freeman's point of view, was any remaining provision for mandatory supply controls; won by the "free market" advocates was the principle that the market-clearing price was to be sought, separate from the issue of income support for the farmers.[10]

However, this was *not* applied to one crucial grain in the total picture—wheat. Here the administration still proposed mandatory controls, and the new law would provide this *only* if a particular event would allow it. First a "wheat referendum" would be held among all wheat farmers, and the controls would go into effect only if two-thirds of those producers voting in the referendum agreed. If it was not approved, a less restrictive program with substantially lower price supports would come into being. As Willard Cochrane put it, "the choice was popularly phrased as $1.00 or $2.00 wheat." The date of the referendum was May 1963, giving ample time for proponents and opponents to lobby their views among the farmer constituencies.

The administration immediately began a major informational drive to encourage acceptance. The USDA contingent seemed quite split on the issue, some advocating outright promotion, others opting for informational efforts only.

Out among the constituencies, opinions fell along the lines of the earlier differences over mandatory controls. The powerful American Farm Bureau Federation, the major representative of the larger farmers, announced right away that it would work for rejection of what had come to be called the "certificate" program (a fixed amount of certificates were proposed for production of a specific amount of wheat, which would be prorated to producers on the basis of acreage allotments).

The Cargill stand was, as before, strongly in opposition to the mandatory features. The task force team chose to concentrate its efforts on what they dubbed the "class problem." Mel Middents commented, "We do not have a surplus of wheat as such in this country, rather we have a surplus of low quality hard red winter wheat in several southwestern states . . . while stocks of hard red winter wheat continue to accumulate, supplies of other, more desired classes, have been reduced drastically." The task force feared that, because of the way exemptions would be treated for smaller farmers, these producers (and others) would turn their production away from wheat to feed grains. As a great many of these farmers were not from the southwestern states, typically they would have been growing soft red winter, hard red spring, and durum wheat—precisely those that were in short supply. A shortage of the soft red wheat could present real problems for domestic millers, as the soft wheats were used almost entirely in the production of cakes, cookies, crackers, pretzels, doughnuts, pies, biscuits, and other quick breads. The quality of the flour was critical, and the inherent quality differences generally allowed no economic substitute for soft wheat. Over and over, the Cargill task force materials emphasized, "There is no surplus of soft red wheat!"

Other critics against voting yes on the referendum now rallied around the issue of the loss of exemption by the small farmers and its effects on the production of the soft wheats. The Farm Bureau charged that the farmers were being forced to surrender their very freedom; one of the Bureau's leaflets shouted, "The real issue in the Wheat Referendum is . . . 'freedom to farm.'" The referendum seemed to offer a Hobson's choice between the administration's program and a much lower price if rejected. However, the opponents reminded the farmers over and over again that if the referendum was defeated, Congress would not have the nerve to allow wheat prices to drop as scheduled but would enact another more satisfactory program.

John Foster, a South Dakota wheat farmer, casts his ballot in the U.S. Department of Agriculture wheat referendum vote, May 1963 (UPI/Corbis-Bettmann).

Shortly after the May 21, 1963, ending date for the referendum, the results were announced by the USDA. A two-thirds positive vote was necessary; the final results showed that 1,222,856 farmers voted and only 47.8 percent of the farmers favored the mandatory quotas. The administration's plan was roundly defeated.

The vote startled just about everyone. *Cargill News* reported on the "bushel of surprises" from the landslide no vote, "coming after a fierce 'running scared' fight by both sides. . . . Within the 'no' vote came an even greater upset: not one of the Big Ten wheat producing states turned in the two-thirds 'yes' votes needed for passage. In retrospect hangs the question, 'how did the super-control idea get so far in the first place?'"

In the chilly aftermath, constituencies on both sides now sobered to the realities facing them. Joseph Alsop wrote in the *Washington Post*, "Farm state Republicans and their allies of the Farm Bureau are belatedly but visibly worried about having 'freed' the wheat farmers at a probable cost of $1.10 to $1.20 wheat. . . . The Kennedy Administration meanwhile is visibly worried about being too coldly negative . . . it is a bit too coldly logical to say nothing to the wheat farmers except, 'You've made your bed, now lie in it even if it means $1.10 wheat.'" Alsop editorialized, "There are strong special and biological arguments *against* letting millions of the smaller American farmers go to the wall . . . it is an unexplained fact of history, but an undoubted fact despite its mystery, that great nations have always tended to decline when independent farmers were driven out by industrial farming." The *New York Times* added, "Even the American Farm Bureau Federation, champion of the free market in agriculture, leader in the fight against controls, does not favor complete abandonment of the farmer." The *Times* editor commented, "With farmers turning thumbs down on high price supports and tight controls, the only permanent solution lies in a return to a free market, while the Government takes steps to spare farms unnecessary hardship in making the transition." Don Paarlberg, a respected Purdue University professor, put it more bluntly, "A deep and grievous error comes from considering freedom to be synonymous with license—the total absence of restraint. A better concept of freedom is that it is closely tied to responsibility. The more responsibility is self-imposed, the less restraint will have to be supplied from the outside." Then he added, "One final word. In the farm policy format of this decade, it is government programs and not free markets that are on the defensive. The regulated portion of agriculture is in deep and costly trouble; the competitive part of agriculture is in better condition."

So winter wheat was planted in the fall of 1963 with a virtually free market price in force. And the critics were correct in their view that Congress would bow to pressure and temper the harshness of such a complete transition; now new farmer-friendly legislation began working its way through Congress.[11]

"Food for Peace"

Once Freeman had lost the battle for mandatory controls, and faced anew with the huge surplus that likely would mount further, the secretary turned aggressively to pushing exports as a salvation. Here a very important federal enactment took a special place. This was the popular, mostly successful "Food for Peace" legislation, passed in 1954 under the Eisenhower administration; its full name was the Agricultural Trade Development and Assistance Act, but it became commonly known by its Congressional number, P.L. 480.

During the Korean War (1950–1954), the grain surplus problem subsided with the wartime demand for feed and food grains around the world. With the sudden end of the war in 1954, President Eisenhower, too, was faced once again with the long-standing bugaboo of surplus grains held by the federal government. Indeed, in 1955 the Commodity Credit Corporation (CCC) held wheat stocks that exceeded the total domestic and export use that year. P.L. 480 primarily was a food aid mechanism, designed to both combat hunger around the world *and* dispose of surpluses. Foreign governments could request authorizations from the U.S. government that would allow them to purchase American farm commodities with American loans. The actual handling of the transactions was left to the foreigners; they would contract with private exporters, who then were paid for the grain directly by the U.S. Treasury. The foreign governments had an obligation to repay these loans, but there were long grace periods and maturities. For a number of the earlier years of the law, the foreign governments could pay in their own currencies (leaving the United States to figure out how to use, for example, millions and millions of Indian rupees). These "soft" currencies could be used in the given country for a number of purposes, including promoting economic development, establishing new markets, purchasing goods and services for U.S. government efforts such as military and embassy supplies, purchasing strategic materials, and educational exchanges.

The private grain trade had mixed feelings about P.L. 480. It was true that major sales were being made under this provision: in those early years, almost all export sales were effected through this mechanism. However, the process was tightly controlled by the CCC, and some of the provisions truly galled the private trade. Cargill took the lead in forcing the hand of the CCC on one of these. At the beginning, the sales were always made at export dockside, a CCC ruling. Cargill wanted to be able to ship straight through from inland terminals so that it could take advantage of economies of performance in the Company's own inland transportation segment of the total grain shipment. Finally, under the diligent pressure of Bill Pearce, the CCC relaxed the dockside provision.

Secretary Freeman now drew heavily on this P.L. 480 concessional sale program, promoting deals widely around the globe, and the grain surpluses began slowly to subside. The total wheat owned by the CCC in 1961 was 1,242,000,000 bushels. This dropped slowly in 1962 and 1963 but fell to 828,000,000 in 1964 and to just 102,000,000 by 1968.[12]

The European Economic Community and Its Common Agricultural Policy

Important as P.L. 480 was in *enhancing* exports, another development in the early 1960s had a massive effect in *inhibiting* American exports of grain. Over the mid-1950s, six strong Western European countries, namely, France, Belgium, Luxembourg, the Netherlands, Italy, and West Germany, built on their integrative linkages in the earlier European Coal and Steel Community to form a new economic community, called formally the European Economic Community (EEC, later the EC) and known more widely as the Common Market. By the time of their enabling Treaty of Rome in 1957, the basic structure of a revolutionary economic union was in place. It involved removal of barriers to trade among the six member nations, the establishment of a single commercial policy toward nonmember countries, and further longer-term coordination in transportation and general economic policies. It also assured the mobility of labor, capital, and entrepreneurship within the Common Market. This far-reaching move by the "Six" had profound implications for the rest of the world.

United States policy strongly supported the EEC efforts, albeit with many caveats when it came to EEC commercial policy toward the rest of the world. However, U.S. enthusiasm for the EEC took a setback in 1962, when the six countries developed their Common Agricultural Policy, colloquially called CAP. Even internally among the six, the effort proved very controversial, for many European farms were inefficiently run by individual families who lacked requisite capital and land. West Germany had been balancing its trade through the importation of agricultural goods from nonmembers on a quid pro quo for its outstanding industrial goods. France was the most efficient agricultural country of the six but was burdened by a huge number of farmers who were a potent political force against anything that appeared to be inimical to their own interests. As a result, under the CAP, high domestic prices were maintained in France and to a lesser degree in West Germany and the other countries. In particular, the policy allowed France, which had its own surplus of wheat, to sell it to the other five Common Market countries without having to fight price-cutting competition from other countries (in the case of wheat, especially the competition from Canada and the United States).

This was accomplished by erecting a system of floating duties on farm imports so that there would be no underselling of whatever the subsidized price demanded. As Dan Morgan put it in *Merchants of Grain*, "This was a time when President de Gaulle [of France] was at the peak of his power and petulance, and CAP made important concessions to France . . . the high duties of the CAP left the Europeans free to pamper their farmers with a generous price-support system . . . it would be difficult to overestimate the political importance of CAP as a postwar European achievement."

Right down to today, it has been the feeling of those outside the community that the farmers of the Six (and later with the additions of the United Kingdom, Austria, Denmark, Finland, Ireland, Greece, Portugal, Spain, and Sweden) were forcing high prices on the rest of the world to continue to subsidize German, French, and the other farmers in the EEC. By 1963, both the administration and the various private agricultural constituencies in the United States were directing sharp criticisms to these unsettling events in Europe, particularly because of major new developments in the General Agreement on Tariffs and Trade (GATT) negotiations.

The GATT, originally initiated by representatives of 23 countries in meetings at Geneva in 1947 (all the major trading partners were there, including the United States), was established to materially reduce tariff and nontariff restrictions on world trade. By the early 1960s, after many separate subsequent periods of negotiation, the membership had increased to over 70 countries, and major trade concessions had been agreed among all these parties. Always one of the thorniest issues was that relating to agricultural tariffs, and here the CAP agreements in the early 1960s exacerbated the situation. A fifth round of GATT negotiations had just been completed in Geneva in 1960– 1962; now what appeared to be a highly significant sixth round was to be held, again in Geneva, and was given the short name "the Kennedy Round" to acknowledge the assassination of the American President (in November 1963). The CAP internal subsidies and external tariffs were projected to be one of the highly sticky issues.

Trade issues remained very sensitive throughout the rest of the 1960s, and reference will be made later to the Kennedy Round efforts, as well as a number of other new grain arrangements. One of the most interesting events came in late 1963 and early 1964, when Russia intruded into the picture in a startling way, proposing to buy wheat from the United States. To put this in context as far as Cargill was concerned, we need to understand what was happening at the same time *inside* the Company.[13]

Two Uneasy Years

All of the turmoil in the farm policy arena triggered reverberations back in the industry. While not all of the larger grain trading companies did poorly in the period 1961–1963, Cargill did. The fiscal year 1961–1962, the first full year under the Kelm administration, was a modest one, with earnings dropping significantly from the previous year (to $3.47 million as against the previous

$5.08 million). The Grain Division had had a good year, accounting for some 77 percent of the total Company profit. But the Feed Division turned in red figures for the first time in many years, and the important Vegetable Oil Division saw its earnings drop significantly. Special Products also showed a loss, as did the Commodity Department. There were heavy nonoperating deductions, particularly as the Belle Isle salt mine construction was stepped up. There had been a number of modest property additions that year; the Baie Comeau and Chicago terminals had been upgraded and a soybean plant purchased in Wichita. The new hybrid corn plant at Pontiac, Illinois, was completed, but overall the Company lost heavily in its hybrid corn efforts. The division's report apologized: "We underestimated the full effects of the feed grain program on our inventory position and then reacted too slowly to those effects when they did become apparent. We simply did not predict the consequences of what was happening while there was still time to take action, which at least would have lessened the year's loss."

In total, it was a disappointing year for Kelm and his colleagues. Although the sales dollars continued their upward climb, rising to over $1.4 billion (a gain of 3 percent over the previous year), the self-congratulatory statement in the annual report that "among the 500 largest industrial companies in the nation, Cargill now ranks 29th" seemed somewhat of a Pyrrhic victory.

The year 1962–1963 was even more mixed. The earnings, at $3.48 million, were just $10,000 over that of the previous year (not including Tradax earnings, which were included this year for the first time in the Cargill, Incorporated, financial statements; the reasons for this will be discussed later in this chapter). Fortunately, the vegetable oil contribution to earnings had increased from $1.97 million to $3.25 million. But the shocker was what had happened in the Grain Division. From a quite adequate performance in 1961–1962 ($2.69 million), its contribution had dropped to just $372,000. Feed was back in the black. Special Products and the Commodity Department once again registered losses.

The Grain Division's annual report opened, "By virtue of a very profitable May, 1963, the Division squeaked through a very disappointing 1962–1963." They had suffered reductions of major proportions in two of their principal sources of income, with gross trading income declining from $36 million to $32.8 million and warehousing income down from $10.5 million to $8.3 million. Yet "in spite of lower gross profit we were unable to reduce our expenses to any extent." Winter wheat had had a very good year (a new record for the Company), but spring wheat was down, as was corn. Oats and barley "proved bitter disappointments this year." And so it was with the other grains traded.

There had been mitigating factors; in particular, a strike of longshoremen in January 1963 had cost the division substantial revenue. As Barney Saunders looked ahead to the next year for his division, he noted, "Because of the poor year and the general depression in the grain division, morale in the

Grain Division is poor. We have already begun planned visits to every one of our offices."

There were major additions to Cargill's physical facilities during this mixed year of 1962–1963. Several elevators had been purchased and a major new elevator leased at Denver. New investments had been made in several smaller companies; one of these, an initial investment in a Peruvian fishmeal operation, was an offbeat but exciting new endeavor (of which more later).

The annual report on the overall Company noted that working capital had increased some $7.4 million in the year. But over half of this increase was due to the merger of Tradax's working capital with that of Cargill; the other source of increase "represented a change whereby slow receivables and related reserve for bad debts plus pre-paid expenses were reflected . . . as a part of working capital. . . . This change in procedure is a proper one from the standpoint of generally accepted accounting principles and it rightfully reflects on the balance sheet important values which by their omission was conservative, but hardly orthodox." The balance sheet *did* seem somewhat less conservative after this "creative accounting change."

When the unvarnished facts of the year's performance were scrutinized, Kelm and his fellow senior managers felt substantial unease, enough that they devoted a significant segment at the board of directors' meetings in the third week of July 1963 to the question "What is wrong?" The directors generally used this very important midsummer meeting to travel together over several days, meeting at some length each day and then observing operations. At the first two meetings on July 18 and July 19, each of the heads of the divisions made special reports to the board, with wide-ranging discussion for each. Then a combination bus and private railcar trip took the board to a new Des Moines soybean plant and the Company facilities in Omaha, Nebraska, and Wichita, Kansas, to see the Cargill people there. On the railroad car to Colorado Springs, longer-range plans, particularly capital investment, were discussed in light of the disappointing results of the fiscal year just finished.

The discussion then turned to the need for the "development of a sense of profit responsibility . . . at all levels of the corporation," with emphasis on establishing "volume and margin standards for each activity in the smallest subdivisions possible" as a means of promoting such a sense. The directors agreed that these standards would be developed both on a break-even basis and on a budget or target basis for each activity. The comptroller was given responsibility for establishing interdivisional pricing and cost allocations, and in general the directors seemed genuinely dedicated to tightening the organization all through the Company.

Back in 1961, the board had established a long-range planning committee, dubbed the LRPC, and this group now made its presence felt strongly with the Grain Division. Kelm pointedly wrote the division heads on August 23, notifying them that the LRPC was now to be composed of a committee of the board itself—exactly composed of members of the executive committee—and that the LRPC would now do a searching study of all divisions. "For the next three years," Kelm wrote, "Cargill will concentrate on our present fields of endeavor in an effort to get all of our present businesses to improve their earnings and get to the 'pleasant to contemplate' position of the most efficient in our chosen fields." To telegraph the sense of urgency, the newly constituted LRPC was to monitor the divisions on a three-month basis.

An attached Kelm memorandum contrasted three approaches to profit improvement: cost reduction by decree, analytical review of operations, and/or search for fundamental changes needed. "We all recognize," Kelm continued, "that two years ago we approached grain division operations with a combination of cost reduction by decree and an analytical review of operations." Inasmuch as this did not seem to help grain division performance, "in future months it is suggested that we take our existing information and imagination to apply analysis to search for fundamental change for our business."[14]

"'Hard Hats' on the air drills for the initial breaking of ground for the Northstar Center were, from left, Erv Kelm, president of Cargill; Mr. Boston of Investor Diversified Services, financiers of the projects; Philip Pillsbury, chairman of the board of Pillsbury Co., Inc.; William Baker, chairman, Baker Properties, Inc., builders of the project; Henry Rutledge, executive vice president of the Northwestern National Bank, another of the principal tenants" (*Cargill News*, March 1961).

"Can Chase Help Us?"

As incisive as this LRPC effort appeared, the most striking single event in the wake of the poor results of the 1962–1963 fiscal year was the decision to turn to the Chase Manhattan Bank, Cargill's long-standing lead bank, for consulting help. For many years, Cargill people had had an almost overweening hubris (certainly, this would apply to John Jr.!). The Company consistently had eschewed taking much advice from anyone on the outside. This feeling always had been particularly strong in relation to using outside consultants. For example, a sophisticated outside effort by Booz, Allen & Hamilton had been presented to the Company in August 1949, covering new concepts of decentralization in the Company. Erv Kelm, at that time head of the Grain Division, was its most vocal critic. The consultants had presented a "basic hedge" analysis, and Kelm faulted it severely as being "hardly to the test-tube stage" and reiterated a view that was held by many in the Company that the consultants "had been learning the grain trade at Cargill's expense."[15]

Now Kelm reined in his own substantial hubris, and asked the Chase group to use its corporate financial research division for a thoroughgoing, independent review of Cargill. The ostensible reason for the request was to have the bank survey the possibility of Cargill's establishing its own financial institution within the Company (a notion that had been raised at that major July 1963 board meeting). But it was patently clear that the analysis was to go beyond the finance function to cover *all* of the business.

The Chase did not disappoint. In late October 1963, the bank presented 39 tightly argued, single-spaced pages, accompanied by eight tabular exhibits with both comparative financial figures and a whole set of ratios (much beyond what Cargill had typically compiled). The report looked into every one of the divisions and followed the consultants' analysis with hard-hitting recommendations. No issue was sidestepped, and the analysis of individual operations was painfully honest. Correctly, no individual names were listed in the report. But responsibility and accountability were crystal clear.

Particularly revealing was the comparison the Chase analysts made between Cargill and a set of composites of the financial statements of a group of companies, several in each of Cargill's fields ("it represents a combination of all of the leading companies in Cargill's lines, rolled into one; it provides a yardstick against which to measure Cargill"). These cross-comparisons were most sobering to the Cargill senior management. Comptroller Bob Harrigan (who had come to Cargill from General Mills at the time of the Booz, Allen & Hamilton report in 1949) took the responsibility for organizing the long document into a four-page memorandum for the rest of senior management. A succinct first page captured what Harrigan saw as the highlights; it read as follows:

1. Cargill more highly leveraged than the composite taken as a whole, with heavy debt concentrated in current borrowings.

2. Growth of Cargill's sales volume . . . steady, but earnings have not kept pace.

3. Net profit has declined—not in every year, but generally over the past five years—in absolute amount, in relation to sales, and as return on both net worth and total capital.

4. Working capital has moved irregularly downward over the past five years . . . failed to match Cargill's growth, and in comparison with the industry composite appears to be substandard.

5. The trend is disturbing, and its causes should be explored and understood so that remedial action may be considered.

6. Although Cargill's capital and debt are clearly out of line, this may be more *effect* than *cause* of the poor earnings.

7. The Company's principal problem is one of operations, rather than of financial structure.

8. Most of Cargill's ills appear to be curable. . . . A careful study by the Company should indicate whether the most serious problems can be alleviated. Our guess [the Chase analysts speaking] is that, at least in good part, they can. The Company has tremendous potential.

Each division came in for frank, searching criticism. The analysts stated at the beginning that "the major problems are clearly in the Grain and Feed Divisions." For grain, the analysts wanted careful studies, elevator by elevator, "to determine which locations are bleeding the Company the most." Clearly, the Chase group envisioned closing many of the elevators, largely because of their inefficiencies. They wanted the Company to move "very slowly" in acquiring or building any additional elevator capacity and wanted the division executives to seriously reconsider the existing policy of trying to fill elevators with Cargill's own grain. In the Feed Division, poultry would be cut back, so would turkey and eggs. Credit terms and capital loans should be curtailed drastically, and consideration should be given to closing some of the plants. Owning rather than leasing of facilities was preferred. Finally, the Chase analysts recommended dropping dog food. Vegetable oil came off relatively well on the analysis; the Special Products Division was urged to abandon seed corn and the Commodity Department to put a larger focus on salt sales. The Cargo Carriers operation was recommended to move slowly in new types of shipping: "Resist temptation." CCI was encouraged to liquidate some of its side ventures. Indeed, as to Cargill's view of CCI, "Do not feel obliged to continue CCI forever." Tradax came in for only a few comments.

The Chase group faulted certain dominant features of a special Cargill culture as being at the root of some of the Company's malaise. "Cargill Management gives the impression of being grain-oriented . . . both a strength and a weakness." This bias toward grain was compounded by an accounting method that did not provide breakouts between trading and storage, and in turn this led to feed and oil not having an adequate basis for comparison. It was necessary for profit-and-loss analysis to include cost of goods sold, margins, and expense, with explicit ratios to sales computed for all major categories. In sum, the Company was not employing adequately the tools of financial analysis that had become widespread in the rest of American industry.

Chase argued that sales growth received an inordinate emphasis and that "this preoccupation with growth and expansion has been more of a factor in management thinking than have considerations of profits." John Jr. had often stated that the family wanted to double the Company every seven years, and Kelm had adopted a similar set of growth goals. The average return on net worth for the Company during the 1950s was 12.2; this had dropped to an average of 6.4 for the years 1960–1962. The analysts concluded that "this industry is not doing as well as American industry generally, and Cargill is not doing as well as its industry."

At the end of the report, the Chase analysts raised a controversial point that seemed tactically far away from the views of both the families and the management—they recommended consideration of a public offering of either common or preferred stock or convertible debentures. This could be done, said the analysts, "without causing the family to lose control." They concluded with a provocative thought: "There is also something to be said for the whetstone effect of having public ownership. A company and its management can be sharpened by being exposed to the criticisms of sophisticated shareholders, stockholders, and . . . the scrutiny of professional security analysts, and submitting to public appraisal in comparison with its creditors and peers."

Once again, this was likely to have been seen as a heretical point of view to most of the Cargill group (family *and* management). Willingness to accept criticism gracefully had never been a tenet of the Cargill culture.

While the Chase report stirred management to make many specific changes that had been suggested, there appeared to be little shaking of the basic Cargill culture itself. In essence, Chase had for the moment taken on the role of a surrogate outside director, a post that Cargill had assiduously avoided throughout most of its history. John Jr. often had spoken of the great values of Cargill's "inside" board, who could meet "on five minutes' notice." But the Chase exercise was painfully close to being a defining moment in that it pressed Cargill management to be more introspective than it had been during many years of self-satisfaction under John Jr. To whet is to "goad, incite." Chase had done just this.[16]

Tightening the Organization

The Chase Manhattan Bank report was a clarion call to Cargill senior management. Erv Kelm and Bert Egermayer visited the bank in New York in late November to discuss the report; this was followed by intensive discussion at the board meeting of December 26, 1963. Back in July, the board had formally constituted the Long-Range Planning Committee (LRPC); at this time, its membership was reconstituted: Kelm was chairman; Fred Seed, Bob Diercks, Whitney Macmillan, and Richard Baldwin were its members (the latter two, respectively, secretary and assistant secretary). At the December meeting, the goals of the LRPC were formally voted; it was to establish specific objectives for each division and provide explicit guidelines for decisions by the finance committee. Clearly, the LRPC was to be the central vehicle for tightening the Company's procedures. A "fact finding and profit improvement" committee had been established back in late 1962 under the chairmanship of Cargill MacMillan, Jr., to look into control of the Administration Division expenses and methods of allocation to individual divisions and subsidiaries, but this embryonic effort now was appropriated by the LRPC.

The series of steps now taken by Kelm and his colleagues was to give many clues to defining Kelm's own imprint on the Cargill culture. In October, the LRPC worked out its own detailed long-range objectives. At the top of the agenda was production of earnings that were "favorable with competition in each of our fields." The Triple A credit rating would be maintained, and facilities research and personnel goals were delineated. Finally, the Company was to "maintain a public image of service to agriculture and of a young, vibrant, aggressive organization—a leader, not a follower."

Following this, the LRPC mandated very specific objectives for the divisions. Market penetration minimums were established (grain, 30 percent; oil, 20 percent; feed, 10 percent). For each there was added the same telling statement: "Costs lower than industry average." Return on investment objectives were spelled out—8 percent for grain, 12 percent for oil, 10 percent for feed, 15 percent for cargo carriers, 12 percent for commodities, 10 percent for hybrid corn—but 20 percent for both resins and fatty chemicals. Interestingly, in the Grain Division objectives, once again appeared the notion of the "endless belt" theory of John Jr.—that Cargill should have control of the movement of grain from the time it left the farmer until it reached the final buyer. This point of view was coming into question from more than a few members of the Company because of its tendency to overcentralize.

In the weeks following, the LRPC had a number of meetings with the divisions, and it is evident from the minutes that remain that these were far more serious sessions than in earlier efforts along these lines. The Grain Division was first and received the most scrutiny. A Barney Saunders report was generally optimistic, with winter wheat demand looking particularly good. An enigmatic comment probably held the key to the division's upcoming year: "Russians may buy after first of year." The outlook for the division seemed to turn on this Soviet possibility: "If the Russians do not buy, we will have a struggle to maintain present P&L balance. If they do buy, the position should improve . . . for a net of about $2.25 million or 6.5—7.0% return on invested capital." The division intended to move aggressively in closing some inefficient plants but also was looking ahead at new efforts, with a rice department suggested first.

The Vegetable Oil Division had an easier time—after all, it was the "star" of the previous year. But it too had some problems, for the Company had found it had been cheated on warehouse receipts for soybean oil in the developing Tino De Angelis scandal.

Anthony "Tino" De Angelis, the self-styled "salad oil king," apparently thought he could corner the market in soybean and cottonseed oil and began buying huge quantities of the oils, storing them in his Bayonne, New Jersey, tank farm. Or so he said! He financed his speculations by selling warehouse receipts for this supposedly stored oil, ultimately over $150 million worth, with most of the financial paper held by an American Express Company subsidiary, American Express Field Warehousing Company. AMEXCO decided in late 1963 to sell this paper, and an audit needed to accomplish the transaction turned up startlingly large shortages of the actual physical product at Bayonne. The De Angelis company (called Allied Crude Vegetable Oil Refining) went into bankruptcy, and De Angelis subsequently went to jail.

Once the De Angelis scam had become fully evident, hundreds of soybean oil processors who had depended upon the De Angelis operation as a storage vehicle for their oil found themselves bilked of very large amounts of this oil. Cargill had possibly massive potential losses here, too. Pete McVay reported, "Have $1.5 million involved. There are two possible ways to collect but these will take time." McVay suggested that this total sum "be set up as a reserve and put below the line so it does not distort current operating figures."

As of this point, Cargill appeared to have lost heavily in Tino's escapade. An Oil Division annual report for 1963–1964 told the story: "In November Tino went bankrupt and oil plummeted to 7¢ per lb. Meal prices had to absorb the decline in oil value. Hence, meal prices rose dramatically." The report ended poignantly, "We view the past year as a sort of arduous shakedown cruise, testing our organization and policies of past years."

The Company took a full write-off of the Allied loss, which came to $1,488,000; 50 percent of the loss subsequently was reflected in oil profits and the other half charged to nonoperating expense. A number of other grain trading companies took heavy hits too, with several of the "big six" (Cargill, Continental, Bunge, Dreyfus, Garnac, and Cook) being hard hit. The Vegetable Oil Division's annual report concluded: "We should not have made any sales to Allied. We made money on the decline. But we would have felt better had there been no open sales. Our losses (totally written off), if any, will be with American Express Warehousing and not with Allied Crude Vegetable Oil." Later, American Express assumed responsibility for the Allied losses and made restitution for some $60 million of the total creditor claims; Cargill received a partial return of its loss.

In the year 1963–1964, Cargill published its first "more-public" annual report, a printed document that went to bankers and selected people in the trade (but not in any way a public document). This public version did not contain any mention of the loss to Tino De Angelis.

Other than this upsetting special problem, the Oil Division looked to be in excellent shape. McVay put a substantial focus on his new efforts in France and "would prefer France ahead of Italy." The minutes noted: "The main concern Pete has is 'are we really prepared to do business in Italy with their ethics and moral attitudes.'"

The same process of analytical examination of each division extended through the rest of the organization. The 1962–1963 results and the subsequent Chase report had lit a fire under everyone.

Perhaps the single most important Company internal document of this period was Kelm's annual letter to the rest of the Cargill organization. This year's letter, dated July 8, 1963, went to "all Cargill office, sales, and supervisory employees." The tone was upbeat, with the accomplishments of the year all noted. Earnings were reported as being up for the year by 20 percent but "with the gain resulting largely from the acquisition of a majority interest in Tradax International, an overseas corporation located in Switzerland." The report discussed new facilities, the research accomplishments of the year, and the "remarkable success" of the public policy study group in respect to farm legislation.

The report then continued with a lengthy set of paragraphs on "increased efficiency and cost improvement." After listing a number of such efforts going on in the Company at this time, the section concluded, "Why all of the stress on costs? . . . It is because we firmly believe that cost improvement is a day-to-day problem and one that can be best licked in your office, your plant, or in your territory. You are closest to the point of expense origination and know best what can and should be done . . . you are in the best position to do something positive. There isn't a thing we do that cannot be done better!"

The last page viewed the outlook for the year ahead, again in positive terms. Once more, the conclusion was centered directly on the Cargill people themselves. "Dedicated, knowledgeable personnel is the answer to almost every management problem . . . in the final analysis it is people that provide the enthusiasm, the direction, and momentum for business success . . . we must consistently strive to create new opportunities to expand and to develop faster so that we need more people . . . not less. You are Cargill's most valuable asset."[17]

Nutrena and Tradax Brought Closer to Cargill

Two mergers in the 1962–1963 period related directly to the issue of tightening the organizational structure of the Company. The first involved Nutrena; this merger was mostly pro forma. The second, involving Tradax, had major substantive implications.

Since Cargill had acquired Nutrena in 1920, that corporation had kept itself separate in a legal sense, operating under the company name Nutrena Mills, Inc., a Kansas corporation. In actual practice, this had been accomplished by a management agreement each year, specifying the services of a general corporate nature that Cargill would provide to Nutrena. There was a management fee assessed by Cargill, based upon two charges, one a percentage of payroll dollars and another a percentage of Nutrena's net worth. In real terms, however, this primarily was treated as the usual divisional allocations from the corporation. From the Cargill management standpoint, there was no real difference between Nutrena and, for example, the Grain Division.

This last statement must be immediately amended in respect to the Nutrena esprit de corps. Nutrena people always had felt they stood at arm's length from Cargill, and the separate value system of a Nutrena approach was clearly evident, particularly strong in the earlier years but in evidence right down to 1962.

The merger was consummated in the board meeting of November 2, 1962, effective at the end of the year. But Jim North, president of Nutrena, had described the essence of the change in a *Cargill News* article in June of that year. North pointed out "this is merely a mechanical change within our corporate family" but that such action "will bring about much simplification in corporate reporting to all of the states, as well as the federal government, preparation, filing and paying of state and federal taxes, economies and uniformity in forms and procedures." North vowed that the Nutrena name would continue to be used vigorously and that, while the name Cargill would begin appearing on some of the Nutrena brands, the whole process would be "orderly and gradual." North wanted to make perfectly clear that "your job is the same, your benefits all continue, your opportunities are as great—we want to grow and grow." He ended, "If you have any question about what this means to you personally—in a nutshell, I can tell you it's business as usual."[18]

The Tradax reorganization was at a different level of complexity and importance. Since its formation in the mid-1950s, Tradax had been owned not by Cargill, Incorporated, but by means of a combination of stock held by members of the Cargill and MacMillan families (including their ownership of the Swiss Salevia Foundation, another shareholder) and nominal amounts by Erv Kelm and Fred Seed from the U.S. company; all these stocks were held individually. At the time of Tradax's formation, it had made particular sense to John Jr. and other members of the family that Tradax be fully a European operation, for the families seriously had contemplated at several points moving most or even all of Cargill to Switzerland.

After almost a decade of operation, the downside of this sharp, almost arbitrary break between the two companies began to trouble Cargill executives. Involved here was considerably more than just cleaning up a few duplications in reporting, as in the Nutrena case. The difficulties lay along a number of lines.

First, Tradax initially had been startlingly undercapitalized, and a degree of this had remained right up to this point. Fortunately, despite this ostensible lack of an adequate capital base, Tradax had had great success. Earnings had been maintained as surplus, rather than being repatriated to the United States, there to be subject to U.S. tax. But this had become an unbalanced capital structure. The Tradax annual report for 1961–1962 put this very well: "Our balance sheet is in good shape from the point of view of working capital, the Company being very liquid. Our European banking friends continue to be concerned, however, with the capital structure of the Company. There is too little in capital and too much in surplus. Our bankers point out correctly that the surplus can be declared out in dividends at any time, and our capital does not provide sufficient protection for them."

Indeed, the investment in 1961 by the common shareholders was only $18,646 out of a capital stock on the balance sheet of $1,376,876. As Hubert Sontheim, a Tradax lawyer (and husband of Marion MacMillan, John Jr.'s daughter) put it, "This is certainly unusual. Remarks in that direction were recently made by Credit Suisse. The Bank expressed some astonishment at the fact that Tradax Internacional . . . did declare dividends on preferred stock even in bad years, while the Company was relying extensively on bank credits."

Beyond this imbalance problem, there were serious organizational qualms about the relationship between Cargill and Tradax. Not only were the incentive and bonus systems of Tradax sharply different from those of Cargill, the lines of organizational authority and responsibility seemed so often to be unclear. Many times Tradax seemed to Cargill executives to be "marching to its own drum," more than occasionally stepping on the toes of a Cargill executive's effort. A Tradax executive later looked back on this tension and commented, "Probably the most serious charge against Tradax and Geneva and the basis for an uncomfortable sense of 'hostility' which seems to be pervading other divisions of Cargill . . . is that it is not a part of the Cargill culture. It is not clear whether the charge is that Tradax has never been part of that culture, or that it has been in the process of breaking away from that culture. In any case, this hostility is widely felt in Geneva today and is disturbing to morale, to say the least."

While these allegations were hard to pin down, it seemed to senior management in Cargill that "the rogue elephant needed to be corralled" (as one executive put it). Operationally, there seemed to be a number of areas, not just personnel policy but in trading operations and others, in which closer linkages could make for a more effective total organization.

Beyond all of these knotty managerial issues, there were underlying tax considerations, too. One of the basic family *and* company goals had always been to minimize taxes. Indeed, this almost primitive dislike of paying taxes had been carried to a fault by Cargill MacMillan Sr. and had permeated both family and Company decision making for many years. With the U.S. tax code changing often and turning in this period more negatively against any tax shelter, it seemed that the existing Tradax posture as a totally European entity and not a division of Cargill was harder and harder to defend.

A plan now evolved to have Cargill purchase from Tradax shareholders enough ownership to guarantee majority control. This would, of course, have tax implications for Cargill but was believed to offer important trade-offs in the process of strengthening the Tradax capital structure. This reorganization plan went through an amazingly complex set of steps; it was not only a tax lawyer's nightmare but also a difficult one to design in terms of the restructuring of management relationships. Detailing each step in this saga here would be counterproductive. Perhaps the best summary statement about the Tradax reorganization was given by Erv Kelm when he wrote in June 1962 (just a month before the final plan was approved), in a letter to the members of the two families:

The plan is simply this: Tradax would authorize additional shares of equity stock in sufficient number and amount so that these newly issued equity shares, when being sold to Cargill . . . would give 55% ownership and control to Cargill, Incorporated. The present holders of Class A, namely The Salevia Foundation, and Class B Common stockholders would keep their present shares until such time as it was decided what disposal should be made of them, if any. The ultimate disposal of the present Class A Common in Salevia and the Class B would depend on what type of a tax bill, if any, is forthcoming from the Congress this year.

Thus, at the present time after Cargill buys this newly authorized stock, Cargill would have 55% ownership and control and if it was decided after the advent of the new tax bill that it was desirable to have Salevia and the Class B Common stockholders make disposition of their stock, Cargill might wind up with either 75 percent ownership and control or 100 percent ownership and control. . . . At the present expected value of equity stock in Tradax, this would require an expenditure by Cargill . . . of about $6,000,000; however, since Cargill would have 55 percent control, our auditors would allow us to consolidate the statements of Tradax into our overall balance sheet and profit and loss, so that this would not affect the working capital position.

While this was the final plan voted by the Cargill board of directors on July 27, 1962, the details in several respects went through further reiterations at later points. The total amount of money paid by Cargill, Incorporated, was actually $6,607,459. The 55 percent ownership did become 70 percent within a few months, as plans were made for phasing out the Class B common stock (the stock held by the families and the nominal shares of Cargill senior management—Erv Kelm and Fred Seed).

The plan was carried out through an intermediary, a Canadian Cargill company named Cargill Manitoba. Classes of stock in Tradax and in Cargill Manitoba had to be adjusted, and there were other complexities relating to tax implications and relationships between the families and the Company. In essence, however, the Kelm statement gave a useful overall "keyhole" view of the entire transaction.

Both further memoranda and many face-to-face meetings would be necessary to make precise these complex arrangements in organizational terms. A Don Levin memorandum in October 1962 spelled out some of the dimensions of the management side of the decision:

... the new subsidiary would operate the business exactly as it has in the past, with the same personnel and from the same locations. The new subsidiary will have to have sufficient working capital to carry the trades and will have to establish bank lines as required. For the latter purpose, the guaranty of Cargill, Incorporated will presumably be available. As operating economies can be worked out, and staff and operating personnel of the Cargill group of Companies can be utilized, appropriate changes will be made in the operating structures and procedures in the international business. From an internal point of view in Cargill, Incorporated the international operations will have a division status equivalent to that of the Grain and Oil Division.

Levin pointed out that Tradax "will operate as an investment company," willing to invest money it might have available in cash and through its borrowing power for facilities of various sorts abroad in which *any* of the Cargill group of companies might be interested.

The announcement of the transition was made to employees in the Company house newsletter, the *Green Wave*, in September; it was terse, stressing only that no changes in the organization of Tradax were contemplated and that Kelm would be elected to the board of Tradax. "Tradax will continue to operate essentially as it has in the past." The significant sum of money that had been transferred from Cargill (including some of its "special reserves") made some senior management members uneasy in freezing such a large amount of capital in an operating company. However, the advantages of a cleaner organizational structure appeared to overbalance any of these concerns.[19]

A Russian Bombshell: Wheat Purchases

The U.S.S.R. had been a minor player in the world wheat arena for a number of years, but after the cold war settled in during the late 1940s, it did little trade with the Allied powers; almost none had been directly with the United States. Tradax, as Cargill's European arm, had done a very small amount of trading with Eastern Europe and Russia. But often as not, Russia was a seller rather than a buyer.

In September 1963, a startling happenstance changed all of this. In the face of persistent rumors of a shortfall in the Russian grain crop, Canada closed an agreement to sell the Soviet Union nearly $500 million worth of wheat, the largest sale of grain for delivery in one year ever transacted. To make matters more complicated, Cuba was to be a direct beneficiary of part of this sale. Canada's Minister of Trade and Commerce, who had negotiated the agreement, noted that the United States had been informed about the segment going to Cuba and that Canada had received no objections.

The huge size of this sale astonished a great many people in the trade. Even

← Breaking Bread Together

↓ On Stage

The Press looks at the Russian Grain Sales.

'WHAT BIG TEETH YOU HAVE'

—Harold Maples, Star-Telegram Cartoonist
Fort Worth Star Telegram

more surprising was a spate of new disclosures about the current state of Russian agriculture. The Soviet grain crop for 1963 was down at least 10 percent, and with Soviet officials being unwilling to cut the wheat and flour allocations for its own people or to lessen its continuing concessionary sales to Eastern Europe and to Cuba, a massive foreign purchase was required. This Russian desire for wheat supplies seemed to indicate virtual chaos in the Russian system, part of which was being attributed to natural causes (drought had been reported in many parts of the country). But many analysts felt that the Soviet agricultural policy itself was a significant problem. The *New York Times* commented, "It reflects serious internal difficulties for the Soviet Union, already beset by its intense ideological struggle with China. . . . Ten years ago this month Nikita Khrushchev won the center of the stage in post-Stalin Russia . . . by delivering a slashing speech exposing Soviet agricultural weaknesses and proposing radical reforms. Since then, Soviet farming has constantly been his main domestic concern. Now Premier Khrushchev has had to take the radical—and for him personally humiliating step—of buying $500,000,000 worth of wheat and wheat flour . . . after all his torrent of words about the 'superiority' of socialist agriculture."

A few days later, rumors began to circulate that the Soviets also were striving to buy wheat in the United States. This would require a sharp change in U.S. policy, which by this cold war period banned the export of any items that would contribute to the strength of Communist economies. However, both Secretary of Commerce Luther Hodges and Agriculture Secretary Orville Freeman supported a policy change. Any sale of wheat would require presidential approval.

Farmers had long opposed trading with the Communist bloc, although now there appeared to be some wavering on this, given the manifestly large wheat surplus and the opportunity to be a party to rising wheat prices. However, the farmers wanted these wheat sales to occur only on their own terms—that any sale be at "our price." This was defined as a sale at the domestic price of wheat, at this time about $1.80 a bushel, which was considerably higher than the current price on the world market. Only by a government export subsidy of some $.50 a bushel could this high domestic price compete in the world market.

Over the succeeding weeks, the debate within the United States raged over whether the country should help the Soviets. Several senators accused the administration of pursuing a policy of appeasement that would intensify the Kremlin's grip on Cuba. (Interestingly, there was bipartisan support in Congress for *each* side of this debate.) The International Longshoremen's Association (I.L.A.) was a particularly vehement critic. Thomas Gleason, the union's president, sent a telegram to the Department of Agriculture stating that "the membership and officials of this Union are baffled as to why our government even contemplates providing economic aid to an ideological enemy who has vowed to bury us economically. . . . The longshoremen of the United States would probably gain more money and wages than any other American working men if the United States decided to trade with Russia. Nevertheless, we are not interested in any of this so-called 'easy money' and are going to object vigorously to loading any such cargo."

In the midst of this brouhaha, the grain companies themselves were presented with a ticklish dilemma. Several middle-level companies, under the leadership of the I. S. Joseph Company, the International Milling Company, and the Archer Daniels Midland Corporation—together with one of the "big six," the Louis Dreyfus Company—invited other members of the industry, particularly the other five of the "big six," to Ottawa, Canada, to discuss establishing a cartel-like entity under the auspices of an obscure, antediluvian law still on the books of the United States, the Webb-Pomerene Act. Passed in 1918, this law allowed exemption from antitrust liability under the Sherman Act for combinations entered into for the sole purpose of engaging in the export trade.

The question of whether a cartel should be used as a trading device with the Soviets was not an irrelevant notion, for Russia used a single state trading company entity (called Amtorg) to make its grain trading decisions; and similarly, Canada did all of its international selling through a public entity, the Canadian Wheat Board. There were very few Webb-Pomerene associations actually in operation; the strong antitrust laws of the United States placed such organizations out of the mainstream of American competitive policy. Still, should the United States use such a single corporation to do its international wheat trading?

All of the major grain trading companies attended the conference, called by Burton Joseph, president of the company carrying his name and the spark plug for the idea. Barney Saunders and Bob Diercks attended for Cargill, and the group, which now totaled around 30 companies, went into intensive private meetings.

Within 36 hours, Cargill and Continental, the two largest companies involved, had pulled out of the negotiations. Cargill issued a public statement rejecting the whole idea because "the Joseph Group could not assure that the wheat would come from current production through the open market," and Cargill could not substantiate claims that the plan had been sought or supported by the administration and Congress. The proposed combine seemed to both Cargill and Continental to rule out normal competition, and both felt that this was neither required nor justified. Cargill's statement concluded, "We are quite willing to compete with all other exporters in filling sales." With its two largest companies unwilling to join, the Webb-Pomerene proposal collapsed.

Now the pace of the pro and con arguments about a possible Soviet sale stepped up. Senator Dodd spoke in the Senate: "It is argued that this is a true horse trade, they get wheat, which they need. We get gold, which we need. What nonsense: Gold means nothing to the Communists; wheat means everything. We do not need their gold, they desperately need our wheat. Let them pay the price for it, not in gold bars but in concessions to the cause of freedom." With wheat prices rising by the day—up in early October to $1.80 a bushel from around $1.60—the view of the President was eagerly awaited.

On October 10, in a major announcement, President Kennedy authorized wheat sales to the Russians totaling $250 million. In his text, the President stated, "This particular decision . . . is not inconsistent with many smaller transactions over a long period of time, [and] does not represent a new Soviet-American trade policy. That must await the settlement of many matters. But it does represent one more hopeful sign that a more peaceful world is both possible and beneficial to us all."

The protocol also allowed sales to Soviet-bloc countries, with Czechoslovakia, Bulgaria, and Hungary already having made such requests. With $60 million in grain sales authorized here, that would bring the total sale to $310 million. Kennedy made clear that the world market price would govern, that the export subsidy paid by the United States was not a subsidy to a foreign purchaser but an aid to American farmers. Kennedy emphasized that "the Russian people will know they are receiving 'American wheat,'" a question that had been raised by opponents of the sale.

The President also implied that the Commerce Department would prevent any company from getting "an excessive share of the sale." A grain merchant commented that he hoped that "the Government wouldn't slice up the pie for us . . . we want to do the business in open competition." (The press was reporting that no single company could take more than 25 percent.)

The *New York Times* commented: "What the President said about the grain transaction suggests that much of the present United States trade policy toward the Soviet Union is obsolete. For years, this country has prohibited sale to the Soviet Union and to Eastern Europe of many goods which the Communist world can buy freely from our NATO allies in Western Europe. It only makes sense that in the wake of the wheat agreement the Senate Foreign Relations Committee is planning to take a careful look at the whole complex of present policies and laws restricting trade with a Communist bloc."

The first company to receive feelers about an Eastern bloc grain sale was Cargill. Early in October, Tradax representatives in Europe learned that Hungary was in the market for several thousand tons of U.S. grain, with payment to be in dollars. Cargill began the negotiations and soon reached an agreement on both quantity and price—provided that the United States was able to issue a license within eight days. The total amount was to be 100,000 tons. John McGrory of the Law Department and John Cole from the Grain Division went to Washington to ascertain the government's attitude toward the sale. "The first formal application," *Cargill News* wrote, "made it evident to the Administration that a decision must be made soon . . . the President and his foreign policy advisors did not want to get into the position of offering grain . . . and then have Russia say she didn't want any. On the other hand, if there was firm desire to buy, a United States refusal could blunt the basic thrust of the Administration's foreign policy [for] East/West relations." President Kennedy privately sounded out the Soviet ambassador to the United States and learned that the answer was yes.

Kennedy had made one further proviso for any possible sale, namely, that the grain moving to the Soviet bloc would be moved in American-flag ships, to the extent that they were available. Just as with the farmers' subsidies, there was a substantial differential on the shipping prices under U.S. flag ships and lower rates from ships of other than American registry. The Hungarians made it clear that they were not going to pay higher rates just to ship on American bottoms, and the deal was temporarily shelved.

In late October, a Russian delegation arrived in the country, ready to buy wheat—but not ready to pay American shipping rates. The I.L.A. allowed that they would load ships to go to the Soviet Union, although Gleason, the dock workers' union president, said the members would load the grain with certain restrictions: "We do not intend to load a ship that flies the hammer and sickle." Premier Khrushchev added his own warnings—that the Soviet Union would not buy its wheat if the transaction had "any strings attached," that discriminatory conditions would not be acceptable to the Soviet Union.

Since 1936, the U.S. Cargo Preference Act had required that U.S. ships transport 50 percent of all exports for which the government had advanced long-term credits or guarantees. This "50/50" rule applied primarily to grains sold under P.L. 480, the "Food for Peace" provisions. In those cases, the foreign buyer, using local currency, paid freight charges at foreign-flag rates, with a premium on behalf of U.S.-flag rates paid directly to the shipping companies by the federal government. The U.S.-flag requirements had never been applied to commercial exports, goods paid for in gold or other hard currency.

Finally, major grain company officers were called to Washington to attempt to resolve the impasse. Erv Kelm represented Cargill, and the presidents of Continental Grain, Bunge, and Dreyfus were also there. Just at this point, Cargill had negotiated a second provisional contract with Hungary, raising the total to 220,000 tons. The Maritime Administration now granted an export license to Cargill for its first 100,000-ton sale, waiving a proportion of the U.S.-flag requirement because of "intensive efforts . . . to obtain American flag shipping resulting in securing only 9,000 tons needed." By the time Cargill was ready to ship its full Hungarian contract for 220,000 tons, some 54,000 tons of the total of 220,000 tons was to be carried by U.S. ships. The *New York Times* headlined on November 7: "Impasse on shipping rates broken—100,000 tons for Hungary licensed." The Cargill contract, for about $7.6 million, included the cost of shipping.

Still remaining was any consummation of a sale directly to the Soviet Union. The situation was complicated in mid-November when the Soviets arrested an American professor visiting in the Soviet Union, Frederick Barghoorn, who was accused of being on an intelligence mission. Immediately, the issue of a wheat sale was thrown in doubt. A week later, Barghoorn was released; Albanian radio accused Khrushchev of having released Barghoorn "because he feared that Moscow's wheat deal with the United States might collapse" and of "backing down before imperialists."

A further complication now arose. The Export/Import Bank had agreed to make regular commercial loans at the existing 5 percent level, but a number of congressmen objected. A bill was introduced by Senator Karl Mundt of South Dakota, a major wheat state, proposing that sales could be made only for dollars or gold. The ban was killed in the Senate by a vote of 57 to 35; a parallel effort in the House also was beaten back, 189 to 151.

As the weeks dragged on, issues relating to the shipping rates continued to simmer. In early December, the Soviet negotiating delegation returned to the U.S.S.R. Bill Pearce was quoted in the national press as believing that this development "did not indicate they have broken off negotiations"—Pearce said that he still was optimistic about eventual wheat sales to the Russians.

Just after Christmas, a breakthrough came for sales directly to Russia. Continental Grain obtained two licenses for a total sale of 700,000 tons of wheat, valued at more than $40 million. Within days, Continental had signed a full agreement with Russia. But by the end of January, once again there was difficulty in contracting for obtaining U.S. bottoms for the huge Continental shipments. At this point Continental requested a partial waiver, and the Maritime Administration agreed, issuing a statement that said in part, "Approximately 76 percent of the portion designated for U.S. flag ships (38 percent of the total sale) will go in American bottoms." The final Continental contract called for a total of one million tons.

On February 6, Cargill too announced a sale to Russia, this time for 700,000 tons of wheat. The sale had been negotiated in Moscow by representatives of Tradax companies from both Geneva and London and called for 500,000 tons of winter wheat for shipment in February and March and another 200,000 of durum wheat for shipment in May. *Cargill News* explained, "The durum, when accepted by the Russians, was a key to the sale, as it had been in the Continental Grain sale, because the Agriculture Department's unusually high subsidy for large quantities of durum enables sellers to meet, in part, at least, the additional cost of the special shipping requirements."

No sooner had Cargill celebrated the exciting sale than the I.L.A. threw a monkey wrench into both the Cargill and Continental efforts. On February 16, the I.L.A. ordered a halt to *all* loadings for the Soviet Union. The partial waiver to Continental had infuriated Gleason and Paul Hall, president of the Seafarers International Union, representing the merchant sailors on U.S. vessels, both on the lakes and inland waters and the oceans. The two men asserted that the original proposal for half of the grain to be transported on

American ships had not worked out in practice—the Continental waiver was a case in point. Gleason suggested that American ships could be taken out of mothballs, if necessary, to provide additional American vessels. Secretary of Commerce Hodges rejected this idea and accused Gleason himself of trying personally to make America's foreign policy.

Finally, nine days later, the dock unions dropped the boycott. President Lyndon Johnson, now in office after the assassination of President Kennedy, agreed that the government would stick by its requirement that 50 percent of the wheat sold would be in American bottoms. "Settlement of the nine-day boycott appeared to be a victory for the International Longshoremen's Association," the *New York Times* stated, but this "did not indicate a government surrender," for the waiver to Continental was retained and the government had made it clear that the door was not closed to further waivers if ship shortages again prevented adherence to the 50/50 requirement. The *Times* concluded: "The boycott was itself an unconscionable act; it would have been disastrous if it had ended in anything more than a restatement of the government's previously fixed policy."

Cargill, faced with no opportunity for a waiver, was aided by a Russian government agreement to allow "deep-draft supertankers," which were unable to enter that country's ports, to anchor offshore and transfer Cargill's wheat to dockside elevators in small boats (with the additional costs of such unloading assumed by the shipowners).

In mid-March, Cargill announced that it not only had met the U.S. flag requirements on its 700,000-ton sale but had exceeded it by chartering 354,500 tons of U.S. shipping. The Cargill shipments were made very much simpler by the supertanker agreement.

Back in March 1963, Cargill had had experience with the supertankers in loading grain to Poland. In the week of March 11, 1963, the merchant ship *Manhattan*, the largest commercial ship ever built in the United States and the largest to fly this country's flag, had arrived at Norfolk to take on wheat. This was the *Manhattan*'s first grain cargo since the gargantuan ship had gone into service in February of 1962. It was 940 feet long with a 132 foot beam, roughly the length of three football fields and the width of one. The vessel was rated at 106,500 deadweight tons fully loaded. It would then attain a draft of over 50 feet. Cargill's Norfolk terminal was able to load only about 22,000 tons of wheat because of the port's lesser depth; the vessel then sailed to Cargill's Baton Rouge terminal to take on another 45,000 long tons, for a total of 67,000, or more than 2,500,000 bushels. This topped the world-record loading of grain by several thousand long tons. Even here the vessel could not be fully loaded because of that deep draft and certainly would not have been able to unload at a Russian port other than by using the offloading small-vessel combination.

The physical loading of the *Manhattan* itself was a major problem, as the

A colossal cargo of 65,550 long tons of wheat for export went aboard the 940-foot-long S/S Manhattan from Cargill's Eastern Region elevator at Norfolk and from the Southern Region elevator at Baton Rouge. An indicator of the ship's size—the largest merchant vessel afloat— is that its cargo would equal more than 1,300 railroad boxcars (Cargill News, May 1963).

ship dwarfed the loading gantries at Norfolk, and the existing spouts would not reach all of the loading areas. Special chutes had to be developed. When the vessel was fully loaded it drew 32 feet, an adequate margin to keep out of the mud, which was 35 feet under the surface. The *Manhattan* and two other supertankers, the *Transeastern* and the *Ocean Ulla*, were later used for further Russian loadings.

Cargill's press announcement highlighted the fact that the Company had met the 50/50 American bottom requirement without asking for any waivers. A statement under Erv Kelm's signature concluded, "We are aware that U.S. ship owners are saddled with higher construction and manning costs than their foreign competitors. But any attempt to overcome this cost disadvantage by simply ordering the use of U.S. flags is self-defeating. The U.S. has vigorous competition from other suppliers of farm products—particularly wheat. If we insist on a premium for our farm exports to cover higher costs of U.S. flags, importing countries with dollars to spend will simply go elsewhere."[20]

The sets of trades accomplished by the two companies—Continental and Cargill—ended by being all that the Russians were willing to buy. Likely they had what they needed at this point. But the long imbroglio over the "U.S.

"Well, she made it to Baton Rouge. The S/S Manhattan, *first introduced in the April issue as she was tied at the Cargill elevator in Norfolk, is taking on 44,250 long tons of wheat in Baton Rouge, to be added to 21,300 received at Norfolk. The full cargo bound for Poland would fill a freight train of more than 1,300 cars"* (*Cargill News*, May 1963).

bottoms" certainly did not help the situation. President Kennedy had promised that no company would get an "excessive share," and later this had been defined by the press as being no more than 25 percent. It ended with Continental having 58 percent; Cargill, 42 percent. But given the skittishness of the Soviets throughout, any effort by the U.S. government to "manage" the percentages could easily have doomed the whole venture. In truth, the sales turned out to be a one-shot windfall. The Russians' crops improved the very next year, and they did not return to the United States for any significant grain purchases for the rest of the decade.

"Comfort Levels" Rise Markedly

It is difficult to overestimate the impact of these Russian wheat purchases on the Company as a whole. After the disappointing 1962–1963 results, a real sense of angst had pervaded Cargill's management. The Chase Manhattan Bank's cautionary, indeed, critical report had come out in the fall of 1963, adding to this anxiety.

By June of 1964, all had changed. Net earnings had jumped to $7.7 million, up from the $4.3 million of 1962–1963 (with Tradax merged, its earnings for the two years are included in both these figures). This was the second-highest return in the Company's history, exceeded only by the $9.1 million figure of 1958–1959. A downward trend that had begun in 1961–1962 now was reversed. The combined profits of both the Grain Division and Tradax accounted for most of the upsurge, with "the Russian business . . . the underlying spark," as the annual report put it.

Barney Saunders wrote in the Grain Division report: "The benefits to our organization by the consummation of this trade are almost incalculable." While Saunders meant this to include the entire organization, it was true many times over for the division itself. "Here is what the Iron Curtain trades did for the division," Saunders continued. "We liquidated a long wheat position at the proper time (which allowed us to go short wheat at the proper time); we liquidated a long ocean freight position at the proper time (which allowed us to go short ocean freight at the proper time)." In addition, Saunders tabulated the "good elevating margins at several elevators," allowing a useful mix on various grades of durum. "We believe our trading income of $30,178,000 to be a new record . . . it should be borne in mind, however, that of this . . . $3,153,000 came from profits in the basic hedge. The bulk of this profit resulted from a long wheat position taken when the Russians indicated buying interest and a short wheat position begun at the completion of the Russian trade."

The Tradax annual report was frank about this propitious move to the short side of the market: "Our close position with the Russians enabled us to predict accurately that they would buy no more wheat after our sale, and, when known, this would cause weakness in the . . . market." Still, "Eastern Europe remains as difficult as ever to extract information [from] . . . we do know that Russia has urgent need to increase sharply her livestock population, so it seems likely that she will import feed grains and also will not be able to supply any of her neighbours, thereby causing them to import from the West." Walter Gage, however, did not foresee any significant purchases of wheat in the upcoming year.

Across the Company, it had been, in the main, a good year for everyone. Properties all over the country had been upgraded, obsolete ones discarded. Cargo Carriers made sizable additions to its facilities, and this included a major Mississippi towboat, which was christened the *John H. MacMillan, Jr.* Working capital for the Company had climbed to over $60 million, for an increase of $2.5 million over the preceding year. The total net sales to customers approached another milestone for the Company by rising to $1.98 billion, a gain of 15 percent over the prior year and almost nudging the two billion mark. The net earnings for the year were equal to 0.40 cents on each dollar of sales, compared with 0.25 cents the year before.

In this first year of the innovation in reporting—the formal "Cargill Annual Report" for shareholders, the Company's major bankers, and other business links—the message was upbeat. The various specifics of the year, always included in the internal annual reports, were summarized for this more public version. It concluded: "Primary objectives for this year are to increase feed sales and earnings, to realize the full potential from salt, fishmeal, and molasses, improve corn belt grain origination, win our court fight with the CEA [a story for the next chapter], pursue further cost reductions, and continue to lead our industry in national and international policy affecting our business." The report was over Erv Kelm's signature, and he concluded, "There is no question in my mind that we have all the resources—the personnel, the will, the programs—to make next year, Cargill's 100th year, the greatest in its history."

Anticipating this anniversary, the editors of *Business Week* had written a comprehensive, quite substantive article on what the Company was doing and where it was going. Its concluding section, entitled "Like Harvard and Yale," presented an intriguing thesis. The editors first discussed "one of the most extraordinary aspects of Cargill," that it had been able to grow so large without recourse to public equity financing and public control. "Several elements," said *Business Week*, "kept the Company private. First, the Cargills and the MacMillans come from Scotch Presbyterian stock that believes in hard work and careful spending. To say that the Company's dividend policy is meager is an understatement. Whitney MacMillan actually calls it a 'negative dividend policy.'" Another element in the Cargill success story that was "absolutely essential," said Kelm (quoted in the article), "was to recruit and hold the best possible people." The management training program established 30 years earlier had been an outstanding success, Kelm being a prime case in point. In order to hold senior management, stock options and other financial carrots had been given, but the real factor had been "to give them every bit as much opportunity for promotion as members of the family. . . . In this lies perhaps the most ingenious element in keeping Cargill private and well managed."

Then *Business Week* recalled how, back in the 1930s, John Jr., Austen Cargill, and Cargill MacMillan had studied organizations like Harvard and the Hudson Bay Company and had concluded that there needed to be a balance within the board itself. "The result," wrote the editors, "Cargill now has a nine member board . . . the non-family management stock elects one director; all the voting stock as a whole elects four directors. This means that as long as the family sticks together it can elect the four." Four additional directors were elected by the Cargill Foundation, a charitable trust, itself managed by one member of the family: one Cargill officer not in the family, one former member of management, and two outside directors. "As long as management is doing a good job," Whitney MacMillan told the *Business Week* editors, "there is no chance for the family to oust it. I think it is a great system; it preserves the best values of our Company. And you know where we got it? From the trustee system that governs institutions like Harvard and Yale."[21]

If there had been any unsteadiness in the Company after the two years of downturn under its new Kelm regime, the results of 1963–1964 gave everyone a feeling of increased stability for the future. Cargill was a much tighter ship at the end of 1963–1964 (if a Cargo Carriers analogy can be permitted). For senior management, it was a more directed, more motivated group; for Kelm, the positive results reaffirmed his basic instincts, his managerial ego.

Truly, angst was out, confidence was in!

CHAPTER TWO

A Return, an Unexpected Result

O ne of John MacMillan, Jr.'s most enduring legacies now came under scrutiny. Back in the late 1930s, when Cargill collectively and John Jr. individually had lost the famous "corn case," the initial antagonist against both was the Chicago Board of Trade (through its Business Conduct Committee). Later, the federal courts confirmed the CBOT ruling. John Jr. maintained that he and the Company both should have won the case. Harboring harsh feelings against the CBOT, he pulled Cargill completely out of the exchange. As time went on, despite the many difficulties that this caused in the Company's trading, John Jr. remained adamantly opposed to going back.

Now Erv Kelm proposed to reverse this long-standing decision. Early in the year 1962, Kelm asked a combined staff and operating committee to look at the advisability of the corporation itself or one of its subsidiaries applying for a renewal of its membership, in the process also contemplating a "clearing" membership at the CBOT. This working group made a strong case supporting the notion, and at the May 1962 board meeting, Kelm appointed an ad hoc board committee to make a final recommendation. Bob Diercks chaired it, and it included Fred Seed, Bert Egermayer, and Ted Young (with Cal Anderson as secretary). Reporting at the July 25, 1962, board meeting, they unanimously recommended moving ahead "at once." Most compelling was the estimate that there would be annual savings of "roughly $350,000." The committee felt that there would be no serious compromise of Cargill's proprietary financial information and saw no other adverse side effects.

Certain caveats were registered, however. First, the Company should take an "active" role. Further, "we must conduct ourselves with discretion in our futures trading, particularly in view of the fact that Cargill's position at any one time could be a substantial part of the open interest." Some members of the operating group felt that it might be good tactics to continue to clear some portion of the Company's trades through other members, "to help conceal Cargill's total position." The board committee recommended otherwise, urging that the membership be in the name of the Company alone.

The full board concurring, the Company moved forthwith to once again become a member of the CBOT. In the process, it also became a member of the Clearing Corporation. This was a separate entity located at the CBOT that provided three critical services. It acted as a surrogate holder of the other side of every futures contract; although there always were two parties for each contract—a buyer and a seller—each dealt only with the clearing house, rather than having to know each one of the individuals or companies on the other side of their contracts. In addition, the clearing-house allocated physical delivery rights and obligations at the expiration of a futures contract, and it insured against defaults. Thus the clearing corporation was a highly responsible and absolutely essential piece of the futures trading effort.[1]

This return to the CBOT after more than two decades of standing aloof now takes on special poignancy, for within the very first year back in the Exchange, Cargill became enmeshed in a major regulatory battle with the Commodity Exchange Authority (CEA), which alleged that Cargill had traded illegally in one of the most important of all CBOT contracts.

The Futures Market

Cash wheat is bought and sold on many commodity exchanges, but mostly at three key places: the Minneapolis Grain Exchange (handling, particularly, high-protein northern spring wheat), the Kansas City Board of Trade (handling hard winter wheat), and the CBOT (handling, particularly, soft red winter wheat). All this cash wheat trading is for spot prices, moving up and down, day by day, in an endless array of prices.

All three of these key exchanges also trade futures contracts for these various types and grades of wheat. Here "contracts" are established on a staggered basis; for the wheats, there will be four separate contracts for each calendar year, one each in March, May, July, and December. For these, the grades are standardized, and the quantity traded for each contract of wheat at the three exchanges is always 5,000 bushels. All of these contracts, just like cash grain, are traded daily, with prices moving up or down depending upon the complex bargaining that goes on each day. The difference between a cash contract and a future is that the former is for specific physical grain, traded and delivered at that price. In the case of a futures contract, these are "paper" trades all during the contract period, up to the point of its specific termination date. Those who hold one or more "buy" contracts are "long" in the market. If the long waits to this termination date, he or she *will* receive physical grain for this. Similarly, those who purchase a "sell" contract are "short" in the market. If a short holds a contract until the termination date, the short is obligated to deliver physical product. Usually, futures contracts are settled before physical delivery, but occasionally actual delivery is required to settle the contract; for example, a long could continue to hold contracts beyond the termination in order to ensure delivery needed for product already sold or for its own further processing, as in crushing soybeans for meal and oil.

Futures contracts can be settled *during* the period before the termination date by an offsetting sale or purchase in a second "paper" trade. Whether one profits or loses in this transaction depends upon the prices in effect at the time of the initial acquiring of the contract related to the price at the time of relinquishing the contract by this paper trade.

One of the key functions provided by the futures market is the ability to "hedge," where this process of acquiring at one point and relinquishing at a later point can be used to counterbalance efforts in the physical market itself and thus give protection against price movements. In a given futures market—for example, wheat—there will be a significant number of individuals and companies using the market as hedgers. In addition, there will be others who will be trading futures, not with any real interest in the physical grain but for the opportunity to make money by speculating on price movements in the futures contract. In any given futures market, there will be a significant number of speculators, likely considerably more than hedgers. (Incidentally, the same basic concept applies to hundreds of other futures markets—in a wide range of agricultural products, foreign exchange trading, and many others; the contracts are described differently and the physical amounts are different, but the principle is the same.)

There is one feature found in agricultural futures that is not characteristic of other futures arenas: most agricultural products have seasons dictated by the weather. Therefore, one of the contracts for a given agricultural commodity will be the last contract of the season—roughly, at the end of the crop that year. That contract will be the "old crop" contract, and the next contract period will be the beginning of the "new crop." Sometimes there can be short-term shortages or overages as the crop comes in that will produce rapid price movements upward or downward. These make for excitement, particularly for the speculators in the market.

The CBOT's May contract for soft red winter wheat is one of the best known of the old-crop endings. Traders look forward to what many of them have dubbed "Miss May." May 1963 was expected to represent one of the wilder ones for CBOT May wheat; in the weeks preceding the May 21, 1963, termination of the contract, there were many cautionary signs about the size of the crop available for sale. At these termination dates of contracts, all contracts that have not been previously liquidated by an opposite and offsetting transaction now must be liquidated, both by the long accepting the product and the short producing the product. Alternatively, one can bargain for a monetary settlement basis, but this will be done directly with an individual on the other side of the market (remembering that all through the contract period, contracts were essentially with the clearinghouse as a holder, rather than with another individual).[2]

Now to the Cargill story.

May 1963—the Company Goes Long

In early 1963, Cargill traders had felt that there would be an ample supply of soft red winter wheat at the end of the crop year and hence had recommended that the Company hedge its inventory by selling May 1963 wheat futures at the CBOT. In early March, this position had risen to more than 8 million bushels. There were no limits mandated by the CEA on the total size of such holdings as long as these were held as a bona fide hedge; however, no single speculator was allowed to hold above two million bushels.

However, in February and on into March, mills in the southwestern part of the United States began to buy soft red winter wheat, an irregular movement for this variety prompted by an unusual combination of freight rates that made it economical to ship from the Midwest to the Southwest. Also in March, Cargill learned that the Spanish government was indicating substantial interest in purchasing large quantities of soft red winter wheat; Cargill expected it would be a strong contender for these sales. This led the traders to liquidate the short hedges and to establish a long position in Chicago futures.

As the days passed, the Company traders' instincts told them that supplies for the May 1963 contract were tightening quite sharply, so they began to add to the long position, registering these transactions as a speculative position because the Company already had ample supplies of uncommitted wheat stocks.

There was an interesting further fact. On April 12, just prior to the time Cargill established its long position in the May 1963 wheat future, U.S. Department of Agriculture (USDA) figures showed that there were 2,804,800 bushels of deliverable-grade wheat stored in Chicago warehouses. Of this amount, Cargill now owned 2,471,000 bushels. "It is important to note here," stated the federal judges in the later U.S. Circuit Court case, "that Cargill was thus in possession of a vital piece of information that other traders and grain dealers in Chicago did not have access to, namely, that it owned the bulk of deliverable wheat in Chicago. While all traders of course knew the total quantity of wheat available in Chicago, only Cargill was in a position to know that it owned the vast majority of this wheat."

A Digression about Previous Dealings in Oats

An earlier exchange of letters between Barney Saunders, head of the Grain Division, and the outside counsel for the Company, John Dorsey, gave an important clue for understanding the problems in May 1963. In May 1959, Saunders had queried Dorsey about Cargill's positions in trading cash oats and oats futures at the CBOT. The May 1959 oats future was an "old crop" situation too, and Saunders was concerned about whether an increased Cargill long position in the May contract would be so large that it might trigger CEA concern. But the reason for the long holdings lay in conventional trading positions, and Dorsey concluded that the proposed transactions were "normal and usual in the course of the operation of a commodity trading and merchandising business" and that this would be seen by Cargill's competitors as normal operations. This satisfied Saunders, and there were no further problems with the oats transactions that year.

Dorsey did comment, however:

The reason you have presented this problem to us for consideration is the fact that on a number of occasions we, as counsel for the Company, have advised burdensome, irksome, and perhaps unnecessary restrictions on the conduct of the Company's futures trading operations. We have done so in an effort to avoid even the possibility of another expensive administrative proceeding with the Commodity Exchange Authority, comparable to the two such proceedings in which Cargill, Inc. has been involved since the past twenty years [he was referring here to John Jr.'s "Corn Case" in 1937 and the Kelm oats trading difficulties in 1953]. In essence we have attempted to guard against any situation in which there could be a possibility of an accusation by the Commodity Exchange Authority that the operations of Cargill, Inc. constituted manipulation or an attempt to manipulate.

Dorsey's letter then went through some of the legal reasoning from past cases about "manipulation," mentioning the difficulties of interpretation involved in this term. "Having in mind these very indefinite and amorphous concepts of what may constitute manipulation," Dorsey ended, "it is, nevertheless, our opinion that the contemplated transactions set forth above would not be held by any reasonable tribunal to be manipulated. . . . During past proceedings and past discussions with the officials of the Commodity Exchange Authority, we have had indications that these officials look with some suspicion on changes of position during a delivery month (i.e., standing for delivery and then going short and making deliveries, or, vice versa, making deliveries and then going long and standing for delivery)." These cases Dorsey felt, *would* be causes for action by the CEA.

This portentous exchange codified for Saunders a key issue at the heart of both the previous corn and oats cases. Manipulation, hard as it was to describe precisely, was to the CEA the most important concern in market transactions, for conscious manipulation of the markets was anathema to the law. Indeed, civil and criminal penalties, both for companies and for individuals, could result from a CEA case alleging manipulation. Cargill's actions as the May 1963 wheat contract moved closer to termination now were to raise such questions in the CEA's eyes.[3]

A Spanish Sale and the Last Day of Trading

On April 21, 1963, just one month from the termination of the May wheat contract, Erv Kelm, Bob Diercks, and Barney Saunders met to review the wheat supply-demand situation. Saunders reported that the supply was going to be "very, very tight"; Kelm responded that Cargill's long speculative position was a good business venture and approved it. A day later, Cargill bought an additional 225,000 bushels of the May futures, which increased the Company's long position to 1,450,000 bushels.

Then the possibility of the major Spanish purchase began to look more promising. In early May, the Geneva office of Tradax informed Minneapolis of their confidence that there would be a tender for the purchase of possibly 50,000 tons of wheat (at a conversion of 36.74 bushels per metric ton, this would be 1.8 million bushels). The Spanish tender materialized, and on May 14, Cargill sold through Tradax 12,500 metric tons of wheat at a price that equaled $2.13½ per bushel, or 10½ cents over the May future. On the next day, Cargill offered 15,000 tons at a price of $2.09 per bushel, or 5½ cents over the May future. Both of these offers were accepted by Spanish authorities on May 18. (These prices, minus the current U.S. subsidy of 62 cents, minus lake freight from Chicago to Cargill's Baie Comeau terminal at the mouth of the St. Lawrence (9¢), brought the price for Spain to the current world price of $1.61 f.o.b. Baie Comeau.) At this point, Cargill increased its position in the May wheat futures to 1,880,000 bushels. Further, Cargill immediately loaded out to a laker all of the Spanish wheat, leaving the Company with approximately 50,000 bushels of wheat in its warehouse as of May 20.

On the morning of May 15, the day following the Spanish sale, Ben Jaffray, the head of the Chicago office, sent a wire to the Wayzata office: "Boys are going hammer May wt smorn. Sug we watch CNS [Commodity News Service] and Dow-Jones and if no subsidy report next couple hours prob shud sow few seeds" (i.e., Cargill should noise the sale around the floor of the Exchange). A subsidy registration or report carried by the Commodity News Service or Dow-Jones would inform the trade that Cargill had sold wheat for export and thus would heighten rumors of a shortage of May wheat at Chicago and drive prices up.

Just before the consummation of the sales to Spain, Barney Saunders checked with Donald Levin, the inside general counsel of the Company. Levin approved the sales and expressed the opinion that Cargill's decisions were legal and proper and further stated that there would be a legal problem only if the Company "would sell wheat out of Chicago at an uneconomic price"—this "would not be legal and proper." The prices to Spain seemed equitable and proper, with the Company making a reasonable trading profit on the sale.

Prices of the May wheat futures, which had shown a downward trend in the earlier days of May now began to climb. On Thursday, May 16, prices were up, closing at \$2.05½ and on Friday rising to \$2.09⅛. According to traders, these rises were in reaction to rumors that wheat would be shipped out of Chicago over that weekend.

On May 20, the Monday after a tense weekend, prices began to rise more rapidly, and Cargill decided to begin liquidating its long futures position. Under Board of Trade rules, the maximum permissible price fluctuation in a given day was 10 cents above or below the previous day's closing price. The maximum permissible price for Monday was \$2.19⅜. During that day, Cargill placed an order with its floor traders to sell 100,000 bushels of futures at \$2.19. The broker was able to sell only 40,000 bushels, and the order was canceled. The close that day was 2.18⅝, an increase of 9¼ cents from the previous day's closing price.

The following day was the last day of trading in the May contract. There was a total open interest (contracts that had not been liquidated) of approximately 8 million bushels. Cargill owned 1,890,000 bushels, or about 24 percent of the total. When trading opened, the May future traded at approximately \$2.22 but then gradually declined until, at 11:02 A.M., it traded at \$2.15¼, which turned out to be the low price for the day. During this period, Cargill purchased another 100,000 bushels of futures, which increased a speculative long position to 1,990,000 bushels, just 10,000 bushels short of the maximum for Cargill's speculative position. In addition to this, Cargill obtained control of another 50,000 bushels, which it agreed to sell for Continental Grain Company's account. Trading in this May future was to cease at precisely 12 noon.

At 11:45 A.M., the future was trading at \$2.20. At this point, Cargill sent six orders to the floor, to sell its futures position as follows:

200,000 bushels at \$2.27

200,000 bushels at \$2.27¼

300,000 bushels at \$2.27½

400,000 bushels at \$2.27¾

500,000 bushels at \$2.28

390,000 bushels at \$2.28¼

These orders were "limit orders," meaning that the sales could not be made until the prices reached the specified price. The maximum price at which the May 1963 future could be sold was \$2.28⅝.

Prices did not reach the limits of Cargill's order until 11:53 A.M. By this time, Cargill's holdings consisted of approximately 62 percent of the open interest. In the following seven minutes, Cargill's broker liquidated 1,625,000 bushels for Cargill's account and prices did indeed reach \$2.28⅝. There was pandemonium on the floor; the confusion over what was happening and the congestion in the attempts to trade were so great that at the close of trading at noon some 420,000 bushels remained open after trading ended, and Cargill had unliquidated holdings of 365,000 bushels.

Shortly after the close of trading, the acting chairman of the Business Conduct Committee of the CBOT talked to Cargill about arranging an orderly liquidation of the Company's remaining long position. Inasmuch as there was an apparent short supply of physical wheat in the Chicago area, he suggested that Cargill offer to sell warehouse receipts to the unresolved shorts in order to clear up the May wheat future. Company officials pointed out that they had only approximately 35,000 bushels of uncommitted wheat available but that they could make substantially greater amounts of warehouse receipts available at a price of $2.28¼ per bushel. They added a proviso that the Company be assured of receiving these receipts back in settlement of its long position, since this wheat was actually needed for delivery on prior commitments. Receiving such assurances, Cargill sold 100,000 bushels of warehouse receipts to various commission houses for $2.28¼ per bushel. These receipts were then tendered to Cargill to satisfy the shorts' delivery obligations, resold by Cargill, and then redelivered to Cargill and other longs in satisfaction of the contracts. This process continued until 370,000 bushels were liquidated by this method. Cargill was thus able to follow this process with a uniform price of $2.28¼ per bushel.

After settlement of the outstanding May futures contracts, Cargill had approximately 88,000 bushels of old-crop wheat remaining in its warehouse. Between June 4 and June 14, it disposed of this wheat at prices ranging from $2.10 to $2.13 per bushel. By all measures, it was a magnificently lucrative trading experience for the Company. After the market closed that day, there was a mammoth celebration by all of the longs who had been so successful; the party also was attended by quite a few of the shorts who had lost in the process, with "Miss May Wheat" toasted by just about everyone.

CEA Charges: Manipulation of Price

But there was a quick aftermath. By early June, the CEA had representatives in Chicago, interviewing widely among CBOT members about what happened in the May wheat contract. With intense investigation going on over many months, it took a full year for the CEA to move. On June 3, 1964, a formal complaint was issued against Cargill, Incoporated *and* four Cargill individuals: President Erv Kelm, Executive Vice President Bob Diercks, Vice President Barney Saunders, and Ben Jaffray, the head of the Chicago trading office of the Company. The respondents, said the CEA complaint, "acted with a purpose and intent of causing prices in the May 1963 wheat future which were arbitrary and artificial and demanded and received such prices . . . the respondents . . . attempted to manipulate and did in fact manipulate the price of a commodity for future delivery . . . in willful violation."

The facts of the case, as related in the paragraphs above, were quite straightforward to everyone, Cargill included. The chronology of the events, the prices at which trading was made, the public nature of the Spanish sale—all these could be clearly substantiated by everyone. This hearing, which became highly complex and very protracted, did not rest on differing interpretations of these facts; rather, it turned on subtle questions of intent and perception and what Cargill officials later called "some fundamental philosophic disagreements with the CEA."

Most of the key arguments were thrashed out during the lengthy proceedings heard by the CEA-appointed referee, Benjamin Holstein. After a number of prehearing conferences, Holstein held formal hearings in Minneapolis, Chicago, and Washington over the year 1966, concluding in November 1966 after 32 days. The record contained 4,715 pages of oral testimony by some 50 witnesses and had over 200 exhibits backing up positions. After many legal skirmishes before and after the hearings, Holstein's recommended decision was published on August 12, 1968.

By this time, most of the key points from both sides had been argued. But there were to be several additional steps in the case after this; first, the case went to the judicial officer of the CEA for decision, then to a federal circuit court of appeals and finally to the U.S. Supreme Court in May 1972, nine years after the events. Holding in abeyance for the moment the actual decision at each of these points, it seems appropriate to first sketch out the basic structure of arguments from each of the two sides.

The government maintained throughout that Cargill had manipulated the price of the May 1963 wheat future by means of a device known as a "little corner" or "squeeze." Most commentators refer to a dominant position in the cash or spot market as a corner; such a position in the futures market is denoted as a squeeze. *Fortune* magazine acknowledged that the definitions were not precise: "Up to a certain somewhat nebulous point, squeezes are not regarded as manipulations, according to the rules of the game." The judges ruling in the eventual circuit court case used the definition of a squeeze given by Senator Pope when he was in charge of the bill that was enacted as the Commodity Exchange Act: "Squeeze (congestion); these are terms used to designate a condition in maturing futures where sellers (hedgers or speculators) having waited too long to close their trade find there are no new sellers from whom they can buy, deliverable stocks are low, and it is too late to procure the actual commodity elsewhere to settle by delivery. Under such circumstances and though the market is not cornered in the ordinary sense, traders who are long hold out for an arbitrary price."

The government's contention in this case and in the earlier hearings was that Cargill had manipulated the market price of that May 1963 wheat future by means of a squeeze. First, Cargill acquired and held a controlling long position; second, there was insufficient supply of wheat available, and what supply there was was controlled by Cargill. Further, Cargill then exacted an artificially high price in liquidation of its futures contracts, all of this intentionally caused by Cargill.

Cargill, in turn, contended that in order to be guilty of manipulation under the Act a trader would have had to commit an uneconomic act—they urged the wording, "the performance of an act which, viewed by itself, is not economically justified, with the intent to influence price and which results in influencing price." The referee discarded this definition, citing a number of cases that made it clear that he believed that manipulation was present when a price was not responsive to the forces of supply and demand, in other words, an artificial price.

He added a telling citation from none other than John H. MacMillan, John Jr.'s father, when John Sr. testified before a congressional committee in 1921: "A manipulator is a speculator who, by reason of the large quantities in which he deals, attempts to force artificial conditions or to aggravate conditions for his own advantage." (The testimony was before the House Agricultural Committee hearings in the 66th Congress in 1921.) The circuit court justice in the current case also discarded Cargill's definition, commenting, "This is a rather novel proposition and we suspect many market traders might be startled to learn that the only manipulators among them are those who fail to make a profit on all of their various maneuvers."

Cargill had put particular dependence on one key case cited a number of times in both the CEA proceedings and in the eventual court case, the Volkart Brothers case, decided in a U.S. circuit court proceeding in 1962. There were many similarities between the Volkart and Cargill cases. In the former, there was a small supply of available, deliverable cotton; and Volkart stood on its long position, more than twice the size of the deliverable supply, into the last day of trading, pressuring the price upward. Volkart, however, had nothing to do with the fact that the available deliverable supply of cotton was small. The CEA had ruled against Volkart; the circuit court case that followed did not support the CEA's findings nor its conclusion that Volkart had manipulated cotton futures prices.

In Cargill's circuit court case, the justices rejected the Volkart decision as a precedent:

Read at its broadest reach, which is the way Cargill reads it, the Volkart decision holds that manipulative squeezes are not prohibited by the Commodity Exchange Act. . . . It is somewhat difficult to discern why the Court reached this result, but apparently its concern was that a contrary result would relieve the shorts of their delivery obligation and transform the futures contract into a gambling transaction. We think this approach disregards commercial reality and the economic functions of the futures market . . . we conclude that if the Volkart decision is to be interpreted as prohibiting regulation of manipulative squeezes, it is not in line with the Commodity Exchange Act . . . and should not be followed.

The justices' opinion spoke specifically to Cargill's emphasis on Volkart: "Cargill was clearly picking and choosing which precedent it would follow . . . and the Volkart decision has been criticized by commentators. . . . Cargill was playing close to the line of even the Volkart decision."

As the Cargill case developed through its three stages (the referee's and the judicial officer's findings, followed by the circuit court case), the final decisions essentially turned on the question of whether a squeeze had been intentionally caused by Cargill. First, the court concluded, Cargill had acquired a dominant long position: "On its face, ownership of 62 percent of the open contracts would appear to be a dominant interest." Further, the justices ruled that there was an insufficient supply of wheat available from sources other than Cargill for delivery on the May future, rejecting in the process the Cargill argument that alternative wheat was available. Cargill had suggested that hard winter wheat could have been brought into Chicago, but the justices ruled that "its price was higher, no premium was allowed for its delivery, and the cost of shipment to Chicago for the delivery on the future was an additional economic impediment to its delivery."

Then the justices turned to the question of whether Cargill had exacted an artificially high price in the settlement of its contracts. First, was the price that Cargill received artificially high? Here the justices relied on three tests proposed by the CEA, utilizing historical analysis of the May 1963 futures prices. The government contended that the record $18\frac{5}{8}$ cents price rise of the future in the last two days of trading was not comparable to movements in the previous nine years, that in fact in six of those years the futures price actually declined. Similarly, the spread between the May and July wheat futures in 1963 increased by a record $18\frac{5}{8}$ cents during the last two trading days and that no comparable movement had occurred during the prior nine years, in seven of these years the spread remaining the same or increasing. Finally, the government contended that the May futures prices were considerably out of line with the Kansas City futures price as compared in those prior years. The justices concluded: "It seems clear that the only reason the price advanced so rapidly during the last few minutes of trading was because of Cargill's dominance of the long interest and the high prices it set for liquidation."

The question of intent was, of course, the crux of the matter. The justices reiterated the fact that Cargill possessed a very valuable piece of information unknown to the trade at large, namely, that it owned "practically all of the wheat available for delivery." As Cargill began liquidating its contracts, the justices saw the Company's behavior as "clearly intentional . . . highly unusual market behavior." In their decision, the justices quoted another interoffice Cargill telegram sent on May 6, which stated: "Excellent wheat summary. Question is how much wheat going to be available June 15 so we can figure old crop needs and what it going to cost our pals." In an interview with Department of Agriculture investigators, the justices' opinion continued, "a Cargill executive said that the Spanish business came about at a good time because without it, if Cargill had 'bulled' the market, there would have been criticism . . . that the sell order was not placed until the last minute because he 'waited and watched because he knew the market was going up.' This was knowledge that other traders did not have."

The justices put particular emphasis on the fact that "Cargill did not sell at the market price but set the market price by reason of its dominant long position in the closing 7 minutes." Finally, the justices made their decision: "The conclusion is well founded that these severe fluctuations were caused by Cargill's manipulative actions and such severe fluctuations constitute a threat to a free and orderly market. . . . We conclude that the squeeze was intentionally brought about and exploited by Cargill."

The Company Becomes a Crusader

Cargill began this saga feeling reasonably confident about the initial advice promulgated by Don Levin that Cargill's actions were legitimate and comfortable about the results of that incredible last day of trading. This confidence heightened as Cargill approached various friends in the trade to testify and some trade organizations to actually file briefs supporting Cargill. The list of brokers and competitors responding positively was long and impressive; it included Dwayne Andreas, at that time president of First Inter-Oceanic Corporation and a former Cargill employee whom John MacMillan, Jr., had once thought would succeed him as president of the Company (see Broehl, *Cargill: Trading the World's Grain* for this story). Even one of the "big six" grain trading companies agreed to support Cargill (although Continental Grain, Cargill's closest competitor, declined).

Three briefs were filed supporting Cargill's side of the argument—from the Association of Commodity Exchange Firms, the Great Plains Wheat Market Development Association, Inc., and, most important, the Board of Trade of the City of Chicago (the CBOT). The CBOT also felt that the Volkart case was the guidepost: "Since 1962, the Volkart case has served as a solitary beacon for commodity traders and commodity exchanges in the murky and treacherous waters of 'manipulation' law." The Exchange went even further than Cargill did, finally concluding that "the state of the law respecting manipulative intent was sealed in Volkart." The CBOT's position was that it was the fault of the shorts, that many shorts willfully neglected to make preparation for delivery and resolved instead to stand by their short futures contracts until the last minutes of futures trading despite the serious risk of defaulting in breach of their contracts and Board of Trade rules. They accused the CEA of "reckless conduct" in seemingly supporting the shorts.

As to Cargill's market behavior, "More is required to establish 'manipulation' than mere proof that the accused knew that his activity would or could influence market prices." Only a reaffirmation of the legal principles presumably found in Volkart "can restore for the commodity exchanges and the commodity industry a confidence and understanding of the respective duties under the Commodity Exchange Act."

Cargill's internal memoranda were cautious and temperate in the early stages; for example, a June 1964 statement concluded, "An orderly marketing system in which prices reflect true values has great importance in our economy. We trust that the Commodity Exchange Authority shares this view and differs with us only in its judgment on whether our activities in May wheat supported this objective." The newly published annual report of the Company in 1963–1964 said only that one of the primary objectives was to "win our court fight with CEA."

By 1965, however, with the extensive industry response apparently supporting the Company, both Cargill's and its supporters' statements took on a more combative tenor. In June 1965, in the monthly letter of the CBOT to its members, their editor called the CEA interpretations "a strikingly different interpretation . . . of the legal principles involved" and went on to hold that the complaint contained "ill-considered legal theories, some of which are being resurrected here after defeat in previous cases." Cargill was in the process of working with *Fortune* magazine for an article giving a major look at the overall Company. In anticipation of this, Don Levin prepared a memorandum about the "fundamental philosophic disagreement" that Cargill had with the CEA. His memorandum ended with perhaps an unintentionally arrogant conclusion: "We must recognize that the CEA is staffed almost completely with long-term Government employees without trade experience, and in many cases embued with economic and political philosophies which are incompatible with the business and political beliefs of Cargill . . . a solution other than litigation or efforts to impose beliefs by new laws might be to attempt to infuse into the CEA, at high levels, persons who have had substantial business experience and who may hold pro-business political beliefs."

Cargill issued a public statement at this time that maintained, "Cargill and those personally involved in this proceeding, of course, are unhappy to be the center of such litigation. In another sense, however, it is perhaps desirable that they are the defendants rather than another firm or individuals who might be less able or less equipped to do what has now become necessary—that is to defend the grain marketing system itself."

The *Fortune* article, which came out two months later, devoted a paragraph to the issue and was generally sympathetic. "Grain traders believe that Cargill had acted strictly within the rules," the article noted. "The Business Conduct Committee of the Chicago Board of Trade declared that it had 'found no evidence that the respondents [Cargill and four of its officers] had manipulated either the cash or future prices, but the case, widely recognized as crucial to the future of commodity-market regulation is still in litigation." The Company also looked for support from friendly political links, particularly from the Minnesota congressional contingent.

In June 1965, Cargill received a request from the Company's two term money lenders, Northwestern Mutual Life Insurance Company and the Prudential Insurance Company, to provide them with a letter outlining Cargill's view of its prospects in the case. Levin's response was upbeat, calling particular attention to the fact that in the Volkart case the circuit court had overturned the CEA's decision. "On the other hand," Levin stated, "the Commodity Exchange Authority seems quite dedicated in this case." Despite the seriousness of the charges, he continued, he expected Cargill to prevail, and "at the worst we would not suffer irreparable economic harm were the maximum penalties, reasonably to be expected, imposed." The 1964–1965 annual report to stockholders came out just at this time and hewed to the optimistic line: "We are well into our trial of the CEA's charges and, enjoying industry's support, we fully expect to win it."

Levin had also been working with one of Minnesota's senators, Eugene McCarthy, concerning the charges against the four individuals (Kelm, Diercks, Saunders, and Jaffray).

In the present proceeding all of the purposes of the law can be achieved without including individuals as respondents. Indeed, the only sanctions which are sought or can be imposed in this proceeding against the individual respondents is to deny them trading privileges on Commodity Exchanges, and since none of the individuals trades for his account such a sanction is really meaningless to the government . . . nevertheless the effect on the individuals can be most serious. If . . . the respondents are found guilty, the damage will have been done. Final vindication after review by the U.S. Circuit Court of Appeals cannot redress the respondents for the ignominy and censure that they will have suffered.

It took two more years before the four individuals learned whether these arguments would have any effect. On August 12, 1968, Referee Benjamin Holstein promulgated his "recommended decision" in a 112-page document. He stressed that this was not a final order, which could be issued only by the judicial officer after the parties had had an opportunity to file exceptions. But his proposed order was a shock to the Company; it stated: "All contract markets shall refuse all trading privileges to respondents Cargill, Inc., Erwin E. Kelm, H. Robert Diercks, Walter B. Saunders, and Benjamin S. Jaffray, for a period of 90 days, such refusal to apply to all trading done and positions held directly by any of the said respondents, and also to all trading done in positions held indirectly through persons owned or controlled by them or any of them, or otherwise." It was a sweeping defeat of Cargill's positions.

The case now went to Thomas J. Flavin, the CEA's judicial officer. Cargill filed extensive exceptions. The CBOT exceptions and those of the Association of Commodity Exchange Firms and the Great Plains Wheat Market Development Association also were forwarded. In addition, Cargill now filed a new motion, for disqualification of Flavin himself. The Company alleged that he would prejudge the proceeding because of a personal bias against the respondents, arguing that a retired employee of the USDA then working for Cargill in Washington, D.C., had stated that he once met Flavin on a bus and that Flavin, upon sitting down with the retiree, made a remark that the retiree remembered as being substantially, "Your Company (or you fellows) have rigged the market again." Flavin refused to disqualify himself, stating that whatever remark he may have made to the retiree was "purely in jest" and "before he had seen the complaint."

Flavin's decision came on August 13, 1970. The order repeated the facts essentially as Holstein had enumerated, went through the Volkart case once more, and chronicled testimony from a number of people supporting Cargill, as well as from government officials in the USDA giving expert testimony. At the end of his report he included this paragraph:

> This proceeding unfortunately has been a protracted one. Cases of this kind are usually lengthy and time-consuming. But there were factors present in this case, not attributable to respondents, which made for unusual delay and are not likely to recur in other proceedings under the Act. The respondents had been under the constraints of the proceedings since the complaint was filed in June 1964. Taking this into consideration, together with respondents' apparent reliance upon the Circuit Court decision in Volkart, *supra*, as legitimizing the conduct and issues, we conclude that the sanctions proposed by the referee should be suspended.

The order itself still stated at the end that Cargill, Incoporated, and the four individuals were to have their trading suspended for a period of 90 days but then suspended the sanctions themselves and concluded: "If any of the respondents is again found to have violated the act, after opportunity for hearing, within two years from the date hereof, the suspended sanctions will be taken into account in determining the sanctions to be ordered in connection with any such violation."

A CEA judicial officer's order has the effect of law, and thus the case was finished unless Cargill wanted to carry it to the federal circuit court of appeals. One of the Cargill law team argued against this possible appeal, holding that Cargill's prospective use of the futures market, "clearly the most important" of the objectives, had been preserved. There might still be some civil liability (for example, Cargill still had a few pending cases from the shorts, alleging damages), but while "this risk still exists [it] does not appear to be great." As to whether the Flavin decision developed a realistic understanding of manipulation, the situation at best was confused. Volkart had set out some fairly understandable guidelines, and the Cargill case "seems to represent a statement by CEA that it will not follow these guidelines. This would probably require Cargill lawyers to advise refraining from some market activity which might well be economic and lawful."

As to the broader reaction, "[the public] does not appreciate the issues involved but probably has reached a conclusion that Cargill's acts were questionable." In respect to any goal of improving CEA supervisory operations, "there has been no change or improvement since 1963." If the case were carried to the circuit court of appeals, a better definition of manipulation might result, possibly a reaffirmation of Volkart. But it was conceivable, he continued, "that the definition could become even less precise." If the Company won the case in the courts, there would be a full public justification of Cargill's actions. If lost, it might reinforce negative judgements. Rather, he proposed negotiations with the CEA, hopefully accompanied by the various industry friends who had supported Cargill, to see if a satisfactory conclusion could be worked out regarding issues such as the definition of manipulation. "I think there is much to be gained through negotiation," he argued, "using the case in its present posture as an example of misapplication of the law and administrative mismanagement."

It was clear that Cargill officials felt, as the same lawyer implied in a separate memorandum, "that the Federal courts have shown a much better understanding of the principles of an open, competitive marketplace than the CEA has been capable of." Beyond this assessment of a likely more positive response from the courts, issues of personal ego were in play here. The four executives felt strongly that they were not guilty, and they wanted open vindication. Finally, the decision was made to go ahead with an appeal to the circuit court of appeals, holding in reserve any of the suggested negotiating steps.

One of the first moves in the defense strategy was to keep the CBOT on their side, with its own brief in support. Bob Diercks and Cal Anderson traveled to Chicago to meet with the CBOT executive committee, only to find that "for some reason they seem somewhat reluctant to proceed." The two Cargill executives made a strong case that the Exchange needed to be there to continue the support of the Volkart decision; finally, the CBOT did submit a new brief. In its opening pages the brief stated, "The Board of Trade's interest in this case . . . is not related to Cargill's guilt or innocence, but rather its fulfillment of statutory duties under difficult circumstances where the CEA feels free to interpret the Commodity Exchange Act as if it were an extra-legal tribunal autonomous and independent of judicial precedent."

The Commodity Exchange Act, in its provisions for review by a U.S. circuit court of appeals, empowered the reviewing court to affirm, set aside, or modify the order of the agency. The government's case was made by L. Patrick Gray III, Assistant Attorney General (and later Attorney General) of the United States. The 121-page brief submitted by Gray was a stunningly documented piece arguing that Cargill indeed had acted with manipulative intent and that the previous Volkart decision was unsound, "plainly wrong." The court, instead, would rely on other precedents more readily accepted as applicable to this case. The Cargill allegation of bias by Flavin was dismissed by Gray with a short paragraph: "Obviously, the statement was a joshing of a friend, not an expression of a view on the merits of the case."

On December 7, 1971, a three-judge panel of the U.S. Court of Appeals, Eighth Circuit, rendered its verdict, in a lengthy decision addressing just about all of the arguments that had been used pro and con in the case. The last line of the decision was "The Order is affirmed." Cargill decided to petition the Supreme Court of the United States on appeal. Five months later, on May 15, 1972, the petition was denied. The May 1963 Cargill wheat case was over.

In the aftermath, the Cargill court case joined a small group of other precedent-setting decisions for future cases of similar nature. Indeed, Cargill and Volkart were often cited together as contrasting opinions. The Company's court decision reaffirmed that the four individuals' proposed constraint on trading privileges *was* suspended. But any thought that this would be now forgotten was rudely shaken when Barney Saunders was queried by a hostile congressman in a House of Representatives hearing in 1972 on sale of wheat to Russia about the two-year length of time that he and the other three were "put on probation." The matter was dropped after just a single question about when the probation period was up, but the mere raising of the issue was quite disconcerting.

The Wheat Case: A Reprise

In retrospect, the case had proved to be a punishing and damaging one for the Company. Cargill had just returned to the CBOT and hardly had had time to work out its office space and public posture when this saga began. The total cost of the case in management time was mind-boggling due to its sheer length, just six days short of nine years from that last day of trading in the May 1963 contract to the Supreme Court denial. Beyond this, however, there must have been a hidden cost, unmeasurable but potentially severe, in that four top Cargill officers, including its chief executive officer, had their personal careers on the line here, while at the same time continuing to make hundreds of key decisions affecting the Company over those nine years. The distractions must have been difficult to overcome.

The case had many similarities with John Jr.'s Corn Case back in 1937–1938, including the fact that both John Jr. at that time and the Cargill officials in the present case never really felt they had done anything wrong. It was true that there was wide support for the principles that had formed the basis for the Volkart case, namely, that as a given contract closed, those on the wrong side of the market and being hammered by adverse price movements needed to remember their well-established, well-known responsibilities to the market to follow through even if in adversity—to put it more colloquially, to "take their medicine like a man." It was an age-old battle in the pits, no quarter asked or given. Great profits had been made over many of these Exchange battles;

great losses, even ruin had often been a companion. The lore and ethos of grain trading truly glamorized the process.

Some considerable part of the wide support for Cargill in this case (a support that simply was not there in the case of John Jr.'s Corn Case) was the feeling that in order to have the commodity markets work well, there had to be this instant price recognition by outcry in the pits and as much unfettered movement as possible. There were controls on this—certainly, the daily limit requirements served as a significant leaven for runaway price rises or falls. It is interesting, though, that with all of this support of Cargill by its trading friends and exchange executives, there never was explicit support of Cargill's methods in that last few days of trading. Palpable was some real fear of unvarnished market power exerted by one of the giants of the industry.

Cargill officials seemed never to have seen this, never had recognized just how powerful a great company could be at the point of the crunch. The Company made the argument, both in briefs and in many memoranda, that (as one memorandum put it) "Cargill's long position was only 3.8 percent of the total open interests on April 16th and went only to 10 percent on May 14th, to 23.6 percent on May 20th, and finally, of course, to 85.5 percent on May 21st." It was the last part of this sentence that Cargill people were not understanding. As Cargill's memorandum stated, "Obviously the percentage increased the last two days of trading as others traded themselves out of the market." The memorandum continued: "How can it be said that Cargill had a 'controlling long position' in this future when its position (except for the last two days) approximated the 10 percent mark. We submit this is 90 percent away from a controlling position."

This thinking fundamentally missed the point. This case was essentially an antitrust case rather than a CEA-type market mechanisms case. In the circuit court decision, the justices stated that while there were no Supreme Court precedents on several of the key questions relating to the Commodity Exchange Act, there *were*, however, a number of such precedents "in the closely related area of antitrust regulation under the Sherman Act." All one had to do was substitute the words "conspiracy to set price," and it was a full-scale antitrust concept. The CEA officials, including the referee and the judicial officer, did not have antitrust as their charge and were not used to dealing in its precedents. The circuit court justices, on the other hand, dealt often with antitrust matters (and at the same time seemed to have a good grasp of the commodity markets, too).

The power of Cargill on that last day of trading truly was overpowering. Further, the CEA referee, its judicial officer, and the courts all had made a believable case that Cargill had planned the coup ahead of time and had engineered it through to the final second of the contract, at noon on May 21. Stories still remain in the Company of Kelm and Saunders standing intently in front of the ticker tapes in Cargill's headquarters in Wayzata, barking orders and making plans all through that morning (while cash transactions were traded directly in the Chicago office, futures transactions were traded by wire from Wayzata). Throughout the case, Cargill officials denied any such intent; but although this argument may well have been true, it was not sustained at the CEA or in the courts.

This case, now known popularly around the Company as "CEA 120," certainly achieved its place in the panoply of Cargill trading stories as one of the three great cases—the Corn Case, the Oats Case, and CEA 120. Further, the results of the case, particularly the circuit court of appeals decision, sent one of the most powerful messages one might imagine in a Company priding itself on individuality and personal decision making. At least in the case of commodity trading and specifically in situations where market power might be construed by outsiders as being inordinate, the Company subsequently has modified its market behavior markedly. This is not to deny that the same sharpness and ability to make quick, purposeful decisions is still fully present; however, one of the watchwords of the Company ever since has been "Don't forget CEA 120."[4]

"Boss Town" of the County

Look back now 100 years. Will Cargill has just stepped down from the McGregor Western railroad car at the tiny wide-place-in-the-road that just had been named Conover, Iowa. It was probably October 1865—we cannot be sure. Will, at 21, was celebrating his majority with his first trip on his own to the end of the new rail line extending out from McGregor, 46 miles to the east on the Mississippi River. The post–Civil War railroad boom had begun with a bang; rail lines were being built west from the great river in Missouri, Iowa, and southern Minnesota. The agricultural frontier now was moving rapidly.

The railroad men broke old villages and made new ones almost by the month. The settled town of Calmar had been bypassed by the builders, who chose to move four miles to the north and west, where a railroad depot was put down in new Conover. "Calmar is to be 'left out in the cold' . . . the cars are not to stop by—only leave the screeches of the steam whistle to edify the people—to remind them that they did not 'shell out' when asked to." (Local citizenry typically was importuned for substantial dollar advances for construction; Calmar apparently didn't listen!) A writer of that day trumpeted that Conover "bid fair to become 'the boss town' of the County . . . like a Pacific Coast mining camp."

Within weeks a whole little town had been cobbled together. The focus was business: three hotels, a dozen stores, "a whole street of warehouses," even 32 saloons. One of those warehouses was Will Cargill's flat house along the railroad track, a simple structure with bins; all that was needed was a

"The town's oldest resident, Frank Bubrick, recalls that Cargill's original elevator stood at the intersection 'just behind the railroad crossing sign,' where hand-fashioned square nails from a long-gone structure can still be found" (*Cargill News,* January 1965).

strong back and a good wheelbarrow to load it full of bagged grain. Will probably lived there, too. Could Will Cargill even have dreamed, sitting in his makeshift office in a corner of the flat house, that there would be a great multinational Cargill, Incorporated, celebrating its 100th anniversary in 1965?

When spring 1866 came, the railroad built on north and west, and Will Cargill moved his operations to Cresco and then to another new village, Lime Springs. Conover now fell like a rock; the stronger businessmen picked up their entire operations (most often including dismantling and reerecting whole buildings) and moved on to Cresco and little Lime Springs. Soon the disparaging name "Goneover" was used for the now-ghost-town Conover. But Will Cargill surely never forgot that first exciting business scene as Conover became another of the boom-and-bust frontier towns of the mushrooming westward movement.[5]

Cargill's Centennial Celebration

Cargill News announced the Company's "Centennial Year—1965" in its August 1964 issue. Only a few companies could claim continuous operation for a full century, fewer still from "so small a beginning to such impressive present size and national prominence." The editors also perceptively noted an even more unique fact: only a handful of companies celebrating 100 years of corporate life could claim an origin west of the Mississippi. By unanimous vote of the board of directors, the calendar year 1965 was declared the centennial year. Late in 1965, there was to be a celebration all through the Company, both domestic and foreign. Before that, *Cargill News* would carry serialized historical stories almost every month. The *News* editor, John Work, also was writing a more substantial book, to be called *Cargill's Beginnings*.

An official emblem was announced in April of 1965, the numeral 100 encircled by a ring of pod shapes, "which might be a sunburst, or flames from birthday candles, or shapes of grain kernels, or drops of vegetable oil, or any other thing the observer prefers." Then, in June 1966, a more permanent Cargill symbol was adopted; Erv Kelm described its circular, C-like shape in a *Cargill News* editorial: "In contrast [with the pre-Anniversary version and its globe and growing stalk of grain], the new symbol is not specific. . . . It is an organic rather than a mechanical shape and thus . . . compatible with all our operations. Its interior shape recalls a seed, a kernel of grain, a drop of liquid (oil, soft water, melted snow, chemicals), all of which are similarly compatible with Cargill activities." Kelm did confess that "I shall miss the Cargill shield . . . unfortunately too complicated and symbolically too specific to fulfill our present needs." This new symbol of 1966 has remained the Company's logo to today.

An employee slogan contest also was announced at the beginning of the anniversary celebrations. The winning person or couple was to travel first class by air to St. Louis, there to begin a five-day voyage in the handsome guest suite of Cargill's mammoth new towboat, the *John H. MacMillan, Jr.*

The Company's centennial emblem (*Cargill News,* October–November 1965).

At the end of this Mississippi River trip, an overnight stay had been arranged in "glamorous New Orleans." Appropriately, the winners were to return to Minneapolis via Chicago, traveling from New Orleans to Chicago on Illinois Central's Panama Limited (within just three years Cargill would initiate the innovative "Rent-a-Train," with the Illinois Central, covering essentially the same route). The winners were announced in the October 1964 *News* (the winning entry was not quite as innovative as the term "Rent-a-Train"; it was "A century serving farm and industry"). A Borup, Minnesota, couple, Lawrence and Pearl Hansen (he was the 15-year manager of the Company's country elevator there), took the trip in November. The towboat trip was the feature, but the Hansens reported, "We even sat for a sidewalk artist in the French Quarter and had our picture painted."

Conover itself, such as it was, was visited by a contingent from the Company. All that was left was a tightly locked one-room "depot" plus a half dozen farmhouses. An elder resident thought he could confirm the location of the warehouse, but it had been gone for just under 100 years, of course.

The culmination was the huge centennial celebration. On October 8, 2,000

Chicago Cargill employees at one of the simultaneous banquets held around the country celebrating the company's centennial year, October 8, 1965 (Cargill News, October–November 1965).

people in Minneapolis gathered, and 3,000 to 4,000 more celebrated at the same time at 19 other parties across the United States. A stunning simultaneous nationwide television linkage allowed everyone to come together at the same time. Among the speakers was a longtime Cargill friend, Vice President Hubert H. Humphrey, who spoke from Washington, D.C. There also were celebrations for several of the overseas offices, although not directly a part of the U.S. events. Humphrey, too, commented on Cargill's "humble beginning."

Everyone likes a party, so of course there was enthusiasm about all of these activities. But there seemed to be something indefinably more than just that; as one reads through all of the *Cargill News* columns, there was a sense of great regard for and pride in the Company, a manifestation once again of the enduring impact of the elusive "Cargill culture." One person at the great party put this in a unique and quite poignant way: "I had mixed feelings of pride and shame as I looked around the crowd during the program and realized, for the first time, that all of the people there had just as much at stake and were as proud of their Company as I was."[6]

A More Substantive Look at This 100-Year-Old Company

What *was* Cargill as this centennial year of 1965 ended? By the end of the crop year 1965–1966, the Kelm-generated recovery had taken hold very well indeed. A major increase in depth was happening all through the Company, both in facilities and in management. The summary statistics in table 1 will show this, at the same time giving the reader the full picture of the units in the Company (including some new names as of 1965–1966).

The overall figures for the total Company for that third year of 1965–1966 testified to Cargill's renewed strength. The net earnings of $16.7 million were more than double those of the previous year and much the highest in Cargill's history. Return on net worth had exactly doubled, to 17.6 percent; the ratio of working capital to total capital invested rose to an impressive 52.4 percent. Long-term debt had increased by a net $6 million, 21 percent of total capital. The summary annual report noted, "The ratio of earnings-times-interest on long term debt jumped to ten times, a very creditable performance."

The Company recorded another milestone this year when dollar sales passed the $2 billion mark to a new high of $2.12 billion, up 13 percent from the previous year. The physical volume of goods sold rose by 10 percent, to 31 million tons. Book values, on an adjusted per-share basis, rose to $54.79 for common stock and $34.80 for management stock. The overall financial and performance figures for the Company surely were fitting partners for the hundredth-year celebration.

Individually, the various divisions, departments, and other smaller groups almost uniformly had done very well, as the figures above show. A bird's-eye view of each of these will help in sketching exactly what was going on in the

TABLE I
Cargill's Share of Net Earnings—($000 omitted)

Division	1965–66	1964–65	1963–64
Grain	2,817	2,208	3,612
Feed	1,028	(116)	180
Food Products	414	(450)	—
Vegetable Oil	7,457	3,101	2,218
Chemical Products	(314)	(275)	130
Seed Department	5	167	101
Commodities	616	(48)	(489)
Cargo Carriers, Incorporated	820	736	590
Tradax	4,234	2,281	1,694
Hens Companies	21	111	—
Shaver Companies	101	—	—
Aliansa Companies	49	—	—
Brazilian Companies	(34)	—	—
Administrative:			
Insurance	204	84	195
Other administrative	(246)	(147)	(76)
Operating income (after taxes)	17,172	7,652	8,155
Nonoperating (after taxes)	(444)	166	(418)
Net earnings	16,728	7,818	7,737
Return on beginning net worth	17.6%	8.8%	9.4%

Company at this 100-year point. In the process, we will pause occasionally for a somewhat more extended view of some of the newer efforts.

Grain Division. New highs were set in trading margins and volume in the Grain Division. Yet expenses kept pace, to substantially reduce the net gain. Following the Chase Bank criticisms of the division for holding on too long to some of its outmoded properties, a major effort had been made over these three years to close smaller and less efficient operations while at the same time making commitments for major new elevators and terminals. The total effective capacity of all terminals, river houses, and line elevators stood at 176.3 million bushels in 1962–1963; this rose to almost 179 million bushels in the following year; for 1964–1965 it was 175 million; and for 1965–1966 it was down to 169.7 million bushels.

For this latest year, the northwest region had six terminal elevators (the huge Port Cargill operation being the largest, with 11.3 million bushels). In the southwest region there were eight (with the Omaha terminal at 8.7 million bushels the largest). The central region had the mammoth Chicago terminal (20 million bushels) and three others. The eastern region counted eight (with Albany the largest at 11.5 million bushels and three Buffalo terminals totaling 12.7 million). The southeast region had just three, Norfolk the largest at

6 million bushels. The southern region included Baton Rouge, at 6.9 million bushels, and nine other terminals. The West Coast region had the Portland terminal at 8 million and the Seattle terminal at 5.8 million, together with three smaller terminals. There were seven river houses, most along the Illinois River and small in size but unique in their function. The line elevators, so important in the early history (when there used to be hundreds) now were down to about 30, most of them refurbished and modern; many older line elevators were finally part of history.

Taking a closer look at the geographical pattern, the division clearly had a strategy in this upgrading process: almost all activities were along major trunkline railroads, reinforcing the traditional lines of export, south to the Gulf, east to the Atlantic, and west to the Pacific. Erv Kelm described this strategy to the *Minneapolis Star* in January 1964, as building "in the stream of marketing. . . . We didn't put any facilities out in the middle of the prairies."

Despite the good but nonetheless modest performance of the Grain Division over the previous half dozen years, the board of directors now promulgated a real surprise—a major commitment in 1965–1966 to purchase land and

Terre Haute grain, soybean meal, and molasses river terminal under construction south of Baton Rouge, Louisiana. Pictured are Commodity Marketing Division vice president Clifford M. Roberts, Jr.; Erwin E. Kelm, chairman of Cargill; and division vice president John P. Cole, who would have operating responsibility (*Cargill News*, November–December 1974).

follow through on major planning for a state-of-the-art export terminal at Houston. One could make a good case that the Houston plan was perhaps the single most important decision made by the board in this period, not just for the Grain Division itself but for the Company as a whole. The board clearly was signaling that the Grain Division was at the center of the Company and that the halting and sometimes unpromising export trade was viewed as improving and deepening in the upcoming years. This was not a "gamble," in the sense of pitching darts at a dart board, but a conscious, rationally analyzed decision. But not until the Houston terminal was in operation a couple of years from then and this strategy became a reality in the existing international trade structure of that time, could this decision really be considered a fait accompli.

The strengths of the Grain Division lay in its depth of trained and motivated people. At the assistant vice president level this was particularly evident—people honed in their skills, eager and ready to take their full part in the potential "grand strategy" that Kelm and the rest of the board seemed to have in mind. There were Gordon Alexander in futures, Milt Bondus and Joseph Bailey in terminal elevator operations, Howard Boone heading the San Francisco copra operations, John Cole in grain merchandising, Tom Connolly in the New York office, Addison Douglass at St. Louis, William Fischer at Portland, Robert Hatch handling coarse grains, Irving Hyland in branch office administration, Benjamin Jaffray in Chicago, Melvin Middents for wheat, Gerald Mitchell in the Buffalo office, and John Rockwell in Kansas City. In addition to these assistant vice presidents, there were several other key operations and staff people: John LeFevre in accounting, J. N. Haymaker in oilseeds, James Howard in oats and barley, Walter Mayhew heading line elevators, D. S. Macgregor at Baie Comeau, and Earle Greene at Winnipeg. So many of these names become important in the next decade.

Feed. Nutrena had been a satisfactory member of the Cargill world since its acquisition in 1920, although the earnings had skidded a bit in this period, particularly with the losses of 1964–1965. The healthy profits of 1965–1966, the best in six years, helped to recoup reputations. In the process, "we devoted our advertising efforts to improving the Nutrena image," stated their annual report, an obvious reference to the evolving consolidation of Nutrena with Cargill and the ongoing concern that the latter name would not overcome the former.

Early in 1964, a new feed-company name appeared on the Cargill books, the "Hens Companies." A joint venture agreement had taken place among Cargill, its foreign subsidiary, Tradax, and Karel Hens, of Antwerp, Belgium, a well-known European feed producer. The arrangement involved several companies in which Hens held interest, including nine feed manufacturing plants and three additional ones under construction, constituting one of Europe's largest feed operations (there were also some poultry operations). Four countries were involved: an operation in Belgium, another in Germany, one in France, and a separate organization in Spain that was later transferred to Tradax. The earnings were small in the two years to this point, and the internal annual report noted, "There was intense debate throughout the year about Hens/Cargill objectives, policies, and means of accomplishments and as a result much confusion and very little progress." Lack of agreement slowed down corrective action in France, and the morale in Belgium suffered as a result of confusion on objectives and policies. Only the Spanish operation seemed to be making progress and decent profits. As to plans, a Turkish poultry development had been proposed, but another section of the Hens annual report cautioned: "Do not consider any more 50-50 partnerships. Someone must have the power to decide—under a 50-50 arrangement that function is not decisive."

Nutrena, not yet involved in this international feed operation in a significant way, did take a technical assistance role in another, later international feed operation begun in 1965, a partnership arrangement with an El Salvador firm, Aliansa, already operating an automated feed mill in that nation. A second feed mill was now being constructed by the partnership in Guatemala.

The deepening of manpower had also given the Feed Division a number of strong assistant vice presidents: Robert Bartikoski in production and manufacturing; E. C. Fuller in foreign feed; Lloyd Smith in administration, accounting, and credit; David Wentzell, general manager of the division; and Clarence Whitworth, director of marketing. Key staff people included James McDougall, manager of research and product development, and J. Wesley Nelson, research director.

Food Products. This was a department rather than a division, and in its second year of operation was now profitable after a considerable loss in the first year. Originally in the Feed Division, this was reconstituted as a separate department and included at this time a group of egg-producing operations in Minnesota, Tennessee, Mississippi, New Jersey, and Texas. Turkey processing had been undertaken during 1965–1966 with the purchase of the Dodgen companies in Arkansas. Assistant Vice President Edward Reynolds headed the department.

Shaver Company. This, again, was a new endeavor as of 1965 and not yet a part of any division. Shaver Poultry Breeding Farms, Ltd., of Galt, Ontario, was a major world supplier of poultry breeding stock; its Starcross layer hens and Starbro broilers "are famous literally the world over" (said the *Green Wave* announcement). Because of Cargill's national and international production of poultry feeds and feed ingredients, the joint venture that was put together with Shaver gave the Company a major new access to the high-quality poultry breeding stock of the world. Cargill's interest was a controlling one; in addition to the Canadian operations, Shaver had major breeding farms in England, Sweden, Germany, Pakistan, Chile, and Japan and was actually doing business in 52 separate countries. Links were immediately put together with the Company's Argentine group (Tradax-operated).

Cargill felt that Shaver, perhaps more than any other breeder, "has the material and versatility to produce whatever local national markets may require or prefer." This even included a new feather-sexing layer "for more primitive markets." The Company expected the Shaver outreach to put particular emphasis on Africa, the Middle East, and the Far East. Cargill personnel were not directly involved yet.

Vegetable Oil. The Oil Division at this point was the Company's star performer. It was expected to be entering a period of major profitability and total contribution to the Company. The year 1965–1966 was the best year for the industry since the late 1950s. Margins were exceptionally good for the early part of the year and above average later. Although the margins per bushel were less than back in the 1950s, the greatly expanded volume and lower plant costs combined to produce excellent dollar profits.

Back in 1960, Tradax had worked in the Netherlands with the city of Amsterdam to establish a grain transfer and storage facility there; the city would build it, and Tradax would guarantee a fixed percentage of usage and provide some management expertise. This was a surprise to many in the Company, for Tradax uniformly had shied away from any project that involved Tradax itself being related to fixed facilities, even by lease. Now the Oil Division had developed its own international outreach with a new joint venture for a soybean processing plant in Spain, at Tarragona. In the year 1965–1966, this embryonic venture had processed some 7.2 million bushels, 40 percent of all soybeans crushed in Spain.

Tensions now appeared between the Oil Division and Tradax in relation to operating responsibilities in Europe. Oil Division management advocated U.S. divisions controlling and operating their own activities overseas as they were now doing in Spain ("Cargill operating divisions experienced and skilled in certain fields should apply those skills and benefit from that experience in these activities everywhere in the world"). And when funds were available for investment in Europe, "let Cargill management make an allocation . . . as it now does in the U.S.," not Tradax.

Tradax also spoke in *its* annual report to the issue of corporate changes: "As suggested a year ago, reappraise the question of internal management, both general and specific . . . it is felt strongly by Tradax management that a definite decision must be made soon . . . the larger we get, the greater the need for a well-defined, carefully thought-out scheme of international management. The lack of it could be harmful in the future." While these words were rather oblique, there was no doubt that Tradax felt some encroachment by the Oil Division.

Flax profits for the Oil Division had dropped over the three-year period considered above, copra even more, showing a loss in 1965–1966. However, Granexport, the Philippine organization acquiring and exporting copra, had done very well. At the end of the year 1965–1966, this group was the second largest exporter from the Islands, buying about 20,000 tons of copra a month through bodegas and agencies. As most of this copra was shipped across to San Francisco for the Oil Division's plant there, the savings of Granexport helped San Francisco's bottom line, too. "We will be as deeply integrated as anyone in the industry," the division's annual report maintained. James Wilson headed Granexport, and Howard Boone ran the San Francisco copra operation.

Vegetable oil management also had been keenly pursuing executive development. At the assistant vice president level were another cadre of able "comers": Samuel Aronoff and R. Ward Watson handled especially flax and linseed; John Haymaker, and James Spicola, soybeans and meal; and John Mogush, soybean oil. Edmund McCoy was manager of accounting.

Chemical Products. This division had suffered two straight years of losses. Although resins had done well, industrial chemicals had fared poorly. For the latter, the plant at Carpentersville, Illinois, was closed "because of plant mechanical problems, plant personnel problems, product quality problems, margin problems, sales problems . . . all in one way or another contributed to the seeming flood of red ink." The plant was going to be started up later in the year as a test to see if it could be made profitable. Arthur Klobe, deputy division head, was the division's single assistant vice president.

Commodities Division. This was a new division, created in 1964 to house the efforts in molasses, salt, and fishmeal. The small salt operation had been enhanced greatly when the Belle Isle deep mine became operative (a 12,050-foot shaft, Louisiana's deepest, had been completed). A modestly profitable operation ensued; the 1965–1966 efforts to sell to state highway maintenance units for road salt were quite successful, and an upgraded salt product had been developed in 1965 that had a rust-inhibiting treatment, giving up to 87 percent protection against automobile rust. It was marketed under the trade name "Carguard," and sales jumped. Molasses sales provided a modest return through this period.

One of the most interesting developments in the Company came with the commodity division's effort at producing and trading Peruvian fishmeal. In early 1963, Cargill joined with a Peruvian firm to establish two new Company subsidiaries in Peru, one to conduct fishing operations for anchovies and the other to produce fishmeal from them. Fishmeal had a very high protein content and was particularly favored as part of the feed mix for poultry.

The fleet of eight fishing boats—equipment operated by Pesquero Delfin, S.A., Cargill's fish-meal operation in Peru—was seldom seen together, except when in dry dock for painting and repair (as shown here in the fall of 1966). The boats went to sea each morning and returned each evening with their catch of anchovetas for the Company's meal processing plant (Cargill News, April 1967).

Peru was one of the great fishing areas in the world; the cold water of the Humboldt Current, a mighty Pacific Ocean "river," sweeps up the west coast of South America from the Antarctic, bringing with it nutrients in sufficient quantity to make marine life abundant off the coast of Northern Peru. There the current meets head-on a southbound current that has water some 15 degrees warmer; this confluence was producing stellar fishing grounds. The new Cargill venture purchased a somewhat antiquated operation in Huacho, about 70 miles north of Lima, together with two 120-ton diesel-powered boats. The first two years of fishing and production were not very effective, but an innovative program of upgrading the plant soon brought efficiencies that were the envy of the industry.

Peru's industry was marked by a large number of small fishing operations and an equally large number of antiquated plants. When Cargill and several other international companies (U.S. and European) came into Peru at this time, the effects on the existing Peruvian plants were traumatic. Some of the latter also modernized; those that did not fell behind quickly. When Cargill developed a pelletized operation in 1965, it was able to eliminate the use of bags as a storage and loading vehicle. This permitted not only bulk storage at the plant but also bulk loading to ocean vessels; thus considerably more product could be loaded aboard far more quickly and in smaller space than the old way of loading separate bags.

This modernization hit the Peruvian fishmeal industry and brought great repercussions. One of the Peruvian partners wrote a Cargill executive, reporting the prevailing attitude of the Peruvian members of the industry toward the international companies and, specifically, Cargill:

The way [the Peruvians] talked about Cargill/Tradax was with the greatest of criticism but always with the undertone of complete respect, admiration and envy . . . nobody can ever say that Cargill has done anything against the law or that we have been out to ruin Peru. The most they can ever say is that we are exceedingly competitive in Peru as well as all over the world. [But] in spite of the fact that we are being recognized as being superior in our approach to production, marketing, and organization and in spite of the fact that we are big and strong and rich, we have not as yet captured the confidence of the average Peruvian producer. . . . Through our display of efficiency we are making ourselves unreachable to the guy down the street who through his lack of sophistication, lack of education, lack of technical know-how and lack of marketing knowledge, simply is afraid of us and is convinced that our overall objective is to eliminate these little guys down the street and set ourselves up in a nice big business to control the Peruvian fishmeal industry.

Now that Cargill was beginning to move into operations in developing countries (El Salvador and Guatemala were additional examples), this undercurrent of nationalistic hostility toward the multinational firm was a new dimension that Cargill had not yet much encountered and was going to be forced to understand.

The Peruvian fishmeal operation proved to be a telling case study of this manifestation, for in May 1973 the government of Peru (a military junta at that time) nationalized all of the non-Peruvian fishmeal industry, expropriating Cargill's and the other new companies' operations completely and forcing Cargill to write off the entire operation (later, partial recompense was made by the government to these various companies).[7]

The Commodities Division was headed by Vice President Maitland "Hap" Wyard; at this point there were as yet no assistant vice presidents. F. Clayton Tonnemaker was manager of salt; Jack Busby, fishmeal; J. Y. Edwards, molasses; and David Bratton, Durabond.

Seed Department. Seed was having its trials at this point; the year 1965–1966 ended with a profit of some $106,000, but returns of 20,000 bushels and product liability claims of $104,000 doomed the year. George Jones was manager of the department.

Cargo Carriers, Incorporated. Earnings of $820,000 were a record for Cargo Carriers, Incoporated (CCI), a somewhat autonomous division, despite the

With the Peruvian fish meal plant pelletized, conveyors speed bulk fishmeal pellets from ship's side to covered warehouse in just a fraction of the time required to move a similar volume of bagged meal (Cargill News, October 1969).

untoward effects of Hurricane Betsy in the New Orleans/Baton Rouge area in September 1965. Sinkings, damage and cargo loss to CCI equipment ran close to $1 million, most covered by insurance (but the business interruption was *not* so covered). Inland waterways profits were good; with the two new, powerful towboats, the *Austen S. Cargill* and the *John H. MacMillan, Jr.*, the Company now confined its fleet to these two, chartering other tows as needed. The Illinois River routes were becoming ever more important, so Cargill started to charter all its Minneapolis tows. Temporary parking of barges "grows more acute as industry takes over more of the river shoreline." Great Lakes shipping for the Company was now almost exclusively charter. For years these charters had been voyage by voyage; now the Company had turned to contracting for a season (or even several seasons). "This concept gives us great flexibility . . . actual rates were well below single-voyage charter rates."

CCI also oversaw two Cargill subsidiaries, Rogers Terminal and Shipping Corporation (stevedoring) and Greenwich Marine, Incorporated (ocean ship chartering). Another new subsidiary had just been formed, Victoria Marine Co., a Liberian corporation, for the purpose of owning and operating ocean vessels. Now Cargill made a momentous decision—to order built for the

Company a 52,500-ton bulk carrier, to be constructed in Japan (delivery about July 1967). In addition, Victoria contracted for a second ocean vessel, a 13,800-ton Japanese-built specialized ship for the Manchester, England, ship canal.

It was a truly exciting year for CCI, and the tone of their annual report mirrored this: "Be daring—new thinking for future growth . . . not content with evolution . . . lead with revolution . . . ruthless discard of the obsolete and imaginative investment in the future."

Under Vice President Clifford Roberts (who had taken over when Bob Burkey had died suddenly), CCI possessed a strong management team: Don Brandenborg was manager of inland waterways, Ray King of cargo procurement, John Finlayson (at Greenwich) of ocean freight, and George Cohee of vessel operations.

Tradax Internacional, S.A. It was the tenth anniversary of Tradax Internacional, S.A. (TISA), a critically important Geneva-based arm of the Company, and its 1965–1966 performance had been stunning. The record earnings ($6.1 million; Cargill share, $4.2 million) came particularly from its wheat trades. Corn trading was good too, and soybeans set its own record. The Russians were in the market in Europe (not the U.S.), and Tradax also made considerable money trading long freight. The Amsterdam terminal showed a modest profit, and Cargill S.A., the Tradax Argentine subsidiary, had increased its earnings over the previous year for the sixth straight time (grain earnings down, feed up, hybrid corn a stellar producer).

Walter Gage had conceived the TISA personnel structure somewhat differently from the Company's domestic pattern. He was chairman, and Brewster B. "Stu" Hanson was vice chairman and managing director. E. T. Petterson was its titular president, with a small office in Panama, the country of record for TISA. There were six vice presidents: N. Leonard Alderson, W. E. Bindenagel, R. Pearsall Helms, Thomas H. G. Huxley, Lowell B. Nelson, and Hubert F. Sontheim. Alan Blair managed the office in the Netherlands (but was moving to Tradax's office in Japan at this time, with Ian Watson returning to Geneva); Peter Brees handled the Belgian office and Hans Jensen the German operation. Michael R. Cross had for many years supported the Cargill outreach in the United Kingdom; when Tradax was formed, he established its office there, with the title of managing director. Because of the extent and complexity of the Argentine operation, its head, Heinz F. Hutter, carried the title of president and general manager, with Antonio E. Marino as vice president.

Administrative Division. A number of important staff responsibilities were lodged in the Administrative Division: public relations, which was quiet in 1965–1966 but gearing up for the Kennedy Round negotiations, joining with

Continental Grain in alternative suggestions for a proposed "World Grains Agreement"; law, which was busy in this period, especially with CEA 120 (the annual report noted, "our philosophy continues to be strong on day-to-day preventive law"); tax, busy too with several IRS audits being handled in tandem; operations research, business research, and communications, all reasonably small operations; labor relations ("in our overall labor relations picture, our general relations with all of the unions seemed to be on a very good basis this year"); internal audit, for which some of the newer egg products operations needed special oversight; and research, with four new resin products and working on new ideas for linseed oil (but "central research continues to be basically 'chemical research' and thereby represents only a small segment of Cargill's total business . . . we should staff ourselves so that we can contribute in the other areas"). For some reason, an operating entity, rail transportation, also had been assigned administratively to the division; the technology of freight operations was changing rapidly with the hopper car (see "Big John" below), and Cargill had begun leasing a large number (400 additional just in the year 1965–1966). James Springrose had just been promoted to vice president of the department.

The remaining member of the division was, hands-down, the most important—finance. Borrowing was extensive in 1965–1966: the peak during the year was about $240 million; the low point, $159 million. The Company borrowed $10 million on commercial paper, but "prudence will require careful consideration of the magnitude of commercial paper borrowing in which we engage. . . . In view of the tight money situation, it may be necessary to use the commercial paper market more heavily than . . . normal." Taking into consideration the outstanding overall financial results of 1965–1966, the finance officers were remarkably positive about the outlook.

In the tradition of Cargill MacMillan, Sr., Cargill prided itself on its finance and overall administrative team. The division's assistant vice presidents were Gilbert Bakeberg in labor relations and Harold Gray in rail traffic; Clyde Hegman was manager and general auditor, John Savage headed personnel, Calvin Smith was manager of data processing, and H. Duncan Watson headed engineering. Other key staff executives were Almon Greenman in business research; Mentor Addicks, engineering advisor (who filled the same role earlier for John MacMillan, Jr.); Samuel Parks, manager of the insurance department; Samuel Mahoney, manager of international telecommunications; James Loeffler, office services; William Mains, manager of printing services; Gerald Joines, personnel department; Sidney Burkett, training; Robert Jacobson, purchasing; and Albert James, vice president and manager of the tax department. Assistant comptrollers included John Byrnes, D. J. Berkley, and Vardin West. Assistant secretaries were Cargill lawyers Calvin Anderson and John F. McGrory. Assistant treasurers (in addition to Parks) were Waldo Hull, Luther Schmeiding, and John Sorenson.

Some Postcripts

THE "BIG JOHN" CASE

In the early 1960s, an innovative new rail freight car had been developed in the industry, a jumbo aluminum covered hopper car dubbed "Big John." This new car came in several capacities; the most common was the size allowing 4,713 cubic feet of capacity, with a tare (empty) weight of 57,500 pounds (28.5 tons) and handling a load of 223,000 pounds (111.5 tons), thus reflecting a gross weight of approximately 280,000 pounds (140 tons). In comparison, the standard boxcar had a gross weight of 128,000 pounds and a tare weight of about 24 tons.

But it was not just the capacity that distinguished it; the ease of loading had changed enormously. Grain must enter boxcars from the center door, with the piping manually carried to the ends and corners of the car and the car unloaded through this same center door. To load the aluminum car, the top watertight hatch covers would be laid back, a spout inserted, and the four compartments quickly filled with grain; to unload, the bottoms would be opened, and the

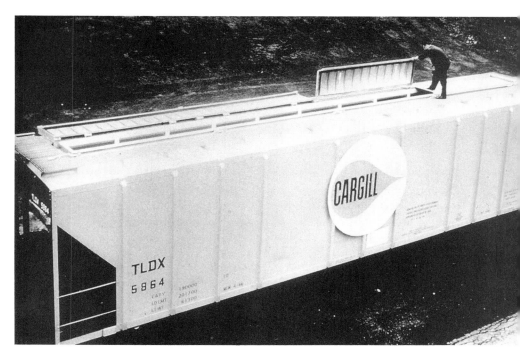

The "Big John" size of aluminum boxcars, c. *1966* (Cargill staff photograph).

grain ran out by gravity. Further, the jumbo cars were free from insect infestation and could be reloaded over and over again without cleaning or conditioning, as had to be done with the boxcar. Aluminum would not rust; therefore, the car required no painting. Further, the four compartments allowed as many as four types or grades of grain to be loaded. Here was a true technological breakthrough of great moment.

In addition, very soon a rate case arose out of the use of the hopper car that promised to revolutionize rate-making concepts also. At least at the beginning, this new rate appeared to alter negatively many of the rates that Cargill and a number of other users had been utilizing, especially to move grain into the southeastern part of the United States. The Southern Railroad, a dominant carrier in that region, had invested in a large number of the new hopper cars and now proposed to the Interstate Commerce Commission (ICC) that rates for their use be lowered but under certain conditions: that shipments would consist of four cars or more and that they travel straight through from certain gateways at Memphis, St. Louis, and Cairo, Illinois, to final unloading at the feed mills, flour mills, poultry plants, and other consumers in the Southeast. Cargill and a number of other competitive shippers argued against the rates (the Southeastern Association of Local Grain Producers, Merchandisers, Processors and Consumers decried the Southern's "peculiar rate-making theories . . . more baneful than beneficient"), and the case was quickly brought to the ICC.

While Cargill had, of course, used rail transportation all over the country, the Company had particularly invested in inland waterway equipment and facilities, as well as depending heavily on trucking. It seemed incongruous that Cargill would be opposing lower rates, given its long-held beliefs in competition and the most efficient transportation. As a major Cargill position paper on rail rate structures stated, "In view of this early interest on Cargill's part in such advanced rail concepts, it is ironic that when the test case came, which was to begin the modern era of rail rates, Cargill for one of the rare moments in its history, found itself at least initially, a protestant aligned against the new concepts which, as promulgated by the Southern Railroad, were aimed directly at operations such as Cargill's barge-truck facilities at Guntersville [Alabama] and Chattanooga [Tennessee] and were bound to give pause to a company which had a massive investment in water-oriented facilities."

The paper told of Cargill's change of heart: "It is greatly to Cargill's credit in these circumstances that it found itself extremely uncomfortable being aligned against what it recognized as long overdue progress from the rail carriers and very quickly Cargill's participation in the Big John case became a rear guard holding action to limit time to develop new facilities to utilize a new rate concept, and indeed to begin innovating all over again in the field of rail transportation." Cargill had little difficulty in recognizing the wave of the future and the long-term implications for agribusiness if the railroads, with

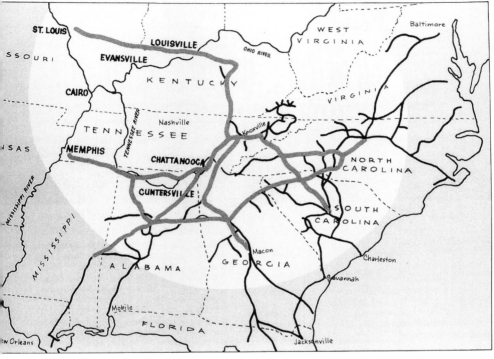

Area affected by Southern Railroad rate case; heavy lines are main routes of the Southern (*Cargill News,* July 1962).

ICC approval, "finally begin to achieve the efficiencies of which they were capable in the bulk transportation of grain and grain products."

However, Cargill wanted to make certain that the ICC did not lock itself into just the gateway cities, as the Southern Railroad wanted; one of the early results of the case was the development by Cargill of its own gateway rail-loading point at Princeton, Indiana, so that Cargill could use the multicar hopper from its own terminal for its shipment into the Southeast. The barge truck terminal elevators at Guntersville and Chattanooga did not go out of business nor did barge operations on the Tennessee cease. But the new rail rates made the decision of how to ship more sophisticated now that it incorporated some highly competitive rail rates along with the inland waterway rates and the trucking tariffs. As the Cargill position paper put it,

With the benefit of hindsight, it is probably true to say that the gloomy prognostications which the opponents of non-transit rates predicted did, pretty much, all take place but, for the most part, they proved less drastic, less destructive and more gradual than courtroom histrionics had suggested . . . a drastic change in rail rates, such as these were, produced reactions by other rail carriers, reactions by truckers and water carriers, reaction by merchants and consumers, nearby and far distant, even reactions by producers of grain; such chain reactions invariably produced new opportunities as well as diminishing old ones.[8]

MOTHER NATURE STRIKES HARD

Hurricane Betsy, in September 1965, was the second hurricane to hit in the Gulf in two years. Just the previous October, Hurricane Hilda had hit southern Louisiana, with heavy damage in the New Orleans–Baton Rouge section. Twenty people were killed, and much damage to civilian housing resulted. Particularly hard hit agriculturally were the sugarcane growers.

Some Cargill installations suffered damage, but it was not as serious as it could have been. Two watchmen for the Company, Frank Rulk and Redester Aucoin, had difficulty taking shelter, finally staying behind a decommissioned tow boat, the *Carcities*, which had been moored hard and fast for use as a shop and work area. The *Cargill News* article in November carried some graphic shots of automobiles inundated and other photographs, but the Company escaped any serious difficulties.

Hurricane Betsy's visit the following year was short but a "wicked one," *Cargill News* noted. Damage to Cargo Carriers equipment was substantial. Barges, even loaded ones, were thrown up on the shore; one disappeared completely. The huge towboat *Austen S. Cargill*, which had been tied up at Point Landing 10 miles from New Orleans, was damaged on one side and lost some exterior fittings. A chlorine barge not belonging to the Company but attached to some CCI barges also disappeared completely. The two missing barges were finally found over a week later, with the help of Cargill people who had rigged up a lightweight diving station to identify both the chlorine barge and the Cargill barge. Not finding the former, of course, would have left a dangerous cargo under the water.

Far and away the most damaging mischief of Mother Nature happened not by hurricane but by flood. The Minnesota River had always been a flood-prone waterway, and Cargill's major complex at Port Cargill on the river (the place where the World War II vessels were built) had had difficulties in high-water years. Even while the big ships were being built there, a flood had slowed down operations significantly.

In April 1965, the Minnesota River suffered its most damaging flood in history. There had been a record-breaking runoff of snow melt, and almost every river and stream in the state had overflowed. Given Port Cargill's vulnerable position on the Minnesota, the Company earlier had protected the whole complex by two miles of permanent earthen dikes, built following major floods in 1962. These would hold against water 17 feet above "normal" flood stage and 1 foot above the previous flood record, set in 1962. Unfortunately, 1965 was destined to be the worst year, and the outer dike finally was overwhelmed by the rising waters. There had been time before this happened to move some equipment and stored commodity products to safety. Erv Kelm summarized the situation in a wire relayed to all Company offices at the height of the danger:

We have suffered some losses at our St. Peter, Minn. hybrid corn plant . . . our LaCrosse elevator has water in the basement . . . our major concern has been over our Port Cargill complex, where flood waters are $5\frac{1}{2}$ feet higher than anytime in history. We were forced to abandon the general yard area where salt, molasses, fertilizer, and other products are stored and handled . . . we simply could not reinforce and increase our other dikes high enough fast enough. It will likely be a month before waters recede so we can fully assess damage and losses. Our oil plant is completely surrounded by water for the first time in history, but we believe we have successfully protected all inventories there. Our major effort has been to protect the many millions of dollars worth of grain in elevator C . . . we believe the flood has reached its peak and will soon begin to recede, but it may be weeks before the plant is out of danger (from collapse of dikes softened by water).

By February 1966, the Company had completed a new, heightened dike. The whole levee had an elevation of 715 feet above sea level, 1 foot above the 1962 crest. The 1965 crest had come up as high as 719.35 feet. Now the levee

Port Cargill complex, inundated by swollen waters of flooding Minnesota river, was cut off from the town of Savage except by boat. Roads, bridges, powerlines, and rail trackage fell victim to waters, which crested at an all-time high of 719.35 feet above sea level, $5\frac{1}{2}$ feet over 714-foot previous flood record set in 1952 (Minneapolis *Star*, c. April 1965).

had been raised to 721 feet. Only time would tell whether there would be a new record breaker coming along in a future year.

Fire, too, was always a threat, although the Company had been quite fortunate in this regard over the years. Still, incidents did happen. In September 1963, one of Cargill's older line elevator properties at Carrington, North Dakota, burned to the ground. The fire, which had started in the cupola, spread through the headhouse and storage annexes within minutes. The loss of the property and grain in store was estimated at about $400,000. It was an old structure, and the Company promptly rebuilt it as a much more efficient operation. Nevertheless, fire always terrifies grain men, not only for the loss of any structure but also for the potential for explosion.

Cargill took a significant initiative in early 1965, when it purchased the Horizon Insurance Company, Limited, of Hamilton, Bermuda. The firm would be operated as a wholly owned subsidiary and was organized "to provide insurance coverage at competitive rates for selective company properties and inventories"; so noted Charles Mooers, the Company's vice president and treasurer. The new company would not offer this insurance to the general public; rather, it would be used as a "captive" firm, to cover only properties of Cargill and its affiliates. Mooers pointed out that the Company would allow Horizon to take "only the better risks—those in which the discrepancy between probable loss and commercial premium is greatest."

Only a fraction of Cargill's total insurance requirements would be underwritten by Horizon. Insurance covering all properties located within the United States were written by a major commercial insurance firm, with 5 percent of the total then reinsured with Horizon. Outside the United States, however, Horizon insured ocean cargo shipped by either Cargill or Tradax, again retaining only 5 percent of the total for its own account and distributing the remaining 95 percent through a group of commercial insurance firms brought together by an insurance broker in Belgium. Samuel Parks, manager of Cargill's insurance department, pointed out that it was routine for many U.S. firms to be partially "self insured." However, as companies grew larger and more diversified, it became increasingly desirable that this self-insurance be made formal. Horizon now could issue insurance policies and certificates, functions that had not been possible under earlier self-insurance arrangements.[9]

How Should the Company Organize Internationally?

The sharp differences expressed in several of the 1965–1966 division annual reports about "who should be in charge of what" in the Company's European operations mirrored some deep-seated, sometimes almost hostile tensions about how to expand international efforts. Some of this appeared to be narrow "turf" infighting by several strong egos. But it was deeper than this—it went to the heart of questions about how to organize a multinational organization.

The decade of the 1960s was a period in which a large number of American companies began to move abroad. Many had had sales and service outlets abroad since before World War II. But the seminal step of graduating from this to having major operations abroad and doing this as a coordinated "multinational" strategy was a much newer manifestation. So often at this point, questions about how to develop the most effective organization to handle this stage would surface. The issue can be posed simply this way: If one were to put a full-scale manufacturing unit in, say, West Germany (as I described in a previous book about Deere & Company going to Mannheim in that country in 1957), would the new German office be more or less a self-standing, decentralized one, fully staffed with the various functions, all reporting to its managing director? Or would each function (or some of them) report directly back to the home office heads of that function? As one began to deal with all the realities of this, further complications would quickly arise. Today management practices on these questions are far more sophisticated, particularly as they began to draw on newer concepts such as matrix theories.

Earlier in the year 1966, there had been a rash of misfires by several Cargill/Tradax entities, each trying to set up new projects in France but each operating mostly alone. Karel Hens had new feed projects in mind and was approaching central authorities in Paris. Tradax had new proposals for French grain, a joint account with J. A. Goldschmidt & Cie in Paris but with field prospects in St-Nazaire. A silo and oil plant project in St-Nazaire had been worked out in Minneapolis, with the assistance of Tradax. There was even a possible hybrid seed plan mooted, with Cargill's research department involved.

All of these initiatives shooting off in all directions disconcerted the French; indeed, there was a press campaign against the oil plant and elevator in St-Nazaire. Tradax lawyer Hubert Sontheim, called in to try to give some coordinated direction, worried that "the Cargill-Tradax companies have thus no control over their 'image' with the French authorities. This might even have a very misleading effect upon Cargill's actual intentions in France." Sontheim emphasized the need for "one spokesman."

Erv Kelm, realizing that the cacophony among all these units was becoming acrimonious, now took a bold step. In preparation for the annual board of directors retreat scheduled for late July, he appointed not one but *three* board ad hoc committees, each given an identical charge "to consider the international question" and each to be ready to present its recommendations at the July meeting. The two executive vice presidents, Bob Diercks and Fred Seed, and Walter Gage, chairman of Tradax (and just elected with Whitney MacMillan to the Cargill board), were the chairs for the three committees. Certainly this decision telegraphed some pointed clues about Kelm's private management strategy. It was a move not without risk, for any wrong signal could quickly exacerbate any factionalism that might be running as an under-

Cargill board of directors in the chairman's office, 1965 (from left, A. G. Egermayer, R. J. Harrigan, J. C. North, Cargill MacMillan, Jr., F. N. Seed, E. E. Kelm, D. C. Levin, and H. R. Diercks (Cargill staff photograph).

current. Looking back at this with hindsight, Kelm seems to have exhibited a strong self-confidence that he could manage any such discussion well.

All the documents submitted to the board by the three committees were thoughtful, detailed analyses. The Fred Seed report was an extension of an earlier version Seed had made at the summer board meeting the previous year; it put special focus on a number of tax concerns as they would be affected by alternative organizational choices. Seed posed a series of questions but did not opt for a particular direction. The Diercks piece was blunter. It called attention to the fiasco in France and continued: "One of the difficulties is that with our headquarters in Wayzata we tend to be provincial in our ways of doing things. This, however, is a state of mind that must change as Cargill grows into a truly world business. With rising nationalism throughout the world, each country we might want to enter has its own regulations and ideas."

Hubert Sontheim, the author of the Tradax report, echoed this concern, citing a private report of European investment bankers after a trip to the

United States: "In many fields, Europe seems incapable to meet the American challenge. We even would raise the question as to just how far the United States will be able to carry their economic expansion abroad without meeting major obstacles, particularly of a psychological or political nature." (Interestingly, a highly influential book had been published right at this time by a French author, Jean Jacques Servan-Schreiber, called just this—*The American Challenge*; the author worried about what he saw as the overwhelming power of the American corporation as it moved abroad.) Sontheim opted again for a single individual, preferably a national, as manager and representative for "any one given country."

Walter Gage was the most direct in proposed solutions. He recommended that "general management of all the Cargill group's affairs outside of North America be concentrated in one place" and that this place should be Geneva. "The same reasons that made it wise to carry on worldwide trading from Geneva should apply with equal force to manufacturing and other activities. It is a matter of geography rather than one of individual capability. . . . We would continue to utilize the technical and engineering skills [available in Wayzata]. Administratively, however, all operations (perhaps excluding Central America) would report to Geneva."

This left the matter, still murky and undecided, to the long-range planning committee for decision. And here Kelm was decisive. In a memorandum under his own signature on August 24, a "statement of policy concerning international goals and organization" was sent to all senior management. First, it made clear that "the top management of the corporation reserves for itself the ultimate direction and control for public relations, governmental relations, finance, salary administration, personnel policies, corporate organization, final review of law, accounting and communications." In the process, he made explicitly clear the prerogative of the chief executive officer.

The next statement, underlined in the memorandum, cut to the core: "*Organization will be product-oriented*" (Kelm's emphasis). Each division was free to "use all talents and know-how" to develop their activities in foreign countries. Each division was responsible for its own profit and loss but could draw on the Company's administrative facilities, when needed, to avoid establishing duplicate staff functions. Where there was more than one project in a country, a single person, if available, would be spokesman "in public and government relations" while being "responsive to the divisions." If not available, the director of administration in Geneva would assume the role, "again responsive to the divisions involved."

As to trading activities, "the corporation recognizes the really major contribution that Tradax has made . . . and wants to continue the present singleness of purpose concept. This is their operational responsibility." In addition, Tradax would provide administrative services as described in the memorandum—"this is their administrative responsibility." Tradax was to be excluded, however, from trading in "North America, Central America, and the following countries in South America: Venezuela, Colombia, Ecuador, Peru and Chile."

Enumerated also were some "special situations." The Geneva law office would have primary responsibility for legal matters in all the Tradax trading operations in Europe and in the Middle East. The profit-and-loss responsibility for the two new ocean vessels would rest with Tradax. As to Argentina, that operation "is meeting our objectives. They have been successful in managing the business on a decentralized basis but still being particularly responsive both to divisions . . . and to the staff." The comptroller's department was given specific assignments here.

Kelm's memorandum was a tour de force, for the moment definitively tying most of the loose ends that had resulted over the recent years of foreign initiatives. It was not going to solve the problems of the future, when an amazing extension of Cargill's foreign thrust would take full hold. In the short run, however, the battles over turf had much clearer guidelines. In particular, the underlined statement, the "*organization will be product-oriented*," laid to rest the issue of whether divisions could aggressively pursue their own projects abroad (they could).

The instant when Cargill became a truly multinational company can be placed right here. The Company had had "listening posts" in both Europe and Argentina since before World War II and had had the semiautonomous Tradax operation in Geneva since the mid-1950s. The Amsterdam terminal and Argentina operation had come along shortly after. But it was at this point, with the Spanish soybean plant, the purchases of the Hens and Shaver companies and the Central American operations, and the expansion plans of 1965–1966, that Cargill moved toward a truly multinational posture. Company managements today generally prefer the word *global* rather than *multinational*, for the latter became a somewhat tarnished word in the hearings of the Senate Subcommittee on Multinational Corporations in the mid-1970s (see Chapter Eight). Being precise, the words typically *are* used differently: *multinational* tends to involve discrete businesses in various countries, whereas *global* connotes knitting those businesses together into systems. At Cargill, the board of directors meetings of late July 1966 and the subsequent Kelm statement provided this multinational watershed and certainly had the beginnings of going global.[10]

CHAPTER THREE

India's Hunger, Beachhead in Japan, a Tragedy

Famine had struck India again. Expected monsoon rains were failing as the year 1965 continued; by December, drought had taken a huge toll on agricultural crops. Already it was apparent: Indian farmers and their families were eating their seed wheat, thereby virtually ensuring that the next crop would be very weak. A cycle that had been seen so many times in India over the centuries seemed now about to repeat.

India had suffered famines since time immemorial. In earlier days, famines came only about every 50 years; but in the nineteenth century, this rhythm had accentuated, and the occurrence in the twentieth century was equally frequent. In those earlier years, the word *famine* had been used particularly to describe situations where there was literally *no* food. In this more recent period, the world's food was typically available "somewhere" in adequate quantity, but the logistics of getting the food to people were horrendous. Even by 1965, only about 11 percent of India's 580,000 villages had reasonably adequate access roads. One village in three was more than five miles from a satisfactory road. Further, the extreme poverty of the villagers made it almost impossible for hundreds of thousands or millions of people to buy adequate food even if it could be made available. As early as the Great Famine of 1896–1897, which was a country-wide calamity, food was "always purchasable in the market though at high and in some places at excessively high prices." But it was quite another thing to afford it.

This evolving Indian famine of 1965 was being played out in the context of food shortages in many other developing countries, some of these quite serious. The culprit here was, particularly, population growth, which was exceeding food output in poorer countries all over the globe. Gunnar Myrdal, the famous Swedish economist, warned that this population growth was being grossly underestimated and that food supplies must be doubled by 1980 and trebled by the year 2000, else "hundreds of millions" faced starvation.

In February 1966, President Lyndon Johnson sent Congress a special mes-

Cargill Addresses World Hunger (*Cargill News*, August 1968).

sage on a national food policy, urging that up to $3.5 billion a year be allocated to combat hunger and malnutrition. As far back as 1959, Senator Hubert Humphrey and others had proposed changes in the basic P.L. 480 legislation; Humphrey wanted a stronger focus on humanitarian food aid. The law was changed at that time to include barter provisions, but it still focused on surplus disposal. By that time the United States was building up too large a local-currency balance in many of the developing countries utilizing this aid. Senator Humphrey put this concern well: "In many countries we have sizable amounts of foreign currencies loaned out as a result of Public Law 480 activity, and we have an equal amount of foreign currencies which lie idle, drawing no interest, losing value through inflation, hanging like a sword over the economy of the country, with no one knowing what will happen to it. . . . Meanwhile, people are in need, schools are inadequate, health facilities are neglected, roads are not being constructed, medical research goes undone." Yet the focus in the United States was still on commercial prospects, with attention particularly to those always-looming surpluses of grain held by the government.

Now Johnson reiterated that the name of the law *was* the Food for Peace Act and vowed to place emphasis clearly on the humanitarian goals of the program. Coupled with this was a critically important and widely urged additional proposal, that the recipient nations themselves heighten their efforts at *self-help*, and to accomplish this they would be aided by technical cooperation from the United States and other developed countries. Many analysts had come to feel that the easy credit and outright grants of food were debilitating the recipients, giving them "Band-Aid" help without pushing them to work harder to upgrade their own productive capacities.

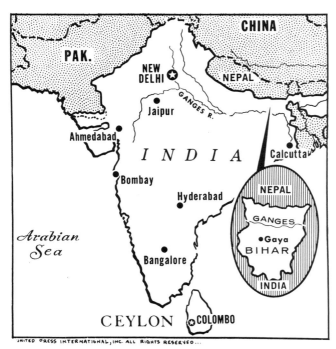

February 8, 1967: "News map locates Bihar State in northeast India, where nearly 29 million people are affected by the drought and its accompanying famine. Worst hit is the Gaya district" (UPI/Corbis-Bettmann).

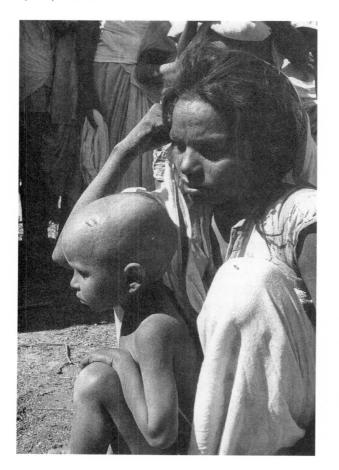

Bihar, India, February 1967:
"Kamli Dussach, whose hus-
band died because he had
nothing to eat for 10 days, sits
idly with her youngest son.
Custom has it when a father
dies the son shaves off his hair"
(UPI/Corbis-Bettmann).

India appeared to many observers to fit this description. Its governmental policy in the late 1950s and early 1960s focused particularly on assuring adequate food at low prices for the huge urban centers, such as the great cities of Calcutta, Delhi, Bombay, and Madras. But a depressed domestic price for grain from the huge imports deadened incentive for India's own grain producers. As one Indian analyst put it, "the American farmers had taken over the task from them." He continued: "the Government of India, distrusting and disregarding the market signals of excessive imports, regulated P.L. 480 imports by the slide rule assessment of 'needs.' This neglect of price trends led to imports far in excess of market deficits; these excessive imports, through price repression, retarded the expansion of cereal production, especially of wheat . . . thereby undermining one of the P.L. 480 objectives, namely, self reliance." Another Indian analyst concurred: "This paradoxical situation is explained by the fact that from the very beginning, P.L. 480 supplies came to be used for providing budgetary support to the Central Government on the one hand, and to moderate on the other the inflationary impact of deficit financing . . . how far was the use of concessional food imports justified for purposes of budgetary support, or to buttress the reckless fiscal policy followed by the government?"

In the 1950s and early 1960s, India had received massive shipments of wheat under both the provisions allowing payment in rupees and in outright food aid grants. Now, under the Johnson proposals, India's totals would need to be greatly increased if the incipient famine was to be averted. An additional 3.5 million tons of grain were added to the 6.5 million tons already scheduled for shipment in 1966. The challenge was to add to already massive imports to defeat the famine yet provide incentives and technical help to Indian producers to become more self-reliant.

President Johnson recommended that Congress enact legislation that would expand food shipments to countries where food needs were growing *and* self-help measures were underway. In addition, he proposed increased capital and technical assistance and a focus on nutrition, especially for the young. Cargill's Joe Bailey, then assistant superintendent of terminal elevator operations, was one of the consultants to Indian port authorities at this time; he reported: "We found very little modern machinery, and most of that in bad repair . . . every bushel removed from the holds of ships is bagged by hand for shipment inland. Hand labor is used everywhere for almost every kind of job . . . there is always resistance to change."

Congress agreed with Johnson on the Food for Peace program, although the strong anti-Communist feeling among some congressmen resulted in the inclusion of a provision banning any aid to a nation trading with North Vietnam or Cuba (a concept that President Johnson opposed).

The food situation in India now became worse, for by mid-1967 the drought had revisited the country for a second year, with its severity centered particularly in the state of Bihar. The *New York Times* reported that "Farmers were selling their children." Related problems of malnutrition, disease, and drinking water shortage exacerbated the situation. The food grains production for the country in 1965–1966 was just 72.03 million tons, compared to the 89 million tons of the previous year. In 1966–1967, with drought continuing, the amount rose only to 74.23 million tons. Total imports of wheat, which had been 3.09 million in 1960–1961, jumped to 6.6 million in 1964–1965 and to 7.8 million in 1965–1966. Now the United States provided an additional 1.5 million tons of food grains, which brought its total grain aid in 1967 to 5.1 million tons. The wheat owned by the Commodity Credit Corporation, which stood at 1.1 billion bushels in 1963, had dropped to 123.6 million in 1967.

Finally, the rains did come and the country could look forward to a good crop. The massive aid programs from agencies all over the world had averted a tragedy. And it was not just that the rains had returned, for the Indian gov-

Breaking local record, U.S.-flag tanker Hans Isbrandtsen *completes May loading of record cargo of white wheat from Cargill elevator at Albany, New York. The shipment totaled 25,300 tons of New York wheat purchased by the India supply mission. Gerald Mitchell, Eastern Region manager, stated that the large shipment was made possible by completion the previous year of a project to deepen the Hudson River channel from 27 to 32 feet. Ships of up to 50,000 dead weight tons could then travel up the Hudson to Albany* (Cargill News, *August 1967*).

ernment turned toward a more free-market approach, giving more generous terms of trade to the farmer. As Harvard economist Robert Paarlberg put it, "Indian production had fallen so far behind internal demand that free-market prices finally stopped their downward slide, and began a sharp upturn . . . it was in response to this 'adverse' development, which directly threatened the objectives of a policy elite still oriented toward urban demands, that Indian agricultural policies at last underwent significant revision."

Just around the corner, too, was a striking new development that had occurred in the technology of grain production, the fabled "Green Revolution." This will be described later in this chapter, when we explore the effects on the world's grain trade of this "sea change" in India's food production.[1]

"Aggressive Diversification"

The unusual demand for food grains militated by the Indian famine afforded great opportunity for the grain trading companies. The effects of this exciting new business milieu were pronounced at Cargill.

When the results of the 1966–1967 crop year were in, the Company's net profit slightly edged the previous year's record—$16.9 million compared to $16.7 million. The Grain Division had had an excellent year; Vegetable Oil, a record. Tradax earnings had been cut in half from the previous year; an Argentine peso devaluation had had some effect, but mostly it was the uncomfortable fact that Tradax had been on the wrong side of the market. There was a "psychological market in U.S. grains during the summer and fall . . . when it was felt by the public that the U.S.A. would run out of grain supplies. . . . Our analysis showed the contrary, and while we were proved correct by the reduced exports from the U.S., it was a long time before public realization of this trend restored some of our losses."

For the overall Company, it was a second very good year, and this now fu-

"Dedication of the new Industrias de la Soja installation at Tarragona, Spain. The official blessing is bestowed by formally garbed Cardinal Archbishop of Tarragona, wearing high gold-and-white mitre. At left (in conversation), general director Joaquin Guardiola; beside him, commercial director Hank Van Veen; at right 'INDUSOJA' board chairman Alejandro Mollinedo" (Cargill News, February 1965).

"Future uses for Cargill computer system and for large-facility equipment now on order are discussed by Cal Smith, data processing manager; Dr. Tom Caywood, training specialist from prominent consulting firm; Jim Cargill, vice president, who directs operations research; and terminal elevator department head Milt Bondus" (*Cargill News,* December 1964).

eled a growing optimism. At the major summer board meeting, discussion reverted again to corporate goals; and while the essence of these goals stayed the same, the enthusiasm of the rhetoric now showed through. Repeated was the basic objective mentioned four years earlier, to be a "young, vibrant, aggressive organization—a leader, not a follower." The return-on-investment goals now were advanced for several of the divisions: grain from 8 to 10 percent, vegetable oil from 12 to 14 percent. Further, for the first time a specific growth goal was set out for the Company as a whole—a minimum 5 percent annual growth. Included also was a Kelm preoccupation, to double the net worth of the Company in 10 years (later, he moved this down to 7, then to 6). Plans to expand overseas permeated the document; in Bob Harrigan's backup detail, he advocated expanding overseas operations to 30 percent of the Company's net worth by 1970.

But was the document motivating for *all* of management? One of the sentences highlighted in the minutes emphasized this: "Are key employees fully informed of our philosophy and goals to achieve maximum challenge and contribution?" More work needed to be done here, thought many. The final line in the corporate minutes for that July board meeting was a self-affirmation that senior management was on the right track: "The aggressive diversification and expansion policies of the Company as evidenced by our recent activities are proper."

A highly detailed finance committee document in November of 1967 spelled out precisely the financial mechanisms that would be used to obtain these goals. Even with the usual financial officer caution, the view here was upbeat, too; it was "an up-to-date review . . . in view of the current rise in earnings." While the guidelines were based "with an eye on the past" they were influenced "primarily [by] the results of the 10-year projections prepared by Mr. Kelm." To put this in a grain trading context, the board was "bullish."2

Innovating in Japan's Backyard

Tradax, rather than the divisions, now took many of the key steps in the aggressive diversification abroad. One of the most far-reaching was in Japan, a country notoriously skeptical of having any outside business intrusion in their own land. Tradax now undertook just such a challenge.

When Cargill acquired a significant West Coast grain trading firm, Kerr Gifford & Co., Inc., in 1953, a link was established with Kerr Gifford's Japanese agent, a British house called Andrew Weir & Co. Thomas Huxley had been a Japanese prisoner of war during World War II and had stayed on after the Occupation as head of the Tokyo office of Weir. Huxley and John Cole at Kerr Gifford had established joint relationships in Tokyo, Huxley handling the importing and John Cole the exporting. The Andrew Weir management had come to feel that trading was not one of their core competencies and inquired whether Cargill would be interested in purchasing the Tokyo office. Cargill agreed to the acquisition, Weir moved its Pacific Rim offices to Hong Kong, and the office was renamed Tradax Japan, Ltd., in 1956. Huxley joined Tradax in Geneva, with Ian Watson coming from Geneva to be the new head of the office.

Tradax wanted particularly to emphasize quantity importing directly into Japan, not just continuing the sundry export business that had been the main effort before. Since far back, Japan had always wanted to trade for its imports on an FOB basis, utilizing its own shipping (or shipping charters) and purchasing or underwriting its own insurance. Tradax, on the other hand, wanted to be able to ship into Japan on a CIF (cost/insurance/freight to destination) basis, so that *it* could make its own ocean transport decisions and its own insurance choices; ship charter had been one of the important Tradax roles over the years, and Cargill's Horizon Insurance operations allowed savings for CIF efforts, too.

Earlier, the Japanese government had allowed full import of wheat with no restrictions; but by the early 1960s, quotas had been established, and the large Japanese trading companies, the *zaibatsus*, had gained a stranglehold over the business. By 1965, the *Asahi Evening News* was commenting about the "tremendous power now being wielded by the 'all round' trading houses" that were dominating the wheat, soybean, and feed grain business.

Japanese shipyards had become the marvel of the world. Several of the great shipbuilding companies, working out of huge dry docks capable of holding as large as a 200,000-ton ship, now produced the most advanced vessels in the world, highly automated with state-of-the-art loading and unloading equipment. On the other hand, Japan's docks and unloading mechanisms on shore were almost primitive; as a marketing publication put it in May 1966, "On one side are the giant trading companies and the 150,000 ton tankers; on the other, the 1.3 million retailers with gross sales averaging only $15,000. Japan's distribution systems run from new-fashioned to near-feudal." Grain coming to Japan, for example, was almost universally transferred from large and medium-sized vessels at buoys in the bays or from small ships at mill berths, at a slow 1,000 tons per day. Literally, there were no modern, fully automated shore installations to match the large, highly efficient grain ships that could be serving the country.

Several of the larger world grain trading companies owned their own ocean shipping at this point. Of the "big six," Louis Dreyfus and Continental Grain were the leaders. Both had started with ownership of reconverted Liberty ships from World War II, and this size of vessel—about 7,000 tons—was dominant for several years after the war. Then Dreyfus began to upgrade its fleet to vessels in the 20,000-ton range. Continental had gone through the same process, although not quite as innovatively as Dreyfus.

Now pressure was building in some quarters within Cargill to follow suit, coming particularly from the CCI group. George Cohee had interested himself in the patterns of Cargill's ocean shipping and had charted statistics on the movement of the Company's grain over a 10-year period. These highlighted just how much of Cargill's grain moved on a fixed route from Baie Comeau to Europe or from Baton Rouge to Rotterdam/Amsterdam. Cohee argued that these figures pointed to a hard core of business that was there dependably, year after year, and that Cargill should have its own ships to handle it.

However, there were vehement objections from other quarters, particularly Tradax. Ocean freight was being traded by Tradax on a significant scale, but Walter Gage, in particular, opposed the notion of purchasing shipping (in line with his overall attitude of Tradax not owning fixed assets). Nevertheless, CCI pushed ahead. Clifford Roberts, its head, made a visit to Japan in the fall of 1965. After a tour of the various shipbuilders capable of producing these highly efficient large ships, he obtained a commitment from Ishikawajima Harima Heavy Industries at Kure to keep a tentative bid open for six months so that Roberts could sell Cargill management on the idea. Despite Gage's opposition, the decision from the board was positive, and Kure proceeded to build the vessel, quickly enough to be launched in the summer of 1967. This was a 55,500-ton dry bulk carrier, some 735 feet in length and 106 feet in breadth, tailored with 6 inches to spare through the Panama Canal. Thus, the ship was a Panamax—the maximum size that could traverse the Panama Canal (the larger 150,000- to 200,000-ton vessels were single-ocean ships). CCI immediately had its Greenwich Marine subsidiary begin the process of crewing and fitting the ship. George Cohee was assigned as head of the project and moved to the Greenwich office in New York City.

Cohee made certain that all of the special needs of grain carrying were met. Later he commented, "To this end the [ship] was able to load grain with more slack spaces (partly loaded) than any other similar size existing vessel. This to allow it to clean out various parcels left in the elevator which would otherwise have to be carried in smaller ships at a higher cost. In the large holds, the [ship] had a down-draft ventilation system to prevent damage to the grain on top due to condensation under the hatch covers, as was experienced with practically all vessels loading in the warm U.S. Gulf and then sail-

Kure, Japan, shipyard, at the launching of the Cargill's Captain W. D. Cargill *(ship is in right foreground, between two other vessels* (Cargill staff photograph, 1965).

ing to colder Europe in the winter." Erv Kelm added, "Because of design, size, and speed, this will be the most efficient grain vessel afloat."

Roberts did not want the name of the vessel to be associated with Cargill so initially had decided on using the same system as with the earlier inland waterways fleet of the Company in naming its towboats after the cities on the Mississippi River, proposing to start a new series with "Bay" as the last word. On Lake Minnetonka, which the Lake Office faced, were Grays Bay, Wayzata Bay, Stubbs Bay, and so on, for a total of over 60 bays, enough for any fleet that Cargill might build in the future. So he had picked Grays Bay, and it had already been painted onto the ship in the Kure yards. Then the families had second thoughts, and decided to name the ship the *Captain W. D. Cargill* after the ship captain father of W. W. Cargill.

Walter Gage, too, had had a change of heart. The ocean freight scene had become more frenzied, with profitable charters more difficult to come by, and it now seemed to Gage to make sense to have Cargill own some ocean shipping. Further, Gage wanted the newly acquired *Captain W. D. Cargill* to be part of the Tradax group, rather than CCI, and he was able to persuade Kelm to support him. Cohee left the Company at this point and grumbled later, "No sooner did I step out the door at Cargill, than some fellow in Geneva noticed that there was a hiccup in the ocean freight market and he re-let the about-to-be-delivered *Captain W. D. Cargill* before she ever got a chance to perform her grain mission. That monumental mistake was compounded by what then became the view of Cargill shipping as practiced in Geneva,

Commodities Division introduction of anti-rust product, Carguard. Special fenders were put on cars lent by Ford Motor Company to be used in Carguard road tests in Iowa. Panels of autobody metal were fastened under the specially made fenders of the cars in the tests, held in cooperation with the city of Davenport. Carguard showed up to 87 percent less rust then those exposed to untreated salt (Cargill News, March 1965).

namely, 'We are in the shipping business' and not 'We are in the grain business.' With that attitude in place, subsequent vessels were built that were semi-suitable for the grain trades and were flexible for other uses, rendering them not especially good for anything."

Interestingly, Cohee's notion of a fully specialized ship had been accomplished by Cargill just at this time, for with the ordering of the *Captain W. D. Cargill,* another vessel was being built for the Company, also in Japan—a 14,000-ton ship that would be specially designed just to shuttle back and forth from North American ports to the Manchester ship canal, to deliver corn to a Corn Products Company subsidiary at that city. The ship, named the *Carchester* after that city, was 496 feet long, with a $63\frac{1}{2}$-foot beam and a maximum draft of 26 feet. Its function precisely met Cohee's definition: "Ironically, we did do for Corn Products Company what we should have done for Cargill . . . the *Carchester* was ruthlessly specialized for that task and no other ship in the world could achieve her low cost of delivering grain into the canal. Corn Products was the beneficiary of that venture and Cargill should have been the beneficiary of many such ventures. An era is gone and an opportunity was missed."

Hindsight is always easier, however. Not only was Cohee indulging a bit in second guessing, so was Walter Gage! In June 1967, war erupted between the Arabs and the Israelis; and during the early days, shipping had been sunk in the Suez Canal, resulting in the absolute closing of the canal (and it was not opened again for eight years, in June 1975). The Tradax annual report for the year 1967–1968 commented, "With the uncertain conditions created by the Arab/Israeli War and the closure of the Suez Canal—the war in Vietnam and the unsettled political situation in various parts of the world—the freight market was even more difficult than usual to read. We were fortunate that . . . we took delivery of the '*Captain W. D. Cargill*' during this period."

Cargill Aspires to Be a "First Mover"

One of the most interesting processes in business is that of innovation, when an organization (often sparked by a single dedicated individual) sees a need that is not being filled and takes the substantial risk to try to meet the need with something new. Economists have dubbed this group or person the "first mover" and have posited that this innovator will have certain first-mover advantages. They would have a head start in developing capabilities and would be able to exploit the cost advantages of scale and scope. Rivals would have to follow with a later process of trying to establish the same end effort that the first mover already had in place. Barriers to entry would have to be met, and this intimidating process might or might not "take."

Just at this time, a group of researchers under the leadership of Everett Rogers was studying this process of diffusion of innovations, pointing out the complexities as the process moved from "early adopters" to the "early majority" and, finally, to "the laggards." In essence, if one could successfully put in place a true innovation, there would be first-mover advantages for at least enough time to make the effort productive and remunerative.

Having had signal success with its Amsterdam terminal (leased from the city), Tradax now began the process of attempting to build (or have built) a similar silo operation in Japan. Lowell Nelson was sent to Japan from Geneva and, working with Alan Blair, now the head of the Tokyo office, began the search for how this might be done. Land was extremely expensive, and the local Japanese firms, both the *zaibatsus* and the smaller warehousing groups, seemed interested but quite skittish about the notion of such a drastic change in existing unloading and storage facilities. Nelson reported back in August of 1965 that his research showed that in "five to ten years, Japan will be the largest importer of free dollar grains in the non-communist trade area"—that estimates for 1974 forecast that grain imports in the five major Japanese ports would exceed 9 million tons. All of this seemed to indicate that the potential for a modern grain transfer facility was opportune. Thus began an intricate process of finding out just how to do this.

At first, Nelson explored the possibility of a large floating transfer facility that would require little or no land acquisition. But this did not prove feasible, nor did the transshipment from large ships to smaller look attractive. A Japanese partner with existing port-side land seemed the most promising. Nelson talked with a number of American companies with Japanese partners and reported back to Minneapolis about his findings:

Negotiations are difficult and run a rocky road. Often one is led to believe that basic agreement has been reached, only to find the next day that your intended joint venture partners have taken another tack. The nod of approval only means the recognition of your statement . . . it is absolutely paramount that all details be specifically spelled out . . . integrity in a partner is the primary requisite. Although [a U.S. company] feel that they have one of the best partners in the industry and one with the highest integrity by Japanese standards, they have deemed it advisable to have Peat Marwick & Mitchell audit the books on a monthly basis. . . . Negotiations can be expected to be slow. The Japanese are great paper shufflers and red tape abounds! This condition is true, not only [with] government agencies, but also dealing with . . . one's partner on both the board and operating level . . . often bills of other subsidiary companies may find their way into your joint venture company, if for any one of a number of reasons it is deemed advisable by your joint venture partners. . . . I was told on more than one occasion that the Japanese are deficient in up-to-date marketing and financial practices.

Now Cargill began to enter just this process. Walter Gage wrote Erv Kelm in February of 1965, "This has been a frustrating affair to try to get underway with any speed, and I fear it will continue to be that way. Our information from many other American companies has shown the same frustration and delays. . . . I think it an excellent idea if you look for yourself on the spot."

As the halting process of searching for a partner dragged on, Cargill's West

Coast group at Portland, Oregon, weighed in with its own worries. Robert Menze wrote, "I suppose our chief concern here in Portland is that we select a partner which will suit our purpose in Japan but not affect, negatively, our export business to the Japanese market generally." Menze preferred a partner that was not a trading firm at all; if no such company was acceptable, "we believe that we would be inclined to line up the small trading firm with relatively small influence and wheat quota. . . . The smaller, less well-established firm possibly would tend to take a less active part in control and policy decisions . . . if we lined up with one of the big firms, we believe we would risk a boycott, or at least a more suspicious or 'cooler' attitude on the part of other big importers. Inasmuch as the Japanese wheat and barley business is subject to Japanese Food Agency quotas allocated to the various firms . . . and which show no signs of being changed or liberalized, we would severely limit our potential volume if we tied our fortunes to one firm in such a way as to prejudice our business with others."

Finally, just such a smaller firm was identified. It was the Toyo Wharf & Warehouse Company, Ltd., established in 1946 as a successor to a previous similar company whose principal business had been transporting cargo between Japan and Manchuria as a subsidiary of the South Manchurian Railway Company. Toyo fit many of Cargill's criteria: It was a medium-sized warehousing company, located in Kawasaki, in Tokyo Bay. The firm had substantial storage facilities, reasonably modern, and its loading and unloading equipment was also adequate (although not large enough for handling one of the Panamax ships). The dockside space was long enough for the larger ships, but if the latter were in the 50,000- to 60,000-ton range, additional dredging would be necessary.

An intricate process of negotiation now began with Toyo. Alan Blair handled the long discussions over big issues and small and soon had to warn the Geneva Tradax group not to make too many direct comparisions between the Amsterdam experience and the Toyo progress. In Amsterdam, Tradax had exclusive use of the facility right from the start; the plan here would involve sharing quarters. The individuals in the municipality of Amsterdam really knew nothing about the practical business of discharging ocean vessels and operating a transfer facility, whereas Toyo had been in this business for a long time and on a large scale. By July, Blair reported to Nelson, "They are already showing some irritation about the catechism to which we are subjecting them. They have not yet gotten to the point of saying 'That is none of your goddamn business.' But they have pointed out that they wrapped up a previous deal of the same size 'without being asked to explain or justify their calculations.'. . . Please do not misunderstand me. I am not suggesting that we should blindly accept all their calculations and sign on the dotted lines, but I feel that our approach should be one of making polite constructive suggestions as to the areas where Toyo Futo might pare down certain cost items."

The plan that was evolving would call for a silo of not less than 28,000 metric tons capacity, Tradax having exclusive use of only about one third of the silo. Tradax would be expected to unload a maximum of 500,000 unit tons per year; if there were additional quantities, Tradax would have to pay an additional fee yet to be negotiated. The wharf would be arranged so that it would take an ocean vessel of overall length of 224 meters (734 feet), with a beam of 32 meters (105 feet) and a draft of 11.5 meters (38 feet). In effect, the dock space and discharging capacity would be designed to handle ocean vessels up to 52,200 tons—a revolution in the Japanese grain discharge business. Discharge rates were to be specifically stated: If the vessel was over 32,000 dead weight tons, Toyo was to guarantee 7,000 metric tons per "weather working day." This dropped to 6,000 metric tons for vessels from 26,000 to 31,999 dead-weight tons and went as low as 3,000 metric tons for vessels less than 20,000 dead-weight tons.

The mechanics of moving this much grain from the ship into the silo and/or coastal vessels, rail, or truck were to be specified, too. Here the quite antiquated small truck and rail car combinations, together with some of the handling methods, made the process of moving the product swiftly through the entire warehouse and out to end users more than usually difficult. For all of this, the Tradax contribution to the joint venture would be 227,000,000 yen ($750,000 per year), making the total Tradax commitment to Toyo over the 10 years an eye-catching $7,500,000.

As the complex parameters of the deal began to be put together, Bob Diercks wrote Nelson, "From the looks of it, I feel even more strongly that this is the only route for us to take if we want to advance in Japan. . . . I admit it is risky, but it is a matter of taking a risk or going backwards."

By November 1966 a simple memorandum of agreement covering the basic issues had been signed. Toyo planned an immediate announcement, and the Cargill senior management in Wayzata wired that this be couched only "IN VERY GENERAL TERMS AND ABSOLUTELY NO SPECIFIC DETAILS . . . SUCH AS TONNAGE GUARANTEE, LUMP SUM PAYMENT, OR TONNAGE EQUIVALENT RATE . . . OR DAILY DISCHARGE GUARANTY . . . INFORMATION OF THIS NATURE MUST BE CONSIDERED CONFIDENTIAL." The final announcement did indeed look very bland, for Cargill remained uneasy about competitive responses, especially from the big *zaibatsus*.

At this point the negotiations had to turn narrowly specific. At so many stages here, the questions evolved around Tradax pushing Toyo for increased efficiencies in the project. Tradax wanted (as one wire put it) to "make a statement" that it was insisting on state-of-the-art technology. As Cliff Roberts averred, in a wire to Blair, "IF PRESENT OLD LINE COMPANIES WON'T PROVIDE THE SERVICES THESE PEOPLE DESIRE THEN EVIDENTLY THEY ARE WILLING TO DO IT THEMSELVES. AS A 100 YR OLD FIRM IN THIS BIZ, I THINK IT IS UP TO US TO BE AHEAD OF THESE NEWCOMERS IN EFFICIENCY AND

Two vessels discharge at Toyo Futo's new grain terminal at Kawasaki, built as a joint venture with Cargill. Shown above is the ship M/S Atlantic City, *unloading across the bridge structure into the terminal; below, the Norwegian vessel* Tonga *sending grain directly to barges in the slip* (Cargill News, September 1968).

THEN WE WON'T HAVE THEM CONSIDERING ENTERING OUR BUSINESS." As Blair and his colleagues looked around among the Japanese feed and grain trading companies, they found several "apathetic and uninterested" in what Tradax and Toyo were doing, but others "alarmed and disturbed." A few of the *zaibatsus* "gave veiled threats" to prevent Tradax/Japan from selling in the channels where they already were established.

Blair wrote a few days later, "A SECOND PHASE OF REACTN TO OUR PRO-JECT IS APPEARANCE OF TYPICAL JPNSE UNOFFCL CARTEL CONCEPT . . . THEY NOW SEE TRADAX KAWASAKI DEAL AS POTENTIAL ALLY IN THEIR WAR FOR SURVIVAL." (These were smaller feed mill customers who felt they needed protection). By January, the opposition seemed to be picking up steam; Blair wired: "RE OPPOSITN TO OUR KSKI PLANS IS GETTG TO BE AS GOOD AS A MYS-TERY PAPERBACK WITH RED HERRINGS GALORE . . . I SUGG WE SOUND THE ALL CLEAR FOR THE TIME BEING BUT KEEP OUR EARS TO THE GRND AWAITG FURTHER RUMBLES."

By February, many of Tradax's proposed "details" had raised hackles among the Toyo people. Some of the most sensitive issues evolved around the Tradax desire to pin down specific Toyo performance in writing. Blair wired: "EVEN AFTER WE WITHDREW CONTROVERSIAL CLAUSE TEN THEY WERE VERY ANGRY INDEED ABT MAJOR CHANGE IN TONE BTWN DRAFT OF END DEC AND OUR FINAL VERSN ON PRINCIPLE THEY CSDRD HIGHLY OFFENSIVE. ALL OUR CLAUSES STATG PENALTIES FOR NON-FULFILMT OF XPCTD PFMANC OF SCALES CONVEYORS ETC. TO A JAPANESE FIRM WITH NO PREV XPERIENCE OF INTERNATNL CAKS SUCH CLAUSES CAN ONLY MEAN FUNDAMENTAL LACK OF CONFIDENCE ON OUR PART IN THEIR ABILITY . . . TS MAY SEEM CHILDISH SENSITIVITY BUT WE GOT A REAL STRONGLY WORDED SPEECH YEST FM —— SAYING SO SHOCKED BY ABRUPT CHANGE IN TONE AND SPIRIT OF OUR RE-LATNSHIP TEY HAD CSDRD DISCONTINUING ENTIRE NEGOTIATIN WITH TRA." Blair concluded: "They prefer a Japanese style—loose and woolly, leaving all possible problems to be amicably discussed as they arise."

And so it was throughout the negotations that spring. Innumerable issues had to be settled, and all through the Cargill correspondence are concerns about the Japanese "extraordinary sensitivity on the matter of their independence" and insistence that "in no circumstance can we dictate to them." The word *stubborn* appears from time to time and the need for satisfying "their delicate pride." This posed a dilemma between the Tradax desire to have everything settled precisely and the Japanese dislike of "encroachment on their autonomy." As Blair put it in one wire, "TROUBLE IS TT BY DEFINITION NO CONTRACT IS POSSIBLE UNLESS THE PARTIES GIVE UP SOME OF THEIR LIBERTIES." Finally, in late March of 1967, the full agreement *was* consummated—the whole project was a "go." The Toyo management made a special trip to Geneva to sign the agreement at the Tradax office and stopped in Minneapolis on their return to Japan. Cargill had become a first mover in Japan.

But had it? Even before the document was signed, the Cargill and Tradax people had been uneasy about whether Toyo might repeat a similar silo project at its facility on the Keihin Canal. Tradax was able to have a right of first option written into the contract, although Toyo was not enthusiastic about giving up any future autonomy.

By the fall of 1967, it was clear that the Tradax/Toyo project had captured the imaginations of many people in the industry, and the latter were moving very rapidly. Blair wrote Stu Hanson in September 1967 about the ferocity of the competitive instinct in Japan: "In many countries, the first man with a good idea can usually develop a profitable business. Japanese Big Business, however, seems very fond of the Irving Berlin refrain, 'Anything you can do, I can do better.' By the time a few competitors get into the act, chances are that nobody makes any good profits."

However, Blair continued, many of the facts as of 1966 had already changed or were in the process of changing. Several of the *zaibatsus* already were taking aggressive steps: Marubeni was developing presumably a premier discharge facility at Chiba, rumors had it that Mitsubishi was going to do the same in Yokohama. Mitsui, "the boldest and biggest wheeler and dealer in the game" (Blair's words), seemed to be biding its time but had just announced a facility to be built five years from this date "which will make everyone else's projects obsolete. I shudder to think what it will all cost, but Mitsui clearly intends it to be the 'biggest and the bestest.'"

The Toyo warehouse technologically was a stellar success. The large Panamax ships could now unload at Kawasaki, and the discharge rates that had so concerned Tradax turned out to be quite workable. The bottlenecks in the transportation from the warehouse out to the feed mills and other customers remained, although the pressure of the state-of-the-art warehouses rapidly being built all over put enough pressure on the internal distribution system to bring about many changes there, too. In sum, the Company was indeed an innovator in Japan, a first mover in the classic sense of the word.

Yet the theory involved in usual first-mover analysis tends to give the company first on the scene a pronounced advantage for a significant period of time. Here the time lapse was very short. Given the high degree of innovativeness and efficiency in the shipyards, it is not surprising that the Japanese could readily adapt such efficiencies to warehousing and to ocean vessel unloading. The response was so quick that the profitability for Tradax in the new 10-year contract was vitiated almost from the start. It had been "a complete change in the nature of Japanese trading," said the Tradax annual report of 1967–1968. Indeed, within a couple of years Tradax had to renegotiate downward some of the terms with Toyo (once again a long, involved process).

It is exhilarating to be a first mover, but the Toyo story is a sobering one in terms of those elusive payoffs presumably redounding from being an innovator. While this Toyo venture did not involve any ownership by the Company—

it was a joint venture in which the Company attained a right to only one-third of the silo that was built—the project provided one of the most trenchant experiences that the Company had had in this period. The special problems in negotiating with a sensitive people, the vivid experience of assimilating the realities of the Japanese business structure, and particularly the sensing of the enormous power of the "all round" trading companies, gave a wealth of lessons for future relations with Japan, a country that would in the next two decades become such a powerhouse for just these reasons. Toyo was a case study in learning.[3]

Cargo Carriers—a "Cash Cow"?

The vignette recounted above about CCI's doing the initial studies, the oversight of the construction, and even the crewing for Cargill's exciting venture into ocean vessels, the *Captain W. D. Cargill*, only to lose control of it at the last minute to Tradax, points up a unique feature of CCI. It always had been the dependable, mundane transportation arm for the Company's inland and Great Lakes transportation. Since back in the 1930s, when John Jr. had moved CCI to the Erie Canal and the Buffalo and Albany terminals had begun to play so large a role, CCI had been an efficient member of the Cargill team. Indeed, its steady profits, enhanced particularly by the fact that the tax laws for marine transportation equipment carried very high depreciation allowances, made CCI a classic example of a "cash cow." John Jr.'s stunning, expensive decision to build the Baie Comeau terminal at the mouth of the St. Lawrence had enhanced all of CCI's abilities manifold. Once Baie Comeau was in place, the trendline of CCI profitability seemed steady and upward; here are CCI's earnings from that late-1950 period:

1957–1958	$ 482,000	1963–1964	$ 590,000
1958–1959	$ 465,000	1964–1965	$ 736,000
1959–1960	$ 572,000	1965–1966	$ 820,000
1960–1961	$ 380,000	1966–1967	$1,036,000
1961–1962	$ 386,000	1967–1968	$ 782,000
1962–1963	$ 428,000		

The *Austen S. Cargill*, which began plying the lower Mississippi in 1960–1961, performed very well; the *John H. MacMillan, Jr.* came three years later and was an even more successful, efficient addition. By 1966–1967, the *Austen S. Cargill*'s cost per ton mile, in mills, was .82; that of the *John H. MacMillan, Jr.* was even lower, .77 (the average for chartered tow boats that year was 1.64). There was a constant search for more efficiency; for example, an ingenious bow steering unit located on the lead center barge, had been developed for the two towboats, "a positive solution to moving larger tows at higher speeds with increased safety and lower costs. It is the talk of the industry." Shades of John MacMillan, Jr., who had developed a similar device for the Erie Canal towboats!

Christening of towboat John H. MacMillan, Jr., *on May 5, 1964, in St. Louis, Missouri. At left Clifford M. Roberts, Jr.; center, Mrs. John H. Macmillan, Jr.; right, Erv Kelm* (*Cargill News,* June 1964).

In 1962–1963, CCI joined with the Hanna ore interests (through a joint venture company, Nipigon Transport) to bring the *Lake Winnipeg* into the Great Lakes–Baie Comeau operations. In its first year, it had three ore and three grain trips. The annual report of 1963–1964 commented, "A definite rate pattern has emerged in both the Canadian and U.S. fleets. The shipper who can adapt to the use of large ships is at a considerable advantage. This requires larger docks, deeper drafts, and faster handling, but the reduction in costs can also be worthwhile. For example, large lakers from Chicago to Baie Comeau are available at 2–3 cents per bushel less than small boats." By that year, the CCI inland waterways operations had moved 1,080,000 tons; the Company's lake shipments had been 135,000,000 bushels. The *Lake Manitoba* was launched in May 1968, and the annual report that year noted: "This vessel will be one of the most modern lakers in operation and will sail with a crew of eight less than the *Winnipeg.*"

But CCI had *not* been as successful with a foray early in the 1960s into chartering ocean shipping. The 1961–1962 annual report told the sad story: "We took the *Electra* on a three-year charter which commenced in February. It was a costly mistake. Soon after the charter started, the market started a steady decline and has reached the lowest level in 30 years. Revenues are now below

Nutrena's dog food finds a ready customer
(*Cargill News,* April 1967).

out-of-pocket ship costs and we are losing about $24,000 per month. Perhaps the market has reached bottom and is on the upswing, but we expect no substantial relief this calendar year." These hopes did not materialize; the next year's annual report continued the sad news: "In regard to the time charter of the *Electra* for the grain division, Greenwich is unable to make delivered sales out ahead for advanced positions that suit this charter. Hence we are most always at the mercy of the spot market." In the third year, the *Electra*, operating on a long-term charter, cut its losses substantially, down to a loss of $38,000, compared with $287,000 the previous year. As Greenwich Marine also did a great deal of its work for Tradax, the untoward losses with *Electra* must have been constant office gossip there and undoubtedly led to the successful raid that Walter Gage made on CCI two years later, when the *Captain W. D. Cargill* fell under the control of Tradax.[4]

Corn Milling: Small Beginnings—but, Wow!

In the May 1967 issue of *Cargill News*, a tiny article not even important enough to be in the index of that issue noted: "Oil Leases New Plant." It chronicled an agreement having been reached for the Vegetable Oil Division to lease the processing facilities of the Corn Starch and Syrup Company in Cedar Rapids, Iowa, effective the following September 1. The plant had been built in 1965 and had the capacity to process 14,000 bushels of corn daily and also to produce starch, syrup, and gluten feed products. The article ended, "This is the first operation of a corn milling plant for Cargill."

Despite the low-key story, the Oil Division annual report for that year seemed more bullish, more lyrical: "The first year is certain to be an eventful one. The plant will be expanded and modified and we have an organization to build for sales, production, and research. We expect to sell starch to the paper and textile trade through Stein Hall, General Mills, and Keever. We will sell the food trade both starch and syrup with our own people. It is our hope that sales will justify an increase in capacity to 25,000 bushels per day before the first of 1968." The next year's report chronicled the first nine months of processing 3.8 million bushels of corn, producing 69 million pounds of starch and 68 million pounds of syrup, plus 50 million pounds of feed corn and 13 million pounds of germ, all at margins per bushel of 92 cents versus costs of 79 cents. "The past nine months have been active, stimulating, and productive," the report concluded, "we have put together a young, eager, intelligent group of people who have made substantial progress in all areas."

Still, this was a "new boy on the block" effort by the Company, a newcomer in competition with some giant members of that industry. Were these "young, eager, intelligent people" in the embryonic corn milling effort going to make it? Hint: In 1971 the Processing and Refining Division had a net profit of $20.5 million; no other division was in double numbers; the corn milling group contributed well over 10 percent of this. A second hint: Corn milling became a separate division in the fiscal year 1973–1974. More on this success story later.[5]

Salt: Backhaul Success

It is a canon of transportation to try to discover a backhaul, if possible, because many transportation routes—air, rail, and water—have traffic that tilts heavily in one direction. Grain is an excellent example here. Grain is grown in agricultural regions, then moved to production centers, domestic and abroad, where it will be converted to its many products. One of the great grain routes in the United States is down the Mississippi by barge—destination: Gulf ports. Then these barges must be sent back up the Mississippi for another grain trip back down. This backhaul was essentially unproductive unless a product could be found to ship *up* the river. Cargill experimented with ideas on this in the early 1950s; CCI's Ray King was given the assignment and soon developed both coal contracts and salt sales. One of the major salt-producing areas was Louisiana, mining salt out of deep mines. By the mid-1950s, there was a Company salt group housed within the Grain Division, buying salt from producers and selling in the North, primarily as road salt. New storage facilities were constructed along the transportation routes, including Chicago, the prime consumer area for road rock salt. Soon molasses also became an important piece of what was now called the Commodity Department. It also was bought, transported, and sold along the same routes, although, as the 1961–1962 report of the department noted, "Common terminals are not used, and each commodity has its own technical problems that are not remotely common to each other."

With the vagaries of trading in the market for all one's product, Cargill now decided it needed to develop its own salt manufacturing competency. In March 1961, the Company announced, jointly with Louisiana governor Jimmie H. Davis, that a major new supply of rock salt from a historic untapped deposit at Belle Isle, near Morgan City, Louisiana, had been purchased. According to Clayton Tonnemaker, Cargill's salt manager, the new Louisiana product would be "as pure as there is," 99 percent sodium chloride. Belle Isle was one of five similar "salt islands" along this gulf coastal area. The Belle Isle underground salt deposit had first been discovered in 1896 by Captain A. F. Lucas, the pioneer geologist who in 1901 had brought in "Spindle Top," one of the most famous oil wells in the development of the vast East Texas oil fields. Lucas had attempted to mine the Belle Isle salt but failed because of shaft flooding.

Now Cargill brought new technology to shaft construction. A 16-foot circular shaft would be developed, the first 300 feet of the planned 1,250-foot depth to be sealed watertight into the salt itself by a freezing process in which a vertical core of earth 40 feet in diameter was literally frozen by mechanical refrigeration, enabling the shaft to be stabilized in the otherwise muddy earth without collapse. The walls of the shaft would then be lined with reinforced concrete as it progressed.

By October 1961, more details became available as the construction continued. The 16-foot-diameter shaft would have 3-foot-thick concrete walls sunk in 7-foot sections. The freezing process had been done with a series of freeze holes in a 45-foot radius around the shaft opening. A liquid calcium chloride line was pumped into the pipes to freeze the ground around the shaft to about minus 35 degrees. The shaft would be extended to 1,250 feet, the level where the mining was to be done. By late 1962, the plant was in operation, and the first six months' production cost averaged $2.93 per ton, considerably below the cost of $5 per ton for salt purchased on the outside. By May of 1963, mining costs had dropped to $2.56 per ton; "a remarkable performance," stated the annual report. The department made modest profits in 1963–1964, then continued upward over the next two years.

At this point, a significant expansion was made in the mining operation, doubling its capacity (after geologists had estimated that the Belle Isle dome, resting some 1,250 feet beneath the bayous, contained enough high-purity rock salt to provide the needs of the entire world for several centuries). Both salt for roads and chemical salt sales were estimated to go upward, to double by 1970. Salt seemed a success at Cargill.

But now a terrible tragedy was to be visited upon the group and the Company.[6]

Fire

Suddenly, at about 11:15 P.M. on the night of Tuesday, March 5, 1968, trouble was reported from the bottom of the 1,250-foot shaft. Twenty-one men were below. *Cargill News* described the tragic events that unfolded from that moment: "Hoist Operator Clemere La Boeuf heard Miner Roy Byron say, 'The shaft's on fire . . . send the North skip [elevator platform] down.' Moments later he heard him again. 'The skip's on fire. Pull it up.' Another voice—he took it to be Foreman Paul Granger—called for help. Then the line went dead."

Hoist machinery had begun raising the down-skip, a carry-all elevator suspended by heavy steel cable. At the same time an identical, counterweight skip started to descend. Before the skips' positions could be reversed, heavy smoke began rising in the head frame above the shaft. The shaft was filling with fire (because salt corroded and weakened any steel beam, Belle Isle had structural beams to guide the skips made of wood, as was the bulkhead dividing the shaft for intake and exhaust of air). The air divider had been chemically treated for resistance to fire. But nothing could withstand the fast-mounting temperatures. "Fire extended the length of the shaft. Heat was intense. The hoist cable went slack, its steel strands melted. Electric lines were severed. The head frame building, like a cap on a chimney, was blackened with soot . . . fire fighters at the mine turned hoses into the shaft . . . pumping equipment drew water from dockside to pour into the quarter-mile deep pit. At the surface, heat and smoke lessened gradually."

Calls by radio went to superintendent Nick Nicola and to Joe Pinkham, the assistant mine superintendent, as well as to the Coast Guard. A call to the nearby Sun Oil refinery brought a pumping unit to the mine by barge. Fire departments were summoned from Patterson, Berwick, Franklin, and Morgan City, mainland towns within a dozen miles of the mainland boat landing at Calumet but distant in time from the mine (it was a 13-mile trip by water to Belle Isle).

Clayton Tonnemaker, head of Cargill's Salt Department, would direct fire fighting and rescue attempts and would remain in charge throughout the emergency. Louisiana's Governor John J. McKeithen assigned Troop C of the state police to maintain approaches to Calumet, to escort volunteers, and to assist at the mine; the governor called on the Coast Guard cutter *Point Look Out* to keep small boats away from the island.

Families of the missing men congregated at the Calumet landing. Wives and children waited silently for news. Elderly men and women, their sons in the mine, asked for details of the work in progress. Cargill's warehouse at the landing was cleared to contain cots and chairs. Anxious families sat speechless or spoke in whispers. From nearby restaurants and homes came boxes of sandwiches, doughnuts and milk. The Red Cross set up cots, brought blankets, served coffee.

Only male relatives who also were miners were allowed on the island. Roy Granger and Preston Romero, both Cargill supervisors, had brothers in the mine; Arthur Olivier, a foreman on the day shift, had a son and three nephews. Shortwave radio was the main link between the island and Calumet—at first a single commercial set, later a more elaborate radio system installed by CCI men from Baton Rouge. Still later, Sun Oil crews helped rig a phone line to the mainland. Calls to the regional office of the U.S. Bureau of Mines in Oklahoma City made clear that mine rescue experts were few in the area. Salt mines were believed relatively safe from fire because they were free of explosive gases, and they were dug into solid material, so cave-ins were unlikely. Calls confirmed that no rescuers could be found in salt mines as far north as Kansas. Regular mining crews, no matter how well versed in standard safety procedures, were not trained or equipped for the hazards of rescue work.

Mine rescue experts were sought from Minneapolis. The Bureau of Mines in Washington pointed the way to two coal mining companies in Kentucky; Island Creek Coal Company in Madisonville, and Pittsburgh and Midway in Sturgis agreed to ask for volunteers among their corps of miners with special rescue training. Almost immediately each reported that a six-man team was assembling. Some 500 pounds of rescue equipment would be sent with each team.

The Island Creek and P & M rescue teams, along with the crates of gear, boarded a charter airplane from Louisville on Wednesday evening. The trip was made nonstop to Patterson, Louisiana, where safe landing on a short airstrip put the crews as near Belle Isle as possible. From the Patterson airfield, the Kentuckians were airlifted by helicopter to a cleared area not 200 yards from the mine shaft. They were deployed just before midnight, less than 24 hours from the first warning. Water hoses to the shaft had been turned off, but traces of smoke still rose in the head frame.

One attempt to penetrate the mine had already been made. Through Wednesday afternoon, Cargill miners had contrived two rectangular cages of steel pipe and angles. The first was discarded untried. When a test drop was made of the second with no one aboard, it lodged 300 feet down and was withdrawn. It too was discarded. A third man-lift was made from a spare fan housing. Welders and metalworkers followed sketches drawn quickly by Doyle Berry, oil field contractor from nearby Berwick, La. Humble Oil's B. B. Box supervised cutting and welding. Pipes were attached to the side and bent inward under the bucket to guide it through timbers and hanging debris. . . .

The mine rescue teams were briefed by study of maps and plans of the mine. Question-and-answer exchange helped them locate underground hazards. Numbers and placement of machinery, vehicles, oxygen tanks, fire extinguishers, water supplies, gasoline, explosives—all had to be known.

Belle Isle, Louisiana: tight fit in bucket. Four rescue crew men begin 1,200-foot drop in mine shaft. Equipment includes hard hat, miner's lamp, face masks with hoses to filtration canister on chest, walkie-talkie. Nearest camera is Roy Capps, Bureau of Mines safety expert from Dallas, Texas (Cargill staff photograph, 1968).

The first descent began at 5 a.m. Thursday. Dilford Holmes and Edward Holeman, both Kentuckians, rode the bucket. It was three-and-a-half feet across and chest deep . . . hung in the shaft on a steel cable brought to the island by barge and installed only hours before.

Both men wore breathing masks and carried oxygen tanks. One held a walkie-talkie radio for contact with the surface. One had a miner's safety lamp on his belt. Its small flame would go out if the oxygen level was too low to support life. The men rode back-to-back, hands raised to fend off the shaft walls and to counter a tendency of the bucket to swing like a pendulum.

The round trip by bucket took an hour and 29 minutes. Holeman was injured when struck on the shoulder by a fragment of salt that fell from the wall. Neither man left the bucket, yet both returned exhausted.

They reported that the heat was intense, the lower part of shaft was completely burned out, higher in the shaft were dangerous remnants of burned timbers, smoldering coals and small flames were visible at the bottom of the shaft, the sound of an idling diesel engine could be heard from the mine. The sump, an 80-foot extension of the shaft below the mine floor, was filled with hot water.

The two men were debriefed by the team directing the rescue; they urged changes to lessen the danger to rescuers. Hard hats were poor protection from falling salt and debris. So much energy was needed to draw steam-laden air through the breathing masks that other efforts were hindered. The bucket did not merely swing—it teetered in response to their smallest movements. Despite use of nonrotating cable, received from the nearby Jefferson Island

The surface operations of Cargill's Belle Isle salt mine, taken at the time of the mine's disaster, 1968 (Cargill staff photograph).

mine of Diamond Crystal Salt Co., the bucket repeatedly rotated a quarter turn, then returned to position.

Routinely, after every debriefing, an initial summary of the team's report was radiophoned to the Calumet landing. All news, good and bad, was first given to waiting families by Evan Williams, a Salt Department product manager. The *Cargill News* continued:

Jobs of building and welding were finishing in hours that would normally take days. As quickly as the first drop was evaluated, the man-lift was removed. Two pieces of steel plate were welded above it to protect against falling debris. Work was begun on another man-lift to backstop the one being used. The new bucket would be deeper and wider with a curved shield overhead and a more stable connection to the cable.

At 11:05 Thursday morning the smaller bucket was maneuvered into place and three men started down. Along with Dilford Holmes and Paul Gregory, rescue team men, went Joe Pinkham, assistant mine superintendent. An hour and five minutes passed before they surfaced. At mine level a line and grappling hook had been thrown and secured. The gondola was pulled to the edge of the sump, clear of the water. One man was helped over the edge to tie off securely. Another dismounted and the pair advanced briefly into the mine entrance. Their companion remained on board, in sight of the searchers and in radio contact with a team member above. Piled debris was found between the shaft and the mine. Some open flame was seen and put out with hand extinguishers. Using a bull horn they called repeatedly into the mine but heard no answering sounds. They established that the missing miners would not be found without searching the mine's interior. For breathing easier, they suggested that a pipe be lowered for pumping fresh air.

Cargill's president, Erv Kelm, arrived on the island; newsmen asked him how long the trapped miners might survive "under optimum conditions." He said: "I'm not an expert on this. I wish I were. With enough air, they can survive. But I'm told we'd better get them up soon." Earlier that day, Louisiana governor McKeithen had spent an hour at the mine. "Everything possible is being done," he stated.

Between completion of the second drop after noon on Thursday and descent of the third at 4:55 p.m. various topside projects had been advanced. A 3-inch oil well pipe was suspended in the shaft to carry air. An ingenious speaker-listening device had been lowered that carried a winking light to be seen and approached by survivors whose movements and voices would be heard above ground. Nearly finished was the fourth cage to be used as a man lift.

Despite their best efforts, workers on the island knew that progress seemed slow to families waiting in Calumet. Five hours had passed since the last try at the mine. Three men, equipped with gas masks and air filtration canisters now were ready to go down. One was Cargill's Jim Gustafson, an engineer trained at Colorado School of Mines; the others were Island Creek's A. R. Blair and Pittsburg and Midway's Jim Reynolds. Even before the official go-ahead was received they climbed in the bucket and started down.

By walkie-talkie they reported that the bucket seemed stable and the rate of descent good. They told the hoist operator to continue lowering. They were on the bottom at 5:12, in 17 minutes. They stayed down for one hour and returned to the surface to report the air pipe attached to a flexible hose, no glowing embers visible and access to the mine better cleared.

The work of the third drop was aimed mainly at creating time so longer searches could be made. The safe limit of gas mask canisters was two hours; oxygen remained near the mine entrance but a dangerous level of carbon monoxide also was measured; physical exertion was extreme; noticeable cooling could not be expected immediately. Until the third drop, most available time was needed to travel the shaft and to debark and embark at mine level.

Later rescue teams not only had more minutes for active search but gained new strength and confidence with the arrival from Vincennes, Indiana, of two Bureau of Mines rescue experts. Clem Dovidas and Don Martin were supervisory coal mine inspectors who had taught rescue procedure to most members of the Kentucky crews. Both intended to take active parts in the rescue. Thursday night, as preparations for the fourth drop continued, Dovidas and three others were at the mine shaft, ready to descend. The *Cargill News* went on:

The fourth drop, like all others, had limited objectives. Friday morning at 12:45 a.m., Dovidas and three veterans of earlier drops—Holmes, Gregory and Holeman—were lowered into the shaft. Their tasks included checking operations of the first air pipe and starting operation of two more air lines, shaft-long columns of coupled oil field pipe.

Here is a minute-by-minute log kept at the top of the shaft.

(Gregory during initial descent) "Conditions appear to be the same. . . . Talkies working better than before. . . . Bucket riding smooth."

(At 220 ft. level) "Better than other bucket. Rides like a Cadillac."

(300 ft.) "Riding smooth. Begin to encounter some water seepage. . . . Now at the end of concrete. . . . Just passed concrete. . . . Condition apparently the same."

(470 ft.) "Riding extremely well. Encounter little clockwise rotation."

(500 ft.) "The diesel engine is still running."

(Steele from surface) "Seven minutes in."

(Gregory below, 500 ft.) "Now at end of other hoist rope. . . . Clem's quit talkin'. We're ridin' smooth. . . . Clem's grading us right now." (Reference to dangling skip cables melted by fire and to Dovidas' familiar role as rescue technique instructor.)

(575 ft.) "Smooth ride. Believe it's better than other cage. . . . Ridin' smooth."

(675 ft.) "Cap light going out. All conditions appear the same. . . . All conditions apparently the same." (The miner's cap light apparently was adjusted, for no further reference was made to it.)

(Steele from surface) "Are you encountering any smoke at all?"

(Gregory, 750 ft.) "No." (Previous trip encountered smoke at this level.)

(800 ft.) "That ole diesel is really runnin' smooth. . . . Temperature gradually increasing."

(900 ft.) "That hoist man's got a magic touch, hasn't he? . . . Temperature gradually increasing . . . 200 feet left to go. . . . Diesel engine loud and clear . . . 150 feet to go. Can see the light on the speaker." (Listening speaker device lowered into the mine.)

(Steele from surface) "Has anything scaled off the side?"

(Gregory, 88 ft. from bottom of shaft) "Negative . . . 84 degree to 89 degree temperature change."

(44 ft. from bottom) "Cage appears to be rotating. (A counterclockwise movement of about one half turn.) Ten feet. . . . Stand by. . . . Easy. . . . Easy. . . . Easy. . . . Two more feet. . . . Whoa. . . . Hold tight."

(Gregory on bottom at 1:03 a.m., 18 minutes after drop began) "Gimme a time check."

(Steele on surface) "20 minutes since you left the top."

(Gregory in mine) "Smoke is less than previous trips. When we clear up we'll take a CO (carbon monoxide) test. . . . Grappling over to side. . . . Preparing to disembark. . . . Diesel engine still running. . . . Smoke considerably less in all directions."

(Gregory, 1:06 a.m.) "Oxygen content good. . . . Holmes is now out of the cage. . . . Temperature now 92 degrees in the bucket."

(Steele from surface, 1:08) "How many are out of the bucket?"

(Gregory) "Only one. Tying off again to get better disembarkation spot. . . . Gonna take a CO check."

(Steele from surface, 1:09 a.m.) "Waiting for a report."

(From below) "Four hundredths with color metric (calibrations on instrument to measure carbon monoxide.) Two on ground. . . . Clem coming out of cage. . . . We're out of the cage. . . . Three men to determine if fire is out. . . . Discharging an extinguisher on some timbers that were going."

(From below, 1:18 a.m.) "Examining the fan now. . . . Fan appears to be in good shape. . . . There was a small fire around the fan and they applied water pressure. . . . Working where the air lock was, by the fan housing."

(From below, 1:20 a.m.) "Examining the motor and wiring in the fan house. . . . Big debris on floor. . . . Standing in middle of old entry roof. . . . Appears to be same as before fire."

(Gregory, 1:23 a.m.) "Fire all out at fan. All of us are together. . . . Other members proceeding toward diesel."

(Gregory, 1:24 a.m.) "Diesel engine is no longer running." (Engine had been turned off by the search team.)

(Gregory, 1:26 a.m.) "Going toward the powder magazine. . . . Oxygen indicator shows O.K. . . . moving air hose to center of entry. . . . Temperature is 90 degrees."

(Gregory, 1:30 a.m.) "Two men departing. Going 'round the corner to explore."

(Gregory, 1:32 a.m.) "Start the air compressor at an idle. . . . We're receiving air. . . . Turn it on. . . . Full force. . . . Good. . . . Try the second one. . . . That'll help too."

(Gregory) "One hour and five minutes down. . . . All were in Doug's sight." (The pivot man was assigned to keep in visual contact with the man in bucket and searching point men.)

(Gregory, 1:52 a.m., one hour and seven minutes after start) "Pull us up. . . . Slow and easy. . . . Pull us up."

(Gregory, 1:59 a.m.) "Stop the cage. . . . Stop. . . . It's swinging."

(Gregory, 2:00 a.m.) "Start pulling. . . . Easy. . . . Easy . . ."

The trip back to the top required $12\frac{1}{2}$ minutes. Total time of the fourth drop was 1 hour, $59\frac{1}{2}$ minutes.

The fifth drop went underground two and one half hours later, with four men aboard. Returning after 1 hour and 38 minutes, the searchers told of a longer probe, but no man-made barricades or air chambers were found. The fifth attempt ended Friday morning at 6:48.

By 10 A.M. on Friday, when the sixth drop began, communications had been improved. CCI men had rigged a telephone link to the bottom; now one rescue man still was needed to keep in touch with the surface, but the former pivot man was freed for further search.

Again, four men went down. Dilford Holmes was team captain. A team member told later of Holmes' tireless pace, deliberate and unrelenting, calculated to cover as much of the mine as possible without either courting exhaustion or wasting a moment of use from filtration canisters. The crew took a zig-zag search course. Before leaving the mine, they had covered from one-and-a-half to two miles of rooms and corridors.

The team returned to the surface at 11:30 a.m. and went to the debriefing room. Their report, as usual, first was radio-phoned to the mainland. There Evan Williams, asked if someone else should inform the waiting families, said, "I've told them whatever good there was. I'll tell them this too."

Newsmen heard him approach and say, "I cannot repeat this but once. It is tragic news. Sixteen bodies have been found on the floor of the mine." No other words were heard. Only sounds of despair.

At almost the same moment, Clayton Tonnemaker, after reiterating the message to those on the island, confirmed that a team was being prepared immediately to descend to search for the other five men. The sixth team later told of discovering the 16 miners 1,700 feet from the shaft, "huddled together, like sleeping children." Because little time remained, they had made no attempt to identify the quiet forms. They were counted to determine how many were missing. The team then moved back to the shaft.

At 1:30 Friday afternoon, with Clem Dovidas leading, the seventh drop was made. Point men traveled in a slightly different direction than the previous team. They were some 1,400 feet from the shaft when the remaining five bodies were found, 600 feet from the first group. Dovidas, like Holmes, ordered no close inspection—only a count was made. The seventh drop returned to the top. At the head of the mine and in the warehouse-refuge at Calumet, hopes that remained were ended by the shortest message of all: "The last five are dead."

When the final tragic report was brought from the mine on Friday by rescue crewmen in the seventh drop, a dismal, potentially dangerous choice remained to be made. Families of the miners and the general public expected and awaited recovery of the 21 bodies. Plans had begun for funerals and burial. But persons familiar with conditions in the mine knew that the risk of being lowered into the shaft was as great as ever, that to recover the bodies would require numerous trips away from the relative safety of air hoses and possible escape, that dependence on self-contained breathing equipment would be absolute, that the mine atmosphere still was deadly.

Under such circumstances, often it is decided that no more risk of life is justified, that descents to the mine would be discontinued, that the bodies would not be removed until air in the mine was cleansed, a matter of weeks or months. Reentry of the mine and recovery of the bodies also was uncertain because those best qualified to work underground—the Kentucky rescue crews and the dozen experts from the Bureau of Mines—were in no way obliged to involve themselves. The Kentucky teams were excluded by mining custom from tasks not directly connected with rescue. Even during rescue operations, they retained volunteers' rights to withdraw. Bureau officials, who willingly entered the mine to aid rescue attempts, were not obligated beyond seeking causes of the disaster. For that purpose, no formal below-ground inspection would be conducted at Belle Isle until the workings were safe. So the decision as to whether or not to recover the bodies was not Cargill's. It was in the hands of others.

An announcement Friday afternoon did not fully answer the question. It said only that drops would not be made before Saturday because the men were exhausted. All but guards and a relief crew returned to the mainland. The assumption that recovery of bodies would begin next day was not questioned.

There were no official meetings of the Kentuckians; there were no apparent differences of opinion; there was no discernible time lag. But when Saturday arrived, the men needed for the recovery operation were there, ready to return to the mine. Their reasons were never fully explained. One said, "We came here to get them out." Another mentioned the families, people who had waited at Calumet, people he had never seen and would never know. He said, "For them it won't be finished until the bodies are buried." Another said, "One day it may be me down there. I'd like to think somebody would come after me." A Bureau of Mines engineer referred to the rescue attempt: "I've never seen an effort to equal it," he said. "Nothing was spared, not time or money or equipment or men. We all feel the same. We don't want to leave the job half finished."

In terms of time and manpower, the largest part of the job was yet to be done. The earlier rescue operation required two and a half days and seven drops, descents by individuals a total of 24 times. Recovery operations took five days in which there were 29 drops and some 135 descents by individuals.

A set of necessary steps preliminary to the recovery were received with understandable impatience by some. The reaction was less from bereaved members of the miners' families, who continued to show strength and patience, than from people more distant—"some newsman anxious to 'wrap up' the incident, some public officials, a few individuals among the public." Despite others' impatience, the men at the mine moved carefully. In a series of 11 drops over Saturday and Sunday, a "safe-air" house was put together on the surface, disassembled (with its parts numbered), and reassembled at the bottom of the mine. A flexible hose attached by a sealed collar passed fresh air into the chamber. Also, one of the mine's diesel-powered vehicles was fueled and its operation checked. A cargo hauler ordinarily used to transfer salt, it would carry men and equipment into the depths of the mine and would return the dead to the mine shaft. To hasten cooling at the fresh-air base below ground, tons of bagged ice were airlifted by helicopter from mainland to mine and packed around steel pipe heat-exchange coils that extended from compressors parked outdoors to air pipe couplings at the shaft opening. The *Cargill News* picked up the story: "One huge contraption, finally abandoned as too cumbersome, was a compartment chest with locking lids to transport bodies through the shaft. The box was 3 feet deep, 3 feet wide and 30 feet long. Its builders planned to lower it from the top after attaching it rigidly under the rescuers' man-lift. Approaching the mine floor, still suspended from the bucket but allowed to swing free, it was to be drawn toward the landing while being lowered until it lay flat. The plan was that, when the lids were latched, the carrier and its cargo would be withdrawn, again as an extension of the man lift."

But cooler heads prevailed. There was too much danger that this unwieldy monolith would become jammed in the shaft, thereby endangering the lives below. The steel chest was abandoned.

. . . economy of time and energy in the shaft and mine were high among priorities. Even with the air room operating, the margin of safety was narrow. Only the most skillful and enduring men were chosen for recovery drops. Most were from the Kentucky rescue crews. . . . Bureau men . . . worked mainly near the shaft landing to man the safe house, maintain equipment and help recovery crews don heavy breathing apparatus.

Actual recovery did not begin until Sunday afternoon. The day's fifth and sixth drops assembled seven recovery crewman at the foot of the shaft. A series of trips began to the distant mine workings that continued through Monday and ended near midnight on Tuesday.

Even the most experienced found the task harrowing. In a half dozen trips, the procedure varied only slightly. Crews rode the diesel carrier to where the dead miners lay. Before each body was moved, its position was marked for later reference by the Bureau of Mines in reconstructing the accident. . . . Return trips brought the dead to the bottom of the mine shaft.

By late Tuesday afternoon, all bodies were near the shaft . . . the man-lift was used. Seven trips were required. Each bore three bodies to the surface and each required a recovery crew man riding the lift and radioing instructions to the hoist operator.

It was nearly midnight Tuesday when the last bodies reached the top. Another trip brought up the recovery team 40 minutes later.

Cargill managers and miners, and no others, received their dead companions as they were lifted from the elevator cage. They accompanied them to a nearby enclosure where tentative identification was made. They stood by as prayers for the dead were read by Father Landry, priest from the Catholic church in nearby Centerville. They carried the dead on stretchers to the boat dock, lifted them aboard the Car-Isle and went with them to the Calumet landing, 14 miles away.

Aftermaths

Inevitably, serious questions needed answers. The U.S. Bureau of Mines report on the disaster stated that "the cause of the fire could not be determined with certainty" but did comment on the inadequacy of fire prevention measures and of the firefighting facilities at and in the shaft. In particular, queries were focused on why there was not a second shaft. The previous August, Cargill had asked a health and safety engineer from the Bureau of Mines to go through the mine step by step and make suggestions for improving safety conditions. Salt mines were not under the jurisdiction of the Bureau; it was Cargill's initiative here. The bureau supervisor made 14 suggestions, one of which was that "a second shaft should be sunk and connected with the workings." By the time of the fire, only one other suggestion—on methods of making blasting primers—had not been put into effect.

The *Cargill News* article discussed these issues frankly. Asked why Belle Isle had one shaft instead of two for ventilation, removal of salt, and transport of men, Cargill officials explained that most new salt mines began with a single shaft. They normally were operated with one until the extent of underground workings made another desirable, usually for adequate ventilation. Other Louisiana mines had "matured" to that point and had second shafts, but many mines in Texas, Kansas, and elsewhere were single-shaft operations. Belle Isle, in operation almost five years, was rapidly nearing second-shaft maturity. Because salt production was greater than originally scheduled, plans to sink a second shaft, originally scheduled for 1970–1971, had been advanced to 1969–1970.

There were recriminations about the lack of the second tunnel; some of the harsher comments came from a Lafayette, Louisiana, newspaper called *True Scope*, dubbed by Cargill's Lafayette lawyer "a 'scandle' sheet" [*sic*]. "There is no excuse," said its editor, "for having only one shaft."

The salt department did well that year; the annual report commented, "Financially the year was an outstanding success; but compassionately, it was the worst year in Cargill history with the disastrous fire." The net earnings for that year were a record-high $970,000.

The mine was immediately repaired, and a second shaft was sunk. By early 1969, it was back in operation. The annual report stated: "The early return to production amazed the entire industry." The insurance settlement for the mine disaster amounted to $3,299,000, less $100,000 deductible. A Company claim of $1,000,000 to cover fixed expense at the terminals was not allowed. The mine costs at Belle Isle rose to $1.49 per ton, an increase of 27 cents, reflecting the lower volume and start-up expense. Production continued to be excellent the following year, and the Company also made the commitment to expand its production facilities elswhere. The Cayuga Rock Salt Company, at South Lansing, New York, was purchased in April 1970, giving Cargill access to the highly profitable northeastern U.S. market. The mining operation itself was on the eastern shore of Lake Cayuga, a double-shaft mine working at 2,400 feet.

By 1970–1971, molasses and salt had been split, with the remaining Salt Department handling salt exclusively. Another significant acquisition also was made that year: a majority position in the Gordy Salt Company, with an evaporated salt plant at Breaux Bridge and a processing plant at Baldwin, both in Louisiana. In June 1972, the Company also entered into an agreement with the owners of Barton Salt Company, of Hutchinson, Kansas, to participate in the management of Barton for three years. This was an operation that developed the salt by evaporation, rather than by deep or surface mining.

A New Calamity

In early March of 1973, a disturbing problem was discovered—water had begun to seep into the second shaft at Belle Isle. Efforts to find and plug its source were unsuccessful, and by the week's end the flow had reached 1,000 gallons per minute. Finally, by virtue of the collapse of the shaft itself, the water flow was stopped. At the top, the surface surrounding the shaft began to crater and slide, taking with it the 60-foot-high head frame, the ventilation fan, an 80-by-40-foot storage building, and numerous supplies. There was no great change at the bottom of the shaft, except for the stoppage of the water. But no one knew how long the collapse-generated plug would hold or what quantities of water might enter the mine if the plug were gone.

When the production crews were allowed to return, a man-made plug was injected into the bottom of the shaft, along the air entry on the lower level. Here drill holes were made at different angles, then filled by a total of 106,500 bags of chemical grout and 180,000 bags of cement. Later a lower level was sealed from the rest of the mine by a concrete wall 22 feet high, 26 feet wide, and 70 feet deep.

Again, the Company was faced with developing from scratch a second shaft, and this was done. Problems of air freshness remained after it was finished, but careful safety procedures, with frequent monitoring of the nitrogen dioxide percentage, made the operation safe. The best engineering advice suggested that the collapsed hole, if not cleared and relined, would never be absolutely secure. The company doing the cement operations therefore began to install concrete linings, with the project calling for a double lining in the upper 390 feet and a single liner through 1,180 feet of the salt dome. "Then," said mine manager Ed Holeman, in a *Cargill News* article in early 1975, "we will have all the good fresh air we want. Our luck will change, production will head up, we will be what's always been intended—the best salt mine in the country."

But this was not to be. It was a mine that was surely plagued, and the miners had to face yet another tragedy. In early June 1979, an explosion occurred deep in the mine. Twenty-two miners were working at the bottom. Fortunately, 17 men made their way out within the hour, but the remaining 5 lost their lives. The explosion was caused by a freak, one-in-a-million happenstance: routine blasting in an underground area had triggered what the U.S. Mine Safety and Health Administration called "an 'outburst'—a sudden, violent release of gases and salt kept under pressure in a geologic formation— that flooded a 500-foot area of the mine." This methane-loaded outpouring was then set off by a spark from a broken electrical cable. The report concluded, "The cause . . . was a general failure by MSHA [the federal agency] and Cargill management to recognize the serious hazards of the blow-out phenomena."

After many months, the mine did get back into operation, but soon it was discovered that there were stability problems in the salt dome itself that might threaten its structural integrity. One study even suggested that eventual collapse of the mine was possible, although it was not imminent.

The Company now gave up. Mining operations were halted permanently at Belle Isle on January 31, 1984. Some 155 supervisory and hourly employees were affected; most were terminated with liberal severance pay.

Belle Isle had ceased to be a mine.[7]

The Green Revolution

Research on food crops of the less developed world had not been widespread prior to this time. There had been some work in Mexico, made possible by the Rockefeller Foundation. In the early 1960s, two new international crop research institutes came into being, the International Rice Research Institute (IRRI) in the Philippines and the International Maize and Wheat Improvement Center (CIMMYT) in Mexico. Both groups began focusing on development of high-yielding varieties of seed. Amazingly, both brought forth highly productive new varieties in the mid-1960s.

India was in the vanguard of the exciting developments for both of these new grains. Both varieties produced dwarf plants, with shorter stems (stronger and less likely to "lodge" or be broken down by wind or rain). Both varieties had highly significant increases in yields. India imported its first dwarf varieties of rice in 1964–1965, just enough to plant 200 acres. The following year some 17,650 acres were planted. In the third year, 1966–1967, at the height of the famine in Bihar and other affected states, some 2,195,000 acres were planted (and this had more than doubled the following year). The new rice varieties needed a "package of practices" to make them work—more fertilizer, assured water, and careful pesticide use. With this, yields could go up by a highly significant amount.

Similarly, India imported the new dwarf wheat varieties from CIMMYT, just 250 metric tons in 1965–1966, used on 7,400 acres. The following year this jumped to 18,000 metric tons of imports, covering 1,270,000 acres, and in 1967–1968 the dwarf varieties were grown on some 7,270,000 acres. For the year 1966–1967, the dwarf wheats had produced 2.87 times the amount that would have been produced by one of the traditional varieties. For rice, the figure was 2.58. In the following year, 1967–1968, wheat varieties increased by a multiple of 3.7, but rice had dropped to 2.2. The total food grains produced in India in 1967–1968, the first year of real impact from the Green Revolution, was 95.05 million tons: a 28 percent climb from the previous year, with a production of 74.23 million tons.

These were spectacular additions to what had been produced in the past, and in a matter of just a few years the two new varieties had revolutionized wheat and rice production in India, as well as elsewhere in the developing world. Area estimates for the free world for acreage planted in the HYVs (high-yielding varieties) were spectacular (see table 2).

Amazingly, in the early 1970s, India became fully self-sufficient in food grains, well short of a decade after introduction of the dwarf varieties into the country. The Green Revolution, as this development became known throughout the world, surely must be ranked as one of the outstanding technological breakthroughs of the world in the twentieth century. The effects on the international grain trade were pronounced.[8]

TABLE 2

Estimated Acreage Planted in HYVs

Crop year	Wheat	Rice	Total
1965–1966	23,000	18,000	41,000
1966–1967	1,542,000	2,505,000	4,047,000
1967–1968	10,189,000	6,487,000	16,676,000
1968–1969	19,815,000	11,620,000	31,435,000
1969–1970	21,551,000	19,104,000	40,655,000
1970–1971	25,256,000	25,294,000	50,550,000

Riding a Roller Coaster: The International Grains Arrangement

All of these high-drama events, especially the Indian famine, the advent of the Green Revolution, and the rise of the Common Agricultural Policy of the EEC, carried the grain companies on a wild ride. It was just at this time, too, that the agricultural negotiations in the Kennedy Round were coming to a head, in particular, the negotiations relating to wheat, which were the most sensitive.

There had been international wheat agreements of varying effectiveness since the early 1930s, with the International Wheat Agreement of 1933. It had never worked well. Importers had sought lower prices and better access; exporters, especially the United States and Canada, sought higher prices and control over the export-import ratios. A more effective organization, the International Wheat Council, was established in 1942 and modified again in 1949. All of this was accompanied by hard bargaining by both the importing and exporting nations.

With the advent of the EEC's Common Agricultural Policy, accommoda-

A presidential visit by President Lyndon B. Johnson to the Cargill facility in Omaha on June 30, 1966, was hosted by Cargill president Erwin E. Kelm, shown here with Nebraska governor Frank Morrison on the right and Omaha mayor A. V. Sorenson next to Governor Morrison. President Johnson spoke to a crowd of about 3,000 persons at the Cargill-leased Omaha city dock; his address, carried by all radio and TV networks, was a major foreign policy statement on Vietnam (Cargill News, July 1966).

tions had to be reached with this powerful body, and it was hoped that the Kennedy Round would be an appropriate forum. Efforts toward a world grain agreement were mounted as a climax of the Kennedy Round. Out of this came the 1967 International Grains Arrangement (IGA), made up of both a wheat trade convention and a food aid convention. American wheat production was down in that year, and prices had begun to rise. Richard Gilmore explained the trade-offs: "Larger importers such as Japan, which had accepted a sharp reduction during the Kennedy Round and the U.K. which had dropped altogether its soybean tariff during these negotiations, were willing to accept an agreement with a higher price floor in exchange for guaranties of a higher minimum level of food imports, especially since the pricing formula proposed was sufficiently flexible to allow importers to profit during a bearish market." The EEC group also seemed amenable to such an agreement, wanting to stabilize wheat prices at a level higher than would have happened in a completely unregulated market. Gilmore noted: "In effect, the IGA established a cartel-like arrangement among exporters, and sacrificed the open trade principles reaffirmed in the Kennedy Round in exchange for more orderly world trading conditions in wheat." A floor was established on world wheat prices, using No. 1 Manitoba wheat as the reference, at $1.95½ a bushel. From this base price the Wheat Trade Convention (WTC) provided for different pricing schedules for each of 14 different wheat types. Temporary adjustments could be made under exceptional market conditions.

The exporters, with Cargill in the vanguard, argued that prices had been set too high, that this particular year was an exception. When 1968 proved to be a high-producing year, the IGA price became increasingly noncompetitive; and countries outside the pact, producers such as the Soviet Union, Hungary, and Yugoslavia, were more than willing to sell below minimum prices. Not only did importers prove disloyal, but exporters did, too. As world prices dropped, American exporters complained about the pricing formula. The United States vowed that the system worked in favor of Canadian and Australian wheat. Further, they said, Australia had been able to use freight differentials to further reduce their prices. In addition, the United States complained that there were other classes of wheat beyond just the 14 and that these were being sold at overly competitive prices compared to the IGA.

Finally, in 1968, an informal caucus of wheat exporters that included the key players—the United States, Canada, Australia, Argentina, and the EEC—decided to develop a more informal system within the framework of the IGA. The Exporters Group, as it became known, became another embryonic wheat cartel, with proposed quotas based on "traditional markets" and several countries advocating rigid use of this mechanism. The United States preferred a system of informal market shares consistent with each exporter's normal market participation. With Canada and Australia joining with the United States in this proposal over the objections of the EEC, the informal system began to be used, with the EEC agreeing to accept the de facto quotas while remaining a nonparticipating member of the Exporters Group.

The system lasted only a few months, plagued throughout by inadequate information about prices and shipments and sporadic cooperation among the participants. The battles over markets continued unabated, and the Exporters Group passed out of the picture by 1971. Dan Morgan commented on the unraveling of the system: "Within 18 months, the IGA had indeed collapsed, the United States, Australia, and other countries had undermined the price floors by increasing export subsidies administratively. The Canadian Wheat Board tried unsuccessfully to hold the line, but rapidly lost customers, and its share of the world wheat market declined from 25 percent in 1965 to 17.17 percent in 1968." John Freivalds seemed to sum up the IGA story by quoting a Washington journalist as having said, "The food aid business in Washington spawns intrigues, rivalries, and a cast of characters which sometimes seems to be drawn from an Agatha Christie mystery novel."[9]

Cargill's 1967–1968 Results: Keeping the Pace?

Erv Kelm had concluded his letter to the stockholders in the 1966–1967 annual report with two ebullient sentences: "Many of the plans and goals we had agreed upon are venturesome and bold. In them are ample opportunities to test our abilities . . . and find the stimulation that accompanies excellence of performance." Now a year had passed, and the optimism had been somewhat tempered. The results of the 1967–1968 year had been excellent but not quite up to the previous year. Sales had set a new record at $2.4 billion, and physical volume had jumped 17 percent, to 36.5 million tons. But the net earnings of $15.4 million were 9 percent below the previous year, "due primarily to strikes and prices in the poultry industry, but were creditable, particularly when compared to competitors." Grain Division earnings were close to the previous year despite a long strike at Baie Comeau and another on the Great Lakes. There were some stars—Cargill in Argentina tripled the profits of the previous year. The new corn milling operation had made a profit (although vegetable oil overall had dropped).

Cargill had done well on international sales. The Company had sold 309 million bushels, up from 259 the previous year. Cargill's total U.S. wheat exports were 31 percent of all wheat exported from the United States, and Cargill had sold more U.S. wheat than the total Canadian wheat sold by the Canadian Wheat Board. West Coast wheat sales were a record 100 million bushels and registered record profits.

Capital expenditures remained high in 1967–1968; the total of $42 million was a record. The corn milling operation at Cedar Rapids, the two ocean vessels, the completion of a soybean plant at Amsterdam, and significant improvements at the Chicago elevator and other additions, both in the United

States and abroad, combined to elicit another statement from Kelm and his colleagues about infrastructure: the core competencies of the Company were to be improved in a major way.

Two capital expenditures in this year were particularly important. First, the Houston export terminal came on line. Its size, at 3 million bushels, was not particularly large by terminal standards, but its efficiency was unparalleled. The Houston operation exemplified a push-button, fully automated operation: incoming truck grain was handled on a 67-foot hydraulic dumper, and incoming rail grain was unloaded via a car dumper (it upended boxcars and poured grain from their open doors). Simultaneously, the big hopper cars were being unloaded over pits. This dumped grain was conveyed to one or another of five elevating legs, four with 35,000-bushels-per-hour capacity and another with 25,000. Outgoing grain, in turn, could be loaded into large oceangoing ships at rates approaching 70,000 bushels an hour.

Interestingly, however, the terminal was incapable of some conventional tasks—it could not load a truck, it could not tap its storage space to fill a boxcar. It could do all of the many jobs expected of plants engaging in export but was not able to fill the endless requirements of domestic millers and other "local" customers. In sum, the Houston terminal was an *export* terminal, no more, no less. This suggested a crucial underlying assumption, namely, that the export trade was going to continue to be a highly significant segment of Cargill grain operations. Certainly, the previous three years of export sales would seem to make that a comfortable statement.

Cargill's Houston export terminal, 1968 (Cargill staff photograph).

The second significant capital expenditure was not in itself a large amount; it was for a 3.6-million-bushel inland export terminal at Gibson City, Illinois. But the significance of this terminal was major, for it was to be the first used for a new venture with the Illinois Central Railroad for initiating a unit train, popularly known as Rent-a-Train (RAT). From Gibson City, grain was to be shipped directly to Cargill's Baton Rouge export terminal. This pioneering venture was an instantaneous success, utilizing primarily the "Big John" aluminum hopper cars (typically the popular four-compartment, 4,713-cubic-foot-capacity size capable of a load of 223,000 pounds). Unit trains of at least 100 hopper cars—115 was a common number—would be sent forward from Gibson City to Baton Rouge, to be returned to Gibson City in five days. The Company was committed to Illinois Central to accomplish a minimum of 56 round trips per year; in this first year of operation, 57 train trips were completed. By the following spring, Cargill had opened a second inland export terminal of the same size at Tuscola, Illinois, and was planning a third terminal at Clinton, Illinois. Once again, this was highly specialized export transport, geared to shipping grain in very large volumes from the Gulf ports. So implicit here, too, was that assumption that the export volume would continue to grow.

There was some caution in Kelm's letter to the shareholders after the crop year 1967–1968; as he put it, "The year has begun with some problem areas persisting." Further, "The year ahead will see higher taxes, lower margins on some products and higher wage rates, higher prices for materials and possibly some strikes." Yet, Kelm averred, "our long range plans are for the most exciting decade in Cargill's history—to do in less than 10 years what took 100 years to do before—to more than double in growth by 1978."

At the four-day directors meeting in late July, the board members discussed once again in some detail the integration of the international investments among the divisions. The major policy statement that Erv Kelm made in August 1966 called at that time "a statement of policy concerning international goals and organization" but now dubbed by Fred Seed colloquially, "the Kelm 'White Paper,'" was reviewed at great length. Seed had prepared an 11-page memorandum, taking up each of Kelm's policy pronouncements one by one. Kelm's objectives were "as fresh as if they were to be discussed today." The white paper delineation of administrative responsibilities seemed to suggest no change (although Seed worried that not all corporation operating results were being reviewed well).

Kelm's earlier statement that the organization would be "product-oriented" now generated renewed discussion. First, Seed suggested that the word *product* be changed to *activity*, as it would "more precisely describe our business." New developments had evolved quite differently, "proof that we have a 'fluid' system." While the businesses in Europe had continued as originally organized, "we have retreated from geographical" in Central America and parts of

South America, as well as Japan and the Phillipines. "We have a combination of the two concepts, tailored to various situations . . . thus, we see evolving a global system with more emphasis on area and our country managers."

Trading activities still had conflicts built into them; a special conference had been held earlier in the year, and prickliness among the grain and oil divisions and Tradax, especially over issues of levy-paid business and the wheat and soybean joint accounts, had been discussed frankly enough to resolve (for the moment, at least) most of the tensions. "A continual free exchange of views and information is critical," Seed intoned.

Seed devoted the remainder of his document to individual situations, some of them quite sticky, for example, differences between Cargill and Don Shaver of Shaver Poultry about the pace of growth in that operation (Shaver wanted to move faster on globally integrated operations). Seed had no overall concluding wrap-up, and the extended discussion itself was summed up in the minutes as holding that the Kelm "white paper" "was still substantially effective and that within such objectives, case by case solutions of specific problems will be continued." Put simply, there was still much work to be done in reconciling conflicting turf battles and the underlying values expressed so cogently by the team of strong-willed senior executives. It would take many years to solve some of these, if indeed they are *yet* resolved!

At this seminal meeting, Kelm also had in mind some realignments of executive responsibilities, "as a matter of planning for succession to the top management of the company." After reviewing the retirement dates for seven key senior managers (himself, Diercks, Egermayer, Gage, Harrigan, North, and Seed), he put the matter starkly: "We must realize that there will be almost a complete turnover of top executives in Cargill in the next ten years." He continued: "I think it is prudent to expose some younger operating people to over-all company problems. . . . We should decide on the next chief executive or executives by 1972. . . . This would give three or four years for a 'break-in' period prior to 'going it alone'" (the word *alone* is interesting here, perhaps reaching back to the time when Kelm later admitted that he felt this way, in 1961 and 1962). Kelm proposd a new title—group vice president—"to provide advanced training spots." Not everyone agreed with this step; Jim Cargill wrote Kelm about his concern that there would be a proliferation of titles. Kelm promised to come forward at a later meeting of the board with the specifics (including a bylaw change that would be necessary).

Kelm followed through at the board meeting of December 17, 1968. Bylaw provisions that had been in effect since 1943 now were amended to provide for the post of chairman of the board of directors and chief executive officer of the corporation—the familiar "CEO" post at the head of today's corporations. Kelm now assumed this post, and Fred Seed was elevated from executive vice president to the position of president. In turn, Whitney MacMillan and Pete McVay were elected to the new post of group vice president for the corporation. Bob Diercks would continue as executive vice president. The charge in the previous meeting in July had been to realign the responsibilities "for succession to the top management," and this had now become clearer with the elevation of Fred Seed to the presidency. Further, Whitney MacMillan and McVay had now moved by virtue of their designation as group vice presidents to a position on the hierarchy just below Diercks. This was the most significant point in the evolution of Cargill's management structure after John MacMillan, Jr.[10]

A poignant confluence of events occurred at this time, for on October 16, 1968, Cargill MacMillan, Sr., died (after having been immobilized by a stroke since 1960). As younger brother of John MacMillan, Jr., he had been the quiet one in the background, proudly following his charismatic older sibling in John Jr.'s many innovative, sometimes quirky ventures. But this modest role from an essentially retiring person was in no way the whole picture. Cargill MacMillan exerted a powerful influence on his brother, perhaps the only person who could bring John Jr. around when his decisions were too idiosyncratic. The two were a very good team, John Jr. full of ideas, brother Cargill leavening John's too-quick mind. Both were Phillips Academy (Andover) graduates; both attended and graduated from Yale University. Cargill also attended Cambridge University in England for one year. He began working for Cargill in 1923, with one of his first undertakings the organization of a statistics department. He was a cash grain merchant for a year or so, but trading and the hurly-burly of the market were not his interests. He gradually moved into administrative positions, becoming secretary in 1926, a director of the Company in 1929, and then a vice president when the Cargill Elevator Company was merged in 1936 into Cargill, Incorporated. In 1950, the title was changed to executive vice president, and in 1957 he became president.

The death of Cargill MacMillan marked the close of a generation. The three family members, John Jr. and Cargill MacMillan and Austen Cargill, with their ties of family blood back to W. W. Cargill, made an excellent management team for the Company. There had been sharp disagreements, particularly over the events of 1925, when the John MacMillan, Sr., family had gained control of the Company. But they were able to work in reasonable harmony, all dedicated to the notion of family ownership and all dedicated also to investing the profits of the Company back into the Company. The death of Cargill MacMillan ended a generation of families in the business, a true milestone for Cargill, Incorporated.[11]

"Serious Difficulties"

Erv Kelm and Fred Seed wrote a joint report to the stockholders after the 1968–1969 fiscal year. The words "serious difficulties" were in its first sentence. After five years of excellent results, the Company had suffered a very weak year. Net profit had dropped from $15.3 million to $8.5 million, a drop of 45 percent in net earnings. Return on net worth declined to 6 percent. While most of the divisions had done modestly well (with Argentina having a superb year), there were two shockers. Tradax profits were down from the $1.8 million of the previous year to just $910,000. Far more disturbing, the Grain Division had dropped from a $3.4 million profit in 1967–1968 to a huge loss of $3.3 million.

The stockholder report chronicled the problems: "Strikes at the Atlantic and Gulf ports and on the Great Lakes, tariff barriers to the imports of grain to the European Common Market, restrictions on the competitiveness of U.S. wheat under the International Grains Arrangement, and reductions in the P.L. 480 program—all combined to shrink export opportunities for U.S. grains. For some of the same reasons, Tradax profits were lower, although its sales were equal to last year."

Barney Saunders began his Grain Division report: "It is an onerous task to record the worst year in the long history of Cargill's grain division." Saunders then listed 14 different "major" problems. Foremost among these, in addition to the ones mentioned by Kelm and Seed, was the division's "failure to achieve our goal in our wheat long position." Stu Hanson, the president of Tradax had commented on the U.S. trading losses in his March 1969 report and added, gratuitously, "We are more than ever convinced that if we were to allocate our administrative expenses to U.S. grains and commodities on a proper cost accounting basis, it would be practically impossible [for the Grain Division] to show any black figures, much less a reasonable return on investment, without a reasonable amount of luck and anticipating flat price market movements." Walter Gage was even blunter in the 1968–1969 Tradax annual report: "It is hard to see in retrospect how *by ourselves* we could have done a better job . . . certainly, we could have reduced a number of these costs . . . if we had had much *closer coordination* with Cargill [the emphasis is Gage's]." He continued: "The only alternative, and one which is very tempting if one doubts the possibility or feasibility of obtaining better coordination from Cargill, would be to adopt the negative attitude of refusing to trade in positions which are likely to be affected by any possible strike. Such a posture would cause us certain problems on filling levy-paid sales, but would certainly produce a much better result for Tradax. Whether it would be better for Cargill and Tradax together of course is open to question."

Later in the Kelm/Seed report, they outlined the plans for the coming year. There was need "to adjust our grain business to changing markets," but the two executives expressed optimism about the division: "Although we know that grain trading will suffer from the almost inescapable reduction in exports from the U.S., your management is convinced that the future is promising. Others are pinched more than we, and some are getting out. Until conditions allow exports to rebuild, we simply will have to dig in, cut costs, innovate and build profits from an increased share of the market. The challenge for both Cargill and Tradax is to use our many resources to widen and sharpen their fields of activity."

The rest of the business, almost without exception, was forecasting major improvements. An old-line feed manufacturing firm, Hales & Hunter Co., headquartered in Chicago and operating throughout the Midwest, was acquired; it would remain a subsidiary of Cargill but be directed by David Wentzell, a Feed Division vice president. Another new subsidiary had been formed in South Korea, a major feed, poultry, and egg organization to be called Korea-Cargill, Ltd. A modern feed plant was being built, as well as a poultry processing and poultry breeding plant. Efforts were also being made to establish a similar organization in Taiwan. The new soybean plant had opened at St-Nazaire, France, and the Company was also exploring land development and had begun to feed beef cattle. Tradax was negotiating with shipyards in Split, Yugoslavia, to build two new bulk ocean carriers of 73,500 tons each. The Company as a whole was moving well.

At the end of that 1968–1969 stockholder report, Kelm and Seed made an interesting statement, one that would have been heretical in earlier years: "There has been a subtle change taking place in our business in recent years. We have been in the food business for more than one hundred years—but in bulk and without Cargill identification. Lately, we have been coming closer to the consumer—with millions upon millions of eggs and broiler chickens, corn starches and syrups and special soy protein products, refined oils, and turkeys. There are almost unlimited opportunities for us to build new businesses and margins in the exciting field of food as we bring our products closer to the dining table."

In April, Kelm had asked the senior management group to make "suggestions for new business opportunities for Cargill." Some 85 items turned up; these were tabulated and the total votes for each determined. They ranged all across the food and agriculture fields; corporate farming garnered the highest number (9), followed by pork and beef processing and marketing (7), fabricated-type foods (TVP etc.) (6), animal health products and insecticides (6), and equity position in foreign flour mills (6). There were some fascinating, offbeat suggestions; for example, franchised restaurants obtained five votes, a computer-sharing service had four, and even a travel agency accumulated three votes. At the tail of the list, with just one mention, were some "sleepers"—the possibility of a Fiberglas boat business, fish farming, an advertising agency, a stock brokerage business, even management consulting. Some 15 of the 85 ideas were assigned to various people for further exploration. The whole effort was an exciting, almost mind-game adventure, and the enthusiasm of the management group seemed to grow apace. Kelm and Seed ended their report to the shareholders with an interesting combination of words, that they were going to pursue the Company's capital investment program "prudently but aggressively."

There remained, of course, the real problems in the Company's flagship Grain Division. Many of the senior management group had serious concerns that the Grain Division (or perhaps grain trading generally) needed major re-tooling. Indeed, there were serious statements by some members of this group that "the Company should get out of grain" (not meant literally, one pre-sumes—the sheer scope of the physical facilities here would require a 'fire sale' to end all). The conventional wisdom and later folklore of the Company at-tribute this notion primarily to Cargill MacMillan, Jr., but there were several others who were equally skeptical about the existing Grain Division perfor-mance. The Long Range Planning Committee now turned to this question.[12]

C H A P T E R   F O U R

Three Strong Years

With the 1968–1969 results telegraphing "serious difficulties," recriminations might have seemed the order of the day. The Grain Division would have been an odds-on favorite to receive the heaviest criticism after just having suffered its huge loss of $3.3 million. But Kelm, Seed, and Diercks rejected outright any "blame game" tactics, choosing instead an "opportunity cost" strategy. Within days of the publishing of the unpleasant 1968–1969 results, Seed wrote an unusual letter to all 11 of the division heads; it concerned the planning of the board of directors meetings to be held in the fourth week of July. In order to "retain heavy emphasis on the future course of the business" Seed encouraged an in-depth forward planning for each of the senior managers, asking them to "assure thoughtful consideration of future economic conditions and their effect on the course of our business" and to "examine the consistency of projections" between and among divisions.

To this end, Seed proposed a set of fresh guidelines. First and clearly foremost, "concentrate only on the future." This must have been a surprising approach for everyone, for he explained, "you will recognize this as a major change; you may assume that everyone will have had an opportunity to study your 1968–69 results." Seed then shifted the focus by interjecting a refinement in the five-year planning cycle, urging all of the division heads "to observe whether we are learning from experience and strengthening our ability to anticipate the future course of our business." He included a syllabus of specifics to be followed.

Seed even cleverly changed the modus operandi of the presentations: "In order to assure a uniform graphic presentation, we ask that you work with the comptroller's department, who will be responsible for preparing such graphs as are needed." Apparently, in some of the previous years' presentations of the divisions, managers had prepared their own dazzling (and lengthy) set of graphics, felt by some of the senior management to stand in the way of getting to informed discussion.

On July 24, Barney Saunders presented the Grain Division's report to the board. He began, "First of all, I would like to applaud the decision not to review last year. For obvious reasons, the grain division would like to forget all about 1968–69 except to attempt to apply the lessons learned to future profits." With the help of John Cole and Addison Douglass, Saunders built a case that the grain industry as it was constituted at that moment "is an example of an overbuilt situation in a declining volume business. As a result, all margins have been drastically reduced as all players fight fiercely for the available business. I believe speculation is rampant as many grain men try desperately to widen margins."

The division now had embarked on a cost control and profit improvement program, he continued, "steadily steering a course toward P&L responsibility. . . . For the first time this year our budget for the coming year is based on P&L budgets by regions." Saunders described a program of automation in some of the older facilities, a realignment of branch offices, and a "short interval scheduling" concept that had been introduced the previous year after working with a consulting group, the Alexander Proudfoot Company. "Their methods caused a drastic upheaval in our plants and offices," Saunders allowed, particularly in the way this was coupled with a "crash program on shrink control."

The division had continued its program of selling unproductive facilities; working with Tradax, it also had developed a new arrangement for levy-paid business in Europe that promised a much closer working arrangement. Saunders explained, "We feel our posture should be to streamline our organization as I have described, to spend money to lower operating costs in our plants where economically sound, to insist on and get more productivity from our merchants and managers, to be ready and able to acquire other grain companies' facilities as they come on the market."

The Saunders presentation was a shrewdly motivating one and seemed to set the stage for the rest of the board meeting that July. While the long-range planning committee, in its September meeting, did postpone the Saunders proposal for additional grain storage at Duluth, saying only that it would "reconsider in December—related to Grain Division earnings," the position of the Grain Division seemed considerably more secure at the end of the year (although controller Bob Harrigan expressed dissatisfaction as late as December with the division's efforts to reduce expenses).[1]

A small but important change was made in the corporate goals at that July board meeting. While the basic corporate goals were retained, they were modified "to stress interest into fields where the Company could use its management skills, expertise, and know-how, without the requirement that it be closely associated with agriculture or necessarily complementary to an existing product or service line." The stimulating brainstorming done earlier in the year about new arenas for Company interests had produced some striking nonagriculture ideas, and some of these seemed ready to be put into practical effect. However, the board members reiterated strong feelings from the past that they not fragment their efforts, "that we only consider entrance into businesses in which we have the potential of being a significant factor." While "generally we insist on at least 51% ownership control . . . we will consider a minority position in sound foreign ventures where the investment clearly will be an aid to and promote our other corporate objectives—particularly our trading activities."

At the end of the meeting, a few members of senior management suggested that a new "planning group" perhaps should be developed. Kelm squelched this immediately: "Cargill has a peculiar advantage arising from excellent informal communication to the top level . . . it would not be necessary to form a special acquisition or planning staff to perform this function." The idea died there.[2]

"Startling" Disclosures

Each fall for a number of years, the Harvard Business School Club of Minneapolis and St. Paul had hosted a blue ribbon dinner at which the club presented its Honored Company Award to a single company chosen that year for the distinction. Cargill had been earmarked for the year 1969.

Interest around the Twin Cities was high, for little was known about the Company even in its own backyard. The *Minneapolis Tribune* caught this rampant curiosity: "It was quite an occasion for the historically circumspect company, which a few years ago told a curious reporter, half-facetiously, that Cargill 'might some day give you its sales for, say, 1903—and maybe the earnings for 1897.'" *Business Week* had characterized this strong Cargill reclusiveness in a major article on privately held companies for its issue of December 9, 1967. The twin values of independence and privacy were stressed by all the companies interviewed; the *Business Week* editors used Cargill as their example of a preoccupation with secretiveness: "Staying private also provides the advantage of secrecy. Many privately held companies avoid going public since they would have to disclose financial data to stockholders—and to competitors. 'The nature of our business is such that competitive secrecy and speed in decision making is vital,' says Erwin E. Kelm, President of Cargill, Inc., the biggest grain merchant in the U.S. Cargill's headquarters, a French chateau 15 mi. from Minneapolis is sheltered from view by wooded hills on one side and by Lake Minnetonka on the other."

Beyond the inquisitiveness at the Harvard Business School Club dinner about Cargill's fabled degree of secretiveness, "not a few brokers admitted they had attended in anticipation Kelm would announce that Cargill was going public." "Not so," Kelm stated right at the start of his speech; and while there was "some resigned disappointment at Kelm's denial of the rumors, it was still an exciting event, like the unveiling of an extraordinary diamond in the windows of Tiffany's in New York. Look, but don't touch."

Kelm *did* surprise everyone—including, prominently, most if not all of Cargill's management and employees (some members of the two families were downright querulous). He started with a blockbuster array of financial information: "In each of the past four years," he stated, "Cargill's sales have exceeded $2 billion; sales in 1968–69 declined nearly $208 million from the previous year . . . earnings were also down from the excellent levels we have had the three previous years. Even so, over the four-year period, net profit has averaged better than $14 million and cash flow has been sufficient to make possible reinvestment averaging $35 million per year." One-fourth of Cargill's capital was invested abroad, and overseas sales had contributed up to $1 billion in one year to America's balance of payments. Working capital amounted to nearly $90 million, although long-term debt was only $55 million. Kelm even added, "The Company's net worth has managed to double every seven or eight years, and today surpasses $150 million."

Now, the revelation of these figures would not be at all startling for any publicly held corporation; indeed, they would be required reporting figures. But to have the privately held Cargill reveal such figures was a major Twin Cities event (even leading to a lengthy article in *Cargill News*, entitled "Financial Facts Revealed to Business Group"). When Kelm reiterated at the end, "We have no plans whatsoever to go public," the finality he expressed (said the *Minneapolis Tribune*) "clearly was a disappointment to the large number of investment bankers who had snapped up tickets to the award banquet with an eye towards handling Cargill's rumored stock issues."

In real terms, the specifics of the speech were not truly "startling." Yet Cargill's chariness in disclosing any financial or operational details about itself had been a tenet of the Company for just about all of its 105 years to this point. The origin of this tenaciously held belief stemmed particularly from the strong feelings of privacy held by John MacMillan, Sr. These were certainly mirrored by the rest of the family of that generation and transferred whole-cloth to Erv Kelm. Kelm himself had had a searing experience in the early weeks, just after the May 1963 wheat contract had come to a head, when government investigators swept through the markets and issued subpoenas widely as the beginning salvo for that long and traumatic case. By the time of this Harvard Business School Club speech, the final results of that case were not yet known, and Kelm and his colleagues fought vigorously and confidently toward the end that they felt was in sight, their own and the Company's vindication.

On June 10, 1963, just after those investigative efforts were loosed on him, Kelm wrote a memorandum to all managers and superintendents of the Company; the subject was "Executive Correspondence." It read as follows: "I have observed that almost all of us tend to retain our personal correspondence virtually on a permanent basis. This practice is extremely wasteful of space and secretarial time. Therefore, I would like you to adopt the practice with respect to your general correspondence to be very discriminating in what you retain in your files. This will be a matter of your discretion, but essentially, I would like you to review your personal correspondence files at least once a year and retain no material more than five years unless it has particular historical significance or is necessary to make future business decisions."

Normally, this would be considered a straightforward communication, designed to cut down on the volume of "dead" records. In this case, however, Kelm's memorandum and other statements and actions by him were read generally among management as encouraging the "skeletonizing" of all management records. Where John Sr., John Jr., and Cargill MacMillan had retained *all* of their correspondence—a fantastic bonanza for business historians and a priceless underpinning for *Cargill: Trading the World's Grain*—now the watchword was "do not retain records." Indeed, Kelm himself left literally no business records from his tenure of employment with the Company. As mentioned in the introduction, this has proved a challenge to historians attempting to piece together what happened to Cargill during Kelm's tenure. It would not be overstating the case to hold that this June 10, 1963, memorandum marked the beginning of a "dry period" in corporate record keeping. Many years later, Kelm remembered and regretted this; "It was a mistake—we threw away the corporate memory." This makes all the more surprising what the newspapers would likely have called the "kiss and tell" evening that Kelm gave the Harvard Business School Club in 1969.[3]

Cargill Seeds in Argentina

In that not-good Cargill crop year of 1968–1969, the year of the nail-biting travails for the Grain Division, there were few performance stars among the divisions. Vegetable oil led; its $5.0 million earnings topped all others, but it was still down from $7.2 million the previous year. The very next division in terms of total profit contribution was not any of the other domestic divisions, nor even Tradax; it was Cargill S.A., the Argentine company. It had registered its own record, almost $2.7 million, over 31 percent of all the Company's profit for that year.

The saga of how this had happened was firmly rooted in the operation's grain, feed, and especially seed businesses. John Jr. had created a presence in Argentina 35 years back, in 1934. Interestingly, the Argentine initiative was born out of an earlier preoccupation with secrecy. John Jr. had sent James Ringwald to Buenos Aires that year as part of an overall import/export strategy; MacMillan described this: "We also wish to buy our foreign grain, such as our Argentine flax, South African corn, etc. f.o.b. steamer and charter the steamers ourselves, as in that way, we can avoid telling the whole world about our every move." Once again, secrecy.

Ringwald began purchasing wheat and flax and particularly became the "listening post" for the Company. John Jr. and his wife visited both Argentina and Brazil in December 1934. A year or so later, John Jr. proposed the construction of new Cargill elevators in Argentina, based on his striking new "big bin" configuration. The Argentine government was to participate but finally backed out, and the idea died. Nothing much happened until just before the end of World War II, when Almon Greenman was sent to Buenos Aires as Cargill's local representative. As it was difficult to do business in Argentina without a formal presence, Cargill S.A. Commercial e Industrial was established in April 1948.

The most promising project was for hybrid seed corn, and at this point a fortuitous connection was made. Antonio Marino, an Argentine scientist, had begun to probe the secrets of hybrid vigor back in 1932, studying under the then-preeminent Argentine geneticist, Dr. Solomon Horowitz, at the University of La Plata's College of Agriculture. By 1935, Marino himself had begun to develop and perfect Argentina's first flint-type inbred hybrid. Then Marino won a fellowship to study plant breeding at the University of Minnesota and there worked under one of the most respected American plant geneticists, Dr. H. K. Hayes, father of Ken Hayes, who was production manager in Cargill's U.S. Seed Department. Marino returned to Argentina in 1944 and became the dean at La Plata. In 1947, Cargill persuaded Marino to join the Company, arranging for the hybrid research and production to be done at Pergamino, in the heart of Argentina's corn belt, 150 miles north of Buenos Aires. By 1949, the Company had sold its first "maize hibrido" seed, a volume at that time of 700 bags of 60 kilos (132 pounds).

This process of cross-fertilization is genetically complex, and isolating the strong genes takes several generations. The effort is made more complex by the fact that a generation must be a full growing season—one cannot just do the crosses and then immediately produce the result (at least this was true in the 1960s; today genome research is much more sophisticated, although cycles still have to be proved by a full growing season).

Wheat is self-pollinating; in other words, it can perpetuate itself in the field generation after generation. However, corn has male and female elements that breed together. In a regular cornfield, the wind carries the pollen from the male tassels to many different female silks. In the hybridization process, the male parts of the female line are either mechanically removed or are sterile to avoid selfing so the plant can be fertilized by pollen from the dedicated male plants.

Dan Morgan, in his important book *Merchants of Grain*, put the special commercial advantage of hybrid corn very well: "The key fact about hybrid seeds is that farmers have to buy new supplies of them every year. They do not reproduce themselves . . . hybrids are obtained by crossing 'parent' plants possessing distinctive traits to get a vigorous hybrid. It is the control of the male and female parent lines that gives any particular firm a monopoly and control over the hybrid seeds it develops. These parent lines are developed separately by company researchers and plant geneticists who know how to isolate and reproduce certain desirable traits . . . it takes at least four generations." This biological fact of life, as Morgan put it, "has made a few companies the sole source of 'hybrid power' for many of the nations" (an extension of Morgan's 'food power' thesis developed in his book).

Cargill S.A. had some early difficulties; in 1950, the Company lost its entire crop from a combination of drought and hailstorm damage. Hybrids were new to the Argentinean farmer; as late as 1957, only 8 percent of all corn plantings were hybrids. By the mid-1960s, this had risen to 60 percent. All through this period, Cargill S.A. was trading grain reasonably profitably and soon began to do quite well in the new hybrid seed corn effort. A sorghum hybrid seed had been introduced in 1962, and new poultry operations also were being contemplated.

One of the key reasons for the Company's success was the arrival on the scene in 1959 of Heinz Hutter. Hutter's overall training in the Cargill organization had been thorough—a classic example of how Cargill was bringing along its younger management team (and in this case all the way to the top; Hutter became president and chief operating officer of Cargill in 1991). He was a German national and had come to the United States first as a Fulbright scholar at Cornell University in a program combining economics and international law. He returned to Germany to work on his Ph.D. but was persuaded to join Cargill's Hamburg office in 1955. There he became a trader, dealing primarily in grains and oil. The Company later gave him short assignments at the Geneva office, then in 1958 to the United States for a year of work, first in St. Louis as a merchant (where he also learned the operations of Cargo Carriers) and next assigned to San Francisco, immersing himself in the minutiae of copra production and trading. He ended in Minneapolis, working under John Cole in the Grain Division's northern region. His training in the United States finished, he returned to Germany. The Hamburg general managership was not yet open; another man was ahead of him.

Both the Hamburg office and the Argentine operations were part of Tradax; now Walter Gage suggested that Hutter go to Buenos Aires as head of that operation. Gage personally loved Argentina and fought to keep the operation viable in the face of considerable opposition from Minneapolis management, which seemed to feel that Argentina would never be stable enough to be profitable. After Gage's next visit to Argentina, Hutter was appointed president of the operation (with Marino as vice president). Hutter had just turned 30 at this point and clearly was the youngest "chief executive officer" in the Company.

The appointment of Hutter by Walter Gage was a stroke of good fortune, for not only did Cargill S.A. thrive during the decade of the 1960s but Hutter himself, with his excellent training in economics and finance, became a special asset for Cargill management in understanding a problem of great concern in Argentina—inflation. In common with many Latin American and other developing countries, Argentina had gone through several periods of galloping inflation in the 1960s. A corporate manager trying to apply conventional standards to a situation like this could have his whole operation decimated by inflationary movements in a matter of months or even weeks. In the U.S. business milieu, inflation was "bad," for managers did not understand the dynamics of mounting inflation, knew that they could be wiped out quickly, and feared inflation as a "black box" that they could not manage. Looking at one's net worth with traditional developed-world analysis could prove to be disastrous, for inflation could rapidly erode cash and other forms of current assets. With interest rates very high in such situations and a surprise devaluation of the local currency always a threat, one had to be highly knowledgeable and alert about interest rate movements and keenly attuned to the relationship between the local currency and the denominators mandated by developed-world hard currencies. Often the ways that one had to look at these volatile interrelationships were quite the opposite of what applied in a developed world with a more stable business environment.

Hutter had this special inflation mentality drilled into him by the constant, day-by-day decisions he had to make to keep his net worth from washing away. He estimated that upward of 80 percent of his time was spent on just this kind of tightrope walking. A Tradax executive described one situation, in the crop year 1961–1962:

Then followed the national elections, with Frondizi's defeat and subsequent ouster, and with that the rapid collapse of the peso. For almost 2 years we had followed a policy of keeping our peso position even and buying exchanges as far deferred as could conceivably be justified by our grain purchases. This paid off very nicely, but it became quite apparent after the elections that we should immediately get short pesos and stay short. Once our short position had been established, our timing on covering proved quite fortuitous, as we about evened up our position two or three times just prior to getting a firmer peso for a short while during which time we continued to buy grain without covering the exchange . . . all in all, it was the type of year that could probably be called most abnormal were it not Argentina, where anything can happen, and usually does.

There were serious losses on occasion; in 1966–1967, Cargill S.A. had operating earnings after taxes of $1.5 million, but exchange losses from a devaluation of the Argentine peso took away all but $509 of it. However, the lessons that Hutter absorbed during his dozen years in Argentina paid off not only for Cargill S.A. but for the overall Cargill organization when Hutter came to the United States periodically to talk through with the rest of the Cargill senior management group what he was learning. The Company was moving significantly into many countries that did not have as strong currencies as the

United States and Western European countries, and this made the Argentinean lessons more imperative. Hutter's help was particularly important to the Company when double-digit inflation hit the United States after the "oil shocks" in the mid-1970s. In February 1973, Hutter was brought to Cargill, Incorporated, in the corporate headquarters in Wayzata as a vice president of the corporation and assistant to the president; the remainder of his career was in the United States.

There was substantial success in the Cargill S.A. feed operations, where it was becoming number one in the country. Poultry became an initiative, too. After the joint venture with Shaver was established, Cargill S.A. began selling both broiler parent chicks and layer parents, as well as commercial layers. In addition, Cargill S.A. itself built a set of complementary poultry processing plants in 1969, "the finest in South America," they averred.

It was in hybrid seed that Cargill S.A. particularly stood out. By the 1969–1970 crop year, at the end of the decade, the hybrid seed department had a profit of $2.9 million from the biggest crop ever in the Company's hybrid maize and sorghum (282,000 bags of maize had been sold, 132,000 of sorghum). "We could have sold at least 50% more maize," their annual report noted; while "the increase in sorghum sales was difficult and had to be achieved by longer payment terms and intensive technical promotion," sorghum still had its first really big year, and "this seed has become as big a profit maker as maize on a per-kilo basis. . . . We hold an outstanding market position in hybrid maize and our production continues to be less than our sales ability . . . we are also the largest seller of sorghum but our quality image is not as good." The report concluded: "No other seed company in South America can compare with us in respect to size, volume, but above all in the scope of our breeding efforts."

Beyond this, there were additional new opportunities for hybrids, particularly with both wheat and sunflowers. The huge success of the high-yielding variety of wheat hybrids in India had now encouraged Marino and his colleagues to pursue their own wheat research. It would take several years before one could anticipate any commercial success, but the program looked promising at this time.

The sunflower research had taken its cue from the Cargill efforts in the United States (discussed below). Wherever it was done, however, the success of any hybrid depended upon the quality of the research that had gone into the variety, which in turn depended critically on having well-trained plant geneticists available for the highly sophisticated, laborious analysis underlying the final hybrid. Antonio Marino was now approaching retirement age, and this fostered questions about who might be a successor to the eminent dean of Cargill S.A. hybrids. An internal report in June 1969 was sobering; while the Company had younger engineers in training, no one was quite ready. "Until such a chain of command can be established," the report continued, "we are

How Hybrids Happen

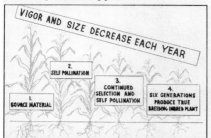

"Source material" plant, chosen for desirable characteristics, is inbred, by fertilizing silks with plants own pollen, to achieve pure strain.

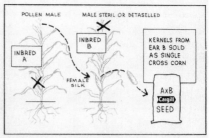

Two inbred lines, prevented by detasseling from self-pollination, are cross bred. "Female" yields single-cross seed from which most vigorous hybrid will grow.

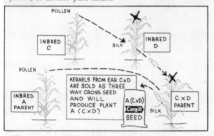

Three-way cross yields more seed because "female" parent is not an inbred, but a single-cross hybrid. Seed incorporates three inbred lines.

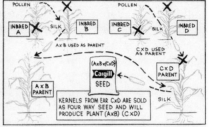

Four-way cross, called double cross, combines four inbred lines and most economical seed production by cross of two single cross hybrid parents.

considering having a highly trained U.S. breeder assume this position [but] the presence of an American in the Argentine research group is potentially a sensitive point for the Company image there. Necessarily, he must be diplomatic, show patience and a willingness to teach, and find it easy to 'go native.' The temporary nature of his position may need to be emphasized through an appropriate title."

The report also spoke bluntly about the unyielding nature of the longer-term dimensions of crossing and testing: "Testing is dynamic and will need to be modified as the program matures. It can be stressed for Argentina to an equal or greater degree than for the U.S. corn belt—there is no substitute for an extensive location, period-years evaluation of experimental hybrids."

The sensitivity about sending an American to Argentina to undertake the Marino responsibility was in line with a larger concern surfacing at this time, both in Argentina and elsewhere, concerning the role of nationals versus expatriates at both the management and ownership levels. In Argentina, demands for "Argentinization" were heard more and more frequently; similarly, in Peru it was "Peruvianization." In July 1970, the entire Cargill board had made a trip to Brazil, Peru, and Argentina; at their meeting of July 26, 1970, the decision had been made to reduce the Company's risk by having Cargill

Peruana pay off external debt as rapidly as possible and "Peruvianizing by adding a partner or partners, preferably inactive." At the May 20, 1971, board meeting, various responses to new Argentinization policies were mulled over; the share capital of Cargill S.A. was increased from $2 million to $10 million by capitalizing earned surplus, and the directors of Cargill S.A. were to subscribe to a segment of common shares of the Company in order to bring about a stronger Argentinean representation. The directors also discussed the merits of establishing a local scientific and agricultural research foundation that would hold some of the shares.

Already in the country there were certain restraints in place, particularly a "buy Argentine" restriction on some purchases and the demand for allocating more bank credit to companies that were "Argentinized." Further constraints could be anticipated that might involve more forced local participation and perhaps even limitations on payment of dividends to foreign shareholders. Certainly, Cargill S.A. had a strong Argentine base due to both the number of nationals in senior management and the spirit that had been built among these people by Hutter and Marino, who had succeeded in developing a special Cargill S.A. culture of honesty and fair dealing in a business environment where these values were not always fully appreciated. The loyalty of the Ar-

Cargill's operations in Brazil, 1974 (*Cargill News*, May–June 1974).

gentine work force was evident throughout, and this would stand in good stead in this particular time of highly nationalistic feelings. Further, Tradax had chosen to plow back a large portion of its Argentine profits in Argentina, rather than repatriate them to Cargill, Incorporated.

Hutter described this in a speech to Tradax management in May 1971: "It made good sense to grow with the host country. If we would have remitted everything we made in the early sixties, we would still be where we were then and would have less than what we now remit as dividends. . . . In South America these last years, the correct philosophy has gained more and more ground that the fact that you make money does not give you the right to do with it what you exclusively want to and/or the fact that you are satisfied with what you make from what you own (land, for instance) does not liberate you from the responsibility to produce more for the country and provide more for its inhabitants. This is the only philosophy which might save us from ultra right or ultra left national socialistic governments." (This did not work, however, in Peru, for, as described earlier, the Peruvian fishmeal operations were nationalized by the Peruvian government in 1973).

Hutter also spoke to the question of size: "We knew that being a foreign company it was obvious that we could not afford to hold too big market shares in one of our by now traditional business lines . . . we are holding at present 40–45% of the hybrid seed market [and] can only afford to grow with the market." In feed and poultry there was room to add to share of market, and there were other agricultural projects, too. "Yet, we must move with care as we are already the biggest agrotechnical concern in Argentina and we cannot invest all our hopefully sizeable future earnings and our strong borrowing power in our traditional sector: agriculture." Hutter suggested a number of nonagriculture possibilities, many of them similar to those advanced by the Cargill senior management a few months earlier.[4]

Working Again in Brazil

Back in 1947, Nelson Rockefeller had approached Cargill about a possible joint venture in Brazil to market grain. Rockefeller's International Basic Economy Corporation (IBEC) had been formed a year earlier to work particularly in Venezuela and Brazil as a Rockefeller family project operating for profit but with the stated purpose of playing a role in developing countries. He had wanted to demonstrate that private capital organized for profit could also upgrade the "basic economies" of the developing world. In Brazil, IBEC had already planned a hybrid seed corn company, a hog production company, a helicopter cropdusting company, and an agricultural mechanization project. Next, Rockefeller wanted to move into grain storage.

After Rockefeller and John Jr. had talked the idea over and taken the measure of each other, Cargill joined as equal stockholder in an arrangement for a

Sewing burlap bags at Jacarezinho, Brazil, feed mill (*Cargill News*, May–June 1974).

new company called Cargill Agricola e Comercial, S.A.; the natural acronym was CACSA. Two country elevators were built in the western part of the state of São Paulo, about 250 miles west of the city by that name; however, they were not well located, and the operation dwindled down, finally going out of business two years later. The IBEC hybrid seed corn operation, on the other hand, was a great success and has continued so up to the present.

At this time, 1967, Cargill again was moving into Brazil. Cargill Agricola, S.A. had been formed in 1965 with the help of Antonio Marino from Argentina and Dr. A. R. Baldwin, the research director of Cargill. The operation was to be modeled after the successful one in Argentina and would have three departments—seed, grain, and feed. Seed came first, with the completion in 1966 of a modern hybrid plant in the central part of the state of São Paulo. An extensive effort was now begun to find hybrids especially acclimatized for the Brazilian environment. A leased feed plant was also established, as well as six interior buying branches for the grain department.

Losses troubled Cargill Agricola for the first three years. All three of the basic operations suffered from that bugaboo of start-up operations, lack of volume. This was put poignantly in the 1968–1969 annual report, when the

Cargill Feed plays a part in a self-help project conducted in the interior of Brazil by Mennonite volunteers. The American church group, working among the poor in two isolated villages, provided some 75 families with six chickens each and a regular issue of Cargill feed for the first four months; thereafter, the laying hens belonged to the families. The families were urged to eat half their egg production—their only protein source—and sell the other half to purchase poultry feed (Cargill News, September–October 1971).

seed department reported, "In retrospect, we probably should have offered greater price discounts, added more salesmen and increased our promotion. On the brighter side, our hybrid won the national yield contest and also the Parana State trials. It is clear that we produced the best quality seed in the market last year." By the next annual report, the managers noted, "The Cargill name is gradually becoming known throughout South Brazil and people are coming to see us about business instead of our always chasing them." Not until the crop year 1970–1971 did Cargill Agricola turn an overall profit, a modest $631,000. That year each of the three segments came through with a positive profit-and-loss statement. However, there was one disturbing comment in the seed section of the report: "Sales were stimulated by a high world price for corn caused primarily by the U.S. blight situation." This unsettling development will be discussed further.

Despite this troubling difficulty from afar, Cargill's Brazilian company seemed off to a solid start. The annual report of 1970–1971 commented that the Brazilian government provided "a favorable climate" for investment by foreigners and that the inflation rate had been brought into control after several years of excess.[5]

Cargill Seeds in the United States

Domestically, Cargill had sold seed under its own name since 1907, when the forerunner of the Minneapolis Seed Company was founded. Over those earlier years, seed had been a minor part of the Cargill operation, being marketed under the name "Crystal Brand." At this point, a whole range of field seed varieties had been sold: timothy, red clover, alsike, alfalfa, white blossom, sweet clover, millets, and others. The Minneapolis Seed Company was phased out in 1936 and a Cargill seed department begun; a new product was added at this point, lawn grass seed. In the early 1940s, Cargill entered the hybrid field once again, continuing the Crystal brand name and using the seeds originally developed by the Universities of Minnesota and Wisconsin. Soon the department began working on its own hybrids at the Company's breeding plots at St. Peter, Minnesota. These used the trade name "Gold Seal." Just after World War II, several small seed companies were purchased, adding depth to the Company's hybrid corn production. Despite a good product, the hybrids absorbed a series of losses during the late 1940s and 1950s.

But then, unfortunately, a "black eye" was given the Company in 1951, when four Cargill employees were found to be adulterating seed and selling it under false pretenses (it was being marketed as Montana alfalfa seed but was mixed with lower-grade Arizona alfalfa). The Company threw itself on the mercy of the court, and the judge accepted a plea of nolo contendere. But the blow to Cargill morale was severe; the Cargill board at this point made the decision to stop all of its field seed production and leave the business altogether. The hybrid corn group was a completely separate endeavor and did continue.

The Seed Department limped along through the remainder of the 1950s and into the early Kelm years. In the 1963 Chase Manhattan Bank consulting report on Cargill, the analysts were harsh on the seed effort: "The Company has been in this business for at least the past fourteen years. In three of the fourteen years (1959–1961), this product was profitable . . . generating $408,000 before tax. In the other 11 years, the Company lost money on hybrid corn, in the aggregate amount of $2,417,000 before tax. There does not seem to be any disposition to discontinue this activity, although Cargill has got out of other special products (viz., fish oil and 'miracle mulch') after shorter periods and smaller aggregate losses." The Chase analysts bluntly concluded, "Before losing any more on hybrid corn, it should get out."

This advice was not taken. There were sentimental reasons for keeping seed—it was a branded product sold widely among farmers and had a modest but definitely positive reputation. In the first two Kelm years, the department lost money again, the reasons apparently rooted in management slips rather than product. In 1963–1964, the group turned its first profit in several years, after "major surgery performed during the year on the sales organization. . . . Looking back, it seems apparent that we went too far in reducing the number of territories and territory managers, leaving some with an area too large to cover effectively. We also lost adequate inventory control during the critical selling periods, and are badly in need of a better means of measuring the trend of demand for specific hybrid numbers in order to balance production with sales."

By the 1966–1967 crop year, the Company had 74 different varieties, a total that included both hybrid corn and sorghum seeds. In this year, the seed group made a major production switch, devoting considerably more acreage to new single-cross varieties. This variety resulted from initial crossing of two "inbreeds," each a variety carefully selected as a potential parent and bred to itself (inbred) for generations until a pure, uniform, predictable seed could be achieved. Then, when two inbred parent strains were crossed, the result was a strong vigorous hybrid offspring, giving farmers high quality and high yield. The superiority of single-cross seed had been known for decades, but only recently had it been possible to produce top-quality single crosses in great enough volume at low enough price to reach commercial farmers (most hybrids were "double crossed" because of their excellent performance and substantially lower cost). *Cargill News* diagrammed this hybrid process in its October–November 1966 issue (see page 149).

For two decades, the Company had pushed the commercial potential of sunflower and safflower production (for its oilseed promise) and had worked with farmers, particularly in the Red River Valley area of Western Minnesota and North Dakota, to take on contract growing for the oil. The Russians were large producers of sunflowers, and Cargill now forged links with Russian seed producers. In 1967, a Russian variety, "Peredovik," had considerable success in the valley; in the following year, three more of their varieties were imported. "Smema" and "VNIIMK 89.31" were excellent yielders with normal maturity; the third, "Krasnodarets," had a lower yield potential but required ten days to two weeks less time to mature.

Cargill's seed research scientists now began to concentrate on the possibility of the Company producing its *own* sunflower varieties. In February 1970, Dr. Freeman Johnson, research manager for sunflowers, announced commercial-scale production of Cargill's own hybrid, which he felt would dramatically raise yields. But the 1973–1974 annual report of the new Flax/Sunflower Department reported: "Our sunflower hybrid on trial on a commercial scale did not produce the major yield breakthrough we are looking for. It is better than Peredovik, but a new Russian variety, Sputnik, shows equal promise." Company research geneticists at the Cargill facilities in Fort Collins, Colorado, also began studying hybrid wheat prospects, building on some of the earlier research done by Norman Borlaug on "dwarf wheat" in Mexico, used so widely in the Green Revolution of India and elsewhere (Borlaug won the Nobel Peace Prize in 1970 for this research).

While the hybrid seed operation was modestly profitable through the late

1960s, it still had problems of excessive seed returns and even some product liability claims. Net earnings for 1967–1968 were $328,000; for 1968–1969, $300,000; and in 1969–1970, a record of $526,000. A warning in the annual report for the 1969–1970 year was a portent of a more ominous problem in the following year: "The 1969 growing season was generally good and would have provided higher yields had it not been seriously affected by yellow blight and eye spot disease."[6]

Blight!

In breeding for better and better hybrids, selection of gene attributes often becomes narrower and narrower. The genetic uniformity of the commercial hybrid corn varieties allowed ever greater yields, but scientists always knew that this uniformity could make a variety susceptible to a mutant strain that could produce disease. Now this happened in the United States. In the same year that Borlaug was granted his Nobel prize, a new mutant strain of southern corn-leaf blight—called by one of those jaw-breaking Latin names, *Helminthosporium maydis*—struck the American corn crop with a vengeance. Betty Fussell, in her classic book *The Story of Corn*, put this well: "The ravages of epidemic dramatized the dangers of sacrificing diversity to yield. Taxonomists and breeders alike now qualify 'genetic improvement' with words like 'genetic erosion' and 'genetic vulnerability.' More and more geneticists agree that the extinction of local corn varieties and primitive races in an effort to 'improve' them is analogous, as Garrison Wilkes says, 'to taking stones from the foundation to repair the roof.'"

Corn farmers had begun the year 1970 with high hopes. Estimates for the 1970 crop had been set at about 4.7 billion bushels, 3 percent above the 1969 level; the Department of Agriculture estimates put the average yield at 80.9 bushels an acre. Then the blight hit, especially strong in the South but with many reports of damage in the Middle West, too, especially in the bellwether lands of Illinois. It appeared that the blackish-brown rot was quite extensive, although it would take several months to determine the damage to the total crop. Estimates ranged from a minimum of 5 percent up to as high as 50 percent, "although the latter estimate is regarded as almost certainly too high." It was obvious that the threat was widespread; all over the cornfields the tell-tale lodging (falling over) of stalks was happening. By late August, there were reports of damage from Texas to Florida in the South and up to Minnesota and Wisconsin in the North. Soon gyrations in the grain futures market built to a frenetic pace on the Chicago Board of Trade.

New York Times writers discussed the underlying genetic problem: "For 25 years, hybrids containing what is known technically as the 'T' cytoplasm for male sterility underwent the tests of time against the challenges of soil, weather, climate, and diseases such as the Southern corn leaf blight. . . . Then with dramatic swiftness the ability of these hybrid corns to withstand the fungi wilted because the fungus itself, impelled by some Darwinian quirk, mutated into a more virulent strain of parasite." The *Times* editors pointed out that the country had millions of bushels of corn left over from the previous year in storage, but if there were several corn crops in succession with this plague, the implications would be most serious.

By September, as the major segment of the crop was harvested, the damage did not look as severe as earlier predicted. But the futures markets seemed not to be reassured; prices continued to move up, pushed particularly, said the *Times,* by "fears that next year's seed corn may not be as blight resistant as earlier reported." At the end of 1970, the results of the crop showed that the total was some 10 percent less than in 1969. The 4.1 billion bushels was nearly 500 million below a year earlier and 650 million below the record crop of 1967. Disturbingly, the corn yields over the country averaged just 72 bushels per acre, down from 1969's 84 bushels per acre.

As farmers contemplated the 1971 crop, the fears that the blight might return dominated their thinking: "The blight spores are there now, dormant, waiting under the snow. Where blight-stricken fields were left unplowed last fall, corn plant residues lay harboring fungus. Where fields were plowed deep

"Again this summer Cargill employed a small army of high school students to rogue and detassel corn plants on 43,000 acres of hybrid seed production in Iowa, Illinois, and Nebraska. Most seemed to like it" (Cargill News, July–August 1977).

to bury the invader, even a small piece of infected trash left at or near the surface can provide enough spores to re-infest the area in a few days, half the
county in a few more." The farmers faced what many felt was a Hobson's
choice: plant larger amounts of corn, which if all was harvested would depress corn prices, or plant at existing levels, then find that the blight reap-
peared and drove the total production way down. The *New York Times* put
the dilemma well: "In principle the solution for the problem . . . is simple; the
breeding of a new variety . . . that will resist the crop destroyer. But at best it
takes several years to breed the needed resistant variety, and there is no guarantee that it will not soon be attacked by another mutant enemy." A report in
early June that the University of Illinois had reported renewed corn blight in
15 different Illinois counties quickly drove corn futures up. By the end of that
month, blight had been reported in 15 states.

A switch by farmers from the male sterile inbreds over to "A," normal-
cytoplasm plants, was stepping up. These would require detasseling, and if
the "A" varieties were used, there would need to be massive work at hand detasseling in the fields. There was some experimenting with the use of the helicopter as a machine-based detasseler, but one thinks of the many thousands of
young high school and college-age men and women who spent their summers
in the cornfields detasseling now being replaced by a machine![7]

Cargill Fights the Blight

Obviously the blight was going to play havoc with the country's seed dis-
tributors. Once it was known that the "T" cytoplasm was the host for the
blight, farmers demanded the "A" cytoplasm seeds. Cargill ended the year
writing off a significant segment of its "T" inventory. The U.S. seed group
immediately ordered 36,000 bags of the "A" seed from Cargill's Argentine operations, helping the latter post a record $4.0 million in seed sales alone. But
the profit for one unit was a loss to the other, the Company's domestic seed
department reporting that "the quality of Argentine seed turned out to be extremely poor—very low germination and vigor. We suffered an inventory loss
of $100,000." The U.S. group also tried to increase its supply of resistant seed
by purchases from Italy, France, and South Africa. When the South African
purchase (45,000 bags) reached the U.S. port, U.S. Customs would not allow
the seed into the country. Finally, the Cargill seed department ordered seed
stock from Company operations in Hawaii to supply seed for 1971 production
planning and for 1972 sales. Despite all of the difficulties, the department did
end up with a modest profit of $365,000 in this difficult year.

Fear of what would happen in the next season dominated everyone's
thinking. But none of the fears of the producer farmers proved warranted;
the season of 1971–1972 was an excellent one. The U.S. corn crop was superb,
a record 35 percent above 1970 and the first in history to exceed 5 billion

At the experimental plant breeding center at Cargill's Pergamino, Argentina, operation, a Cargill plant breeder from Grinnell, Iowa, is in discussion with Doctor Antonio Marino, "the father of Argentine hybrid seed corn."

Hybrid seed corn being airlifted 6,300 miles and two seasons south, from the Midwest corn belt to the Argentine pampas in an operation that promised some relief in 1971 from 1970's corn-blight worries. Cargill, Inc., jetted blight-resistant variety to its thousands of acres of breeding and production fields in Argentina to catch up with springtime in the Southern Hemisphere. Multiplied there some 250 times, the corn seed was returned after harvest in February and was available to corn belt farmers by March 1971 (Cargill staff photograph, c. 1970).

bushels. Harvested acreage was the most since 1960, and there was a heart-warming 21 percent jump in yield, to a record 87 bushels per acre. Of course, this brought lower prices, but no one was complaining. There were significant sales to Russia, and the Argentine crop was not competitive this year, making it an excellent export season for Cargill's domestic company. Still, the bugaboo of surpluses continued to intrude into good news. The crop had exceeded domestic and export requirements by some 600 to 700 million bushels, and the carryover was expected to nearly double the year-earlier total of 663 million bushels.

The Company's domestic operations did very well in the crop year 1971–1972, despite having to write off more "T" inventory, amounting to some $1.2 million, and to settle additional product claims of some $200,000. The reasons for the outstanding year were very much tied to the purchase of a major new addition for the Seed Department, a well-known firm called P-A-G. There is a special story connected with this acquisition.[8]

"Market Domination" in Seed?

In the late 1960s, in an expression of renewed confidence in the Seed Department, the Company's long-range planning committee (LRPC) had authorized the department management to search for a medium-sized hybrid company to buy—a "hunting license," said the annual report of 1967–1968. In the next year, a good prospect surfaced—the P-A-G division of W. R. Grace & Co. This was an old-line firm formed in the 1930s as an outgrowth of the famous Pfister Corn Co. By 1943, it had become Pfister Associated Growers, a cooperative owned by franchised producers of Pfister seed. Grace acquired it in 1967.

A step usually taken by the lawyers in such a "horizontal" acquisition is to query the antitrust division of the U.S. Department of Justice about whether the latter saw any reason to constrain the deal because of possible antitrust implications. There *was* a dominant producer in hybrid corn, but it was not - P-A-G. The DeKalb Seed Co. held 25 percent of the market at that time, by far the largest in the industry. The Cargill/P-A-G combination, according to the Cargill Seed Department, had the market share shown in table 3.

TABLE 3

Cargill Seed Department Market Share

Company	Corn belt	14 states where Cargill had substantial sales	Total U.S. market
Cargill	3.2 %	3.21 %	2.50 %
P-A-G	6.04	5.96	5.09
Combined	9.24	9.17	7.59

This seemed to the lawyers of both companies to show modest totals, in no way appearing to threaten market "domination" (it certainly was far below that of Cargill's Argentine operation). To everyone's surprise, the Department of Justice *did* see a problem, or at least indicated that they would put a "hold" on the deal until their lawyers had had a turn at the figures. This forced the Seed Department to look again at their figures, and to their consternation, they found that a computing error had inadvertently biased the totals upward. Their report to the FTC explained: "the computations were based upon U.S.D.A. 1964 planting rates . . . after discussing current harvest rates (plants per acre) with state agronomists in Illinois, Iowa, Minnesota and Nebraska [we] have determined that the 1964 planting rates compiled by the U.S.D.A. were approximately 25% lower than current rates for corn belt states and approximately 15% low for non-corn states." New computations were submitted; they lowered the corn belt total to 7.29 percent, the 14 states total to 7.21 percent, and the U.S. total to 6.0 percent. The Department of Justice agreed that the new computation was accurate and withdrew its concern. In the process the embarrassed Seed Department had learned a lesson in doing its homework! But all was well—the merger was approved.

In that first year of the merger, the Cargill side of the seed business lost $403,000. However, P-A-G sales produced a pretax profit of $2.8 million. Total Cargill/P-A-G sales volumes set new records with a total of 1 million bags, 629,000 produced at the P-A-G operations.

The P-A-G acquisition brought some difficulties along with its high profits. The Seed Department's annual report commented: "Because of the acquisition, it was necessary to completely reorganize both research and development groups. Some unforeseen changes included two key men who resigned, plus two deaths, and also two long-term disabilities. These . . . caused much concern. Now most everyone is settled down and plans are proceeding." The Seed Department management pushed hard that year to consolidate the various seed businesses within Cargill under one operating unit (presumably theirs). "This has many pro's and con's," they reported, "but the advantages outweigh the disadvantages. With units operating in Tradax, P&R, commodity marketing, producer marketing, research, and seed presently involved, we feel that a central coordination would greatly benefit Cargill . . . and still have the profit autonomy that the respective operating units desire." The board, however, was not willing at this time to undertake such a substantial restructuring, built around the Seed Department. Its "track record" just was not there.[9]

A Seed Sale to Iraq Has Unfortunate Results

Two successive droughts had hit the country of Iraq in 1969 and 1970, and many of its people were bordering on starvation. The ruling Ba'ath party, which had seized power in a coup d'état in 1968, now wanted to placate the peasants by ordering expensive high-yielding "miracle" wheat from Mexico, where Norman Borlaug had pioneered the dwarf varieties. Edward Hughes, writing in the London *Times*, told of the events: "30,000 or 40,000 tons of seed would have been ample, but Iraqi officials dreamed of a spectacular crop. They ordered 73,000 tons of Mexipak. Cargill, an American grain firm, got the bulk of the order—63,000 tons." The Iraqi government specifically wrote into the contract that the grain was to be treated with a methyl-mercury fungicide in order to ward off the possibilities of various rusts, smuts, or blights that might infect it. Both the United States and Canada had banned use of the methyl-mercury dressing for seed, as there were severe environmental effects from mercury poisoning. Indeed, in 1953 and for a few years after, a number of people in the Nigata/Minamata Bay of Japan had been poisoned by eating fish that had consumed high concentrations of methyl-mercury from waste dumped by plastics manufacturers. In that disaster, some 93 people died, and 23 infants had suffered prenatal damage to their central nervous system. Iraq, too, had had earlier tragedies—both in 1956 and again in 1960 Iraqi peasants had been poisoned by mercury-treated seed.

Cargill's segment of the sale, a very large amount by any standards, was a Tradax contract with Iraq, with arrangements made through the Tradax North American unit, Cargill America. Ten or more cooperatives in Mexico were involved in the contract; each applied mercury to its seed, all done under the supervision of the Mexican national government institution, Productora Nacional de Semillas. The seed was loaded out of the west coast port of Guaymas, in Sonora State, beginning in mid-July and finishing in early September. All of the wheat arrived at the Iraqi port of Basrah by early October.

The story of its arrival in Basrah was told by Hughes: "Having ordered far more wheat than was needed, the authorities thought to curry favor with the peasants by distributing it free of charge . . . when word of the handout spread, farmers rushed to sell their own wheat stocks before prices fell; with empty bins they could claim more of the imported grain." But this meant that the peasants would have to fall back on the new seeds, both for their baking needs and for the next year's planting. The Iraqi government, remembering past disasters, devised a safety program that involved government aircraft dropping warning leaflets and depended on a team of high-ranking officials imposing tight discipline at the Basrah docks. But the supervising team left after about four weeks, and the whole process became very much relaxed. The grain had been shipped in plastic bags weighing 50 kilos (110 pounds each); these heavy bags were quickly split open and rebagged into smaller lots, and the peasants used all sorts of subterfuges to obtain as much of this seed as they could carry away.

The original plan had been to have the seed arrive in time for the planting season, but October was past this time, so the temptation was to use it for human consumption. Each original bag was clearly identified with large signs stating that it was "unfit for human consumption," written in both English and Spanish (few in Iraq could read these languages). Further, all the seed had been dyed a deep red, almost purple, signifying that it was not to be used for feeding animals or for human consumption.

The peasants, however, washed off the red dye and, after feeding some of the grain to their animals and noting no ill effects, began using it for their own bread baking. With bread a very important part of the daily diet, this meant the immediate ingesting of large quantities of the seed, now milled by the peasants into flour. Mercury is a particularly insidious poison in that its effects are not seen immediately. Later those animals that had been experimented with became ill and were quickly sold by the peasants to the nearest abattoir, where the animals were prepared to be sold off for others to use.

By the end of the year 1971, large numbers of people who had eaten the treated grain were stricken with mercury poisoning. By mid-January 1972, it was a national epidemic. Belatedly, the government demanded that all seed be returned. But all this came too late. The people themselves, with suspicion of a government trick to gain back the grain, continued to eat it or sold it to other unsuspecting villagers.

Over the spring of 1972, there was a huge international outcry about what was happening in Iraq. In the United States, Senator Gaylord Nelson of Wisconsin appeared before the Senate Commerce Subcommittee on the Environment to testify on proposed amendment of the Federal Environmental Pesticide Control Act in 1971. Nelson articulately and unceasingly pushed for strict regulations in the use of pesticides and advocated furnishing more detailed information to foreign governments, including test data, all of which also would go to appropriate international agencies. Nelson, in his many public statements about the Iraqi case, seemed frequently to make mention of Cargill as the company under whose auspices the sale had been made. The fact that the Iraqi government had asked for the mercury-based fungicide and that the Mexican government had labeled all of the sacks with the statement in English and Spanish "not for human consumption" (accompanied by large skull and crossbones on both sides of the sack) generally was not mentioned in the story. Use by the Iraqi peasants had occurred despite the orders by their own government (belated as they were), with the villagers all too innovative in ways to circumvent the restrictions.

Cargill found itself in the middle of a ghastly proliferation of errors. It had been a substantial sale—the 60,000 tons had brought close to $2 million. The Tradax annual report of 1971–1972 commented, "No blame has been attached to us in this catastrophe. On the contrary, a letter of appreciation for prompt and correct execution of our contract was recently offered to us by the Ministry of Agriculture [of Iraq]." But it was an unsettling experience for the Company to endure.[10]

Dedication to Training, Generation Two

On March 17, 1972, Julius Hendel died. Encomiums were widespread; *Cargill News* memorialized him as "the scholarly elder statesman of the U.S. grain industry." Julius Hendel had been a unique force at Cargill. Born in Russia, he had emigrated to the United States in 1914, in time to attend Cornell University before leaving with the U.S. Army to fight in five separate campaigns in France during World War I. He came back to finish his Ph.D. at Cornell, then joined Cargill in 1922. Hendel likely was the first in the U.S. grain industry to hold a doctorate in fields related to agribusiness. While his first job at Cargill was a technical one—to set up the grain laboratory—he rapidly gravitated toward the exciting, complex grain trading side of the business. He and John Jr. were close colleagues, mentors to each other. Many of the great exploits of Cargill in the grain pits were masterminded by these two.

The other dimension of Hendel's role at Cargill was in training. In the early 1930s, he had instituted a college graduate training program, taught predominantly by himself—"Julius's Kindergarten." Erv Kelm, Fred Seed, Bob Diercks, and Walter Gage were four of the many of his early "graduates." At that time, the program was highly rigorous, involving long night sessions of complicated economic and agricultural strategies, with written tests at the end. In the first years, it was held in an ornate room in the building where Cargill had its offices, one that was beautifully decorated with gold foil on the walls. Thus, the group garnered the moniker the "Gold Room Boys," a special, privileged elite of Cargill's management, destined for the upper reaches of the Company.

Hendel handled all of Cargill's marketing operations during the period 1944–1955. In that latter year, he resigned early from the Company, pushed out in part by some hostility among the younger members of the trading group, who disliked Hendel's second-guessing them. Indeed, John Jr. himself had grown away from Hendel (see references to this in Broehl, *Cargill: Trading the World's Grain*). The end of Hendel's career at Cargill was more than a little unfortunate.

In retirement, he pioneered as founder and first president of Experience, Inc., a management counseling group for new entrepreneurs, with the counseling cadre made up particularly of past-60 experts from business, university, and government. His second career was equally distinguished.

Of all of Hendel's many talents at Cargill, the establishment of the unique training program, known throughout the industry, was undoubtedly his greatest. His ability to teach the grain trading subtleties was legendary; he "Cargillized the industry," said one respected analyst. But by 1955, when Hendel left, the training program was a pale version of its virile antecedent. It had become the trainee Corporate Orientation Program (COP), at that point a 12-week combination of orientation and training but soon shortened to 8

"1965—Still active at 70, Doctor Julius Hendel discusses operation of 'long dreamed of' enterprise, Experience, Inc., a unique [business] counseling firm founded four years ago and staffed by scholars and businessmen who are 'retired in name, but not in deed.' With him is Henry E. (Hank) Schroeder, longtime Cargill employee, who retired in 1963 and promptly became office manager for Experience, Inc." (*Cargill News*, May 1965).

weeks and later to 6 weeks. In the more recent period, the program involved only 3 weeks training before full time work in an individual division. John Savage, who headed the function in the 1950s, felt that a fresh approach was needed and instituted the soon-famous (in Cargill) Stillwater conferences. These were conducted for several years, beginning in 1949, at the Lowell Inn in Stillwater, Minnesota. Professor Kenneth Andrews of Harvard Business School used Harvard case studies very effectively, and a number of senior management went through these experiences; some half dozen conferences were held in the 1950s. Seed, Kelm, Diercks, and others all had attended one of these.

But there was a hiatus in the late 1950s, when there was little senior management training going on. One of the first efforts that Kelm brought to his own regime was to reinstitute a similar management training session. Stillwater was a remembered name; the sobriquet for these sessions soon became even more so. Andrews was unavailable for these new sessions, so the Company turned to Ben Tregoe, one of the principals in the firm Kepner, Tregoe Inc. Tregoe had developed a unique problem-solving concept; Cargill was the first to apply it. At the heart of the program was an organized, analytical ordering of objectives on a "must/want" hierarchy. With the use of a wheel diagram, Tregoe carried the participants through a logical sequence of decision making, stressing the thought process needed to complete each step. Tregoe called the experience his "Apex," named after the hypothetical company he used as illustrative material. Whitney MacMillan and Jim Cargill, together with other senior management, attended the first Apex, and Kelm, Diercks, Barney Saunders, Pete McVay, and Cargill MacMillan, Jr., among others, attended the second.

Tregoe next developed a full set of case materials for a second program, this time involving a hypothetical company called GENCO ("The General Company"). What Tregoe had done was to adapt the Apex program, which was built for senior management, to GENCO, which primarily was a premier middle management training effort. The training director for these early years was Ed Winters, with help from Gerald Joines, the personnel director. Soon a young man, Sidney Burkett, was brought in to do some of the GENCO teaching, and subsequently he headed the management training functions of the Company for a number of years. GENCO became an outstanding success for Cargill during the 1960s and even beyond; indeed, it led Cargill back into the mainstream of management training effort.

The Apex/GENCO "language" became part of the managers' vocabularies, heard all through the Company. Memos and wires between offices began

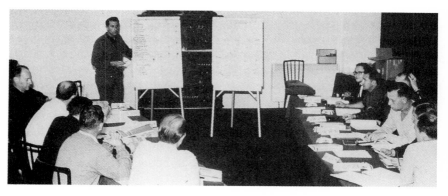

The popular GENCO training sessions are taken to the Tradax organization in Geneva by Cargill training director Sid Burkett (standing). Shown, clockwise from center background, are Burkett, Rene-Blaise Thiebaud, Len Alderson, Winn Wyman, Kay Darting, Rhoef Hoeffelman, Leo Vermeeren, Tjeerd Postma; left, nearest camera, Bill Picullel, Mike Sladek, Ron Hurren, Ken Deters, and Pierre Junod (Cargill News, March 1967).

Tradax Annual Meeting, 1966 (Tradax staff photograph).

to suggest that particular problems be "put on the wheel"; managers would ask whether hoped-for results were "musts" or merely "wants." It became a language that had the same meaning in English as in French, German, or Spanish. Stu Hanson, by this time president of Tradax, put it this way: "The 'common language' aspect is one main reason for exposing as many of our people as possible to GENCO. Our business is worldwide, with many languages and traditions, yet plans and problems must be communicated clearly among Tradax members wherever they are."

A second major thrust in training at the Company took place in the late 1960s with the advent of a Management by Objectives program, called colloquially at Cargill and around the country (where it was used widely) an MBO. The term presumably was coined by Peter Drucker in his pathbreaking book of 1954, *The Practice of Management*; however, MBO concepts had been around for a long time. Essentially, the MBO had been used as an appraisal and planning device, its featured step usually a one-to-one dialogue between a subordinate and a supervisor, discussing individual goals and goal achievement. This, in turn, produced feedback and performance evaluations.

If GENCO was popular all through the Company, the MBOs were not nearly so well accepted. People did want to know what was expected of them and how they were doing, the feedback. Yet in practice the process itself was not totally effective. First, there was a great deal of paperwork involved in preparing for these face-to-face meetings. Second, it was questioned whether MBO conferences should in and of themselves be used for salary increases, transfers, or promotions or, alternatively, used essentially as coaching and feed-back mechanisms. Third, there was a certain artificiality about the conferences. Burkett put it this way: "I came to believe that many managers simply were un-comfortable in having a face-to-face discussion with subordinates. As a result, they were either giving it a superficial treatment or avoiding it completely."

The skepticism expressed about the Cargill version of the MBO, felt widely around management circles in the Company, is well illustrated by an exchange between Heinz Hutter, at that time still heading the Argentine operations, and a Tradax senior manager in Geneva, Pearsall Helms. Beyond just the is-sues of the MBO, these blunt viewpoints testify strongly to the tensions exist-ing between the home office and field about the extent of management decen-tralization. Hutter wrote in May 1971:

You know I am not a great believer in MBO . . . here are some of my principal objec-tions . . . Managing by Objectives is a living thing, which has to be practiced every day and adapted to the daily change of business life . . . yet the MBO, imbedded in a yearly object setting and appraisal of fulfillment of these objectives, presumes that our goals will stay static for one year. . . . This is complete irreality [*sic*] . . . goals established, even by the individual himself, fall practically always into categories known to be ac-cepted by management or . . . imposed by management. . . . The goals we rate perfor-mance on are basically the goals of management and not of the individual. This gets us into the kindergarten approach of the *reward and punishment process.* No wonder most grownup people hate this schoolboy reliance on a teacher's grade or react childishly with or against it. We must get away from the vicious circle of reward-punishment based on some doubtful goals written on a piece of paper sometime ago. *Tying up a program which is supposed to help the man to become a better man for himself and there-fore also for the Company, with salaries increases and/or bonuses is a deadly mistake* . . . the best correction of an error or a change in goals is made when all the evidences of a failure are *immediately* on hand, i.e. when the mistake is made, not six, eight, or twelve months later. When learning by feedback is impossible and resisted . . . the type of MBO appraisal does not take into account the importance of group achievements. The reason for an organization to exist is to achieve more together than each could alone. Why then emphasize and reward individual performance, based on static job descriptions and/or goals . . . these systems like MBO, if worth anything, are good for a sub-standard manager to give him a weak crutch, but they will curtail and tie down the efficient work of above-mediocre managers. I believe in group work, group spirit, group effort, daily feedback and correction, possibilities to identify and for realizing one's own potentials for continued self development. . . . To achieve this, we should not and cannot use cute gimmicks to replace managerial quality [his emphasis].

Helms responded equally frankly:

Aren't we more apt to achieve this energy which you would like to see if each individ-ual clearly understands his own job? No intelligent person would attempt to establish individual objectives without reference to group and company objectives . . . why should agreeing upon objectives provide a manager with a weak crutch? When you say that you are not a great believer in MBO, either in the form in which it is presented or in the way it is practiced in most companies, I take it that your objection is one of form rather than substance. It is quite apparent that you are both objectives and results oriented but you don't like MBO. Is this because you feel that MBO attempts to structure something that should be allowed to remain informal? . . . Surely there is nothing improper or prying for the Salary Committee to ask that this reporting be done somewhat more formalized and documented so they can be sure these exchanges are indeed taking place. If you were a member of that Committee and were called upon to approve salary increases and bonuses for a world-wide organization would you not want something upon which to base a judgment?

Hutter responded:

NO, I would *not* want these formalized statements if I were a member of the Salary Committee, for the simple reason that I could not judge an otherwise closely known person on this basis. . . . I realize that if I would not know them closely, these forms would mean nothing to me and knowing them closely as I do, these forms add nothing to my knowledge. I shiver for the Company and/or the person, if these forms are used to establish bonuses and/or salary increases . . . that is why we apparently differ in our opinion about the task and responsibility of the Salary Committee . . . the Committee, in my modest opinion, does not *give* salary increases; it has the responsibility to *approve* them. The manager knows his people, makes his recommendations to me, or I to Gage, or Gage to the Salary Committee. The Salary Committee should then establish whether the recommended salary is correct with respect to the general levels of salary established . . . *that should be all*, as they do not have the intimate knowledge of the man in order to judge him. . . . Yes, Pearsall, you are correct. I feel that MBO tries to structure something which cannot be structured.

At this point, Bob Diercks, as executive vice-president, also responded to Hutter:

If all our managers were Heinz Hutters, I guess we would not need MBO procedures. Or, in all fairness to our many other capable managers, if all our businesses were in developing areas, where we have a fast growing, energetic, innovative group of people who can see the quick response to their efforts and the leadership under which they are operating, we would not need such a system. But the facts are that we are not always blessed with that situation. We have some managers who are faced with economic situations where all the management tools we can give them are needed . . . obviously, our managers have different degrees of capabilities. Anything we can do to help them become better managers should be done. This is the reason we have for those who see a need for it such programs as Management by Objectives, the Managerial Grid, Tregoe's problem solving system, the GENCO program and others. All of these have components in some degree to improve communications, get everyone involved in an understanding of what we are trying to accomplish and get the whole team dedicated to those objectives.

With the GENCO sessions focusing particularly on an individual's problem-solving abilities, it was felt that a more group-oriented approach was also needed; this led to the Managerial Grid, which focused more on finding solutions, comparing these with expert analysis, then defining management styles and developing personal growth plans. In the early 1970s, another key training effort was mounted, the Profession of Management Seminars (PMS), developed by an outside consulting organization, Lewis Allen Associates. The Allen teaching emphasized the weaknesses of what he called "the natural leader," who tended to be reactive to centralized management, to take intuitive action, to control by observation, and to communicate by telling. This would, according to Allen, create a "corridor of crisis," with personnel dissatisfaction, proliferation of organizational levels, multiplication of assistance, lack of management depth, and increased expense. What was needed was a move to professional management, with balanced authority, planned action, formalized organization, multiple channels of communication, and control by exception.

PMS became the third program in the triumvirate—one could proceed from GENCO, take the Grid program, then follow this with PMS. All of these, in turn, aided the MBO appraisal process, which was reevaluated in the 1970s to become MBO II. One problem, always, was the need to take managers away from their jobs for such efforts. Most managers welcomed learning more about their own work, and all three programs were well received. Yet the issue of the time commitment to take such training always seemed to intrude, a constant battle for the trainers to overcome.

With these three training efforts of the 1960s and early 1970s, coupled with the initiation, then redevelopment of the MBO appraisal process, the dedication of the Company to relevant and effective management training seemed to be back on track as a new generation of strength. One of the legacies of the Kelm administration was this renewed dedication. Kelm himself had been through the programs, believed in them, and supported them. He commented in 1967 about his first GENCO experience:

The most striking insight was recognition of how many important decisions—in business, government, and personal life—are made with inadequate information, uncertain goals, and, in some cases, a backward logic that begins with the wish to do something, then seeks for reasons why it needs to be done. . . . This doesn't mean that all decisions made without benefit of GENCO or Apex are poor decisions, or that decisions after such training necessarily are good ones. It does mean that even the most logical businessman may be unaware of the mental processes that result in correct decisions, and so may profit from studying these processes. . . . The course was an exciting intellectual experience . . . we discovered that discipline increased, the new methods *were* used, and the results were advantageous.

Whitney MacMillan was a particularly strong advocate of training and remembered the GENCO exercises emphatically as being one of the key features of his own management development. As the Company leadership changed in 1977 to that of MacMillan's tenure, training was once again a central focus, as it had been in the early years of Julius Hendel.[11]

Bomb Threats

The country's tensions over the Vietnam War had turned more violent across the United States after police confrontations and crowd injuries in Chicago during the Democratic National Convention in late August 1968. While the eternally famous Woodstock Music and Art Fair in August 1969 was peaceful, by late 1969 there were beginning to be major antiwar demonstrations. An early manifestation occurred in the first months of 1970 with the beginnings of a nationwide set of bombings. The perpetrators were alleged to be members of the Weathermen and the Students for Democratic Society (SDS), but certainly other factions were also involved. New York City took the brunt of the initial bombings; when a four-story brick townhouse in the city was hit by three explosions and a subsequent fire and an ensuing death, "copycatting" began to take effect. Colorado had 24 fires and explosions in a 45-day period in February and March. Several courthouses around the country were bombed, and explosions in mid-March at IBM, Mobil Oil, and General Telephone and Electronics Corporation showed the corporate world that it was not immune—was, indeed, a target. The New York Police Department reported that on one day alone in mid-March they had received 185 bomb threats, bringing the total for the first two weeks of that month to 1,416. Now bombings spread all over the country—in Seattle and Louisiana and Chicago. Bombs even exploded simultaneously in two separate department stores in Whitehall, Ohio.

In August, Minneapolis was introduced to the same treatment when a violent explosion ripped the old Federal Office Building, which had been headquarters for military inductions in the area. No one was injured, but the damage was extensive. In early September, three explosions within 38 minutes injured three persons in St. Paul. "The Police said the explosions might have been diversionary tactics for an attempted bank robbery," the *New York Times* reported, but this did not give much solace to the Twin City residents.

Corporate managers around the country began taking strong measures to protect their employees and their plants. "Any company with its head bolted on right has a bomb security program," stated the executive director of the American Society for Industrial Security. "Many are also working out detailed bomb search and evacuation plans for use if their offices are threatened," the *New York Times* noted, in a major article on corporate fear of sabotage.

These kinds of emergency planning paid off in a major way on September 11, when a bomb threat was telephoned, warning Minneapolis police that an explosive device had been planted somewhere in the North Star Center. In the 15-story Cargill building in this complex, procedures had been set up to deal with just such an emergency. *Cargill News* told the story: "Even as the alert was being passed to Department Managers, police and security officers were scouring stairwells and other exit routes to make sure they were clear and safe for use. Only then were runners (actually very fast walkers) dispatched to each department on every floor to tell monitors—already aware that evacuation was imminent—to begin moving people out. Personnel's Dick Lamberton, who stage-managed Cargill's exodus, emphasized that the operation was deliberately low-key and matter-of-fact. "Within twelve minutes from the signal to the evacuation, all Cargill's 650 employees and 2200 others were cleared from the building to the street."

"Police and North Star security officers quickly found what appeared to be a sewing machine repairman's kit in the North Star parking ramp. . . . Examination of their find by police bomb squad officers revealed a booby-trap device set to go off if the bag was opened in the usual way. However, by cutting along the side seam, they determined the contents to be 20 pounds of dynamite. A special bomb disposal truck was used to deliberately explode the bomb inside an open-top steel container reinforced by sandbags."

The fear of a bomb was made even more personal in June 1976, when several mail bombs were sent to the Cargill mailroom (and to a number of other companies around the country), including one package for a member of one of the owning families. Finally, a single person living in Texas with a grudge against corporations was arrested. There were also fears of kidnapping, particularly exacerbated for the grain trade by the snatching of two of the Argentine members of the Born family, the owners of Bunge y Born. This story will be told in a later chapter.[12]

FBI director Clarence Kelley holds a letter-bomb model in Washington, D.C., similar to those sent to Cargill executives (Associated Press, June 15, 1978).

"Three Strong Years"—the Substance

The 1968–1969 fiscal year ended on a discouraging note—certainly the situation felt that way to the Kelm team. Earnings had dropped sharply, and the flagship Grain Division had had a huge $3.3 million loss, its worst ever. There seemed a malaise in the Company, a loss of momentum, just like in the 1962–1963 crop year. But in that earlier year, recovery came almost immediately, and solidly. The same pattern now repeated itself, with three years of outstanding performance, each one a record from any previous year; the trend line also was sharply upward, as shown in table 4.

As always, this performance involved a complicated set of "strengths and weaknesses/opportunities and threats"—what today management specialists call the "SWOT analysis." A brief SWOT for these Cargill entities over the three years will bring us up to date. In the process, we will familiarize ourselves with new names for the new activities that make up this now more complicated company.

Sometimes, name changes can be a catalyst for change. In February 1970, the Grain Division was renamed the Agri-Marketing Division, with molasses and some marine products departments added from the old Commodities Division (which was being eliminated). Salt, which had been part of the Commodities Division, now stood as a separate department. The Vegetable Oil Division was renamed the Processing and Refining Division.

TABLE 4

Earnings Trends, 1969–72 ($000 omitted)

Division	1971–72	1970–71	1969–70
Commodity Marketing	$8,481	$7,468	$478
Feed	1,284	1,167	1,255
Poultry Products	(471)	(1,330)	1,716
Processing and Refining	18,117	20,510	14,352
Chemical Products	760	657	383
Seed Department	1,253	365	526
Salt Department	608	1,300	1,175
Commodities	—	—	570
Cargo Carriers	1,648	804	453
Tradax	10,386	6,899	3,179
Cargill S.A.	1,224	4,604	2,664
Cargill Agricola S.A.	219	631	(151)
Hens Companies	191	(1,522)	(20)
International Feed	358	47	39
Shaver Companies	63	290	433
Horizon Companies	642	612	366
Administration and Non-Operating	(4,513)	(4,477)	(3,251)
Net earnings (after taxes)	40,250	38,025	24,167
Return on beginning net worth	19.3%	22.2%	16.3%

The "Agri-Marketing" term quickly fell out of favor, and the division became known right away as the Commodity Marketing Division (CMD). CMD now began a slow process of recovery, ending the crop year 1969–1970 with $478,000 profit (with depreciation at $3.8 million, the total cash earnings had reached $4.3 million). Export earnings were up; in calendar year 1969, Cargill again was at the top of the industry with a very strong first, having increased volume to 31.8 percent of total U.S. exports (Continental's share had declined to 20.3%; Cook, with 12.7%, had taken over third place from Dreyfus and Bunge). One of the keys to CMD's modest recovery lay in the "major progress the last year toward the ultimate goal of meaningful responsibility profit centers. . . . We have been striving toward the goal of better budgetary controls and we can already see the merits of this technique."

The next year for CMD was a record, $7.5 million earnings after taxes. This was the year of the southern corn leaf blight, but the disaster for others actually helped the division because it "caused wide price fluctuations and generally higher prices, both of which worked to our advantage." Spring wheat was the key to the division's results; the total sales volume of over one billion bushels was the first to pass this signal step. In the proposed plans for the following year, the division pushed hard for a better terminal in the Louisiana Gulf. Bunge was building a new elevator near Cargill's Baton Rouge facility, and Continental was involved in a massive and expensive modernization; "we must build or lose our place in the export grain business."

The next CMD crop year, 1971–1972, continued a record performance, with earnings now at $8.5 million, a remarkable performance considering that there were serious strikes on the East and Gulf coasts and on the West Coast. "The strike in Chicago . . . left our plant as the only operating facility [and] afforded us a fine profit opportunity. As a consequence, for the first time in several ILA strikes, we had net gains rather than disastrous losses." Still, elevator expense was rising sharply, and "too many of our plants, large and small, are out of date." Once again, there was a plea for a "hard decision" on a modern, efficient elevator at the Louisiana Gulf: "We have slipped badly behind our major competitors at the Gulf; all of them have the capability of unloading more barges than we and at a cheaper cost. In addition, we are on the wrong side of the river for our rented train and Baton Rouge collects dockage and wharfage which fees could be ours if we had our own port. Our plan would be to use Baton Rouge I for soybean accumulation and longterm storage and to use Baton Rouge II [the proposed new facility] for our regular turnover of business." Nothing was done on this matter, an unsettling omen for the future.

CMD had acquired (by lease) one major new export terminal when the Port of Seattle built a modern 68–silo terminal with a capacity of 4.2 million bushels; it came onstream in early 1971. The Seattle terminal had one remarkable feature—it had one of the deepest drafts of any port in the world. This was spectacularly illustrated in 1975, when the supertanker *Archon*, a VLCC (very large crude carrier), made a stop at Seattle for a grain cargo that turned out to be the largest dry cargo ever assembled aboard a ship. The *Archon* left for Pakistan with a load of white winter wheat weighted down with 112,258 long tons, drawing a prodigious 55 feet, 8 inches of water (the loading facility at that spot in the port was 76 feet deep). The *Archon* broke the old record of the *Manhattan*, when it had loaded the Cargill shipment in April 1967. The *Archon* had been on its maiden voyage from a Japanese shipyard and was moving toward the Persian Gulf to pick up an oil cargo when diverted to load the grain. Interestingly, the *Archon* arrived at the Columbia River to take on the first segment at Portland (also at a Cargill elevator) and an additional amount at Kalama. That loaded the ship with as much as it could carry across the Columbia Bar, so it headed for Puget Sound to take on more grain at Tacoma and then top this off at Seattle. The marine editor of the *Seattle Post Intelligencer*, Don Page, pointed out "the *Archon* will find no such depth as our 76 to 78 feet where she is going. At Karachi the great ship will have to anchor off shore and lighter the cargo in. She will lie there roughly two months disgorging the record load it took her three-and-a-half weeks to take aboard in the Northwest."

These three fine years for Cargill had also been helped greatly by two mainstays in the Company, the Processing and Refining Division and Tradax. The former had two record-breaking years, followed by a fine third year. In that

Two employees at one of Cargill's Philippine copra operations, Granexport. A heavy husk protects the coconut shell during its growth process; after harvesting, the nut is opened with a knife in a single blow at the separating line, called the equator. Once opened, the nuts must be dried promptly to prevent contamination by bacteria or mold (*Cargill News*, January 1966).

second year there were unusually good margins in both the United States and Europe, setting new peaks for earnings and crushing volume. Corn milling continued to grow rapidly, with a 50 percent increase in that big second year. Copra was a fine performer in all three years, helped greatly by its new Illigan terminal in the Philippines.

Tradax had three great years; again the second year was the best. Earnings that year doubled those of the previous year, and there was a 26 percent increase in sales volume. "Corn blight scares and rather widespread drought conditions offered tremendous opportunities for sharp price movements and increases in European imports."

There also was a major increase in the Tradax ocean fleet. Six "mini-bulkers," smaller vessels of the size of the earlier Liberties, were ordered to be used for coastal shipping in western Europe—from the Baltic and the Atlantic into the Mediterranean. All carried European names—*Amsterdam*, *St-Nazaire*, *Ghent*, *Tarragona*, *Geneve*, and *Hamburg*. All six were in operation by the crop year 1971–1972 and proved to be profitable and logistically useful vessels for Tradax. In addition, two large new ships, at 73,000 tons, were ordered from a shipyard in Split, Yugoslavia. These were to be OBOs, ships that could interchangeably handle ore, bulk, and oil. This flexibility was at some cost as cargos moved from one category to another but was more adaptable in the cutthroat field of chartering. The first of these vessels was delivered early in the 1971–1972 crop year (but late in terms of the shipyard's promise); it was named the Carlantic (and thus became the second Cargill vessel under this appellative; John Jr.'s World War II vessel, the first built by Cargill, had the same name). The other vessel, delivered later in that year, was named the Carbay. The shakedown for the Carlantic was not good; there were several accidents, and the ship was off-hire for 91 days. The Carbay was delivered in much better condition and also was chartered, still with some lost time. To look ahead for a moment to the very next year (the crop year 1972–1973), "the OBOs presented us with most of our problems. In early July the time charters refused to perform further on both the Carlantic and the Carbay and we had to take back these two vessels from their very profitable contracts. Then a few days later, the Carlantic was involved in a fire, resulting eventually in a proven constructive total loss. Arbitration on the Carbay is still pending and we are rebuilding the Carlantic with the insurance proceeds. The Carbay was tramped on the spot market most of the year and finally time chartered for a period of five years." In sum, the mini-bulkers were a great addition, the OBOs not nearly so effective.

The combined net profits of all the Tradax-managed groups, which included Argentina, Brazil, England, Thailand, and the two grain operations in France and Spain, totaled $17.5 million, a record over the entire Tradax history of 16 years. It provided a return on beginning net worth of 47.3 percent and included a record sales volume of 17.7 million tons. However, reading the

Wartime submarine pens store beans at St-Nazaire plant. A pair of aerial photographs, one from the 1960s and one made early in World War II, show these pens, then being built by the German navy and now used for soybean storage by Cargill. The later photograph (above) shows the soybean processing plant of Soja France, S.A. In the center foreground beyond are the massive concrete pens, heavily walled and with 18-foot-thick bombproof roofs, in which German submarines were docked and outfitted for raids against shipping. Below, in an early wartime reconnaissance photograph the sub pens are seen, left of center. Shown also in the wartime picture is a huge dry dock (right, near bottom of photograph), once used to service the luxury liner Normandie and during the war the only facility in western Europe able to receive and repair the German battleship Tirpitz. The submarine pens were refurbished and equipped by Soja engineers to have a storage capacity of 30,000 tons of soybeans (Cargill News, August 1970).

Tradax annual report for 1971–1972, the outlook seemed less promising: "The world economic situation continues to deteriorate. Although there was some recovery in the U.S, economies in the E.C.C. countries began to slow down and Japan experienced a relatively severe domestic depression. . . . In South America, Brazil was the only bright spot as inflation was held at 15% . . . Argentina provided a sorry contrast with a generally sick economic and political climate and a 50% inflation rate." It was a year of "continual currency crisis."

Looking through the rest of Cargill's listings of operations, feed had been steady during the three-year period. Chemical products had an upward trend line. Salt had done well for the first two years but fell off badly in 1971–1972. Cargo Carriers had a large jump in earnings in that third year, and the new International Feed Division had moved up very substantially. Its annual report separately covered the feed operations in Honduras, El Salvador, Guatemala, Korea, and the new operation in Taiwan; all of these were well in the black. The feed operations of Cargill S.A. in Argentina and Cargill Agricola in Brazil were reported in their country's totals; again, both were in the black for the three years. When one looked globally at the Argentine operation, its total operating earnings after taxes had moved steadily upward to new records in each of the three years, but in 1971–1972 there was a startlingly large exchange loss offset (operating earnings of $6.5 million, less exchange losses of $5.3 million, for net earnings in dollars of just $1.2 million).

The Hens companies, operating in four European countries, had a very mixed picture. Good reports came from Spain, France, and Belgium. But there were very large losses in Germany, worsening over the three years, caused, said the annual report, by the "egg disaster." In 1971–1972, the ownership in the Hens companies had been redistributed, with Cargill now taking 75 percent ownership in France, 85 percent in Germany, and 25 percent in Belgium. Tradax continued to hold 52.5 percent ownership in the Spanish operation. The Shaver earnings were down, reflecting generally poor conditions in the poultry industry in 1971–1972. The Poultry Products Division, which included just the U.S. poultry operations of the Company, had shown substantial losses in that year and a better figure but still a loss in 1971–1972. The poultry industry in both the United States and Europe was unprofitable during this period, with softer-than-expected demand and overproduction.

Cargill Performance versus the Industry

Perhaps because of the overall performance of the Company in that record year of 1970–1971 (net earnings of $38 million, with a new record of return on beginning net worth of 22.2%), the Company decided once again, as it had done periodically over the years, to measure itself against several of its food processor competitors. It had chosen these companies in the past as being comparable in part because it was simply impossible to make comparisons directly with the major grain trading companies; the high degree of secrecy among all of these precluded any kind of realistic measurement. Cook Industries, which was the upstart new company in the "big six," *was* a publicly held corporation, and some comparisons could be made there. But the key one was that between Cargill and Continental. Thus, in the early 1970s, comparisons were made by the Cargill financial analysts not only with the six companies that were major food processor competitors but also directly with Continental, made possible by a fortuitous event, the acquiring by the latter of a majority control of Allied Mills, a publicly held company, which thereby allowed a small window of additional facts about Continental, too.

The Seven Major Food Processors

Results for 1970–1971 were mixed for the seven major food processors (Cargill, Allied Mills, Archer Daniels Midland, Central Soya, General Mills, Pillsbury, and Ralston Purina). The report began: "All-time record earnings were reported by Cargill and General Mills, and Archer Daniels had its second-best year. The other companies suffered declines in earnings, due primarily to adverse conditions in the poultry industry." The authors noted that General Mills had been added, "not because its activities are so comparable with Cargill and the others—but mainly because of the high interest in their results." The authors laid out the seven companies' "yardsticks of performance" on three key factors: growth, profitability, and earnings per share.

The authors then editorialized on the various factors. For sales growth, they pointed out that while Cargill had a mere 58 percent growth over the five years studied, which "compares rather badly with sales gains of 120% reported by Allied Mills, 108% by General Mills, and 93% by Archer Daniels, we find that Cargill's increase of $1,200 million in sales for the period is larger than the entire sales of the other companies, with the exception of Ralston. . . . We in Cargill are inclined to de-emphasize the importance of sales. Actually, our sales vigor is one of our greatest strengths—and it is particularly impressive to the outsider." On earnings growth, the authors were quite self-congratulatory, noting that Cargill's profit growth of 270 percent "represents an outstanding performance." Archer Daniels was second, General Mills was third, and the others were far behind. "Cargill's earnings per share have consistently been higher and reaching the height of $20.03 per share for the current year completely overshadows the performances of the other companies. This is undoubtedly the most impressive comparison included in the report." As to return on total capital invested, "again, Cargill is the overwhelming leader . . . on the basis of cash earnings, Cargill leads the field with an attractive return of 24.1%—almost double the cash returns reported by the other companies." On earnings per share, Cargill ranked second, below General Mills.

The authors waxed lyrical on their overall performance rankings: "Cargill

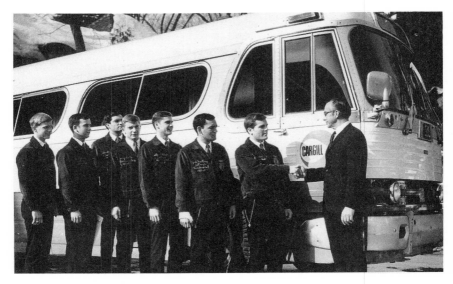

Future Farmers of America national officers for 1968–1969 were guests of Cargill during their nationwide tour. After visiting the company's Wayzata office and lunching with President Fred Seed, they boarded a Cargill bus for a trip to Minneapolis. Shaking hands with Seed is Jeff Hanlon, National FFA president. Others, left to right, are Tom Meium, Tom Johnson, Lowell Catlett, Jerry Batte, Glen Weber, and Joel Martinez (Cargill News, June–July 1969).

again wins the number one spot by a wide margin. Out of six measurements, Cargill scored first place in four of the yardsticks—no other company had more than one first." The report enumerated each company's performance:

1. Cargill—A 270% growth record in earnings per share, an increase of 116% in net worth per share, and the highest return on total capital—all combined to give the first place ranking to Cargill.

2. General Mills—The second position belongs to General Mills by virtue of its increase in earnings per share for the past year and its second and third rankings in sales and earnings growth. Its return on capital, however, was a poor fifth.

3. Ralston Purina—Ralston had no first place points, but ranked second for its return on capital. It fell to fourth place in the rankings on earnings and sales growth.

4. Archer Daniels—Earnings growth for the five years was a healthy 211% on a sales increase of 93%. Although making some progress, the return on capital remained below 10%.

5. Central Soya—Earnings per share were up only 7% for the five-year period and this year's results were down 24% from a year ago.

6. Allied Mills—1970–71 earnings were down 62% and the return on capital dropped to 4.2%—thus breaking a four-year span of improved results. The only bright spot is a sales growth of 120% for the five-year period.

7. Pillsbury—Growth reflects a frustrating sales increase of only 51% and a 28% decline in earnings over the five-year period. This year's earnings dropped 46% compared with a year ago and the return on capital was a disappointing 3.7%.

It *was*, of course, a very good year for Cargill to take such a comparison; the 1970–1971 record performance would likely look fine indeed in any kind of company comparison. Kelm and his colleagues had earned their kudos. On the other hand, the Tradax prediction for the upcoming year was quite cautionary. So the age-old question remained, "Can we keep this up?"

Cargill Passes Continental?

Continental Grain Company, which had had a minority interest in Allied Mills for a number of years, chose in 1972 to become majority owner. With the public debt of Allied Mills requiring disclosure, enough new knowledge of Continental Grain was released to allow the Cargill analysts to make some explicit comparisons for the very first time.

There were many caveats about the figures. The Cargill analysts enumerated these:

It is assumed that the financial figures include Allied Mills but that foreign investments and profits are not included, as explained below. . . . We had available the consolidated balance sheet of Continental Grain and also firm figures on Allied Mills. By subtracting Allied Mills from the consolidated figures, we arrived at a residual balance sheet which we believe reflects the financial interest in the grain operations of Continental. On this basis, the net worth applicable to grain operations is computed below:

		$ *000*
Consolidated Net Worth 3/31/73		126,542
Less: Net Worth applicable to Allied Mills		50,752
Net Worth applicable to grain opns.		75,790
Less: 1972–73		37,000
Net Worth applicable to grain opns. 3/31/72		37,790
Cargill CMD Net Worth:	5/31/73	75,930
	5/31/72	58,636

The above comparison confirms our evaluation of the relative net worth of the Cargill and Continental Grain operations. From these figures we also concluded that the consolidated balance sheet provided us applied only to domestic or northern hemisphere operations of Continental. We would guess that the combined domestic and foreign activities of Continental would show a much larger net worth than indicated above.

From this skeletal but analytical comparison, it seemed possible that Cargill had passed Continental sometime in the immediate period before this analysis was done. The supporting figures attached showed that the analysts believed the total capital invested in the combined Allied Mills/Continental Grain set of companies to be $584.9 million. On May 31, 1972, at the end of Cargill's fiscal year, its total assets were $792.4 million. Total sales for Cargill in that year were $3.5 billion, and for Continental Grain they were $2.9 billion.[13]

Still, Kelm and Seed were cautious about their comparison with Continental and on the overall outlook in their annual letter to shareholders, on August 4, 1972: "The pace of our growth is exciting and gratifying, but again, it is only realistic to caution against assumptions of an unvarying level of earnings or rate of growth. For example, just as last year, insufficient acreage for soybean production is expected to keep prices high, crushing margins low, and to restrict traditional growth in the soybean processing industry. There is no immediate prospect for improvement in the forces that increasingly have restricted exports of U.S. grain to members of the European Common Market. At home, efforts to protect U.S. jobs by distorting trade through quotas and other devices could have a crippling effect on our markets abroad." Not a scenario for rosy optimism about the future!

However, said Kelm and Seed, there was "one recent favorable development in trade." This was "the agreement for supply of United States food and feed grains to the Soviet Union. We have already begun to participate in sales to Russia under that agreement and we fully expect that volume to grow."

But would this be enough?

CHAPTER FIVE

A Surprise: The Russians Again Buy Grain

Momentous geopolitical events were unfolding in the country in early 1971, affecting the decades-long cold war relations with both the Soviet Union and the People's Republic of China. President Nixon, long a cold-war warrior, sensed that the moment had arrived for U.S. overtures toward both countries. In late February, the President addressed Congress, stating his belief in a possible dialogue with China. By mid-April, Chinese premier Chou En-lai had reciprocated. Then, on June 11, 1971, Nixon captured world headlines, issuing an executive order that ended the 21-year embargo on trade with Communist China; at the same time, he announced a decision to suspend the earlier "cargo preference" requirements imposed by President Kennedy in 1963—that 50 percent of all grain shipments to Communist countries (e.g., China, the Soviet Union, and Eastern Europe) be carried in U.S.-flag ships— provisions that had seriously inhibited sales of wheat and other grains to those countries. Now a wide range of nonstrategic items could be exported to China and the Soviet Union—indeed, *all* controls on Chinese imports were lifted. Crowning these economic moves, Nixon also announced that he himself would visit China forthwith.[1]

In addition to scrapping the shipping requirement that "one-half be in American bottoms," President Nixon acted under authority granted him by the Export Control Act of 1949 to eliminate an old rule requiring special export licenses for goods sold to the Soviet Union. Also removed were any such restrictions for the other Communist Eastern European countries, as well as for China. (Such special licenses were still to be required for North Korea, North Vietnam, Cuba, and Rhodesia.)

This change in the licensing mechanisms vis-à-vis the Soviet Union included a notable change in practice. Until that time it had been required that a planned export to the U.S.S.R. be reported to the government prior to shipment; now that notice was not needed until the point when the shipment was to be made. This loosened reporting requirement was to loom large one year later, in the

1972 wheat and corn sales to Russia. First, however, came the feed grain sales in the weeks following Nixon's promulgation of this new arrangement.[2]

Cargill and Continental Score Again

Cargill's Commodity Marketing Division in Minneapolis had had only minimal relations with the Soviet Union since back in 1963, the year when Cargill and Continental Grain made the startlingly large wheat sales to the U.S.S.R. Fortunately, Tradax, Cargill's semiautonomous European entity in Geneva, was not subject to the U.S. licensing constraints and had continued to maintain links with both the Soviets and the other Eastern European countries. The 1965 Tradax annual report to its shareholders noted: "The Eastern European market has been closed to U.S. wheat because of flag preference on shipping. Russia alone bought over 3 million tons of wheat from Australia, Argentina, France and Canada. Fortunately, acting on behalf of Cargill as a broker, we sold 200,000 tons of Manitobas [Canadian spring wheat] to Czechoslovakia and 120,000 tons to Russia." Indeed, over the period from the 1963 sales by Cargill up to this point in 1971, Tradax had continued to trade grain with Russia and the other Eastern European countries and in 1966 established a special department for this, with Dr. Michael Sladek as its head.[3]

After a September 1971 visit to Russia by a U.S. Department of Agriculture (USDA) feed and livestock team, its members reported heightened Soviet interest in building a livestock and feed economy but registered doubt that Russian grain production alone was going to be sufficient to support this. Cargill and Continental—the two companies selected for the 1963 wheat sales—now were asked by the Russians to send representatives to the U.S.S.R. to explore further possibilities. The USDA had large supplies of two of the feed grains, barley and oats, held under its own title in storage. Corn particularly was sought by the Soviets, so the USDA laid out a proposal to the two American companies that required a package of the three grains. The Commodity Credit Corporation (CCC) would sell barley and white oats to the companies for export elsewhere on competitive bids, but allowing in the process the export to Russia by the companies of one metric ton of U.S. corn (and/or grain sorghum) from private stocks for each metric ton of barley or oats purchased.

As in 1963, once again Continental scored first, with a series of negotiations that produced, finally, a sale of 900,000 metric tons of barley and oats and an equal amount of corn. Cargill had sent a negotiating team to Moscow in early October 1971, prepared to offer the barley, oats, and corn package for as many tons as possible. Eventually Cargill too was able to connect, selling the Russians 300,000 tons of CCC-owned barley and oats and also committing to selling an equal tonnage of corn from U.S. free market stocks.

But there was a complication for both companies. The International Long-

"Cargill grain division executives at a two-day, end-of-April meeting in French Lick, Indiana. On hand were all the division's regional and branch managers, the headquarters administrative staff from Minneapolis and representatives of Cargill, Limited, the company's Canadian subsidiary. Shown in the front row, from left to right, are: Charles W. Mooers, Minneapolis; John Rockwell, Kansas City; Irving Hyland, Buffalo; Howard Boone, San Francisco; A. H. Douglass, Norfolk; C. MacMillan, Jr., Chicago; W. B. Saunders, H. R. Diercks, M. D. Wyard, Thomas Hall, Minneapolis; Carl Swanson, Louisville; Wm. F. Drum, San Francisco; Glenn A. Pritchard, Columbus; Gerald Mitchell, Milwaukee. Middle row: Donald Peck, Albany; J. R. Kinney, Champaign; C. D. Siegfried, Sioux City; J. N. Haymaker, Minneapolis; Richard Mikkelson, Vancouver; Earle Greene, Winnipeg; Lloyd Graving, Baton Rouge; William M. Berger, Chattanooga; Gilbert Booth, Montreal; Lee D. Canterbury, Memphis; C. D. Roberts, Indianapolis; Dudley Russell, Marietta; Robert Morgan, Fresno; William Cox, Wilson; John E. LeFevre, Minneapolis; C. M. Roberts, Jr., St. Louis. Back row: Gordon Alexander, Minneapolis; Cary Humphries, Philadelphia; John Finlayson, New York; Robert Cowdery, Des Moines; Ace Cory, Omaha; Lawrence Elfelt, Los Angeles; Truitt Kennedy, Fort Worth; Kenneth Lenhart, Maumee; W. L. Larson, Buffalo; Harold Johnson, Minneapolis; William Ritchie, Baltimore; J. H. Cunningham, Chicago; Donald Kleitsch, St. Louis; Dart Smith, Cedar Rapids; R. T. McIntyre, Peoria; Milt Bondus, Minneapolis" (Cargill staff photograph, c. late 1950s).

shoremen's Association (I.L.A.) was bargaining for new contracts for the East and Gulf coasts at this same time; negotiations were tense and not being resolved. Unfortunately, the I.L.A. once again brought up, essentially as a bargaining chip, the question of shipping in U.S. bottoms. The Soviets, in turn, became intransigent, refusing to pay more than world market value for both the grains and the ocean freight. At Cargill's Houston terminal, an I.L.A. picket line was thrown up against the bulk grain carrier SS *Theomana*, a foreign carrier standing ready to load grain for shipment to Russia. Cargill petitioned and obtained a Taft-Hartley Act injunction; the port was reopened, and the union grudgingly agreed to load non-U.S. ships. Clarence Palmby, assistant secretary of the USDA, who had been the driving force in the early contacts with the

Soviet Union, tried to put a positive twist on the settlement: "It is interesting to note that when the first vessel left our ocean-going port, New Orleans, the name of the vessel was the S.S. *World Neighbor*, purely by happenstance."[4]

While this agreement on shipment stayed in place reasonably well over the fulfillment periods of the two companies' contracts, the complicated story of the sale had received a wide public press, not all of it positive. In early December 1971, the Subcommittee on Livestock and Grains of the Committee on Agriculture in the U.S. House of Representatives held hearings on many aspects of the sale. The USDA had sold its CCC-held barley and oats at a subsidized price to the two companies in order to have these prices become equated to the prevailing world market price. The total cost of these sales to the companies was just over $50 million; the CCC received approximately $44.8 million for the grains, a loss of approximately $5.3 million. (The world market price in barley was particularly difficult to assess, however; one of the congressmen on the subcommittee stated, "I was told that the way that they arrive at the world price of grains is to take the temperature in London and add it to the temperature in Chicago and divide it by that of Copenhagen and then add the last three digits of the ship in which it is to be sold and that is the price of grain for that day.")

There was considerable public criticism that somehow the United States was "subsidizing" the Russian livestock industry (as one congressman on the committee put it, "In effect, the U.S. taxpayers are being asked to finance a sort of international food stamp program to improve the diet of the disadvantaged citizens of the Soviet Union"). Palmby responded that the taxpayer was benefiting in several ways—the government was "getting rid of some inventory," it was saving storage costs, and "over a period of time, the taxpayer puts out less money for production adjustment in this country, so that we do not need to pay for so many acres being diverted. . . . The taxpayer benefits on all counts."[5]

Once again, as in 1963, concerns were raised in the hearings about the fact that only the two largest of the grain trading companies, Cargill and Continental, were involved. Palmby responded that the process had not been a closed bidding, that anyone who had a contract to export corn had been eligible to bid. One of the congressmen asked again if it was in the best interest of the United States to subsidize the Russian livestock and poultry industry; the influential corn belt newspaper, the *Des Moines Register*, was one of many that responded: "We'll answer that, yes. It is definitely in the U.S. interest to encourage expanded livestock production . . . not only as a potential market for feed grain, but also as a means of encouraging the consumer movement in Russia. The more the Russians concentrate on better living standards, the better for world peace."[6]

All of the shipments of the feed grains to Russia had been concluded by the end of the fiscal year 1971–1972. This had been an excellent year for Cargill, with net earnings increasing 6 percent, to just over $40 million. The Russian sales were mentioned in the Company's annual report as a "recent favorable development." The Tradax annual report called this Soviet initiative "a bright spot on the horizon" but concluded that "Russia remains the big question mark. There are some suggestions that losses due to winterkill were exaggerated earlier."

Startlingly Large Deals Are Struck

Despite the concerns of several congressmen in the feed grains hearings in December 1971 that the Russian sales by Cargill and Continental were, as one congressman put it, "a one-shot deal," there began to be telling signs that the Russians intended coming back for more grain—from the United States or elsewhere. Clearly, the Russians wanted to stay in the "livestock economy" over the long term, to fulfill their promises to their people of more meat, milk, eggs, and other upgrades to the Russian palate. Coincidentally with this, a renewed pattern of weak harvests in the U.S.S.R. had surfaced. There had been a disastrous harvest in Russia in 1963 (the year of the very large grain sales by Continental and Cargill); there had also been a weak harvest in 1969. Ambitious grain production targets were embedded in the current Soviet five-year plan—the goal for the plan was an average grain output each year of 195 million metric tons. In 1971, only 180 million tons had been produced. In early 1972, the Soviet Union was hobbled by an unusual cold wave, triggered by a deep southward movement of Arctic air. Even the Black Sea and the Caspian Sea had ice covers that required the mobilization of ice breakers to open ports such as Odessa (Baltic Sea ice breakers being diverted to the Black Sea). The snow cover had been thin during this winter, and by early February 1972, the *New York Times* reported barley, rye, and wheat particularly hard hit. Because of these crop setbacks, the "Soviets may buy U.S. grain."

The potential for new sales seemed corroborated later that month, when Russia purchased 130 million bushels of wheat from the Canadian Wheat Board (with promises for 55 million bushels in addition). In early April, U.S. Secretary of Agriculture Earl Butz left for Moscow with a delegation of USDA and other governmental officials (the ostensible reason for the trip to return a similar visit that the Soviet Minister of Agriculture, Vladimir Matskevich, had made to the United States the previous December). Butz met privately with Leonid Brezhnev, the Soviet Communist Party leader, the first American official to do so since Nikita Khrushchev was ousted from power in 1964. The rare 90-minute audience with Brezhnev quickly fueled public speculation that a major agricultural prospect was in the making. On Butz's return, he predicted possibly a $200 million grain sale annually in the years ahead. If such major grain sales were to come to fruition, at least all parties concerned had been alerted.[7]

The Russians Want Credit

The Butz delegation encountered one large hang-up in their negotiations in April with the Soviets—the latter wanted special credit terms. This added a complication, as Butz put it in testimony to a later congressional investigating committee: "If we had had a choice, we would have much preferred to reach a trade agreement in Moscow in early April during my visit. This would have made the news available to all U.S. farmers before the wheat harvest had begun. However, the Soviet Union was asking for credit terms which we could not legally offer and which we are not making to other nations that have been long time customers for our wheat and feed grains. We could not do that."

This momentary impasse soon led to further concern at the so-called summit meetings in Moscow in the last week of May, led in this case by President Nixon himself. While an important maritime pact was signed at this session, the question of the grain sales was still up in the air, the Soviets agreeing only to cash purchases of approximately $130 million but unwilling to commit themselves further.

A high-stakes game was being played out over these potential grain sales. The Americans, on the one hand, saw major budgetary savings if such grain sales were made. The USDA staff estimated that if there was a one-year contract, a savings of $1.5 million would result from each one million tons purchased for cash, just from storage costs alone. These savings, they said, would rise substantially in the case of a two-year contract, with $40 million additional assumed as savings in set-aside payments for farmers. (However, the USDA report did not take into account some potentially negative implications, such as the effect of grain sales on export subsidies, on the domestic prices of commodities, and on transportation and shipping facilities.) There was also speculation in the press that the United States was attempting to use the grain sales as a lever to persuade the Soviet Union to pull back on support of North Vietnam in that war.

The Soviets, from their side, knew that they likely faced a major disaster in the crops of 1972. But since the early Cold War days, the Russians had been devilishly secretive about their agriculture. While the U.S. agricultural attaché in Moscow *was* allowed certain travel privileges in the country, these were circumscribed enough to make it quite difficult to tell what was happening in the vast reaches of the Russian countryside. Senators Hubert H. Humphrey and Henry Bellmon later corroborated the Soviets' reluctance in a "trip report" of their field visit in December 1972 to the U.S.S.R. and Poland as members of the Joint Economic Committee of the U.S. Congress: "The U.S. agricultural attachés even though understaffed and under severe travel restrictions, continued to do a commendable job in reporting Soviet crop conditions during 1972. Difficulties in timely availability of Soviet crop information in the United States last year were largely due to Soviet disclosure policy, processing of current Soviet weather data in the United States, and deficiencies in the Soviet agricultural reporting system." (There was a generic problem here, too—the U.S.S.R. acreage was double and the yields half of those of the United States, so minor fluctuations could be multiplied by a large factor. Also, Russian feed conversion was much lower than in the United States, so each animal unit meant more grain units.)

The messages in the spring of 1972 were definitely mixed. The Earl Butz prediction of a $200 million sale in April had mentioned only coarse grains and soybeans—where did wheat stand? Significant winter weather damage to the wheat crop had been reported as far back as March by the USDA (although "less severe than in 1969, the most recent year of abnormally heavy winterkill"). The U.S. agricultural attaché's trip in late April revealed that "winterkill was minimal" in the northern Caucasus and that total acreage was being expanded in the Ukraine "to offset winter losses." However, the attaché estimated more somberly on June 26 that one-third of the winter grain acreage, some 27 million acres, had been lost due to winter weather conditions. The whole Soviet livestock and related programs seemed at risk. Although it was only incompletely seen in the rest of the world, the Soviets by this time knew that their entire effort to upgrade the Russian people's diets was in jeopardy.[8]

In late June, the Soviets sent a high-level bargaining team, led by Minister of Foreign Trade Nikolai S. Patolichev and First Deputy Minister M. R. Kuzmin, to test wills with a team of the U.S. government headed by two powerful people, Secretary of Commerce Peter Peterson (who was also U.S. chairman of the U.S.–U.S.S.R. Commission) and Secretary of Agriculture Butz. As the Peterson-Butz team began negotiations with Kuzmin and his colleagues, the latter made clear that the Soviets now were willing to accept regular CCC credit terms for any such credit sales.

At this same time, the State Department notified the USDA that a second team had arrived, made up of Soviet specialists in grain purchasing, maritime shipping, and financing. This group was led by N. A. Belousov, chairman of Exportkhleb, the Soviet government trading agency, and included L. N. Kalitenko, the director of the grain department of that agency.

The results of the first of the two-pronged set of negotiations was announced with fanfare on July 8 by President Nixon in a simultaneous press release at the President's Western White House in San Clemente, California, and at the White House by Peterson and Butz. A three-year grain agreement had been consummated by the United States and the Soviet Union, totaling $750 million of U.S.-grown grains, for the period August 1, 1972, through July 31, 1975. These grains were at the option of the Soviets; they could be wheat, corn, barley, sorghum, rye, and/or oats. Under the agreement, the Soviets were to purchase at least $200 million of U.S. grains for delivery during the first year. It was the Soviets who had blinked first on the credit issue. As part of the agreement, the United States would make available credit through the CCC of up to $500 million, with the standard CCC terms used for other countries to apply.

The press releases ended with the expected rhetoric about the potential benefits of the huge sales: "Agricultural experts estimate that about 3,000–5,000 additional jobs are created for each $100 million of grain exports. Since at least $750 million is involved it could be estimated that a range of 22,500–37,500 man years of work for U.S. workers [is] involved in this deal."⁹

Present also at the White House press conference was Henry Kissinger, Secretary of State. He too stressed the benefits for the American people: "It will provide grain farmers with a boost in income . . . provide jobs for Americans involved in shipping the grain, including longshoremen, seamen, exporters, railroad and barge line workers [and] will reduce the costs to taxpayers of storage, handling, and other charges associated with maintaining commodity stocks."

All the statements by Kissinger, Butz, and the others were vague about just what grains were involved. There was a one-line mention that "the purchases and sales will be as negotiated between the Soviet Union and the U.S. and the U.S. private commercial exporters," but there was no mention of the other negotiating team that was in the country from Russia, the Exportkhleb group that was to bring about the actual sales. Butz did mention in his prepared release that "if the Russians were to take this entirely in corn, it would be the equivalent of 550 million bushels of corn. That is 10% of our total production last year, a heavy record production year in 1971, to give you some idea of the magnitude of this." After mentioning corn, he allowed, "They won't take it all in corn—the Russians had a bad wheat year. Last Winter in the Steppes east of the Ural Mountains where they had severe winter killing of wheat, they had several weeks of sub-zero weather with no snow cover. Mr. Matskevich, the Minister of Agriculture . . . made no effort whatsoever to hide that fact . . . likewise made no effort to hide the fact that they had a short wheat crop. . . . It is obvious they are going to have to buy wheat beyond that for which they have a commitment from Canada."

Questions from the press centered particularly on the effects of the agreements on consumer prices and on whether the unions would load the grain if the 50-50 ratio of U.S. bottoms was changed. Peterson noted that he had seen Thomas Gleason, president of the longshoremen's union "as recently as yesterday" and that the unions would "cooperate," not only for national security and national economic reasons but because of jobs for longshoremen and seamen.

Only one questioner dealt with the negotiations on the purchases: "In the last three days while the Soviets have been here, two companies in particular have bought more than $200 million worth of grain and the general impression was that it was being purchased for the Soviet Union deal. Were these people privy to this information before the deal was signed?" Butz replied, "If they were privy to this information, it is only because the Russians had contacted them. Whether they had contacted them or not, I have no idea. That is entirely between the Russians and those from whom they buy the grain. . . . From this point on, the Russians buy this grain in this country like any other commercial purchase—they buy it in the private grain trade market from whomever they want to buy it at whatever price they need to pay to get it."[10]

But there was going to be a very important story emanating from these briefly mentioned negotiations between the "private commercial exporters" and Exportkhleb.

"The Russians Are Here"

Just as in the 1963 wheat sales and the 1971 feed-grain sales to Russia, Continental Grain Company and particularly its chief executive officer, Michel Fribourg, became the central actors in the evolving events of June–July 1972. In the 1963 sales, only Continental and Cargill were involved; in the 1971 feed-grain sales, the two companies likewise took all the sales, Continental once again being the first seller and the leader in total sales.

Michel Fribourg long had had a close relationship with the Russians, visiting Moscow many times after the bellwether 1963 sale. In the 1971 feed-grain sale he took a dominant role once again. The Russian delegation's head for these negotiations was the aforementioned Nikoli Belousov, the head of Exportkhleb. James Trager, author of a chatty book on these Russian grain sales entitled *Amber Waves of Grain* (its subtitle, incidentally, is *The Secret Russian Grain Sales That Sent American Food Prices Soaring*), recounted an undocumented story about these two men: "In the summer of 1971, when the U.S. feed grains had been under discussion, the Russians became obstreperous in the hotel they were occupying in Cannes on the French Riviera. When they were asked to leave, Fribourg chartered a yacht and carried on negotiations at sea. Off Corsica the yacht was hit by a gale so fierce that the ship nearly foundered. Michel and Nikoli, the capitalist and the Communist, shared an experience that gave them a bond that went deeper than a mutual interest in grain." Whether this story was true, it *was* a documented fact that Belousov did contact Fribourg first among the grain trading companies.[11]

Another fact, analyzed and debated at great length in subsequent congressional hearings in both 1972 and 1973, needs now to be added: Clarence Palmby had left his position as assistant secretary of agriculture to become a vice president under Michel Fribourg at Continental Grain. Palmby was grilled about this change of employment in both of those hearings; according to his own testimony, he first met with Michel Fribourg in late January 1972, once again in February, and finally in an important meeting in early March.

At this meeting, Fribourg had given Palmby a job description of a post of vice president at Continental. Palmby told Fribourg he was in no position to talk about such a role but within a few days purchased an apartment in New York City with the help of real estate recommendations from Continental Grain. When Palmby accompanied Butz to Moscow in early May, he had not yet told the secretary that he was considering leaving the department. Palmby did notify Butz shortly after the Moscow meetings, and Fribourg made Palmby a formal offer. Palmby's resignation was effective on June 7; on June 8 he joined Continental, as vice president of market development.

On June 29, Nikoli Kalitenko, the second-in-command for the Russian buying team, called Continental Grain at the company's offices in New York from a hotel in Washington. Michel Fribourg, Bernard Steinweg (Fribourg's brother-in-law and a senior vice president at the company), and other top officers of Continental were in Paris, for the Continental annual international meeting. "Had we known what was to occur," Steinweg told a later congressional hearing, "we, of course, would have remained in New York; but no official of the company authorized to negotiate with the Russians was in the United States when they arrived." Steinweg rushed back to Washington, where he quickly learned that the Exportkhleb representatives wanted Continental to make firm offers on 3,650,000 million metric tons of hard winter wheat, 350,000 metric tons of soft white wheat, and 3,000,000 metric tons of yellow corn. "They said the corn to be purchased from Continental represented their total needs," Steinweg later told the congressional hearing, "and the wheat was the single lion's share of their needs." When, the following morning, the Soviets added 500,000 tons of durum to their request, Steinweg called Fribourg back from Europe. A major bargaining meeting was then scheduled for the afternoon of July 3.

At this point, the Continental executives urgently needed an answer from the USDA to a critically important question: Would the department continue its policy of (Steinweg's words) "maintaining the then current world price of wheat"? What Steinweg was referring to here was a long-standing USDA policy of export equalization, whereby the higher U.S. domestic price (due to domestic price subsidies to farmers) would be supplemented with an "export equalization" that would bring the domestic price down to the world market price (the latter, of course, being allowed to stay low by the quite large payments by the French government and other countries in the European Common Market subsidizing their farmers). Consequently, the Continental officials arranged a meeting for the morning of July 3 with Carroll Brunthaver, the successor to Palmby as assistant secretary of agriculture. Steinweg recounted the meeting: "I told him we had been contacted by the Russians, told him the specific amounts of wheat they wished to purchase from us, and told him they wished to purchase corn from us in an amount comparable to the feed grains they had purchased from us in 1971. I also repeated what the Russians had told us about the wheat purchase representing the 'lion's share' of their needs and the corn purchase being all of their needs." Brunthaver was not able to answer the Continental query on the spot but in that same afternoon reported back that the USDA was indeed willing to continue its policy of maintaining the current target prices of various classes of wheat. Apparently, this was an open-ended promise, as no quantity limits were placed by Brunthaver.

Negotiations with the Russians, still private, now went forward rapidly, with meetings all through the remainder of July 3 and on into July 5. At this point, Continental reached an agreement and signed a preliminary memorandum for the 4 million metric tons of wheat, as well as 4.5 million metric tons of corn. Steinweg later stated that he contacted Brunthaver on July 6 and told him that Continental had consummated these sales. All this had happened before President Nixon's announcement on July 8. On July 10, the day before the signing of the formal contracts, the Russians also purchased 500,000 tons of durum wheat and an additional 500,000 tons of milling wheat (and another 500,000 of milling wheat on July 17). In total, Continental had sold 4.5 million tons of corn and 5.5 million tons of milling and durum wheat; the milling wheat was to come totally from the United States, some of the durum could be sourced from another country, as could some of the feed grains.[12]

Belousov had persuaded the Continental people to believe that he was buying grain only from them, and he cautioned everyone at the meeting on the need for absolute secrecy. The Russians had cleverly kept all their sales intentions from every one of the parties they dealt with in the July bargaining. As to secrecy, it was to the great advantage of any party involved, for if the sales became known, the market would have reacted almost instantly. Each one of the several eventual sellers was vulnerable here, as each finally made firm commitments for huge shipments of commodities they did not own, and they would be in an exposed, "naked" position until cash grain and futures that would fit delivery schedules could be purchased. The worst possible contingency for any seller is to have the market "spooked" by a "limits-up" rise in prices. Amazingly, this whole fabric of secrecy stayed in place all through the month of July.

Cargill's Struggle for Sales

Now Cargill was next. If Continental's bargaining with the Soviets had proceeded expeditiously, Cargill's had not. The Company had its first hint of possible Russian sales on June 28 at a retirement party in Washington for Clifford Pulvermacher, who was leaving his post as general sales manager of the USDA's Export Marketing Service. (Pulvermacher had accompanied Earl Butz and Clarence Palmby to Moscow in April, where the first clue of this Russian interest surfaced. Pulvermacher's resignation was effective June 30;

on July 24, Pulvermacher accepted an executive position with Bunge Corporation, the U.S. affiliate of Bunge y Born, the Argentine grain trading company, another one of the "big six" multinational grain trading companies.) Pulvermacher was highly regarded in the industry, so a number of Cargill executives attended the party—Melvin Middents, Clifford Roberts, Daniel Amstutz, James Hessburg, Robert Hatch, Robert Kohlmeyer, and Thomas Connolly. When Pulvermacher saw Mel Middents, he told him, "the Russians are here."

Acting immediately on this skimpy but startling information, Middents called Walter "Barney" Saunders, who already had booked for a Saturday departure to Russia. Saunders immediately canceled his plans, called Leonard Alderson and Michael Sladek at the Tradax office in Geneva to come to Washington, and departed for the capital himself. Late the next day, Erv Kelm received a call in Minneapolis from Kalitenko; the two arranged for a meeting in Washington on Saturday morning, July 1. Kelm, too, came immediately to Washington. On the basis of just this information alone, the Company traders purchased 500,000 bushels of wheat and a like amount of corn, in a combination of cash and futures, and reduced its short milo position by 300,000 bushels. In addition, a 200,000-bushel short soybean position was changed to an 18,000-bushel long position. These were, to be sure, open-ended, "naked" positions but based on expected sales and thus one side of an evolving hedge, not an outright speculation that would need to be reported to the Commodity Exchange Authority (CEA) in the required weekly CEA report. The actions were, as Walter Gage in the Company's Tradax office in

TABLE 5

The Grain Trade's "Big Six" Totals for U.S. Grain Exports, Fiscal 1971

Company	Volume (Millions of bushels)	% of Total
1. Cargill, Inc.	453.7	28
2. Continental Grain Co.	341.9	21
3. Cook Industries	257.5	16
4. Bunge Corporation	134.0	8
5. Louis Dreyfus Co.	107.7	7
6. Garnac Grain Co.	92.0	6
All other companies	211.4	14
Total	1,598.20	100

Source: "Cargill, Inc." case 4-578-088, Intercollegiate Case Clearing House, Harvard Business School, 1977, reporting figures supplied by North American Export Grain Association. *Note:* does not represent total volume of U.S. grain exports, only the volume of NAEGA membership; as each exporter reports both sales for direct export and sales to other exporting firms for export, individual totals may involve minor overcounting.

Geneva later put it, "second nature to a commodity trader [for] the first people to act on a trigger are the ones that do the best. . . . If you wait very long, the market prices have gone up to the point where perhaps it's still worth getting into but not nearly attractive as very early in the game."

On Friday, June 30, Barney Saunders confirmed the Saturday meeting, but the Russians "refused to tell Barney what they wanted to talk about." On that day, too, Middents told Brunthaver about the Russian invitation and the fact that "we had no awareness of what was involved." The company's net position at the end of that day was 3.8 million bushels of wheat long, 2.7 million bushels of corn long, and about 1.5 million bushels of Canadian barley long.

The meeting with the Russians on Saturday, July 1, was full of ominous surprises. The people present were Belousov, Kalitenko, and Pavel Sakun (a member of the Soviet Ministry of Foreign Trade) for the Russians and Kelm, Saunders, Sladek, and Alderson for Cargill. The Russians first expressed interest in buying corn but at the same time referred time and again to the toxicity problem stemming from corn mold. They would not talk quantities but did say they wanted low-moisture corn. Saunders said Cargill could meet this. At that point, the Russians took a five-minute break in another room, returned, and "gave us kind of a brush-off speech." The group recessed for lunch.

At lunch Kalitenko asked one of the Cargill people how much barley Cargill was long. The Cargill reply was quick: "None of your business." One of the Russians replied, "Remember this when you ask similar questions of us."

After lunch, the Russians suddenly announced the termination of the meeting. Cargill asked whether they should stay in town, and the Russians said no, "the Cargill group might as well go home." Barney Saunders remembered the Cargill team's shock: "They walked out of the place, and we thought the end of the world had come." So the Cargill party returned to Minneapolis that evening, deciding that the Russians were in the country to buy corn and that Cargill should go long. The 3.5-million-bushel long position on June 30 was expanded to 8 million bushels by July 3.

As agonizing day upon day progressed, Cargill heard nothing—indeed, for nine days they could not ascertain even where the Russians were. All through this period, rumors surfaced of large sales by Continental; even Greenwich Marine, one of Cargill's transportation units, reported large bookings—especially Great Lakes bookings—of freight. Cargill still assumed the Russians were looking for corn. The Cargill executives were dismayed at what seemed to be a shutout.

Then, on Monday, July 10, early in the morning, the Russians called Minneapolis with a summons. The Cargill party left Minneapolis later that morning and met the Russians in New York at 4:30 P.M. Belousov gave Saunders five minutes to write down what Cargill wanted to sell. Saunders asked, "What grains?" The Russians said, "Let's start with wheat." The dickering soon led to specifics: 12 percent protein wheat, no more than 250,000 tons/month shipment, for eight months. Saunders quoted a price of $60.05 per metric ton. Kalitenko countered that the market was at $59.40. Through most of the discussion, the Cargill team thought they had one million tons of business at $60.05, but the final figure turned out to be $59.525. When one of the Cargill team queried about corn, the Russians said they would call.

The next day the Russians went over the contract with the Cargill team; the latter queried if Cargill could appoint the stevedores at competitive rates, rather than the lower flat price of the Russians. The following day, the meeting began badly. One of the Cargill members asked if the Russians would accept the American premium for stevedoring. When the Russians heard this, they jumped up in anger; one of them said that "this was the last business Cargill would do with Exportkhleb." In the process, they showed Cargill a contract they had signed with Cook Industries that same day for 600,000 tons at $59.525 (Cook was the Memphis-based member of the "big six" and the only publicly held company of these six). The Russians then "delivered a heated lecture that ran on for about an hour." One of the Russian team pointed out that a Japanese firm had come in, given the Russians a pencil and a piece of paper, and told them to write the quantity and price they desired. Belousov finally signed the Cargill contract and said, "If we ever trade again, I will first give you a lecture." There was no further discussion about corn, and the Cargill team felt that the Russians had already bought all they wanted. The Cargill group returned to Minneapolis the following day feeling on the one hand that they had pulled off a stunning deal—a one-million-metric-ton sale of wheat. Yet the Russians' harshness in the last meeting gave everyone pause.[13]

As Cargill struggled in the succeeding days to cover its exposed position in wheat (Cargill had been going long primarily in corn), the markets seemed not to be much affected. The announcement of the grain deal on July 8 had piqued traders' interest, and prices had risen sharply on July 11 but then dropped back. The influential *Southwestern Miller* (later that year renamed the *Milling and Baking News*) in Kansas City put out a daily market quotations card dubbed Sosland cards, after its editor, Morton Sosland. The July 13 card talked of "heavy futures activities and ship chartering again confirm mammoth, but as yet unconfirmed, sales of wheat and other grains to USSR." But the card the next day talked of estimates mostly around a total of 2,750,000 metric tons of wheat. Even that amount would be, the card said, "unprecedented."

Others of the "big six" were also in the act; much more had been going on, and the only ones knowing this in its totality were the Russians. The latter had met with Louis Dreyfus Company the very day that Cargill had made its 1-million-ton wheat sale, and this French-based group had sold the Russians 750,000 metric tons. The following day, the Russians closeted themselves with Cook Industries, consummating the sale of the 600,000 metric tons that they had earlier flaunted to Cargill.

On July 20, Cargill's Barney Saunders had finally been able to get a meeting with the Russians alone, to better explain Cargill's stevedoring rates (Cargill had included a "facilities charge," whereas the others had not; when this charge was factored in for the others, Cargill's offer "looked very good") and to further explore "the anger or unease that the Russian's felt with any Cargill/Tradax people as negotiators." Saunders broached the possibility of Cargill going to Moscow at a later date and also invited the Russians to Minneapolis. On that same day, the Russians had met separately with Continental, buying an additional 850,000 metric tons of hard winter wheat and 150,000 tons of soft white wheat. It was a busy day for the Russians, for they also met with Garnac, another "big six" multinational grain trading firm linked with the Andre Group from Switzerland, and a sale of 200,000 metric tons had resulted. The next day the Russians left New York for Moscow. No one—none of the executives of the six competing grain trading companies nor anyone in the USDA—knew that the Russians had purchased by this point 4.5 million metric tons of yellow corn and 8,050,000 metric tons of wheat. If, as the *Southwestern Miller* stated, a total sale of 2,750,000 metric tons of wheat would be "unprecedented," a total sale of over 8 million tons of wheat and 4.5 million tons of yellow corn would seem to have been superlatively unprecedented.

However, the market seemed not to believe even the *Southwestern Miller*'s rather bullish figure. One trader was reputed to have said at this time (mid-July), "How much of that Russian business can you believe? All I know is we're getting a bumper crop. It's always a matter of supply and demand, and this year there is certainly no lack of supply. I'm selling futures, not buying." On July 5, cash wheat stood at 1.52\frac{1}{2}$; the December wheat futures price on the Chicago Board of Trade was 1.55\frac{7}{8}$. By July 28, the cash price had risen to only 1.58\frac{1}{2}$, with the comparable December futures were 1.60\frac{7}{8}$.

But the Russian bargaining team had returned to Moscow to find out that the agricultural news was increasingly distressing. Except for some fields in Kazakhstan, the Soviet wheat fields had received very little rain. There was a dry wind blowing over much of the territory; the dust rose and the wheat wilted. So sometime in late July, Belousov, Kalitenko, and Sakun were ordered back to America for more wheat. On July 27, 1972, the State Department advised the Department of Agriculture that visas had been issued to the three, the purpose being "to negotiate with Continental Grain."[14]

A Next Tranche

The Russians' offer was really offer*s*—and they happened quickly. The bargaining team was the same, Belousov, Kalitenko, and Sakun. The visa officer's comment was correct—the three met first with Continental Grain. To the latter's surprise, the discussions (on July 31, 1972) were about feed grains. It took only a few hours to reach agreement, the Russians buying 1,750,000 metric tons of corn as well as 100,000 metric tons of grain sorghum and 100,000 tons of North American barley. Bernard Steinweg conducted the negotiations; later he told a congressional committee, "I was shocked to learn that the Russians did make substantial wheat purchases from other companies during this visit, since there was no suggestion of this in their conversations with us."[15]

But the Russians were still in search of wheat. On the day of Continental's sale, Dreyfus was able to sell the Russians 1.5 million metric tons of hard winter wheat. On August 2, Garnac sold 350,000 metric tons, and that same day, Bunge won a contract for 600,000 metric tons. Two days later, Cook Industries sold an additional 300,000 metric tons of wheat and added 1 million metric tons of soybeans.

Cargill, the other member of the "big six," had been contacted by Kalitenko on July 31 by telephone. Barney Saunders was told that "we would like to buy 3–3½ million tons of wheat and 500,000 tons of sorghum." When the Cargill bargaining team came to New York later that day, they surprised the Russians with a report prepared by Cargill's Mel Middents concerning the government's supply position on hard red wheat. Middents had reported that the CCC actually held in storage 60 million bushels less of winter wheat and 60 million more of spring wheat than the CCC had thought earlier. Saunders opened the meeting that afternoon; worried about the possibility of runaway, panic buying, he tried to meet the issue frontally: "We're concerned that you will buy more winter wheat than the U.S. has. Will you give us a guarantee that you will not buy more than 7 million tons of winter wheat and certain quantities of other wheats?" The Russians, clearly not much concerned about the fallout in the United States, replied bluntly: "No guarantees." According to the Cargill records of that day, however, the Russians "were . . . impressed with the presentation." Despite this sidetrack, the Russians pressed Cargill to put together an offer. That evening the Cargill negotiators tendered their offer: 500,000 tons of winter wheat, 400,000 tons of white wheat (Pacific Northwest wheat), and 1 million tons of spring wheat. But the team was discouraged by the course of the day, feeling that the two parties were too far apart on price.

To their amazement, the meeting the following morning resulted in a quick sale to the Russians of a full 1 million tons of hard wheat at just about the price Cargill had originally proposed. After a celebratory luncheon, the Russian bargaining team began to discuss with Cargill further purchase of spring wheat. The Russians seemed quite preoccupied about the ergot problem that often affected spring wheat. This worldwide fungal disease can affect rye plants and other small grains and grasses. Winter wheat (because of its weather cycle) was almost never affected, but spring wheat was a possible candidate. Animals grazing on ergot-infected fields often would sicken. Humans were especially sensitive to the ergot alkaloids—muscle pain, numbness of feet and legs, headache, nausea, vomiting, diarrhea, and dizziness could result and, if large quantities were ingested, even death. Russians remembered the devastating effect of ergotism, or as they called it then, "St. Anthony's Fire," on the armies of Peter the Great in 1722, as he massed his Cossacks at a critical juncture in the war against Turkey. By the thousands, Peter's crack troops died from ergot in their bread.

American farmers and plant scientists together had developed simple techniques to neutralize any ergot symptoms. Fortunately for Cargill, the Russians had brought two technicians whose primary role was to learn what the Americans were doing to eliminate the ergot problem. Despite the Russians' unease about the ergot, they still wanted a decision from Cargill right away, promising that "they would work only with Cargill on spring wheat." The Cargill team made a firm offer on the spot, for a reply by August 11.

Earlier, the Russians had asked Cargill to entertain the two technicians, a cereal chemist and a plant breeder. Now the entire Russian bargaining team was flown by Cargill from New York to Fargo, North Dakota, to visit North Dakota State University. There the Russians were shown how the Americans handled an ergoty wheat problem. The university's seed plots were inspected and a country elevator visited, followed by a flight to Fort Collins, Colorado, for further expert testimony.

Cliff Roberts remembered one incident that seemed to epitomize the Russians' deep suspicions about the United States: "We took them on a trip around the countryside and they pulled a surprise on us—they said, 'let's go to that farm.' We responded, 'Okay, we'll go to the farm.' They wanted someplace where we wouldn't be putting on a planned demonstration. Well, we met the farmer, and they couldn't believe that an American farmer could be this prosperous and have this amount of equipment and machinery and everything else that wasn't a put-on job. It really boomeranged in our favor because the farm we drove into totally unannounced was a grain farm and the farmer was very good about it. They shook their heads. They really did. They were trying to pick out a surprise farm—they are suspicious, always thinking you're going to set them up for something like that. They couldn't believe that you could just pick out any old farm and get a perfectly cordial reception."

At the end of the whirlwind trip, the Russians seemed to have had their concerns about ergot satisfied. On August 8, the entire Russian bargaining team was flown to Duluth, Minnesota, to see the port and then on to Minneapolis for the contract signing itself. The next day the whole group returned to New York.

Nothing further transpired on the spring wheat offer—August 11 passed without any contact from the Russians. A week later, the Russians called Cargill's New York office to say that they did not have time to discuss the offer. Not until August 28 did Cargill hear further; a telex came from Moscow suggesting that the Russians still wanted to discuss the offer. Cargill responded that the offer had expired "by its own terms." So the total sales in Cargill's second tranche was just the quickly reached one-million-metric-ton sale of winter wheat.[16]

Secrecy was still the watchword in this second visit by the Russians. Only they knew that they had purchased an additional 3,750,000 metric tons of wheat, together with substantial quantities of soybeans and yellow corn and smaller purchases of barley and sorghum. Roberts recounted the psychology: "On this side you had private companies dying for more business and going through rotten, slow times. You've got a USDA dying to get the surpluses out, dying to clear up this heavy weight on the market. So the Russians had a perfect setup. If they could keep us guessing, if they could keep us in the dark, if they could prey upon our anxieties, both the private companies and the USDA, we were a perfect setup for them to buy grain cheap. And they did it—did it brilliantly."

T A B L E 6

How the Companies Fared in the Russian Grain Purchases of July–August 1972) (Metric Tons)

Wheat, all varieties		
Continental Grain	5,500,000	
Dreyfus	2,250,000	
Cargill	2,000,000	
Cook	900,000	
Bunge	600,000	
Garnac	550,000	
Yellow corn		
Continental Grain	6,250,000	
Soybeans		
Cook	1,000,000	
Barley		
Continental Grain	100,000	
Sorghum		
Continental Grain	100,000	
Total metric tons, all grains	19,250,000	
Total bushels, all grains	724,910,709	
Individual company totals		
Continental Grain	11,950,000	62.1%
Dreyfus	2,250,000	11.7
Cargill	2,000,000	10.4
Cook	1,900,000	9.9
Bunge	600,000	3.0
Garnac	550,000	2.9

Source: Russian Grain Transactions, hearings before the Permanent Subcommittee on Investigations of the Committee on Government Operations, U.S. Senate, 93rd Cong., 1st sess., July 20, 23, and 24, 1973, p. 218.

When the July and August sales were totaled, the Russians had firm commitments from the six grain trading companies for 19,250,000 metric tons of grain — almost 725,000,000 bushels (see table 6). For anyone connected with the grain trade, this would surely have boggled the mind, and the fallout from this amazing set of events boded to be great.

The overwhelming 62 percent going to Continental Grain, once it became known in the Senate hearings, was a great surprise for many analysts, for U.S. Secretary of Commerce Luther Hodges had espoused a formula back in the 1963 wheat sale to Russia that no individual company should garner more than 25 percent. Of course, those 1963 sales involved only two sellers, Continental and Cargill, each taking roughly half. The Soviets then, and again in 1972, called the shots. U.S. antitrust policy was not of any concern to them.[17]

The Markets Wake Up

No matter how clever the Russians had been in covering their tracks, the mammoth figures of the July grain sales began to leak out, albeit with understated figures. Editor Mort Sosland's *Southwestern Miller* headlined in its July 25 issue that the U.S.S.R. wheat purchases were "believed to exceed 100 million bushels." The actual figures, hidden in the secrecy, were over 400 million bushels of wheat and an additional 246 million bushels of corn. Sosland revised his figures upward to 150 million bushels the next week when he reported the return to the United States of the Soviet buying mission. The influential trade paper must have had wind of further purchases, for Sosland wrote the following week that, with the additional buying, sales were now estimated to be around 400 million bushels.[18] Actually, by that time the Russians had contracted for over 700 million bushels.

The grain market, so surprisingly sluggish all through the period of the July Russian sales, now began to react. On July 4, the December spring wheat futures on the Chicago Board of Trades (CBOT) closed at 153⅝; Kansas City's exchange had December hard winter wheat at 147¼. By July 28, several days after the Russians had returned to Moscow, the CBOT price for December wheat was just 160⅞, Kansas City had risen a bit to 159¾. One week later, on August 4, Chicago's close was 178¼ and Kansas City's 176¾; by August 11, the CBOT December futures had risen to 187½, and Kansas City's to 188½. On the last day of the CBOT December futures, December 18, the price stood at 260¾ (the contract high had been even higher, 272¾). Kansas City wheat was just behind with a contract-ending close of 258½ and a contract high of 275. Much the same pattern had occurred with corn, although somewhat muted; the December futures price on the CBOT had stood at 127⅜ on July 4, remained almost the same at the end of the Russians' second buying trip (the August 11 price, 127⅞), but rose to 163½ close to the end of the calendar year. Truly, the secret was out.

A cacophony of voices now clamorously arose from all those believing themselves injured by the rapid price rise. A *Wall Street Journal* article on August 15 summed up the conflicting tensions raised by the sales in its headline: "Slicing Two Ways: US-Soviet Grain Deal Could Lift Bread Price and Increase Subsidies—But the Sale Also Will Spur US Economy, Aid Barges, Rails, Elevators, Farmers." The effects on the price levels and therefore on food prices were particularly intrusive. This quickly brought the Office of Management and Budget (OMB) of the Executive Office of the President into action. The OMB had the responsibility of exercising budgetary control over the funds of both the Department of Agriculture and the CCC. The agency was the administration's guardian of price levels, always alert to a possible domestic inflation. An increase in the price of domestic wheat would not only have major effects on end users but collateral influence on other commodities. Further, the OMB recognized that the price rise that had occurred would have an immediate effect on the export subsidy to be paid to the grain companies, which had a direct impact on the USDA budget. These export subsidy payments for the Russian grain sales now became the first cause célèbre of the 1972 Russian grain sale.[19]

Export Subsidies Are Terminated—Not Cleanly

The grain trade ruefully had learned, in connection with the feed grain sales to Russia in 1971, that the word *subsidy* carried markedly negative connotations to many in the general public (in the 1971 case, the government had been accused of "subsidizing" the Russian livestock industry). It is, however, legitimate not to call the export payments "export subsidies." In reality, they had been used as equalization payments, bringing domestic grain prices in line with lower world grain prices on export sales in order not to disadvantage American producers. If the U.S. domestic prices were below the prevailing world price (not, to be sure, the more typical case), exporters were required to make payments to the government to bring the domestic price in line with the higher world price (thus not profiting on the differential between the two prices). This actually had been the situation earlier under the International Grains Arrangement; Cargill, in later congressional testimony, noted that it had made such payments in the period September 1969–September 1972 of approximately $80,000.[20] In the period of the Russian grain sales, however, the U.S. domestic price had been held at a higher level by substantial government subsidy payments to farmers (for them, the term legitimately applies); the U.S. price now was above the world price, and the equalization payments went to the American grain exporters for the subsidy-heightened prices they had paid or were to pay to the farmers when they bought from the latter.

At the beginning of the period of the Russian grain sales, as noted in Table 7, the export equalization rate had been under $.10. Domestic prices began to

TABLE 7

The Progress of the U.S. Export Subsidy Rate for Hard Red Winter Wheat[1], July 3–September 25, 1972 (Prices per Bushel)

1972	Kansas City futures closing price — Price	Future month	USDA estimate to deliver Gulf	USDA estimate delivered shipboard at U.S. port	Export subsidy rate[2] I[3]	Export subsidy rate[2] II	Export target price I[3]	Export target price II
July 3	$1.44\tfrac14$	7	$0.24	$1.68\tfrac14$		$0.05		$1.63\tfrac14$
July 5	$1.45\tfrac12$	7	.23\tfrac12	1.69		.06		1.63
July 6	$1.47\tfrac58$	7	.23\tfrac12	1.71\tfrac18		.07		1.64\tfrac18
July 7	$1.46\tfrac34$	7	.23\tfrac13	1.69\tfrac78		.07		1.64\tfrac18
July 10	$1.49\tfrac38$	9	.23\tfrac12	1.71\tfrac78		.09		1.62\tfrac78
July 11	$1.54\tfrac34$	9	.23\tfrac12	1.76\tfrac14		.13		1.63\tfrac14
July 12	$1.55\tfrac12$	9	.21	1.76\tfrac12		.13		1.63\tfrac12
July 13	1.56	9	.20\tfrac12	1.76\tfrac12		.13		1.63\tfrac12
July 14	$1.52\tfrac34$	9	.20\tfrac12	1.73\tfrac14		.10		1.63\tfrac14
July 17	$1.53\tfrac34$	9	.20\tfrac12	1.74\tfrac14		.11		1.63\tfrac14
July 18	$1.55\tfrac78$	9	.21	1.76\tfrac78		.13		1.63\tfrac78
July 19	$1.57\tfrac14$	9	.22	1.79\tfrac14		.15		1.64\tfrac14
July 20	$1.55\tfrac58$	9	.22	1.77\tfrac58		.14		1.63\tfrac58
July 21	$1.54\tfrac14$	9	.22	1.76\tfrac14		.13		1.63\tfrac14
July 24	$1.56\tfrac14$	9	.22\tfrac12	1.78\tfrac34		.14		1.64\tfrac38
July 25	$1.56\tfrac58$	9	.22\tfrac12	1.79\tfrac18		.15		1.64\tfrac18
July 26	$1.55\tfrac38$	9	.22\tfrac12	1.77\tfrac78		.14		1.63\tfrac78
July 27	$1.54\tfrac18$	9	.22\tfrac12	1.76\tfrac58		.13		1.63\tfrac58
July 28	$1.55\tfrac12$	9	.22\tfrac12	1.78		.14		1.64
July 31	$1.57\tfrac14$	9	.22\tfrac12	1.79\tfrac34		.16		1.63\tfrac34
Aug 1	1.58	9	.22\tfrac12	1.80\tfrac12		.16		1.63\tfrac34
Aug 2	1.58\tfrac14	9	.22\tfrac12	1.80\tfrac34		.17		1.63\tfrac34
Aug 3	1.66	9	.22	1.88		.21		1.67
Aug 4	1.74	9	.21	1.95		.31		1.64
Aug 7	1.84	9	.21	2.05		.31		1.74
Aug 8	1.84\tfrac12	9	.19\tfrac12	2.04		.31		1.73
Aug 9	1.76\tfrac34	9	.19\tfrac12	1.96\tfrac14		.31		1.65\tfrac14
Aug 10	1.81	9	.21	2.02		.36		1.66
Aug 11	1.82\tfrac14	9	.22\tfrac12	2.04\tfrac34		.36		1.68\tfrac34
Aug 14	1.87\tfrac12	12	.17\tfrac12	2.05		.36		1.69
Aug 15	1.85\tfrac14	12	.17\tfrac12	2.02\tfrac34		.35		1.67\tfrac34
Aug 16	1.87	12	.17	2.04		.36		1.68
Aug 17	1.89\tfrac12	12	.18\tfrac12	2.08		.38		1.70
Aug 18	1.91\tfrac14	12	.19	2.10\tfrac14		.38		1.72\tfrac14
Aug 21	1.91\tfrac12	12	.19	2.10\tfrac12		.38		1.72\tfrac14
Aug 22	1.93\tfrac14	12	.18\tfrac12	2.11\tfrac34		.38		1.73\tfrac34
Aug 23	1.96\tfrac14	12	.18	2.14\tfrac14		.38		1.76\tfrac14
Aug 24	1.95	12	.17	2.12		.38		1.74
Aug 25	1.92\tfrac34	12	.17	2.09\tfrac34	.47	.38	$1.62\tfrac34$	1.71\tfrac34
Aug 28	1.93\tfrac14	12	.17	2.10\tfrac14	.47	.37	1.63\tfrac14	1.73\tfrac14
Aug 29	1.96\tfrac14	12	.17	2.13\tfrac14	.47	.35	1.66\tfrac14	1.78\tfrac14
Aug 30	1.97\tfrac14	12	.17	2.14\tfrac14	.47	.32	1.67\tfrac14	1.82\tfrac14
Aug 31	1.95	12	.17	2.12	.47	.30	1.65	1.82
Sept 1	2.00\tfrac14	12	.17	2.17\tfrac14		.30		1.87\tfrac14
Sept 5	2.01\tfrac12	12	.17	2.18\tfrac12		.30		1.88\tfrac18
Sept 6	2.00\tfrac14	12	.17	2.17\tfrac14		.30		1.87\tfrac14
Sept 7	2.00\tfrac18	12	.17	2.17\tfrac38		.29		1.88\tfrac14
Sept 8	2.01\tfrac38	12	.17	2.18\tfrac38		.30		1.88\tfrac38
Sept 11	2.04	12	.17	2.21		.29		1.92
Sept 12	2.09	12	.18	2.27		.28		1.99
Sept 13	2.07	12	.18\tfrac12	2.25\tfrac12		.26		1.99\tfrac12

TABLE 7 (continued)

1972	Kansas City futures closing price		USDA estimate to deliver Gulf	USDA estimate delivered shipboard at U.S. port	Export subsidy rate[2]		Export target price	
	Price	Future month			I[3]	II	I[3]	II
Sept 14	2.11¼	12	.18½	2.29¾		.25		2.04¾
Sept 15	2.19⅛	12	.19	2.38⅛		.25		2.13⅛
Sept 18	2.29½	12	.20	2.49⅛		.23		2.26⅛
Sept 19	2.26½	12	.20	2.46½		.21		2.25½
Sept 20	2.20¼	12	.20	2.40¼		.19		2.21¼
Sept 21	2.18¾	12	.21	2.39¾		.14		2.25¾
Sept 22	2.22⅝	12	.21	2.43⅝		.00		2.39½
Sept 25	2.18½	12	.21	2.39½		.00		2.39½

1. No. 2 hard red winter, ordinary protein, f.o.b. gulf/east ports.
2. Rate announced effective 3:31 P.M. that day applicable through 3:30 P.M. the following day.
3. On August 25, 1972, Agriculture announced a two-tier system that provided a special subsidy rate of $0.47 a bushel through September 1 for contracts entered into prior to August 24, a subsidy in later sales at new rates that did not maintain the $1.63 to $1.65 base.

Source: Wheat and Wheat Flour Export Programs Payment Rate Announcements and wheat market information and subsidy work sheets, Export Marketing Service, Department of Agriculture. Reprinted in Russian Grain Transactions, hearings before the Permanent Subcommittee on Investigation of the Committee on Government Operations, U.S. Senate, 93rd Cong., 1st sess., July 20, 23, and 24, 1973, p. 219.

rise all through July (as the congressional chart shows), from 144¼ to 157¼ for the near-term Kansas City futures price.

The export equalization payment rose from $.05 on July 3 to $.16 on July 31. Then, that first week of August, with the second tranche of Russian purchases, the Kansas City futures price rose markedly, to $1.84½ on August 8. The equalization payment on that date was $.31. As domestic grain prices rose further and further during the first half of August, the equalization rate jumped upward, reaching $.38 on August 24 (in effect, world prices were not rising as fast, despite Russian purchases from other grain-producing countries, too).

A harsh complicating factor now intruded—the government's budgetary structure began to erode. It was not just that the export equalization rate itself had gone up sharply in those first three weeks of August; the additional fact was that the number of bushels on which the equalization payments would be made was becoming astronomical. With the final figure of the Russian wheat purchase totaling over 444 million bushels of grain, the average payment— about $.30 in this period—would require well over $133 million just for the Russian sales (and the equalization payments would continue to be paid on U.S. wheat sales anywhere else in the world, too).

The OMB now pressed hard on the USDA, fearing not only the large budgetary "hit" but also that the continuance of the subsidy would quickly contribute to domestic inflation by forcing an increase in the domestic price of wheat, with collateral effects on other commodities. On August 25, USDA officials made the decision to phase down the payments, even if the actual differential continued higher. In doing this, the department clearly intended to move to a zero equalization position, a goal that became a reality on September 22. The grain trade industry had to be notified about this change, of course. The way that this was done soon caused a small tempest in its own right.

Two-Tier System and Telephone Calls to the "Big Six"

The mechanism chosen for phasing out the subsidy established a two-tiered arrangement. Charles W. Pence, Grain Division director in the Export Marketing Division of the USDA requested the "big six" companies on August 24, 1972, to be in Washington the following day. At the subsequent meeting, the six companies were told that as of the close of business on August 24, the department's export payments would no longer reflect U.S. export price levels. The companies would have a week to register any contracts written before August 24, and for these the old subsidy rate (at that point $.47 per bushel) would apply. For sales after this date, a smaller equalization payment was to be made—on August 25 it was $.38, and it dropped steadily through the succeeding three weeks to zero on September 22. Later that day, Pence also notified other smaller grain trading companies of the decision. Whether Pence had made these moves correctly was later to come under considerable question.[21]

At the time of the first Russian sales, after Brunthaver had assured Continental that the export equalization payments would stay in place, the USDA had asked the grain companies to cover in an "orderly" fashion; as a result of the admonition, several of the companies (Cargill included) had prolonged the duration of some of their positions, so with this abrupt turnaround by the USDA, substantial money was lost by the companies when they could not cover these open contracts rapidly enough. As Cargill later put it, "the gradual collapse of the export differential to a 'zero-subsidy' level by September 22 only widened the difference between price levels at which Cargill was to deliver hard winter wheat and price levels at which Cargill had to purchase wheat in domestic markets. . . . On September 1, Cargill was still short . . . more than 15 million bushels. That short position was not covered until September 21, and it had to be covered in a market where domestic prices continued to climb while subsidy levels dropped."

As more and more details of the Russian sales became known, the public outcry rose. This was a presidential election year for the country, and politics began to infiltrate almost all public issues. The Russian grain sales had raised concerns about the effects on consumers and on farmers, and this galvanized a number of congressional leaders interested in the upcoming election. On

August 29, the National Farmer's Union issued a statement alleging a "cozy" private club atmosphere that had been created "by grain trade officials moving in and out of the Department of Agriculture" and by the grain trading companies making "windfall profits." On September 1, the *Washington Post* weighed in with a major editorial focusing particularly on the subsidy payments, calling the way Pence had announced the changes in the subsidy rate a "very curious feature." At this point, presidential hopeful Senator Pierre DuPont of Delaware called publicly for an investigation, approaching the General Accounting Office (GAO) of the federal government to be the investigator. Surprisingly, given the fact that neither branch of Congress had yet looked into the matter, the GAO accepted the request.

Senator George McGovern, from the wheat state of South Dakota, was already thinking of a campaign for the presidential nomination of the Democratic Party (and subsequently did become the party's choice). In early September, McGovern accused the Nixon administration of "a conspiracy of silence" about the sales "to exploit unsuspecting American farmers" and talked of "inside information" being available to a small group of grain exporters, alleging that the "grain buyers and the grain speculators . . . bought futures and capitalized on this rising market and then made a killing when the grain was shipped in August and September." Several other congressman vied for attention with additonal allegations.

Cargill now took an important step, one unusual for the Company, namely, to reply publicly to the allegations, "with no attempt to speak for other exporters or the USDA, but concerning only Cargill's role." The press release on September 8 stated: "Those attacks must be branded as unfounded, uninformed, in many cases patently absurd and, overall, extremely damaging to the open, competitive U.S. marketing system, which serves every element of the agricultural community so well." Contrary to any "advance information," there was no time in Cargill's negotiations with the Russians when the company was "so fortunate to obtain nor were the Soviets so foolish to offer information relating to the total amount of wheat, the classes of wheat or the prices the Soviets were willing to pay. To this date, Cargill does not know the total quantity of wheat, the dates of delivery, the classes of wheat involved or the prices at which it was sold." The only such information relied on "was the well-known intention of USDA to employ the export subsidy to maintain the world wheat price at the two-year-old target level of approximately $1.63 per bushel for hard red winter wheat at Gulf ports. In fact, USDA deviated from that policy, leaving those who had not already covered on their sales in serious jeopardy of 'windfall losses.'" As to windfall profits, "one can only lament the apparent lack of understanding or appreciaton for the world's most efficient and competitive marketing apparatus, the risks (and resulting secrecy) that prevail because of the fierceness of that competition, and the massive investments in facilities required to make such grain movements possible at slim profit margins." This spirited defense of Cargill's role in the overall grain sales to Russia was a change in the Company's usual low-key public relations efforts.

The press release was not widely reported—indeed, it seemed to fall on deaf ears. One national publication *did* respond. The Company had shared some of its data with *Business Week,* and the editors wrote: "Only one trading company, Cargill, Inc., has sought to counter what the industry considers an unfair indictment. Summoning newsmen to its Minneapolis headquarters this week, Cargill rolled out facts and figures to prove that it had not made a windfall from advance information on the Russian deal. Cargill had neither a short nor long position in the commodities market when the deal was announced, a company spokesman declared. Further, Cargill believes it was 'screwed' by the Agriculture Dept. When it sold Russia grain on July 10, the company was left 30-million bushels short. It expected that Agriculture would raise the subsidy as usual to keep domestic and export prices on a par, but instead the subsidy was drastically reduced."

The influential *Washington Post,* in a featured editorial on September 1, seemed to capture the majority feeling when it advocated that "the whole relationship between the U.S. Department of Agriculture and the trading companies now needs to be spread out in the public view." The editors continued: "The Department has shown itself extraordinarily protective of the trading company's profit throughout this sale . . . the circumstances plainly invite a Congressional inquiry."[22]

Such an inquiry came quickly. On September 14, the Subcommittee on Livestock and Grains of the Committee on Agriculture of the House of Representatives opened hearings on the "sale of wheat to Russia." Ahead, many lingering questions would be addressed concerning the effectiveness (or lack thereof) of disclosure all through the summer saga, the validity of employment of key individuals—Palmby, Pulvermacher, Brunthaver, and others—moving back and forth between industry and the USDA (the so-called revolving door syndrome), and the effects of the sales on a wide variety of interest groups—the grain trade industry, the farmers, a host of shipping entities, the consumer, the government itself (especially with the effect on its budget for agriculture). Given the ever-heightening political tensions anticipating the November presidential election, the hearings promised many fireworks.

Path of Disclosure or Lack Thereof

By the last days of the presidential campaign in early November 1972, the effects of the huge grain sales had begun to impact the entire American economy, with the steep rise in grain prices already bringing a significant upward push on wholesale and retail prices in the food arena. The affected consumer was also a voter, so much political rhetoric was expended on the inflationary implications of the sales. Another large voting bloc, the farmers, also began to view the sales with misgivings. Although the huge sales of American grain were giving a sharp boost to the farm economy, the Russian purchases themselves, accomplished with so much secrecy, had apparently caught many farmers by surprise. In particular, wheat farmers in the Plains states and the Southwest, having already harvested their winter wheat crop by the summer of 1972, had begun to sell their crop in large quantities prior to the full disclosure of the Russian sales in mid-August.

For all these reasons, the path of disclosure during the July–August period of the sales now became one of the central concerns of the hearings. Butz was the committee's first witness and gave a spirited opening statement. After his return from the April meetings in Moscow, Butz began, he explained the Russian interest in buying grain "not just to grain companies, or just to farmers, or just to each other. We told it to the world in speeches and statements that were generally released and widely disseminated." As to the first set of negotiations in July, "the Soviets may have had an idea that they were about to enter the market in a major way. If such is the case, they may have contacted individual grain companies with respect to cash purchases prior to the completion of official conversations with the U.S. Government. In this way, the companies may have known that the Russians were contemplating large purchases. If this is the case, we did not know about it, either from the Russians or the companies. . . . Nobody knew then—neither the Department of Agriculture nor the trade—just how much the Russians would buy. The export traders were not telling each other just how much the Soviets were booking with them. The exporters did not tell the Department of Agriculture nor were the Russians talking."

While no one could dispute that Butz had made many statements about potential Russian sales over these weeks, the last part of the statement—namely, that "the exporters did not tell the Department of Agriculture"—was passed over without much comment by the subcommittee questioners. Carroll Brunthaver, the assistant secretary for international affairs and commodity programs of the USDA, was also grilled by the subcommittee members but again was not asked about his substantial contacts with the companies during those early and mid-July days.

If the House subcommittee let this matter slide, this was certainly not so of a Senate investigation 10 months later, in July 1973. At that time, the Permanent Subcommittee on Investigations of the Committee on Government Operations of the U.S. Senate held hearings on the Russian grain transactions. The subcommittee chairman was Senator Henry Jackson, and he began immediately to discuss Continental Grain's contacts with Brunthaver in testimony solicited from Bernard Steinweg, the senior vice president of that company. Steinweg categorically stated that he had told Brunthaver of Continental's consummated sale of 4 million metric tons on July 6. Brunthaver, in his testimony later that day, said that "the statement by Mr. Steinweg to the effect that he told me that an actual wheat sale had been made was very puzzling. It is particularly confusing when he indicated that the information was not confidential. I do not recall receiving any such information and have reason to doubt that it was ever communicated to me. In the first place, why would he give me such information and risk public disclosure of the magnitude of this transaction to commodity speculators and to their own competition. . . . I do not recall any such call and I have reason to doubt that a call was made to inform me that an actual sale, and specifically an actual sale of a specific amount, was ever made." Jackson continued to press Brunthaver, and Secretary Butz intervened: "You are trying now to intimidate the witness here." (Jackson, incidentally, responded: "That is an unbecoming statement of you, Mr. Secretary.")

Jackson, not satisfied with the answers he received in the hearing, later in the fall asked Steinweg, Brunthaver, and Secretary Butz to make sworn statements about what was actually said about Continental's sale of July 5, 1972. In a lengthy sworn statement, Steinweg continued to maintain that he had made explicit statements about the sale. Brunthaver's sworn statement was less unequivocable: "It is entirely conceivable that one or more of the conversations dealt with this matter. In any event, I do not recall specific quantities of durum or other wheat being mentioned to me by Mr. Steinweg, and I don't think it happened. Certainly, I have no recollection of any conversation during this period with Mr. Steinweg or anyone else from Continental that actual sales were made to U.S.S.R." Jackson had not been able to get an earlier statement from Secretary Butz and asked once more; this time Butz replied, "Although there had been rumors and news reports of sales of U.S. wheat to the Soviet Union during the preceding two months, Assistant Secretary Brunthaver and I did not learn of the dimensions of the July 5, 1972 sales by Continental Grain Company until September 19, 1972 when Mr. Clarence D. Palmby, Corporate Vice President of Continental Grain Company, testified [before the 1972 House subcommittee]. . . . At that time, Mr. Palmby testified that Continental Grain Company had signed on July 5, 1972 a preliminary contract with Exportkhleb, the Soviet purchasing agency for grain, for the sale of 4 million tons of wheat." There the matter was left.[23]

The Special Importance of the July Sales

The sharp increase in prices of wheat and other grains after the August return of the Russians tended at the time to mask the enormous importance of the July sales. By the time the Russians had left for Moscow on July 21, they had already purchased over 8,000,000 metric tons of wheat, over 68 percent of the total purchases for the entire July–August endeavor (the total purchase of all grains by this point was 12,550,000 metric tons, over 65 percent of all grains bought during this period). Continental's Bernard Steinweg, in his testimony before the Senate committee in 1973, played down his company's role in bringing about the sharp rise in prices: "It is a matter of public record that the sharp advance in domestic wheat prices occurred as a result of this second round of wheat purchases, in which Continental did not participate. The market rose dramatically only in response to the news that the Russians had suddenly returned to this country and had purchased substantial additional quantities of wheat." This seems a disingenuous argument, given the fact that Continental alone had sold some 5,500,000 metric tons of wheat and an additional 4,500,000 tons of corn (in other words, 68 percent of all the wheat sold in July, almost 80 percent of the sum of all grains sold).[24]

The statements of the USDA officials (Secretary Butz and Assistant Secretary Brunthaver) and ex-officials (Clarence Palmby and Clifford Pulvermacher) also appeared disingenuous to the House and the Senate committees. The public posture of the Agriculture officials, espoused by Butz and repeated by the others, was that the transactions were a private matter between the Russians and the private companies, that this was the way the enterprise system should be working, and that the USDA would not want to intrude into this equation. In truth, Agriculture had a vested interest in not allowing prices to rise rapidly, given that the wheat export differential payments would rise too and that the USDA would be paying large additional amounts of taxpayer's money for the subsidy. The "secrecy," from the department's position, was to protect the USDA subsidy exposure more than the companies' exposures. From the companies' standpoint, the fact that the sales involved such huge quantities put them in the difficult position of trying to gain long positions in the futures markets as quickly as possible but not to act so precipitously as to put a "bullish" tilt to the markets by a runup in price.

Indeed, in the 1973 Senate hearings, further facts had surfaced indicating that when all six companies had presented the required weekly reports to the CEA on their hedged and speculative positions, they had given misleading figures. A misstatement on these reports potentially carried both a civil and a criminal penalty if such a statement had been made deliberately to mislead. This had been picked up by the CEA and, in its own investigation, the CEA examiners charged Continental Grain and Dreyfus with "willful" violations; Garnac and Bunge agreed to "cease and desist" from such practices. Cook Industries and Cargill were not made subject to any CEA administrative action.

The Senate committee, not satisfied with the CEA actions, now asked the Department of Justice to investigate further the mismatch between the reports and the realities of the sales on the part of all six companies. It would have been prudent practice on the part of all the companies to keep the huge amounts of the sales as privileged information until such time as the sales had been hedged. As reported by the Department of Justice investigator, Continental had submitted inaccurate reports "from Continental's internal security procedures which were employed to keep the details of Continental's sale secret from the rest of the world." But the investigator concluded that "the inaccurate reports in no way adversely affected the Government and in fact could have operated to Continental's disadvantage." Cargill answered that

the terms and conditions under which the Soviet buyer was willing to purchase wheat were substantially different from the custom of the trade within the United States for F.O.B. Contracts. The Russian buyers have a history of requesting special terms—however, not always the same special terms. The precise terms under which they would purchase could never be fully ascertained until such time as the completely written document was placed before them for signature and they would carefully examine whether or not the written document conformed with their wishes. . . . Thus because of the substantial quantity of grain that was subject to the negotiations and the immense dollar risks involved, Cargill in no way considered, from a standpoint of prudence, that a sales agreement had actually been fully consummated with the Russians until August 9, 1972. The consideration by Cargill as to whether it had an enforceable contact with the Russians is not only reflected in its CEA reports, but on its own internal long and short audit. It did not enter into its own long and short records the August sale until August 9, 1972.

After finishing its investigation, not only of Continental and Cargill but of the other four companies, the Department of Justice concluded that "the FBI investigation of the matter did not disclose a basis for criminal prosecution." Continental had stated that it had been "their desire to keep the transaction from all lower level personnel in hopes that it would not reach the market immediately." As all of the companies' actions were based upon certain internal record keeping protocols, the Department of Justice concluded that "the criminal sanctions of the Commodity Exchange Act do not cover internal record keeping" and that a criminal violation of the Commodity Exchange Act "requires proof that CEA reports were willfully falsified." Such proof was not forthcoming from the CEA investigation, the FBI concluded, relative to either Continental or the five other grain companies investigated. "In point of fact, the reports as to all six companies, which were referred to the Department of Justice, were to the effect that individuals knowledgeable concerning the Russian sales were far enough removed from everyday CEA reporting procedures that they did not realize that their internal security measures would result in inaccurate reports."[25]

A "Revolving Door" Controversy

One of the early testifiers in the September 1972 hearings of the House subcommittee was Weldon Barton, the assistant legislative director of the National Farmers Union. Most of his testimony centered on the possibility of conflicts of interest when grain trade officials moved back and forth between their companies and positions in the USDA. Barton bluntly stated that "there is reason for strong suspicion that inside information was available to at least some wheat traders. . . . Former high officials of the USDA who went to the grain trade this year, including Messrs. Clarence Palmby and Clifford Pulvermacher, could bring with them to Continental and Bunge information on which excessive profits could be realized." At this point, Barton entered a chart into the record showing Cargill's Bill Pearce having gone to the White House in February 1972 as deputy special representative for trade negotiations (with the title of ambassador), and the movements of Palmby and Pulvermacher were highlighted, together with Carroll Brunthaver's link to Cook Industries (he had come from that organization in January 1969).

When it was Palmby's turn for interrogation, he laboriously went through the chain of events leading to his change of employment from the government to Continental Grain. As to the accusations that his involvement in the conference in the Soviet Union in April 1972 had given him inside information that he was alleged to have passed on to Continental, he said, "Any such statement is an outright lie. . . . I categorically state I took no active part in Continental's negotiations with the Soviets in its recent sale. . . . Still other statements have been made that I somehow or other had prior knowledge of the Soviet's intention to purchase grain from the United States and promptly carried that information to my new employer. This also is an outright lie." Palmby then elaborated further on exactly what he had said at various stages of the negotiations with the Russians. As for his influence as a fresh Continental executive in the actual Soviet–Continental sales discussions, he was only "an observer " and had no direct involvement in the negotiations.

In those 1972 House hearings, Secretary Butz was vehement in his response to the allegations concerning Palmby and Brunthaver. "Yesterday I spoke at the International Plowing Contest in Southern Minnesota, the home state of some of the men on this committee. The site of this contest is just 2 miles from Clarence Palmby's home farm where he grew up. His aged mother lives just a half mile from the site of the plowing contest right now. And they showed me Monday afternoon's paper up there which had a great headline about the Presidential candidate who when there chose that particular spot to impugn the integrity and the character of Clarence Palmby right in his home territory and to infer that he had been engaged in some kind of illicit deal."

Time magazine featured the Palmby–Pulvermacher testimony in its issue that week. But the representatives on the committee seemed satisfied with the testimony they had already heard. However, when the Senate took up the issue in its hearings in July 1973, Palmby was once again called as a witness. Prior to these hearings Senator Henry Jackson, chairman of the subcommittee, had requested a formal investigation by the Department of Justice. Just before the hearings opened, a lengthy memorandum was forwarded from Joseph T. Sneed, the deputy attorney general of the Department of Justice, clearing Palmby of any conflict of interest in the negotiations; he added, "no other known actions taken by Palmby subsequent to his employment with

Fribourg even remotely appear to violate 18 U.S. 208." Similarly, Pulvermacher's "known contact with various government employees subsequent to his
employment with Bunge were investigated with negative results. And his actions on behalf of Bunge failed to reveal a violation." In sum, Sneed unequiv-
ocably cleared both Palmby and Pulvermacher.

Secretary Butz did not seem as histronic in the Senate hearings in 1973
when asked about the presence of Palmby at the Moscow meetings. Butz admitted that while he did not want to "impugn the honesty, integrity or ability
of Mr. Palmby . . . I regard him as extremely capable and honest, had I known
he was going to go with Continental or any grain company, I would strongly
have counseled against his going to Moscow just because of the very appearance of collusion." [26]

Three years later, in the presidential campaign of 1976, candidate Jimmy
Carter made one of the central planks of his campaign the issue of "sweetheart arrangements between regulatory agencies and the regulated industries.
. . . The revolving door between them should be closed." After his election as
President, he continued his exhortations against undue influence from situations involving such a revolving door. In a major series of three articles in
1977, the *National Journal* treated the issue at length; once again, Clarence
Palmby's name surfaced, despite the fact that his two long examinations by
the House and Senate committees back in 1972 and 1973 had appeared to put
the issue at rest. In citing Palmby's name, along with a number of others, the
National Journal author categorized their actions as "perfectly legal but
dubious moves . . . a litany of cases for anyone reviewing the revolving door
issue."[27]

Were the Farmers "Cheated of Profits"?

If a farmer sells his harvested grain crop at or near the point of physical
harvest, he is "taking his profit" at that point. He knows his production costs
and makes a decision to sell at a margin that he thinks is his best maximization, given expectations of the future. If he holds his grain (either in farm
storage or at an elevator under his own name and paying storage rates), he is
making a judgment that he can gain a larger price sometime in the future. He
is at this point a "speculator" (unless, of course, he hedged this grain, but few
farmers use a hedge as a means of locking in price). Farmers very often hold
their grain in such a "naked" position, with the hope that prices will rise beyond that of their cost of storage.

When the 1971–1972 winter wheat crop began coming to the market over
the spring and early summer of 1972, first in the southern climes — Texas, Oklahoma — and then, later, Kansas wheat, many sales were made shortly after
harvest. The wheat crop was predicted to be a record one; prices had been
soft over the previous year. Farmers do keep up on USDA and other agricul-

tural news, and it would have been difficult to find a farmer who had not read something about the drought in Russia and the possibility of Russian purchases in the world market. But there were many winter wheat farmers who felt that the domestic overhang was the crucial factor and that therefore prices might weaken; therefore, they should sell early. The huge Russian purchases, once they hit the market in August 1972, threw this scenario into confusion.

Were these farmers "cheated" by lack of information from the USDA—lack of disclosure of the size and scope of the sales? This became one of the themes of the public response to the Russian grain sales as it evolved over the late summer and fall of 1972. Senator (and presidential aspirant) George McGovern sided strongly with his own constituents, and some of his most vitriolic invective in his early September blast at the overall wheat sales was reserved for the theme of the farmer as victim. "Many unsuspecting farmers from early-harvest states sold their wheat at July prices, about $1.32 per bushel, unaware that if they held their production, prices would rise to current levels of about $1.65. . . . Why did the Department of Agriculture join in a conspiracy of silence with the giant exporters? Why were the farmers the last to know how big the Soviet purchases were when they could have used that information to hold their wheat for a better price?"

The House subcommittee hearings in mid-September reiterated the same charges. The committee's chairman, Representative W. R. Poage of Texas, first cited an example of "my man down in McLennan County, which is way down in Texas," who had normally sold his wheat in June and in the spring of 1972 had sold his wheat "at an average of $1.20–$1.30." Poage continued (in addressing Carroll Brunthaver, the assistant secretary of the USDA), "It is obvious that you concerned yourself and made plans to see that the Grain Trade was not mistreated. Now, I think it is just as important to give some thought as to how we are going to prevent this thing from becoming a serious detriment to the farmers of Texas and Oklahoma. . . . I hope that the Department will come up with some suggestions of their own."

Countering this, Representative Keith G. Sebelius of Kansas, asked that an article in the *Kansas City Star* of September 17, 1972, be written into the record; it elaborated on another farmer's experience, a Kansan. The farmer frankly stated that he too had sold early but that "the typical wheat farmer in the High Plains is a gambler" and that "those buyers and shippers are in the know quicker than our own government. Those accusations [concerning farmers being taken advantage of] are wrong, but then this is a political year." Several other wheat-area congressmen supported the view of many farmers that they did not have adequate notice. Sebelius commented, later in the testimony, "I want my farmers to get more for their wheat and they are getting more for their wheat and they are going to get more for next year's. . . . It seems to me we have a lot of people running for Congress around this hearing." Secretary Butz added, "Farmers knew as much as anybody else."

This view seemed finally to prevail at the hearings, namely, that, while it would have been profitable for the wheat farmers to have known earlier in 1972 of the potential Russian sales, they had had the potential for information and made their own individual judgments and, further, that farmers were going to be gaining much advantage from the future of grain sales resulting from the Russian initiative. A subsequent effort by Senator Hubert Humphrey (Minnesota) and Lloyd Bentsen (Texas) in the Senate Agriculture Committee to somehow compensate those farmers who sold early failed a vote in the committee. The issue of farmer victimization now seemed to fade away, not only in the hearings but in the subsequent period.[28]

Travails of the Wheat Export Subsidy Program

The longest-lasting issue stemming from the House hearings in September 1972 was, by all odds, the wheat export subsidy effort of the USDA. Some parts of this were rather transitory, in particular, the alleged "disclosure" slippages of Charles Pence, the director of the Grain Division of the USDA. On August 24, Pence had first made calls about the upcoming changes in the subsidy program just to the six companies involved in the Russian sales. The next day, he contacted other grain trading companies but did not make calls to farmer groups, those in the domestic grain trade, or others. The press had highlighted this as a potential failure to be evenhanded on disclosure. Pence was queried about whether this gave advantage to the six companies present at the meeting; the congressional committee members present seemed to accept the statements from Pence on their face that this was not so. A subsequent Federal Bureau of Investigation report corroborated Pence's conclusion, the bureau stating that "the information was widely disseminated throughout the grain trade and grain traders took no significant market actions because of the information, therefore, the information was not market-sensitive when it was released."[29]

With so many congressional and executive branch hands on the investigative tiller, the Government Accounting Office (GAO) efforts came to have the most solid analytical base and the most lasting impact. In effect, the GAO had been asked to oversee most aspects of the USDA efforts on the Russian sales, in accord with their mandate under the Budget and Accounting Act of 1921 and the Accounting and Auditing Act of 1951. In a series of sharply worded reports, beginning with an interim report in November 1972, followed by a major report in July 1973 and a follow-up report on accomplishments after 1973 published in March 1976, the GAO laid out explicitly its views on the way the USDA had handled the export subsidy program. The 1976 report began bluntly: "Agriculture has not made a systematic evaluation of the former Wheat Export Subsidy Program, as recommended by GAO in 1973." The USDA *had* initiated a variety of audits, selective studies, and advisory position papers concerning the subsidies; the GAO faulted all of these. The USDA had reported in December 1972 that $2.7 million in subsidy offers had been incorrectly made to exporters; in August 1974, the department disclosed that some exporters had improperly used tolerance and other provisions of the subsidy program to their advantage and that the USDA had brought $8 million in claims that were still being negotiated in 1976. Further, when the USDA reviewed a controversial aspect of grain exporter selling, namely the use of sales through foreign affiliates, only two such transactions had been considered questionable in the USDA's eyes. The GAO found the USDA research to be superficial, short of what GAO felt necessary. Calling the USDA's efforts "limited, fragmented, and generally inadequate," the GAO investigators urged further efforts.

In both the 1973 and 1976 GAO reports, this issue of grain exporter reliance on foreign affiliate transactions seemed to loom as the largest concern. The USDA (in the GAO analysts' view) had held that "the subsidy program was designed to interfere as little as possible with normal commercial transactions, that no other country precludes transactions between affiliates of international grain corporations and, finally, if the United States did not permit its exporters to use the same competitive devices as their competitors, its exporters would be handicapped, while foreign exporters would benefit proportionately." In the 1976 report, the GAO put its view of the USDA agricultural policy thus: "Agriculture's current policy supports a market-oriented, full-production position, maximization of exports, and minimization of government involvement and opposes export subsidies to meet world market conditions." Clearly, the GAO took exception to what they felt was a hands-off view of the USDA about foreign affiliates: "The multinational nature of the grain trades suggests that companies that export from the United States are not operating solely as U.S. corporations. It also supports the contention that multinational organizations that export from a variety of national origins can use their elaborate affiliate relationships to maximize their market position and subsidy eligibility."[30] This issue later came to a head in another set of congressional hearings in 1976, the Church (after Senator Frank Church, its chair) Subcommittee on Multinational Corporations, to be discussed in a later chapter.

A Fall Season of High Politics

Political tensions attendant on the national presidential elections coming in November 1972 now heightened immeasurably, the grain companies being pulled into some of the discussions as pawns. During the House hearings, indictments of seven men had been handed down by a federal grand jury on charges of having conspired to break into the Democratic National Committee's headquarters in the Watergate complex on June 17. As the House subcommittee hearings on the grain sales to Russia ended on September 19, Senator McGovern hit hard on the Watergate issue, at the same time demanding the suspension of Earl Butz and others involved in the wheat negotiations until a further investigation had been conducted. In this same week, Vice President Spiro Agnew made a misstep by stating that President Nixon had ordered the Federal Bureau of Investigation to conduct an investigation of the grain sales. Nixon had to follow through after the public statement by Agnew, although, as the *New York Times* put it, "he had no intention of ordering such an investigation . . . that the Vice President's announcement came as a complete surprise to the White House."[31] Cargill's September 8 press announcement, made at that time in response to Senator McGovern's first set of attacks on the grain sales, had seemed to garner no interest at all. Perhaps the statement was too long on assertions and self-congratulation and too short on specifics; the House subcommittee hearings that started just a week later seemed to capture all the stage at the time. One of the issues that Cargill had addressed in that earlier memorandum was the question of so-called windfall profits. "The fact is," the release had stated then, "Cargill itself cannot possibly know whether it made money or lost money on these sales until the last shipments are completed in mid-1973. In any event, we anticipate a net profit of less than one percent of sales price—a level unthinkable in other businesses that are less competitive."

The notion that there were windfalls continued to persist, however. Cargill officials knew that, at least for their own company, this was far from the truth; by October, it was clear that for the actual Russian sales themselves the net of the two huge sales was going to turn into a loss. At this point, the Company decided to take an unprecedented step of releasing their private purchase and sales data ("for the first time in its 107 year history," the subsequent press release noted). Peat, Marwick, Mitchell & Co., the company's outside auditors, were asked to independently examine the entire period covering the two Cargill sales to the Russians, including all relevant materials, such as Cargill's day-by-day requests for subsidy payments from the CCC (in effect all purchases and sales of hard winter wheat between June 1 and September 20, 1972). The CPA firm laid out a detailed statement, dated November 1, 1972, of how they went about the assignment given to them by the Company. Their three-page step-by-step procedures included steps taken within Cargill to ensure that the trading statements given to Peat, Marwick by the CMD were "presented on a basis substantially consistent with that of the Company's audited financial statements on which we had previously reported." Peat, Marwick made comparisons between Cargill's records and those of the USDA "acceptances of offer to export wheat" and built a day-by-day register of all hard winter wheat sales. They obtained copies from Cargill of the sales contracts with the Russians, verified precisely what the price structure was and then developed a statistical analysis of the total sales as of September 30, 1972. Their conclusion projected a loss on the sales of the 73,487,400 bushels of hard winter wheat of $.009 per bushel (see table 8). In sum, the CPA firm projected a composite loss to Cargill for all of the Russian sales of some $661,000.

The Company's press release on the Peat, Marwick report averred that constant repetition of the allegations of windfall profits "has given them the appearance of fact. Indeed, many branches of the news media now treat the charges as fact." For example, an October 15 release by a nationally syndicated Washington reporter stated, "The grain exporters include Cargill, Inc., which has recently reaped windfall profits from the controversial Soviet grain deal." It was "incredible," said the company release, to observe all these allegations of windfall profits "in the total absence of any input pertaining to costs." Further, the press release noted, "three members of the House subcommittee . . . Rep. Graham Purcell (Dem.), Chairman of the Subcommittee; Rep. Bob Bergland (Dem.); and Rep. Paul Findley (Rep.)—stated publicly that no evidence of illegal activities had been uncovered." A substantial portion of the public "continues to believe there was a scandal, in which Cargill was involved," the writer continued. The Peat, Marwick figures "will convince even the most committed critic that there was no inside information, favor, windfall profits or other questionable activity. . . . What they reveal is the company's willingness to take an unusually large risk in order to perform our normal marketing function, which is to buy grain at time of harvest, dry it, clean it, store and preserve it, transport it and sell it at times and places of need throughout the world, through facilities requiring tremendous financial in-

TABLE 8

Cargill, Incorporated, Statistical Analysis of Russian Hard Winter Wheat Sales as of September 30, 1972

Income from sales	Per bushel
Sales (73,487,400 bushels)—average price, FOB Gulf, adjusted to ordinary protein	$1.621
Subsidy-weighted average (including subsidies identifiable with sales to Russia) of Gulf/East Coast subsidies booked during four months ended September 30, 1972	.334
Projected income per bushel	1.955
Acquisition costs: Purchases—weighted average of contracted purchase adjusted to ordinary protein, domestic price, current shipment, delivered Gulf basis	2.009
Operating expenses—elevator, office, and overhead	.025
	2.034
Less hedging gain—four months ended September 30, 1972, based on total bushels traded	.070
Projected acquisition cost	1.964
Projected loss	$.009

Source: Peat, Marwick, Mitchell & Co. to board of directors, Cargill, Incorporated, 11/1/72, CA, 3E8B.

vestment." The press release, signed by President Fred Seed, frankly elaborated the underlying rationale for the press release: "Our primary aim . . . is to provide the facts to refute the allegations that have unfairly tarnished our business and professional reputation, our position in the community and the morale of our employees."[32]

This time the results of the press release were considerably more positive. The Company's detailed memorandum became widely reported all over the country, most often with enough of the facts present to give an accurate feeling for Cargill's position. The *New York Times* headline read, "$661,000 Loss Reported by Cargill in Sale to Soviet—Price Rise after Contract Signing and Failure of U.S. Subsidy Program to Keep Pace Cited by Grain Dealer." Many dozens of newspapers, throughout the wheat belt and around the rest of the country, reiterated the same message (and there were variations—the *Aurora (Illinois) Beacon News* asked, "What windfall?" and the *Illinois State Journal* in Springfield flatly stated, "Cargill treated unfairly"). A number of papers mentioned that Cargill's complaints of having its reputation damaged had been made "with justification." Some editors made comparisons between Cargill and the other five of the "big six." The *Minneapolis Tribune* editorialized, "Cargill's documentation to refute that charge leaves other exporters in an awkward position. . . . But if the critics were wrong in the case of that exporter, their charges against the others remain in limbo. That will probably continue to be the situation unless the other exporters publish similar information, which they are not required to do." None of the other five did, in point of fact, publish any such figures.

By November 8, the presidential elections had been concluded, with incumbent Richard Nixon the winner. The *Gulfport (Mississippi) Herald* editorialized about the reasons for his victory, recounting the "bitter campaign with many charges of 'political immorality' against the Administration." The *Herald* continued: "The Russian wheat sale was also supposed to be a scandal until an audited report from Cargill, Inc. showed it lost about $6.6 million. False accusations were widely broadcast." The *Spokane (Washington) Spokesman-Review* reiterated the same theme: "Now, maybe the other companies succeeded in having windfall profits that didn't result in substantial losses, but for Cargill anyway, the charges of unconscionable profits, inside information, and government collusion must make mighty wry reading." The influential *Rocky Mountain News* (Denver) accurately portrayed the difficult situation Cargill had been put in by the sales: "Cargill obviously didn't go into the deal to lose money, but it turned out this way because the Russian contract (surprisingly big) along with other commitments caught the company when it didn't actually have enough grain on hand. News of the Soviet deal sent wheat prices up and the company had to buy at higher prices than were offset by U.S. government subsidies to meet the contracts. The report sounds like the McCoy, in the absence of any evidence to the contrary, and Cargill takes a long-range view of it—while it lost money on this specific deal, the increased sales will benefit all agriculture, including Cargill, the company aptly reasons." Secretary Butz wrote Fred Seed the day after the elections, "It took a lot of courage for you folks to put out the information that you lost almost a cent a bushel on the wheat you sold the Russians . . . your release certainly gave the lie [to] the pernicious charges . . . about exorbitant profits made by 'the big grain corporations.'"

Only a few newspapers seemed skeptical; the Hammond, Louisiana, *Star*, for example, noted editorially, "Well, auditors can arrange figures to reflect something less than a precise clear picture—so we're left to wonder about the full real truth about these grain deals." Most of the influential analysts from the national press, however, appeared to have been impressed with Cargill's forthrightness. The *Tulsa (Oklahoma) Daily World* gave the company full credit for its disclosure: "This may not be the first time Cargill has been caught short, but it's the first time in the 107 year history of the privately owned company that officials have bared their records to refute charges of having had 'inside information' resulting in 'windfall profits.'"[33]

Cargill's news release (on November 2) was made more complicated by another press release just one day later, by the federal GAO. This investigative agency had just received its commission a few weeks earlier from several members of Congress to examine the implications of the wheat sale; at this point, on November 3, it chose to make what it called an "interim staff report." Cargill was rightly concerned that this might vitiate the Company's message, for the GAO news release received headline attention all through the press. Fortunately, however, the GAO's own wording of its release included a sentence that stated "one of the six, Cargill, Inc., of Minneapolis, stated publicly Thursday that it lost $661,386 on the deal." The thrust of the GAO interim report was addressed to the question of whether the Soviet Union had been able to buy the grain too cheaply and whether the USDA had needed to pay as much subsidy costs as it did. No judgments were made by the GAO at this point about whether the six grain export concerns had received favorable treatment by the government in arranging the sales.[34]

Hassles about Shipping the Wheat

The huge Russian purchases of grain during that summer of 1972—over 19 million tons in July and August from the United States along with large purchases from Canada, Argentina, and elsewhere around the world—now needed to be transported from the sellers to the buyers. The logistics of this unprecedented amount of grain to be moved physically inevitably led to many problems. First, it had to be shipped from inland storage to the ports—Great Lakes, eastern, and particularly Gulf ocean terminals. Here, Cargill's facilities were superb, with its large barge fleet, railroad hopper holdings (some owned, most leased), and its exisiting unit train arrangements with the Illinois Central Railroad and others. The upgrading of the Company's terminal facilities all through the 1960s now was to pay off handsomely. The Duluth terminals had over 13 million bushels of capacity Chicago had 21 million. The Houston terminal, at a 4,500,000-bushel capacity, though smaller in total size, was Cargill's most efficient and newest terminal and would be the workhorse for Cargill's shipments to Russia. Inland terminals at Omaha (8.5 million bushels), Kansas City (3.3 million bushels), and the two initiating points for the Illinois-based Rent-a-Train—Tuscola (4 million bushels) and Gibson City (3 million bushels)—gave excellent feeder linkages. There were many other terminals in the system that would handle some of the Russian sales, too.

Ocean shipping appeared readily available. Cargill itself owned a small tonnage; Tradax (the European subsidiary) owned some additonal shipping and did substantial chartering. However, both of these Company shipping units participated in only a miniscule way in the Russian grain shipments, almost all of which would be moved by ships from all over the world under charter, with a substantial amount to be transported by Russian ships owned by the Soviet state itself.

Right at the beginning, a flap arose over the ocean rates for the Russian grain cargoes. Shortly after the August sales, U.S. and Soviet officials negotiated a tentative agreement on such rates. At that time, the Russians agreed to a rate of $8.05 per ton from Gulf Coast to Black Sea ports, the world rate at that time being from $5.50 to $6.50 per ton. But public realization of the scope of the Russian purchases brought a rapid escalation in world rates—by mid-October most rates already were up to about $9 per ton, with some ships reportedly getting even $10 per ton. When the Russian representatives came to Washington in late September to sign the shipping agreement, the U.S. negotiators demanded a renegotiation, as they naturally feared that if the Russians once again bested the American negotiators, the public outcry would become overwhelming. So the American negotiators, as the *New York Times* bluntly put it, "reneged" on the agreement.

While the Soviet officials were quite irritated about this, they wanted to keep the overall arrangements in place and finally agreed to a renegotiation that would set the rate at either $8.05 or 110 percent of the world rate, whichever was larger. In other words, if the world rate was $10 per ton, the Soviets would pay American ship owners $11 per ton. Inasmuch as the cost of shipping in American carriers was about $21 per ton, the federal government agreed to subsidize these shipowners for the difference (initially, the Maritime Administration estimated that it would require a $20 million subsidy; later they admitted that this federal subsidy outlay would be more than $60 million).

Another provision of the renegotiated agreement was that the Americans were to be guaranteed a third of all the cargo traffic under the accord, with

The first Russian ship since World War II to call at a Gulf or East Coast port, the M/V Kasi-mov, took on 11,500 tons of wheat at Cargill's export terminal in Houston on November 6, 1972. Captain V. Strunets of Leningrad is at right; center, Fred Seed, president of Cargill; at left, Konstantin Tretjakov, the Commercial Counselor of the Soviet Embassy, Washington, D.C. (UPI/Corbis-Bettmann).

another one-third to be shipped by Russian-owned vessels and the other one-third from general world shipping. An additional accord provided that 40 ports in the United States and 40 ports in the Soviet Union would be open to regular merchant traffic (with the only condition for the use of the ports a four-day notice). The agreement still restricted ships that had called or were to call at Cuba, North Vietnam, or North Korea from U.S. ports. Soviet ships that had called at Cuban ports would not be allowed to load government-financed cargoes, such as grain backed by the CCC, but they would be allowed to pick up privately financed goods.

Collateral to this critical agreement was an understanding with the International Longshoremen's Association (I.L.A.) that they would not oppose working the Soviet flag vessels (the I.L.A. had jurisdiction over East Coast and Gulf ports but not the Great Lakes ports). There had been some picketing of the Russian ships at several ports in late September (the union demanding that five prisoners of war be released by North Vietnam for each ship loaded); but once the agreement was in place, the I.L.A., together with the National Maritime Union, the Seafarers International Union, the Marine

Engineers Beneficial Association, the American Radio Association, the Radio Officers Union, the Staff Officers Union, and the Staff Officers Association, all agreed to abide by the loading protocols.

The reaction to the shipping accord was mostly sighs of relief, although the *Journal of Commerce* carped that "still and all, the end result of a proliferation of these deals will be a gradual stifling of competition, or at least of the competitive urge that has so long characterized the world's carrying trades." The *Washington Post* pointed out that "some sources in the shipping industry suggest that it would have been much better to put an absolute rate into the agreement rather than the rather vague formula that was arrived at." There were some fears at the beginning that the Russians might not have unloading capacity to handle such a massive movement into their ports. But as the shipments picked up speed all through the rest of the year, while rail shipping capacity was under very tight pressures, the overall expected shipment patterns worked out reasonably well. By December, Cargill had loaded five Russian vessels at the Gulf Coast ports, the first since World War II. The M.V. *Kasimov* was pictured in the *Cargill News* of January–February 1973, complete with the smiling captain, V. Strunets, next to Frank Hemmen, the Company manager at Houston, and Haslan Johnson, the elevator manager.

By mid-March 1973, the *Journal of Commerce* was highlighting the "slow start that the US-flag ships had made in hauling their assured share" and that the Americans' total would be well under the one-third guaranteed to U.S. flags. Because of heavy port congestion, the entire 19 million tons did not clear U.S. ports by June 30, as originally hoped (there had been sharp pickups in other export programs, notably the P.L. 480 grain sales). In March, the first of the Russian-flag ships scheduled to enter the St. Lawrence Seaway had arrived, with 20 to 30 Russian ships per month expected over the spring and early summer of 1973. Cargill's Commodity Marketing Division (CMD) report at the end of the crop year (May 31, 1973) pointed out that "the transportation snarl was horrendous . . . without our own hopper car fleet and train-load movement of grain, we would have had an impossible year." (The fact that Cargill commanded "train-load" movement with the Rent-a-Train unit train inevitably tightened the availability of boxcars for general car-by-car shipping; the whole question of the boxcar shortage in 1972–1973 was investigated later by the Interstate Commerce Commission. More on this in the next chapter.)

The combination of Cargill's huge purchase volume, the rising markets, and all these logistic delays found the Company by spring with thousands of open purchase contracts for many millions of bushels, most priced far below current markets, a situation boding disaster if the contracts were reneged on. However, to quote the CMD report, because of the "basic honesty of American farmers," together with assiduous diligence on the part of the Company merchants, "we suffered remarkably little loss from contract defaults."

In sum, Cargill's mammoth sales of grain to Russia were consummated with signal success, although with minimal profitability. But overall the crop year 1972–1973 was an unprecedented one in so many ways and provided the company unprecedented profitability.[35]

The Remarkable Record Crop Year, 1972–1973

The year was "a milestone which will long be remembered as one of the finest performances in the history of Cargill." So stated the annual report to the stockholders. For the fourth consecutive year, the Company had surpassed all previous records, with net earnings climbing to $107 million. It was a tremendous gain from the previous year's record earnings of just over $40 million—a 160 percent increase. Earnings for the year gave a return of 43.8 percent on beginning net worth (19.3 percent the previous year), the volume of goods climbed 30 percent to 62.3 million tons, and sales increased 54 percent to a new record of $5.3 billion. Had the Company been publicly held and listed in the Fortune 500, it would have ranked 14th in sales in the nation, just behind United States Steel Corporation and ahead of Westinghouse Electric. CMD's Barney Saunders described the 12 months: "It was a year of record profits, record dollar sales, record tonnage, record margins, record problems, record expense, record traffic jams, record prices and controls, record aspirin pills, and many record performances by a record number of people." The stockholders' annual report captured the year in a paragraph: "Against a background of worldwide crop reductions the greatly increased demand for food, feed grains and protein supplies sparked a situation which truly sent shock waves around the world. Pressure of demand created critical supply shortages and unprecedented high prices for agricultural products—not only in the U.S. but on a worldwide basis."

Tradax executives Walter Gage, Brewster Hanson, and Leonard Alderson, in keeping with that company's more free-wheeling approach, gave a more speculative touch to their report. World crop conditions had shown wide variance, with severe production losses not only in the Soviet Union but in India, Australia, South Africa, the Middle East, and the Sahara basin. The early buying by the Soviets (by this time cumulating worldwide "to almost 29,000,000 tons") had set off a rapid escalation in all agricultural commodity prices to "practically historic highs." Simultaneously, the general economies of the world's developed nations revived; world trade burgeoned, bringing ocean freight rates sharply upward. Compounding the economic tensions were a series of monetary shocks and devaluations (the dollar itself suffering finally).

Herein, the three Tradax executives surmised, had lain promise: "These events produced tremendous problems and inordinate risks, but also gave us new opportunities for profit. Larger and more flexible position limits were established and a continual reassessment of relative profit potential was more important than ever." (As Walter Gage put it later, "that's one of the advantages of being by ourselves over here . . . we didn't have to go to the Finance Committee to get permision to do this, that and the other thing.") It was "the biggest bull market that any of us had ever seen [and] we took much larger flat price and premium positions than ever before." Tremendous nerve had been needed: "Perhaps the greatest danger to the profitability of our operations lay in the temptation to take our profits and even up, rather than continue to back our judgment and analysis. Fortunately this temptation was resisted and we made a trading profit of $60,174,000 . . . the risks were accepted."

The CMD group at the Cargill parent in Minneapolis seldom took speculative positions on one side of the market—the Company's basic concept of trying at all times to be fully hedged still remained. But the huge sales and the rapidly rising market forced many short-term naked positions. Their report put this well: "Looking back, it is easy to follow the pattern of ever ascending focus. During the year, however, it was far more hair-raising to maintain the large and risky long positions that rewarded us so well." The CMD executives said in a different way just what the Tradax officers had expressed: "It is a tribute to the growth and maturity of Cargill that we accepted these risks."

One of the dilemmas in the intimidating "naked" positions after the huge August sale to Russia of one million tons of winter wheat was how quickly Cargill could "even up." The year-end report on winter wheat noted that "it can now be shown that the conduct of covering our large short position judiciously in August and September, rather than charging the market in panic, saved and made the corporation a great deal of money." (Although, as noted earlier, the abruptness of the USDA phase-out of the export equalization payments *did* catch Cargill and others.)

Any doubt that the two sales of one million tons each to the Russians had indeed been at a loss was dispelled by the CMD report. Cargill had traded almost 280 million bushels of winter wheat in total, 73 million of this to the Soviets. With the losses on that sale, the overall trading margin was just 1.0 cent per bushel, lowest of all CMD's 13 grains reported (the winter wheat margin had been 2.1 cents the previous year, 4.2 cents for the 1970–1971 crop year).

In early 1974, the GAO, asked by the investigating House of Representatives committee to prepare a separate report on the exporters' "profits" on the Russian sales, corroborated that of the five members of the "big six" that had shared detailed statistics with the agency (Louis Dreyfus Corporation had refused GAO access). Two firms reported profits: one of 2 cents per bushel and one of 0.3 cents, with the other three reporting losses of 0.9 cents (Cargill), 1.5 cents, and 1.9 cents.

The 133 million bushels of spring wheat had traded at 6.5 cents in 1972–1973; the Company's 569 million bushels of corn brought 2.4 cents per bushel; and the all-time record 307 million bushels of soybeans, an impressive

8.3 cents in the face of shortages in overall supply. Cargill's "total grains" traded in as a huge 1.6 billion bushels; its combined trading margin for all of this was an excellent 4.2 cents per bushel.

The faster track at Tradax had generated some even more astounding trading margins and some significant lacks, too. Overall, it had traded 23 million tons of commodities (about 850 million bushels); its overall profit on this, at $60 million, was some $2.60 per ton (roughly 7 cents per bushel). Some 6.7 million tons of world wheat had been traded, with a margin of $1.47 per ton, about 4 cents per bushel; the European Common Market trades in wheat, barley, and maize summed to $2.50 (6 cents per bushel) and soybeans to a record $4.52 (12.3 cents per bushel).

Tradax's long positions in these key grains underlay the cumulative performance. "It was in wheat that we decided to place the Company's major long position, " their report stated. "We were a little hesitant in building up the long as we believed the C.C.C. when they told us that they would hold the world price of $59.00 per ton. The scale of Russian purchases soon rendered this impossible and between August and January our wheat long varied between 200,000 and 450,000 tons. The bulk of our wheat profit came from these long positions."

In October, Tradax analysis indicated "a potentially very bullish situation" for soybeans. Longs were put on, taken off, then put on again over the next few months. "Tremendous swings occurred in the flat price, spreads and premiums, so that the risks were high, but so was the profit opportunity for those on the right side. . . . We estimate that we made $9,000,000 on flat price positions, $6,000,000 on spreads and $3,000,000 on premiums." The soybean section concluded with kudos for both the Wayzata CMD group and the European oil plants; the "remarkable results" would not have been possible without "perfect cooperation among the three sets of merchants."

As expected, soybean meal also traded very profitably, although "the volatility of the market was if anything more pronounced." Their positions were turned constantly, "always being in the market . . . anything that looked cheap we would buy and we always had a price at which we were prepared to offer against consumer demand."

Not everything came up positive for Tradax, as significant losses were sustained on trading ocean freight, for "losses on shorts to difficult destinations ate up most of the market appreciation in the overall long position as inventoried." Tradax-owned shipping did well, however, despite collisions suffered by the *Ghent* and the *Tarragona* mini-bulkers and a devastating fire that totally destroyed the *Carlantic*. The latter was fully covered by insurance, to be sure, but "a tremendous amount of time was spent with the salvage association and the underwriters." Finally, however, Tradax did decide to rebuild the vessel.

Jim Spicola's Processing and Refining Division also set new records for profits and volume. He too spoke of the high risk in the year, but opportunities also were "substantial . . . if one was in step." They were, as the $23.8 million total profits testified. Soybean was the star, and flax did well too; but copra and corn milling were down, as was flour milling.

Prices on soybeans and soybean meal were unbelievably high, and export demand was unprecedented. Spicola enumerated the complicated brew in the situation as it stood in May 1973: "Rising demand for protein, stimulated by increased meat consumption in the developed areas of the world; a substantial reduction in the supplies of fishmeal from Peru [the anchovy catch had fallen precipitously, due to a shift in the warm Pacific 'El Niño' current, driving the fish beyond reach of the Peruvian fishing fleet]; devaluation of the U.S. dollar; a poor sunflower crop in Russia leading that country to buy a million tons of soybeans from the U.S.; U.S. soybean production well below desired levels; all combined with a speculative fever the likes never before witnessed, drove soybean meal markets to levels never considered possible."

Less than a month after this May 31, 1973, closing of Cargill's books on the spectacular crop year, the soybean speculative situation caused the Nixon administration, already shell-shocked by the effects of the Russian grain sales, to totally embargo all soybean exports. The repercussions were profound. The next chapter will chronicle this evolving saga.

CHAPTER SIX

Years of High Drama

Businesses receive important feedback each year, when the annual report brings the "results" of the previous fiscal period. Cargill's figures on May 31, 1973, gave for the first time a clear view of that profoundly important year. Just about all of the Russian grain sales of the previous summer had reached their destination, and although new hearings were already scheduled by the Senate subcommittee for July (and would continue on into October), the effects of those sales and the rest of that fiscal year were now spelled out clearly by the Company's annual report. The impact of that greatly heightened profit for the year—a stellar $107 million, far and away a record—became a portent for the near-term future.

How Much in Dividends?

This stunning amount now raised several questions. An immediate issue was how much to pay in dividends on the various classes of the Company's stock. The special preferred and the preferred stock carried fixed returns; there was no problem there. The other two classes of stock, the common and the management shares, had rates to be fixed each year by the board of directors. The policy in previous years for these two more entrepreneurial of the four classes of stock had been highly conservative. From back in the 1930s, in a doctrine first enunciated by John MacMillan, Sr., and Austen Cargill and later corroborated by John MacMillan, Jr., and Cargill MacMillan, a dominant percentage of the earnings always had been put right back into the business. The dividends paid ever since the 1930s to this date had been nominal, almost token. The Cargill and MacMillan families had had disagreements on a not inconsequential number of issues over these years, but dividend policy had never been one of them.

The most recent written policy on this sensitive matter had been enunciated in a July 1964 meeting of the board of directors, with the family input to this decision coming from the next generation (of those earlier generations, only Cargill MacMillan, Sr., was still alive, but he was not involved in decision making due to the tragic stroke he had suffered in 1959). In this meeting, the board discussed a memorandum, "Management/Stockholders Relations and Objectives," written by President Fred Seed. The minutes reported: "James R. Cargill acted as spokesman for stockholders while Mr. Seed presented the concepts and comments of the management group." The relation of the families to the business again was examined, and "it was determined that no disagreement in respect to objectives exists." The directors then promulgated a new policy "of increasing the Common and Management stock dividends by ten cents per share for each $2,500,000 of earnings over the first $5,000,000 of annual earnings after taxes." The matter would then be reviewed annually.

The policy stayed in place all through the 1960s; indeed, it was referred to explicitly in the board minutes of December 5, 1970, before that year's dividend was declared. Dividends that year had risen to 25 cents, but with profits of over $24 million, the formula was far under its limits. Dividends for the two classes were 40 cents for 1971 and 1972 (profits, $38 million and $40 million). For 1972, the formula would have allowed within the policy a dividend of up to $1.40 (this itself would have been a modest dividend in most companies).

So what would be the dividend percentage for the unprecedented $107 million figure of 1973? There had been a 4-for-1 stock split in July 1973; now, despite the significant jump in earnings from the 1972 figure, the answer came unequivocally: the dividend was set exactly the same as the previous year. In other words, taking into account the stock split, the dividend on the common and management stock was the equivalent of 10 cents per share. If earlier dividend declarations had been "modest," this declaration of 1973 was closer to minimal![1]

This was a modern reiteration of what John MacMillan, Sr., Austen Cargill, and later John MacMillan, Jr., and Cargill MacMillan, Sr., had long preached: plow profits back into the business. But the reasons for this were more complex than appeared on its face. Because the families owned virtually all of the common stock, this was building each family's capital position without current personal income tax effects. To provide current income, the family members in the business (Whitney MacMillan, Jim Cargill, and Cargill MacMillan) earned senior management salaries and shared in the bonuses tendered to other senior management in profitable years. W. Duncan MacMillan received an equivalency as president of Waycrosse, the family company. Inasmuch as at this time dividends were taxed as "unearned income" at a higher rate than earned income, the incidence of taxation was reduced.

One difficulty with this was that family members not in management did not share, except in increased book value of their stock (which was illiquid outside the Company). In later years, the very modest dividend policy was to cause considerable dissension because of this.

Deepening Management

The outstanding performances of individuals in those event-filled days of the fiscal years 1971–1973, attested to so eloquently by the division reports in those two years, highlighted once again the critical importance of management as the key ingredient in corporate success. During that time, the Company's top management and board looked especially at management incentive. This first took focus at the board meeting of July 1, 1972, when the directors developed almost a "laundry list" of methods that might "provide recognition to various individuals and . . . motivate individuals to achieve." Congratulatory letters from the president for good work were to be used, special study groups were now planned to focus on specific projects (mentioned were the corporate personnel department, new businesses, and future office building arrangements), and the chairman and the president agreed to appoint a rotating group of worldwide managers to meet once a year for two or three days with a prearranged agenda to "concentrate particularly on the future of Cargill." Erv Kelm suggested that this group's first subject "might well concern itself with people motivation." Finally, it was agreed that the long-range planning committee should "more actively solicit reports . . . from managers of outlying activities."

The bonus system and its relationship to the Participation Allotment Plan (PAP) was discussed; both received strong support. Erv Kelm, however, did request the board "to consider the merit of placing an ultimate limitation on all fringe compensation, including PAP, bonus and phantom stock at an amount equal to 150 percent of base salary."

This caution also extended to adding new management candidates for management share ownership. Despite provisions in the charter and bylaws for a more expanded shareholding by management, the families had persuaded Kelm to restrict it, and this practice of constraining management ownership was to continue over the next two decades. Family lawyers had argued their belief that the new Model Securities Act being advanced by Harvard Law School authority Louis Loss would restrict private companies to 300 shareholders before being required to go public. But it later appeared that Loss had nothing like this in mind—the "300 limitation" was just a phantom. The fact remained that any discussion of increasing management shareholding was suspect as far as the families were concerned.

At the July board meeting the following year (July 25, 1973), the issue of recruiting future managers from the pool of new college graduates was examined. A board committee was appointed to structure a more effective system, "to attract the best possible people from a limited number of schools." The board felt that a small number of schools (the number 10 was mentioned) should be concentrated on, "rather than many schools." Consulting relationships between Cargill management and key professors would be encouraged, and a careful system of tracking hires would be conducted, with three review points of one, two, and four years after hire. Finally, the directors "re-emphasized continuation of the policy of promoting from within Cargill," a policy that had been one of the strongest tenets throughout the years.

The process of making PAP allocations now came under scrutiny again. PAP allocations earned bonuses in stock as well as cash; and because earnings per share had risen sharply after the 1972 Russian sales, this meant that management would get more actual stock than anyone had anticipated. A disconcerting thought surfaced at this time: "It was concluded that some PAP allocations appeared excessive." In the discussion, the directors noted that "in the past no allocations had ever been reduced or withdrawn"; now it was "the consensus of the directors that allocations that appeared excessive should be reduced to approximately 1,500 working shares, but that individuals having an excessive allocation should be given the opportunity to purchase shares representing the excess allocations at book value." The board's salary committee was charged with the responsibility of recommending to the directors at the next meeting "those persons whose allocations should be reduced and the amount of the reduction." At this next meeting (August 14, 1973), the PAP program again was discussed; recommendations were made for specific PAP allocations, but no mention was made of any cutting of "excessive" allocations.[2]

The "pressure-cooker" days of 1972 and 1973 quickly brought major changes in management's structure—and its philosophy. The board itself had dropped from its 13-member size in 1969 and 1970 to 11 for the next several years. Jim North and Bert Egermayer went off the board in 1970, Bob Harrigan in 1972. The latter was replaced by Jim Spicola in 1973.

The Cargill board of directors as of August 14, 1973, was as follows:

General directors
  H. Robert Diercks
  Erwin E. Kelm
  Whitney MacMillan
  W. Duncan MacMillan
  M. D. McVay

Special directors
  James R. Cargill
  Walter F. Gage
  Donald C. Levin
  Cargill MacMillan, Jr.
  James R. Spicola

Management director
  Fred M. Seed

Major new responsibilities also arose. Erv Kelm triggered some of this with his recommendation in the July 1972, board meeting that management should be "more liberal in electing Divisional Vice Presidents"; the board concurred, with a consensus that corporate vice presidents should be directors, heads of operating groups, or heads of major operating divisions. Kelm also disclosed at this meeting his plans in regard to realigning operating responsibilities in divisional structures "in view of corporate growth." A schedule was mandated for this new structure, with the soybean operations to be realigned in June 1973 and a number of other divisions in June 1974. This reorganization implanted considerably more decentralization within the organization, with more autonomous responsibilities for the heads of the various divisions.

In late 1971, Bill Pearce, who had been the Company's vice president for public relations, resigned from Cargill to accept a high-level post in the administration of President Nixon: deputy special representative for trade negotiations in the President's executive office. The assignment carried the rank of ambassador. *Cargill News* noted that upon completion of his duties there in 1973, hopes were that Pearce would return to Cargill. John McGrory was to serve as executive supervisor of the public relations department while retaining his existing assignment as assistant general counsel of the Company.

Two months later, in March 1972, a milestone in management succession—Julius Hendel's death—occurred. His was a special link to the past; colleague and confidante of John MacMillan, Jr., Hendel had been a unique force in the Company's trading ("the Dean") and in its training ("he Cargillized the industry").

The deepening of top management continued with the appointment, in January 1973, of Mel Middents as a division vice president in the Commodity Marketing Division. In May 1973, three senior vice presidents were appointed: Jim Cargill, Cargill MacMillan, Jr., and Don Levin. Then, in July 1973, the entire management structure was reorganized to, as Erv Kelm put it, "enable the company to expand its contribution to agricultural processing, handling and marketing of bulk commodities at a time when world dependence on the U.S. for efficient production and distribution of food is increasing rapidly." The internal announcement in the *Green Wave* put particular emphasis on the demands for "diversity."

Three new corporate groups were formed, each reporting to one of the two executive vice presidents, Whitney MacMillan or Pete McVay. A processing group was established with Jim Spicola as group vice president; a marketing and transportation group was to be headed by Barney Saunders; and the feed, seed, and poultry processing group was to be led by Heinz Hutter. The processing group included both domestic and international soybean crushing operations, corn and flour milling, and the copra, flax, and protein products activities of the Company. New corporate vice presidents were named in the processing group—Don Leavenworth, responsible for domestic soybean crushing; Hank Van Veen, heading international soybean crushing; and Gerry Mitchell leading the milling division (for both corn and wheat). Cliff

Roberts was to be corporate vice president in the Commodity Marketing Division. Maitland "Hap" Wyard remained president of Cargo Carriers, Inc., and John Cole continued as president of the Western Hemisphere trading company, called Cargill Americas.

Following is the full cadre of the senior management group that had carried the Company through the unprecedented two-year bulge in growth (as elaborated in the board minutes of August 14, 1973).

Erwin E. Kelm	Chairman of the Board and Chief Executive Officer
Fred M. Seed	President and Chief Operating Officer
H. Robert Diercks	Vice Chairman of the Board
Whitney MacMillan	Executive Vice President
M. D. McVay	Executive Vice President
James R. Cargill	Senior Vice President
Donald C. Levin	Senior Vice President
Cargill MacMillan, Jr.	Senior Vice President
Heinz F. Hutter	Group Vice President
W. B. Saunders	Group Vice President
James R. Spicola	Group Vice President
Calvin J. Anderson	Vice President and Secretary
A. R. Baldwin	Vice President
Arthur H. Klobe	Vice President
Donald H. Leavenworth	Vice President
Gerald M. Mitchell	Vice President
C. M. Roberts, Jr.	Vice President
Calvin L. Smith	Vice President and Controller
James V. Springrose	Vice President
D. O. Wentzell	Vice President
Hendrik Van Veen	Vice President
John F. McGrory	General Counsel
B. S. Jaffray	Treasurer
John P. Cole	Division Vice President, Commodity Marketing Division
Addison H. Douglass	Division Vice President, Commodity Marketing Division
James A. Howard	Division Vice President, Commodity Marketing Division
Melvin H. Middents	Division Vice President, Commodity Marketing Division
George L. Jones	Division Vice President, Seed Department
Edward E. Reynolds	Division Vice President, Poultry Products
John C. Savage	Division Vice President, Administrative Division
F. Clayton Tonnemaker	Division Vice President, Salt Department

With these major promotions came many other increases in responsibility for persons farther down in the organization. For example, in the *Cargill News* of September–October 1973, the promotion of Evan Williams as assistant vice president in the Salt Department was announced, and John Erickson and Victor Anderson were appointed assistant general counsels. Allen Housh and Ernie Micek became assistant vice presidents in the processing group. Vardin West was appointed an assistant vice president in the Administrative Division. All through the organization such upgrading of responsibility was occurring. [3]

Loosening Constraints

Already, the excellent profitability of the previous two years ($40 million in 1970–1971 and $42 million in 1971–1972) had allowed major capital expenditures. Indeed, these two years of high earnings already had militated a much higher level for the recycling of profits, given the agreed-upon minimal dividends. Now the $107 million earnings of the stunning fiscal year of 1972–1973 heightened the pressure on management to "put these funds to good use." Given the precept of plowing earnings back into the business, where should these earnings be invested, and what constraints should guide this?

Back in the 1960s, when profits were more modest, Erv Kelm optimistically had predicted in the board meeting of May 10, 1965, that net worth of the company would be doubled within 10 years of that date. The other board members agreed that this "was not overly optimistic and might indeed be on the conservative side." Nevertheless, despite this optimism, there had been cautious investment guidelines in place at that time. In a major study of proposed financial guidelines in November 1965, Albert Egermayer's finance committee report noted that "the determination of optimum working capital for a company such as Cargill is a delicate matter." Having too much working capital "is patently an improper use of the company's resources," but having too little entailed the risk of "impairing vital short term credit facilities." The committee advocated "a cushion, looking ahead to the possibility that earnings may not always be satisfactory."

A guideline had been put in place at that time of 1.50:1 for the working capital ratio, but this had not been achieved in any one of the previous seven years (the average over those years was just 1.37:1). This persuaded the committee in 1967 to conclude, perhaps a bit pragmatically after the fact, that 1.40 was indeed "a realistic standard." Egermayer did point out that in the previous 10 years up to 1967, the Company had allocated approximately 65 percent of cash earnings for capital expenditures, retaining 35 percent for working capital and dividends.

Now, in July 1973, the ebullience of the times seemed to persuade most of senior management that "looser brakes" for financial policy were in order. Don Levin, the Company's chief financial officer, concluded as to the working capital ratio that "a guideline range provided a better financial reference point than an absolute ratio." The board then agreed upon a surprisingly bullish 1.20–1.40:1 range. Levin also proposed that a liquidity ratio be established—the ratio of liquid assets (i.e. cash, drafts, and invoices in the process of collection and inventories) related to notes payable to banks. The directors adopted a range here, too, between 1.10:1 and 1.25:1. They also further concurred that "the annual discipline of having no unsecured borrowings at the end of the fiscal year be continued."

Levin, however, wanted a further constraint and proposed that "with respect to funded debt and earnings-times-interest, guidelines should also be adopted." The directors agreed that pretax earnings plus interest on funded debt should cover interest on funded debt four times (with mortgage debt on vessels not included within the funded debt ratio.)

In sum, this seminal discussion at the July 1973 board meeting added further refinements on the constraint system in place while at the same time reflecting the highly optimistic feeling of the board about the Company's prospects after three excellent years.

The first barge built by Cargo Carriers, Inc., in its new facility at Pine Bluff, Arkansas, was launched before 400 enthusiastic onlookers at ceremonies on January 18, 1974. The jumbo barge, 200 feet long, 35 feet wide, 12 feet deep, and weighing 280 tons, was capable of carrying 1,500 tons of grain, salt, coal, or other dry bulk commodities (Cargill News, January–February 1974).

"No Dabbling in Small Ventures"

The directors next turned to discussion of specific investment opportunities. Guidelines on these, too, had been evolving over the past decade. A July 1967 board meeting argued for supporting "aggressive diversification and expansion policies . . . as evidenced by our recent activities." A July 1969 meeting expanded corporate goals to "stress entrance into fields where the Company could use its management skills, expertise, and know-how without the requirement that it be closely associated with agriculture or necessarily complementary to an existing product or service line." However, in order not to "fragment our management efforts," the board placed a caveat that "we only consider entrance into businesses in which we have the potential of being a significant factor." While "we insist on at least 51% ownership control, we will consider a minority position in sound foreign ventures where the investment clearly will be an aid to and promote our other corporate objectives—particularly our trading activities." This seemed to expand a 1964 definition that, while foreign partners might be needed, "except in special circumstances the corporation should have control of the foreign venture."

In the July 26, 1970, meeting, the board expounded an interesting but somewhat fuzzy concept of foreign investments: "Each investment, whether in the United States or abroad, should be looked at on its own merits in comparison to alternative investments. . . . Instead of merely comparing investment opportunities in the United States against foreign investments, the comparisons should initially be against alternatives within specific areas such as United States, Europe, Spain, Central America, Latin America, and Asia and then compared against investment opportunities outside the above-named areas." Projected returns required from higher-risk countries "should be substantially higher than the rate of return required for more stable countries."

While the Company did engage in some truly pioneering ventures abroad, more often than not, "pioneering" was taken to mean that Cargill should not risk much money. The result was often an insignificant market penetration, lacking resources of money and people. As one executive remembered, putting it colloquially, "the Japanese ate our lunch in Asia."

In the July 1972 meeting, the directors first spoke boldly to the always-present swings in the business cycle: "The cyclical nature of a business by itself should not be a reason to either accept or reject a potential business." Then the board returned to its effort to more precisely define the optimum size of a new endeavor: "Cargill should not enter businesses where there was relative ease of entry and where there was rather rapid market response to product production. Cargill should avoid operating in businesses where a small operator with low capital investment and personal labor input might well have the advantage." They continued with what appears to have been an unintentionally cautious constraint: "Cargill should look at businesses that require more substantial capital input which satisfy a basic and continuing need that may appear to others to be declining. Such businesses, bought well and managed well, can produce a more than satisfactory return on invested capital."[4]

It was at this point that Pete McVay made the trenchant observation that was debated over and over in this period of burgeoning expansion. He observed in the meeting that, in entering new areas of activities, "we should look for major areas of activity, i.e., 30 to 50 million dollar projects." Each new venture should be approached carefully and prudently, but there appeared a consensus at the meeting that "there should be no dabbling in small ventures." The hurdle rate was, indeed, then set at 30 to 50 million dollars—quite in excess of any of the new projects in the previous period. McVay's point, however, was compelling: small projects dissipate energies; large projects can provide a true critical mass.[5]

New Acquisitions, New Directions

A first sharp departure from the Company's traditional activities came internally, just prior to the Russian grain sales of 1972, when the Company added financial services as a Cargill initiative. This involved attracting customer investors, acting as their brokers, and also involving Cargill itself in the financial markets. Kelm and others felt strongly that the Company should not be trading on its own account and at the same time giving advice and service to customers; so this activity evolved into two separate entities, Cargill Investor Services, and the Financial Markets Group. Both became permanent, important additions to the Company.

Just at the point when the Russian grain sales of 1972 were being negotiated, the *Green Wave* of August 4 announced two acquisitions destined to take Cargill into uncharted territory—one to purchase majority interest in Impact, Inc., which held 54 percent of C. Tennant, Sons & Co., the other to purchase the assets of Burrus Mills, Inc. Tennant would now take the Company into metals trading; Burrus, into flour milling.

Tennant had its earliest existence in New York City in 1825 (as James Lee & Co.) importing chemicals; in 1845 it became the agent of a British house carrying the Tennant name. Later, Tennant bought James Lee, and the firm turned to considerable trading in ferromanganese, antimony, graphite, sheelite, and wolfram ore. After World War II, tin, copper, and manganese ore became dominant. By the time of the Cargill acquisition, Tennant was importing a wide variety of other products, including kapok, menthol, pepper, and cinnamon, as well as exporting plastics and industrial chemicals.

Tennant became a responsibility of Tradax, which purchased the remaining shares for 100 percent ownership; the total cost for *all* the shares came to $5,950,000. Earnings were modest in the first year, but in 1973–1974, Tennant "turned in its best year in history . . . in spite of disastrous losses in speculative

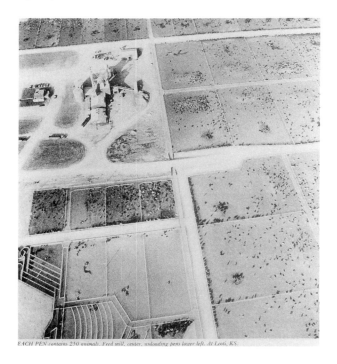

EACH PEN contains 250 animals. Feed mill, center, unloading pens lower left. At Leoti, KS.

Three custom cattle-feeding lots in the Panhandle of Texas and a fourth in southwest Kansas were the concern of Cargill's Caprock Industries, headquartered in Gruver, Texas. The operations had a total capacity of 155,000 head. Pictured here are the pens at Leoti, Kansas (Cargill News, January–February 1976).

trading positions exceeding $6,000,000 in copper, silver and zinc." This was certainly a remarkable feat, but such a huge speculative loss gave Tradax executives pause. In 1978, the international headquarters of Tennant was moved from New York City to the Cargill Office Center in Minnetonka, Minnesota.

Burrus Mills had its main operations in Dallas, with a flour mill, a corn mill, and a milo mill, together with a terminal; there were two other terminals, one at Fort Worth, the other at Amarillo. The mill at Fort Worth was one of the largest in Texas. The firm had been in milling since just after the Civil War. Gerald Mitchell, who had the executive supervision of the new member of the Cargill family, stressed the opportunity for the Company to "learn about the flour industry." The lessons stuck, and with the addition in early 1974 of Ross Industries, Inc., operator of several flour mills in Kansas, flour milling became a significant Cargill activity. (The costs here were just over $2 million for Burrus, $8.4 million for Ross).

An exotic addition to Cargill's panopoly was accomplished in 1973 as

Tradax built and then managed a Holiday Inn in Ghent, Belgium. It opened in May 1974, "with restaurant and bar sales well in excess of expectations." There were even thoughts of opening other motels in both Belgium and the Netherlands. But continuing low occupancy rates soon brought losses, and the operation was sold back to Holiday Inns, Inc., in the fiscal year 1978–1979. Most Company management breathed a sigh of relief—being a hotelier was just too far afield. Indeed, mention of "Holiday Inn" later became synonymous with "folly" around the Company! But it *was* an initiative mentioned by more than one person when Kelm had solicited "new directions" in 1969.

Equally offbeat was Cargill's small effort in solid waste recycling and disposal, with the purchase in 1974 of Aenco, Inc., of New Castle, Delaware. At this point the 26-person operation served only that one city, but the firm also was attempting to innovate by developing a new rotary air classifier and a composter. With only modest success, the operation was sold in 1979.

Another initiative in 1974 took Cargill into peanuts, with the purchase of

"Garbage is the challenge; Aenco firm in Delaware seeks answers." Cargill took a role in one of newest of new industries—solid waste recycling and disposal—when it acquired Aenco, Inc., operating a plant at New Castle, Delaware, servicing a suburban population of 450,000 in an area 30 miles across. A landfill near Delaware Memorial Bridge generates heat and in cold weather attracts thousands of gulls; the fill does not need covering earth because edible material is absorbed, mainly by paper (Cargill News, May–June 1975).

Sylvania Peanut Company, of Sylvania, Georgia. Early efforts under the Commodity Marketing Division (CMD) were unprofitable—"frustrating," said CMD's annual report. The operation continued to limp in the mid- and late 1970s but stayed on the Company roster to achieve later success; the Company has continued to be a force in peanut production.

The year 1974 also witnessed Cargill's entry into commercial feedlot production with the purchase of Caprock Industries in the Texas panhandle at Gruver. Three custom cattle feeding lots in Texas and one in southwest Kansas had a total capacity of 155,000 head. Operations were profitable from the beginning, with a record year of earnings of $3,983,000 in 1977–1978.

There were three acquisitions in this period of the mid-1970s far exceeding the purchase prices of the others mentioned above: the aquisition of a major portion of Peavey Company's Canadian operations in 1974 ($28,200,000), the purchase of North Star Steel Company in early 1975 ($56,963,037), and the acquiring of Hohenberg Brothers Co. in late 1975 ($70,000,000). These were truly within Pete McVay's hurdle rate of $30 to $50 million and would certainly qualify for his dictum, "not dabbling in small ventures."

Cargill was already a presence in Canada, through its subsidiary, Cargill Grain Company, Ltd. Peavey wanted to pull away partially from Canadian grain handling. The sale brought to the Company 286 country elevators and a terminal elevator at Thunder Bay, Ontario. In addition, Cargill also acquired Peavey's National Feeds and Live Stock, Limited, which operated a retail feed business in the four western provinces and a hog breeding plant in British Columbia.

Perhaps the most striking of all of Cargill's acquisitions in the 1970s was the offbeat (for Cargill) new purchase in the mini-mill segment of the steel industry. These small steel mills had metamorphosed from the huge, old-style steel mills (many of which had become moribund). Now scrap only was used; it was melted and conveyed to casting machines, which altered its liquid condition through cooling in a water spray to "yellow-hot" billets. These were reheated and sped through rollers to form customer-requested sizes. The mini-mills had revolutionized the industry.

Cargill now bought a majority interest in a modern young firm, founded in 1967—the North Star Steel Company. Duncan MacMillan, head of Cargill's family company, Waycrosse (the former Cargill Securities Company), had identified the opportunity. The first endeavor was only for a small plant in St. Paul, but this rapidly grew to a major Cargill activity with the acquisition in early 1975 of the Iowa Steel Mill of Wilton, Iowa, just being built. Soon a plant was opened in Duluth to make steel grinding balls for the taconite industry. In late 1977, the Company began the construction of another new mill, in Monroe, Michigan; when it was operational, the Company's annual steel production would exceed one million tons.

By this time, Cargill had acquired all of the stock of North Star (it was merged into Nutrena Mills, then renamed North Star; the name "Nutrena" still stayed in the Feed Division lexicon of products, of course, but it was still a tug to see the name "Nutrena Mills" disappear after so many years).

Erv Kelm described the mini-steel plants as "just another commodity activity," and Pete McVay, one of the initiators of the effort said, too, that the processes involved were analogous to soybean processing, although the product and the machinery were very different indeed. Perhaps Kelm and McVay were trying to counter any opposition from board members that the Company was moving in a nonagricultural, noncommodity direction. But it certainly was!

North Star began its Cargill operation with a spectacular year in 1974–1975, posting profits of $10.4 million; its return on net worth was 56.3 percent. The next two years recorded small losses, as the organization brought a new plant into operation at Wilton, Iowa. From this point, North Star Steel lived up to its name, going on to become one of the true stars of the Company.

Hohenberg Brothers Company was a closely held cotton merchandising company with offices in Memphis, Tennessee, and operations also in Alabama, Texas, and Arizona. When Cargill acquired it in late 1975, it was just four years away from its centennial. Brothers Adolph and Morris Hohenberg had come from Germany in 1879 to establish a general store in Wetumpka, Alabama. Lending to farmers, they often received cotton in payment. Trading cotton soon became the brothers' obsession, and operations extended all over Alabama and then to Dallas. Headquarters were moved to Memphis in 1933. Acquisition by Cargill left the firm in place as a semiautonomous unit, each company contributing to the other. President Julien Hohenberg told *Cargill News*, "We had an acute need for Cargill's systems of reporting and accounting through computers." Cotton operations contributed $3.5 million in profits its first year (1976–1977), fell off to $2.4 million the next. It, too, has had a secure place in the Company over the succeeding years.[6]

The Soybean Embargo of 1973

By January 1973, prices for the various wheats had come back toward the levels prior to the Russian sale. Cash wheat in the third week of January stood at $2.58; the near-term futures were similar. There was little doubt, on the other hand, that the massive export sales through that previous six months had drawn stocks down dramatically. By early March, the farmers were said to be planning record acreage. Still, it startled almost everyone in the trade to hear the government announce that its own grain holdings were just about sold out; a *New York Times* headline trumpeted: "U.S. Government to Leave Business within Ten Weeks—Free Market Is Due" (the word *leave* was a bit misleading—the government really was reducing its holdings to near pipeline levels). The ending "marketing year" stocks of government-owned wheat were estimated to be 439 million bushels, down from 863 million in the previous year.

One of the results of the Russian sales was a marked rise in food prices, part of a large jump in the cost-of-living index. While some of this upward pressure on prices was certainly the effect of these sales, inflation had been looming since the year 1971. Indeed, on August 15, 1971, the government had actually imposed a 90-day freeze on prices and wages but had exempted *all* raw agricultural products. This so-called Phase I was replaced at the end of the 90 days by Phase II, which set guidelines of 5.5 percent increases for wages and 2.5 percent for prices. Once again, raw food products were exempt at the first point of sale. Inflation did seem to cool coincident with the drop in wheat prices, and on January 11, 1973, a new phase, III-A, was announced. Mandatory controls were ended, replaced by a totally voluntary system.

But these plans soon went awry with new inflationary pressures, and on June 13, 1973, the Nixon administration announced Phase III-B, another price freeze (of 60 days), to remain in place until Phase IV controls could be drawn up. At the time of this announcement, the President warned that new export sales might be limited but that the United States would honor existing export commitments.

One highly visible element that appeared to be pushing this inflationary uptick was the sharp rise in soybean prices. Even as voluntary controls were being instituted in January, soybean prices were surging, particularly for old-crop beans. By the first week of February, the price of the near-term futures contract was over $5, a new historic high (the spurt fueled by rumors that the Soviets were in the market to purchase additional soybeans because of their smaller-than-expected sunflower seed crop). A month later, in the first week of March, the price had risen to $7, nudged again by a large order from the Soviet Union.

One of the central lessons of the 1972 Russian grain sales was just how little the federal government really knew about the industry's sales plans. Over and over, outside experts trumpeted the shortfall in government information. Many suggested the adding of specific reporting requirements by private industry. In late April, Carroll Brunthaver, the Assistant Secretary of Agriculture, announced what the *New York Times* dubbed "an unprecedented reporting system," one that mandated weekly announcements on grain and soybean sales by American traders. There was a catch, however—the exporters would not be required to report their sales until 21 days after they were made, "meaning the public may not learn about big new deals much faster than it did last year" (so editorialized the *Times*). Brunthaver explained the 21-day delay as "necessary to give the companies some time to buy the grain they agree to sell." If deals were reported immediately, Brunthaver maintained, market prices could be pushed up before the traders acquired grain to "cover the sale," and this might reduce total export sales. This seemed déjà vu to some critics.

The spectacular price advances for soybeans continued into June; on June 4, the July futures contract jumped by 80 cents a bushel to a record $12.12 (it had been $3.27 one year back). It was at this point that President Nixon announced Phase III-B, with its 60-day price freeze. The President's message, said the *New York Times*, "spurs confusion of traders—commodity dealers are in a quandary." As prices fluctuated wildly in the commodity pits, the Commodity Exchange Authority (CEA) requested the Chicago Board of Trade (CBOT) to suspend trading for a day. But the CEA had no real authority to suspend trading in *any* commodity; the CBOT temporized, and the chaos in the markets continued.

Finally, on June 27, the government moved decisively. Secretary of Commerce Frederick B. Dent imposed export controls on both soybeans and cottonseed and the meal and oil produced from them. The embargo, said the *New York Times*, "cast a deep gloom over the nation's commodities exchanges and prices of almost all raw materials were marked down in lackluster dealings." Particularly upsetting was the fact that the embargo reached back to sales already on the books as of June 13; this was perceived as a breach of faith by foreign customers, especially the Japanese. Secretary of Agriculture Earl Butz apparently grudgingly had agreed on the necessity for the embargo, but "the Street" had heard considerable talk about his possible resignation because of it.

Part of the concern about the wisdom of the embargo lay with the conflicting information available to the government at that time. Richard Gilmore had been a legislative assistant specializing in trade for Senator Hubert Humphrey (and was later, in 1976, the staff professional for the Senate Foreign Relations Subcommittee on Multinational Corporations—the Church Committee, responsible for extensive hearings on the grain trade). He later wrote in his book, *A Poor Harvest*:

There were . . . sharp discrepancies in the figures gathered by various agencies . . . the figures on soybean inventories furnished to John Dunlop . . . director of the Cost of Living Council, ranged from 245 million to 265 million bushels with roughly the same spread for soybean crush. The Commerce Department had concluded on 15 June, on the basis of its own analysis, that carryover stocks would be depleted by 31 August and that there would be a shortfall of 1.26 million metric tons in soybean meal. The Department of Agriculture, on the other hand, estimated the end of August soybean inventories at a relatively comfortable 45 million bushels and the corresponding soybean meal inventory at 765,000 metric tons, while forecasting a bumper crop in September. Such discrepancies produced nine different estimates of the quantity of soybeans available for export and might, in a different atmosphere, have challenged the need for an embargo. What they served to highlight, even then, was the inadequacy of the government's information about exports and its nearly complete dependence on the industry for that information.

The Export Sales Reporting System was part of the problem, because the sales reported seemed to exceed the soybean and soybean meal supplies. The trade understood this, knowing (or at least assuming) that this should work itself out through cancellations, delays, and so on. But the Department of Commerce and the White House failed to grasp this commercial reality.

The Nixon administration, so badly burned in public opinion by the "grain coup" of the Russians in the previous year, was not ready now to take any chances. The Department of Commerce viewed the situation with alarm, and its predilections held sway, resulting in an embargo. In almost any circumstance, such an action is a many-edged instrument, with unexpected eventualities often coming into play. The Nixon decision to ban the exports caused an immediate outcry abroad; with the United States producing some two-thirds of Western supplies, the move was seen all over the globe as a manifest threat to international livestock production. The Japanese were particularly disturbed, for the soybean was a vital ingredient in virtually every Japanese meal, and 98 percent of Japan's supply came from the United States. Not only would the various foreign buyers suffer short-term price escalation, but their very dependability of supply now was in question.

While the actual embargo lasted just a week (to July 2), to be replaced by a system of export licenses, the damage to the belief in U.S. dependability was severe, particularly because the embargo had reached back to include contracts that Nixon publicly had "sanctified" in his June 13 speech. As *Milling and Baking News* put it, "The embargo and licensing scheme . . . came as a particular shock in light of the President's assurance in his June 13 address that the nation would honor its commitments while limiting exports. This thought has now been interpreted to mean that nation-to-nation commitments would be upheld, but that private contracts would be abrogated."

The European Economic Community agriculture commissioner, Pierre Lardinois, flew to the United States to argue that American consumers were being given preferential treatment over traditional customers in Europe. "We are really angry at Nixon-san," said Hiroshi Higashimori, the secretary-general of the Japan oilseed processors association. President Georges Pompidou of France personally complained to President Nixon; the *New York Times* commented editorially, "At the apex of the French power structure the lowly soybean is regarded as of more symbolic importance than the sordid Watergate mess."

The Japanese were the most vehement. A high-level mission headed by Secretary of State William Rogers went to Tokyo in mid-July to attempt placation. In early August, Japanese premier Kakuei Tanaka visited Washington; he and his aides received "reasonable assurances" that the soybean controls would be lifted by the early fall. The Commerce Department later replaced the outright embargo with a "cut across" permitting partial shipments and then allowed the full amount of soybeans committed for the month of September to be shipped, but the long-term damage had been done. In a small article hidden away in a back section in the *New York Times* of August 8, 1973, a prophetic news note recounted, "Brazilian farmers are turning from their usual crops needed on the home market"—from corn, cotton, wheat, and even coffee to the "magic" soybean. By mid-September, the *New York Times* stated, "from Europe's viewpoint, the soybean crisis has ended . . . but confidence in the U.S. as a reliable, cheap supplier is lacking."[7]

How the Industry—and Cargill—Handled the Soybean Crisis

During this tension-filled period encompassing the Russian grain sales and the soybean embargo, one might readily have believed—from statements of the public press, government officials, and congressmen—that the individual grain trade companies, especially the "big six," were privy to "everything" and that there was a conspiracy among these grain traders to hide the facts and trade for themselves from preferred positions. Given the arcane nature of the world grain trading venue, with so many different countries involved, one can appreciate why this feeling might have grown so strong at this time.

In truth, by mid-1973 this presupposition had proved to poorly describe the true situation. The relationship among the "big six" traders and their counterparts was also hampered by lack of full knowledge and their desire to cover real supply for soybean crushers (themselves included). There *was* confidentiality of information, each trader against all others. While this confidentiality was understood particularly well by the government administrators at the Department of Agriculture, both they and their counterparts at the Department of Commerce were frustrated by their joint inabilities to garner adequate information. As one Commerce official put it in the midst of the soybean entanglement, "I was presented with a choice of attempting some consultation with the Trade, and running the risk of criticism for the very fact of having consulted with the Trade, and insulating myself from the criticism, but having to move forward in this position of vast ignorance or only the knowledge that we in Government could put together."

This same frustration about not knowing what was going on faced the individual grain trading groups. Again, nowhere is this better illustrated than in the soybean embargo itself. It seemed clear to everyone in the early months of 1973 that old-crop 1972 supplies of soybeans were tightening (the skyrocketing prices noted earlier in this chapter offered telling proof). Grain trading companies are not speculators but middlemen at the interface of providing supply to end users. In Japan, the *sogo shosha*, the trading companies of the huge Japanese *zaibatsus*, were buying heavily all through the first months of 1973. Fearing a shutdown of the American supply lines, they had adopted a preemptive strategy in order to cover their import requirements. As the wild events leading up to the embargo and the institution of the embargo itself played out, the *sogo shosha* clearly had overbought their needs, a strategy that had left them by luck in a comfortable position as the summer tensions built up and prices mounted.

This gave them an opportunity, if they so chose, to make a huge profit by reselling the contracts. Richard Gilmore told of the denouement:

The Sogo Shosha found the temptation irresistible. With their associated processors and feed manufacturers at home well-supplied and a minimum spread of $100 per ton between current market prices and their original purchase price, the Sogo Shosha went for the windfall. They had no trouble finding customers: American companies were only too happy to buy back their contracts from the Japanese at a price below what they would have had to pay on the U.S. spot market prior to the embargo, had they been able to find so much as a seller. U.S. buybacks from the Sogo Shosha in May were on the order of 70,000 metric tons per week. This volume of purchases continued at roughly the same level until the embargo.

But in the process, the Japanese companies had overplayed their hands, for when the embargo was replaced by the licensing system, not as many soybean shipments were to be allowed. This precipitated a crisis in Japan as Japanese carryover quantities dipped very low. The *sogo shosha* were required once again to go into the open market, forced in many cases to purchase Canadian rapeseed (a less desirable substitute) in order to barely squeak through the remainder of the old-crop year.

Cargill's actions in the saga of the soybean embargo later garnered a very high profile because of a special circumstance. In June 1976, Senator Church's hearings on multinational corporations, after having treated several other industries, focused on "international grain companies." Cargill was

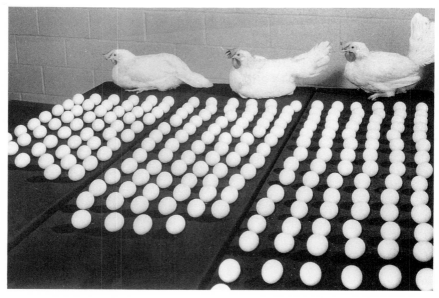

Three "sisters" produced these strikingly different totals of eggs during a 100-day test period at Cargill's Nutrena research farm at Elk River, Minnesota. The one on the right (99 eggs) had the advantage of a special egg-egging formula that soon would be available to help any hen anywhere boost her output (center hen laid 76; the one on the left, 56) (Cargill staff photograph, c. 1961).

chosen to testify. The Company's posture was very different from that in the period immediately after the Russian grain sales, when Cargill had released its self-congratulatory press release that had been so poorly received. In Bill Pearce's absence as trade negotiator for the federal government, John Mc-Grory and Robbin Johnson had moved senior management further along the learning curve toward a professional stance for public affairs, which all three men so eloquently had been advocating. In June 1973, the old name of the de-partment was changed to "public affairs"; at the same time the 15-year use of Carl Byoir & Associates as outside public relations counsel was terminated. Johnson spelled out a broader perspective on the interface of the Company with its publics in a major speech to the processing group in December of that year. Accuracy and integrity were the pillars, with "the corollary to accu-rate information [being] complete information."

Always this was to be accomplished through and with these operating men; this had proved successful, as John McGrory told a meeting of the Long-Range Planning Committee: "Working with operating division person-nel . . . we have generally been regarded as the most persuasive, articulate member of our industry in terms of dealing with government, scholars and press analysts—not press sensationalists." Bill Pearce returned to the Com-pany early in 1974 to head the public affairs group (as a corporate vice presi-dent) and pushed resolutely to senior management an agenda of accurate, complete information with true integrity. By 1976, under this rubric of open-ness, the Company's testimony before the blue-ribbon Church multinational subcommittee turned out to be a tour de force (an important story in itself, to be recounted in Chapter Eight).

One of the questions addressed to Cargill at that time related to this soy-bean embargo period. The Company laid all its figures about its own actions on the table and accompanied them with a detailed and articulate factual analysis of exactly why it had taken these steps. Cargill was a major soybean crusher in the United States, as well as a significant crusher in Europe and South America in its Dutch, Spanish, and Brazilian operations. In addition, the Company traded soybeans and products widely around the world, both through the Minneapolis oilseeds group and by Tradax personnel in Geneva.

Seeing the tight supply situation in the spring of 1973, Cargill told its asso-ciated European processing plants to acquire beans "sufficient to cover their maximum theoretical crushing capacity for the crop year 1973–1974." Ship-ments were to be spaced evenly, priced on the basis of the weighted average f.o.b export price for soybeans shipped in the month preceding. The way these purchases were priced was extraordinary, for both the buyer and the seller gave up merchandising flexibility in order to ensure regularized use of export facilities on the one hand and regularized supplies for processing plants on the other. Transportation congestion and market uncertainties had per-suaded the Company not to use the futures market to hedge market price risks.

President Nixon, in putting in place the startling new set of price controls on June 13, 1973, made the public announcement late in the afternoon by Minneapolis time. Immediately, Cargill responded, contacting all overseas offices through its peerless communications system. "The problem was we needed 'contracts' on the books," a Company senior lawyer remembered, "but contracts needed a 'price' to be valid, and no one knew how to come up with proper prices for what could be far-in-the-future delivery. . . . Since we had advance notices, though less than one day, we put on extra contracts [mostly with affiliates]. . . . Later on, after the delivery dates became much more nearby and more closely in line with normal delivery dates, the contracts were amended to reflect more normal pricing, more typical pricing."

In reviewing its outstanding export commitments up to that point and by matching these against its maximum theoretical crushing capacity at the European plants, the Company found that the total supply under contract would be more than the actual crushing under normal conditions. Minneapolis senior management recommended that the plants reduce their purchases by the amount of overlap between theoretical and practical crushing requirements and 28 million bushels were canceled by mutual agreement on June 20. These cancellations were fully reported to the government that day.

Cargill entered the fall of 1973 with this set of what Company officials dubbed "formula-priced sales" to its affiliated European soybean processing plants, expecting a crush through the summer of 1974 of about 57 million bushels. As the situation over the fall turned to more ample supplies and more normal markets, additional cancellations were made (11 million bushels in September, almost the same amount in October, and 7 million in November).

The Company statement to the Church subcommittee explained this: "Cargill's reluctance to engage in unnecessary cancellations is reflected in the decision announced on July 30 [to] offer unilaterally a 'deferred delivery privilege' to its foreign soybean and soybean meal buyers, if they prefer to accept deferred delivery to forced reduction and shipments." Many, in fact, did accept the deferral. The notion was unique enough for a separate article by the *New York Times*, commenting on Cargill's special "service . . . for foreign buyers who were caught in the Government's control program."

Company people nevertheless chafed under the complexities of the licensing program. The processing group's 1973–1974 annual report stated: "This problem became so gross it was necessary for us to send a person to Washington to do nothing but make license applications and update weekly reports. We found it most desirable to have personal contact with the Department of Commerce people in order to speed up the process of getting export licenses—but the Company was able to get through the fall period with a minimum of ill feelings on the part of its customers."

The number-one customer was, of course, Cargill itself, with its own crushing operations. And the crop year produced some outstanding results. Domestic soybean crushing accounted for an amazing $48.5 million after taxes. The annual report explained: "Government price and margin controls added another complicating dimension to an already challenging year of margins, ranging from 5¢ to $1.50 per bushel. Aggressive programs when margins widened paid off handsomely." Jack Haymaker reported on domestic crushing:

A 500,000 bushel . . . crush for a major refiner that helped solve his price control problem gave us a dollar a bushel margin on beans we feared might be subject to loss on the steep inverse. Some of the fear psychology carried into nucrop [new crop], enabling us to sell large quantities of export meal at very high historic basis levels as well as good quantities of domestic meal at a basis that really wasn't warranted by the feeding prospects in the face of ample supplies of nucrop beans. We then proceeded to buy our fall bean inventories at historically cheap fall accumulation levels in spite of greater than normal farmer holding . . . and a higher than normal f.o.b. export bean market.

On the international side, the Dutch operation made some $10.6 million; Brazil was in second place at $4.2 million. Tradax (Geneva) commodity trading did well for the year; the rice accounts were at the top, contributing $14.7 million profit out of a total for all commodities of $38.2 million. The soybean complex made its own contribution to this, but the Tradax annual report documented some serious problems. The embargo brought "chaos"—the "vast sums of money in question strained business ethics and morality to the utmost. This precedent cast a cloud over trading strategy in all commodities, which will probably be with us for a long time." The authors elaborated upon this later in the report: "This year the 'honourable' character of the business suffered. Defaulting became common practice. Soybean meal traders and shippers looked for and used the flimsiest excuse imaginable not to perform when it best suited them rather than to abide by contract terms or to jump entirely out of contracts [and] there were numerous cases of falsified bills of lading and quality certificates." A gloomy note closed their account: "We had an excellent position prior to the embargo, but afterwards never really got back on track again."

The embargo was traumatic for just about all parties involved. The government garnered much hostility for its overall price control effort, especially Nixon's second "freeze," which was greeted with derision by many. Herbert Stein, chairman of the Council of Economic Advisors, was quoted as having told the President, "You can't step in the same river twice," to which Nixon reputedly replied, "You could, if it was frozen." The analogy did not really seem to fit.

The long-term implications of the embargo were far more serious than had been guessed at the time. The Japanese aggressively turned to alternative sources of soybean supply, Brazil being a favorite choice. Fortunately for Cargill, the Company now was well geared to serve this, with its own Brazilian soybean processing and merchandising businesses; Company executives in Brazil even considered instituting their own production operations, perhaps to grow not only soybeans but other agricultural products.

Some critics faulted Cargill (and others) for, as one writer in the *New Republic* put it, "using the embargo to promote expanded production in Latin America in order to compete with the American export market and increase corporate independence from the U.S." The soybean boom that had begun in the late 1960s *had* led a number of the grain traders—for example, Bunge's subsidiary Sanbra, Continental, Cook, Anderson-Clayton, and Dreyfus—to build in Brazil. The fact that several (including Cargill) had used U.S. government loans and guarantees (through the Overseas Private Investment Corporation [OPIC]) antagonized the American Soybean Association, among others, which felt that the government was subsidizing its competitors. These arguments were protectionist ones, of course, flying in the face of the world-trade, free-market philosophy of this and many other multinational industries.

Nixon's soybean embargo seemed overly self-serving for the United States in the eyes of many of the long-standing, loyal purchasers from abroad. While Cargill came out well for the year in its soybean crushing and trading, the travails of doing business under a governmental system that changed frequently, coupled with the residual hostility from the general public stemming from the Russian grain sales of the previous year, made the soybean embargo a star-crossed endeavor.[8]

Required to Report—but to Whom?

Assistant Secretary of Agriculture Carroll Brunthaver's innovation (established in April 1973), with its tepid requirement that sales were to be reported to the USDA at any time within 21 days following, seemed too ineffectual to satisfy the USDA critics. Now the Department of Commerce stepped into the vacuum with its own reporting requirement, using its statutory authority to invoke export controls given by the Export Administration Act. Agriculture, too, had been working on a new set of provisions but was rudely sidetracked in the July 1973 Senate hearings. Senator Henry Jackson took Earl Butz to task on this: "Mr. Secretary, you had almost a year of trouble. You had the problem on shipping, the problem in connection with some farmers not knowing and others getting the advantage. Why did it take 10 or 11 months to get even a voluntary system in effect?" Butz replied, "Primarily because, as you said, Mr. Steinweg [the Continental Grain vice president] pointed out this is highly confidential material for each individual company. It is the way the American business enterprise works. . . . Sometimes the market goes down . . . it's why the private companies have their own crop reporting estimate services, so they can anticipate the U.S.D.A. crop reports." Butz, it seemed, wanted only a voluntary system and was not moving rapidly even on this.

After Commerce mandated its own system on June 13, 1973, the USDA once again took some initiative, and in the new Agriculture and Consumer Act of 1973 (P.L. 93-86) instituted a system of mandatory reporting. All exporters of wheat, flour, feed grains, oil seeds, and cotton were to report all sales over 100,000 tons within 24 hours of their completion.

Supplies tightened once again in the fall of 1974, and exporters were required to obtain *prior* approval for any sale of over 50,000 tons in a single 24-hour period or of over 100,000 tons in a given week. Then Russia came back into the market, reportedly attempting to purchase as much as 3.4 million tons of corn and wheat. Secretary of Agriculture Butz and Secretary of State Kissinger both preached restraint to the Soviets. But President Ford seemed to panic and called into his office representatives of Continental Grain and Cook (who were to be favored with the deal) and asked them to suspend their sales until the United States could review sales commitments. Richard Gilmore told the story:

The executive officers of the two companies, however, went away with different interpretations of the government's order. Cook maintained that what had been requested was a universal sales suspension. Steinweg of Continental claimed that the agreement affected only sales to the Soviet Union. Their different understandings resulted in a big loss for Cook and a windfall for Continental, since the latter, according to [Cook president] Ned Cook, executed a sale to Iran that Cook had refrained from making in an effort to keep its part of a gentleman's agreement worked out in the White House. Whichever version of the White House meeting is correct, the incident underscores the fact that in 1974 the system was working no better than it had in 1972–73.

By 1975, the pressure to exert tight supply management had tapered off as supplies of grain grew enough to make global scarcities less likely. By October 1975, the government had been persuaded by the private sector that, indeed, a relaxation would contribute to heightened foreign business (the reporting system was not completely eliminated; it was left that any sale of over 100,000 tons had to be reported within 24 hours). The trade disliked even this, feeling that it restricted the free market too much. There was always the fear that information would leak out and prices get away from the sellers before they could hedge in the markets. In the end, as Gilmore wrote, "the prior approval system proved unworkable not only because it cramped industry's free-wheeling style, but also because even a voluntary enforcement system raised questions about preferential treatment of certain companies and certain business practices."[9]

Inflation Becomes a Bugaboo

The huge expansion of U.S. wheat and feed grain exports in 1972, followed by the startling escalation in soybean prices in the first six months of 1973, had a profound influence on food prices and therefore on overall inflation in the country. World grain production fell relative to expanding demand as adverse weather conditions were faced not only in Russia but in South Asia and in sub-Saharan Africa. Meanwhile, consumption jumped, and most developed countries experienced strong economic growth throughout 1973, keeping demand high.

Moreover, successive devaluations of the dollar had made U.S. grains relatively cheaper abroad, which produced the effect of softening the impact of higher prices there. In the United States, grain reserves had been sharply reduced due to a system of acreage set-aside programs with direct cash payments to farmers, which had been substituted for the previous method of stockpiling large amounts of grain. This policy change was not as flexible, for it did not allow shifts into production-oriented approaches until reserves had declined to extremely low levels. Through the year 1973, the Consumer Price Index rose 8.8 percent, and the Wholesale Price Index rose some 15.5 percent. The impact of food prices on these overall increases was highly significant—farm prices jumped some 45.8 percent in early 1973. Along with this was a very sharp acceleration in wholesale prices for crude oil; on October 17, the Arab oil-producing nations imposed an embargo on crude oil to the United States in retaliation for the latter's support for Israel in the 1973 Arab-Israeli war. The embargo was not lifted until March 1974, and in the five-month period of the embargo, oil prices skyrocketed.

In the European Economic Community (EEC) and in Japan, policies designed to insulate consumers from price changes now were put into effect. For example, the EEC variable levy was allowed to decline to zero in December 1973 and subsequently became an export tax. The effect was to keep surplus grains within the EEC. Internal consumption was subsidized, contributing to tighter supplies elsewhere. Fortunately, as the year 1973 ended, prices were moderating all through the commodity markets.[10]

The roller coaster ride during the crop year 1973–1974, with the soybean imbroglio, the Arab oil boycott, and the threats brought by high inflation, nevertheless produced an excellent year for the Company. Profits doubled, to $212 million. The commodity group exceeded previous earnings substantially; although volume was down, margins widened to reflect increased seasonal demands and uncertainties. Soybean profits were at a record high; corn milling, copra, flax, and flour milling all contributed. Feed did well, except for poultry. The annual report to the stockholders summarized: "We were able to employ investments we have made in the past decade in people and facilities both at unprecedented profits to the company and in a major contribution to the nation's economy in a period of stress."

Allegations of "Boxcar Blackmail"

In that first 18-month period after the unprecedented U.S. grain sales to Russia in July and August 1972, staggering problems had surfaced in moving that huge amount of grain from the farms to the ports and into the ocean shipping waiting for it there. Even if everything had worked perfectly with that 30-million-ton surge, the very magnitude alone would have challenged everyone along the route.

But there were further complications. First, the shipping accord with the Russians about the percentages of Russian and American bottoms had come several months late. By the time the agreements had been signed, in December 1972, 10 months of grain movement had to be compressed into approximately 5. A second severe problem occurred immediately after: major flooding of key rivers in the Midwest all through the spring of 1973. Barge traffic on the larger rivers, particularly the Mississippi, was severely curtailed, throwing added traffic to already burdened railroads. Then, when the Arab oil embargo began later in that year (October), the costs of fuel for the third arm of grain movement—the truck—rose precipitously, once again affecting the complex competitive relationship among these three transport competitors. Clearly, the railroads were to take the brunt of the movement in the crop years of both 1972–1973 and 1973–1974.

In many respects, the railroads were ill-prepared for this. A number of the midwestern and Plains states railroads—the so-called Granger railroads—had slipped into slim margins, with some close to bankruptcy. The strict rate regulation placed upon the railroads by the Interstate Commerce Commission (ICC) constrained rate flexibility. A report in July 1974 by the Federal Railroad Administration put this problem well:

In times of enhanced demand, the rates charged by carriers hauling commodities not subject to uneconomic regulation by the Interstate Commerce Commission are quickly raised to a level where physical shortage [of equipment] is no longer relevant—the market clears at the new price level . . . the pricing mechanisms used by carriers of unregulated commodities encourage maximum flexibility.

In the case of railroads, however, the inability to adjust rates to reflect change in demand poses severe problems for the carriers in meeting shipper needs with responsive and flexible transportation. Particularly in the rail movement of bulk agricultural commodities, the lack of a responsive pricing capability means that little or no demand restraints operate to smooth or regulate the flow of such large-volume commodities as grain. . . . The net result is that little incentive is afforded grain marketers to develop storage and movement combinations to utilize off-peak transport capacity, and post-harvest car shortages frequently occur when movement requests exceed available local or regional equipment availability.[11]

However, there was one key innovation in rail grain carrying that was to exert a profound influence on the situation. This was the unit train, popularly known as the Rent-a-Train (RAT).

Cargill's pioneering RAT with the Illinois Central Railroad had been an almost instantaneous success. This innovative concept utilized primarily the "Big John" aluminum-covered hopper cars discussed in Chapter Two. The cars most widely used were the popular four-compartment, 4,713-cubic-foot capacity, able to carry a load of 223,000 pounds (111.5 tons). Unit trains of at least 100 hopper cars—115 was a common number—were sent forward from

Gibson City, Illinois: Erwin E. Kelm (left), president of Cargill, Inc., and William B. John-son, president of Illinois Central Railroad, at historic ceremonies marking the inaugural run of the "Rent-a-Train," the nation's first. Kelm presented Johnson with a check for $66,666, representing the first month's rental payment (Cargill staff photograph, November 1968).

the Company's new 3.6-million-bushel inland export terminal at Gibson City, Illinois, to Cargill's export terminal at Baton Rouge, Louisiana, and were returned to Gibson City within five days. The Company was committed to Illinois Central to accomplish a minimum of 56 round trips per year; in its first year of operation, 57 train trips were completed.

This had not been easy to accomplish, as it required a steady volume of incoming grain, and as a Cargill background paper reported, "The problem is buying sufficient grain to meet a unit train schedule in the face of producer psychology which told producers that a pretty urgent buyer was in the market who had to fill a train against some severe penalties." But this was a challenge that readily could be met by building good farmer relationships. By the following spring, Cargill had opened a second inland export terminal of the same size at Tuscola, Illinois, and was planning a third terminal at Clinton, Illinois.

So successful was the RAT idea that there was an immediate competitive response by other grain companies in conjunction with other railroads. By April 1969, just seven months after the inaugural train from Baton Rouge, another RAT had been established by the Norfolk & Western Railway to go

"Rear platform remarks are made to press and visitors by Cargill's President Kelm and Illinois Central's President Johnson. Parlor and Pullman cars shortly were picked by fast Panama Limited for the trip to the Gulf" (*Cargill News*, December 1968).

from Gibson City, Champaign, and Homer, Illinois, not to a Gulf port but directly to Norfolk, Virginia. This new rate contract even eased the requirements for minimum numbers of trips, in this case cut from 54 to 10.

Within a year, these rates to the East had spread to origins in Ohio and Indiana and put the Gibson City and other Illinois origins under heavy competitive pressure. Cargill quickly changed its plans for the proposed Clinton, Illinois, terminal, scrapping it in favor of a terminal at Linden, Indiana, to be an originating point for shipments east to Norfolk. Interestingly, Cargill could quite handily compete with itself there, for the Company also had a well-positioned export terminal at Norfolk. It was a hurly-burly period for RAT competition, but the bottom line was that the system had become an outstanding success. This success, however, was focused particularly on the three states of Illinois, Indiana, and Ohio. The states of Iowa and Minnesota were not in the running, and therein a simmering controversy began to build.[12]

Small-Quantity Problems in Iowa

The railroads serving Iowa, faced with the increasing RAT efforts in their neighboring states with traffic to the East, chose a strategy that subsequent events would prove to be "too little too late." The Rock Island Railroad was the first Iowa carrier to attempt a RAT; its original proposal in May 1970 was protested, and it did not become effective until June 1971. Fatally, the Rock Island did not elect to use a 100-car unit but instead a 54-car train. Even this had an optional rate level for two cuts of 27 cars and actually allowed some smaller multiples. The Rock Island alone served an incredibly large number of mostly small Iowa country elevators—some 853 had licenses. Most of these would require much modernization to make them effective, even at the load level of the smaller unit trains. Then, in July 1972, the other two principal Iowa carriers, the Chicago & Northwestern and the Milwaukee Road also came into the picture, being granted two rate levels, available to 50-car and 25-car units. These latter rates became effective only after July 1972.

This was just at the point of the Russian grain sales, and the requisite modernizations, difficult as they would be to accomplish, had just begun. This obvious case of piecemeal modernization by the three carriers might have worked had not the Russian sales intervened. Technological innovation already had taken place all over among farmers and middlemen, including, somewhat belatedly, those in Iowa. Rapid modernization also had been occurring at many country elevators across the country in order to be able to serve unit trains. However, this was *not* happening among the Iowa elevators, and the owners now paid the price in their efforts to manage the Soviet purchases. Wheat exports had jumped from 632 million bushels in the crop year 1971–1972 to 1.186 billion in 1972–1973. Soybean exports also gained substantially that year, and corn exports had almost doubled, from 796 million bushels to 1.3 billion bushels. The unit train was ideally suited to handle this huge additional volume.

Jim Springrose, Cargill's vice president in charge of transportation, testifying before a subsequent House of Representatives committee, illustrated the gap between RAT and the old way: "Railroad equipment used in single-car service can average about 55 miles per day. By paying greater attention to car control, utilizing modern computer techniques and refining scheduling . . . Cargill has been able to increase that average to 90 miles per day. . . . By combining hopper cars in multiple-car shipments of unit trains we have been able to triple that latter figure to 280 miles per day per car." The unit train could be kept moving more of the time (it had been estimated that, historically, railroad cars were actually moving, either loaded or empty, only about 10 percent of the time).

By 1973, there were some 204,270 covered hopper rail cars, just over 60 percent owned by the railroads themselves and 40 percent by private shippers.

By this time, Cargill had a fleet of 1,073 of these hopper cars, most of them of the "Big John" size; it did not own any of these but leased them, primarily from the Pullman Transport Leasing Company, with a 12- to 15-year contract at just over $200 per month per car (during the heavy-use period of the Russian shipments, the lessor was able to add a lease maintenance escalation clause to cover the excessive wear and tear). With all shippers and carriers looking for the most efficient way of shipping, when new equipment became available, preferences toward sending these new units to the unit train operators was common.

This tilt toward the unit trains, both for obtaining new equipment and for existing hopper-car allocation, quickly impacted negatively on the smaller shippers—assuredly for those who still were loading just a few "free-running" cars at a time and even for those (as in Iowa) who were putting together unit trains of 25 to 50 cars. Rumors quickly circulated that farmers selling to these elevators were being asked to absorb a discount, said sometimes to be as high as 25 cents per bushel. Further, premiums were alleged to be pushed upon the country elevator by the larger shippers in order to assign a car to them. Cases of such "boxcar blackmail," as the alleged practice began to be called, surfaced all over the Midwest but were particularly focused in Iowa and southern Minnesota. Farmers and small elevator operators felt they were being crunched by the market power of the larger shippers.

In particular, the "big six" grain trading companies faced much hostile opposition, given the context of the times. With the Watergate hearings now in progress and the investigative reporting of the press combining with keen congressional interest in instituting additional hearings of various sorts, it is not surprising that such an inquiry now focused on the transportation equipment shortages.[13]

A New Player—the House Committee on Small Business

In late July 1973, Representative Neal Smith, the chairman of a subcommittee on "special small business problems" in the House of Representatives, convened hearings related to the "marketing of grain and other commodities." Three days of these hearings were held in July, three more in September, and three more in October.

The focus in these first hearings primarily was on the functioning of the futures markets. Smith made clear in his opening statement his concern about the possible existence of manipulation and squeezing and the relationship of these alleged excesses to the Commodity Exchange Act. His primary constituency seemed explicit when he stated that his goal was to "investigate to see whether the purpose of the Act is being frustrated to the disadvantage of the innumerable small businesses engaged in agriculture in the processing and distribution of agricultural products." The subcommittee also promised to look into the lack of transportation facilities, which, Smith maintained, "are so limited that grain cannot be delivered in fulfillment of a contract," with "many businessmen having to store their product at great cost to themselves considerably beyond the date when a market was available."

As part of these hearings, Cargill was asked to testify and agreed to do so. Continental had also been asked but declined; according to Smith, "they chose not to appear voluntarily." Smith added, "We do have subpoena power, and if they have any information we need, we will get it [in June 1974, almost a year later, Clarence Palmby did testify for Continental]. But I do want to compliment Cargill for voluntarily coming and wanting to help us round out this record."

Jim Spicola, Cargill's group vice president for the processing group, carried the main testimony for the Company. Most of his comments and the questions addressed to him by subcommittee members focused again on the commodity markets and on Cargill's proposals for a "strategic agricultural commodity reserve" for the country as a whole, an impressive, rather longer-range notion but not high on anyone's agenda at this time. Strangely, there were just a few questions on the transportation shortages of early 1973.

The focus, however, changed markedly by the time the subcommittee reconvened for a second and third set of hearings in the period May–July, 1974. By this time, the transportation log jams and the ensuing slippages, together with the increasing number of accusations of discrimination against the small shipper, turned the hearings in both of these sessions explicitly to transportation. Several days of hearings were held in the field, at Des Moines, Iowa, and Omaha, Nebraska. "Especially in this time of high petroleum prices and short petroleum supplies," Smith stated at the beginning, "we must strive to use our most efficient modes." There were not enough railcars and "tremendous underutilization" of those already in use; congestion at several of the export ports was severe, especially at Houston, Baton Rouge, and New Orleans. Smith charged the subcommittee to search for suggestions "to alleviate current transportation bottlenecks and decrease the cost of movement."

A litany of complaints ensued. The rail bottlenecks, in particular came in for violent criticism. During most of this entire period, there had been significant congestion in the Kansas City, Missouri, railyards, which had led to worsening problems at the Gulf ports themselves. Two General Accounting Office (GAO) investigators had been deputed to the subcommittee and had made several field investigations of the port of Houston. In early 1973, it had rained there a great deal, even snowed three times; and by July, Houston had received 18 inches of rain above normal. This prevented the loading of ships and caused softening of the railbeds under the heavy traffic, thus reducing speeds. "When the grain shipments began to congest and a car shortage developed," the investigators noted, "the railroads began to use open top hopper cars for grain shipment with the approval of the shippers. This proved to be a big mistake, primarily because of the extremely wet weather experienced by these cars from the origin to the port destination. In some cases, these cars sat for over a month before being unloaded. Therefore, the grain became too wet, crusted, and even sprouted. These cars were extremely difficult to unload . . . had to be unloaded manually and only a few were unloaded each day." The chaos compounded, eventually causing the Port of Houston to endure a number of rail embargos, promulgated by the Car Service Division of the Association of American Railroads. Each embargo further backed up Kansas City and other intermediate points.

All of these glitches in the previously smooth-running inland-to-Gulf movement of grain put pressures back on the individual shippers, with the shortages of railstock making the competition between and among individual railroads and grain shippers like Cargill and between and among country elevator shippers ever more intense. The unit train being far more efficient in moving grain, the superior bargaining power of major shippers like the "big six" grain companies became more evident. Jim Springrose, in his testimony representing Cargill, put the issue frankly:

Greater efficiency in origination of grains by country elevators is needed. More careful scheduling of delivery and loading at internal transfer points is needed. . . . In our experience, many country elevators are moving quickly to capture these many potentialities by making needed improvements. At the same time, there are some locations which are unable or unwilling to adjust and face these difficult choices. In approaching this question, I think it is fair to ask what best serves the long term interests of American farming. Farmers have been increasing their productivity at $2\frac{1}{2}$ times the rate for manufacturing industries. Domestic processors and merchandisers, as well as exporters, are committing capital and expertise to serve better America's vast productive potential. Should these efforts and plans by farmers, processors, and merchandisers be frustrated by those avoiding responsibility such opportunities entail?"[14]

In the 14 days of intense exchanges before the subcommittee, multiple complaints about the efficacy of the rail transportation system surfaced. The railroads' dilemmas absorbed the lion's share of the testimony. Their capital deficits were decried, their deteriorating roadbeds and faulty equipment recounted. Both the railroads and the Interstate Commerce Commission were taken to task by several witnesses for what some believed to be excessive abandonments of trackage. Small-town or out-of-the-way shipping points had seemed to be shunted aside in the rush for abandoning "low traffic" points of origination. The railroads were faulted by many of these same shippers for allowing the sharp upswing in privately owned railcars, which were a particular manifestation of the RATs. Even the USDA, the perennial friend of the farmer, was faulted by the latter for grabbing too many boxcars in order to ship their own CCC-stored grain. The sharp trend upward in shipper-owned railcars by the private grain companies, both owned and leased, was a particular focus of significant parts of the testimony.

Throughout these two provocative sets of hearings, the theme of efficiency provided a major touchstone. The great success story of the RATs was cited over and over in the hearings, particularly aided by the positive thrust given them by Jim Springrose's seminal statement.

But many times, too, his thesis was referred to with concern and even fear. The fact that the very large grain companies—the "big six" in particular—were the protagonists of the RATs added a further concern linked to the same kinds of fears raised by the Russian grain sales two years previously. In their final report, the subcommittee articulated an ambivalence that seemed to be felt by many in the hearings:

The economies of scale heretofore discussed involve mammoth operations from high-speed loading facilities in the grainbelt, use of jumbo covered hopper cars in continuous unit train service, an operation of huge export facilities at ports, all of which seem ideally suited for the huge grain shipper, primarily the private grain company. But what of the small shipper, the local elevator operator and small farmer? Obviously he can supply neither the capital nor the amount of grain needed to take advantage of these new marketing concepts. Is he doomed to extinction because of the marketing innovations which permit a giant marketer to move his grain to a port for 10, 20, or 30 cents per bushel less than the individual entrepreneur?

The subcommittee's final statement put their concerns well:

The Subcommittee is heartened by the innovations . . . in the grain marketing system, as they hold out great promise as methods to transport ever-increasing amounts of grain at a lower cost. . . . The subcommittee is, however, greatly troubled by the control which the giant grain companies are acquiring in this entire chain. It is the largely unregulated giants, about which little is known, which control some 90 percent of the grain business; it is the same companies which are acquiring their own fleet of barges and railcars; it is these same companies which are constructing the subterminals in the Grain Belt and the port facilities needed to handle such large and repeated shipments and it is these same companies which already account for about 1/2 of the existing elevators and elevator capacity at major ports.

Admittedly, the grain companies cannot be said to be dominating all of these links . . . to some extent they have been forced or at least encouraged to become more dominant because common carriers did not expand facilities and equipment enough to meet the demand, but they are expanding in each of them and it appears to be economically feasible for them to continue to do so until they do achieve the feared dominance.

At that point, what will become of all the small business grain producers and marketers? Unless in some way they are able to participate in the "new system" and reap the advantages of the lower cost rapid transportation involved, how will they be able to compete with the giants?

Just as in the Senate and House investigations of the Russian sales, another competing governmental agency had been asked to separately assess the boxcar crisis. It was none other than the ubiquitous GAO. Back in March 1974, Montana representative John Melcher, a member of the House Committee on Agriculture (but not the Subcommittee on Small Business) had requested the GAO to ascertain whether there had been discounting in the boxcars, whether the "Interstate Commerce Commission should be doing something it had not done," and whether the Elkins Act (prohibiting rate discrimination) had been violated. The GAO was put in a delicate position here inasmuch as it did not have legal authority to audit records of private sales of the companies involved and therefore was not able to verify alleged concessions or discriminations between railroads and grain shippers. The GAO did interview some country elevator proprietors and also looked at the ICC's efforts to develop a rate structure for the unit trains. All this, however, was really the purview of the ICC rather than the GAO, and the latter backed off.[15]

The chairman of the ICC, George M. Stafford, had taken a major role in the House hearings, particularly because many of the practices in car allocations and other related matters had been set in place at the beginning by an ICC rate-making decision. Stafford promised that the ICC itself would take up such issues as the Iowa and Minnesota small shippers' allegation that discounting had been forced upon them by those who controlled the boxcars and who were presumably extracting such monies for use with the RATs.

The House subcommittee itself was limited in what it could promulgate as remedies. It had some words for several other federal agencies in its conclusions, but the primary focus was on the ICC. The ICC was urged to look again at its definitions of RAT size constraints and those other features that provided continuity to the unit train notion. The ICC's regulations on allocations were to be looked at and the discounting issue to be addressed. Stafford had seen to the initiation back in July 1974 of an ICC investigation, *Ex Parte No. 307*, described in its title as an "investigation into the distribution and manipulation of rail rolling stock to depress prices on certain grain shipments for export." This case now became the defining one.[16]

Settling the "Boxcar Blackmail" Issue—Ex Parte No. 307

Beginning in November 1974, the ICC's Bureau of Enforcement began extensive field investigations of the "blackmail" complaints. In early March 1975, at a public prehearing conference, an attorney for the bureau told the attorneys for the respondent railroads and larger grain companies that were parties to the rate case that "evidence indicates there has been discounting on grain tariffs. . . . These may or may not be unlawful [but] . . . testimony from grain shippers included the charge that all the exporting companies were 'extorting' them."

A *Journal of Commerce* article then identified the companies: "Grain exporters involved . . . are Bunge, Cargill, Central Soya, Continental Grain, Louis Dreyfus, and Cook Industries." The implication laid by the ICC's attorney was that *all* of these grain exporters were involved in illegal discounting. The prehearing findings were picked up widely by the press; the *Des Moines Register*, in a lead editorial, called it "gouging grain farmers" and charged that

Earl Butz "in his passion for the free market" had been "turning over the control of grain exports, marketing and prices to the four or five dominant grain companies, to the disadvantage of farmers."

Unfortunately, the ICC's Bureau of Enforcement was unwilling to name its informants. The railroads and grain companies finally used provisions of the Freedom of Information Act to bring this into the open. Forced by this legal request, the ICC brought into the hearings in late July 1975 a series of sworn statements that alleged, as the *Washington Post* put it, a "situation where the major grain export firms have managed to gain control of a significant share of available freight cars. . . . Unable to get box cars for grain and unwilling to let the crops rot in elevators, Midwest producers have been forced in many instances to sell grain at a discount to big grain firms—just to get it moved." The *Washington Star* added, "The discounting practices have been uncovered in Indiana, Illinois and Iowa and involve at least eight grain merchandising companies." The *Star* once again mentioned, prominently, Bunge, Dreyfus, Continental, Central Soya, Cargill, and Cook and added Lincoln Grain Inc. and Taber Co. The "insatiable" demands of the unit trains were mentioned in several of the articles.

But as the case moved into formal hearings and the ICC commissioners themselves began to sift the evidence compiled by the Bureau of Enforcement, it began to appear to the commissioners that a great many of the allegations of the elevator operators were not, indeed, overt discounts, illegal under the law, but normal competitive bargaining relationships dictated by the period of boxcar shortages. It seemed equally evident that there was also some actual discounting going on. The commissioners needed to sort out which was which.

Cargill officials felt certain that the Company had done none of this discounting. Jim Springrose, in his sworn statement in the hearings, made this abundantly clear: "Cargill applied normal marketing principles to the changing situation and the market facts it faced in 1972/74. I do not know how it could have functioned differently. It did not 'discount,' it did not 'black market,' it did not 'manipulate rolling stock to depress prices.' It merchandised grain. I do not know how to say this any differently nor how to make the facts any clearer."

He continued:

The Bureau has alleged a number of instances where exporters or processors who leased their own equipment purchased grain and made a specific charge per bushel for furnishing equipment which was written into the contract variously as "equipment usage," "minus 10 equip.," "10 car usage," "3 ¢ Disc for leased hops," etc. This was not a Cargill practice and Cargill did not use its leased cars in this manner. There are further allegations by the Bureau that certain exporters or processers were purchasing single cars of grain or small multiple car groups (I use this term to distinguish it from unit trains) in carrier equipment, which they furnished, paid less than they, or someone else, was offering for grain to sell unfurnished equipment. In the case of all these practices in connection with single cars or small car groupings Cargill's records indicate that it never followed any of these practices.[17]

As the case moved through many months of tortured testimony, a split opened up between the commissioners and their Bureau of Enforcement. As the commissioners put it in the final decision of the case, "From the outset . . . we note that a substantial number of allegations of abuses have not been demonstrated on the record. On cross-examination and further analysis, many of the complaints of elevator operators remain unsubstantiated or have been shown to be unfounded insofar as actual economic harm is involved." Cargill had had just one discounting allegation raised against it, involving a cooperative country elevator in Joice, a village of 231 people in north central Iowa. The commissioners concluded: "Single cars which Cargill did have available were placed to serve its own elevators and were not doled out to small country elevators. The matter of the one allegation by an elevator operator of discounting involving Cargill has already been discussed in full and resolved by us in Cargill's favor."

Still left was the more crucial question of possible constraints to be put on the unit train concept itself. Here the Bureau of Enforcement had taken some strong stands, stands that Cargill and other private carriers felt were highly threatening to the success of RAT. Cargill had had prepared (under the eloquent hand of Assistant General Counsel Victor Anderson) a lengthy, articulate brief about the issue of the unit train; it was a fitting role for the Company, as it had pioneered the concept back in 1968.

Anderson drew a careful distinction between the development of the unit train in Illinois, Indiana, and Ohio as "matured" systems (defined by Anderson as "a geographic area which has made the necessary adjustments to its grain loading facilities to make optimum use of unit train tariffs made available by the rail carriers serving the area") and those of many parts of Iowa and Minnesota. The Iowa unit train efforts, which had moved ahead more slowly and therefore were found wanting during the 1972–1974 period of extreme boxcar shortages, were compared by Anderson in 10 separate examples of "what was going right" in the Illinois–Indiana–Ohio region during the shortage period. In Iowa, there had been too few unit trains operating and (as mentioned earlier) these were of smaller size, 25 to 50 cars.[18]

This had changed by 1975: "Cargill is totally persuaded that Iowa has achieved the status of a matured unit train system and that that status alone, would, in fact, account for its better, and comparatively trouble-free 1975 performance." The ICC commissioners agreed with this, the final decision stating, "It was a healthy system and one which flourished because of the absence of artificial restraints, and where disproportionate premiums or values were not being placed on ownership or control of rail cars."

The Bureau of Enforcement had proposed several critical changes in the car allocation policies; especially limiting was a proposed rule that would deny the right of ordering cars to anyone except elevator operators. The commissioners rejected this notion, stating in the final decision, "It has been shown on this record that effective unit train operation can only be carried out by the exporters themselves. Most unit trains have operated in this matter both for the logistical as well as the economic considerations involved."

The commissioners bluntly criticized their own bureau:

Opponents of the Bureau's car distribution plan point out that plans for the distribution of grain cars exist on all railroads, and they are working, although they may not be reduced to writing or be as rigid and formalized as the Bureau would prefer. Unlike the Bureau's proposed plan, they were drafted by people knowledgable in railroad operations and familiar with problems likely to be encountered by railroads and each meets the particular needs and requirements on an individual railroad and its customers. The problem the rules are meant to correct no longer exists and is not likely to recur.

Another of the bureau's proposed rule changes would have canceled the so-called consecutive trip requirement, thus threatening the unit train operator's ability to set up unhindered a multiple-trip relationship with the carrier. Both the carriers and the shippers argued vehemently that if this stability over time was not present, the whole unit train relationship would fall apart. Here the commission struck a balance between the two sides:

Pre-hearing press

'Black Market' In Grain Cars
Des Moines Register

'Black Market' for Rail Cars?
The Florida Times-Union Jacksonville Journal

Black market in freight cars for shippers probed
TWIN FALLS, IDAHO TIMES NEWS

ICC Probing Boxcar 'Blackmail' By Major Grain Companies
BOULDER, COLO. CAMERA

Cargill denies rail car juggling
St. Paul Pioneer Press

ICC probers say big grain companies hoard freight cars
MINNEAPOLIS TRIBUNE

Agency Orders Probe Of Boxcar 'Rake-off'
Omaha World Herald OMAHA, NEBR.

ICC probers find large-scale black marketing of grain cars
Des Moines Register

Grain Exporters Control Boxcars
Washington Post

Post-hearing press

Grain giants clear on rail leasing
LAFAYET JOURNAL COURIER

Cargill among firms cleare
WAHPET(NEWS

Grain Firms Are Cleared
OMAHA, NE WORLD-HEF

5 grain firms cleared in rail shipping scandal
Chicago

Black Market Allegations Groundless
CLARKSVILLE LEAF-CHRON.

Five grain firms cleared of 'black market' ch
JACKSONVII JOURNAL

ICC Clears Grain Firms Of Rail Deal
Omaha Wor OMAHA,

Cargill cleared
St. Paul ST. PAUI

Clear big grain firms of shipping allegations
PONT: LEADE

We recognize the benefits generated by these consecutive-trip provisions. In return for the steady stream of tonnage, volume shippers are granted rate reductions on the basis of the efficiencies inherent to scheduled movements of large volumes of traffic. . . . Consecutive-trip provisions offer the prospect of improved car utilization and reduced port congestion." However, a five-trip limitation was justified "because it allows a volume of traffic sufficient to generate the efficiency as a unit-train operation but guards against abuses in car distribution practices. . . . The lawfulness of consecutive-trip provisions should be conditioned upon the carrier's retention of the power to interrupt unit-train operations in periods of emergency car shortages. . . . Carriers whose volume or multiple-car tariffs provide a shipper with a consecutive-trip option for unit-train operations beyond 5 trips will be required to cancel such provisions without prejudice.

Altogether, the ICC gave a strong endorsement for the unit train, its Bureau of Enforcement views to the contrary notwithstanding. Elimination of the consecutive-trip requirement would have been the death knell of the RAT. The carriers and the shippers felt they could live with the rule; it was to be used only in severe emergency situations. The ruling would not affect cars owned outright by the shipper or leased from car companies (Cargill had a substantial fleet of such leased cars).

Springrose reflected on this in a later *Cargill News:* "We are confident that the need to break up unit trains in order to obtain single cars will not arise. . . . What the tariff modification ordered by the Commission has done is to give the carriers the ability to satisfy themselves that their allocations of cars between unit trains and other shippers is fair and lawful in times of car shortages, and to take remedial action if they conclude it is not fair."

An appealing postscript in further defense of the unit train had been appended to Cargill's brief by Anderson and subsequently picked up by the national press: "Here is a tiny wild flower of thought which springs up, unbidden but irresistibly, as wild flowers do, outside the formal garden of this brief. . . . Possibly it is in the category of an idea whose time has not yet come, but once, in a world of less than carload rates, carload rates, too, were in that category. And who, if not the Commission, can successfully nurture such tender plants and make today's struggling wild flowers into tomorrow's staples." *Railway Age* featured the quote in a prominent sidebar on the day the decision was announced, commenting, "There is no immutable law requiring that passage through a legal brief be like passage through a near-impenetrable jungle, a jungle unrelieved by even a bit of beauty."

Of the "big six" companies, only Cargill and Dreyfus received a complete bill of health in the case. At its end, the commission held only Continental Grain over for further investigation (along with the Illinois Central Gulf Railroad). For Cargill, the "boxcar blackmail" case was over.[19]

Indian port

CHAPTER SEVEN

The "Grain Scandal"

"The charges of a 'Great Grain Robbery' and of 'boxcar blackmail' were disquieting, but to Cargill management they reflected more a misunderstanding of events than skepticism about the integrity of the industry itself. A series of grand jury indictments in New Orleans beginning in 1974, however, triggered more fundamental questions in some observers' minds." So began a 1977 Harvard Business School teaching case on Cargill. It *was* the greatest challenge to face the grain trade industry in many a year.

Initially, these indictments centered on private grain inspection agency employees, accused of accepting bribes from shipping companies (not grain firms) in return for certifying vessels as fit for grain loading. Then further evidence turned up of misgrading and misweighing of grain at several grain company elevators in the New Orleans area, involving state of Louisiana (but not federal) inspectors and some of the employees of the grain firms themselves. Grain inspectors were alleged to have issued certificates that did not accurately describe grain being loaded on vessels for export. This seemingly had resulted in delivery abroad of grain of below-grade quality.

A short digression will be useful for the reader in understanding the relationship between mixing and grading. The U.S. Grain Standards Act assigns different numerical grades to grain on the basis of certain factors that affect its value: minimum test weight (and protein content for some grains) and maximum limits on tolerances for moisture, damage, dockage, and foreign material. Every grade of grain carries with it an allowance of a certain amount of dockage and foreign material, less for higher-valued grades. For example, if the contract grade allowed a maximum of 3 percent of foreign material, it would be perfectly legal and universally practiced to mix down to grade—mix, for example, an equal amount of grain carrying 2.5 percent with an equal amount of 3.5 percent to produce an overall grade of exactly 3 percent. Normal mixing and blending would readily handle this; the ability to mix and blend enables an elevator to buy widely different qualities of grain and yet match them to the needs and demands of users, thus allowing the elevator to pay a premium for good-quality grain while providing a market for lower-quality grain at only a modest discount.

What was *illegal* was to attempt to deliver to a buyer grain not up to contract grade or actually to adulterate grain by deliberately *adding* foreign matter (e.g., street sweepings, sand, gravel, etc.). Now it was alleged that export elevators were adding other lower-priced grain, grain fractions (e.g., rice hulls), elevator sweepings, and dirt to make sure that shipments of U.S. export grains contained the maximum weight (thus the maximum bushels) while staying within the allowable amounts of dockage and foreign material. Foreign buyers were said to be threatening to purchase grains and oilseeds from other countries unless the practices were stopped.[1]

Cargill officials had their first inkling of an incipient problem of their own in February 1974, when an informant advised them of a possible fraud/theft operation at the Company's Baton Rouge export terminal involving the inspection of inbound shipments (the alleged fraud favoring the inbound shipper—i.e., cheating Cargill). Earlier, Cargill had quietly called in private investigators at the Houston terminal; these people now were asked to go to Baton Rouge. In March 1974, one of the private investigators was requested by the Houston District Attorney's office to brief a group of FBI agents in the workings of the grain business. Then, in May, Cargill officials and one of the private investigators were asked again to meet with a group of FBI agents; in the course of the conversations, the agents informed the Cargill group of a major investigation they were conducting all through the Louisiana port operations. The agents expressed unfamiliarity with the operation of export elevators and so were given a "thorough tour of our facility, from top to bottom (under guise of writing a story, John Work, editor of the *Cargill News* in attendance for cover)." After this early May meeting, Cargill officials continued to provide additional information to the FBI as requested.

As the Company lawyers began their own investigation of Cargill's Baton Rouge terminal, they became quite disconcerted about what they found. For years, inspections at the facility had been done by a combination of a few federal inspectors, on duty primarily in the daytime, and a larger group of state inspectors. The problems concerned the Cargill terminal employees' interaction with the second group, the state inspectors, particularly at night.

There was no evidence that a Cargill employee ever had paid off any inspectors (four or five years earlier, so the grapevine told, one inspector solicited a bribe but was "turned down flat"). Rather, it was a pervasive ethos of "good old boy," a way of life that fed on reciprocity and favors, ethics being dictated by the situation: "You scratch my back and I'll scratch yours." Some argued that it was a Louisiana hangover from its heritage of French law. In any case, precise legal specifications from the "book" were probably not a way of life for some, indeed many, locally raised inspectors. Inspectors had fallen into allowing slipshod practices, particularly on the percentage of foreign matter in outbound shipments. Some elevator personnel were a party to this. Minor favors in return had been dispensed from time to time—a few football tickets, some metalwork construction of barbecue pits, and fish-frying burners put together by the terminal shop and made available to the inspectors.

Most of these were in the nature of the age-old small-favor "greasing of the system," allowing, for example, the foreman not only to mix up to full component of foreign matter (3% was allowed) but sometimes likely exceeding this figure in a small way. All of these practices, nevertheless, were completely against both oral and written Cargill policies. It was particularly upsetting to Cargill's investigating team to learn that after an earlier discovery of such slippages the terminal management was advised to discontinue a number of the practices but some had not done so, had actually decided deliberately to go against the advice and continue the pattern. It was naturally to the advantage of the foreman to send out each loading with the maximum number of bushels while meeting grade, but this was being accomplished by significant mixing anomalies on more than just an occasional basis.

Once again the corporate policy was enunciated, now with additional strong admonitions from the legal department. This time the practices stopped.

If Cargill's infractions were not egregious enough to concern the outside authorities, the same was certainly not true in other parts of the industry. By early August 1974, a federal grand jury in New Orleans had indicted elsewhere six government-licensed grain inspectors on charges of bribery to approve ships to store or export grain; another inspector had been indicted for issuing a false certificate for a vessel he had not inspected and for subsequent perjury to the grand jury; the president of a ship-cleaning company and the company itself were indicted for paying bribes to inspectors; and a marine surveyor had been indicted for perjury in denying that he had received bribes in connection with his ship examinations. A total of 10 indictments, with 210 counts, had been issued, after FBI and U.S. Department of Agriculture (USDA) joint investigations. Belatedly, the USDA issued supplemental procedures regarding cleanliness examinations of grain ships.

But this was only the proverbial tip of the iceberg. Most of the early cases had involved inspection of ships, with a focus particularly on the period after the July 1972 Russian grain sales, when the huge influx of grain came to the Gulf ports. With the costs very high to ocean ships for demurrage while waiting to load at the elevators and with all sorts of shipping being called upon to load grain, the temptation to short-circuit the inspection procedure was always present—and succumbed to in a number of instances.

Later in the year, the federal investigations broadened to include the grain companies' grading and weighing procedures. All the grain companies with terminal facilities in New Orleans, Baton Rouge, and Houston were now subjected to intensive interviews, accompanied by a searching examination of all records. Cargill was included in this assiduous investigation by the FBI agents, the Company now being put at arm's length by the latter (indeed, there were enough late-night calls by agents at various employee homes to elicit a Company complaint).

In January 1976, three grain inspectors employed by the Baton Rouge Port Commission and assigned by the commission to Cargill's export elevator were indicted for taking bribes of some $67,000 from an elevator company in Louisiana that had been shipping through the Cargill terminal. The indictment alleged that the three consistently upgraded shipments of soybeans, receiving bribes based upon 25 percent of the increased values. The three inspectors pled guilty to reduced charges. Cargill, not involved in this in any way, was the unknowing victim.[2]

The Controversy Broadens

As the investigations moved from the narrower issue of ocean shipping cleanliness to practices on grading and weighing, the discussion suddenly mushroomed into the national press and then to Congress. In early May 1975, the *Des Moines Register* instituted a series of articles on the "grain inspection fraud." An editorial on May 6 began, "Foreign buyers of United States corn, wheat and soybeans often have complained about the quality of the goods they received and paid for. Especially in the past 15 years of growing demand for feed grains and soybeans, European buyers have objected to the cracked kernels, dirt, sand, and insects in U.S. export cargoes. . . . It appears that more than poor grade standards have been behind the poor quality of grain exports. James Risser of our Washington Bureau reports a scandal of sizable proportions in the grading and inspection of grain for export."

The issue was picked up by Senator Dick Clark of Iowa, who, in an extraordinary speech on the floor of the Senate on May 10, 1975, made the following charges: (1) that major grain-exporting companies might have been paying cash bonuses or kickbacks to grain elevator operators who deliberately shorted their shipments; (2) that major grain companies profited from the sale of these excess stocks; (3) that the quantities of grain involved could be massive; (4) that there were a number of practices available to elevator operators, from "tipping" scales to mixing or blending below grade to misrepresenting loadings to bribery of inspectors; and (5) that while the major exporters were only indirectly involved in a bribery scandal, they were directly enmeshed in the bonus fraud. Further, Clark alleged, the "big six" grain companies accounted for about half of America's grain-exporting capacity, and as these companies moved grain toward the ports, they gained more and more control, which, in Clark's mind, increased the possibility "of their involvement in this particularly damaging form of corruption." The breadth of Clark's charges stunned the industry.

The alleged involvement of the "big six" was picked up by the *Des Moines*

Register, which headlined an article in mid-June: "Big Grain Exporters Shrouded in Secrecy." All over the country, the press featured detailed articles on "the scandal." What had seemed at the start a set of factual accounts of limited criminal activity now had ballooned to sweeping indictments of the overall grain marketing system.

With issues of this apparent seriousness, congressional hearings followed almost immediately. The Subcommittee on Foreign Agricultural Policy of the Senate Committee on Agriculture and Forestry, chaired by Senator Hubert Humphrey of Minnesota, began hearings on June 19, 1975.[3]

By late May, Dan Morgan's articles in the *Washington Post* were enumerating complaints from the Soviet Union, from Britain, from Italy, from West Germany, and from India about the substandard grain being received from the United States.

In this same week, the *New York Times* reported that two of the "big six" grain companies were reportedly under inquiry, together with a domestic grain elevator operation owned by Serafino Ferruzzi of Ravenna, Italy. Cargill, knowing it was not itself the subject of any probe, stated its noninvolvement publicly for quotation in an issue of a Minneapolis paper at this time.[4]

With the burgeoning publicity, Cargill now decided to institute a major task force within the company, to look into every possible relationship to see exactly where Cargill stood on each. Sixteen persons, most of them senior management, were appointed to the newly composed Grain Irregularities Task Force. Bill Pearce acted as the committee executive director, and there was wide representation from senior management in the Grain Division. They were Jay Berkley, Maury Brannan, Ron Girouard, Bob Hubbard, Heinz Hutter, Rob Johnson, Hank Kaufmann, Whitney MacMillan, John McGrory, Mel Middents, Gerry Mitchell, Pete Reed, Cliff Roberts, Barney Saunders, Jim Spicola, and Roy Wallace.

Each person on the task force was given specific assignments for study, and extensive reports were called for from various offices of the company, both in the United States and abroad. It was patently the most far-reaching Company-wide study performed in many decades.

First, the quality complaints from overseas were looked at carefully over the summer and fall of 1975. The USDA had compiled a list of these foreign-buyer complaints for the years 1971–1975; Cargill was mentioned in seven on this list. The Company immediately requested the full files on each from the USDA's Office of Investigation. Only six of the files could be located.

Two complaints related to shipments of grain sorghum to Africa, where the receivers of the grain alleged that there was infestation from weevils and other insects. However, when Cargill sent samples from the Ivory Coast to the Agricultural Research Center in Beltsville, Maryland, the Board of Appeals and Review at the Center found no evidence of insects.

Another shipment, to England, concerned a complaint of lower protein content. Once again, the USDA disposition found that the samples "sustained the original finding." Another case, involving a German shipment, also related to protein content; in this case, no destination samples had been taken, and the USDA concluded: "We are unable to offer a definitive reason for the differences in the protein results obtained at origin and at destination. The difference may have been due to a use of different samples at origin and destination, different sampling and testing methods, . . . variations in the lot or a combination of these factors."

Several sets of complaints came from India, again relating to infestation, but the USDA reported, "There is no documentation in the file of lab analysis or any other official form attesting to the infestation of any of the vessels." An Italian complaint argued that there were damaged kernels in a yellow corn shipment. Cargill's Norfolk terminal had graded these as having 5.6 percent damaged kernels, while the Italian analysis showed a range of 18–25 percent. The conclusion from this case was that the export inspection certificate "represents the quality at the time and place of loading and may or may not represent the quality of the grain at some future date or at some other place where it is unloaded."

Another Italian case, which occurred in June 1975 after the sharp fall in grain prices over the previous months, challenged Cargill's standards for No. 3 yellow corn. The captain of the ship felt that the port inspector's grading was incorrect and urged the Italian company to demand that USDA inspectors meet the ship in Venice when it docked and inspect the cargo for a second time (his complaint was stated to be "very strongly worded"). The USDA did indeed take such a sample (it had a team in Europe at the time) but would not release the findings to the Italian buyer, claiming that this would violate USDA policy for confidential reviews. However, the USDA records of the inspection when the vessel left confirmed the initial grading of the corn.

This was one of several cases in a larger set of disagreements between American shippers and Italian buyers, the latter refusing to pay for a number of shipments. A long article in late June in the *Wall Street Journal* was headlined "Foreign Fuss About U.S. Grain Quality Involves More Than Inspection Problem." The editors mentioned for the first time the influence of sagging prices and their effect on buyer complaints. This situation had been exacerbated by poor growing and harvesting weather in 1974, which had led corn and soybean shipments to be more susceptible to breakage in handling. The effects of the soybean embargo had resulted in a sharp drop in prices during the 1974–1975 marketing year, catching many foreign buyers in high-priced contracts. "Now, with prices materially lower, many foreign buyers are using complaints about grain quality as an excuse to void money-losing contracts." One grain dealer was quoted in the article: "There's no doubt about it. Some countries would like to use quality complaints to get out of what have become not-so-good trades." Nevertheless, as the article pointed out, there was more slippage in the American inspection system after the huge Russian grain sales had begun to push on the market.

The Italian Grain Association at that time even addressed a petition to Ambassador John A. Volpe, the American ambassador to Italy:

Considering the relationship of friendship and collaboration between our countries and, in particular, the close commercial relations in respect of above mentioned imports in Italy of U.S. yellow corn, I beg your Excellency to please intervene at your earliest possible convenience with the federal and state competent authorities of your country, more particularly with the Department of Agriculture, so that they take with a maximum of rapidity and severity the necessary measures to ensure that shipment of the grain in question be effected with goods of quality corresponding not only to the specifications provided by the official standards established by your government but also to the traditional intrinsic quality of U.S. products so as to allow the regular performance of contracts in Italy without creating continuous and increasingly serious disputes and litigations with the receivers and the consumers.

A Cargill wire from Tradax in Geneva chronicled the other side:

IF U HEAR ANY STORIES ABT MASSIVE ITALIAN DEFAULTS TSY—THEY'RE FOR REAL. WITH EXCEPTION OF———ALL ITALIAN IMPORTERS HV SENT TELEXES TO THEIR SUPPIERS SAYING IN EFFECT THEY WILL NOT TAKE FURTHER SHPT OF US CORN NOR SBM [soybean meal] DUE TO POOR QUALITY OF TS SEASON'S SHIPTS. EACH HAS HIS OWN SPECIAL WORDING—THE MILDEST BEING———WHO WILLING TO TALK ABT IT—THE STRONGEST BEING———WHO WILL ONLY PAY SPOT MKT VALUE AND———WHO ABROGATES ALL CAK [contract] PERIODS BELV ITALIANS MORE OR LESS BORROWING THE IDEA FROM RUSSIAN WHO PROTESTED US 3 YC [yellow corn] TS SEASON S CROP. BUT OBV W/O WHOLESALE DEFAULTING ON ALL CAKS. UNDERSTAND ON 10 MAY A FORMAL ITALIAN PROTEST ON QUALITY WAS SUBMITTED TO US EMBASSY IN ITALY AND SOME TALK OF US FEDERAL INSPECTORS BEING SENT TO ITALY TO TAKE A LOOK. WE FAVOR AND STRONGLY RECOMMEND IT BE MADE CLEAR TO USDA/SB COUNCIL/ ETC. TT ALL TS IS RESULT OF UNFAVORABLE ITALIAN MKT SPECULATION AND IS NOT A QUALITY ISSUE. WE ARE GG INSIST ON CONTRACTUAL FULFILMENT OF ALL CAKS OR SELL OUT/ARBITRATE.

There was no doubt about a groundswell to renege on unfavorable contracts (and thus to violate one of the most basic of tenets in grain trading, "my word is my bond"). Whether there was also a deterioration in the shippers' quality standards is very difficult to determine 20 years after the fact. The answer probably lay somewhere between the two sets of views.

Italian/American grain trading remained a source of tension all through the latter half of 1975. There had been similar problems with some Turkish buyers during this period, with some unilateral cancellations of contracts and continuing complaints about quality.[5]

Fred Seed Speaks

The cacophony of charges raining upon the industry, surely quite disconcerting to Cargill employees, now persuaded senior management to make a statement to everyone in the Company. From President Fred Seed, it read in part as follows:

June 16, 1975

To All Employees:

Serious charges have been made in Congress and in the national press about irregularities in vessel inspection and in grain weighing and grading at some ports. These charges range from bribery of inspectors and weighmen—which our own investigation of our port facilities indicates Cargill is not involved in—to mixing and blending practices that are important features of normal commercial activity. . . .

While we do not know all of the facts, Cargill shares with farmers and foreign customers . . . [a desire to see] that all necessary steps are taken to eliminate irregularities where they are found and to restore confidence in the grain marketing system. . . .

The charges of a "grain inspection scandal" rest on evidence that federally licensed grain inspectors and weighmen may have intentionally misgraded or misweighed grain shipments. Such practices—if committed—would prove very damaging to the grain industry. They undermine foreign confidence in U.S. grain exports and willingness to rely on U.S. inspections.

All grain going to overseas customers is sold on the basis of weights and grades established by inspections *as the grain is loaded on ships* [my emphasis]. These inspections may be performed by individuals licensed by the U.S. Department of Agriculture or directly by USDA employees; . . . the overseas buyer assumes the risk of deterioration in transit. Our obligation as exporter is satisfied by supplying a certificate showing that the shipment met contract specifications at the time of loading. Allegations of scandal threaten the integrity of weight and grade certificates on which exporters like Cargill must rely in enforcing outstanding contracts. . . .

Many foreign customers are complaining about the quality of U.S. grain shipments. Such complaints underline the seriousness of the current problem, but they may also result from factors totally unrelated to accurate grain inspection.

Seed then described the drop in world prices and noted the fact that many valid extant contracts for delivery involved commitments made in good faith at the higher prices. He continued:

Large losses on these contracts could encourage some overseas buyers to raise questions about the condition of grain delivered and about the integrity of origin grades in an effort to avoid taking delivery.

The coincidence of these factors promises continued controversy. No one suffers more than Cargill from lack of confidence in the marketing system. For more than a year we have known of and cooperated with authorities in their investigations of grain inspections at the Gulf. Congressional interest is more recent and extends to much wider issues. Hopefully the result of these investigations will be a better grain marketing system and renewed confidence on the part of customers for American grains.

Sincerely,
Fred M. Seed

Cargill Tries an "Op Ed"

The *New York Times* had just begun experimenting at this time with an interesting new editorial device, the "Op Ed" section opposite the editorial page, where a particular person could make a statement in his or her own interest, to be commented upon by the editors in the opposite-page editorial column. The *Minneapolis Tribune* agreed to try the device with a Cargill entry about the grain irregularities. It was to be signed by Barney Saunders, group vice president overseeing grain trading.

As this was to be Cargill's first public statement on this issue, many drafts were considered before an acceptable version was ready. The final product mirrored the Seed letter of a month earlier, emphasizing the importance of integrity in the grain system and discussing all of the reasons why mixing and grading could have variations. The activities that were illegal were decried, and once again Saunders spoke officially for the Company: "Cargill has not been involved in any of them."

The Company got a bit more than it had bargained for in the *Tribune*'s editorial companion. "We welcome Saunders' comment that his company has not been involved in such practices," it began. But the editor emphasized the widespread cases and added that "determining just who has abused the inspection system would not, in our view, settle the matter." The *Tribune* advocated a federal inspection system and implicitly criticized Cargill and Continental Grain Company, as privately held companies, for having "no obligation to say much about their operations." The focus of the editorial reinforced its title, "Investigating the Grain Trade."

Most disconcerting, however, was a prominent mention in the article of an expected shortfall in the grain harvest in the Soviet Union and reports surfacing once again of massive U.S. grain sales. As to the 1972 sales, only "some" of the questions about how the U.S. conducted its grain sales had been answered. In the final analysis, the Op Ed article raised more questions than it answered.[6]

The Russians—Again!

The rumors were true. Once again, Russia had fallen behind on its grain needs and was in the market. This time, to quote from Dan Morgan's extensive story of this 1975 sale, there was to be no "buying spree" like the 1972 exploits that had caught the Americans napping. "That had been an audacious Cossack raid"; now the tactics were to be those "of a night infiltration."

The negotiations this time were held in Moscow. Four days after the Op Ed editorial, the nation's papers headlined a huge "73-million bushel" sale of wheat by Cook, which had sold the Soviets 2 million metric tons, using its export company. By the next day, Cargill had done the same, using Tradax for another 1.2 million tons. USDA officials stated that these were only the first of what was expected to be larger sales; a week later, Continental Grain had sold an additional 5.6 million metric tons, in this case a combination of corn and barley. Australia also sold 750,000 tons of wheat; the Canadian Wheat Board, another 2 million tons.

With the press reports mushrooming by the day, most comparing the sales with those in 1972, Secretary of Agriculture Earl Butz felt compelled to respond. He flatly averred that the total of all the sales would not raise U.S. prices: "Some people who don't know wheat from chaff are drawing ridiculous conclusions." But price rises by the milling industry and much public outcry disputed the Butz analysis.

At this time, several arms of the federal government advocated a "grain power" concept to President Gerald Ford and his staff. The essence of this argument, told well by Dan Morgan in a long excerpt in *Merchants of Grain*, involved bargaining U.S. grain for Soviet oil—in effect, demanding from the Soviets concessions on oil prices in order to be willing to sell the U.S.S.R. grain. Extended negotiations took place in Moscow between representatives of the "grain power" faction (particularly pushed by Secretary of State Henry Kissinger) and the Soviets. But the Russians, said Morgan, "were not bluffing. It was evident that their hand was strengthening. For one thing, the old-boy network of Soviet and Western grain merchants was busily sweeping the world for every available particle of surplus grain. The Americans had regained control over U.S. exports, but they could not control what the multinational grain houses did elsewhere. Powerful as the U.S. Government was, it had little power to control what Cargill, Continental, or Cook did in Europe, Australia or Argentina." The Ford administration had asked the American units of the grain companies to voluntarily hold off on further sales; when this did not seem to stem the tide of sales by other countries, grain sales by the United States were once more "temporarily suspended" on August 11, 1975.

Then an unexpected event occurred to complicate the issue: AFL-CIO president George Meany publicly stated that the International Longshoremen's Association (I.L.A.) would refuse to load grain for Russia until the administration had acted to protect domestic consumer and shipping interests. President Ford asked for a meeting with Meany, but the truculent labor leader would not back down. The press responded with an outpouring of vitriol against Meany and the I.L.A. The *New York Times* castigated "the AFL-CIO and its rapacious maritime unions [who] have made a messy situation messier by reasserting their right to dictate foreign policy by economic might." The *Baltimore Sun* called it "George Meany's demagoguery." A federal judge issued a temporary injunction against the dockworkers in the Gulf areas of Louisiana and Texas.

January 23, 1973: the first Russian ship to visit Albany since War World II, the M/S Kom-somoltz Latvii, *takes on 23,000 tons of wheat under the trade agreement reached by the United States and Russia in 1972. After loading, the ship returned to its home port of* Leningrad (UPI/Corbis-Bettmann).

Finally, the unions reversed their boycott after President Ford promised to arrange a new long-term purchasing and shipping agreement with the Soviet Union. After much pressure, on October 20, 1975, a five-year agreement was reached with the U.S.S.R. It committed the latter to purchase 6 million metric tons of grain per year (representing about $1 billion in annual exports). It could increase this quantity without consultation by up to 2 million metric tons in any given year, unless the U.S. government determined that the country had a grain supply of less than 225 million metric tons. All purchases were to be made at prevailing market prices, and the parties agreed to space their purchases "as evenly as possible over each 12 month period." A maritime agreement was also concluded, and a face-saving statement was made on the "grain power" issue, with both governments committing to "mutually beneficial terms for a 5-year agreement for the purchase of Soviet oil." It seemed that now, for the first time since 1971, there was a more regularized and more open way of handling grain sales to Russia.[7]

However, the new flap about further Russian grain sales had served just to add to and deepen the mistrust and outright hostility toward the grain indus-

The press views George Meany's role in the Russian grain sales.

"Dis is y'captain speakin' . . . bring th' Ship of State about!"

try itself, particularly the "big six" companies. All through this saga, from the initial sales by the U.S. grain companies in Moscow, through the George Meany/I.L.A. boycott of shipping to Russia, to the final denouement leading to the momentous five-year pact, the Senate subcommittees on foreign agricultural policy and on agricultural production, marketing, and stabilization of prices had continued their joint hearings. Laid on the record were example after example of slippage in the grain inspection system, in the grading practices of the companies, and in the loading of ocean shipping for foreign buyers. The industry's ethics seemed to many people to be in full disarray.

Reaffirming Cargill's Integrity

Shortly after the announcement of the five-year pact, two major internal steps were taken by the Company. In August 1975, Fred Seed had retired as president of the Company. Whitney MacMillan was elected by the board as the new president; Erv Kelm remained chairman and chief executive officer. This marked the first time since 1960 that a member of one of the two families (Cargill and MacMillan) had assumed a position of this breadth of leadership within the company.

Over many years, Whitney's father, Cargill MacMillan, and Austen Cargill had assumed the roles of the conscience of the Company, to leaven the more entrepreneurial thrust brought so strongly to Cargill by John MacMillan, Jr. Now Whitney MacMillan chose the occasion of the tensions of the fall of 1975 from both the Russian sales and the grain irregularities hearings to reaffirm the corporate values that had made Cargill so distinct in the industry. No further explanations or justifications for corporate practice were in the statement—it was a straightforward, unambiguous restatement of the Company's policy, with five explicit emendations by MacMillan of what this meant. Here is the memorandum in its entirety:

November 5, 1975

Fellow Employees:

During the past year, all of us have been made aware through the news media of various illegal or questionable corporate practices, ranging from illegal campaign contributions in the U.S. to payoffs made to foreign officials. Grain industry firms have been charged with bribing weighers and inspectors at U.S. Gulf export elevators. Such events compel me to reaffirm certain corporate policies of Cargill as they apply to all of our activities around the world.

Our corporate goals and objectives state: "Continue to make certain that all employees of the Cargill Companies recognize and adhere to the principles of integrity which have always been basic to our philosophy and upon which the Cargill Companies' reputation is founded.

1) This means we have a deep responsibility to conduct ourselves and our business under the highest standards of ethics, integrity, and in compliance with the laws of all

countries and communities in which we have been granted the opportunity to perform our services.

2) This means should there be a question concerning a particular practice, open discussion will surely resolve the issue. If a practice cannot be discussed openly, it must be wrong.

3) This means business secured by any means other than legal, open, honest competition is wrong.

4) This means if a transaction cannot be properly recorded in the company books, subject to an independent audit, it must be wrong.

5) This means that Cargill does not want to profit on any practice which is immoral or unethical. Should we discover our business being done in any other than an absolutely proper manner, disciplinary action will be taken.

A company with a good reputation is a good place to work. Cargill has enjoyed 110 years of a fine reputation built on integrity. We must maintain our honor and self-respect as a basis of our continued growth and pride in the Cargill Companies.

Sincerely,
Whitney MacMillan

Several new concepts were contained in this statement. First, there were to be, from this point forward, no "secrets" within the Company about grading, weighing, and loading practices (or for that matter, any other internal practices). Such secrets had been unearthed in the earlier investigations by the Company legal department of the practices at the Baton Rouge elevator, where, even after having been given explicit statements not to shade grades, Company personnel had continued to do so. The statement reaffirmed the principle that all company practices must be subject to record keeping and independent audit. Finally, disciplinary action would be taken if there were *any* violations.

In effect, the essence of the renowned and revered competition of the grain trade was ringingly restated, but explicitly this was to be "legal, open, and honest" competition. The last sentence of the statement repeated once again what had been the belief pattern for over a hundred years, that honor and self-respect were the essence of the Company.[8]

The Cargill Affirmative Action Program

The USDA had taken much criticism during the grain irregularities investigations. Its oversight of the grain trade industry in general and of the inspection system it managed in particular had been judged by many to be insufficient. Indeed, several of its employees, including a few in management levels, had been culpable enough in the missteps that had been uncovered to be asked to resign.

Now the department chose to move decisively in certain arenas in order to bring more control into the process. The flagship for this was to be the "affirmative action program" (AAP) (in this instance referring to antitrust concerns). Each of the grain trading companies (with an emphasis on the larger, especially the "big six") was to be asked to construct and then have approved an AAP that would address the firm's own specific situation and contain a set of precepts for control that the firm would agree (in writing) to abide by in future actions.

Cargill took this matter very seriously, and the board of directors instructed the Grain Irregularities Task Force to come up with Cargill's specific plan as soon as possible. Early in 1976, the task force sent its final program directly to the board, which formally accepted the plan in a special meeting called on March 16, 1976. Cargill was to obtain grade by licensed inspectors on all grain received and shipped at its export elevators. A compliance officer was to be appointed, to review and strengthen auditing procedures, specifically with the assistance of an independent CPA firm. The Company was to increase the frequency and detail of existing audits and was to identify shortages and overages and explain them in company records.

Further, the Company was to inform the auditors of all customer complaints, was to avoid conflicts of interest with private agencies performing official inspection and weighing services, was to use "reasonable precaution" to protect the quality of grain in the process of loading vessels, was to open its records to the USDA's auditors, was to improve the security of all scales and have them tested and adjusted quarterly, was to seek a qualified independent agency to supervise all inbound and outbound shipments at the export elevators, was to evaluate the use of independent draught surveys and discuss with the USDA the practicability of using them to identify substantial weight discrepancies, and was to follow up with both the weighing agency and USDA all shortage complaints. Finally, Cargill agreed to "terminate employees who plead guilty or are convicted of violating the U.S. Grain Standards Act, the U.S. Warehouse Act, or state and Federal laws governing grain weighing, except where they acted in good faith, reasonably believed they were following instructions or came forward voluntarily with evidence."

With most medium-sized and large grain trading companies each working on such a compliance plan, Cargill was the first to voluntarily come forth with a final version. Indeed, the USDA stressed the voluntary nature in its press announcement, although not mentioning that four other companies—Bunge, Archer Daniels Midland, Mississippi River Grain Corporation, and Garnac— earlier had signed AAPs, but in each case mandated to them under court orders linked to charges involving these four firms.

The press picked this up, however, the *Washington Post* commenting that "Cargill has not been mentioned in widespread charges of grain handling irregularities." The *Minneapolis Star*, in a more detailed statement, quoted

Cliff Roberts, head of the Commodity Marketing Division (CMD), as saying that "evidence uncovered so far suggest that Cargill's existing system of internal controls has worked well" (one would have needed to add, "the Louisiana terminals' slippages to the contrary notwithstanding"). Yet, Roberts continued, the Company had agreed to "additional procedures" because "it believes that a visible, positive effort will help restore public confidence in the integrity of the grain-weighing and inspection system." In a lengthy editorial in an industry publication, *Feedstuffs*, the editor commented, "the giant grain firm [i.e., Cargill] has taken the initiative to defuse some of the industry's critics, who see the only solution to the recent grain exports scandals in a federalized inspection system."

Sorting out the actual steps to take in the Company's AAP was not completely unambiguous. Jay Berkley, appointed the Company's compliance officer, called a meeting right after the announcement of the program by the USDA. General Counsel John McGrory gave a detailed presentation of the obligations that were imposed on Cargill by the program. The Company could not excuse "overages" that were within "tolerances" since there was no agreement with the USDA on tolerance ranges. "Problems must be identified, and followup must occur immediately." Second, McGrory noted, auditing work would not necessarily uncover all of those activities that if disclosed would be illegal. "Therefore, in implementing this agreement we need to pay attention to actual practices in weighing and grading grain at our elevators. . . . We need to ensure that grain inspectors do not resolve all doubts about quality conservatively . . . that is *against* the house. At the same time, we cannot take advantage of sloppy inspectors to our benefit . . . in other words, we need to adhere to the spirit as well as the letter of this agreement." McGrory put this point bluntly: "We also need to sensitize our superintendents, merchants, and elevator managers to their legal requirements and to the new 'atmosphere' that prevails in the industry."

Bob Hubbard, manager of operations in the CMD, stated: "Our goal in loading out grain should be to come as close to grade lines as possible without intentionally exceeding them." In weighing, tolerances should not be set to favor the house. "The problem, however, is in judging where to set the scale's zero tolerance within the full range of weighings that the scale must perform. In other words, a zero tolerance for a 50,000 pound truck may necessarily involve some discrepancies for 70,000 pound trucks." Hank Kaufmann commented, "Guidelines on some kind of quality problems will be extremely difficult to develop. There are elevator practices that can yield grain lots of a specific quality, which quality cannot be maintained for more than a temporary period."

A number of meetings were held over the spring and summer of 1976, clarifying the AAP. In June, an extensive report was made to the USDA on Cargill's efforts. In the covering memorandum to the members of the task force,

Jay Berkeley noted: "Our most serious problem seems to be the continued malfunctioning of the scales at Houston. This problem has been with us for a long time, and we must do whatever is necessary to really fix the scales. . . . There is a big credibility gap among our customers about Houston weights, and we need to correct the situation as quickly as possible." In late June, Berkley wrote the director of the USDA grain division, "We have concluded that a complete overhaul and modification of these scales is necessary. . . . A capital expenditure has been approved for this purpose [and] we have scheduled implementation for the first week of September." By the end of the year 1976, Cargill's compliance efforts were fully on target. In the process, Cargill had significantly enhanced its industry reputation.[9]

Are "Overages" a Sign of Cheating?

In the early stages of the grain irregularites saga, the focus had been on efforts of the inspectors of the grain—federal, state, and private—to obtain bribes from ocean shipping officers and from grain elevator operators and on the seeming "sweetheart" interactions between inspectors and elevator personnel in shading the quality and/or quantity in grain loading. By the time the Senate subcommittee had begun hearings, the focus had shifted more pointedly to the actions of the grain-trading companies themselves.

One of the most consistent complaints against export terminal operators was that of "shortweighting." As the subcommittee and General Accounting Office (GAO) investigators began to dig into company records, patterns of "overages" began to surface. Terminals kept records of inbound and outbound shipments by weight and grade. If, in a given period, there was an accumulation of grain in excess of the difference between inbound receipts and outbound shipments, there was an overage. As the investigators sifted through detailed statistics for all the industry's export terminal operations, widespread overages were seen. Several natural reasons might allow this to occur—moisture absorption in the export terminal, humidity conditions, and so on. There were also possibilities that a deliberate pattern of shortweighting was being performed by the terminal—loading ships at tolerances below the one tenth of 1 percent allowed by standard practice in grain scale accuracy.

In December 1975, a shortweighting charge was brought against six employees of Bunge Corporation; one of these had been a vice president. Verdicts of guilty were reached against the defendants; the company had pleaded no contest on the same charges and had been fined $20,000. One of the six men paid a small fine of $500; the others were put on probation. In March 1976, two more major grain trading companies, Garnac Grain Inc. and Archer Daniels Midland Company, also pleaded no contest to charges of shortweighting over a four-year period; each company paid a fine of $10,000, the maximum penalty under the existing law. No company officials were found guilty in these particular cases.

Then, in May 1976, a major case occurred, this time against another of the "big six," Cook Industries. Grain irregularities had first surfaced there in January 1976, when three USDA officials had paid a surprise visit to Cook's Bayside elevator at Destrehan, Louisiana. A Polish supertanker, the *Rysy II*, was being loaded with yellow corn. During their inspection, a "Keystone Kops" incident occurred, when the three became locked inside one of the tanks. One of the three managed to escape by wriggling through a small hole and released the other two. The newspaper accounts made it seem as if there had been a possibility of deliberate mischief by the company.

When the subcommittee had its next set of hearings, in March 1976, the president of the company, Edward W. Cook, was asked by Kansas senator Robert Dole about the lock-in. Cook answered, "Well, they got out . . . but you would think somebody had gone out and segregated the inspectors and purposely closed the hatch on them. . . . Nobody is trying to lock anybody up. It is like the fellows out in the West with Indians behind every rock. It is just not that way."

But there were more serious concerns involved here—whether Cook had been pursuing a policy of deliberate shortweighting. After the hearings, the company was indicted for such efforts, which the court alleged had occurred on 37 separate instances. The company pleaded no contest to the charges, and the maximum fine was levied, in this case $10,000 for each of the 37 instances, a total of $370,000. At the same time (early May 1976), Mississippi Grain Elevator Inc. at Myrtle Grove, Louisiana, was fined $60,000 after pleading no contest to six such counts. Later in 1976, four men who had been vice presidents at Cook, together with a former elevator operator, were indicted by a federal grand jury, were found guilty, and paid small fines.

At this same time, Continental Grain Company also was indicted for similar examples of shortweighting. In Continental's case, it was alleged that the scales at their Westwego, Louisiana, export elevator had been "adjusted" so that outgoing grain appeared to weigh one-twentieth of 1 percent more than its actual weight—a small amount but one that added up to about 100,000 bushels of grain per year, according to the company's own figures. Continental was indicted on 50 counts of violating the Export Administration Act and pleaded no contest in early May 1976, paying a fine of $500,000.

These total amounts were large, but they represented a large number of counts, where the individual fine for each was $10,000. Some of the national press decried what they felt were the low levels of these fines; the *Des Moines Register*, in an editorial entitled "Not Much Deterrence," called these "slap-on-the-wrist" efforts and advocated "stiffer penalties for violators."[10]

Finally, Cargill Also Is Drawn In

Throughout all of 1974 and 1975 and into 1976, Cargill had been the only one of the "big six" maintaining export elevators in the Gulf not to be drawn into the grain irregularities cases. In January 1976, a single case involving a Cargill terminal occurred: three civil service employees of the Greater Baton 'Rouge Port Commission, licensed by the USDA as inspectors and working at the Cargill elevator in Baton Rouge, were indicted on charges of defrauding the government and taking a total of some $67,000 in bribes. Once again, Cargill itself was not involved; the bribes came from a Port Barre grain company that bought soybeans from farmers and sold them to Cargill, delivering by truck. As the *New York Times* put it, "Cargill was a victim of the activity, since Cargill paid the country elevator for grain that the inspectors graded as being of a higher quality than it deserved." Once again, Cargill received similar positive comments from the press, as it had through the period from 1974.

But two events in May of 1976 shattered any possible complacency that Cargill employees might have felt about the Company never being drawn into the grain irregularities allegations. The first involved India.

INDIA SUES FIVE COMPANIES, CARGILL INCLUDED

The widespread publicity given to the irregularities in weighing, grading, and loading in the export terminals now led a number of purchasers to enter suits against the firms involved in the shipping. On May 3, 1976, the government of India, with its Food Corporation of India unit as a party, filed suit against five large American grain companies, charging fraud in grain shipments over a 15-year period and seeking $215 million in damages. Five identical complaints were made against Cargill, Continental Grain, Cook, Dreyfus Corporation, and the Minneapolis-based Peavey & Company, alleging that the grain shipments were not the same as the contract provided but instead "were inferior and of lesser value . . . in that they were short weight, of lower grade and quality and were infested or contaminated." There already had been evidence in the Cook Industries case that Cook employees (wrote a *Wall Street Journal* editor) "were instructed . . . to short weight ships as much as 1.5% if their cargoes were destined for Mediterranean, Mideast or South Asia ports." Later in 1970, the indictment charged, instructions were given "to increase the short weighting to 3% for vessels going to Pakistan, India and other countries that didn't have weighing facilities."

India's unloading facilities *were* notoriously primitive; unloading was most often by hand (the grain in sacks), with considerable spillage and lack of care in the process. Trying to establish any kind of post-unloading judgment would be extremely difficult for all of the five companies. The situation was further complicated by the fact that almost all of these shipments were accomplished under the P.L. 480 "Food for Peace" program, which provided for concessional sales to developing countries in great need of food aid.

While the testimony in the Cook case did seem to indicate some advantages taken by Cook, the Cargill executives felt certain that Cargill had not consciously done anything of this nature. The India suits were seeking damages of $75 million each from Cargill and Continental, $35.5 million from Cook, $26.25 million from Dreyfus, and $3.5 million from Peavey. Given the great difficulty in ascertaining exactly what happened after the fact, the case seemed almost untryable. Fragmentary information came from the current Singapore director of the Western Wheat Associates (WWA), a multicountry entity representing shipping countries, indicating that the WWA had been inspecting for 15 years wheat imported into India from all origins, and that the U.S. shipments met or exceeded the loading grade in all cases; he felt the claim was "inspired by a Russian communist faction in the Indian government that forced the Gandhi government to proceed with claims." This statement, too, would be difficult to substantiate at this late date.

A preliminary decision by a U.S. District Court judge in January 1978 ruled that the statute of limitations had not expired; the case was then to go to jury trial, with Cargill's amount now expanded to $175 million for the alleged defrauding of India on 700 separate grain shipments since 1961. But the case never came to trial, as the government of India settled for a nominal sum of $250,000, largely to cover their court costs to that point.[11]

OVERAGES HIT THE PUBLIC PRESS

The other "shoe that dropped," in early May 1976, again involved the longstanding issue of overages. It was a subject that the Cargill Grain Irregularities Task Force had spent much time studying. In November 1975, Bill Pearce had written the team, "There have been several recent indications that investigators are concentrating on 'overages' and that this may be the next important avenue of attack."

Overages and weight pickups had never been deliberately covered up. Nor were they fully disclosed, for the accounting system in place was designed to check shrinks, not overages. Normal shrink losses were built into the system, so final figures were net gains or losses, not "gross overages" or "gross shrinks." When overages were first reported in the Gulf, management was confident that a gross inbound to gross outbound comparison would reveal a shrink, not an overage. However, such was not the case. Notwithstanding all normal shrinkage, more grain appeared to have left the elevators than entered the elevators. Company officials were at a loss for an explanation.

So Pearce asked Jay Berkeley, Bob Hubbard, and Hank Kaufman for further reports on aspects of the issue. At the subsequent meeting, in late November, record-keeper Rob Johnson wrote, "At several stages in the investigation, the OI [the USDA's Office of Investigation] expressed approval of our controls and of our division of responsibilities. They seem to feel that that division helped prevent collusive activities while retaining broad oversight and awareness." Johnson continued:

Among the points made in the overages discussion were the following: (1) Cargill's weight pick-up was not covered up—it shows up clearly in our records, which implies lack of misdealing; (2) these weight pick-ups continued even after full knowledge of Federal investigations (in fact, the only change we instituted was in our instruction manual to make clear that 'tolerance' on weight is not to be taken by the house); (3) we should attempt to explain specific instances of sizable weight pick-ups in terms of the changes that occurred in that period of time and grain handled (e.g. more unit train movement of grain from the North); (4) we should also check to see whether there are shortages around a particular weight pick-up, either in time or in other commodities—implying an offsetting loss; (5) our own rules for checking our weight discrepancies indicate that our focus is on *accuracy,* not gain, since—for each elevator—the same weight pick-up as weight loss will trigger a closer look and (6) experiences of weight pick-up can be correlated with either modern, recently constructed elevators or with extensive investments in modernization of older facilities.

The task force concluded that the Company's overages were legitimate and explainable.

The first hint of Cargill's being linked publicly to the overages issue came in an article in the *New York Times* on February 19, 1976. Interpol, the international police organization, had had a meeting back in November in France; one of the nine American delegates had made statements at that time that "1.5 to 2 percent of all export of wheat, soybeans and corn in the last five years had been stolen." The delegate went on to detail methods, including forged certificates, tampering with weight machines, and account sheets that had been fraudulently altered. "I suppose, to get the message across, you'd have to dramatize it with pictures of starving children," the delegate continued. "Most of that grain was stolen from poor countries. Every time somebody short-weights a shipment to those countries, some children don't eat."

The *New York Times* writer then added that overages had been found in a number of large American grain companies, "including the three giants of the industry, Cargill, Inc., the Continental Grain Company and Cook Industries, Incorporated. . . . This is the first time that Cargill has been mentioned in this connection."

The juxtaposition of the Interpol delegate's accusations of fraud and the mention of the three companies seemed to imply that Cargill was guilty of these fraudulent practices just because it showed overages in its accounts. Cargill had attempted to defend itself in the article: "A spokesman for Cargill said today that the Company was aware of the overages and asserted that they occurred normally, and 'regularly appear in our accounting records,' usually as a result of moisture gains when grain is transported from cold, dry climates to warm and moist regions, such as the Gulf area. He said new dust control measures had increased the gain in inventory weights in recent years. 'There are also underages in some facilities,' he said."[12]

In early May, the *New York Times* returned to the allegations, this time with explicit figures and an eye-catching headline: "U.S. Agents Hint $45 Million in Excessive Grain Inventories of Three Companies." The article detailed a report of the USDA's Office of Investigation (OI), which alleged overages at Cargill of $23.8 million (covering the years 1969 through 1974), $16.9 for Continental, and $5.5 for Cook for the same period. There was no analysis by the OI as to what this meant. For Continental and Cook, the OI report did imply short weighting; for Cargill, the report (said the *New York Times*) stated "only that an investigation had been conducted to determine the Company's 'inventory position.'" All through the long article were references to the continuing "wide-ranging Federal investigation of corruption in the grain industry."

This time Cargill officials were truly shocked, given the strongly positive signals from the OI just a few months earlier. The Company now made the decision to respond publicly. An important letter to all Cargill employees over the signature of chief executive officer Erv Kelm was circulated. "Some will interpret the report as evidence that irregularities are involved," Kelm began, even though no charges had been made by the OI. "The OI's most serious error was its arbitrary assumption that two-tenths of one percent of all grain received by export elevators is lost in handling." Modern equipment utilized by Cargill had reduced such transferring losses at its major export terminals "to a small fraction of this amount by careful management and extensive investments we have made to improve their engineering and the design and grain handling equipment." Nearly half of the OI's estimate of the overages was attributed to this assumption.

Kelm explained further that the U.S. Warehouse Act required all companies at all times to maintain stocks on hand at least equal to outstanding warehouse receipt obligations. Kelm continued, "To be sure we meet this requirement, a margin of safety is incorporated into accounting estimates of losses incurred each time grain is handled in a licensed elevator. As a result, there is more grain in the elevator than shown in inventory records." Therefore, Kelm maintained, the OI had significantly exaggerated the incidence of actual overages. Further, the OI had totally ignored any shortages; "to regard one as significant and ominous and to ignore the other," Kelm maintained, "raises serious questions about the objectivity of the whole effort."

Kelm devoted a whole page to a thorough discussion of the issue of weight gain. Moisture pick-up had been found to be a major source of weight gain. Part of this could happen when grain was washed to remove smut or when water-soluble fumigants were added. Further, changing conditions of temperature and humidity were even more significant sources of added weight. Grain originating in colder, drier areas—for example, in the Midwest—could gain significant weight from condensation and absorption of moisture by the time it was loaded in a vessel in a warm, humid port area. In earlier times, most of the grain moved from interior to export points was transported in barges and rail boxcars that took more than a week to complete the movement. At this point, however, an increasing amount of grain was being moved from the interior to export points in covered hopper cars; the RAT's would arrive less than 48 hours after loading.

Cargill had commissioned extensive laboratory tests, conducted independently by Dr. Clyde Christensen, a University of Minnesota professor, and these had verified the Company's hypotheses. This was a straightforward laboratory test—the long time lag from the actual Cargill shipments to India would have made it very difficult to examine actual shipping dates, points of origin, arrival dates and relative temperatures or humidities.

The Christensen research was printed in full in the August 10 issue of *Milling and Baking News*. In an editorial in the same publication, the editors, under the title "Laying Overage to Rest," noted that "the indisputable conclusion from all this is that efficient systems of delivering grain to Gulf elevators and handling within the facilities will more often than not also result in a build-up of moisture and a significant pick-up in the weight of the grain. . . . The probes thus far have largely neglected the role of moisture pick-up. . . . The investigations may have been just as shoddy as the illegal practices the industry and all involved yearn to see eradicated."

All of these considerations, Kelm averred, seemed to be either little understood or ignored by the OI, and this was complicated by the fact that no interviews were held with Cargill personnel to obtain this kind of explanation. "It is not my purpose to offer a final judgment on all of Cargill's operations," Kelm concluded. "The best we can do now is to reaffirm what we expect of Cargill employees at all levels and to assure, through our affirmative action program, that in all our activities we meet the highest possible standards. This, of course, is what we are doing."

To be sure, the Kelm explanations were not shared by everyone. Indeed, in a major front-page *Wall Street Journal* article on July 1, 1976, concerning Texas grain elevators then coming under scrutiny, Attorney General Gerald J. Gallinghouse, who had spearheaded the Louisiana investigations was quoted: "The key thing to remember is that grain doesn't grow in these elevators . . . if there's any logical explanation for these overages, we haven't heard it. You can cut it thick; you can cut it thin. I don't care how much you cut it, it's still baloney."

However, the Gallinghouse view was not shared by the USDA. Two weeks after the *Wall Street Journal* article, Bill Pearce received a call from John Knebel, the Undersecretary of Agriculture. Knebel had seen Kelm's letter to Cargill employees and was "troubled" (so reported Pearce). Knebel held that the Kelm piece was "the most rational explanation of overages I've ever seen." Knebel expressed concern that the department's investigators had released "raw numbers, unrefined," and that they seemed to be "chasing the wrong rabbits." If Cargill had been overstating handling losses in order to be certain that it met U.S. Warehouse Act obligations, the department was hitting Car-

September 26, 1975: "Washington: Gerald Gallinghouse, U.S. Attorney in New Orleans who headed an investigation of grain inspection scandals in Louisiana, told a Senate agriculture subcommittee yesterday that 52 indictments returned so far will probably be followed by a 'substantial number of very significant additional cases'" (UPI/Corbis-Bettmann).

gill with "the back side of the broom," and this was not fair. Knebel stated that he was prepared to go on record with this view.

In a meeting with Pearce a week later, Knebel repeated that the OI had released "raw data," with no explanation and that, as a result, "bad conclusions" apparently had been drawn. There was some confusion a few days later when Secretary Earl Butz seemed to support the OI investigation, but the matter rested at this point. Congress was turning its concerns to legislation on new grain standards, and the issue of overages began to fade away.

On August 30, Bill Pearce and John McGrory were able to obtain a face-to-face meeting with Secretary Butz, along with Undersecretary Knebel and the general counsel for the USDA, James Keast. Pearce's memorandum to the files on the meeting noted that "Butz expressed deep concern about the Department's role . . . that he was concerned that 'there are people in the Department who, when faced with criticism, try to shift the blame to others—in this case the grain trade.'" When Knebel suggested that the department needed more evidence on moisture pick-up, Butz replied that the Christensen data "looked to him like solid technical evidence." At the end of the meeting, Pearce reported, "Butz stated that he feared that the Department was responsible for serious and unsupportable charges against the trade (assuming that what we had told him could be verified). He instructed Knebel to investigate the matter immediately and if he finds that our position is borne out, to write both to the Attorney General and appropriate Congressional committees setting the record straight on the matter of overages." This seemed to end the matter.[13]

A New Grain Standards Law

From the start of the grain irregularities saga in early 1974, there had been many concerns about the two laws that governed the inspection, weighing and grading of grain. Back in 1916, Congress had passed both the Grain Standards Act and the Warehouse Act; in the legislative discussions at that time there had been some support for actual federal intervention, but a system of state and private inspection with oversight by a federal inspection agency had resulted, to become the pattern all the way through. The Warehouse Act had been amended in 1931 to guarantee the supremacy of federal regulations over conflicting state regulations, and the Grain Standards Act was amended substantially in 1968. Despite these amendments and revisions, the regulatory approach had remained unchanged—federal licensing of employees of state or private grain inspection agencies and of warehouse operators, leaving essentially a supervisory role for federal officials.

This had led to a polyglot system, where each state had its own separate inspectors under separate systems, although all were under the general supervision of the USDA. It was really a two-tier system, as the laws allowed profit-making firms also to take on the responsibilities of inspection, with costs to be defrayed by charging a fee. There was always the option in the case of disagreements to request a federal inspector to perform an on-site appeal inspection, even to have the sample mailed to a federal laboratory for final determination. This system had proved to be reasonably inexpensive and expeditious but left many possibilities for a less than arm's-length relationship between the grain trading companies and the inspectors, state or private. The two-plus years of hearings, indictments, convictions, and general public distrust of the system had led to widespread demands for changes in the laws themselves.

All through 1976, such possible changes were debated in both the U.S. House of Representatives and the Senate. Politics intruded prominently, with many states wanting to preserve their own political system and the grain trading companies expressing many divergent notions (although coming together at least on preserving the historically flexible system). Even President Ford had difficulty in deciding how strict he wanted to be, given that his vice presidential running mate, Senator Robert Dole of Kansas, wanted a tighter version than did the President's own Secretary of Agriculture, Earl Butz. Nevertheless, by late September, all the various versions had finally been melded to allow passage of a new U.S. Grain Standards Act of 1976.

The compromise version tilted toward the version with less control. At the ports, private grain inspection agencies were eliminated, replaced with federal inspectors at most ports, state inspectors at a few. A new federal Grain Inspection Service under the USDA was established, and larger grain exporters were to be registered, with this registration revocable for violations of the grain inspection law.

Registration was not popular with the exporters, for it required disclosing more information on ownership than previously. Given the privately held structure of many of the companies (five of the "big six," for example), their hostility toward "telling all" was not surprising. There were large family fortunes involved here, which, in times of terrorism, were best kept private. Kidnapping was particularly on executives' minds after the seizure of Jorge and Juan Born in Argentina in September 1974. The kidnappers of the two scions of the Bunge y Born grain trading group in that country (the parent of the American Bunge), reputed to be Montonero terrorists, exacted a ransom of $60 million, as well as promises that the Bunge group would give free food and wide publicity to the Montonero credo. The two Borns were then freed, unharmed. Cargill had been concerned about kidnapping as early as July 1973, when the board discussed what was happening in Argentina. In June 1974, Erv Kelm invited senior management executives and their wives to a private session at the Company's Lake office, where an FBI agent was to discuss security in families. "Cargill's size and recent profit performance have received some attention from the media during the past year. The public availability of this information . . . increases the corporate and personal risks . . . of which you should be aware."

In two of the key exporting states, Louisiana and Texas, inspection now would be taken over completely by federal inspectors. State inspection could continue at ports in several other states, including Washington, Virginia, and Minnesota, where no corruption had been involved. Reasonably rigid restrictions were put on conflict of interest possibilities between any private agency and the grain trading firms using its services. These provisions could be waived for grain exchanges, chambers of commerce, and boards of trade that already had their own inspection agencies. The new service was to be under the USDA but with substantial independence from the Secretary of Agriculture, for the administrator of the new service would be appointed by the President and confirmed by the Senate.

Senator Dick Clark, the Iowa Democrat so strongly involved in the hearings, felt that the compromises in the final act were too substantial; the *Minneapolis Star Tribune* reported, "As for Clark's desire to take nothing now in hopes of winning bigger in the future, Senator Hubert Humphrey of Minnesota [said] 'you can never be sure about next year.'" Perhaps Hubert Humphrey's ending comment could serve well as the overarching thought for the whole grain irregularities legislative effort: "He said he has learned to 'harvest the ground that has been plowed.' You can always 'go back for more later' if the situation looks promising."[14]

"Welcome to Pearl's Kitchen," Pearl Bailey tells Ed Reynolds (out of picture on left), vice president and general manager of Cargill's Paramount Poultry Products department. TV commercials starring Bailey were filmed in a New York studio for airing there starting February 19, 1974 (Cargill staff photograph).

. . .

Despite the turmoil in both crop years, 1974–1975 and 1975–1976, Cargill's financial results had been excellent. Indeed, the $218 million in net profit in 1974–1975 once again set an all-time record. The commodity group had its second best year; some futures trading was down, as were salt and barge earnings. The processing group continued at a high level, though below the previous year's peak. Especially successful were soybean crushing and corn milling. Feed achieved record earnings—volume down but margins up. Poultry production suffered. Chemical products had its seventh straight record year. Several of the new acquisitions had shown promise—Sylvania Peanuts, Aenco (solid waste disposal), Cargill Leasing. Indeed, the $181.3 million in capital expenditures and the $47.6 million to acquire new businesses totaled to a new investment record for the Company, "tangible evidence of our confidence in the future," said Kelm and Seed in the annual report.

The earnings for 1975–1976 were less, although almost $179 million. Commodity marketing had been set back by the moratorium on sales to Russia, and there were other declines in that group. In processing, soybean crushing was down, milling up. Tradax had excellent results, so did feed. In general, it was a fine year, with capital expenditures a healthy $229.8 million (and new acquisitions coming in at $91.7 million).

Over the four years 1972–1973 through 1975–1976, Cargill had earned over $700 million. It had put back into the business for capital expenditures and acquisitions (using its massive cash flow) an amazing $775 million—three-quarters of a billion dollars. It was not just that these total sums were quantitatively substantial but that the qualitative changes had been so significant. There simply was no doubt that Cargill was a markedly more complex agribusiness firm after these four years; further, the Company's very definition of this term had widened almost beyond the understanding of those who thought they knew the Company well. By this point Cargill was involved not only in all of its traditional agribusiness efforts but was adding new ones—flour milling, peanuts, cattle feeding—as well as making its own barges (at Pine Bluff, Arkansas), underwriting insurance, leasing heavy equipment, providing investor services, making steel, and learning solid-waste recovery.[15]

But management really did see synergies among all these—saw most of them as the processing of commodities and all of them as linked (perhaps the one signal exception being the Holiday Inn endeavor in Belgium, which stayed in Company hands only a few years; the hotel industry was never to be tried again). Management had deliberately, self-consciously moved the Company to a more multinational, more varied, more publicly attuned business corporation.

One of the strongest contributing factors allowing the Company to undergo extensive refurbishing, upgrading, and additions to existing physical facilities, while at the same time diversifying its efforts was the willingness of the owners (and management) to accept very modest dividends. In December 1974, the rate had risen from the equivalent of 40 cents per share to 70 cents, after a 4 for 1 split; it stayed right there for the next two years. So almost all of the earnings were plowed back into the business.

Still to come was one more public challenge to the values, indeed, the very ethos of the Company. This was Senator Frank Church's Subcommittee on Multinational Corporations and United States Foreign Policy. We turn now to this story.

CHAPTER EIGHT

The Multinational Hearings

W hen either the Federal Trade Commission (FTC) or the Department of Justice speaks, business listens, often quite anxiously. The purview of both agencies is antitrust policy and related concerns about various "restraints of trade" (the key legislation for this from the Sherman Act of 1890 and two pieces of legislation passed in 1914, the Clayton and Federal Trade Commission Acts). Enforcement of the Sherman Act is the exclusive responsibility of the Department of Justice, which deals with allegations under the act relating to conspiracies in restraint of trade and monopolies. These are particularly serious charges, carrying potentials for heavy civil and even criminal penalties by the courts. When Justice speaks, industry listens.

The FTC's particular focus is on practices in restraint of trade, such as price fixing and price discrimination, and the effects on competition from proposed corporate mergers. While the FTC does not have the power to exact criminal penalties on individuals, it can issue "cease and desist" orders that are enforceable in court. Its role, particularly in passing on mergers, is always a special concern, for the commission's power includes outright prohibition of this key corporate device for growth. When the FTC speaks, industry also listens.

So a pathbreaking speech in October 1974 by James T. Halverson, the director of the Bureau of Competition of the FTC, captured full attention in the grain trade. The speech was given before the Antitrust Law Section of the Ohio State Bar Association and carried the arresting title "FTC and the Food Industries—1974's Major Antitrust Emphasis." He disclosed a new FTC initiative—the "National Food Program." Its objectives: to identify anticompetitive conditions that might be interfering with the free play of competitive forces and (in his words) "resulting in higher prices for consumers."

Halverson maintained that the FTC had been guilty of "an ad hoc 'mailbag approach' . . . a proclivity to bring cases which either were trivial or represented at best a non-optimal use of our manpower." The agency had been reactive, primarily depending upon the "mailbag" of complaints *to* them. Now they had determined to subject the food industries to coordinated, sharply focused scrutiny. The "recent skyrocketing prices" that had stemmed from the Russian grain sales and other forces were now to be examined, so that the FTC could "discover whether these factors . . . are now being used as convenient excuses for raising prices, maintaining high and noncompetitive price levels, and engaging in anticompetitive activities."

There was to be a special focus on commodities, "particularly staple agricultural products . . . involved in a world trading market." It was this, said Halverson, that augured "possible use of traditional antitrust enforcement tools." In sum, the grain trade was to go under the FTC microscope of intensive investigation.[1]

Five days later, Cargill's president, Fred Seed, received a disconcerting letter from the assistant director of the Bureau of Competition of the FTC, which included (in a 12-page single-spaced letter) a stunningly comprehensive list of questions to be answered. A description was requested for "each entity, plant and office" of the Company. Full stockholder lists were to be sent. Income tax statements and "all supporting schedules and other material" were to be compiled, covering the years 1965–1973. Charts and tables of organization were to be included, with a list of all foreign and domestic acquisitions and dispositions for the years 1960–1974. Also, all joint ventures were to be elaborated, again for the years 1960–1974.

All memberships in any form of trade association were to be spelled out. For each grain that the company sold domestically, in export, or in foreign countries, an extensive table was to be prepared detailing all sales by categories, both in dollar volume and in bushels. All speeches, testimony, or written statements delivered by "any director, officer, or employee of the company" to trade associations, cooperatives, financial analysts, congressional committees, state regulatory bodies, state legislatures, and the like, were to be sent. Examples of all standard forms used by the Company (sales contracts, purchase contracts, etc.) were also to be forwarded. All reports sent to the Department of Agriculture were to be listed; likewise, the same list was to be compiled of contacts with the Department of Commerce. All reports to commodity exchanges were to be included.

Further, specific details were requested concerning electronic data processing equipment and information systems. All of the Company's grain elevators were to be listed, with details of their size, classification, and bushels of throughput. For those facilities handling railroad cars, similar details were also required. For each separate function of the organization—purchasing, transportation, operation of foreign entities, and so on—the Company was to provide the name of a specific person in the organization whom the FTC could contact.

Most of the material was to be sent to the FTC within 30 days; for some of the more complex requests, a 60-day window was allowed. Meanwhile, the Company was to retain all documents in its possession, suspending all records destruction programs until further notice. Remembering that the Company was at this very time involved in the "boxcar blackmail" and grain irregularities cases, each demanding major responses, the FTC request put great demands on Company management.[2]

As the Cargill people rushed to assemble these data, on what one Company lawyer called a "priority-crash basis," they were taken aback in early December with the arrival of a second letter from the FTC. The agency also had decided to investigate "soybean marketing and related activities." In addition to a number of the items requested in the first letter, now all soybean trading records for the years 1970–1974, in great detail, were requested. Processing figures for conversion to soybean meal and oil were to be delineated. Gross margins were to be provided for all sales, overall financial statements for the period 1965–1974 were to be included, and modes of transportation for all of this described. Now the "search, find and report" efforts had to be doubled.[3]

Cargill's Attempt to Take Over the Missouri Portland Cement Company

The FTC inquiry was not a complete surprise, for Cargill had recently garnered substantial attention from the agency in the process of a tense effort to acquire a new company in a new industry. In August 1972, just after the Russian grain sales, the Company had established a Salt Expansion and Diversification Group with the goal of expanding into an industry similar to salt with respect to at least two of the department's skills of production, marketing and distribution. After considering coal, cement, lime, chlorine, kaolin, aggregates, zinc, fluorspar, asphalt, potash, phosphate, and caustic soda, the group rated the cement industry as its number-one acquisition prospect. Distribution and marketing were similar to that in the salt industry, and cement had the unique advantage of being seasonally opposite to salt. Demand and prices had been trending upward for the cement industry; it was a capital-intensive, basic industry that would enable Cargill to utilize its transportation expertise; and it would fit Cargill's international commodity efforts.

Some 31 of the 51 U.S. cement companies were actually contacted by letter, and some negotiations had transpired with several of these. Most were reasonably small; if Cargill was to purchase one, it would be a "toehold" effort (as a circuit court of appeals judge later called this approach).

Rather than this, the Company finally decided to make a bid to acquire a considerably larger company, the Missouri Portland Cement Company. The executives of this firm quickly rejected a Cargill bid out of hand; the effort would have to be a hostile takeover. In mid-December 1973, Cargill made a tender offer for their stock; and when the tender expired, they had acquired some 19 percent of Missouri Portland stock. The cement company fought back, petitioning a U.S. District Court judge for a preliminary injunction preventing Cargill from proceeding with a further tender offer. The central argument of Missouri Portland was that Cargill's acquisition, if allowed, would be anticompetitive, leading to economic concentration and therefore violating the monopoly constraints of the Clayton Act. The district court judge ruled in their favor and issued the injunction.

Cargill then took the case to the circuit court of appeals, and in a widely reported case, circuit court judge Henry Friendly spoke for the three judges and reversed most of the decisions of the district court judge. The case was a complex one, involving both issues of securities regulation and some dozen different aspects of monopoly theory. Friendly saw Cargill's entry into the cement industry as "beneficial to competition," for "the vices of an oligopolistic market lie in price and other agreements among the oligopolists, often impossible to prove—or what amounts to nearly the same thing—their slothful acquiescence in a state of affairs beneficial to all." Acquisition of one of the oligopolists by a more efficient company intent on acquiring a larger market share would break the explicit or implicit agreement or the condition engendered by the sloth. As Friendly put it, "Introducing a bull into a china shop is a good way to break through the comfortable vices of oligopoly."

The FTC's Bureau of Competition thought otherwise, attacking Cargill because "its large barge operations could also provide a significant competitive advantage in transporting cement." But another branch of the FTC, its Office of Policy Planning and Evaluation, disagreed: "This appears to be offered as a reason why the acquisition should be attacked . . . we take it Cargill's barge operations . . . which are alleged to be increased by the acquisition, are forms of efficiency. If this is the case then it appears that these acquisitions are being attacked because they create efficiency. . . . As Judge Friendly points out, the introduction of efficient firms, especially into a oligopolistic market, will *promote* competition." The position paper ended its lengthy analysis: "As to the Cargill matter itself, we strongly recommend that no additional resources be expended on this case."

Unfortunately for Cargill, the Bureau of Competition viewpoint held sway. In late October 1974, just a few days after the bureau had sent its letter asking for the details of Cargill's operation, it issued a proposed complaint against Cargill, alleging that the acquisition of Missouri Portland by Cargill was "anti-competitive." The FTC's proposed complaint sought to force Cargill to divest itself of its shares of Missouri Portland and also to prohibit it from acquiring Portland's cement production facilities for 10 years without prior FTC approval. On February 7, 1975, the FTC joined the issue by promulgating this as a formal complaint.

In late August of that year, Cargill gave up the battle to acquire Missouri Portland, selling its shares to H. K. Porter Company, in the process going on record that it was "no longer seeking control of Missouri Portland." The *Wall Street Journal* commented, "After expending all this energy, it obviously wasn't easy for Cargill to abandon the plans."

But the reasons for the Company's about-face were more complicated than this. The Securities and Exchange Commission would require additional disclosure of Company finances if a second tender were made. The earlier financial revelations to counter the criticisms of the Russian trades had unsettled a number of people in the corporation, the family owners in particular. Because the family interests in Cargill were such a large part of the Company's net worth, financial disclosure of Cargill was also financial disclosure of their wealth. It was just at this time, in the face of the industry's increasingly negative profile from the Russian sales, the soybean embargo, the allegations of "exporting the nation's food supply," and sharply rising food prices, that there had been threats of terrorism against companies and individuals in the grain-trading industry (for example, the September 1974 kidnapping of Jorge and Juan Born in Buenos Aires). Cargill had even decided that it was necessary to conduct private sessions on security for a group of family members and senior executives (this paid off in the prompt discovery and neutralization of the letter bombs received by both the Company and a family member in June 1976). With the Company having just come through another record year, a number of family members questioned the wisdom of possibly increasing the personal security risks of the families in exchange for a hoped-for better public understanding of the Company.[4]

Inasmuch as Cargill now finally drew away from the takeover effort in the cement industry, had the FTC forsworn its spotlight on Cargill? The Company had taken heart from the FTC's Office of Policy Planning and Evaluation statements in December 1974, praising Cargill's efficiencies that might be brought to the cement industry and seeming to criticize the FTC's own Bureau of Competition for holding "that these acquisitions are being attacked because they create efficiency . . . we do not think that it is good policy to attack business transactions because they are likely to give firms competitive advantages based on efficiency" (quoting once again Judge Friendly's decision). This influential arm of the FTC even had recommended that the agency's Bureau of Competition drop the case altogether.

Such tension between the two FTC arms was reminiscent of the same kind of strained relations between the Interstate Commerce Commission's Bureau of Enforcement and the commissioners themselves in the "boxcar blackmail" case. It was not at all uncommon for the enforcement division of a given federal agency to take a much stronger posture than the commission overseeing the overall effort; the latter, by nature of its broader charge, was more likely to take a compromise view, considering all conflicting parties involved.

In the boxcar case, the Bureau of Enforcement seemed also to be saying that, inherently, consumer interests were better protected by many competitors, so most consolidations were bad, ignoring the efficiencies brought by consolidation and their likely lower consumer costs.

Yet despite the high credibility of Judge Friendly's powerful words and the added support of the FTC's Office of Policy Planning and Evaluation, the FTC still *did* decide to continue its investigation of Cargill, and the Company had no choice but to fulfill its requirements to forward more requested data to the FTC. The *Des Moines Register* commented that the FTC lawyers and economists were focusing on "operation of the Big Grain trading companies in and around the commodity markets, and their relationships with each other and with the big commodity trading brokerage firms." Further, the *Register* vowed, the FTC was looking into the "revolving door" nature of employment in the industry—in government and then back into the industry—and that the FTC was also interested in possible indirect control of country elevators by the larger firms.

The FTC, according to the *Register*, had a special concern about the overall government entity regulating commodity trading, now to become a new agency called the Commodity Futures Trading Commission (CFTC), replacing the Commodity Exchange Authority (CEA) in April 1975, after fresh legislation was passed. In the extensive hearings leading to this change, the FTC had seemed skeptical of this "freshman" enforcement group as not being independent enough from the commodity exchanges themselves, so this, too, was to be made a peripheral function of the grain industry investigation.[5]

Cargill had long maintained a cooperative relationship with the antitrust division of the Department of Justice; its interaction with that agency during the latter's earlier questioning of a Cargill soybean plant acquisition in Iowa in 1963 was a good case in point. But links with the FTC were not as strong, and all through the spring of 1975, Cargill waited for the FTC's "other shoe to drop."

Senator Church's Unpleasant Surprise

One of the longest-standing investigative committees of Congress during the 1970s was the U.S. Senate's Subcommittee on Multinational Corporations, operating under its Committee on Foreign Relations. The chair was Senator Frank Church of Idaho. In the period from early 1973 until this point of Cargill's evolving FTC relationship (in July 1975), the subcommittee had made spectacular charges against a wide range of American multinationals concerning their behavior abroad.

In its early days in 1973, the subcommittee had taken up the International Telephone and Telegraph Company's machinations in Chile, where clandestine efforts were being made in opposition to the newly elected president of Chile, Salvador Allende. The Central Intelligence Agency (CIA) had been involved with this; so had ITT. This was followed in 1974 by revelations against the actions of seven of the major multinational oil companies in their links with Iran and Libya, in activities in Bolivia, and in efforts related to the Arab oil boycott. Early in 1975, the subcommittee (again in operation) looked at the relationship of another oil company with Italy. The boycott by Arab groups against companies doing business with Israel also was closely examined. By mid-1975, the subcommittee was examining the multinational operations of several of the major aircraft companies, with a particular focus on bribes and other questionable sales practices in bringing about large aircraft contracts with foreign countries—Indonesia, Saudi Arabia, Japan, and even the Netherlands.

The public press had been filled with these disclosures; the so-called Church Subcommittee had gained a high profile and succeeded in bringing to public attention a wide range of private practices by multinational corporations that seemed to be inimical to the public good of the country. In sum, the Church Subcommittee had put its finger on a whole series of shady practices, just about all of which had turned out to be both accurate and needing amelioration by some form of congressional action. The subcommittee was indeed a formidable adversary![6]

There had been rumors through the spring of 1975 that the large international grain-trading companies were an early upcoming target for the subcommittee. Cargill now became the first to learn that this was reality. On July 23, 1975, the Company received a call from Richard Gilmore, who at this time was staff consultant to the subcommittee. He began by relating that the subcommittee was considering an "investigation of the grain trade mainly from the vantage point of multinational corporations." All the major grain companies were to be contacted; Cargill was first. Gilmore promised that "he did not intend this investigation to be a witch hunt. He was personally trying to do an objective job." No plans had been made as yet by anyone to hold hearings; there were alternatives, which "might include a formal staff study or no action at all."

The subcommittee's staffer enumerated a laundry list (just "partial," he noted) of the subjects he was interested in examining. He emphasized that these items were not to be seen "as an exhaustive list." It was a demand much more complex than that of the FTC—and more murky as to the motives. Company officials did agree that all of the FTC questions seemed to fall within a legitimate set of bounds for that agency. But in dealing with a congressional committee, the ground rules shift considerably. The short-term topicality often matters much more to the congressional committee; the vagaries of public opinion and the winds of change often govern where a committee's staff will go. Initial questions such as those posed by Gilmore often would hide (unintentionally or not) the underlying thrust of the investigation.

Gilmore's questions lay in 11 different categories; here is the list (as compiled by Robbin Johnson):

(1) the role of subsidiaries in shipping and handling grains from both U.S. and foreign origins; (2) the scale of our grain shipments; (3) detailed information concerning our export contracts, transshipments, contract cancellations and volume of exports; (4)

how we charter ships and . . . how we move grain; (5) our participation in P.L. 480 shipments . . . are they handled in a different way; (6) inspection, blending and related issues, including an "exhaustive" list of foreign complaints on quality (some of which involved Cargill) and short weighting (on which he could not recall complaints concerning Cargill); (7) hedging or covering of sales in Milan and other international or speculative markets; (8) how much of our operations are affected by OPIC [the Overseas Private Investment Corporation] and EximBank [the Export-Import Bank] and . . . subsidies we receive for shipping from the Maritime Division; (9) how Cargill [analyzes] statistically world crop production and supplies; (10) our operations in Canada, Brazil and Western Europe . . . and experiences [with] wheat boards, export subsidies, variable levies, etc.; and (11) our use of unit trains and related discounting practices.[7]

Gilmore also addressed the question of the inviolability of any Cargill records that might be tendered to the subcommittee. They would, he promised, "respect confidential business material." But if there was an instance where he thought a company was "attempting to extend the shield," he would negotiate this assurance. Cargill's skepticism about whether the system was leakproof showed in Johnson's report: "Essentially, he was saying that his track record and the rules of confidentiality should give us some confidence that he and the subcommittee could preserve legitimate confidences." *Some* was the operative word.

The complication of having two separate entities of the federal government investigating the Company now rapidly worsened with the entry of a *third* group. On October 6, 1975, Senator Church requested that the General Accounting Office (GAO) join the research process, to produce "information on marketing systems of principal grain supplying countries." The GAO analysts took this to mean a study of the grain trading efforts in Argentina, Australia, Canada, and the European Community, as well as soybean marketing in Brazil. Church made it clear to the GAO investigators that this should not "preclude Subcommittee staff from their own access to individuals involved in grain marketing."

Soon the GAO appeared at Cargill's own door for help on their efforts. The Company agreed to put the GAO analysts in touch with key people in the U.S. grain trade who would know these sections of the world (Cargill operated in each one) and also was persuaded to set up a general briefing for GAO on the overall grain marketing structure. In addition, Cargill would introduce the GAO to important nationals in all of the countries in question.

As Cargill set about making information available to these three separate assiduous investigators, Company officials tried to sort out the relationships involved. An internal memorandum caught this perplexity: "There is no sensitivity in supplying the GAO questionnaire. Information provided to the Federal Trade Commission, on the other hand, is very sensitive in several areas . . . several of the FTC questions overlap questions that Gilmore addressed to us directly." One alternative was to supply the subcommittee less sensitive answers for those questions that seemed to overlap both the FTC and the subcommittee requests. There was a further possible strategy of supplying to the subcommittee all the FTC information requested. But some of the subcommittee's questions "involved disclosure of financial or operating data of great sensitivity and material we have historically refused to disclose in the past." Just how to sort out these nuances was to occupy Company management over many months.

Finally, the Company developed a set of "basic" answers that could be readily shared with the three agencies, leaving a smaller subset concerning, particularly, Cargill/Tradax relationships. Even some of these were reasonably straightforward, and decisions subsequently were made to share them with the subcommittee; but profit-and-loss relationships between Cargill and Tradax, explanations of the corporate structure, elaboration of Cargill's short- and long-term lines of credit and breakdowns of Cargill/Tradax earnings into domestic, export, and non-U.S. origins were considered by management to be too sensitive to share publicly. Drawing a precise line as to just what truly was Cargill's own proprietary information and what was legitimately public information continued to be a puzzle up to the June 1976 hearings at which Cargill was subsequently asked to be the first grain company witness.

Late in August 1975, Gilmore recast his earlier questions in a more narrowly specific frame, this time ending up with a total of 25 questions. He now was interested in specific cases, for example, requesting detailed chronological sequences in a current sale to the Soviet Union and inquiring about details of another sale, to the People's Republic of China, where there were some questions concerning rejections and cancellations. Complex questions about ownership of elevators, barges, and ocean shipping and more queries concerning credit lines were added. Specifics of Cargill's Brazilian operations were requested. Finally, a number of Gilmore's queries concerned Cargill/Tradax interactions. Detailed profit figures continued to be requested for these.

Not only did Gilmore want Cargill's response to the GAO questionnaires but he also "would like a copy of the material we submitted to the Federal Trade Commission in connection with their investigation of the grain industry, especially as that information related to parent-affiliate relationships." In late October, Gilmore complained to Cargill about how slowly responses were being made. Robbin Johnson, charged with the responsibility for the answers, replied to Gilmore, "I was surprised that you thought it possible that we might be dragging our feet. I suspect that we gave you the most detailed, open and complete backgrounding of any of the grain firms you visited. . . . I suspect that we will end up providing you with a better understanding of our business than others." (By the time of Gilmore's first trip to Cargill, in late August, he had already visited Continental, Bunge, Dreyfus, Garnac, and Cook and was headed to see Archer Daniels Midland after the Cargill stop.)[8]

The Russians Queried

Just after his threat to "light a fire," Gilmore and his associates on the sub-committee staff left for a long investigative trip to Europe. First on the docket was Russia. Gilmore himself visited the Soviet Union between November 23 and December 1, 1975, shortly after the five-year grain agreement had been reached between the United States and Russia (the events leading up to this, including the short embargo, were described in the preceding chapter). Gilmore requested estimates of current Soviet grain needs and apparently was given figures showing Russia's own production at even less than had been estimated a few weeks earlier. Gilmore queried the Russians about ongoing shipments and deliveries and found conflicting responses concerning capacity of the ports, railroads, and barges in handling large quantities of grain. Some officials seemed to imply congestion at the ports and railcar shortages.

This led Gilmore to some conclusions that later became quite controversial. Gilmore stated (in his later trip report): "The most noteworthy aspect of my discussions concerning exports was the impression Soviet officials conveyed of a determination to keep exports at levels not drastically different from earlier years. They were indifferent as to whether or not these exports would have to come in part from foreign sources." Further, "I was told that the same companies who are the major sellers of grain to the USSR are also exporters of Soviet grain to other parts of the world." This led Gilmore to the conclusion that "if Soviet claims about their stocks and exports are correct, then the United States may find itself in the awkward position of having signed an agreement . . . which assists the Soviet Union in stock replenishment and its own export program. . . . The United States could end up protecting Soviet leadership from any public admissions of failure in their own planning and production process. Freeing Soviet supplies for export by means of increased, relatively cheap imports of U.S. grain may also be a boon to the U.S.S.R.'s political and economic standing."

All of this became public in Gilmore's trip report, published on April 1, 1975. Senator Church immediately made a public statement for his Subcommittee on Multinational Corporations (MNC), seeming to imply that large quantities of U.S. grain shipped ostensibly to the Soviet Union itself was really being stored in Western Europe for resale: "For all we know, the Soviet Union may be storing U.S. grain in elevators of American companies in Amsterdam, Rotterdam or Hamburg. This grain may never end up in the Soviet Union, but instead may be exported as Soviet grain to other destinations." The newspapers picked this up quickly; one reporter quoted "a high White House official" as saying that "Government officials have known that some Soviet grain exports were being handled by American-based companies."

The word *some* gave the clue here. In truth, while modest amounts of grain on the way to the Soviet Union had been stored in Western Europe because of the jam in Soviet unloading facilities, it was not a regular practice of any American company to store large quantities of grain for the Soviets or to act as the Soviets' sales agent for U.S.S.R. sales elsewhere.

By the time of Church's news release, he had determined upon holding public hearings on the multinational grain trading firms (it looked as if Cargill was to be the "star witness," inasmuch as Gilmore and his associates had spent most of their time with the Company). Church stated in his announcement concerning Gilmore's trip report, "The issues raised in this report will be a matter of further inquiry when the Subcommittee holds public hearings on its investigation of U.S. multinational grain companies."

These hearings were held in June 1976, becoming what most people considered to be the most important single public airing relating to the grain trade that occurred all through this high-profile period in the early and mid-1970s. But the issue of the multinational companies storing and selling Russian grain was on its face a nonissue. There was a tangential reference to this in the hearings, during the Cargill testimony, turning up no evidence, and the issue was completely dropped. The damage to the credibility of Gilmore and his staff associates was not minimal.[9]

Swiss Authorities Intrude

After his Russian trip, Gilmore and his associates turned to questions relating to Western European grain trading practices, with particular scrutiny of Cargill's Tradax operation in Geneva, Switzerland. That country's very strict rules about foreign governments conducting any business on Swiss soil now came into play. Indeed, the relevant provisions under Swiss law involved very harsh penalties for any infraction (as these were seen by Swiss authorities' eyes). Not only were there civil penalties involved but also severe criminal penalties.

The previous year, the subcommittee had run into difficulties with these Swiss regulations in conjunction with other investigations. The answer at that time had been to interview outside the country, and this was the solution eventually determined in Cargill's case. On January 27, 1976, Gilmore and his legal counsel met with Leonard Alderson, the senior vice president of Tradax, accompanied by Hubert Sontheim, the general counsel for Tradax. The session was held across Switzerland's border, in Divonne-les-Bains, France. A wide-ranging discussion ensued. The focus was particularly on the Tradax organizational structure. At two important points, when Gilmore asked for specific statistics on Tradax sales to Eastern European countries and on a set of questions relating to the Tradax involvement in a French government-sponsored grain-selling consortium, France Cereales, Sontheim had to reply, "We will have to check whether this information can be supplied without violating Swiss legislation."

After the meeting, Tradax outside counsel worried that "it would appear that the representatives of Tradax have in several instances been drawn into discussing specific business done with, or business practices specific to, certain clients in a way which goes beyond [what] the guidelines supplied by the Federal Attorney General's office would have recommended as safe." Nevertheless, the discussions themselves had been planned to be wide-ranging, and Cargill had been forthcoming in its responses. Much more on these Tradax relationships and ways of doing business were to become central in the hearings themselves (see below).

This important meeting in France on January 27 carried Cargill further along the route of sorting out the questions relating to how much the Company was willing to divulge. This process of "discovery" continued all through the winter and spring, leading toward the long-awaited, much-feared hearings with the subcommittee. The pace became quite frenetic in the immediate weeks preceding the scheduled hearing date of June 24.[10]

The GAO Report Informs

The next event, awaited with concern, was the publication of the GAO study covering the overall grain marketing systems of Argentina, Australia, Canada, and the European Economic Community (EEC), as well as the soybean marketing system of Brazil. On May 28, just a few weeks before the hearings were scheduled, the report was made public. Although the grain companies expected fireworks, it turned out to be quite straightforward and noncontroversial, with its strong, factual base serving as a useful underpinning for the upcoming hearings. The "big six" grain companies were not mentioned in the report, with one exception. A short paragraph did note an Export-Import Bank loan of $86,000 to an affiliate of Cargill, made in 1973 to purchase processing equipment for the Company's new Brazilian soy meal and oil facility. In addition, a $2.5 million loan by OPIC for the same facility also was discussed.

The report additionally described the political tensions in Brazil attendant to the marketing of the 1974 soybean crop, with most of the charges directed at the international companies (but only in a general way). A Committee of Investigation of the Multinationals had been formed by the Brazilian government to look into the "overtones" of the international companies. The GAO investigators concluded, however, that "the principal theme was that Brazil at this stage of its development needs the capital and technology . . . and that the government has the necessary tools to ensure that the actions of these companies comply with the national interest."[11]

The Heady Days of June

By June 1, dates were set for the Church Subcommittee hearings. The opening session was to begin on June 18, and according to Senator Church's initial letter to Erv Kelm, Cargill was to testify that day. But the subcommittee staff later changed this arrangement; the staff itself would take up the whole first day, then on June 23, "a farm group Nordlicht [Gilmore's associate] refuses to identify" would take the day, with Cargill following the next day, June 24. June 25 was to have testimony from a USDA witness on the companies' role in exports. Then on June 28, there would be a panel of "big six" executives (Kelm was asked by Church to be with this group, too). Last, "one more day of hearings is likely to be scheduled" beyond the five specified.

Cargill now entered into a frenzy of preparations, trying to meet the subcommittee staff's continuing pressure for more information, at the same time attempting to hold back on what the Company felt were confidential matters. A delicate dance of memoranda and telephone calls ensued between Nordlicht, Gilmore, and Cargill's Robbin Johnson, who was the funnel for all of the Company's correspondence.

Nordlicht continued to push Johnson on matters relating to Tradax organization. In particular, the two subcommittee staffers were trying to sort out in their minds the relationship among the three key Tradax companies—Tradax Geneve S.A., the Swiss company, and the two Tradax companies chartered in Panama, Tradax Internacional S.A. (TISA) and Tradax Overseas S.A. (TOSA). Both the subcommittee men had formed the impression that Cargill was in the process of reorganizing the three Tradax companies, but the precise basis for this and the reasons behind it were not clearly identifiable from the Cargill answers to them.

The reasons for the Company's reluctance to spell out the situation completely became clearer in a critically important "executive session" on June 14, just four days before the actual hearings were to open. This meeting divided into two parts. The first was between the subcommittee staffers and their lawyers and Cargill and its lawyers, just these two groups. The second part of the executive session was to be with the MNC staffers and all the other "big six" grain companies involved in the hearings (and also to include the Archer Daniels Midland Company).

Senator Percy Urges a Change of Heart

There was one important prior meeting that much influenced Cargill in how it handled itself in this executive session. On June 10, Bill Pearce and his colleague Bob Fahs (from the Washington office of Cargill) were accorded the opportunity to meet with Senator Charles Percy, one of the members of the subcommittee. Pearce outlined to Percy the Company's central concerns: "lack of certainty about the scope of the subcommittee's inquiry, the apparent bias of the subcommittee staff and Senator Clark and the special concern private companies in this business have about confidentiality." Senator Clark had been vocal in castigating the grain companies from his very first speech in the grain irregularities issue; Cargill had been particularly taken aback by his comment on March 11, 1976, concerning the "giant multinational grain companies," which he said "have cheated farmers and foreign customers alike. And they have brought shame and dishonor to the American system of doing business."

Percy admitted that he himself had been concerned about "a very biased and political subcommittee" and that he had "done his best to blunt the blatantly political attacks on business and bring some sense of balance." He promised to do his best "to prevent harassment of our witnesses . . . no appearances 'en bank' for photographers and no demagogic charges if he can avoid them."

However, on the question of confidentiality, Percy "cautioned us that we have a problem in this regard . . . a great deal of progress has been made depicting the grain trade as a group of a few, highly secretive companies with divided interests . . . that it will be important to be as forthcoming as possible." Percy exhorted Pearce and Fahs to "give serious thought to being more willing than we have to release information about our business . . . we are an important public business and notwithstanding private ownership, we should understand the need to take the public in our confidence if we want their support in continuing this system." But this was a message that several of the family owners and many of the executives did not want to hear.

The Executive Session

The session was "executive" only in the sense that the public was not privy to the proceedings. Otherwise, it seemed just like a hearing itself. Senators Clark and Percy chaired, the Church Subcommittee staff (particularly its lawyers) conducted the questioning, and the Cargill executives all were testifying under oath. The issue of confidentiality permeated the meeting. Cargill was pressed to explain why such secrecy was required; Cargill's answer: it was needed because of the desire of the Company to protect its innovations—its "new ways." Company witnesses elaborated by describing extensively Cargill's groundbreaking decision to put the Baie Comeau export terminal at the mouth of the St. Lawrence River.

But the subcommittee lawyers chose, instead, to talk about Tradax and its three companies, for it seemed to them that this was another example of "new ways." Why, then, "is the fact that you are contemplating changes in your organizational structure so sensitive to you at this point . . . what I don't understand is why is the fact that Cargill conducts a significant, large part of this business through these subsidiary parts to their corporations in and of itself a matter of such sensitivity?" Senator Clark posed a blunt question: "Aren't you in the process of reorganizing?" Cal Anderson, vice president and secretary of the Company, responded, "No." Clark pressed again: "You are not in the process of reorganizing any of your structure in the company in a basic way?"

Anderson allowed, "Well, we are in a constant state of modification in the organization." Clark pushed again, and Anderson did admit that "what I would call from an ownership point of view a change was made virtually at the time of your letter of inquiry, which made it difficult to respond precisely to your question." The subcommittee lawyer pressed Anderson once again: "But really, is what comes out of this that the central reason for this organizational structure, isn't it really to minimize U.S. tax liability?" Anderson replied, "Well, obviously the purpose is to permit the earnings to be retained to the maximum extent possible. There is no particular commercial advantage in organizing the business in an area that is going to pay unnecessarily high taxes."

In truth, Cargill *had* made a major organizational change in Tradax just a few days before the executive session. The reasons were quite separate from the hearings and *were* related directly to taxes. The full story did not come out at the executive session but had to await the subcommittee questions and Cargill's answers in the open hearing itself. Two other subjects were touched on briefly in the executive session, one relating to the so-called DISC (Domestic International Sales Corporation) provisions of federal law offering tax incentives to expand exports and the second being the 1973 soybean embargo and its effects on the individual companies involved (see my discussion of this in Chapter Six). Both of these matters became clearer in the actual hearings.

One other very important event transpired just at the end of the second half of the executive session. Senator Percy had not been present for part of Cargill's session but returned in time to speak once again about confidentiality:

I would have to say to the grain companies, I think you have to make your minds up that there is either going to be heavy Government regulation of the industry, or public information put out. I would rather, if I were you, go the route of public information. Lay it all on the line. Let information be out there. To the degree that we can protect trade secrets in confidentiality, the overriding concern is . . . to maintain competitive position. Times are different today and I do think that you will have to make your minds up. A lot more information will have to be known about how the company operates, and then it has to be justifiable the way the operation is carried on.[12]

The First Day: Newspaper Headlines

Now the time had come for the hearings. Richard Gilmore and Ira Nordlicht conducted the entire first day's proceedings (June 18). Their opening statements telegraphed what appeared to be their strong, personally held thesis, namely, that the larger international grain companies had conspired to set prices both in Europe and in the United States. In the former, as the staffers described it, the companies dominated the price information flows and the actual price setting, particularly related to the "levy" prices established in the EEC. In the United States, prices were set by actions of "cash closing committees" on the exchanges (the subcommittee focus here was on the Minneapolis grain exchange). Permeating the testimony of Gilmore and Nordlicht was the implication that unreliable price information deliberately had been introduced into these venues and that this had allowed the larger grain companies to manipulate price, more or less in concert.

Cargill had been warned by Nordlicht just two days before this hearing that the MNC subcommittee staff planned to introduce a memorandum written by a federal government employee, Alan Trick, who in 1967 was the U.S. agricultural officer in Hamburg, Germany. Trick had seemed to imply that incorrect price information had been submitted at times by the companies. Senator Clark, as chair, summarized the testimony given by Gilmore: "This system has remained basically the same for a number of years. In 1967 our agricultural attache in Hamburg kept for two years records of the information that these grain companies provided both to the EEC committees and to him. He found that these were not in agreement, and he concluded . . . that there was a regular pattern and practice of these major grain companies giving false information, and thereby adversely affecting [EEC] committee prices."

Clark then made the link between Europe and the United States: "This in turn affects the prices on American markets as well . . . to the advantage of these major grain companies individually or collectively . . . the exchanges in this country—[using] the Minneapolis exchange as an example—the pricing there, the closing prices are determined by a number of major grain companies themselves in these committees."

The headlines the next day were striking. The *Journal of Commerce* said, "Grain Firms Charged with Price Manipulation." The *Washington Post* went one better with a half-page picture of "investigator Richard Gilmore testifying" and titled this article "Grain Traders Lied, Probers Say."

The second day of hearings, five days later (June 23), featured the farmers' side of agricultural pricing, with testimony from the commissioner and the deputy commissioner of the state of North Dakota and a group of North Dakota farmers. The focus was on how the farmer was disadvantaged, at the bottom (as the commissioner, Myron Just, put it) of the "pyramid of power." In North Dakota, there had been efforts to develop a wheat pool (they called it the North Dakota Farmers Steering Committee), but they too were at a disadvantage in dealing with the huge grain firms.

Once again, the focus of the session turned to the setting of grain prices. A small-town North Dakota elevator operator testified that the major grain companies seemed to be in collusion in setting the prices they paid; he alleged that the firms were making offers to buy that were identical, firm to firm, "over 90% of the time." Senator Clark queried, "How can they call you up and all of them—if I understand what you are saying—offer you exactly the same price on many occasions?" The elevator manager replied, "Well, to us, it's obvious. They decide what they are going to price it at."

Not unexpectedly, the newspapers picked this particular part of the hear-

ings to highlight; the *Minneapolis Tribune*, for example, headlined: "N.D. Elevator Man Alleges Collusion on Grain Prices." The *Des Moines Register* reported: "Identical Bids by Big Grain Firms Charged." Earlier, the *Register*, reporting the first day's accusations, pinned the alleged manipulations directly
to four companies: Cargill, Continental Grain, Bunge, and Louis Dreyfus.
One of the radio stations in Minneapolis used a short clip: "The Minneapolis-
based Cargill Company is among those reportedly involved in international
grain manipulation and antitrust violations."

A New York City station carried a short rebuttal from Secretary of Agriculture Earl Butz: "There is tremendous competition among those companies
and the margins which they get from the business on which they have to bid
are very competitive margins. Anybody who says that they manipulate grain
prices simply is demagoging the issue." But the Butz words seemed lost in a
deluge of negative publicity.[13]

The third day of testimony was Cargill's, just one day after the "farmers'
day" on June 23. It had become clear that Cargill was to be the only grain
company to be examined in detail; this had been one of the Company's fears,
that it alone would be on the stand. Now Cargill was to defend itself—and the
industry.

Cargill on the Stand

At the executive session, the Church Subcommittee staffers had insisted
that the chief executive officer of the Company had to be present at the hearings to lead Cargill's presentation. So Erv Kelm, as chairman and CEO,
"made a rare public appearance" (as the trade journal *Feedstuffs* put it). He
first asked Barney Saunders to make the Company's opening statement.

Saunders went directly to the heart of the subcommittee allegations, initiating a blunt discussion of the implications that the staffers had drawn using
the 1967 memorandum of U.S. agricultural attaché Alan Trick, quoted by the
staffers as implying that the larger multinational grain companies had been
manipulating the levies of the EEC. Reminding the hearing's participants of
the provocative headlines after the staff's testimony (e.g., "Probers Charge 4
Grain Firms Manipulate Prices"), Saunders maintained that the subcommittee staffers were wholly incorrect on four key points: "First . . . the Dutch
Committee gathering the price information for transmittal to EEC officials
was made up of importer, broker and consumer representatives. No grain
shippers were on it." Further, the committee decisions had to be unanimous,
and "we told the subcommittee staff this during their visit to our offices this
summer."

Second, the staffers had implied that the situation in 1967 was the same as
in 1976, but in actual fact price unification had been achieved on July 1, 1967,
just five months after Trick's memorandum. Third, prior to this, Tradax and

other U.S. firms were being boycotted by the German importers and could accomplish only a minimum of levy sales. Finally, the suggestion by the staffers that false prices were affecting U.S. prices was "implausible," as the EEC "only publishes the variable levy, in units of account . . . prices are not disclosed." As to Tradax itself, Saunders continued, "it does not report to Cargill and Cargill is not aware of the offering prices Tradax reports to European price-gathering bodies."

In sum, Saunders averred, "the staff members unfairly drew conclusions from a system that no longer exists, incorrectly identified U.S. firms as potential beneficiaries, and stated a connection to U.S. domestic market prices that is sheer fantasy."

This pungent statement seemed to sting Clark; a give-and-take with Saunders followed. After several exchanges, Clark asked, "You're not disagreeing with the nature of the interpretation of the Trick memorandum?" Saunders replied, "You bet we are!" Clark: "But you did not do that at that time [referring to the previous summer's meeting with the staffers]." Saunders: "Well, we didn't know about the Trick memorandum then" (fortunately, Stu Hanson, Walter Gage's second-in-command in Geneva, *had* known Trick and had wired Minneapolis with clarifying information). There the matter rested, with Clark ending, "Well, I think you have raised a number of valuable questions and interesting questions. . . . Rather than spending the remaining 1 hour and 10 minutes on this question, I would like to ask you questions about your basic statement. . . ." Thus, the exchange about the famous Trick memorandum (or perhaps "infamous" is a more apt word) ended as substantially a repudiation of the staff's research credibility and was widely reported in the press as such.

A similar rebuke was given a few minutes later in the hearings, when the North Dakota elevator operator's allegation of "offers for grain being collusively identical 90% of the time" was examined. Saunders explained the process of putting out bids, each company vying for a price acceptable to the elevators (and farmers). "When all of us that are trying to buy . . . start bidding in the marketplace, we are soon told that we're not paying the market. And so we either have the choice of paying the market or not buying any grain; so that the chances are, late in the afternoon, or maybe even an hour after our bids go out, we will be paying the same as our competitors, if we want to buy his grain. If we don't, we won't."

As to collusion, Saunders stated, "I would like to extend an invitation for you or a member of your staff to sit in on any one of our offices, whether it's in North Dakota or Illinois or any other place, and just find out how competitive our business is because it's a dog-eat-dog competitive business if there ever was one." Senator Percy corroborated Saunders: "In the hearings of the Permanent Investigating Committee about the oil companies, I was enraged that there could be collusion [however] there wasn't a shred of evidence at the end of all of these hearings that there had been. The market forces were actually operating . . . to the extent that you have a dog-eat-dog business . . . the better we like it . . . the more pressure you are under, the more the competitive marketing system is working."

Percy was enough concerned by the North Dakota allegations now to do some research of his own among his constituents in Illinois. In a bit of irony, he telephoned Senator Clark the next day, asking him to have his (Percy's) statement entered into the *Congressional Record*. It read in part: "As part of these hearings, a number of witnesses have made allegations that there may be collusion in pricing on the U.S. grain market. Since this testimony was not documented nor in line with my own general perception of this market, I took the opportunity last night, Thursday, June 24, 1976, in Galesburg [to consult] with a group of outstanding members of the central Illinois agriculture community. They uniformly felt that the grain companies and grain markets in Illinois are highly, in fact intensively, competitive and they want less rather than more government intervention, regulation and control." Percy included in the statement the views (by individual name) of six of the farmers.

The influential trade journal *Milling and Baking News* was more disparaging of the accusation: "Even though a lot of ridiculous thoughts came from the Senate subcommittee hearings prior to the Cargill testimony, the most ludicrous of all reflected the charge that the major grain companies are somehow in collusion in establishing domestic and foreign prices. . . . The grain business is an industry that in its lack of collusion literally makes the market function. That is the point that Cargill made so effectively. . . . It is a point that other grain companies and the industry at large will have to make more often if the image of the grain trade is ever to match reality."[14]

Will Large Profits Be Misinterpreted?

If Cargill had intended to hold as confidential its profit record for the exceptional years 1972–1976 (and right up to the opening of the hearings this had been undecided), the friendly but persistent exhortations of Senator Charles Percy to be as forthcoming as conceivably possible finally persuaded the Company to include audited figures for net profit for all of these years. These were announced in the hearings themselves; more important, the Company made the decision on June 23, just a day before its testimony, also to publish widely (in a press release devoted just to this) the key profit figures for the 1973–1974 fiscal year ("$212.5 million on sales of $9.1 billion"), for 1974–1975 ("$218.4 million on sales of $10.9 billion"), and for 1975–1976 ("$179.026 million on sales of $10.795 billion"). There—the deed was done!

Agreeing that "tax costs were important in locating our international trading principal in Panama," Saunders strove to put this in perspective in his prepared statement: "Cargill's effective worldwide corporate income tax rate has averaged 39% over the last 5 years. In that period Cargill has paid $358 million in U.S. income taxes which is 33 percent of our worldwide income for that period. This compares favorably with the weighted industry average for major industrial concerns, which paid a worldwide rate of 44 percent and a U.S. rate of 24% in 1975." At this point, the Company submitted detailed tabular statements from its audited annual reports for the years 1970–1971 through 1974–1975, adding also the unaudited figures for 1975–1976. They showed that Cargill had paid an effective U.S. tax rate for the six years of from 44.4 percent to 52.6 percent; the average was 49.6 percent.

A detailed table was included, showing the corporate federal tax burden for several major industrial companies; the worldwide rate ranged from Western Electric's 16.4 percent and Westinghouse's 20.6 percent to General Electric, 36.3 percent; DuPont, 38.4 percent; and General Motors, 47.1 percent. Of the 14 industrial companies in the table, 9 had paid a percentage under that of Cargill. Later in the hearings, Senator Percy responded more generally about Cargill's income tax payments: "For the benefit of those in the room who do not have copies of these, the testimony that's been given is quite accurate. These are audited reports. A six-year average for worldwide income indicates an average of $229 million; earnings after taxes $144 million, which is a 37.1% rate; and the U.S. taxes, even more important to us, indicate a 6-year average of 49.6%, which in my judgment puts you considerably ahead of the average in companies. So, . . . in my judgment you're paying a full fair share of U.S. taxes; and concerns that we might have had that I expressed to you, I think personally, are fully answered by these statements."

Tradax Revisited

Given Cargill's sketchy performance at the executive session concerning the organization and operation of Tradax—the sharp questioning by the Church Subcommittee lawyers had produced only partial responses—the Company team changed its tactics here, too. Perhaps influenced once again by Senator Percy's admonitions, they decided to provide clearer answers than at the executive session. Saunders wasted no time in getting to the crux. Further details now were submitted specifically about Tradax organization structure. In a cogent letter to Ira Nordlicht, the associate counsel of the subcommittee, Robbin Johnson described in detail the changes that had just been made by the Company in the overall organization of the Tradax companies, enumerating precisely the reasons why this was done. The heart of the letter was as follows:

Until most recently, all international grain trading activities were performed by Tradax Internacional, Tradax Export, or Tradax Overseas, all organized in Panama and all functioning under Management Agreements with Tradax Geneve. Tradax Geneve allocated the management fees to the three companies managed by it, on the basis of . . . tonnage.

Tradax Internacional engaged both in international commodity trading and shipping, and its income was tax deferred until dividends were remitted. . . .

Tradax Export is . . . primarily engaged in the exportation of U.S.-origin agricultural commodities. The income from such activity is tax deferred until dividends are remitted, so long as its earnings are invested in export trade assets.

Tradax Overseas, now inactive, was a partly owned subsidiary of Tradax Internacional which engaged primarily in the trading of Latin American-origin agricultural commodities. Its earnings were also tax deferred until dividends are remitted under Subpart F of the Code. Tradax Internacional's share of the earned surplus of Tradax Overseas has been fully remitted to Tradax Internacional through dividends.

Recently, Tradax made a major readjustment with respect to both its capital positioning and its business activity. Such changes were made with reference to tax considerations and a more general business need. The tax considerations arose out of changes made in the U.S. tax law with respect to shipping income as well as the obligation to invest earnings in export trade assets, which limited the future growth of Tradax Export. The business consideration arose out of increasing demands for capital-intensive projects outside of the United States . . . to position capital in order to serve such demands, enhance financial flexibility and yet minimize specific country sourcing dependency.

It was determined . . . to increase the capital of Tradax Export through a substantial investment by outside interests, to centralize all agricultural commodity trading and shipping activity in that corporation and for it to be managed by its own management subsidiary, Tradax Gestion, under a contract similar to the contract between Tradax Geneve and Tradax Internacional. . . . Jointly owned and capitalized by Tradax Internacional and outside interests . . . the earnings of Tradax Export will continue to be tax deferred until dividends are paid . . . thus be able to maintain competitive equality with foreign-based trading and shipping firms.

Tradax Internacional itself will retain a pool of capital which, along with project oriented term debt, will permit orderly and rational growth without placing capital demands on Cargill, Incorporated in the United States. Cargill's share of the future earnings of Tradax Internacional will be currently taxable to Cargill.

The key to this entire change lay in Johnson's sentence concerning Tradax Export, "now jointly owned and capitalized by Tradax Internacional and outside interests." A significant change in the federal tax code had been made in 1975. Prior to this time, international trading companies had been able to defer taxes on income from transactions abroad under certain conditions. A variety of arrangements had been used by Cargill to enjoy tax deferral; some involved collateral record keeping demands and artificial splitting of organizational responsibilities that sometimes became onerous in their own right.

But all such exceptions had been eliminated inadvertently through a legislative glitch, as Cargill's Bill Pearce outlined to the subcommittee in his testimony in the hearings:

[They] were eliminated at the conference level without the opportunity for hearings. . . . We argued, and others argued at the same time, that it was very important to provide a continued opportunity for U.S. owned companies with [foreign-based subsidiaries] to continue to operate on an equal tax footing. The Congress accepted that. The House report accepted it explicitly. However, . . . the way that tax bill was put together in the rush to complete it, the language chosen to cast the new exemption was in exclusionary terms. It implied—and the Treasury has since adopted the position—

that in essence it's limited to trade in third country agricultural products *which do not compete with the products of this country* [my emphasis]. In other words, it is a very limited exception from the current taxation.

Pearce outlined his view of the seriousness of the loss:

If Cargill as an American-owned firm operating foreign subsidiaries in the commodity trade cannot compete on an equal tax footing . . . that business is going to pass beyond the tax jurisdiction and control of the United States. . . . [But] it is exactly the competition, exactly our participation in competitive business from which the United States draws its most important advantages [as] source of information about third country transactions on which it has very little other source. . . . Our ability to take part actively in competition involving trade from Argentina, for example, to Western Europe, gives us a better idea [of] what kind of pricing is involved. . . . It brings us to the bargaining table where grain is being bought in this world.

Thus, a way out of this dilemma had just been consummated by Cargill. If an international trading company (such as a number of the Tradax organizations were considered to be) was owned at least 50 percent by owners from outside the United States, the deferral would remain. In order to qualify for this new exemption, so narrowly framed by the Internal Revenue Service, Cargill had sold a half interest in Tradax Export to the lead bank for Tradax in Geneva, Credit Suisse. The bank was actually to hold a minority of the common stock and all of the preferred stock, the combination to give them exactly half of the voting stock. It was this change that was being effected in late May 1976, just at the time the MNC subcommittee was demanding all of the information about Tradax. On June 24, the day that Cargill testified before the subcommittee, this last piece of information was also released.[15]

Johnson sent a second letter to Richard Gilmore, delineating the amount of deferred taxes that Cargill had taken under the DISC legislation (the Domestic International Sales Corporation provision allowing abatement of 50 percent of export profits under certain conditions of export enhancement). DISC had achieved considerable notoriety in the Russian grain sales of 1972, when several of the "big six" grain companies, including Cargill, had claimed deferred taxes on those parts of the Russian sales initiated abroad. There had never been much public information on which companies were using the DISC provision and how much tax deferral was being accomplished. Now Cargill had made the decision to release specifically its deferred tax amounts since the act's initiation. In 1972, the figure was $162,000; in 1973, $1.049 million; in 1974, $2.712 million; and in 1975, $12.024 million.

There already had been substantial discussion in governmental and congressional circles about the lesser need at this point for DISC, and proposals had emerged for phasing out the tax deferrals. Cargill's substantially increased figure for 1975 caught the attention of the MNC subcommittee; Senator Percy sharply queried Cargill management about this in the hearings themselves: "I support a DISC very strongly. But I did it . . . based on the fact that there ought to be additionality [i.e., adding to exports]. I did not want any windfalls going to companies, for them just to get a windfall for doing . . . what they were going to do anyway. It ought to be additional export. And that is why I was really concerned when I saw a figure of $15,947,000, which, as I understand it, is exempted from U.S. tax liability for DISC, for Cargill, for the years 1972 through 1975." Percy then added, "Despite that exemption you are paying a very, very full share," referring again to the Company's overall tax burden, discussed earlier in the hearings.[16]

Along with the DISC letter, the Company also sent two new tables of figures from audited Cargill annual reports relating to total taxes paid by Cargill, Inc., together with an extensive set of statistical and financial materials, to include both those already sent to the subcommittee and those not yet released. But it still seemed that the subcommittee staff and the senators were confused as to whether Tradax income was included. Senator Clark asked, "Now, I notice in your opening statement . . . you say Cargill's effective worldwide corporate income tax rate has averaged 39 percent over the past 5 years . . . now when you say Cargill Inc.'s and consolidated subsidiaries, this does not include all of the income on Tradax Internacional or your Panama subsidiaries does it?" John McGrory, Cargill's general counsel answered promptly, "Yes, it does, sir." Senator Clark: "It includes everything?" John McGrory: "Yes, that is right."

It was clear in the detailed materials submitted by Cargill that Tradax was able to shelter a very large percentage of its earnings in a given year. In 1973 some 97.6 percent was U.S.-tax deferred; in 1974 this figure was 71.8 percent, and in 1975 it was 86.1 percent.

The Tradax board of directors called attention to this significant amount of deferred earnings in their 1975–1976 annual report: "The Finance Committee needs to keep in mind at all times the large amount of liquid assets now reposing in Tradax Internacional S.A. In the short term, these funds will be used to replace short-term bank loans and any excess in bank deposits and other short-term instruments. Our long-term objective should remain the suitable investment of these funds in operating facilities throughout the world, with the exception of the U.S.A. . . . The use of these funds . . . should mean that Cargill, Inc. should not have to export any capital from the U.S.A. for a number of years . . . building up Cargill's domestic capital."

Senator Clark seemed to feel that having a subsidiary like Tradax gave Cargill a chance to circumvent the reporting law. John McGrory responded that he considered this was less likely than "with a foreign parent who has an American affiliate." Clark pressed McGrory: "In accordance with the law, you could sell to Tradax Internacional and in turn sell to the Soviet Union without reporting prior notice—or without falling within the jurisdiction of the law." McGrory: "That's not correct." Clark: "But you could sell to Tradax without including the understanding that it was going to the Soviet Union." Mc-

Grory: "The special terms required by the Soviets would place us in the position of knowing that destination, and we would be required under U.S. law, presently, to report that." Clark: "So, it's impossible for you to do it in any way practically?" McGrory: "No, it's possible for Tradax, without making a contract to Cargill, to do that. *But we do not do that without reporting*" (my emphasis).[17]

Saunders had emphasized the "intense competition" in the American grain marketing system; this had provided the incentive for continuing innovation that reduced marketing costs. The earnings analysis took off from this. Since 1971–1972, grain exports had increased by over 25 percent, and margins rose. "Cargill was positioned to retain much of this increased margin because of substantial investments it had made in the second half of the 1960s. . . . Our decision to make new investments in grain handling facilities . . . involved significant risks. At the time the return on our investments in grain marketing ranged from a low of minus 7 percent to a high of 8.6 percent." (Recall the story in Chapter Three of the pitched argument in 1968 as to whether Cargill should "get out of the grain business altogether"). Indeed, world grain exports had declined from a high of 109 million tons in 1965 to 91 million tons in 1968.

The Company's decision to assume these risks was in contrast to the attitude of the Canadian grain marketers, "where a government board dominates marketing and where elevator operators receive fixed fees for their services. In the late 1960s grain companies in Canada faced the same realities as their American counterparts. Returns on existing investments were extremely low, prospects . . . were dim. Faced with the facts . . . Canadian elevator operators simply were unwilling to assume the risks of expanding their facilities. . . . [In the Russian purchase bulge] the Canadian marketing system was simply unable to accommodate the surge."

To put it in another way, Cargill was practicing an advanced example of the "first mover" thesis discussed in Chapter Three (the Tradax effort in the mid-1960s in Japan), that the "early" innovator—early in this case in a chronological sense—was able to gain a competitive edge and reap the solid profits of the pickup period. "The opportunity to earn wider margins on increased volume encouraged large investments . . . despite uncertainty about their future earning potential when investments were committed."

Pete McVay, in a widely remembered speech on Cargill's "capital investment philosophy," given to the Commodity Marketing Division management a few months after the Church Subcommittee hearings, deepened this concept: "We bought more capacity with each capital dollar than our competition. It is our tradition. We built plants for capacity and for performance . . . the musts, not the wants . . . we did not add very much of the 'it would be nice to haves' or 'it's so convenient' kind of equipment. . . . The result—we out-earned competition by twice measuring profit per bushel processed and up to 5 times measuring profit on capital invested."[18]

At the end of Cargill's day of testimony, there was some evidence that some of the "other grain companies" might also heed the exhortations of Senator Percy for more openness about themselves and step forward in the hearings with more facts. Indeed, *Feedstuffs* editors wrote on June 28: "There was speculation following the Cargill testimony that Continental Grain Co. executives were sufficiently impressed with the way Cargill approached the problem to be strongly inclined to follow suit as early as sometime this week. Such a step would probably involve testimony from Continental president Michel Fribourg."

The Church Subcommittee Calls It Quits

The string of embarrassments that the Church Subcommittee staff had taken during the third day of the hearings (the Cargill day) now led the senators to determine upon a strategic retreat. The press of business in the congressional schedule at this point was extremely heavy; if the MNC subcommittee hearings were to continue as planned, it was to be a balancing act for all the legislators involved. Given the disarray of the staff after the Cargill day, the decision was taken to postpone the remaining two days scheduled (one was to be a panel of chief executive officers of the "big six," the other a USDA administrator).

Senator Clark ended what was now destined to be the final session with a direct query to Saunders: "I assume the committee would like to have you back with regard to the so-called Alan Trick memorandum." Clark had intimated during the hearings that he would attempt to recall Trick, by this time an agricultural attaché in Moscow, for personal testimony. But it never happened. Trick himself now seemed to disdavow the implications that the MNC staffers had planted (the memorandum itself was reprinted in the final proceedings of the hearings). But it was clear that the hearings were finished.

The press reaction to the hearings was in the main quite critical of the subcommittee. The industry organs were relieved, indeed gleeful. The editor of *Feedstuffs* wrote, "The grain trade has followed the week of hearings very closely, and by the end of the week seemed to feel that it had been largely vindicated. The trade has maintained all along that the hearings were hardly more than a witch hunt by Sen. Dick Clark." That magazine's Washington reporter added: "The victory, for lack of a better term, is especially sweet on two counts: First, Clark is a hot and persistent critic of the industry, and will embarrass it any way he can, and second, the trade was uncommonly leery going into the hearings over just how well it would fare. As it turns out, Clark has been able to come up with little to raise Cain about. . . . Part of the trade's elation is thanks to Cargill, whose executives decided to let down their corporate financial hair and came out looking solid and respectable."

Milling and Baking News also gave considerable credit to Cargill for its "stunning effort to lay to rest the innuendoes emanating from the subcommittee." Their editorial writer gave particular kudos to the Company for sharing publicly its earnings and tax data. The *Journal of Commerce*, generally considered to be one of the most objective of the business press, summed up the premature suspension of the hearings, "It is widely said here that the subcommittee canceled the hearings due to the senators' embarrassment over inadequate staff investigation before making charges." A prompt disclaimer by the European Community Commission within the week that the Trick memorandum did not have its facts correct added to this perception.

Not everyone saw it this way. In an article in the *New Republic*, "Cargill's Private Empire," perennial critic Joel Solkoff wrote: "The investigation is temporarily suspended—with the five other companies and governmental officials yet to testify. Perhaps the Cargill disclosures have already revealed too much. . . . The new Senate leadership may decide not to resume the hearings for fear of offending the powerful grain dealers."

Ralph Nader (in his 1986 book with William Taylor, *The Big Boys: Power and Position in American Business*) faulted Cargill's apparent openness, calling it "still the classic example of defensive disclosure. . . . Cargill decided on a brilliant response. It offered to disclose information nearly all of which is routinely available from a public company. . . . The timing of these disclosures worked as much in the company's favor as the disclosures themselves, according to a source close to the subcommittee. Although standard practice called for documents to be submitted forty-eight hours in advance of a hearing, Cargill delivered much of its material less than twenty-four hours before the public session. . . . Still more information arrived the very morning of the hearing."[19]

The Federal Trade Commission Backs Off

It was not just that the MNC subcommittee hearings were petering out; it now appeared that the FTC also had lost interest. Several factors had come into play here. Looking into the future, many companies in this period were developing (or in many cases, renewing) detailed "antitrust compliance programs" for their own organizations, designed to alert all their employees as to exactly what the laws required.

Cargill lawyers had pored over the Company's own compliance program at great length in this period, sharing the final draft widely among senior managers. The Sherman Act, the Clayton Act, and the Federal Trade Commission Act were the subjects of examination, and a set of specific hypothetical case situations (featuring a mythical "Company A," selling "widgets") gave reality to the document. Cargill's program covered not only U.S. regulations but also those in the EEC. A detailed article in *Business Week* in January 1975 chronicled dozens of such corporate efforts and listed the editors' "Ten

Don'ts of Antitrust." These diligent efforts by corporations to develop compliance programs were wise management efforts, for the interpretation of the laws had become extremely complex.

Cargill took one other important step that embraced both FTC concerns and the basic antitrust policies of the Department of Justice: in March 1975, the Company commissioned a major independent study of the grain trading industry. The principal investigator was Dr. Richard E. Caves of Harvard University's Department of Economics. Additional consultants came from the Harvard Law School, the Harvard Business School, and Stanford University's Food Research Institute. Caves had a national reputation in the field; his book *American Industry: Structure, Conduct, Performance* had already gone through four printings as a key contribution in the Foundations of Modern Economics series.

A nine-chapter draft manuscript ensued, "Competition in the Grain Trading Industry," and its essence was excerpted in a shorter version under the title, "Organization, Scale, and Performance in the Grain Trading Industry," reprinted as the 546th paper in the long-standing Discussion Paper series of the Harvard Institute of Economic Research.

Caves long had been much interested in the grain trading industry, "the intellectual attraction being that economists have given little attention to competition in the sort of trading and arbitrage activities that Cargill carries out." An adaptation was necessary, he posited, "because the standard concepts addressed themselves implicitly to a commodity-producing industry." But in a commodity-trading industry, "the functions of arbitrage, ownership, and physical possession are independent of one another." Therefore, scale economies could exist independently of physical facilities. Further, the time span over which pricing decisions were made was extremely short.

It was clear, he held, that the industry evidenced some oligopolistic tendencies—the fact that there was a "big six" of very large firms was well known. But the trading activities themselves were not geographically constrained "and so are subject to relatively low concentration in the U.S. national market." The concentration that the "big six" had in elevators and transshipment facilities was generally of "limited economic relevance because of the substitutability between channels of distribution from a production point or accumulation to a consumption point." Not only that, storage facilities at different points along a distribution channel competed with one another. "Thus, we can observe moderately high concentration of facilities at individual inland and export terminals but cannot attribute much significance to it." Cooperatives, with organizational characteristics and tax status different from commercial firms, were present, but these had differing behavior.

As to the industry's market conduct, it was notable for the low potential it provided for the recognition of oligopolistic interdependence. The futures market could be taken as purely competitive, and the pricing of cash grain

"*Mary Benson is manager of Cargill's new commodity handling complex at Duluth . . . the world's busiest inland port. Cargill's installation is that port's finest and fastest export facility. . . . Past her window roll trucks and trains from as far west as Montana, hauling wheat, soybeans, barley, corn and other grains and such commodities as soybean meal, alfalfa pellets and sugar beet pellets. Mary Benson is in charge of the whole Duluth operation*" (Cargill News, May–June 1977).

"basis" and prices in the futures market were "moment-to-moment deci-sion[s] resting on each dealer's current trading position and conjectures about the future." Almost inherently, each rival was incapable of coordinating with his competitors.

With the evidence pointing to a largely competitive market structure and conduct, Caves continued, "The presence of large traders at high concentra-tion export sales [did allow] scale economies in coordination and risk-bearing that are due to the characteristics of information as an input." There were also scale economies in physical facilities, transportation and storage. Therefore, Caves concluded, the large scale of the principal grain trading firms seemed to result from those scale economies involving the coordination of information and risk. "The large grain traders are not vertically integrated in the conven-tional sense; rather, their individual facilities and divisions tend to interface with competitive market prices. . . . Profit margins in large-scale trading de-pend not so much on the volume traded as on the incidence of disturbances that create opportunities for a good deal of non-routine arbitrage."

In the concluding chapter of the draft, Caves made his point explicit: "It is not apparent that this industry poses any problems for public policy toward competition. The absolute size of the larger firms does not appear to be asso-ciated with a systematic market power. No economically relevant markets ap-peared to be highly concentrated." Caves wrote Cargill lawyer Linda Cutler, after the study was completed, that "my study has basically confirmed the 'house view' of how the industry operates." With Caves and his consultants having the reputation of being impeccably independent, the picture of the in-dustry as being a highly competitive one despite the seeming dominance of the "big six" gave a powerful reinforcement to what members of the industry had been saying for a number of years (witness the many exchanges in the Church Subcommittee hearings, exemplified particularly by Senator Charles Percy's comments after he had discussed competition among his constituents in the farming communities of Illinois).

Whether it was because of these preventive initiatives in the grain trade in-dustry (Cargill's being an appropriate example), the FTC too decided to ter-minate its investigation of Cargill. In April 1979, the Company received a terse letter (directed to Whitney MacMillan as president), noting that the agency "has conducted an investigation involving your alleged violation" and that "upon further review . . . it now appears that no further action is war-ranted." While "the investigation has been closed . . . the Commission re-serves the right to take such further action as the public interest may require."

Roger Burbach, writing in the *Progressive*, had another hypothesis as to why the FTC's scrutiny of the grain trade fell apart: "The Federal Trade Com-mission initiated an investigation of the major grain companies to determine whether they had conspired to hinder competition. The companies adopted a shrewd strategy for handling this challenge: Rather than try to withhold information, many of the companies deluged the FTC with reams of documents and papers. An official of the National Grain and Feed Association . . . boasted that his organization alone had sent the FTC a mound of papers six feet high. . . . The FTC is unable to get a handle on the operations of the companies, and it now appears that the government will take no legal action." His argument seemed a bit farfetched, given the assiduousness with which the FTC had pursued Cargill for "more records."[20]

So the market behavior/merger concerns generated by the FTC were gone. However, Cargill was indicted in this same period by a federal grand jury for a Sherman Act antitrust violation in the resins industry and pled *nolo contendre* to the ensuing misdemeanor complaint issued by the Department of Justice in 1978 (this case will be analyzed in a subsequent volume).

Assessing the Subcommittee on Multinational Corporations Hearings

"If there is one subject that practically everyone in breadstuffs probably could agree upon, it is that the grain segment of the industry has an image that could use a great deal of burnishing." So said *Milling and Baking News*. Cargill had indeed burnished the industry's reputation "in no uncertain terms," continued the *News*; "the now-suspended hearings provided an essential and important lesson. This lesson was given by Cargill."

At the end, it *was* just Cargill. Without further hearings, the incentive on the part of the other companies to make their own affairs more public vanished. If Continental Grain had been "strongly inclined to follow suit," now it was not. Cargill had vocally expressed that being the only company to make its data public was "especially unfair" (enunciated in the executive session). A case can be made that probably most of the "confidentiality" was overblown, at least as far as being forced into giving "secrets" to competitors. The revelations about the complex organization of Tradax and its convoluted ways of doing business were of limited help to competitors. A better case can be advanced that the very complexity of Tradax made it easy for outside critics to misuse facts and twist stories—and this was a legitimate fear.

Going through the tortuous FTC/Church Subcommittee saga forced Cargill to do an enormous amount of preparation. And the Company *was* extraordinarily well prepared. It had done its homework on itself and so could make the rapid shifts on data release on a very short timeline without the concern that some byway had not been fully explored and its exposure would cause unexpected trouble. The amount that the Company management learned about itself was a stong plus from the experience.

One truly unique input cannot be overemphasized in its importance to the overall events. This was the special contribution of Senator Charles Percy at a critical moment in the story. Percy urged Cargill (and later, the rest of the companies) to be more open with the public, not just as a tactical measure but because (his words) "we are an important public business and notwithstanding private ownership, we should understand the need to take the public in our confidence."

Old ideas *do* die hard, and the feeling was strong among the five companies of the "big six" that were privately held that it was somehow "snooping" by the public (and government authorities) to want to know about their *private* affairs. Percy was gently saying that they were just too big and wielded too much market power to have this argument stand up to scrutiny. As discussed in a previous chapter, this was precisely the problem when Erv Kelm and his colleagues were so certain that they had not violated the law in the 1963 May wheat case. They were likely right on the narrower issues of CEA rulings; but it was really a case of market power, in effect an antitrust issue, upon which the judge made his decision against the Company.

Cargill took a major step, under Percy's urgings, in making public so much data on its operations, on its earnings, and on its tax burden. The sloppy staff work by the Church Subcommittee tactically changed the whole tenor of the hearings. But it was really more than that: it was a perceptive recognition of the public role of the Company, a "sea change" in thinking. This was not the last of Cargill's nor the industry's claims for confidentiality as "privately held" companies. But a major step had been taken (for better or for worse, depending upon whom one talked with).

As the industry moved through the Russian grain sales, the soybean embargo, the "boxcar blackmail" imbroglio, the grain irregularities tensions and, finally, the FTC/Church Subcommittee investigations, it became ever more obvious that each of the "big six" handled its corporate goals and objectives in separate ways. The value structures of each were disparate. The fact that three of the six were non-U.S. was one cause, but so many other beliefs and personal outlooks of individual managements added to this dissimilarity.

For Cargill, the heritage of John MacMillan, Sr. and Jr., of Austen Cargill and of Cargill MacMillan, had produced a truly unique corporate culture. We will be looking at this more carefully in the next chapter. But it is worthwhile to note here how important the MNC subcommittee hearings turned out to be for the honing and refining of this culture in the 1970s and 1980s, especially so for the marked change in public awareness noted above. To this should be added the ascension of Whitney MacMillan as chief executive officer of the Company (in 1977) and the impact of his clear enunciation of corporate values, which he stated in November 1975. This would now be tested in a further case, involving irregular payments by corporations (including Cargill) abroad.

The Knotty Question of Bribery Abroad

Doing business abroad involves grappling with the mores and practices of widely differing cultures. More than a few American beliefs about probity in commercial dealings do not mesh with given countries' ways of conducting such business. Bribery to obtain business—or alternatively, extortion against the one purveying the business—is often an accepted way of life.

Examples of these on a small scale, what is often dubbed the "grease" of the system, have produced many euphemisms around the world. The Near East *baksheesh* (tip, gratuity, alms) is so widely used that it is listed in Webster's dictionary; in Italy it can be called *un allettamento* (an attraction); in Mexico, *mordida*. The Spanish term is *unto amarillo* (gold-colored grease). *Cumshaw* is pidgin English for "tip," said to be derived from *kan shieh*, Mandarin Chinese for "grateful thanks."

Sometimes these terms also are used to describe much larger monetary amounts that could hardly be considered just grease.

In the Watergate scandal, the special prosecutor discovered illegal domestic political contributions to the 1972 reelection campaign of President Richard Nixon. Subsequently, a number of prominent American corporations, and in certain cases their senior executives, were prosecuted and convicted for these violations. At the same time, the Securities and Exchange Commission (SEC) began an investigation of these improper payments and the associated concealment.

In the process, the SEC broadened its inquiry to include improper payments abroad. Disclosure, one of the ongoing devices used by the SEC, also was required in these cases (there were a few exceptions, where companies involved argued successfully in court that disclosing individual names would be too devastating; the State Department even intervened in a case to quash some disclosures on the grounds of national security).

This information on bribery and extortion abroad was widely used by Senator Church's Subcommittee (see above). With new legislation for a "Foreign Corrupt Practices Act" being advocated widely (and eventually passed on December 19, 1977), several other congressional committees and other federal agencies also entered the fray.

One of these was the Internal Revenue Service (IRS), which from the beginning had been looking into the tax implications (the IRS agents being particularly interested in whether bribes were being charged off as legitimate business expenditures). Involvement of the IRS also satisfied some critics' views that the SEC investigations failed to monitor privately held companies. Cargill, for example, came under SEC purview only when it was involved in a merger effort, as in the Missouri Portland case mentioned earlier in the chapter; on the other hand, Cook Industries, the only publicly held "big six" grain trading company, was minutely investigated by the SEC in its probe. (On April 5, 1976, Ralph Nader made an appearance before the Senate Banking Committee, which was considering new bribery legislation, specifically to complain about Cargill, which would not be covered if the SEC were to administer the new legislation.)

In early April 1976, the IRS announced a massive tax evasion investigation, with its particular targets a group of 1,200 major corporations, all routinely audited by the agency. Eleven questions about possible bribes, kickbacks, and other illegal payments were to be asked of all these companies. The *Minneapolis Tribune* quoted an IRS spokesman: "If they lie, they'll have problems; if they don't answer, they'll have problems. . . . We're asking these people now everything but the color of their underwear." Among the 1,200 corporations was Cargill.

Revelations Abound

As the Company began its very substantial discovery effort to fully answer the IRS's "eleven questions" while at the same time making its final preparations for the upcoming June appearance before the Church Subcommittee, the revelations of several hundred of the other companies being investigated by both the SEC and the IRS began to reach the public. The SEC, for example, gave the Senate Banking Committee a long list of household names among American corporations that had disclosed "questionable" foreign payments, ranging from Smith International, at $13,349, to Lockheed Aircraft at $25,000,000 and Exxon at $56,771,000.

Roderick M. Hills, the SEC chairman, elaborated six different practices considered by the SEC to be questionable: (1) phony "bonuses" to company employees in order to make illegal domestic political contributions; (2) payments from revolving cash funds at a foreign subsidiary to make illegal domestic and foreign political contributions; (3) secret kickbacks on purchase or sales contracts made through foreign-bearer stock corporations or foreign subsidiaries; (4) funds passed through foreign consultants for illegal political or commercial payments; (5) money paid to consultants or commission agents, with inadequate documentation of purpose and value; and (6) money paid directly to foreign officials for favorable business concessions.

The SEC also described the ameliorative efforts being taken by many of these firms. Some had instituted disciplinary action, including demotions and terminations. Several corporations received resignations from senior executives. Of the 109 cases analyzed in one study, five of the companies had instituted efforts to sell foreign subsidiaries following disclosure of questionable payments.

Cargill Discloses Its Irregular Payments

In early March 1977, the Company made its final report to the IRS on the eleven questions, and on March 16 released a brief public statement. "Unusual payments" had been made during the period June 1, 1975, to May 31, 1976, totalling "about $5 million." None involved illegal political contributions, just over $16,900 was "in connection with U.S. domestic transactions . . . none was paid directly or indirectly to any federal, state or municipal employee, nor did any part . . . relate to any government contract." The Company also declared in its public statement that it believed that "little or none" of its admitted payments involved any U.S. tax liability.

The remainder of the Cargill payments had been made in foreign countries, the total payments just short of $5 million. No details on individual cases were included in the Company's news release. The *Wall Street Journal* explained: "Being privately owned, the company doesn't have to make a publicly available statement on payments as required of companies subject to regulations of the Securities and Exchange Commission."

The Company privately explained to the IRS that in all the cases where questionable payments had been made to foreign companies it did not want to include the name of the company, the name of the recipient, or the country in which the recipient resided because disclosure would result in designating the country, which in turn would, because of the nature of the transaction, designate the individual. The amounts did not have any effect on the computation of U.S. tax, and further, the Company was concerned about the welfare of persons who had made or received the payments and worried also about embarrassment that might be caused to the governments of the countries involved. Finally, there was the concern about Cargill's future ability to be able to transact business in and with the foreign countries involved.

However, the *Minneapolis Star* included a short paragraph of detail on one particular case. While it did not involve bribery per se, it had been discovered internally by Cargill officials in the process of researching the eleven questions. The *Star*'s revelation had not been in the Company's press release; the reporter's statement read as follows: "It was also learned that some Cargill affiliates in Spain kept two sets of books to avoid a portion of that country's income taxes. Cargill said that it has ended the practice, which reportedly has been widespread among companies in Spain."

This was the only mention at this time anywhere in the public press, in the Twin Cities or nationally, of this specific case. The reason became evident later in a story that became a cause célèbre, going through a series of daunting federal court hearings before its final disposition in August 1983. The reason for the uniqueness of this case lies in the following incident; the text included here is from the federal district court judge's decision in December 1979 in a case brought against Cargill by the IRS:

On February 14 and 15, 1977 [the] head of [Cargill's outside counsel] met with several persons at the request of [the] general counsel for Cargill. The participants . . . included two auditors from [Cargill's auditing firm] and a tax attorney from Cargill's legal department. The meetings arose out of Cargill's responses to the Eleven Questions. . . . Discussed at the meetings were activities of two of Cargill's subsidiaries [in Spain]. . . . Following the meetings, [Cargill's general counsel] requested that [the

Hugh storage bin at Port Cargill, in Savage, Minnesota, was built to store grain during a time of large surpluses. Reputed to be the largest single bin in the world, with a capacity of about 6 million bushels, it was emptied early in 1976 as the surplus dwindled (*Cargill News,* May–June 1976).

outside counsel] summarize his notes at the meetings in typewritten form . . . and sent a copy to the Cargill corporate offices in Minneapolis by a messenger provided by a delivery company hired by [the outside counsel].

Without authority, the messenger who was to deliver the questioned document . . . opened the taped envelope and examined the document in a men's room. The informant, who holds a journalism degree and is a sometime reporter, photocopied the document and proceeded to deliver the resealed envelope containing the original document to Cargill. . . . The informant then delivered a photocopy to [the] *Minneapolis Star* . . . the *Star* informed Cargill that the newspaper had a copy of the questioned document. . . . Upon learning of the *Star*'s journalistic coup [Cargill] informed the IRS that a document had been stolen, and that if the IRS received it, it should be aware that the document was privileged [i.e., the doctrine of lawyer-client privilege].

On March 16, 1977, the informant arranged a meeting with [a special agent of the IRS Intelligence Division] and handed [the agent] a copy of the questioned document, a magazine article about Cargill and a listing of Cargill executives and their duties. . . . On May 19, 1977, [the IRS] personally delivered . . . tax summonses [to Cargill] that require[d] the production of documents and the giving of testimony by and from Cargill.

After the summons was served, Cargill representatives surmised that the IRS probably possessed a copy of the questioned document, because the language of the summons tracked the language of the document. . . . From March 15, 1977, . . . until September 7, 1977, . . . the IRS engaged in misleading conduct. On several occasions, IRS agents denied that the IRS possessed a copy of the questioned document. Not until September 2, after the IRS received the informant's consent [to reveal his identity], did it reveal that it had a copy of the document. On May 8, 1978, the IRS commenced these actions to enforce the summonses.

This federal court decision specifically addressed the issue of whether the stolen document could be declared by Cargill a "privileged document." Despite the theft and despite the complications of notice to Cargill by the IRS that it *did* have the document, in a complex opinion the judge ruled against Cargill. The document was not "privileged"; it was an "opinion work product," and the IRS summonses were enforceable—the document was a public document.

The case itself, relating to the tax liabilities of Cargill for actions in the two Spanish companies, continued through November 1981, when Cargill pleaded guilty to charges that it understated its income by more than $6 million during the fiscal years of 1975 and 1976. The company paid the back taxes and a modest fine of $10,000. The government agreed not to bring criminal tax charges against Cargill or its employees related to ongoing investigations of company tax returns from 1972 through 1978.

The case was widely reported throughout the public press and damaged the Company's reputation. In particular, Whitney MacMillan's clearly enunciated statements of corporate values seemed compromised. Ralph Nader and William Taylor, in their book *The Big Boys*, used the stolen document to recount an earlier incident relating to MacMillan's view of the evolving situation in the Spanish company: "Then-president MacMillan went to Spain [circa June 1976] and met with the executives . . . 'Whitney took a strong stand there,' the memo noted. 'This is when they told Whitney that the . . . operations were more expansive than we thought. Because of this, Whitney took a strong position. . . . [Cargill official] Jay [Berkley] said there would be no more purchases of companies . . .'"

Assuming Nader and Taylor are correct in their dating of this meeting in Spain, this puts it some six months after MacMillan's blunt letter to Cargill's "fellow employees," decrying "various illegal or questionable corporate practices" present in some American businesses and ending with five explicit, no-nonsense precepts that MacMillan felt defined "the principles of integrity which have always been basic to our philosophy" (the letter is printed in full in Chapter 7). In particular, MacMillan reminded Cargill employees again that "if a transaction cannot be properly recorded in the Company books, subject to an independent audit, it must be wrong." The Spanish case must have been upsetting to him, particularly since most of the news articles reporting Cargill's admission of a $5 million total for "unusual payments" also mentioned this earlier MacMillan statement.

Once the story of the pilfered document became public knowledge and the government won the right to use it in the courts, the tax case was sent to a grand jury. At this point, the Company faced a profound dilemma about what to communicate to their employees. Much of Cargill's evidence was constrained by being involved in the case. Further, there was concern by many in senior management that (as one put it) "somebody in the government bureaucracy or judicial hierarchy has decided to go on an ego trip and/or make a name for himself in the persecution of big business," and almost any disclosure could be overblown and misinterpreted. Given the extensive press stories on the eleven-questions disclosures and those earlier in the MNC subcommittee publicity, this reaction was perhaps understandable.

On the other hand, as Heinz Hutter put it (after an extensive field trip among Cargill people in August 1980), "All of them voiced great concern that they might get up one morning and might have to read in the newspaper or be confronted by a customer with further details and information on the subject without being properly prepared for it or without having any well founded comments and/or explanations." But at this time, after several drafts for an employee letter were discussed, it finally was decided not to make *any* such statement.

This situation changed once the case had concluded. The public announcement of this, in mid-November 1981, was followed by a terse, 12-line *Green Wave* "special announcement" to employees, explaining that the Company had pleaded guilty to two counts in the filing of the tax returns for 1975 and 1976 and that the Company had been fined $5,000 on each count. Neither the country nor the companies involved was mentioned; the charges had arisen "out of the handling, for tax purposes, of a series of transactions among affiliated firms abroad." When the Company "discovered the error through its own audit and legal review," additional taxes were found to be due and were "promptly paid. . . . Regrettably, this does not alter the fact that we failed to meet our obligation to file complete and accurate returns when they were due."

On the same day, Whitney MacMillan sent a full two-page letter to Cargill managers, stating, "I suspect that the *Green Wave* announcement will leave questions in your mind and in the minds of people who report to you." This time the explanation was more complete: "Nothing about this case is simple, but in short, we failed to treat part of the proceeds generated by certain sales of corn and soybeans by foreign affiliates as 'constructive dividends' subject to current taxes." The entire second page was devoted to a statement of the underlying Cargill values at stake. Here the thread of MacMillan's 1975 statement once again came through clearly:

. . . it is very tempting to make excuses for our actions. But in this case, I think that would be a mistake. Every taxpayer has the affirmative obligation to ensure that his tax return is complete and accurate. For a company like ours, the tax implications of all transactions, however complex, must be understood and communicated to everyone involved to ensure that our tax returns are complete and accurate. The results of our failure . . . are the fines assessed today, potential civil penalties and embarrassment to us all.

How did it happen? It happened because our system failed to bring together people with full knowledge of the transactions and those with the expertise . . . to ensure their proper handling. . . .

So, where do we go from here? We've learned from this experience. We've made changes. We have put in place controls that we believe are effective. I am confident that this problem will not recur.

On the other hand, I am also confident that we will encounter other, equally unexpected problems as our business grows and becomes more complex. . . . We will have to anticipate these problems and deal with them more effectively.

MacMillan ended his statement with a pointed caveat reminiscent of his 1975 words: "Systems don't manage our business, people do. In the end, it's our decisions and actions that will make the difference." This time, MacMillan was speaking as chief executive officer, not as president (Erv Kelm had stepped down in August 1977, MacMillan then becoming CEO). We will look more closely at this evolving Cargill value structure in the final chapter.[21]

"Soviet Graindoggle"

Had not the Russians agreed back in 1975 to regularize their purchases of grain from the United States over a full five-year period, buying at least 6 million metric tons every year, but checking with U.S. authorities if the purchases were to go over 8 million? As part of the agreement, U.S. grain experts were to be allowed greater on-site visitations; further, CIA satellites were to be free to monitor overhead. The plan had worked well in 1976—the Russians apparently did not need huge additions to their domestic supply.

But in 1977 the tidy agreement fell apart. In early September, the USDA forecast of the Russian grain crop had "remained unchanged at 220 million metric tons." However, as *Time* magazine put it, "Agriculture Department inspectors visiting the U.S.S.R. were taken out to collectives to see sturdy stands of corn and wheat fields that they now know to have been exceptions." Further, the CIA's photo interpretations had gone awry because of what *Time* called "bad 'ground truth' data—information from the observers *escorted by the Russians*" (my emphasis).

In sum, what the USDA interpreted as a good Russian crop turned out to be very much below expectations. On November 2, 1977, Chairman Leonid Brezhnev announced in Moscow that Soviet grain production was expected to be a shockingly small 194 million tons. More startling, Brezhnev estimated that Soviet grain import requirements from all sources would be in the range of 20 to 25 million metric tons for the upcoming 12 months.

There had been earlier intimations of this situation. Wheat average prices had begun to go up—soft red winter wheat at Chicago had averaged $2.08 a bushel in August and rose to $2.59 in November. Trade sources noted that the Russians were contracting for substantial additional shipping. Rumors had been rife that purchases had been consummated privately with members of the "big six" grain companies. By late November, *U.S. News and World Report* was predicting another "grain robbery." *Time* called it a "Soviet grain sting." It was the *Christian Science Monitor* that coined the term "graindoggle."

The Russians had stayed within the letter of the law on the agreement. Their early, quiet buying had been in Europe, from the foreign subsidiaries of the "big six" and others, where contracts were typically made for delivery that did not specify country of origin (perfectly legal for the subsidiaries). When the Soviets came to the quarterly meeting with the United States on the agreements, they requested—and received—permission to raise their totals by 15 million tons. By the time of Brezhnev's announcement, Russia had most of its grain, "bought cheap" again.

A number of U.S. congressmen jumped to the attack. Kansas senator Robert Dole called for hearings to investigate the ability of the USDA to predict the size of the crop. George McGovern, the South Dakota senator, echoed the demand. Iowa representative Jim Leach stated that "in all probability" Cargill was one of the major participants "in a secret grain sale." (A newspaper headline seemed even more definitive: "Cargill in on Grain Deal: Leach"). Once again, Cargill officials felt themselves unfairly under attack for the perfectly legal, highly successful—but highly controversial—activities of its semiautonomous subsidiary, Tradax.

Despite the federal reporting requirements for export sales, it was still difficult to tell just how much grain was going to the Soviet Union. For example, on the "Report of Export Sales and Exports" to the USDA, Cargill stated on October 31, 1977 (just before the Brezhnev announcement of lowered expectations for the Soviet crop), that only 433,000 metric tons had been booked for the U.S.S.R. In the same report, the sales to 'unknown' destinations were 3.7 million metric tons.

Again, most of Cargill's sales to Russia were transactions accomplished by Tradax, which had no reporting requirement to the U.S. government. In the summary annual report of Tradax, its management reported, "We were particularly successful in being the major commercial supplier for the Soviet Union." Commodity trading margins were up from the previous year—maize from $9.3 million to $12.3 million and wheat from $10.2 to $13.1 million (soybeans, however, lost some $11.5 million, when "both flat price and premium judgments proved incorrect"). On the other hand, "the Argentine option on the large Russian maize volume was a great money-maker."

In a major statement in the Company's *Public Affairs Newsletter* in late November 1977, the case was made once again for allowing Tradax to remain unfettered: "At present, the Export Sales Reporting System (ESRS) does not require foreign firms—even if they are affiliated with U.S. firms—to report sales of U.S. grain." While an argument had been advanced that these firms should be drawn into a reporting system, this would be "fraught with problems." Indeed, it would be destined to fail, stated the *Newsletter*, for "in today's world marketplace many major grain sellers lie beyond the U.S. law." This would include, the authors stated, the Japanese trading firms and others, and they would operate outside the scope of any reporting system. "So, reporting rules divert business from the United States to other origins and from

U.S. affiliated companies, subject to U.S. reporting requirements, to non-U.S. firms not subject to these requirements."

On the other hand, there would be "real value in enabling U.S.-affiliated foreign trading companies to operate on an equal footing with non-U.S. concerns because their U.S. parent companies have substantial investments in grain-handling facilities to serve American farmers, so they have an incentive to ship American grains on sales whenever possible. This is not necessarily true of non-U.S. companies." In place of any reporting requirement, the Company advocated heightened cooperation between the major trading firms and the government in the process of assessing world crop and market developments.

The issue of a "graindoggle" began to subside, however, after the first of the year 1978. The average price of soft red winter wheat in Chicago rose to $3.68 by November of that year (and ballooned to $4.39 by July 1979). The consumer price index rose some 6.5 percent in 1977, 7.8 percent in 1978. Food and beverage prices lagged in 1977 and were slightly above the average in 1978. Still, grain production was excellent, and farmers received good prices for the crop. The Russians imported about 14.6 million tons from the United States in 1977–1978 and about 15.7 million tons in 1978–1979. Even with these higher numbers, the supplies on hand appeared to be adequate to meet other anticipated domestic requirements and maintain a sufficient carryover into the next period. In sum, while the ingredients for a renewed confrontation between the grain trading industry and its publics seemed to be in place once again, perhaps to repeat the 1972–1973 tensions, the effects on the consumer this round were not so pronounced as to keep the pot boiling.

Although the Russians once more had shown themselves master tacticians at the business of grain trading, the reporting requirements were not changed at this time. It was not an economic but a political issue that was to bring one of the greatest confrontations between the two countries vis-à-vis grain trading: the U.S. embargo of grain sales to Russia in 1980 in retaliation for the Russian invasion of Afghanistan. This major development will be an interesting early story for a next volume of this Cargill historical series.[22]

The Farmers Pull a Surprise

Since 1775, when that small band of embattled farmers stood their ground against the British at Concord Bridge, the producers of this nation's food supply have been known for their independence, perseverance and stubborn pride. On December 14, 1977, modern counterparts of the Massachusetts Minutemen proclaimed their own rebellion. Armed with placards rather than muskets, American farmers fired media volleys that—if not heard "round the world"—echoed loudly from Capitol Hill to Pennsylvania Avenue.

Farm strike is what they called it. Their threat: not to buy, sell nor plant. Their battle cry: "Hell no, we won't grow." The action that resulted was probably one of the most curious movements in the annals of American agriculture and labor.

The dramatic hyperbole of the *Cargill News* writer certainly was matched by the realities of the farm strike. The notion of a strike "grates on the independent nature of farmers," the *News* stated, "and recalls old feuds with organized labor." But by the end of the harvest of 1977, the farmers began to comprehend fully the results of the excess farm production worldwide of the previous two years. Exports had slackened, prices had continued to drop, and net income in the United States for the 1976–1977 crop year was expected to plunge to a level of $20 billion, some 50 percent below 1973. Of course, that was the record year when prices had doubled subsequent to the 1972 Russian grain purchases. After that record year of 1973, a bullish euphoria had spread among a great many farmers; and in the face of soaring farm land prices, they had expanded their acreage in a frenzy of purchases. Further, this same expansionist-minded segment of the industry had often coupled its land binge with an equally bullish purchase of high-ticket equipment. With the sagging prices of 1976 and especially 1977, this put an unbearable squeeze on farmers' finances. "The high base of the early 1970s gave us some false dreams," a farmer reported to *Business Week* in December 1977, "and we are just awakening to the fact that we are back to the 1960s level of modest farming profits instead of enormous wealth."

So the high protest level of farmers was concentrated not among the marginal farmers who were hanging on but directly on the large-farm, mechanized segment, many of whom were newer entrants into the farming fraternity. Many banks in the farming areas had abandoned past cautionary financial constraints and had lent large sums for this land/equipment boom. Now the denouement had arrived for both farmers and bankers, caused particularly by the famine in cash flow.

Sometime during the early fall of 1977 — *Cargill News* spotted it as being in September at the Branding Iron Café in Campbell, Colorado — a group of farmers put together a loosely knit organization they dubbed the American Agricultural Movement (AAM). Soon plans were made for the strike, to feature "tractorcades" and rallies in a number of places in the farming areas. Support for the movement was sporadic, varying by state and by type of farmer. Most of the activity was concentrated in Texas, Georgia, Kansas, and the Dakotas, with less interest in California, Iowa, Wisconsin, Minnesota, Ohio, Illinois, and New England. Wheat farmers seemed more enthusiastic than the corn belt farmers; dairymen and livestock producers were more removed. Some drought in the Southeast had put farmers there under additional pressure; relatively, the Midwest was doing better.

Nevertheless, there was indeed a movement. The organization, if that is what it could be called, had no permanent leadership; and the federal government appeared to vacillate on its own position, with Secretary of Agriculture Bob Bergland particularly on the fence. By December 1977, at the point when the "strike" began, tractor motorcades hit the nation's capital, with accompa-

"True grit was common among farmers who drove from distant fields through all weathers to protest and add spice to Washington traffic." The farmers' strike, spring 1978 (Cargill News, May–June 1978).

nying live animals and other striking publicity sorties. "Though its leadership is fragmented and its goals are not clearly defined," Senator George McGovern of South Dakota commented, "it is evident to me that we are not far from the 'farm holidays' days of 1932."

The demands of the group were specific and controversial. The main goal of the strikers was "full parity." Parity typically was defined as the relationship of prices received for agricultural commodities to prices farmers paid for their production needs and living expenses. For many years, the base for determining parity had been the years 1910–1914, a period generally considered to be the golden age of farming. Parity thus became the buying power of a bushel of wheat, corn, or other commodities at that time. Of course, conditions in the years 1910–1914 truly had become outdated; with all the amazing productivity changes on the farm, the hours a farmer spent to produce that bushel of grain had changed radically. Both the USDA and most farm economists had branded this mechanistic form of describing parity as outmoded. Secretary Bergland, in the January 1978 annual convention of the American Farm Bureau Federation, said it was not the government's role to ensure 100 percent parity for agricultural products nor to assume responsibility for the risks involved in farming. In his view, only with huge government intervention could a parity concept be made a reality.

In addition to the central demand for parity, the AAM advocated four other steps: a policy board of farmers within the USDA itself, the allocating of grain markets among farmers based on historical production, the prohibition of agricultural imports at any point when parity dropped below 110 percent, and the storing of any farmer's overproduction at that producer's expense.

As the strike began, on December 14, 1977, the leaders exhorted all farmers, "Don't buy, don't sell, don't plant." Some called it a "plowdown." At this point, the tactics were expanded to include stopping trains and trucks thought to be carrying farm products, blockading grain imports and cattle from Canada, and also protesting at entrances to domestic meat packing plants. Substantial picketing and closing down of grocery stores, bakeries, and food processing plants also occurred. There were even sporadic threats to plow up planted crops themselves. Among the agribusiness-related organizations approached by the farmers were country elevators and terminals of the grain-trading companies.

Cargill soon was accosted. It was a scattered effort, affecting only some 15 or so locations, mostly the Company's country elevators. Some managers were asked to stop shipping, some to stop receiving, and others to shut down completely. Cargill management debated the pros and cons of the issues at length and eventually developed a uniform statement of response that could be articulated at any of the Company's locations that might be affected. It read as follows: "We respect the right of farmers to withhold purchases and sales to dramatize their concerns about farm prices. At the same time, we respect the decision of other farmers to continue normal business operations. It is not our purpose to take sides in this dispute. Our job is to provide services to farmers who need them as efficiently, effectively and productively as we can. We intend to meet this responsibility."

At four locations, the situation facing Cargill was more complicated. In Portland, Oregon, the Company's CMD export elevator (Terminal 4) was closed when longshoremen refused to cross a farmer picket line. The same thing also happened at the Seattle CMD truck-rail elevator at Pier 86. The next day, however, the longshoremen were back on the job after an arbitrator ruled that the farmers' picket line was not to be honored because it was an "informational" and not a "legal labor picket." At Cargill's Princeton, Indiana, CMD terminal, pickets paraded for a week, talking to drivers of arriving trucks and then later taking a harder line by attempting to block movement entirely. The usual daily flow of trucks, ranging from 50 to 100, was slowed to a trickle, until an informal agreement in a major snowstorm closed the elevator for a day. Princeton manager Jim Williford reported later to *Cargill News*: "Actually we got quite a bit of sympathy from farmers. They are an independent bunch and wanted to make their own decisions. So they respected our position and thought we were doing the right thing to continue to do business."

The *News* also carried the story of another "besieged manager," Bill Fielding at the Burrus flour mill in Saginaw, Texas. Strikers had blocked the mill's access road, and the Company had asked for and received a temporary re-straining order. While the order listed only two persons' names and was not enough to disperse the group, the presence of Texas Rangers and highway pa-trolmen seemed to encourage strikers to negotiate. "We met late in the day with strike leaders and city officials," Fielding reported, "and agreed not to load trucks overnight. We told them frankly that we weren't planning to load trucks anyway, but they were looking for a way to get out and still save face." The farmers did go home, somewhat mollified.

Cargill president Pete McVay made a major address about the strikers' de-mands and stressed to them that Cargill's and the farmers' interests were truly identical, to be "partners in building world markets." Cargill had been urging improvements in multilateral trade agreements that would provide freer ac-cess to world markets for grain production. The Company, he stated, be-lieved that the solution lay in expanding these markets, not enclosing them until the prices reached a level tied to some parity concept. The Company was sympathetic to the need for some kind of income support for troubled farm-ers, but believed that support prices should not be so high that they restricted consumption or encouraged farmers overseas (e.g., in Brazil, Argentina, or Australia) to make capital investments and expand production that they might not otherwise have done, thereby becoming new competitors for American farmers.

By February 1978, the farmers had begun concentrating their efforts on congressional office buildings and the administration building of the USDA, putting pressure on Congress for new legislation. "It was a new experience for Congressmen and bureaucrats to meet dirt farmers in their offices and meet-ing rooms," Willard Cochrane, the well-known agricultural economist, com-mented. The AAM advocated a series of target prices that startled both con-gressmen and bureaucrats. Senator Edmund Muskie of Maine argued on the floor of the Senate that their "three-headed monster" would add billions to the federal budget. The USDA released an extensive statement on the AAM proposals, estimating that food prices in the fourth quarter of 1978 would go up by 20 percent if the parity provisions were instituted literally.

As the hearings before the Senate's Agriculture Committee continued through February and into March 1978, various farm groups testified, includ-ing not only the AAM but the National Farmers' Union, the National Grange, and several regional groups. The leaders became more and more adamant about their demand that 100 percent of parity at the initial point of sale be adopted as new legislation. "Attempts to point out the problems of passing such a bill in a largely urban Congress," Garland West of Cargill's Washington office reported, "were categorically rejected by the crowd. . . . The farmers preferred to continue giving long, flag-waving, philosophical statements of the economic dangers facing the family farm."

But the arguments *were* being made to a Congress that was highly sensitive to farm price escalations, having just revisited the issue of the Russians getting the best of American negotiators on fresh grain sales to that country. The scales were tipped against the strikers.

Cochrane summarized the basic issues of the debate that winter as embracing three propositions: (1) the government of the United States stood willing to provide farmers with a price-income support floor to keep the farming industry from falling into a deep economic depression; (2) the government of the United States stood willing to provide all farm operators, except the great corporate enterprises, with a modest income supplement and many and varied kinds of technical and financial assistance; but (3) the government of the United States would *not* grant farmers the program devices, the monopoly power in the marketplace, to enable them to push up farm product prices significantly and hence increase retail food prices significantly. This latter action could not be taken. Food prices represented the cutting edge of the general price inflation, and to give farmers the programs and the power to push food prices upward by a significant amount would be to exacerbate general price inflation and to infuriate millions of urban consumers.

This was precisely what finally happened. The government was willing to provide "fail-safe" provisions to keep the farmer from disaster. It was willing to provide both income supplements and technical backup, but it was unwilling to give the farmers (in this case, exemplified by the AAM) the actual power to force parity into place.

There was further farm legislation that winter, but it was a token addition to the existing Agricultural Act of 1977. The fall of the flexible parity bill was a bitter defeat for farm-strike activists. *Cargill News* commented: "The impact of the strikers' demands on the nation's economy would have been too great."

The more gradual process of the grain price cycle righting itself had begun to take place, with grain prices already rising substantially since the early AAM movement in September 1977. One anguished striker, in Washington at the defeat of the flexible parity bill, told *Cargill News*: "It's just like a crop failure—we'll go back and start working on another bill." But Congress had spoken definitively, and the issue really was over.

CHAPTER NINE

The Cargill Culture—a Reprise

When John MacMillan, Jr., died in 1960, the 95-year legacy left by just three chief executive officers, each a member of the Cargill or MacMillan families, came to a close. In this unbroken span of years a significant, powerful corporate culture had been put firmly in place. How had Erwin E. Kelm affected this in the next 17 years, with his stewardship as chief executive officer (CEO)?

There is often a temptation to clothe a corporate culture around the single persona of the CEO, the whole organization as a simplistic extension of the "long shadow" of the CEO. More than infrequently, these executives *do* put in place strong values that permeate the organization; still, a host of people in an organization, senior level and otherwise, also affect it importantly.

Both of these statements are true for Cargill. All through the years, there have been strong individuals in key posts throughout the Company. Indeed, that is one of the most noted elements at Cargill—the widespread presence of strong-willed, independent, and self-motivated senior management, backed by loyal, intelligent, and hardworking subordinates and line employees.

Having said this, we return immediately to the overriding impact of these three men—William W. Cargill, John H. MacMillan, Sr., and John Jr. Seldom in American business history has an organization been more influenced by three such men. Perhaps the "long shadow" overly mythologizes the story, but there is little doubt that the forceful culture of Cargill stems profoundly from these three men.

W. W. Cargill was a product of his times and provided the entrepreneurial zest and enthusiasm that brought great growth to what soon became a far-flung grain trading system. Early on, he sensed the need for vertical integration, and the grain companies flourished. But his nongrain efforts had not been as well chosen; when he died in 1909, a financial crisis ensued. Son-in-law John MacMillan, Sr., was able to rescue the Company; pervasive additional values were set in place under his tenure. He fostered new management principles most advanced for his time, particularly focusing on modern accounting methods. MacMillan had a courtly, open way of dealing with his colleagues, inspiring confidence and engendering quick loyalty. One could make a mistake and be forgiven, provided the lesson was well learned.

John Sr. was no innovator; he wanted steady growth and no deep swings. Caution and conservatism—these were his bywords. All the members of both families seemed to share "an overwhelming anxiety for security" (John Jr.'s own words). Likely it was John Sr. who most deeply felt this need, although both John Jr. and brother Cargill MacMillan strove hard in the 1930s and 1940s to take portions of the company abroad, in part because it was a very important strategic move for the business but also because they feared the insecurities of the 1930s very deeply. Initial moves to establish Tradax in Montreal were made because of "the grave consideration of safety for our principal, and Cargill and I feel very strongly that we would be infinitely safer there than here" (again, John Jr.'s words). This would be a means to protect a portion of the Company's capital in the event of "some disastrous social upheaval in the United States" (Cargill MacMillan). The bedrock Cargill values of integrity and honesty were particularly the product of John Sr.'s complex, believable convictions.

But after his heart attack in the early 1930s, John Sr. turned inward, fearful, perseverative. Now it was 1960, and the seminal qualities put in place by John Sr. had happened many years back. Only the older members of the Kelm team knew him when he was functional and important. Kelm and Fred Seed joined the Company in the early 1930s, two of the first members of the fabled Cargill training program run by Julius Hendel; this was precisely the time that John Sr. was becoming narrowly introspective.

So it was John Jr. who dominated—not Cargill MacMillan, not Austin Cargill, the son of W. W., except as good friends and solid alter egos for "Junior." John Jr. became a legend in his time, an icon that provided one of the most striking role models among business management of his day. Dynamic, articulate, fast speaking and fast paced, innovative, and creative, he looked to the future and was opportunity-cost oriented, a motivator of men far beyond that overused cliché. Dominating, indeed domineering, concerned too often about social position and the "best" schools, he was always scrupulously honest by his own standards but, as his nephew Whitney put it, "sometimes running down the side of the field instead of the center."

This complex man was an amalgam of a widely varying set of traits, an overwhelming number of them positive but some significant negatives, too. John Jr. came up through a different set of experiences in the business, interlaced particularly with a fine-tuned sense of haggling that gave him a trading mentality, a combative bargaining basis for his business life. He never lied (that would have been anathema), but he always wanted to best the other side and be able to say, "Weren't we clever." *Fortune* magazine called him "a contentious, abrasive, uncompromising free enterpriser."

The *Fortune* editors correctly noted that younger brother Cargill MacMillan gave John Jr.'s leadership "moderation and balance." Cargill MacMillan was quiet but not retiring; he was willing to be blunt with John Jr. when necessary; for example, "Just received your proposed memo . . . I like it but still wish caution. Impression one gets where too radical ideas are too hurriedly presented." Austen Cargill, too, had a special input, always speaking for and representing in himself the human qualities of the business.

"John Jr.," *Fortune* posited, "was the kind of creative goad that every company destined for greatness must suffer at some time in its career—an impatient, imaginative eccentric who would never let well enough alone." John Jr.'s strong will and highly successful—almost overly successful—stint as the youngest major in the U.S. Army in World War I gave him a view of authority that was overweening at times. John Jr. analyzed his own approach in an amazingly frank statement quoted in his house organ, *Cargill News*: "Either way you like it—a man of strong opinions or an opinionated man, I see things in black and white. If there are shades of gray, I have no time for them." He did not admit to quirkiness, though he noted, "There are some who say I am eccentric; they are wrong but they're again welcome to their opinion." *Cargill News* added: "He summarized himself in a note to his son in the Army, in 1952; when recalling his days as a 23-year old major of artillery, he added, 'it is doubtful that I know any of your generals. The officers I knew in World War I are nearly all dead or retired. I circulated in rather exalted circles, age considered. After all, I was considered precocious.'"

John Jr. had strong personal prejudices; for example: "We have also to be sure that our people have adequate self-discipline. We have had some extraordinarily brilliant people who have been in Cargill who should have gone places. But the first thing we knew, some of these weaknesses turned up—alcohol, women, finances, or perhaps they were just too fat." As a retired Cargill executive once commented, "attempts at despotism represent, as it were, the drunkenness of responsibility. It is where men are overwhelmed with the difficulties and blunders of humanity that they fall back upon a wild desire to manage everything themselves." There was some of this in John Jr.

This was the legacy handed to Erwin Kelm with the sudden death of John Jr., which had followed just months after Cargill MacMillan's totally disabling stroke (and three years after the death of the popular Austen Cargill). Both the Company's president and its chairman and CEO were gone in a matter of months. Kelm was to succeed. He now had to step into these shoes—certainly a large order for any person.

The Kelm Years

Kelm succeeded in this challenge, beyond even the most optimistic expectations. The term is apt—these *were* the Kelm years, for by the end of the period 1960–1977, Kelm had put his own mark on the Company in a major way. Kelm did not shake the tradition—that was not his style. Rather, he implanted a set of his own values onto those of his predecessors, deepening but not supplanting the corporate culture he had been handed. In so many ways, the Cargill of 1977 was reminiscent of the Cargill of 1960 (as, indeed, the Cargill of 1997 is reminiscent in its dominant features of the Cargill of 1977—but that is another book!).

An important thing had to happen here at the start of Kelm's regime, relating to the families. While he was the fourth CEO by succession, he was the first nonfamily person in charge of the company in its entire 95-year history. There were five young family members in their 30s in the next generation who also were employees of the Company—in one case, as head of a closely related organization, Cargill Securities Company (later renamed Waycrosse), the joint family management company. The five were Jim Cargill, son of Austen Cargill (thus actually third generation from W. W.); Cargill MacMillan, Jr., and Whitney MacMillan, sons of Cargill MacMillan; and John Hugh MacMillan and W. Duncan MacMillan (the one heading Cargill Securities), sons of John Jr. Given the visceral feeling of the preceding generation that Cargill was a family company (John Jr. had vigorously opposed any common stock holdings by members outside the family, developing a preferred stock form for those outside the family who originally had held some shares of the initial common), would this group of five next-generation young executives choose to exert proprietary rights, not just for stock but for top-level management positions?

The answer to this sensitive question came immediately—no. With initial counsel, particularly of Terry Morrison, the caretaker chairman of the company in the first two years of the Kelm regime, these five young men met privately to develop an analytical scale of measurement of what their various (and varying) objectives would be for "their" Company. They adapted a point scale stemming from the Company's Ben Tregoe management seminars just coming into being at that time and concluded that their number-one objective was "best management to the top." They eschewed any patronage power play and opted for, as one analyst put it, "climbing the ladder of meritocracy rather than riding the escalator of nepotism."[1]

The five young men went further; in the joint letter quoted in Chapter One, they explicitly abstained from an early appointment of any one of them to board membership ("if a young man goes on the Board, and he turns out be a poor choice, the Board is likely to be stuck with him for many years . . . older men generally have more to offer"). This effort by the five was a preemptive blunting of what had been an earlier effort by John Jr. to bring the next generation of management onto the board at an early age. So the open spot on the board brought by John Jr.'s death was subsequently filled not by one of the five young men—earlier, John Jr. had advocated this—but by the appointment of Sumner "Ted" Young, a longtime family confidant and Company lawyer.

Young wrote Hugh MacMillan at that time, "I think the smartest thing you boys ever did was to refrain from taking top-management positions in the Cargill organization when C. Mac. became incapacitated, and when your father died. That served notice on the world that these top positions were not pre-empted for family occupancy; that the family was not going to allow itself to take positions in the hierarchy for which it was not fully trained."

There has been much writing among analysts of business history about the so-called Buddenbrooks syndrome, the name coming from a famous book by Thomas Mann chronicling the rise and fall of a German family that had built a flourishing business in the 1870s and had seen this patrimony wither away as the succeeding son and grandchildren of the founder grappled with the business without much success or ability. Mann wrote a number of these dark, brooding novels of social realism, commenting on the foibles of all-too-human people struggling to deal with their own egos.[2]

The "Buddenbrooks effect" is a somewhat simplistic commentary on a quite complex and nuanced story. In its simple form, it advances the thesis of "shirtsleeves to shirtsleeves in three generations"—the hardworking first generation of a business is followed by a more workmanlike but adequate second generation. But by this time, with the wealth building up in the business, the third generation is more interested in spending the proceeds than in putting time and effort into the business. It *is* a suspect idea as far as trying to generalize about the patterns of family businesses. Some do have substantial trouble in succeeding generations and eventually go under. Others, like Cargill (and John Deere, in my earlier book) grow and prosper over generations, Cargill being particularly good at sensing the right time to move from family members to non-family, then back to family and, in the current generation, back to non-family (Whitney MacMillan, son of Cargill MacMillan, became CEO of Cargill following Kelm; when MacMillan retired in 1995, the chairmanship returned in its sixth generation to again a non-family member, Ernest Micek).[3]

In a special sense not immediately apparent, it really was not correct to characterize Cargill MacMillan, Sr., as being "gone" from 1960 onward. "Mac Sr." did not die until 1968. Rendered almost completely speechless, he nevertheless was able to take in at least some part of the news of the Company through the eyes and mouths of his two sons, Cargill MacMillan, Jr., and Whitney, even though he had so little cognitive ability remaining that the reciprocal feedback to the sons was not of truly substantive nature. Yet it was not only a satisfying ritual for all of the family and for Cargill MacMillan himself, it was also a symbolic relationship with the Company that he had served so well. More than one of the senior management later expressed the feeling that no one wanted to "disappoint Mac Sr." after John Jr. was gone. Cargill MacMillan seemed to act as an invisible leaven, a constraint on actions of those in management still in full control of their faculties and active in management decision making, a role model even beyond the stroke.

Two Decades: Preparation, Fruition

For our perspective in assessing the changes in the Cargill culture over the 17 years of the Kelm watch, it will be helpful to provide here in this final chapter a brief summary of the most consequential events in that evocative period.

The 1960s were generally upbeat but with several nail-biting undulations. Kelm's first two years started slowly, with a most troubling sharp downturn in the flagship Grain Division. Losses in this group in the 1962–1963 crop year brought swift cuts in their hoped-for expansion plans. The Long Range Planning Committee (LRPC) came into its own at this point, mandating some draconian cost cutting for the division and generally tightening the Company all over.

Primarily because of the Grain Division dip, Cargill at that moment took an unprecedented step—a consultant was asked to take a full look at the organization and report back. The Chase Manhattan Bank, the Company's lead bank, agreed to the assignment and returned two months later with a wide-ranging, biting report. A number of divisions in the Company were brought to task, especially the Grain Division, of course, but with pungent criticisms liberally scattered about for other groups. Many of these negative judgments of the bank stemmed from some underlying Chase beliefs about Cargill: the Company was too concerned about growth per se, not enough about the ultimate endgame, profits. Financial ratio comparisons between Cargill and a composite of a set of companies in the Cargill orbit showed that Cargill was below the average and apparently not paying much attention to the lessons that loudly spoke from these ratios. An implicit undercurrent in many of the Chase remarks was that Cargill people were overly self-satisfied, not self-critical enough, perhaps a bit more arrogant than was good for them.

In the process of suggesting that it might be worthwhile for the Company to "go public" by issuing common stock in the marketplace (a notion given short shrift by both management and family), the Chase analysts propounded an important concept that would keep coming back to remind management in later periods. This was the admonition that the Company ought to subject itself to one or another form of what Chase called "the whetstone effect." To whet is to sharpen, to hone, in this case by a process of independent, outside criticism and evaluation. An independent board of directors might provide this; certainly, the public ownership would do so in a major way. While this latter notion never was seriously considered, the reluctant step of allowing an outside disputation about company business and company results did produce more self-criticism than had been typical under John Jr.'s leadership.

Two good years followed in 1963–1965; then there were three straight excellent performances, and the jarring Chase report faded into the mists. The mid-1960s was a period of record-breaking growth and results; net earnings in the crop year 1965–1966 reached a figure of over $16.7 million, almost double the previous record in 1958–1959 of $9.1 million. The next year was just above this, and the third, 1967–1968, just a few thousand below. All three years saw constant refurbishing of existing facilities and the opening of new ones; and there was expansion on a significant scale abroad, not only in Europe (with the Hens operations established in four countries there) but also in Latin America, including Central America. The Argentine operation came into its own in this period, by the end of the decade contributing in a major way to the Company's profitability.

One interesting move involving an effort at innovation occurred in Japan in the mid-1960s with the development of a grain unloading facility in conjunction with a Japanese partner. Negotiations were difficult but successfully concluded. Cargill had become a "first mover"! But within months, the powerful Japanese trading companies saw the evidences of Cargill's very efficient operation, and they themselves duplicated the efforts, vitiating Cargill's longer-term potentials. Yet the innovational thrust of Cargill's effort made the whole project worthwhile as an excellent learning experience.

A new Oil Division effort, to enter corn milling, quickly grew to be a Cargill powerhouse. The years up through 1967–1968 were forward-looking and exciting, with a philosophic commitment to growth. Kelm's own strategic principle was at work here; he had come to the conclusion that not only was growth going to be accomplished most importantly by taking operations abroad but that this growth was going to be fueled by exports from the United States, especially grain exports, particularly wheat, corn, and soybeans. Therefore, Kelm reasoned, expansion internally within the United States ought always to have in mind the export routes within the country. Better equipment for inland waterways and the Great Lakes was accented in this period; movements into the southeastern United States not only served new domestic markets but opened opportunities for exports. Upgrading of elevator and terminal locations was typically accomplished along those major trunk routes—railroads, waterways, major highways—that could be used quickly in case of significant increases in exports. Clearly, it was "growth with a purpose." In the process, Kelm provided everyone with a clear vision of where he wanted to take the Company.

Farm policy would be a critical ingredient in whatever export possibilities evolved. Grain surpluses had hung over the market, exacerbated by the ongoing subsidies granted to the American farmer. The Kennedy administration, beginning in 1961, was dedicated to continuing the same effort to control the supply side of the equation, requiring land set-asides and other mechanisms for holding down supply. Secretary of Agriculture Orville Freeman sent clear signals that he planned to push for maintaining this market-constraining approach. While this was marginally acceptable to certain farmers, most corn, wheat, and soybean producers opposed such limitations, and certainly the grain trading companies felt strongly otherwise. If the world markets could be shaken free from price management, letting the free interaction of supply and demand control, the overall strength of the world markets could be heightened. A complication here was the agricultural policy of a new entity in Europe, the European Economic Community (EEC), as it developed its own Common Agricultural Policy (CAP) among the original six countries (later several more were added). They planned to maintain a high support price within the six countries via subsidies and sell into the external market at the lower world prices.

The grain companies earlier had kept a fairly low profile in dealing with the U.S. government on farm policy. Now this changed. Cargill took the lead, forming an internal task force that worked assiduously within the circles of policymakers (government, industry, farmers) to modify the old, long-standing supply management policies. Melvin Middents, a vice president in the Grain Division, developed a plan that would partially separate the subsidy given the farmer from the market price itself. The so-called Middents Plan was folded into the American Farm Bureau Federation suggestions, eventually to become a feature of a quite new approach by Congress in the farm bill of 1963. It provided for the subsidy to be paid separately, directly to the farmer—not quite a complete decoupling of subsidy from price, for the amount still would be linked to the total bushels sold by the farmer, but it represented an attempt to break the old nexus between subsidy and market price.

This surprising entry of Cargill into the battles relating to farm policy was led by a young Cargill lawyer, William Pearce (later a vice chairman of the Company). He had been appointed director of public relations (later called public affairs); his work with all of the farm policy stakeholders soon made Cargill a key player in the public policy arena. Cargill continued this more public, more involved brand of public affairs all through the remaining Kelm administration. By the end of the Kelm years, Cargill had become the most visible and active in the industry (although to call it the "spokesman" would have stretched the facts for this still-fragmented, secretive group).

Working with the government in policymaking seemed not, however, to make Cargill officials more receptive to the various positions and actions of government officials. The Company management had appeared almost implacable antagonists of the government agencies they dealt with, not only all through the earlier years of John MacMillan, Jr., but also all through the Kelm years. This animus particularly was directed at the regulatory agencies and seemed to find its most vivid and hostile expression in Cargill's relations with the Commodity Exchange Authority (CEA), the federal agency that supervised—and chastened if necessary—the grain trading industry. John MacMillan, Jr., had become enmeshed with the CEA back in the late 1930s when allegedly attempting to work a corner in the corn market. The Chicago Board of Trade ejected Cargill from membership, the CEA charged Cargill with the attempted corner, and eventually the Company and John Jr. were found guilty of the offense. It was a large black eye for Cargill.

In the early Kelm period, the Company once again ran up against the regulatory power of the CEA. Kelm, Bob Diercks, Barney Saunders, and Ben Jaffray had been centrally involved in the May 1963 wheat contract on the Chicago Board of Trade. Supplies were very short, demand was skyrocketing, Cargill had a very large amount of the total wheat available at the termination day of that contract. The CEA saw this Cargill involvement as an attempt at a "little corner," or what euphemistically was called in the trade a "squeeze." The CEA brought a manipulation charge against Cargill, which the Company, believing it had every right to act as aggressively as it did in that contract, fought tooth and nail. Previous precedent-setting cases, particularly one called Volkart, were used by Cargill as buttress for its position. The Company publicly vowed, "We expect to win this case."

They did not. The CEA ruled against Cargill, and the Company took the case to the circuit court of appeals, finally even to the Supreme Court of the United States. But the justices also agreed with the CEA and in rather decisive language castigated Cargill's actions in the contract. Kelm and the other three Cargill officers were found guilty, as well as the Company. Once again, it was a black eye for Cargill.

There was another unsettling setback at the end of the 1960s with the crop year of 1968–1969. In that year, a series of internal inefficiencies and even a few mistakes within the Grain Division, coupled with a set of market-based grain problems, resulted in an alarming performance by the Grain Division, which had done quite well since the earlier setback in 1963. A very large $3.2 million loss was registered; sags in some other divisions combined to bring about a decline in Cargill net earnings from the previous year's $15.3 million to only $8.5 million for 1968–1969. Once again, the LRPC committee reacted with a concerned and aggressive effort to bring about better controls within the Grain Division and urged renewed vigor and push by the division for the following year. Fortunately, it *was* just a one-year blip—the following year, 1969–1970, resulted in a record-breaking $24.2 million in net corporate earnings, by far the highest the Company had ever experienced. Nevertheless, the two Grain Division backslides in the 1960s gave some members of management such concern as to advocate "getting out of grain." While this was not meant literally—Cargill *was* a grain trading company—the essence of this comment was their preference to phase back those parts of the business involving direct grain trading, to put resources elsewhere. Kelm made it clear that this was not *his* view, and the Grain Division continued its premier role in the Company's belief structure—grain was still "king."

The 1970s—Halcyon, Then Turbulent

The last few years of Erv Kelm's tenure as CEO of Cargill were tumultuous ones. After a modest, peaceful start for the decade, in 1972 a stunning development occurred: the Russians wanted to buy grain from the United States—in massive amounts. The huge sales in the fall of 1972 changed the map of grain trading forever. The physical amounts were gargantuan, with two grain companies, Cargill and Continental, dominating. Cargill's net earnings for that one crop year, 1972–1973, jumped from the $24 million in 1970 to $107.8 million in the 1972–1973 crop year. This was quickly followed by two more record years, with $212.5 million net earnings in 1974 and a historic 1974–1975 figure of $218.4 million. By any standards, this was not just a very good trend line up, it was a discontinuous, mind-boggling increase that was far above anything seen to that time. Continental Grain had the same discontinuous jump upward. The other four of the "big six" of the industry also posted record-breaking earnings. It was a period wholly without precedent.

It was a time also for overall tensions in the American economy. The secret, almost instantaneous nature of the first sales in 1972 was quickly followed by multiple effects throughout the American economy. Inevitably, the vast amounts of grain going to just one customer would bring a lessening supply for other users. Result: price pressures upward. The bugaboo of inflation quickly appeared and was made far worse by two "oil shocks" during the 1970s. The first, in 1973, was brought about by the narrow supply management by the petroleum-producing countries, even involving for a while their oil boycott. Oil prices went through the ceiling, and inflation jumped even more. There were even special grain trading dimensions of this boycott effect. When President Nixon instituted a short-lived boycott against exporting of soybeans, it had both mammoth effects on soybean prices and seriously sharpened hostilities from the rest of the world toward the U.S. government's position and, collaterally, the grain trading companies' actions during the boycott. These events had worldwide implications, and the period 1972–1976 was one of high tension in the world of agriculture and agribusiness.

Compounding all of this, an ugly set of miscues and scandals struck the industry, its own fault because of the actions of a number of grain trading companies. In shipping the massive amounts of grain to Russia, there soon were shortages of rail cars around the United States, and there began to be some favoritism and under-the-table relationships involving shippers struggling for help. A lengthy set of governmental hearings was held on the issue of so-called boxcar blackmail. Even more serious, this was followed by scandals in weighing and shipping, particularly from the Gulf ports, where some grain trading warehouse managers and state grain inspectors were found to be in collusion to allow shoddy shipments to pass through the inspection process.

Cargill, now so much an industry leader, was obviously going to be one of the central companies investigated. However, in the boxcar blackmail hearings, Cargill was one of just a few of the companies totally exonerated from the illegal practices. In the "grain scandal" concerning the export warehouse failings at Gulf ports, Cargill was the only member of the "big six" that was not found guilty in any of the court cases that ensued. This was not to say, it must be noted, that Cargill did not have some significant infractions of its own, and these turned up in Cargill's own rigorous internal investigations. Nevertheless, in hearings on both issues, the position of Cargill was clearly the most exemplary of the major companies.

Because of Cargill's preeminent role in the industry, it was the first (and eventually the only) grain trading company called to testify in a new set of Senate hearings in 1976 concerning the operations and possible failings of the multinational corporations of the country. The senators conducting the hearings carrying this "multinational" label already had concluded investigations in a number of other industries and had turned to the grain trade in 1976. In a protracted set of proceedings, Cargill was the first called upon to testify. Sena-

High art is accidental at the Leslie Salt Company's evaporating ponds in San Francisco Bay (*Cargill News*, November–December 1978).

tor Charles Percy, one of the members of the Senate subcommittee, who wanted the grain trade industry to be more open about its business in order to allay the mushrooming suspicions that the general public seemed to have about this secretive industry, urged Cargill to open its books for a more analytical view by the general public. Cargill did so, albeit reluctantly, and it proved to be a very important positive development. The charges by the staff of the Senate subcommittee against Cargill and the industry proved to be overblown, indeed, faulty, and the hearings cumulated to a great victory for Cargill, once again with a full exoneration.

So Cargill came through the public investigations of the industry with an involvement that turned out in the main to be quite positive. This period of investigative zeal by congressional committees was particularly an outgrowth of the profoundly important Watergate hearings, and all of American business felt under some considerable siege during that time. The grain trade industry had certainly had its "day in the sun" with its set of hearings. By 1976–1977, most of this had been resolved and the issues had subsided, but those years were tense ones for Cargill management, as they were throughout business. By the crop year 1976–1977, the Company's net earnings had dropped to a good but not spectacular $110 million, the next year it was $121.4 million, and it rose in the first year of the Whitney MacMillan era to $178 million. Performance of the industry in the early 1970s was spectacular without precedence; now the agricultural world settled back to a more normal pattern.

Diversification, Becoming Global

In the 1970s, the Cargill board of directors, in the face of this stunning cash flow and the net earnings coming into the organization, chose to remain modest in its dividend policy. Certainly the strong backing of the senior members of the two families in this decision was pivotal. The concept of plowing back earnings into the business remained firmly in place.

But what an enormous amount of money to recycle! The amounts were so much more than had ever been contemplated, the challenge to management to make good use of this money was itself unprecedented.

In the 1960s, "growth" dominantly had been the refurbishing and renewing of domestic facilities lying along export routes, in Kelm's anticipation of a more than usual increase in export sales. This included some movement into new industries (e.g., corn milling, poultry, insurance). That earlier view was prescient, its wisdom reinforced many times over when the Company reacquired its secretive, unruly customer, the Soviet Union, once again. Major outlays resulted from this business, and the projects that ensued lay all over the world. If not yet fully there, the Company was "going global"—as early as 1972 the *New York Times* headlined a major piece on the Company, "It's Said, 'The Sun Never Sets on Cargill'" (the text modified this to "never sets on Cargill *corn*"). The pace of upgrading and diversification took a discontinuous, giant jump upward. Capital expenditures during the seven-year period from 1965–1966 through 1971–1972 averaged $32.9 million per year; in the five-year span from 1972–1973 through 1976–1977, the average was $150.4 million ($229.8 in 1975–1976 alone). These amounts were stupefying to the industry; *Business Week* wrote in 1979: "One Dreyfus executive laments: 'Cargill is spending at a rate that no one could hope to match.'"

Indeed, these astronomical amounts were making the board of directors more than a bit uneasy. The minutes of their July 31, 1975, meeting noted that "Long-Range Planning Committee allocations totalled $391,000,000 for 1975–1976. [These] would cause working capital to fall below the target objective of $480,000,000, even assuming a 14 percent earnings and the successful placement of long term debt. Therefore . . . capital expenditures should not exceed $340,000,000." It was at this point that the board decided "that further allocation should not be made to the steel industry until more experience had been gained in this industry."

Further, it was not just that these amounts were very much higher; there was also a recycling into new, often very different activities, with the attendant risks of startup in unfamiliar ground (but Pete McVay warned that "we have the capacity to destroy ourselves if we put all the money earned back into the businesses that produced it . . . businesses are cyclical and expansion in good years would generate plants far beyond the economic need and only make the depression worse").

So the Company moved into flour milling; took on peanuts, cotton, and metals trading; and became a significant force in cattle feeding. A momentary exposure to the hotel industry with the Holiday Inn in Ghent, Belgium, and an equally short involvement in coal mining soon faded away. Similarly, the small inroad into solid waste processing and disposal was found not feasible and was dropped. One of the largest projects in total dollars was also an odds-on candidate for moving farthest afield: purchase of the mini-steel operations of North Star Steel Company; this became an outstanding success.

By this time, it was not infrequent that customers using Cargill services or products would not really know they were being served by Cargill. The *Wall Street Journal* caught this anomaly in 1975: "Many farmers who knew Cargill as a grain trader weren't aware that the Company was a producer of hybrid seeds and animal feeds that they had been using for years." The *Journal* editors noted that Cargill made barges, underwrote insurance, and leased heavy equipment, was into peanuts, flour milling, solid-waste recovery, and even cattle feeding. Bob Diercks said, "One of our strengths is our attitude that if we can do it, let's try it."

How to achieve a balance between domestic and foreign investment and among countries abroad commanded much attention. By July 1976, as assistant controller Bob Lumpkins (later to be vice chairman of the Company) pointed out, "We have become capital-rich overnight." He estimated that Cargill would have $250 million to invest annually; he did not want the 60 percent domestic to 40 percent international ratio to tilt any more toward the latter ("very few foreign countries are as attractive as the U.S."). Lumpkins was particularly uneasy about sending more money to Geneva: "Tradax continues to control most of the foreign projects work, and they remain trading-oriented. In fact, their opportunistic approach tends to prevent them from developing a long-term investment strategy . . . we will not get the foreign funds invested wisely without substantially more involvement and/or responsibility from the U.S. management organization."

The board voted a few days later that "if the net worth of corporate activities in any single country exceeded 8% of total corporate net worth, there should be a review by the full board of directors." But this soon appeared too limiting; and in July 1978, they decided that "while investments should not be made disproportionately in one country or area of the world, no specific guideline should be adopted for any country or by geographical area. Rather, investment opportunities should be pursued on a worldwide basis."

Some of this new money *was* used for heightened trading, of course. But the notion of purchasing or buying into physical facilities abroad now became an important thread. Even Tradax, so chary earlier of owning *anything*, had built warehouse facilities and shipping and was involved substantially in Argentine agricultural operations in addition to the earlier, more traditional grain trading there.

Increasingly, outside analysts began to focus on Cargill's "long run" view and to make the connection that it was the *privately held* company that was better suited to give credence to not having to face stockholders and the financial press every quarter. The Cargill and MacMillan families had known of this advantage for many years—both John Sr. and John Jr. spoke of it often. But it was Kelm who gave it a new operational reality in the early 1960s with his introduction of the five-year rolling budget.

By the 1970s, there was an even further look into the future; as Dwayne Andreas, chairman of Archer Daniels Midland (and a former Cargill man once picked by John Jr. as a possible Cargill president) later put it, "It's not unusual for them to look 10 years ahead and have unlimited patience. . . . They're natural long-range thinkers." Cargill's Barney Saunders (also a later vice chairman) added another dimension: "One advantage of taking the long look is we're willing to take a chance. . . . When we developed this rented train from central Illinois to the Gulf . . . it required us to build two very fancy, very expensive grain elevators that, if the concept hadn't worked, would be just white elephants. Fortunately it worked, and now there are I-don't-know-how-many of these subterminal elevators in the Corn Belt. But we proved it to the world because we were willing to take the chance that we might have to write off those two elevators if [it] just wasn't valid."

A corollary of this was Cargill's willingness to pick up a company at the bottom of that industry's cycle and take a number of loss years before the cycle turned back, "in the belief, " explained the *New York Times*, "that there are big payoffs if one rides out the bad phases of the cycle."[4]

Organizational Déjà Vu

The geographical spread of these new capital projects in the 1970s inevitably led also to more complex organizational relationships, occasionally contentious, between Minneapolis and the operations in the field, especially abroad. In particular, the push-and-tug between corporate headquarters and Geneva continued almost unabated. Tradax had been close to autonomous at its start but had been pulled back into the Cargill orbit from an ownership standpoint early in the 1960s. During both the remainder of the 1960s and the 1970s of the Kelm years, there were many turf arguments between Tradax and Minneapolis and between other operations abroad and Minneapolis about how to organize, who was to lead, who was to command resources, and so forth.

In this period a seminally important single story chronicles this tension very well. In 1968, polemics between international management and the domestic leadership in Minneapolis and between and among each of the divisions became so strong that Kelm mandated a special board meeting on the subject. Individual papers were prepared and argued by Fred Seed, by Bob Diercks, and by Tradax officials representing Walter Gage. But despite these three articulate papers, the issues remained quite muddy, the answers still far from clear. Finally, Kelm stated that he himself would craft his own paper on international organization.

The long-awaited memorandum was issued in late 1968 and quickly achieved a patina that subsequently led it to be known around the Company as Kelm's "White Paper." Writing bluntly and unambiguously, Kelm reinforced his belief that managers of individual product areas should feel free to go abroad with their own separate projects, that geography was not going to be the dominant thread for organizing an international project. Tradax, for example, would not automatically be the final authority on a project that was in its arena (particularly Europe), that a division with a particular project could take it to one of the European countries more or less on its own (here we simplify a complicated story; see my discussion in Chapter Three).

This definitive Kelm policy statement served as the guiding principle all through the hurly-burly period of the early and mid-1970s; the pace of the business, especially in 1972–1976, was so frenetic that any attempt to legislate major organizational devices could have been profoundly disruptive. The issues themselves continued to be debated, of course, and nowhere more seminally than in a series of exchanges in 1972 between Pete McVay and Heinz Hutter (both men later to hold the Company's presidency).

McVay's paper stressed experience, "the soundest single block on which to build." The "exceptional experienced leader" was the key. Because "it takes most of us an important part of a lifetime to learn *one* business well . . . specialization and singleness of purpose" was crucial. "It is good that *some* top management will remain generalists, but it is essential that our major activities . . . be represented by the most qualified person available in the field. . . . *Development of opportunities should not be limited to the experience and imagination of personnel at a specific geographical location.* . . . I have concluded that more desirable objectives can be obtained with a minimum of management tiers, *using a structure that emphasizes a functional alignment*" (McVay's emphasis).

Hutter responded, admitting that he was "influenced" by the earlier successes of decentralization in Argentina:

The functional organization is the usual form for small and medium size organizations . . . *functional* means centralized, *divisional* (for instance, geographical) means *decentralized.* Any manager who thinks he can run a big enterprise . . . exclusively centralized and goes on worrying about the so-called one penny decisions, etc., will, in his hunger for power neglect his actual responsibilities, jeopardize the development of new general managerial human material . . . and in the long run, cost the enterprise great amounts of money. . . . The more we decentralize, the better advice from and controls at top management must be in the form of a staff organzation and probably of an interwoven functional structure which works *with and through* the division or geographical heads. . . . If we have a single business in a country, I fully agree with your solution . . . when we have diversifed operations in one country, we need a strong national head . . . all the national operations run by him and united under his hopefully competent leadership.

By that time, the influence of geography inevitably was in the picture in an organization as far-flung as Cargill now had become—a product manager had to understand his territory, likely with considerable help from the "locals." Thus, it seemed a natural evolution to some form of matrix of geography, product, and function—some combination allowing a flexible, multidimensional decision-making process. Cargill began to study more seriously how other companies were sorting this out, for example, the quite formal matrix system that was being developed at Westinghouse Electric in this period. However, Company management eventually decided to "let the pot boil"— allow any new system to survive on its own. This was put frankly by the board in its meeting of July 26, 1978: "It was recognized that a matrix organization had evolved which, while it posed and indeed institutionalized certain conflicts, nevertheless seemed to be working in a satisfactory manner. The Directors were not in favor of an immediate change." This seemed, however, to allow some drift; Hutter commented later, "We may have gone too far in matrixing and layering. Whoever is responsible for outputs *must* have full control over inputs. We must avoid second guessing and long distance remote control."

Kelm's predilections remained with "product" as the controlling thread:

"We thought of regions, but I think to run the Company it was better to have like businesses under one management rather than regionalized. . . . I think looking down to the people below, they would like to be working for something more substantial than a sector . . . more of a line responsibility." Incidentally, while Kelm seemed to tilt here toward the more centralized, he was not speaking of a line organization built on a solely top-down mentality, as was in evidence in John Jr's earlier days; by this time Kelm and almost all of senior management were dedicated to, as a board "corporate guidelines" paper put it in July 1977, "decentralized decision-making to the greatest degree practical to stimulate interest and facilitate the growth of the individual." It still remained, though, just how to define this; later, after the Kelm years, there were some significant modifications of Kelm's "product line" basis for international growth.[5]

Was the "Cargill Culture" Still Relevant?

With the kind of growth and diversification of the late 1960s and early and mid-1970s remaking Cargill closer to a global company, the faces of Cargill had become geographically diverse, its cadre of men and women now represented by many, many nationalities. Was the Cargill of 1960, at John Jr.'s death, with its strongly embedded Midwestern Cargill culture, still the same in 1978, after Whitney MacMillan became Cargill's fifth CEO?

The question almost answers itself. Cargill now began to have large numbers of newly hired employees with strong national linkages in countries not only in the traditional locations in Europe but elsewhere on that continent, as well as extensively in Latin America and significantly in Asia. In the excellent crop year 1965–1966, the Company had a grand total of 5,632 employees; this had grown to 8,000 the next year, just over a quarter of them abroad. By the year of the first big Russian grain sale (1972–1973), the total had advanced to 14,500, almost 41 percent abroad. In the year 1978–1979, Whitney MacMillan's first full year as CEO, the grand total was 32,530, about 34 pecent abroad.

The 1960 Cargill culture extended on a plumb line straight back to W. W. Cargill in the 1860s. The figures in the preceding paragraph detail a striking growth in this most immediate dozen years, in particular because so many operations in new cultures and significantly different kinds of businesses had been added over such a short time span—indeed, almost abruptly. This presented a great challenge to senior management of just how to transmit this abiding historical culture to such a far-flung panoply of operations.

Stu Hanson reflected on this difficulty in relation to Tradax in a major paper, "Elements of Geneva Climate" in 1982: "Probably the most serious charge against Tradax and Geveva and the basis of the uncomfortable sense of 'hostility' which seems to be pervading other divisions of Cargill, both in the U.S. and in Europe, is that it is not a part of the Cargill culture." (One senior manager in Wayzata put this bluntly: "Tradax was clannish, operated as a clique.") Hanson assessed the Cargill culture as "a communal mind-set, a matter of knowing where you fit, where you and the organisation came from and are going. Living within this culture can be both exhilarating and secure-making. As they say, you can revel in the group spirit. You can compete [with colleagues] inside the company, knowing that you will all be judged by the same standard. These are exciting words, and they are meaningful . . . Geneva personnel do feel a part of Cargill . . . they are longing to participate more deeply in the corporate culture . . . [there is] a deep fear of being fur-ther isolated from the Group. They want to belong . . . to be a part of the family!"

Yet despite these consequential difficulties, as one looks at the Company of 1978 and, particularly, goes below the surface to the underlying values of the corporation—the belief system of Cargill—it appears that those ideals and standards that differentiated Cargill so sharply from any other company in its industry were still in place just as indelibly as they were in 1960. This was par-ticularly so for the longer-standing domestic operations, somewhat less so for the foreign (the newer ones, but also, apparently, some older ones such as Tradax). Heinz Hutter's powerful personality had carried the Cargill threads all through the Argentinian and Brazilian companies. Indeed, it was through the charisma of key Company senior managenment throughout both the do-mestic and international operations that the culture was transmitted; the board of directors as a body had held formal board meetings in a number of foreign venues, in the process splitting themselves into smaller teams and fan-ning out to all the operations in the particular area being visited. In 1977, the board concluded that for management abroad it was "important for executive growth, particularly for those employed by Tradax companies, to gain experi-ence in the United States," and they instituted a more regularized process for a "Cargill exchange program," under the direction of Barney Saunders. In-deed, there was wide recognition among senior management of the power and efficacy of that strongly held Cargill culture—and its lack in some places.

Still, these instances where the culture was not as strong *were* the exception and need to be kept in perspective. Pete McVay put this well in his retirement piece in *Cargill News* in 1984: "I do suggest that there is less backstabbing, throat cutting, second guessing, seeking advancement by pushing others down than in any other corporate environment that I am aware of. There is good will, respect, willingness to help, desire to teach and share knowledge, and in general, pleasure in associating with each other . . . one of Cargill's greatest assets. Many of us have spent our career with Cargill for this reason more than any other."

What were some of the specific features of this Cargill culture?

First, it matters a great deal that this is a grain trading company. The word *trading* is the operative one and defines a whole lore of the industry, a fabled,

"Cargill's Office Center . . . is a carefully planned and eminently practical solution to corporate problems that have emerged in the last few years . . . accommodations in the mid-town Cargill building had become cramped. Some divisions and departments were split among the downtown office, research building, salt house and headquarters Lake Office . . . locating the new Office Center near the existing headquarters office emerges as the best solution. What resulted is a most humane of buildings—bright and spacious within, shaped without to fit the hills and woods" (*Cargill News,* January–February *1977*).

special, lightning-fast, high-risk function that is carried through every day, indeed, minute by hair-raising minute in many cases, by a group of men and women who plan the process of buying grain, moving it, storing it, and loading it out for resale in wide numbers of channels. To be a trader is to be someone special in this industry, a person with the ability to bargain and to apply psychology to this process, a person who often makes decisions on very short-term frames (although this short-term focus has to be congruent with the longer-term strategy to make it viable for any successful company).

In the past there were fabled speculators on the exchanges, those like Joseph Leiter, James Patten, and Arthur Cutten, who would attempt to corner the market and, as *Fortune* magazine put it in a wonderful article in 1949 on "the grain traders" (which included, incidentally, extensive coverage of John MacMillan, Jr.), the old group of speculators could "shake the economic pillars of society." There still are modern-day speculators at the exchanges—they need to declare themselves as such with the Commodity Futures Trading Commission (CFTC, the successor agency to the CEA) in order to be able to trade.

These speculators are not the people we are talking about at Cargill and the other grain trading firms; the Cargill people and their counterparts are professional traders. Their primary function is to buy and sell grain, and the essence of Cargill is its desire to be premier in trading/handling the *physical* commodities. This is almost universally accompanied by sophisticated efforts to hedge the risk, generally by taking opposite positions in the futures market. Grain trading companies like to say that they are fully hedged every second. In an interesting article about Cargill in *Forbes* in 1978, the authors related, "Cargill . . . sells rather than speculates . . . it is a highly conservative and safe approach from which Cargill never strays."

Yet this oversimplifies the actual reality of trading physicals. In the process of developing all of the hedges and straddles that are necessary, infinite variations in timing and in amounts and other dimensions of the sale are possible. Companies like Cargill, in the process of protecting their exposure in these physicals, are always taking positions in the real sense of the word. Occasionally, in the face of strong market signals, the assuming of a position on one side of the market will verge toward a nominally "naked" position, with similarity to a speculative stance, although within the legitimate definition of a hedge position; profit taking directly on this hedge will possibly be a result. Company officials could conceivably also choose to do some outright speculating but then would be required (earlier by the CEA and now by the CFTC) to so state when they did (the 1963 wheat case brought Cargill to the point where its total contracts in May wheat approached the limit number allowed as a speculator, which they had so declared themselves). Cargill trading almost universally has been as the professional trader, although Tradax, in its European operation through this period, had taken speculative, "naked" positions at several points.

All of this trading is an art—it involves strategic and psychological moves in the market built of subtle and complex tactics. For those who are given this uncommon charge, there seems almost always a sense of excitement and personal hubris. At Cargill, this is fundamentally so. To be a trader at Cargill is to be at the heart of the business, to be one of that select fraternity given the personal responsibility to make decisions that stand at the center of what Cargill considers itself to be. There are clear implications that trading is only for the few—for those who can react very quickly, taking most often a short-term focus on matters and acting decisively.

Kelm was a clever, able trader in his time and taught a whole new group his skills. The four men involved in the CEA case for the landmark 1963 May wheat contract and particularly two of them, Kelm and Barney Saunders, were once again the prototypical traders and, at least according to the CEA and the federal judges, attempting one of the more esoteric of the grain trading tactics, a squeeze at the termination of that contract. Of all of the senior management group, Kelm was the preeminent trader, of the likes of John MacMillan, Jr., and Julius Hendel (who were, of course, his mentors).

There were a number of others in that senior management group of Kelm's that came strongly out of a trading background, most in the Grain Division but a number from the Oil Division, too. Remembering that it is not such a sharp dichotomy that one could automatically class one person as trader and another as not, still, the trading function with its attendant trading mentality has characterized the Cargill culture since way back in the early days of John Jr. and Julius Hendel, on up to and including the Kelm years.

At times the romantic literature about the grain trading function makes the trader out as a hard-driving, corner-cutting "buccaneer." Indeed, that exact word has been used rather frequently in articles about the grain trade; a 1965 article in *Minneapolis* on Cargill wrote of "their philosophy, 'the buccaneer spirit'"; a 1975 *Wall Street Journal* article devoted a whole paragraph to this very same "buccaneering spirit." The editors wrote, "A former Cargill grain trader rejects any suggestion the buccaneering spirit is dead at Cargill. 'I think events of recent years show there's still an attitude that if the business is there, let's grab it and worry about the consequences later.'"

The spirit of being a sharp, aggressive trader *is* a part of Cargill, but the word *buccaneer* really misses the point. The Cargill traders are involved preeminently with position risks; as they look at the business this way, they tend to put more emphasis on *competitiveness*, rather than any kind of buccaneering—it is more the desire to win than the desire to risk all that captures Cargill's spirit.

This leads directly to a second bedrock Cargill value—integrity. One key caution must be used in that interface between competitiveness and buccaneering. The latter can often involve tactics of evasion, subterfuge, and unfortunately, sometimes downright dishonesty. Any such connotation would be anathema to Cargill. Indeed, the integrity of the Cargill people all through the years has been a mark of distinction of the Company, widely reported on from the outside. As one perceptive Minnesota analyst, who knew the Company very well, put it, "Competitors, for all of their pecking away at Cargill's edges, acknowledge a profound respect for the Company and for its honesty. When there had been grain scandals over the years (on short-weighting and so on), Cargill's name has been conspicuously absent from the lists of those culpable. 'They're too big to need to be dishonest' says one grain man. 'It's a risk they couldn't hedge against.'"

John MacMillan, Jr., focused over and over again on this value; he wrote in *Cargill News* in 1951: "Our reputation for integrity has assured our customers of integrity of products and of contract and has not only assured our receiving the preference from a host of customers but has carried us through several tight squeaks. Integrity is the back-bone of our credit which makes it possible for us to borrow many times our working capital. Without this credit, we would be unable to engage in many of the activities which are now the cornerstone of our very existence. Anything which reflects on this integrity directly jeopardizes the safety of the entire business. Integrity, therefore, becomes of paramount importance to all of us." Barney Saunders analyzed this in an article published in the early 1980s: "One of the things that all of us are indoctrinated with from the day we come to work for this organization is the ethical practices of our business. Those of us that have traded grain realize that our word is our bond, and Cargill wouldn't have been in business for over 117 or 118 years if they were not very, very ethical."

These statements are perfectly congruent with the actions of John Jr. in the famous corn corner in 1937 and in the 1963 case against Cargill, where the CEA and the federal judges ruled that the Company had attempted a squeeze. In each of these instances the Cargill executives' actions were based upon what they and their lawyers felt was the current interpretation of the law. There was simply no implication whatsoever that anyone had been dishonest or that there had been any fabrication or deceit used by Cargill. Yes, Cargill traders pride themselves on the so-called buccaneer tradition. But this means exclusively that they are trading competitively in a fast-paced environment, not that *any* shortcut would ever be countenanced.

There has been an aplomb, a collectedness about Cargill people through the years—*Fortune* called it "audacity," "smartness," "aggresiveness"—that gives them a high degree of self-confidence. Pete McVay, at his retirement in 1984, remembered that when he came to the Company "there was an air of excitement and a spirit of aggressive competition, even cockiness. The 1937 corn case had just been completed. There was some criticism of that activity. Some were embarrassed by it. John Jr.'s statements as reported by the press surely would not give comfort to today's public relations department. . . . It was one of the reasons I came to work with Cargill. Leadership with that kind of spirit appealed to me. Cargill was respected by competitors, but not necessarily liked or appreciated. They were making too many changes and upsetting customs and long-established patterns of businesss. *I was proud to be a part of the organization*" (my emphasis).[6]

The training function at Cargill has had much to do with this and generally has been superb over the years (although not always). One of the unique marks of Cargill was its early training program, where that special group of college graduates was trained by Julius Hendel. Kelm and Fred Seed were two of the first graduates of this program. Additionally, promotion from within was a strongly held tenet; seldom was anyone brought directly into management from the outside (a potent motivational device for the Company, although having the downside of missing some of the "whetstone" from fresh faces).

Cargill's long-standing problems with the narrow loyalties and competitiveness on the part of the divisions continued to intrude into this promotion process, for these tended to block cross-division transfers, especially for the division's best people. Kelm worked hard, but not completely successfully, to smoke out any division manager's overprotectiveness; he complained, "If you ask for his superstar, he won't let him go."

Company efforts to maintain its training thrust have continued down through the years. In more recent times, training executives in the Company report that sometimes both middle and senior management are so busy that it becomes difficult to persuade them to take on a somewhat lengthy personal commitment to training. Sometimes this seemed to be a matter of abiding self-confidence—"I don't need this training—I *know* how to manage." Heinz Hutter said the same thing in a different way in a recent article in a Minneapolis newspaper: "Professors don't train managers—managers train managers." Thus, a "Cargill MBA," a combination of formal education and on-the-job training—"Once people join us they become part of the process and the culture."

One article on the Company in the early 1980s stated, "Cargill's competitors are divided: some say that the training isn't so good anymore; others say it can't keep pace with the Company's spreading horizons. Either way, they see (or, perhaps, wish to see) Cargill managing less well." But a closer look at the training function would seem to corroborate its continuing excellence at Cargill. There seems no disagreement at all that the training is proper and worthwhile, a fundamental dimension that deepens management. Training has emphasized a highly analytical view of the management process, and Cargill is known throughout the industry as "doing their homework" superbly.

But this can sometimes breed an overweening hubris, a feeling that "of course Cargill is right." Erv Kelm demonstrated some of this in his remarks over several years in the annual report to the stockholders about the 1963 May wheat case. Kelm confidently stated in the annual report itself that "we feel we are right and we *will* win the case." When the case was lost, it was a terrible shock.

Cargill people sometimes find it hard to admit that they are wrong. Even when they change course, they tend to rationalize that they had been right all along but now "it is time to change." This is, of course, an illustration of trading—a position for the moment is "right," but events can change and one must always be ready to take the new "right" position.

An earlier manifestation of this was management's unwillingness to use—indeed, its hostility against—outside advice. Consultants always had had a difficult time establishing credibility with the Company and sometimes were not able to. During the late 1960s and into the 1970s, more use was made of outside consultants, for example, the involvement several times of the well-known Harvard economics professor, Richard Caves. But the outside professional consulting firm was often viewed askance, accused of "learning on the job" and recycling what management had told them back to them.

Kelm had been one of the most vocal skeptics in an early use of a consulting firm, Booz, Allen & Hamilton in the late 1940s. As he diplomatically put

it then, "It is recognized that the BAH crew members have acquired considerable knowledge of Cargill accounting and operations during the past year."
Now, in the early 1960s, Kelm, as CEO, had initiated the use of another firm
to mastermind what he felt was a long overdue cost-cutting effort. Cutting
costs is never popular, and squawks reverberated in the halls. Once again, it
was "paying them to learn on us." While Kelm gave some lip service to these
complaints and did finally agree to terminate the consultants before the projected end of their assignment, he later revealed his underlying strategy: "It
worked out because it got us going and doing the job ourselves." Kelm
likened the difficulties that a CEO often has in overcoming inertia and getting
things moving as "beating on pillows," and here the consultant was a catalyst.
Still, Cargill preferred to "go it alone," and this sometimes heightened insu-
larity, validating the credibility once again of the "whetstone" effect advanced
by the Chase analysts back in 1963.[7]

One of the features of an industry culture that over the years had been so
pronounced was the high degree of secrecy exhibited by just about all of the
major grain trading companies. In trading, a primary rule is not to tip one's
hand by premature disclosure of strategy and tactics. This has fostered secrecy
down to the smallest details about the trading. Erv Kelm put this succinctly
when interviewed by *Business Week* about the special features of a family business: "The nature of our business is such that competitive secrecy and speed
in decision making are vital." Whitney MacMillan told the *Chicago Tribune*,
"In the part of business we're in, patents are not available, concepts get transferred very rapidly." One unnamed Cargill executive put this to *Business Week*
more bluntly: "Our strategy is the only proprietary part of this business—the
lead time we build, keeping our competitors in the dark, is a big edge."

But secrecy also fostered problems, indeed, a backlash. "I'd have to rate the
grain exporting companies a close second to used-car dealers in terms of poor
public image," the *Wall Street Journal* quoted a grain merchant as saying (in
1975, at the height of the "grain scandal" hearings); the authoritative *International Directory of Company Histories* commented, "Cargill's low profile has
created no reservoir of favorable public opinion in difficult times." Asked in
1975 by Whitney MacMillan to enumerate the "most significant problem areas
which can adversely affect Cargill's operations," Heinz Hutter named as his
second concern "the continuously growing impression of the tremendous
size of Cargill, mainly, but not exclusively, [with] one main client of ours, i.e.,
the American farmer, who by nature is small in size and must feel crowded."

Cargill's alleged "secrecy" was accented by its corporate headquarters in
Wayzata—the "Lake Office." The setting and the ambience led business reporters into flights of hyperbole: it was "a vast giant in the Minnesota
woods," on "baronial grounds—the woods are silent, the summer air is still, a
narrow road rises gently to the hills." One comes to the 64-room "replica of a
French chateau, sheltered from view by wooded hills on one side and by Lake

Whitney MacMillan; M. D. "Pete" McVay (Cargill staff photographs).

Minnetonka on the other . . . "set back hundreds of yards from the main road" in a "walled private courtyard." Inside, "it is tastefully furnished with antiques and given a homey touch by fireplaces that burn brightly on the brisk days of autumn and winter," "a cocoon of secrecy—surroundings fit for pondering, reflecting and digesting." The board room "doubles as part of the office of Erwin Kelm . . . distinguished for its elegance . . . portraits of prior presidents, all of them either Cargills or MacMillans . . . gaze down on Kelm [who] says that at times all this scrutiny makes him 'a little nervous.'"

Over the years, especially the difficult early 1970s, there was a cutting edge to these comments, combining to imply a secretive, uncommunicative organization, hidden to the world in the isolated Lake Office. Then a new Office Center was opened on the same property in 1977, to house some 1,250 Cargill employees (most from the Cargill Building in downtown Minneapolis), and the Company-visitor interactions vastly multiplied. Public reaction to the new complex was generally quite positive, although there was some carping by the Minneapolis city fathers and the press about the loss of a downtown cadre of this size. Media coverage of the Lake Office turned noticeably more positive, enough so for *Cargill News*, in a full-issue story in 1979 on the chateau and its occupants, to be able credibly to headline one of the sections of the issue "Business Writers Charmed by Lake Office."

In the Kelm years, Cargill *did* become relatively more open. In 1963, the Company published for the first time a printed annual report to the shareholders. While this had limited circulation, it did go to bankers and other companies and individuals directly relating to Cargill. In this sense, it was not a fully public document but certainly not hidden from view. One of the watersheds in Cargill's attitudes toward its own proprietary business facts came in the Senate multinational hearings in 1976. It was just before these hearings began that Senator Charles Percy of Illinois had talked privately with Cargill management, cautioning them bluntly that "a great deal of progress has been made depicting the grain trade as a group of a few highly secretive companies with divided interests," that the Company ought to "give serious thought to being more willing than we have to release information about our business," and that "we are an important public business and notwithstanding private ownership, we should understand the need to take the public into our confidence if we want their support in continuing this system." While this was not a message that some of the family and senior management wanted to hear, the Percy advice did help persuade the Company at the hearings a few days later to reveal specific profitability and related financial statistics.

For a great many who watched the grain companies, this emerging openness was a surprising and exciting change in an industry pattern. In a major article on Cargill in 1978, *Forbes* magazine wrote, "This reticence caused problems for Cargill whenever suspicions arose about profiteering in the grain trade (who *was* this shadowy, private company?). Intelligently, Cargill management has become progressively less secretive. In 1972, for example, at the time of the huge Russian grain sales, Cargill held a press conference to disclose that, far from profiteering, it lost money on shipping grain to Russia. In 1976, to the delight of curious competitors, Cargill gave detailed data on its operations to the Senate subcommittee on multinational corporations."

(Old ideas die hard, however; in 1987, Cargill filed a prospectus in Europe for a large Eurobond offering and found that this required substantial disclosure of its finances. The press descended on the Company, and Whitney MacMillan was quoted by *Forbes* as saying to the journalists, "We would have preferred you were not here. This is an experiment. We didn't realize the reporting requirements. If we did, we wouldn't have done it").[8]

The "big six" in the Russian grain sales of 1972–1975 had lost one of its members altogether; Cook Industries, the only publicly held of the six, had suffered a combination of substantial federal fines and tax penalties from the grain scandals and very heavy trading losses. Their traders had speculated in soybeans, and the market had turned on them. Cook took a net loss of $81,051,000 for its fiscal year 1976–1977 and had been forced to sell off piecemeal all of its grain trading terminals and elevators, resign from the Chicago Board of Trade clearing corporation, and pull out of grain trading completely. (Most of the properties went to two Japanese trading companies, Mitsui and Marubeni, giving that country further bridgeheads in the United States.) With Garnac falling back to a smaller role, grain trade analysts now

denominated the world grain trade as having the "traditional 'big four'"—
Cargill, Continental Grain, Bunge, and Dreyfus.

These four (and Garnac, too) always had been private companies, owned in
most instances by one or two particular families. The family corporation is a
good fit for the parameter of secrecy. As the *Business Week* article quoting Kelm
noted, family companies throughout industry tended to be more private, more
independent, and therefore appeared to be more secretive. The private corporation does not have to publish many facts that the public corporation is required to do. Cargill continued as a family corporation in the Kelm period, and
this group of people in the two families remained fiercely devoted to privacy.
Wealthy families almost always tend to feel this way, for the threats of kidnapping and other untoward events make them very skittish about revealing any
personal information. This would seem to be a natural feeling at any time but
was particularly so in the late 1960s and early 1970s, when there were letter
bombs sent to the Company, including one to a family member (and two
members of the Bunge y Born grain trading family kidnapped in Argentina).

Often, when the two families involved in the ownership of Cargill were
mentioned, questions popped up about Cargill "going public." One of the
problems of a closely held corporation is the difficulty of egress, as owners
find it difficult or even impossible to sell their stock. At several points during
the Kelm administration, most notably the speech before the Harvard Business School Club of Minneapolis in 1969, outside observers of Cargill seemed
to smell a move to have the Company taken public. This never happened, of
course, and on into the next decade of Cargill, beyond Erv Kelm, the same
question kept surfacing: whether Cargill "might finally be going public."

In 1993, to briefly look ahead into this period, a major decision was taken,
to allow a partial egress for members of the family via an employee stock option plan (ESOP). Each of the family owners, several dozen by this time, had
the right to tender partial amounts of shares, which would then form the base
for the ESOP. Some 17 percent of the total extant common stock *was* tendered, and while the Company had not literally "gone public," there now
would be a much wider base for the ownership of the Company through stock
held by the ESOP. Stock could not be sold, in turn, to the general public, so in
this sense it was a limited change in direction. However, it has heightened employee interest and provided a new dimension to that whetstone element that
was desired by the Chase Bank analysts back in 1963. In the year following the
establishment of the ESOP, the Company also broadened its board of directors to include additional younger members of the family, as well as a set of
five outside board members. Once again, the whetstone was in play.

The concept of an ESOP is built around the values of Company employee
loyalty; certainly, one would expect an ESOP plan to do this. Thus, the ESOP
seemed ideally suited for Cargill, for the pattern of company loyalty over the
years had been outstanding. Employees at the Company took great pride in

their organization, embraced the Company's vision/mission, and enjoyed the freedom, camaraderie, and team spirit that came from competing and winning. They felt that they were recognized for their efforts. Finally, they apparently did feel that the pattern of employee benefits and accoutrements were satisfactory, but it certainly was not the pay or even the benefits that was keeping employees at the Company (employee attitude surveys in this period consistently gave this dimension mixed marks).

So it was Cargill's underlying belief system that was the tie that bound. The employees had bought into it and "owned" it; they respected management for its competency and for being professional and dependable. Pete McVay seemed to capture this feeling in a speech to senior managers in May 1977: "We want our plants and facilities to reflect the kind of a company and the kind of people we are. We are *productive, inventive, efficient*, Spartan, if you will, but good citizens. We are embarrassed by sloppiness and carelessness—indifference—lack of discipline. *But* we are equally embarrassed by extravagance, opulence, pretentiousness, and waste."

All of this seemed to generate a high degree of personal achievement motivation, and the result was a source of great satisfaction. Especially, employees felt that they were recognized for their efforts. Erv Kelm, in speaking before a Company business management program in 1973, stated: "It is not idle flattery nor exaggeration to say that you are the people who make this Company what it is. No amount of planning or policymaking by the directors has any meaningful substance until you put it to work and make it happen. Our staff could not exist without the excellent performance of you in the line, although, I am sometimes tempted to think that the opposite—all line and no staff—might work quite well indeed. Perhaps for the short run, anyway. . . . It seems to me that it would not be immodest for any of us to feel that 108 years of accomplishment is a pretty good record for any organization to proud of."

An early 1980s article in *Corporate Report—Minnesota* talked about the Company's continuing high level of employee loyalty: "On one thing there is universal agreement: there *is* such a thing as the 'Cargill Man.' Oh, there are some women in the Company, but it's men who run the place—if for no reason than that there haven't long been many women in the field and that a Cargill career tends to be a slow ascent. But the descriptions one hears of employee loyalty to Cargill are remarkably consistent; 'you come out of there with Cargill tattooed on your ass,' says one observer from academe. You're Cargill now and forever. I can't think of another company that has this kind of image.'" A quotation from *Cargill: Trading the World's Grain* is worthwhile to repeat: One younger executive, leaving the Company, wrote to his superior: "There is something about a spirit in Cargill that exists in few other firms . . . several people told me that they thought I had Cargill stamped all over me and could never rub it off. I am finding that it is very difficult to make the change." John Cole, one of the newer senior managers, commented on this:

"As most of you know, I came to Cargill with the purchase of Kerr Gifford. At the time of this purchase, I had no intention of staying with Cargill. It did not take very much exposure to Cargill's management, however, to convince me that here was a forward looking company which had the capacity and vision to shift with the ever-changing business situation, and which would remain in the forefront regardless of the vagaries of politics and the weather. It is important to me—and to all of you—to know that this same vitality still exists."

This is not to say that Cargill executives go around each day fulsomely praising all the employees. Indeed, one of the interesting idiosyncrasies of the Cargill culture is the fact that praise is not often given; it is just assumed that everyone is to do their very best, and so be it. Perhaps that makes the praise when it comes even more effective; at any rate, making the assumption that everyone is working up to their potential is certainly a piece of the Cargill culture.[9]

Transition, Family Leadership Again

The transition at Kelm's retirement in 1977 merits close attention, for it represented a move back to a family member as CEO. On December 14, 1977, Whitney MacMillan assumed that role.

The year 1977 was relatively calm after the severe traumas of the Vietnam War, the oil shocks, Watergate and its investigative mania. The grain companies had been caught in the eye of a storm in the period of the Russian grain sales (to be sure, this was a storm in part their own making). The Russian grain sales were a watershed. Born in secrecy—the Russians made that so— the results were not only spectacular for the industry in terms of profitability but brought many burgeoning effects, some untoward. Most prominent were the rapid rise in prices and their impact on the economy when combined with the oil shocks. The enormous logistic problems of moving those huge quantities of grain to the Soviet Union had led to boxcar shortages—the "boxcar blackmail" issue. Then there had been the extensive investigations of the industry stemming from the "grain scandals" at the Gulf ports during this period. Finally, there were the high-profile multinational hearings, part of a larger pattern of investigation of many other industries.

By 1978, when Whitney MacMillan was CEO, it did seem that a lull had settled over the agricultural scene; business was just average and farm policy not particularly sensitive for the moment. But *Business Week*, in a long article on Cargill at this time, did not see it quite that way. "A *deceptive* calm [my emphasis] blankets the world's grain markets. . . . Yet at its headquarters, Cargill Inc. the nation's largest privately owned company and the world's biggest grain trader is quietly but aggressively preparing for a brand-new era. For Cargill, the next few years may be every bit as turbulent as the period following the 1972 Russian wheat deal."

This article appeared in April 1979. Less than nine months later, in January

1980, arguably the most important single event to strike the grain trade in the seven-plus decades of the twentieth century occurred when President Jimmy Carter prohibited any grain sales to Russia in retaliation for the Soviets' invasion of Afghanistan. This high-profile act of attempted "food power" had profound effects on the grain trading already in process between the grain companies and the U.S.S.R. and led to traumatic longer-run repercussions. A complex story, it should serve as an exciting and important opening for a next volume of the Cargill history.

Clairvoyant the *Business Week* editors were not. Literally, no one could have predicted the Soviet embargo and its subsequent detrimental effects on U.S. grain exports. As *BW* put it in the Cargill article in 1979, "Now, another round of explosive growth in grain trading could be in the offing, accompanied by substantial new risks that are forcing Cargill to plan for a boom that might just as easily turn into a painful bust." While this explosion did not ensue, the editors did foreshadow the evolving changes in demand around the world; they saw increased buying from the developing countries and especially from Asia (but overall demand for U.S. grains was somewhat down in the early 1980s). More competition was evolving from other grain and food processing companies: "several new rivals have jumped into the business to join the traditional Big Four—Cargill, Continental Grain, Bunge and Louis Dreyfus" (they mentioned Peavey and Pillsbury; Philipp Bros., the metal-trading arm of Engelhard Minerals & Chemicals; two of the Japanese *zaibatsus*, Mitsui and Mitsubishi; the German-based Alfred C. Toepfer; and Farmers Export Co., a trading venture founded in 1968 by six U.S. farm cooperatives).

Cargill seemed well prepared for these challenges. Most of the senior management had stayed in place during the Kelm years—a whole cadre of like-minded people who worked together very well as a team. The tensions about international organization were important, but in the final analysis all these people, too, accommodated and worked together. Just a few of the Kelm team were gone; Fred Seed had died, John Savage had retired, Clayton Tonnemaker had resigned. All the rest of the elective officers in the listing in Chapter Six were still on board, many, of course, with enhanced job responsibilities. And a substantial nucleus of new senior managers also was in place. There were 2 new vice presidents: William Pearce (public affairs and labor relations, later a vice chairman) and Cary Humphries (coal, salt, and Car-Ren) and 11 new division vice presidents: Gordon Alexander (administration), Gilbert Bakeberg (administration), D. J. Berkley (administration), F. E. Steinbach (administration), I. M. Hyland (insurance), Robert Hubbard (commodity marketing), E. W. MacLennan (Pan American), Howard Boone (Pacific processing), Ewald Gustafson (processing, plant operations), R. W. Watson (processing, flax), and Evan Williams (salt). This cohesive, intact team (with the additional group of appointive assistant vice presidents) was living proof of the loyalty and corporate longevity of Cargill people.

Cargill's board of directors traveled to Perthshire, Scotland, in July 1977. In the front, Duncan MacMillan, Cal Anderson, Walter Gage, Erv Kelm, Cargill MacMillan, Jr., Bob Diercks, Pete McVay, and Jim Cargill; in the back row, Heinz Hutter, Bob Hanson (not a board member), Don Levin, Whitney MacMillan, Jim Spicola, Cal Smith, and Barney Saunders (*Cargill News,* July–August 1977).

The period 1960–1978 marked an ascendancy of management within Cargill. Not only was its chief executive officer a professional manager, so too was the entire cadre, family senior management included. There was much concern through all of the period about motivating senior management well and questions about management compensation; the several mechanisms that were to accomplish this dominated many board of directors meetings. Indeed, there seemed occasionally almost a preoccupation with management compensation (however, given the wide excesses of today on this issue, this seems in retrospect not quite so introspective).

If this be Cargill's "generation of the manager," the compensation of the senior management team did not in any sense run away. First, the family members still in the Company (Jim Cargill, Whitney, Cargill Jr., Duncan and Hugh MacMillan) were stockholders with definite ideas about who should get what. Some of the more analytical discussion of management-directed stock and bonuses held in the board were triggered and led by family. Ownership had not abdicated.

There was another factor that needs mention in this regard: the so-called Minneapolis effect. The Twin Cities represents the heart of Midwestern values and culture (even Cargill's humor was simple and uncomplicated; for example, the *Cargill News* of May–June 1972 contained a small article on the play of words in people's names as they related to agriculture; mentioned were Fred Seed, Lorraine Rice, Marlon Oates, and Bill Korn). The Twin Cities had not been an arena for outrageous management salaries (especially outrageous salaries of CEOs); thus, the general feeling among Twin City businesses that modest and defensible salaries should characterize the cities. Excesses surely would be noted by the strong Minneapolis press, and they would not go down well, not only with business peers but with the general public.

The deliberate structuring of the board itself early on into three director segments representing, separately, common stockholders, management, and the employees (as indirectly represented by the Cargill Foundation) gave practical effect to discussions of this type among various stockholders. The Foundation in this period did not, however, represent the general public in a significant way; the contributions during the mid-1960s were quite modest, with $200,000 in gifts in four of the years, dropping down to $100,000 in two of the years, and having only one year at $300,000. In 1971–1972 this rose to $400,000, in 1972–1973 to $1 million, $2 million the next year, $1.3 million in 1974–1975, and $1 million in 1975–1976. In these last two years there were also significant contributions from individual divisions, over $3 million just for these two years; the board's contributions committee also made significant grants, on an ad hoc basis, for "large rifle shot projects . . . relatively few in number" (the wording from a 1975 board meeting). It should be noted for the record that the contributions in the 1980s and the 1990s were quite substantially over anything of this level.

The Company had moved a significant way toward a public conscientiousness, a willingness to testify, to open its books, to communicate with its stakeholders, especially the farmers, and to take a role as one of the preeminent corporations of the United States. There seemed little question now that Cargill was number one in the industry; it likely had passed Continental Grain sometime late in the Kelm period (it was never easy to ascertain this, as Continental was one of the most secretive in the industry; as late as August 1973, after the Cargill internal analysis (mentioned in Chapter Four) that appeared to show Cargill as the larger, each company continued to nominate the other in the public press as "largest"). Still, from a narrowly entrepreneurial corporation under John Jr.—freewheeling, private, reclusive, unwilling to communicate—Cargill had matured to be more in the nature of a public corporation in its responsibilities.

Walter Gage retired at the same time that Erv Kelm did; certainly, the absence of these two closely tied men marked the passing of an era. Gage stayed on the Cargill board until 1980, but Brewster "Stu" Hanson took over as CEO of Tradax. Kelm himself retired completely, also being required by age to give up his position on the Cargill board of directors. The board numbered

13 at the time of the Kelm/MacMillan transition: longtime members Jim Cargill, Bob Diercks, Gage, the three MacMillans (Cargill Jr., Whitney, and Duncan), and Pete McVay, together with newer members Hanson, Heinz Hutter, Don Levin, Barney Saunders, Cal Smith, and Jim Spicola.

From far back, Whitney MacMillan by many marks had appeared to be the logical person to succeed Kelm as CEO. The decisive, defining moment really came at the point in 1975 when MacMillan was chosen as president and chief operating officer. Although one member of one of the families registered some reservations about the choice, there was no doubt about whom Kelm thought should succeed him (and it was crystal clear to all of the board that the choice was to be Kelm's in the final analysis). Kelm vividly remembered this moment two decades later and stated unequivocally, "I would have chosen Whitney even if he had not been a member of either of the families." A *St. Paul Pioneer Press* reporter quoted a source in the grain trade: "Kelm was not there just to hold it together until a family member was ready. They're too big, too professional and too successful to do that." (Kelm did find, however, the decision in appointing Fred Seed instead of Bob Diercks as president in 1969 a more difficult one, where "I might have made a mistake . . . he was more mature and he had a good mind, a very orderly mind. But we needed original ideas . . . during this time when our earnings were going up we *had* to have ideas.")

Pete McVay, the hard-driving, somewhat outspoken member from the Oil Division he so fiercely protected, moved up to president and chief operating officer; Bob Diercks continued as vice chairman, the position he had held since 1971. These three—MacMillan, McVay, and Diercks—formed a triumvirate that MacMillan called "the office of the chairman." *The Chicago Tribune* emphasized the "newly formed" character of this combined office. The *Tribune* also took the occasion to comment, "Although Cargill would have ranked 12th if sales were compared with the 500 largest publicly held companies in this country, the grain exporter would be 40th if compared by profits." Cargill did emphasize the long run and was willing to take the small margins marking the grain trade. Just as the Chase analysts commented in 1963, Cargill seemed to pay more attention to the growth in net worth than in the inherent profitability of the Company. Cargill MacMillan, back in the late 1950s, had wanted to reach $100 million in net worth by the anniversary (and did); Kelm stated in the mid-1960s that he wanted to double net worth in seven years (they did, and many times over in the early 1970s with the Russian grain sales).

Business Week commented specifically about Cargill's transition in that major article on the Company in 1979:

Until a few years ago, the Company was dominated by officers from the trading side of the business, while the "processing and feed people were almost a lower caste," recalls one former executive. Now that is changing; the differences between the two camps are exemplified by the disparate backgrounds and experience of Chairman MacMillan and President McVay. MacMillan, 49, is a trader. After graduating from Yale, he worked his way up as a vegetable-oil merchant and later as a grain trader. McVay, on the other hand, is the first executive from the processing side of the business to reach the presidency. He is a livestock specialist . . . seems to embody the new wave of management at Cargill. It is more operations-oriented and technically trained; some of its members are MBAs and, many were educated in the Midwest—contrasting sharply with the liberal arts graduates of Harvard and Yale picked in the 1950s and 1960s to become Cargill's elite coterie of grain traders. In the recent moves at Cargill, outsiders see the ascendancy of the technical camp generally and McVay in particular. "McVay is the brains behind it all," says one Cargill alumnist. "He is the guy who is setting strategy now."

The article went on to question "if this is so," and one might be a bit wary of the sharp dichotomy between MacMillan and McVay characterized by the *Business Week* writer. Nevertheless, the thrust of the comment that the Company was turning more toward the processing and technical side of the business had some merit.

By the time of the transition, Cargill was widely acknowledged by the public press as number one in the industry; *Business Week*, in a major article on the industry in early 1979 credited Cargill with 25 percent of the United States exports; "Continental Grain Co. of New York, is next with about 20%." The *Business Week* editors stated that Cargill's "350 elevators, 500 barges, 5000 railcars, and 14 ocean-going vessels give the Company a big lead over second place Continental in grain-handling and storage facilities." With Cargill spending at the annual rate of about $150 million to expand its grain-handling capacity by 50 percent in 1984, the Dreyfus executive mentioned by *Business Week* was probably right that Cargill was moving at a pace that no one was going to match. Still, those newcomers mentioned by the editors already were bringing more competition (a few years hence any article on newly powerful competitors would likely also have included Archer Daniels Midland and ConAgra). *Forbes*, in a 1978 article, designated Cargill "the largest privately held corporation in the United States." Incidentally, the *Forbes* editors seemed to get carried away with one of their analogies, dubbing the Company the "dowager of the grain industry." Somehow, this seems about as far as one could get from describing Cargill!

The *Forbes* writers in this 1978 article added their voices to the point that Cargill had become concerned about how little the public *did* know about the Company. In 1977, Cargill commissioned a survey of how farmers assessed Cargill. It turned out that while 94 percent of farmers were aware of the Company, only about 49 percent were familiar with what it did. Even among so-called opinionaters—politicians, businessmen, lawyers, journalists, who were also interviewed (the term was the advertising agency's)—only about half were even aware of Cargill, and only 12 percent were familiar with its operation. Worried about this, Cargill launched an ambitious $2 million corporate institutional advertising program in May 1978. The focus was on its role

What every city slicker should know about soybeans.

There's a lot more to soy than sauce.

Last year, America's farmers grew $10 billion worth of the amazingly versatile soybean. It helped put meat on your table, paint on your walls, and medicine on your shelf.

And, as America's largest agricultural export, it helped pay for petroleum and other needed imports.

PACKED WITH PROTEIN.

Soy flour contains four times the protein of wheat flour. When added to baked goods, it improves their nutritional value.

GETTING OUT THE GOOD STUFF.

Soybeans are loaded with proteins and edible oil. To separate these valuable components, Cargill processes soybeans into flour, meal, and oil. These, in turn, are used in a long list of products including animal feeds, margarines, salad dressings...even baby foods.

DEFLATING INFLATION...

By using more efficient methods, Cargill has been able to hold the line on its cost of processing a bushel of soybeans. As a matter of fact, since 1950 Cargill has held increases to less than one-fifth the increase in living costs. And price competition among soybean processors assures that these economies are shared with both the farmer and consumer.

GOBBLERS GOBBLE IT UP.

Soybean meal is the major protein source for poultry and livestock feed.

America's bountiful soybean supplies mean more efficient production of meat and dairy products for everyone.

Cargill is a major processor and worldwide marketer of soybeans, meal, oil, and feed. The more efficiently we do our job, the more we benefit farmers and consumers alike.

CARGILL

HELPING MAKE BOTH ENDS MEET.

One of Cargill's informational advertisements, 1978 (Cargill News, July–August 1978).

as a middleman, with the theme, "Cargill is helping make both ends meet." A clever advertisement was headlined: "What Every City Slicker Should Know about Soybeans."

The 1977–1978 annual report to the shareholders, the first one signed by Whitney MacMillan as chairman, commented on the campaign: "This year . . . the board of directors approved an expanded public education program; included are a one-year experiment in institutional advertising on television, radio, and in magazines; two newsletters—one informing Cargill managers of developments in Washington affecting our business and the other giving our views on them; and a monthly newsletter on Cargill's activities that is sent to reporters and editors at publications and broadcasting organizations important to us. While the industry as a whole will benefit, we think our leadership role in this area will be recognized."

Cargill in general and Kelm in particular had been groping for a better explanation of Cargill's natural product mix. In the late 1980s, the Company would hire a professional consultant who would lead them to a much better understanding of the concept of "core competencies" and how to describe these in regard to a statement of company goals and objectives. Kelm mentioned more frequently in the 1970s that Cargill was doing more "branding" and that the Company was "capability driven." In this, he was striving to understand the notion of moving up the value chain, a term and concept that was not yet in use at that time.

In 1975, the board of directors once more codified its corporate goals and objectives and for the first time published them in the *Cargill News*. The lead for the article said, "The following paragraphs are the most recent statement of Cargill's managerial goals and objectives. In the past, they have been distributed mainly among company managers. In these trying times, however, it seems appropriate that they should be seen, and studied, by all Cargill employees."

The statement was the most comprehensive and wide ranging that Cargill had ever done. It contained 16 different goals, a number of them put in writing in this fashion for the first time. Erv Kelm had stated in the early 1960s that "it goes without saying that the Company's integrity is important" and had explained this further in a speech in the Company's Business Management Program in February 1973: "You will note that Cargill's corporate objectives are silent on ethics. We assume our people know that lying, stealing and cheating are not acceptable. We speak only in a general way of the image that we wish to present, for that image will generally reflect what we actually are." In contrast, the *Cargill News* iteration stated the question of ethics flatly as its very first point: "Continue to make certain that all employees of the Cargill Companies recognize and adhere to the principles of integrity which have always been basic to our philosophy and upon which the Cargill Companies' reputation is founded."

This was followed with statements about "reasonable and improved corporate earnings and the upgrading of facilities." Later in the piece, there were more explicit statements about working conditions and the importance of safety practices (the board had expressed concern about Cargill's safety record in this particular period). The Company was to "continue to develop and administer a total pollution control program consistent with the objective of being a good corporate citizen, complying with the spirit as well as the letter of the applicable law and regulations." In this regard, the Company was to "seek specific ways to contribute to improving the quality of life of the communities of which we are a part and encourage individual employees to follow a similar objective."

The statement reaffirmed Cargill's concern about providing better nutrition for the people of the world; on employee relations, the Company wanted to "seek more ways and means to identify with our people." The Company would "continue to support the principle of decentralization . . . and develop managers experienced in more than one function, and who can manage effectively in a number of areas." This latter had been an ongoing battle in the Company during the Kelm period; in John Jr.'s regime, often managers stayed in one function all of their lives, with the inevitable provincialism and turf consciousness.

Included again was a statement about hiring, training, and promoting; but this time there was specific mention of these being "without regard for race, color, creed, or sex." This was followed by several paragraphs concerning competitiveness. Once again, a Cargill tenet was repeated: "We will maintain our reputation as an innovative and aggressive competitor," and "we will continue to . . . be an articulate spokesperson in the development of public policies worldwide which support the public interests and our continued growth and development." "We recognize that we are no longer solely agriculture-oriented and will seek opportunities outside of our traditional businesses so long as certain requirements are met." Finally, the Company wanted to be able to use its existing knowledge to compete, with costs and market penetration better than the average of the competition, and stated that "we must foresee becoming as competitive as the best in the field." The business should be a growth business, which would "present a growth possibility greater than population growth."

With this goals statement firmly in place and articulated widely among all Company employees, Whitney MacMillan's memorandum to all employees (November 5, 1975) about ethics and values takes on added meaning. This frank and open evocation of MacMillan's thinking, reprinted in its entirety in Chapter Seven, made explicit five key precepts: (1) that the Company had a "deep responsibility" to operate under the highest standards of ethics and integrity, in "all countries and communities"; (2) that "open discussion" would resolve questions of any given practice; (3) that any business obtained by any means other than legal, open honest competition was wrong; (4) that if this business could not be properly recorded in Company books and independently audited, it was wrong; and (5) that disciplinary action would be taken for anything immoral or unethical. MacMillan was a student of the management process by this point, and his efforts in the late 1980s and early 1990s to restructure the Company were a later result of this burgeoning interest. With Erv Kelm's retirement, it was now to be MacMillan's watch—to continue to champion this philosophy.

In July 1979, a "Future Strategic Profile" was formally reduced to writing for the first time, a document that was to have a time perspective of five to seven years (the next one *was* seven years later, in 1986). It codified and made more specific both the 1975 goals statement and a July 1977 restatement of "corporate guidelines" by the board. Of particular importance in this 1979 profile were nine "strategic basic beliefs," as follows:

1. Ethical legal, and responsible business conduct. Integrity/honesty.

2. It is important to have market dominance/leadership in the business.

3. Private ownership allows and encourages growth through reinvestment of cash flow.

4. We are committed to financial strength, AA credit rating.

5. We are managers, not investors.

6. We will stick to what we know.

7. We are risk takers, not risk avoiders.

8. The world is our oyster.

9. We will maintain a low public profile.

These, then, were the operative catechisms for Whitney MacMillan as he headed off on his voyage as the fifth chairman and CEO and the third MacMillan to head Cargill, Incorporated.[10]

The Kelm Years—an Afterword

Hubert Sontheim, John Jr.'s son-in-law and the Tradax general counsel, reflected with me on the Kelm years: "The Chinese have an aphorism that each generation wants to rewrite history. However, Kelm and Morrison respected the existing structure, and Kelm often said, 'Don't drop a going boat.'" At the start of Kelm's period "times were lean, and it helped for the new team to get its feet on the ground and make a little money." Sontheim then paid a special accolade to Kelm that seems to capture beautifully the Kelm era: "Erv Kelm was the 'Leonardo da Vinci' of the Company. He exuded confidence and he was a visionary."

As one looks back over the 17 years of Kelm's leadership, the Sontheim accolade seems well corroborated. Kelm had been a premier trader early on. His trading instincts carried him into what was perhaps his greatest mistake in his term as CEO, the decision to follow through on the squeeze in the May 1963 wheat case. However, Kelm had taught himself over those early years in the 1960s to be a professional manager. John Jr. had really thought about organizational structure and had often spoken about its problems, but his vision on this front was not as good as in others, and he never was able to break away from his own views of organization and his certainty of being right that had been imprinted on him so vividly by his experiences as the youngest major in the U.S. Army in World War I. His way of command was very different from that of Kelm's.

Kelm was a true leader—there was no doubt about who was the CEO— but he led by consensus and suggestion (he sometimes called this "the English system of muddling through"). "I had a policy of letting everybody have their say, then we would move ahead. . . . I was quick in deciding in those days—I don't think I would have been too good a second man." Kelm had the ability to step into an argumentative discussion at just the right time, often with a pungent one-liner (as with the 1969 battle about "getting out of grain," after the Grain Division had posted a huge loss; Kelm vehemently opposed this and at a critical moment stated, "You don't kill your grandmother." The debate suddenly was over, and the Grain Division survived to later post its huge profits in the Russian grain sales).

Yes, Erv Kelm was often inarticulate, gruff, and uncommunicative. But his senior management colleagues had an enormously high regard for him, and his leadership and innovativeness over the 17 years was a tour de force for the Company. The legacy to Whitney MacMillan, a person who had a very close mentor-student relationship with Kelm, was now quite secure.

Cargill, Incorporated, and Subsidiaries

Net Earnings and Net Worth, 1961–1979
($000 omitted)

Fiscal year ending 5/31	Net earnings, Cargill's share	Net worth
1961	5,088	70,716
1962	3,474	72,527
1963	4,276	82,428
1964	7,737	89,208
1965	7,818	94,875
1966	16,728	109,982
1967	16,867	126,542
1968	15,339	141,021
1969	8,474	148,093
1970	24,167	171,576
1971	38,025	208,714
1972	40,250	246,308
1973	107,846	352,392
1974	212,490	567,214
1975	218,397	781,411
1976	178,883	957,856
1977	110,132	1,074,132
1978	121,429	1,177,763
1979	178,107	1,349,793

Notes

1. An Attack of Angst (pp. 4–47)

1. For the history of the Company prior to 1961, see Wayne G. Broehl, Jr., *Cargill: Trading the World's Grain* (Hanover, N.H.: University Press of New England, 1992).

2. Cargill MacMillan on Austen Cargill, March 24, 1944, Cargill Archives (CA hereafter), 47-01.

3. The first of the extensive "family meetings" of the next generation was April 11, 1961; family objectives rating scale in the meeting of May 18, 1961 (also meeting of July 17, 1963). The process was repeated over a number of later meetings; also September 28, 1964, March 11, 1969, November 11, 1971. Meeting of family with Erwin Kelm, April 21, 1961, and attached memorandum of that date; meeting with H. T. Morrison, April 27, 1961. Also Morrison to Kelm, April 25, 1961 (with two attached memorandums). Early thinking of family group in an internal memorandum, "A Timely Statement from Ownership to Management," dated May 18, 1961, discussed orally with management. Also "Family Statement to Morrison and Kelm," n.d., circa May 1961, MS collection, James F. Cargill (secretary pro tem for the family group).

4. The key case in the rye encounter, *General Foods Corporation v. Brannan, Secretary of Agriculture*, October 9, 1948, 170 F. 2nd 220. For a discussion of the entire experience, see Broehl, *Cargill: Trading the World's Grain*, op. cit., pp. 652–61. For oats case, see Commodity Exchange Authority, *In re Cargill, Incorporated and Erwin E. Kelm*, Docket No. 58, June 11, 1953, CA Law B-12, 514-1; complainant, George E. MacKinnon, U.S. Attorney, District Court, District of Minnesota, Fourth Division, *United States of America v. Cargill, Incorporated and Cargill Grain Company, Limited*, Civil 4849, February 20, 1954; Broehl, op. cit., pp. 754–62. Cargill MacMillan stroke, John MacMillan, Jr., to William W. Cargill, August 9, 1960, CA Lake 16.

5. H. Terry Morrison, "Integrity," *Cargill News*, July 1961.

6. Georgina Hamilton McGillivray, "The President Speaks," *Cargill News*, September 1961.

7. *Cargill News*, January 1961.

8. University of Chicago attitude survey, *Cargill News*, August 1961.

9. Willard W. Cochrane and Mary E. Ryan, *American Farm Policy, 1948–1973* (Minneapolis: University of Minnesota Press, 1976, p. 79).

10. Ibid., pp. 40–45, 189–90, 207–11; Willard W. Cochrane, *The Development of American Agriculture: A Historical Analysis*, 2nd ed. (Minneapolis: University of Minnesota Press, 1993), pp. 146–48. William R. Pearce to grain division branch managers, March 8 and September 25, 1962, CA 5H5F; M. H. Middents, "Analysis—Food and Agriculture Act of 1962," ibid. "Cargill Bill," *Wall Street Journal*, November 7, 1975. Payment-in-kind, Calvin Anderson to R. C. Woodworth and others, May 14, 1962, CA 6W5B; John F. McGrory to M. H. Middents, June 28, 1962, ibid. U.S. Department of Agriculture, "Long Range Feed Grain Program," November 23, 1962; Pearce, "Feed Grain Legislation," Annual Marketing Seminar, Minneapolis Grain Exchange, August 29, 1962; ibid. "Recent Commodity Legislation from the Standpoint of the Grain Trade," Annual Convention, Grain & Feed Dealers National Association, March 15, 1965, CA 5E4F. See also *Cargill News*, September 1962; *Cargill Crop Bulletin*, February 23, 1963. "Savvy negotiator," *Wall Street Journal*, November 7, 1975.

11. "Wheat—1964 and Subsequent Years," January 30, 1963, CA 5H5F; "Soft Red Wheat and the 1964 Referendum," CA ibid.; Pearce to grain division branch managers, March 8, 1963, ibid. For results, *Cargill Crop Bulletin*, June 20, 1963; "The Wheat Vote," *Cargill News*, June 1963. Don Paarlberg quotation, *Successful Farming*, June 1963; "Only solution," *New York Times*, May 26, 1963; "go to the wall," Joseph Alsop, *Washington Post*, May 27, 1963.

12. "The Evolution of Public Law 480," undated Cargill internal memorandum, circa 1976, CA 3F7B; Robbin S. Johnson, testimony before the Foreign Agricultural Subcommittee, Senate Committee on Agriculture, Nutrition and Forestry, April 5, 1977.

13. There are numerous references to the establishment of the European Economic Community; see, especially, Susan M. Collins and Barry P. Bosworth, *The New GATT: Implications for the United States* (Washington, D.C.: Brookings Institution, 1994). Factual references here taken from *Encyclopedia Americana*, 1995 ed., 14:606, 17:705. Dan Morgan, *Merchants of Grain* (New York, Viking Press, 1979). For "Kennedy Round," see Chapter Three of this book.

14. As of the 1962–1963 figures, the Tradax merger with Cargill, Incorporated, brought the latter's share of Tradax net profit to the Cargill net ($712,000 is added, bringing the total to $4,196,000); this was not done in the 1961–1962 closing, which reported a net profit of $3,474,000. For 1962–1963, subtract the $712,000, or $3,484,000. Walter B. Saunders, *Annual Report, Grain Division, Crop Year 1962–1963*, section I. Quotation on "change in procedure," *Cargill, Incorporated and Subsidiary Companies*, Annual Report, section C, p. 3. "Sense of profit responsibility," *Minutes of the Board of Directors*, July 26, 1963, p. 12–58. "Pleasant to contemplate," Erwin E. Kelm to all division managers, August 23, 1963, CA 5K6B.

15. Report on accounting decentralization, Booz, Allen & Hamilton, "Interim Report: Accounting System Installation," September 30, 1948, CA 56-05; Kelm response in his letter to Cargill MacMillan, May 25, 1949, ibid.

16. Alex H. Ardrey, Jr., "Report on Cargill, Incorporated to Mr. Charles Cain, Jr., Executive Vice President, Chase Manhattan Bank," October 18, 1963, John Peterson MS collection, CA; Robert J. Harrigan, "Chase Manhattan Report on Cargill: Highlights," November 5, 1963, ibid.

17. "Leader, not follower," internal memorandum, E. E. Kelm, October 24, 1963, CA 5K6B. "Costs lower than industry," F. M. Seed to Long Range Planning Committee, December 2, 1963, CA, ibid. "Russians may buy," ibid., December 23, 1963. For "Tino" De Angelis scam, see Peter Z. Grossman, *American Express: The Unofficial History of the People Who Built the Great Financial Empire* (New York: Crown Publishers, 1987); Edmund K. Faltermayer, "The Future of American Express," *Fortune*, April 1964. Sentencing of De Angelis, *Wall Street Journal*, August 18, 1965, July 19, 1966, January 11, 1967. Writeoff of Allied loss, "Cargill, Incorporated, Summary Annual Report, 1963–1964," p. C2; see also Annual Report, Oil Division, 1963–1964, p. VC4. Tax implications, Long-Range Planning Committee (LRPC) meeting of March 20, 1964, CA 5K6B. Erwin E. Kelm, "Report to All Cargill Office, Sales and Supervisory Employees," July 8, 1963, CA, John Work MS. For Cargill explanation to its bankers, see Albert Egermayer to James W. Bergford, Chase Manhattan Bank, January 2, 1964, CA 5K2F; the Chicago Board of Trade reaction to the scandal is in the H. Robert Diercks MS, ibid.; see also Warren W. Lebeck, secretary, to members, April 23, 1964; Robert Liebenow, president, to editor, *Life* magazine, April 14, 1964, re the magazine's article of April 3, 1964, CA 5K2F.

18. The full Nutrena merger proposal was enumerated in the board of directors minutes of November 2, 1962, pp. 12–26, 27; the *Green Wave* announcement of May 28, 1962, described the move as "the beginning of gradual steps to merge." James North statement from *Cargill News*, June 1962.

19. "Concerned with the capital structure," Report to Shareholders, Tradax Internacional, S.A. and Subsidiaries," June 30, 1961–May 31, 1962, p. 5. "Did declare dividends," Hubert F. Sontheim to Donald C. Levin, December 9, 1961, John MacMillan, Jr. MS collection. For the first plan, Erwin E. Kelm to Shareholders of Tradax Internacional, S.A., January 9, 1962; see also of this date, "Memorandum Re Reorganization . . ." and "Memorandum Re Cargill, Incorporated Proposal to Acquire a Seventy-five Percent Equity Interest in Tradax . . ." The "Proposed Revision of Articles of Incorporation of Tradax . . ." and a "Memorandum Re Reorganization of Tradax . . . ," relating to the Class "A" and Class "B" and the First, Second and Special Preferred, dated February 15, 1962. The Erwin Kelm description of the revised plan is in his letter to Cargill MacMillan, Jr., Whitney MacMillan, John Hugh MacMillan III, Duncan MacMillan, Marion and Hubert Sontheim, James R. Cargill, and Fred Seed, dated June 12, 1962, CA 6O8F. The final

plan as submitted to the shareholders of Cargill, Incorporated, is in the minutes of July 27, 1962. Description of the management effects in "Memorandum Re Proposed International Organization," written by Don Levin, October 9, 1961, CA 6O8F. The reorganization was announced to Cargill employees in the *Green Wave*, September 28, 1962. On tax effects for Class "B" shareholders of Tradax, see Donald Levin letter, February 8, 1963, CA 6O8F. Quotation on Cargill culture, "Elements of Geneva Climate," Brewster Hanson MS, November 26, 1982.

20. Two excellent *Cargill News* articles give the chronology of the Russian sales of 1963–1964: "Grain for Soviet Bloc—Cargill's Role," November 1963, and "The Great Russian Wheat Deal," April 1964. The Canadian wheat sale, *New York Times*, September 17, 1963; "serious internal difficulties," ibid., September 18; Thomas Gleason, "object vigorously," ibid., September 28. Citation for Webb Pomerene Act, 15 USCS 61; Cargill press release at CA 5B1F; *New York Times* report, September 27. Senator Dodd, "they get wheat," ibid, October 4. President Kennedy announcement and press conference, ibid, October 10; "what the President said," ibid; Thomas Gleason, "hammer and sickle," ibid., October 16; Kelm to Washington, ibid., November 5; Bill Pearce statement, ibid., December 1; Continental sale, ibid., December 27. "Not an ILA victory," ibid., February 27, 1964. "Cargill will meet quota," ibid., February 28. See also *Business Week*, October 5, 1963, and February 2, 1964; *U.S. News & World Report*, October 28, 1963, and February 17, 1964.

21. *Business Week*, January 4, 1964.

2. *A Return, an Unexpected Result (pp. 50–92)*

1. An entire chapter in Wayne G. Broehl, Jr., *Cargill: Trading the World's Grain*, op. cit., is devoted to Cargill's 1937 corn case; see, particularly, the notes on pp. 935–941. The two key cases were *Cargill, Incorporated, Complainant v. the Board of Trade of the City of Chicago, respondent,* Commodity Exchange Authority Docket No. 6, August 16, 1940, and *Secretary of Agriculture, Complainant v. Cargill, Inc., Cargill Grain Company of Illinois, John H. MacMillan, Jr., E. J. Grimes, Julius Hendel and Philip C. Sayles, Respondents,* CEA Docket No. 11, i, March 7, 1940. For citations covering the rye and oats cases, see chap. 1, note 4. Reentry into the CBOT is first discussed in the board of directors meeting of May 22, 1962; a five-person committee chaired by Bob Diercks was established. This committee's report of July 17 was accepted at the board meeting of July 27; announcement was made in the *Green Wave* of September 28.

2. For explanation of the "clearinghouse," see Theodore R. Hartley chapter in Perry J. Kaufman, *Handbook of Futures Markets* (New York: John Wiley and Sons, 1984); for CBOT clearinghouse, see *Commodity Trading Manual* (Chicago: Chicago Board of Trade, 1985), chap. 4.

3. "Irksome restrictions," John C. Dorsey to W. B. Saunders, May 11, 1959, CA 5L8B, Dorsey and Whitney MS, Box #2, C5135 subs.

4. "Nebulous point," *Fortune*, August 1949. For early CEA interest in the Cargill activities in the May 1963 wheat future, see, for example, "Interview of Roy C. Loftus," June 26, 1963, CA, Dorsey and Whitney MS, op. cit.; press release, "Cargill and Its Position in Chiago May Wheat, 1963," CA 5B1F. Cargill long position "only 3.8% on April 16th," from "Memo on Cargill Case," circa June 1964, CA 5L8B. The CEA complaint became "CEA 120," dated June 3, 1964; see *Wall Street Journal*, June 8 and June 9, 1964. "Ignominy and censure," Donald C. Levin to Sen. Eugene J. McCarthy, March 16, 1965, CA, Dorsey and Whitney MS, op. cit. "Ill-considered legal theories," "Monthly Letter to Members," Board of Trade of the City of Chicago, June 15, 1965, ibid. "Imbued with incompatible philosophies," Levin memorandum, April 2, 1965, ibid. Query by term note holders, Levin to E. E. Kelm and others, June 16, 1965, ibid. Quotations from *Southwestern Miller* in its issues of June 8 and 15, 1963. "Refreshing the White House contact," Levin to John G. Dorsey and others, August 4, 1965, CA 5L7B. Comment about upcoming *Fortune* magazine article, Levin to Diercks, September 3, 1965, CA 5L8B. For first CBOT brief as intervenor, see Philip F. Johnson to Calvin Anderson, September 20, 1965, CA, Dorsey and Whitney MS, op. cit. "Power grab," Levin to John C. Dorsey, October 22, 1965, CA, ibid. The *Fortune* article, "The Two-Billion-Dollar Company That Lives by the Cent," is in its December 1965 issue. Lists of those testifying for Cargill, Jaffray to Diercks, circa July 1966, CA 5L7B. For Cargill's arguments that the four individuals should not be part of the case, see "Proposed Findings, Conclusions and Argument Submitted to Referee Benjamin M. Holstein on Behalf of Individual Respondents Kelm, Diercks, Saunders and Jaffray," CEA Docket 120, CA

5L7B; see also internal memorandum "Case for the Cargill Individuals," circa 1964, CA, Dorsey and Whitney MS, op. cit. For the early CEA arguments (prior to referee decision), see Earl L. Saunders, attorney, CEA, "Complainant's Reply Brief," August 1, 1967. The "Recommended Decision" of Holstein is dated August 12, 1968. "Cathedral appearance," Oral Argument before Thomas Flavin, judicial officer, December 9, 1969, p. 9. Decision of the judicial officer, *In re Cargill, Incorporated [and the four individuals] CEA Docket 120, Decided August 13, 1970, 29 A.D. 880.* "Public against us," August 21, 1970, CA 5L7B. Reluctance of CBOT to file second brief, Cargill wire, Anderson to Diercks, Saunders, and Jim Howard, March 11, 1971, ibid.; final brief sent, "Memorandum of the Board of Trade of the City of Chicago as Amicus Curiae," April 28, 1971. Brief of the government, L. Patrick Gray, Assistant Attorney General, August 13, 1971, CA 5L7B. Circuit court case, *Cargill, Incorporated, et al. v. Clifford M. Hardin, Secretary of Agriculture, Thomas J. Flavin, Judicial Officer by Appointment of the Secretary of Agriculture, and the United States Department of Agriculture, Respondents*, U.S. Court of Appeals, Eighth Circuit, December 7, 1971, 452 *Federal Reporter*, 2nd ser. 1154. Denial of writ of certiorari by U.S. Supreme Court, 406 U.S. 932, 32 L. Ed. 2d 135. "Volkart case" *Volkart Brothers, Inc. v. Orville Freeman*, U.S. Court of Appeals, Fifth Circuit, December 5, 1962, 311 F. 2d 52. Questions re dates of probation, "Sale of Wheat to Russia," Hearings before the Subcommittee on Livestock and Grains of the Committee on Agriculture, House of Representatives, 92nd Congress, 2nd sess., September 14, 18, 19, 1972, pp. 249–251. For post-case citations of the Cargill circuit court decision, see *Robert Lagorio, et al. v. Board of Trade of the City of Chicago, et al.*, U. S. Court of Appeals, Seventh Circuit, February 13, 1976, 529 F. 2d 1290; *Howard, Weil, Labouisse, Friedrichs v. Insurance Company of North America*, U. S. Court of Appeals, Fifth Circuit, August 15, 1977, 557 F. 2d 1055; *Philip Smith, et al. v. Richard C. Groover, et al.*, U. S. District Court, N.D. Illinois, E.D. February 22, 1979, 468 F.Supp. 105; *Neil Leist et al. v. J.R. Simplot et al.*, U. S. Court of Appeals, Second Circuit, July 8, 1980, 638 F. 2nd 283 and 101 S. Ct 1346. One of the best comparisons between Cargill and Volkart is in *Indiana Farm Bureau Cooperative Association v. Commodity Futures Trading Commission*, CFTC Docket 75-14, March 1, 1983, 1983 CFTC Lexis 489.

5. For the story of Conover and Calmar, see Wayne G. Broehl, Jr., *Cargill: Trading the World's Grain*, op. cit., pp. 3–18. "Boss town," Charles H. Sparks, *History of Winneshiek County, With Biographical Sketches of Its Prominent Men* (Decorah, Iowa: Jas. Alex. Leonard, 1877).

6. Centennial slogan, *Cargill News*, August and October 1964; Conover visit by Company officials, ibid., January, 1965; centennial parties, ibid., October–November, 1965. "Pride and shame," ibid. Centennial book, John L. Work, *Cargill Beginnings . . . an Account of Early Years*, privately printed, 1965.

7. "Out in prairies," *Minneapolis Star*, January 4, 1964; "little guys down the street," H. H. Hessler to Clifford Roberts, September 13, 1968, CA 3E1B.

8. The "Big John" case, "Grain in Multiple-Car Shipments—River Crossings to the South," Investigation and Suspension Docket 7656, January 21, 1963, 318 I.C.C. 641. For early Cargill view, "The Southern Rate Case: A Nationwide Bombshell," *Cargill News*, July 1962. Quotations from "Development of the Grain Rail Rate Structure, 1930–1975," Cargill, Incorporated, draft MS, n.d., CA 6V7B. See also "Hopper Cars Are Great Advantage," *Cargill News*, January 1964. "Peculiar rate-making theories," Background Memorandum, Southeastern Association of Local Grain Producers, Merchandisers, Processors and Consumers, n.d., CA 5I5F.

9. "Hurricane Hilda," *Cargill News*, November 1964; "Hurricane Betsy," ibid., October–November 1965; Port Cargill flood, ibid., April 1965; dike repair, February 1966.

10. The international organization reports were discussed at the board of directors meeting of August 4, 1966; the matter was referred to the Long-Range Planning Committee. The reports presented were H. Robert Diercks, "International Organization," circa July 1966, CA 6O8F; Fred Seed, "Foreign Operations and Organization," July 15, 1965, ibid.; Hubert F. Sontheim, "International Organization," July 14, 1966, ibid. See also Walter F. Gage to E. E. Kelm, February 25, 1966, ibid. The final Kelm statement, "International Organization," August 24, 1966, CA 5K4B. For the difficulties with the French plans, Sontheim to Donald C. Levin, February 23, 1966, CA 6O8F. See also "Precis—Organizing for World Wide Operations," *Business International*, special report, n.d., A. C. Greenman to Kelm, July 29, 1966, ibid.; B. B. Hanson, "Tradax Developments and Progress—Plans and Outlook for the Future," address at Grain Division meeting, circa April 1964, CA 3E1F.

3. *India's Hunger, Beachhead in Japan, a Tragedy (pp. 98–139)*

1. On India's history of food insufficiency, see B. M. Bhatia, *Famines in India* (New Delhi: Konark Publishers, 1991); quotation on Great Famine of 1896–1897, p. 8. On causes of Indian famines, with focus on the monsoons, Michelle Burge McAlpin, *Subject to Famine: Food Crises and Economic Change in Western India, 1860–1920* (Princeton, N.J.: Princeton University Press, 1983). "Slide rule assessment of needs," R. N. Chopra, *Food Policy in India: A Survey* (New Delhi: Intellectual Publishing House, 1988), p. 144. "Selling children," *New York Times*, December 12, 1966; President Lyndon Johnson proposal for new "Food for Peace," ibid. February 9, 1966; Gunnar Myrdal on food needs by the year 2000, ibid., March 16; on impact of famine in state of Bihar, ibid., April 19, 1967. On Indian farmers' role in prices, Robert Paarlberg in D. Gale Johnson and G. Edward Schuh (eds.), *The Role of Markets in the World Food Economy* (Boulder, Colo: Westview Press, 1983). The problem of India's rural roads, William E. Hendrix and others, "Accelerating India's Food Grain Production," *Foreign Agricultural Economic Report No. 40* (Washington, D.C.: Economic Research Service, USDA, 1968), pp. 14–15. "Hanging like a sword" in *Food for Peace 1954–1978—Major Changes in Legislation*, Subcommittee on Foreign Agricultural Policy, Committee on Agriculture, Nutrition, and Forestry, U. S. Senate, 96th Cong., 1st sess., April 26, 1979, p. 7. See also Gunnar Myrdal, *Asian Drama: An Inquiry into the Poverty of Nations*, 3 vols., (New York: Pantheon, 1968); Fred H. Sanderson and Shyamal Roy, *Food Trends and Prospects in India* (Washington, D.C.: The Brookings Institution, 1979).

2. See Robert Harrigan, "Corporate Goals," memorandum to board of directors, July 18, 1967 (and his earlier draft, March 30, 1967), CA 6O8B. Finance Committee report is part of the board minutes, November 13, 1967. "Aggressive diversification . . . proper," board minutes of July 27, 1967.

3. Power of "all-round" trading companies, *Asahi Evening News*, April 23, 1965. "Near-feudal," in "Japan: Contrasts in Physical Distribution," *Marketing Information Guide*, May 1966. Vessel *Captain W. D. Cargill* described, *Cargill News*, September–October, 1966. George Cohee to Whitney MacMillan, September 19, 1991, CA 3F5F. For a discussion of "first mover" advantages, see Alfred D. Chandler, Jr. *Scale and Scope: the Dynamics of Industrial Capitalism* (Cambridge, Mass.: Belknap Press of Harvard University, 1990). Thomas K. McGraw (ed.), *The Essential Alfred Chandler: Essays toward a Historical Perspective of Big Business* (Boston: Harvard Business School Press, 1988), pp. 492–94, 497–98. For diffusion theory, Everett M. Rogers, *Diffusion of Innovations* (New York: Free Press of Glencoe, 1962). Initial feasibility study, Lowell Nelson to Walter Gage and others, December 11, 1965 CA, Toyo file #2, June 1966; "a rocky road," Nelson to Donald Levin, December 1, 1965, CA 6V5F. "Frustrating affair," Gage to E. E. Kelm, February 16, 1966, CA 5L8B. Profile of Toyo Wharf & Warehouse Co., Ian Watson to Nelson, March 17, 1966, CA 5L8B. For specific details of the Toyo final negotiations, see the final agreement of March 27, 1967, CA 6V5T; comparisons with the Amsterdam operation (IGMA), Blair to Nelson, July 11, 1966, CA 5L8B. "Taking a risk," H. Robert Diercks to Nelson, July 27, 1966, ibid. For questions on charges beyond the 500,000-ton-per-year maximum, see Blair to Toyo Wharf & Warehouse Company, September 22, 1966, ibid. "Very general," wire of November 25, 1966, to Blair and Tradax/Geneva, ibid; this agreement was dated November 23, 1966, ibid. "100 year old firm," Clifford Roberts wire to Blair, November 25, 1966, CA 5L8A. "Cartel concept," Blair wire to Wayzata and Geneva, December 12, 1967, CA 6V5F; "red herring," ibid., January 26, 1967; "loose and woolly," ibid., February 7, 1967. Contract is dated March 23, 1967, CA 6V5T; signing in Geneva and trip to Wayzata, Sei Sugano to John F. McGrory, May 8, 1967, ibid. "I can do better," Blair to B. B. Hanson, September 5, 1967, CA 5L8B.

4. Financial figures from CCI annual reports. "Electra costly mistake," annual report, 1961–1962; "definite rate pattern," ibid., 1963–1964; bow steering, ibid., 1964–1965 and *Cargill News*, December 1966. See also *Cargill News*, September–October 1968.

5. See, especially, Nancy Restuccia, *It's More Than Just a Place to Work: An Anecdotal History of Cargill's Corn Milling Division, 1967–1987* (Cargill, Incorporated, 1987); *Cargill News*, May 1967.

6. For the early history of the efforts to develop a backhaul for the Company's Mississippi River barging, see Wayne G. Broehl, Jr., *Cargill: Trading the World's Grain*, op. cit., pp. 742, 779, 880. The announcement of the purchase of the Belle Isle property, *Cargill News*, April 1961; construction, ibid., October 1961; expansion, ibid., October–November 1961.

7. Excerpt from *Cargill News* on the Belle Isle fire, April–May 1968; there was extensive newspaper coverage of the fire and its immediate aftermath. The New Orleans *Times-Picayune*, March 9, 1968, contains the verbatim report of the Bureau of Mines inspector, CA 6V5F. The report is entitled "Final Report on Major Mine-Fire Disaster, Belle Isle Salt Mine, Cargill, Incorporated, St. Mary Parish, Louisiana," dated March 5, 1968, and issued by District D of the Bureau of Mines, CA 5C1B. See also "Cargill Should Be Shut Down Until Safe," *True Scope* (Lafayette, La.) circa February 23, 1969. For an excellent description of the subsequent seven years of Belle Isle, see "Belle Isle Mine Digs Salt, Sinks Shaft, Hopes for a Change of Luck," *Cargill News*, January–February 1975; the 1979 explosion, ibid., May–June 1979; the Final Report of the U.S. Mine Health and Safety Administration, June 8, 1979, CA 5L7B; quotation from U.S. Department of Labor, MSHA, press release, May 1, 1980, CA 5C1B. The permanent closing, *Cargill News*, January–February 1984. Cayuga Salt acquisition, *Green Wave*, April 2, 1970; Gordy Salt, ibid., August 4, 1971; Barton Salt, ibid., June 9, 1972; Watkins Salt, ibid., December 29, 1976; Leslie Salt, ibid., March 27, 1978.

8. Dana G. Dalrymple, *Imports and Plantings of High-yielding Varieties of Wheat and Rice in the Less Developed Nations*, Foreign Economic Development Report 14 (Washington, D.C.: U.S. Department of Agriculture and U.S. Agency for International Development, 1972), and*Measuring the Green Revolution: The Impact of Research on Wheat and Rice Development* (Washington, D.C.: Foreign Development Division, Economic Research Service, USDA and AID, 1975); Dana G. Dalrymple and James R. Sayre, *Indexes of Agricultural Development: Less Developed Countries, 1970* (Washington, D.C.: Foreign Economic Development Service and AID, 1971).

9. For Cargill's and Grain and Feed Dealers National Association's opposition to International Grains Arrangement, see the testimony of William R. Pearce and his position paper for the Association in *International Grains Arrangement of 1967*, hearings before Subcommittee of the Committee on Foreign Relations, U.S. Senate, 90th Cong., 2nd sess., March 26, April 4 and 9, 1968, pp. 43ff, 118ff. See also Grain and Feed Dealers National Association, "Appraisal of International Grains Arrangement," January 2, 1968, CA 5H6F; W. R. Pearce, "Remarks," U.S. Foreign Trade Outlook Session, National Foreign Trade Convention, November 20, 1968, CA 5E1F. For an excellent overall summary of international grain agreements, see Richard Gilmore, *A Poor Harvest: The Clash of Policies and Interests in the Grain Trade* (New York: Longman, 1982), pp. 181–97; see also Dan Morgan, *Merchants of Grain*, op. cit., pp. 182–83, 186. "Agatha Christie mystery novel," John Freivalds, *Grain Trade: The Key to World Power and Human Survival* (New York: Stein and Day, 1976), p. 158.

10. Excerpts from Cargill annual reports, 1967–1968 and 1968–1969. For Houston terminal, *Cargill News*, June 1968. Unit train history, Interstate Commerce Commission *Ex Parte 307*, "Investigation into the Distribution and Manipulation of Rail Rolling Stock to Depress Prices on Certain Grain Shipments for Export, 357 ICC 819, July 18, 1977; for Cargill's early experience, "A Background Paper Setting Forth Cargill's Basic Position in Regard to the Issues in Ex Parte 307," CA 6W7F; testimony of James P. Springrose in *Small Business Problems Involved in the Marketing of Grain and Other Commodities*, hearings before the Special Subcommittee on Small Business Problems, Permanent Select Committee on Small Business, House of Representatives, 93rd Cong., 2nd sess., June 11–July 31, 1974, p. 1104; *Cargill News*, October–November 1968; December 1968; April–May 1969. The "white paper" of Kelm is "International Organization," August 22, 1966, CA 5K4B; the following memoranda were background papers for the board meeting of July 31–August 1, 1968: Erwin E. Kelm, "Divisional Officers," June 28, 1968; ibid., "Planning for Realignment of Executive Responsibilities," June 28, 1968; Fred Seed, "Integration of International Investments between Divisions," July 3, 1968, CA 6O8F. "Proliferation," James R. Cargill to E. E. Kelm, March 23, 1968, ibid. See board minutes, December 17, 1968, for bylaw changes re new senior executive titles and the appointments to these posts.

11. For biographical note on Cargill MacMillan's death, see *Green Wave*, October 16, 1968.

12. "Serious difficulties," *Cargill Annual Report*, 1968–1969; "impossible to show black figures," "Tradax Operating Results to Date and Projected Earnings for 1968–1969," Long Range Planning Committee meetings, March 1969, CA 5K4B; "couldn't have done better," Tradax annual report to shareholders, June 1, 1968–May 31, 1969. Erv Kelm memorandum asking for suggestions for possible new endeavors, March 18, 1969; compendium of suggestions at Long Range Planning committee meeting of April 21, 1969; 15 top choices in memorandum to the committee from A. R. Baldwin of that date, CA 5L7F.

4. *Three Strong Years (pp. 141–82)*

1. Instructions for board of directors meeting, Fred Seed to division heads, July 8, 1969, CA 5K4B; Barney Saunders remarks at the July 24, 1969, meeting, CA 5K4F. Long Range Planning Committee minutes, CA 5L7F. Robert Harrigan dissatisfaction in his letter to the Grain Division of December 8, 1969; see J. P. Cole and I. M. Hyland to Harrigan, December 18, 1969, ibid.

2. Discussion of corporate goals was at board of directors meeting of July 31, 1969, *Minutes,* pp. 15–19, 20.

3. The Kelm memorandum on "Executive Correspondence" was written to "all managers and superintendents," and dated June 10, 1963, CA, Robert Woodworth files, Lake 6, 1963. Quotation from *Business Week* article, "Keeping Their Success in the Family," December 9, 1967. Newspaper articles on the Harvard Business School Club of Minneapolis and St. Paul award banquet, *Minneapolis Star,* October 30, 1969, and *Minneapolis Tribune,* ibid. See also *Green Wave,* October 31, 1969, and *Cargill News,* November–December 1969.

4. "We can avoid telling the whole world," John MacMillan, Jr., to Ed Grimes, May 4, 1934, CA 35-07; "hybrid power," Dan Morgan, *Merchants of Grain,* op. cit., p. 314; "anything can happen," Pearsall Helms, Tradax Annual Report, 1961–1962, p. 4. Antonio Marino replacement, "Hybrid Corn Research and Development—Nature of Some Company Crop Research Problems in Argentina and Brazil," n.d., circa June 1969, CA, Heinz Hutter MS, CA; "grow with the host country," Heinz Hutter speech to Tradax management, May 1971, ibid. On Argentinization, Calvin Anderson memorandum, May 17, 1971, ibid. On inflation, see Heinz Hutter, "Speech Delivered at Innisbrook, Florida for Poultry Products Department Meeting," June 29, 1974, ibid.

5. For early International Basic Economy Corporation joint venture, see Wayne G. Broehl, Jr., *Cargill: Trading the World's Grain,* op. cit., pp. 722–23.

6. Alfalfa adulteration case, Broehl, op. cit., pp. 749–50. Russian sunflower seed exchanges, *Cargill News,* August 1968; announcement of Cargill variety, Public Affairs Release Book, February 1970, CA 5C8F. See also A. Richard Baldwin, "Economic Significance of Sunflowers in World Trade," paper presented to the Fourth International Sunflower Conference, Memphis, Tenn., June 23–25, 1970, CA 5C8F; "Report on Sunflower Project," September 1967, CA, Heinz Hutter MS.

7. Betty Fussell, *The Story of Corn* (New York: Alfred A. Knopf, 1992), p. 93. "Darwinian quirk," *New York Times,* August 23, 1970; "next year's seed corn," ibid., October 3, 1970; "blight spores there," ibid., February 7, 1971; "another mutant enemy," ibid., April 18, 1971.

8. South Africa imports, February 3, 1971, Public Affairs Release Book, January–March 1971, CA 5C8F; imports banned, March 17, 1971, ibid. Argentine and French imports, ibid., March 5, 1971.

9. P-A-G market share calculations, "Memo for the File re Proposed Acquisition of P-A-G," January 28, 1971, CA Law 1–637.

10. Edward Hughes, "Pink Death in Iraq," *Times* (London), September 9, 1973, reprinted in *Readers Digest,* November 1973. For Cargill analysis, Bob Fahs to John F. McGrory, March 30, 1972, CA 5G5F. See also *New York Times,* July 19, 1973. For mention of Cargill, see "Statement of Senator Gaylord Nelson on H.R. 10729, the Federal Environmental Pesticide Control Act of 1971 . . . before the Senate Commerce Subcommittee on the Environment," June 15, 1972. See also Leonard M. Mayer to McGrory, April 20, 1972, CA 5G5F; H. Rustam and T. Hamdi, "Methyl Mercury Poisoning in Iraq," *Brain* (1974): 97, 499–510; Laman Amin-Zaki and others, "Intrauterine Methylmercury Poisoning in Iraq," *Pediatrics* 54 :587–95; The Use of Mercury and Alternative Compounds as Seed Dressings: Report of Joint FAO/WHO meeting (WHO Technical Report Series No. 555, 1974).

11. Julius Hendel death, *Cargill News,* March–April 1972. For history of Cargill's training programs in the 1960s and early 1970s, Sidney Burkett, "Musings on the Growth of the Organization/Employee Development Function at Cargill," n.d., CA 4C6F. See also William R. LaFollette and Richard Fleming, "The History of Management by Objectives," *CPCU Journal,* 35: 225–27; the authors attribute MBO to Peter Drucker's 1954 book, *The Practice of Management.* For views of Cargill MBO, see Heinz Hutter to R. Pearsall Helms, May 14, 1971; Helms to Hutter, May 25, 1971; H. Robert Diercks to Hutter, June 11, 1971, CA, Heinz Hutter MS.

12. Minneapolis bombing of Federal Building, *New York Times,* August 18, 1971; St. Paul bombing, ibid., September 2, 1970. The quotations on the Cargill Building evacuation, *Cargill News,* October 1970. Letter bombs, *Minneapolis Tribune,* June 15 and 16, 1976.

13. Comparison of "seven food processors," CA 3C4B; "Financial Review of Continental Grain Company," ibid., 1 5N1B.

5. A Surprise (pp. 183–224)

1. For specific items included in President Nixon's executive order, see *New York Times*, June 11, 1971. The embargo on trade with Mainland China had been imposed by President Harry S. Truman when China entered the Korean War; the shipping rule that 50% of all shipments of grain to the Soviet Union had to be in U.S.-registered ships was promulgated by President Kennedy in 1963 (see note 20 in Chapter One). For analysis of the negotiations between Secretary of State Henry Kissinger and International Longshoremen president Thomas W. "Teddy" Gleason, see Dan Morgan, op. cit., p. 197.

2. The licensing requirements at this time were contained in the Export Administration Act of 1969. For a discussion of the change in reporting requirements in 1971, see Tyler Sanford Biggs, "Political Economy of East-West Trade: The Case of the 1972–1973 U.S.–Russian Wheat Deal," Ph.D. diss., University of California–Berkeley, 1976, pp. 131–32; James Trager, *Amber Waves of Grain* (New York: Arthur Fields Books, 1973), p. 19.

3. Tradax International S.A. and Subsidiaries, report to shareholders, June 1, 1964–May 31, 1965, p. 3., CA.

4. Statement of Clarence D. Palmby in *Sale of Feed Grains to Russia*, hearing before the Subcommittee on Livestock and Grains and the Subcommittee on Department Operations of the Committee on Agriculture, House of Representatives, 92nd Cong., 1st sess., December 8, 1971, pp. 2–14. For the October discussions between the government and the Longshoremen's union, see *Southwestern Miller*, November 16, 1972, and Morgan, *Merchants of Grain*, op. cit., p. 190. The actual grain negotiations were reported in *Southwestern Miller*, November 9, 1971; Michel Fribourg, president of Continental Grain, and Fred Seed, president of Cargill, were quoted in the article.

5. Rep. Eligio de la Garza (Texas), *Sale of Feed Grains to Russia*, op. cit., p. 19.

6. *Des Moines Register*, November 21, 1971, quoted in *Sale of Feed Grains to Russia*, op. cit., p. 24.

7. On Russian crop failure, *New York Times*, February 6, 1972, and March 4, 1972; Russian grain purchases from Canada, ibid., February 29, 1972. See also Mary E. Wilson, "U.S. Agriculture's Stake in Improving Trade with the USSR," USDA, *Foreign Agriculture*, June 12, 1972, and March 20, 1972. The Earl Butz report of possible "$200 million sales yearly," ibid., April 13, 1972. The progress of the mission and its result are analyzed in detail in the Butz testimony in *Sale of Wheat to Russia*, hearings before the Subcommittee on Livestock and Grains of the Committee on Agriculture, House of Representatives, 92nd Cong., 2nd sess., September 14, 18, and 19, 1972, pp. 5–6, 210–14. See also the detailed chronology provided by Clarence D. Palmby in *Russian Grain Transactions*, hearings before the Permanent Subcommittee on Investigations, Committee on Government Operations, U.S. Senate, 93rd Cong., 1st sess., part 1, July 20, 23, and 24, 1973, pp. 14–21.

8. "If we had had a choice . . . ," Earl Butz's testimony, *Sale of Wheat to Russia*, op. cit., September 14, 1972, pp. 6–7. For President Nixon's visit to Moscow, *New York Times*, May 26, 1972; the Maritime Pact was signed there on May 29, 1972. The progression in the winterkill during the spring of 1972 is documented in the Palmby chronology in *Russian Grain Transactions*, July 20, 1973, pp. 14–21. For the Humphrey/Bellmon report, see "Observations on Soviet and Polish Agriculture, November–December, 1972," a trip report by Hubert H. Humphrey and Henry Bellmon, U.S. Senate Committee on Agriculture and Forestry, 93rd Cong. 1st. sess., January 11, 1973 (see also report to Joint Economic Committee, "Observations on East-West Economic Relations U.S.S.R. and Poland," February 16, 1973).

9. The White House fact sheet, "Agreement between the Government of the Union of Soviet Socialist Republics [and] the Government of the United States of America with Respect to Purchase of Grains by the Soviet Union in the United States and Credit to be Made Available by the United States," July 8, 1972. See also *New York Times*, July 9, 1972; news release of Claude Clifford, USDA, July 14, 1972. Press conference remarks from "U.S.–USSR Grain Purchase Agreement," *Weekly Compilation of Presidential Documents*, week ending July 15, 1972. Full texts of Peter G. Peterson–Earl L. Butz press conference in *Russian Grain Transactions*, July 20, 1973, op. cit., pp. 232–41.

10. Butz, "I have no idea," ibid., p. 236.

11. James Trager, *Amber Waves of Grain*, op. cit., p. 28.

12. Clarence Palmby was questioned on his resignation from the USDA and subsequent employment with Continental Grain Co. in *Sale of Wheat to Russia*, September 14, 18, and 19, 1972, op. cit., pp. 192–225. Bernard Steinweg testimony, *Russian Grain Transactions*, July 20, 23, and 24, 1973, pp. 51–90; "lion's share," pp. 55–56. Steinweg statement of his conversation with Carroll Brunthaver on July 6, ibid., p. 56.

13. The chronology of the July 1972 Cargill negotiations with the Russian mission is described in the testimony of Walter B. Saunders, *Sales of Wheat to Russia*, September 14, 18 and 19, 1972, op. cit., pp. 226–66 (also reprinted in *Russian Grain Transactions*, part 2, October 9, 1973, op. cit., pp. 291–305). See also "Narrative," n.d., CA.

14. "How much . . . can you believe?" James Trager, *Amber Waves of Grain*, op. cit., p. 48. Visas "to renegotiate with Continental Grain," in *Russian Grain Transactions*, July 20, 23, and 24, 1973, op. cit., p. 20.

15. Bernard Steinweg testimony ("shocked to learn"), *Russian Grain Transactions*, part 1, July 20, 23, and 24, 1973, op. cit., p. 57.

16. For documentation of the Cargill negotiations, see note 13, above. Ergot problems are discussed in G. L. Carefoot and E. R. Sprott, *Famine on the Wind* (New York: Rand McNally, 1967). See also John G. Fuller, *The Day of St. Anthony's Fire* (New York: Macmillan, 1968); James Trager, *Amber Waves of Grain*, op. cit., pp. 68–69; Frank J. Bove, *The Story of Ergot* (Basel: S. Karger, 1970).

17. James Trager, *Amber Waves of Grain*, op cit., p. 27.

18. "U.S.S.R. Wheat Purchase Believed to Exceed 100 Million Bushels," *Southwestern Miller,* July 25, 1972; "U.S.S.R. Negotiates for More Grain," ibid., August 1, 1972; "Massive Additional Wheat Purchases by U.S.S.R.," ibid, August 8, 1972. Sosland later reported (in his issue of October 3, 1972) that he had been receiving unsolicited telephone calls form a mysterious stranger calling himself "John Smith," who seemed unusually prescient about the Russians' intentions. Over many weeks, Smith's calls, alleged by him to be originating from London, had made predictions on the size of the Russian sales that subsequently were corroborated by the facts. Sosland had no way of knowing who Smith was or what persuasion he spoke from and was wary of trusting him. Nevertheless, Sosland related, he *did* incorporate some of the Smith "predictions" in the *Southwestern Miller* articles, although keeping them conservatively stated. See the issues of July 18 and 25 and August 1 and 8, 1972, for these predictions; the full story of Smith, "Publication's Editors at Center of Wheat Intrigue," is in the October 3 issue (note that *Southwestern Miller* became *Milling and Baking News* on October 3, 1972). See also *New York Times*, October 21 and 27; James Trager, *Amber Waves of Grain*, op. cit., pp. 47–67.

19. For initial OMB role in early August 1972, see *Russian Grain Transactions*, part 1, July 20, 23, and 24, 1973, op. cit., pp. 14–21; the chronology of OMB involvement is elaborated, ibid, p. 20. William A. Morrell, former assistant director of OMB, testified in these hearings (pp. 202–11).

20. W. B. Saunders, *Sale of Wheat to Russia*, September 14, 18, and 19, 1972, op. cit., p. 236.

21. "News Release from Pete du Pont" (Senator Pierre du Pont), August 29 and September 6, 1972; news release, National Farmers Union, August 29, 1972; "A Private Club for Grain Exporters?" *New York Times*, August 30, 1972; "Ex-Aides' Role Hit in Soviet Grain Deal," *Washington Post*, August 31, 1972; "A Few Questions about the Grain Deal," ibid., September 1, 1972; "GAO Will Probe U.S. Sale of Wheat to the Soviet Union," ibid., September 7, 1972; "McGovern Alleges Grain Sale Abuse," *New York Times*, September 9, 1972, "U.S.–Soviet Deal on Grain Becomes Campaign Issue," ibid., September 10, 1972; Cargill announcement of September 8, 1972, in *Green Wave*, September 12, 1972; "The Anatomy of a Subsidy," *Journal of Commerce*, September 13, 1972; "Wheat Subsidy Debacle," *New York Times*, September 13, 1972.

22. Hard winter wheat prices for 1972 from *Commodity Year Book* 1973. (New York: Commodity Research Bureau, 1973), p. 367. Senator George McGovern press conference, *New York Times,* September 9, 1972; *Minneapolis Tribune*, ibid. Cargill's W. B. Saunders was queried about this statement concerning grain still held locally in his testimony before the Subcommittee on Livestock and Grains; see *Sale of Wheat to Russia*, op. cit., p. 245. Asked if "this benefit which resulted then was not accruing to exporters but to local interests in rural areas," Saunders answered, "That is correct." "Cargill believes it was 'screwed,'" *Business Week*, September 30, 1972.

23. Secretary Butz, "we did not know about it," in *Sale of Wheat to Russia*, September 14, 18, and 19, 1972, op. cit., p. 7. Bernard Steinweg, "spoke with Brunthaver," in *Russian Grain Transactions*, op. cit., part 1, July 20, 23, and 24, 1973, p. 56. Carroll Brunthaver, "doubt that a call was made," in *Russian Grain Transactions*, ibid., pp. 97, 101. Affidavits from Steinweg, Brunthaver, and Butz in *Russian Grain Transactions*, op. cit., October 9, 1973, part 2, pp. 252, 255, 257.

24. "Continental did not participate," Bernard Steinweg testimony, *Russian Grain Transactions*, op. cit., part 1, July 20, 23, and 24, 1973, p. 57.

25. For Department of Justice positions on CEA investigation of the six companies concerning form 204 (weekly report on cash and futures positions), see *Russian Grain Transactions*, op. cit., part 2, October 9, 1973, pp. 260–75; quotation from Exhibit 25I, letter of Henry E. Peterson, Assistant Attorney General, Department of Justice, to Senator Henry M. Jackson, September 4, 1973. See also testimony by Alex C. Caldwell, administrator of the CEA, *Russian Grain Transaction*, July 24, 1973, op. cit., pp. 163–201. Cargill reply, Exhibit 25G, pp. 271–72. In July 1972, the American Bakers Association reported to the CEA that it believed there was a manipulation of the September 1972 wheat futures on the Kansas City Board of Trade, allegedly done by the six grain trading companies "to influence the wheat export subsidy rates." The CEA's regional administrator investigated and found that "the price action . . . reacted the same as the other Kansas City wheat futures. In fact, the advance in the September future was less than that which occurred in the other futures." The administrator of the CEA, Alex C. Caldwill, disagreed and sent the case forward to the Attorney General for possible investigation by a grand jury. The Attorney General declined to act, and the Senate Subcommittee report (*Russian Grain Transactions*, op. cit., part 2, October 9, 1973, pp. 275–81) stated later:

> In regard to the conclusion of the CEA Administrator that the investigation showed that wheat futures were 'intentionally' raised to affect the USDA subsidy rate, the subcommittee staff found that CEA personnel had failed to inform themselves as to how the subsidy rates were published and how the grain companies registered for the subsidy. In the staff's opinion, this was crucial in any investigation to determine manipulation to affect the subsidy. In the opinion of the staff, the CEA investigation to disclose alleged manipulation to affect subsidy rates was completely misdirected in that the trading days selected for examination were not the trading days on which manipulation to affect the subsidy would have occurred.
>
> Furthermore, the recordkeeping failures of members of the Board made it difficult, if not impossible, to develop evidence of manipulation. The CEA failed to monitor the operations of the Kansas City Board of Trade members to assure that the recordkeeping was in good order.

The case completely died after that.

26. Testimony of Weldon V. Barton for National Farmers Union, *Sale of Wheat to Russia*, September 14, 1972, op. cit., pp. 92–112; chart, ibid., p. 95, was "supplied by the Agri-business [*sic*] Accountability Project. See also Martha Hamilton, *The Great American Grain Robbery and Other Stories* (Washington, D.C.: Agribusiness Accountability Project, Washington, 1972). "His aged mother," testimony of Earl Butz, ibid., p. 20. *Time* magazine article, "Campaign Fodder," September 18, 1972); Palmby was interviewed by Walter Cronkite, *CBS News Report*, September 27, 1972, CA 3E4F, "Jackson Committee" file. Quotations from Joseph T. Sneed, "Investigation of Matters Related to the United States–Soviet Union Grain Sale Agreement," *Russian Grain Transactions*, op. cit., part 1, July 20, 23, and 24, 1973, pp. 242–46. "I would strongly have counseled," Earl Butz testimony, ibid., p. 120.

27. The three articles in the *National Journal* on the "revolving door" were in its November 19, 1977 issue; Clarence Palmby mentioned in "The Revolving Door—It's Tricky to Try to Stop It," pp. 1798ff. President Jimmy Carter quotation, ibid.

28. Representative W. R. Poague on "my man down in McClennon County," *Sale of Wheat to Russia*, op. cit., September 14, 18, and 19, 1972, p. 90. "Kansas Farmers Stoic—Can't Win 'Em All in Wheat Game," *Kansas City Star*, September 17, 1972, is reprinted in ibid., pp. 143–46. Representative Keith G. Sebelius, "lot of people running for Congress," ibid., p. 191. Vote for additional compensation, *Washington Post*, September 21, 1972. Earl Butz, "farmers knew," *International Herald Tribune*, September 11, 1972. Cargill press release, September 8, 1972, CA.

29. See testimony of Charles W. Pence in *Sale of Wheat to Russia*, op. cit., September 14, 18 and 19, 1972, pp. 73–77. See also "Butz, Aides Deny Knowing of Any Grain Export Tip," *New York Times*, September 15, 1972; "Butz's Agency Says Aide Notified Grain Exporters," ibid., September 16, 1972. The Federal Bureau of Investigation report is in *Russian Grain Transactions*, op. cit., part 1, July 20, 23, and 24, 1973, p. 246.

30. Comptroller General of the United States, report to Congress, "Russian Wheat Sales and Weaknesses in Agriculture's Management of Wheat Export Subsidy Program," July 9, 1973; "Agriculture's Implementation of GAO's Wheat Export Subsidy Recommendations and Related Matters," ibid., March 3, 1976. "Limited, fragmented, and generally inadequate response," ibid., p.6; "market-oriented, full-production position," ibid., p. 7; "interfere as little as possible," p. 17; "use their elaborate affiliate relationships," ibid., p. 17. For discussion of GAO's earlier "interim report," see *New York Times*, November 4, 1972.

31. Senator George McGovern on suspension of Secretary Earl Butz, *New York Times*, September 18, 1972. Vice President Spiro Agnew's assertion concerning proposed FBI investigation, ibid., September 20, 1972. "Agnew error," ibid., September 21, 1972. See also "Agnew Disputes Account of Wheat Inquiry Origin," ibid., September 22, 1972.

32. "To Board of Directors, Cargill Incorporated, " Peat, Marwick, Mitchell & Co., Minneapolis, November 1, 1972, CA. Cargill, Inc., "The Russian Grain Sales and the Role of Cargill, Incorporated," November 1, 1972, CA. Cargill's press release was dated November 2, 1972, CA. See also Steve Schiffman, Carl Byoir & Associates, Inc., "Cargill Reveals Loss on Wheat to Russia," CA, 3E8B; *Green Wave*, November 2, 1972.

33. For press reaction see, especially, *New York Times*, November 3, 1972; "Cargill Treated Unfairly," *Springfield* (IL) *State Journal*, November 20, 1972; "What Windfall?" *Council Bluffs Nonpareil*, November 29, 1972; "Sounds Like the McCoy," *Rocky Mountain News*, November 8, 1972; "supposed to be a scandal," *Gulfport Herald*, ibid.; "Charges against others," *Benson Monitor*, November 10, 1972; "Auditors can arrange figures," Hammond *Star*, November 7, 1972; "First time in 107 year history," *Tulsa Daily World*, November 20, 1972.

34. For GAO "interim report," see *New York Times*, November 4, 1972; for verbatim use of GAO news release, including paragraph on Cargill losses, see, for example, *La Crosse (Wisconsin) Tribune*, November 5, 1972; *Olympian* (Olympia Washington), November 5, 1972.

35. "Reneged," *New York Times*, October 15, 1972; this article also enumerates the final agreement reached (the 40 ports in the United States are listed here). See also *Journal of Commerce*, September 18, 1972. I.L.A. demand for prisoner release, *New York Times*, September 26, 1972. "Absolute rate," *Washington Post*, November 17, 1972. "Stifling of competition," *Journal of Commerce*, October 18, 1972.

6. *Years of High Drama (pp. 229–65)*

1. For discussion of dividend policies in the generations of John MacMillan, Sr., John, Jr., Austen Cargill, and Cargill MacMillan, Sr., see Wayne G. Broehl, Jr., *Cargill: Trading the World's Grain* , op. cit., pp. 226–28; 362–63; 816–19. For policy of 1964, minutes of Board of Directors, July 20. See also Fred M. Seed to Board of Directors, December 15, 1970.

2. See Robert L. Lumpkins, "Participion Allotment Plan (PAP) — Notes," March 27, 1973, Lumpkins files. See Board of Directors minutes, July 29,1975, for the reaffirmation of the Incentive Compensation Plan Fund and the exact provisions of its various components: the Cash Bonus Plan, the Participation in Equity Growth (PEG) Plan, the Performance Share Units (PSU) Plan, the Stock Bonus Plan and the Participation Allotment Plan (PAP). The Company's management incentives were discussed again in the board meeting of July 25, 1977; the document "Corporate Incentive Program" was incorporated in the minutes.

3. In "Corporate and Division Goals and Objectives," October 1, 1973, decentralization was once again formally reaffirmed: "We will continue to support the principle of decentralization of operating management wherever practicable." See *Green Wave*, June 25, 1973.

4. Albert G. Egermayer for the board of directors, November 13, 1967, minutes of board; "guideline range," minutes of July 24, 1973; "aggressive diversification, " July 17, 1967; "not closely associated with agriculture," July 23, 1969; "CMD and Tradax goals stated separately," July 21, 1971; "cyclical nature," July 27, 1972.

5. "No dabbling in small ventures," minutes of board of directors, July 24, 1973.

6. Material taken from *Division Annual Reports* and *Summary of Division Annual Reports* for the Company.

7. Quotations from Richard Gilmore, *A Poor Harvest*, op. cit, pp. 147–48, 149–50, 152. "Grain Surpluses Almost Sold Out," *New York Times*, April 23, 1973; "unprecedented reporting system, ibid., April 22; new inflation measures of President Nixon, ibid., June 14; "dealers in

quandary," ibid., June 15; halting of soybean trading, ibid., June 22; for embargo effects, ibid., June 28 and 29; "private contracts abrogated," *Milling and Baking News*, July 3, 1973; "angry at Nixon-san," *New York Times*, July 7; French president Pompidou's complaint, ibid., July 12 and July 18; shift to soybeans in Brazil, ibid., August 8; "confidence is lacking," ibid., September 4. For underlying issues of inflation I have drawn on Joel Popkin (ed.), *Analysis of Inflation: 1965–1974*, National Bureau of Economic Research, Studies in Income and Wealth, Vol. 42, (Cambridge; Mass.: Ballinger Publishing Co., 1977); Dale Hathaway, "Food Prices and Inflation," *Brookings Papers on Economic Activity*, 1 (1974): 63–116; Michael R. Darby, "Price and Wage Controls: The First Two Years," in Karl Brunner and Allan H. Meltzer (eds.), *The Economics of Price and Wage Controls* (Amsterdam: North-Holland Publishing Co., 1976).

8. *Multinational Corporations and United States Foreign Policy,* hearings before the Subcommittee on Multinational Corporations of the Committee on Foreign Policy, U.S. Senate, 94th Cong., 2nd sess., part 16, June 18, 23, and 24, 1976; Cargill testimony, pp. 99ff; embargo, pp. 160–62 and Appendix, pp. 214ff; cancellation question, pp. 242–48; formula price discussion, p. 246. "Deferred delivery privilege," Cargill news release, July 30, 1973; public response, *New York Times*, July 31, 1973; "Send person to Washington," Cargill Processing Group, 1973–1974 Annual Report, part 2, CA 5N3F; Tradax Internacional S.A. and Subsidiaries, Annual Report to Shareholders, 1973–1974, CA 5N6F. Robbin S. Johnson, "The Role of the Public Affairs Department in Cargill," Processing and Refining Group, December 6, 1973; John McGrory quotation, ibid., p. 7. See also *Green Wave*, June 4, 1973 and January 8, 1974; *Cargill News*, June–July 1974. Joel Solkoff, "Cargill's Private Empire," *New Republic*, December 18, 1976; John Freivalds, *Grain Trade*, op. cit., p. 118; Dan Morgan, *Merchants of Grain*, op. cit., p. 326.

9. "Why did it take 10 or 11 months?" *Russian Grain Transactions,* op. cit., part 1, July 23, 1973, pp. 125–26; John J. Walsh description of chronology of Departments of Commerce and Agriculture reporting systems, ibid., part 2; pp. 281–82. "System proved unworkable," Richard Gilmore, *A Poor Harvest*, op. cit., 153; Dan Morgan, *Merchants of Grain*, op. cit., pp. 294–95. The story of the Cook/Continental meeting with President Ford is also recounted in *New York Times*, October 9, 1974. For a chronology of reporting requirements, see Charles O'Dell, Grains Program Area, ERS, CED, USDA, reprinted in Harvard Business School, "Continental Grain Company—Export Controls," 4–375-182, 1974, Exhibit 1.

10. Barry Bosworth and Wayne Vroman, "An Appraisal of the Wage-Price Control Program" in Joel Popkin (ed.), *Analysis of Inflation: 1965–1974* (Cambridge, Mass.: Ballinger Publishing Company, 1977), pp. 80, 99. See also Cargill memorandum, "Review of Grain Developments in the 1970's and Implications for the Future," CA 3F7B.

11. "Grain Transportation Problems, Responses of Federal Railroad Administration, Department of Transportation, to Inquiries of the Subcommittee on Special Small Business Problems, House Select Committee on Small Business," July 31, 1974, in *Small Business Problems Involved in the Marketing of Grain and Other Commodities, Vol. 2:, Transportation*, part B, hearings before the Subcommittee on Special Small Business Problems, Permanent Select Committee on Small Business, House of Representatives, 93rd Cong., 2nd sess., June 11, 14, 25, 26, and 28, July 25, 29, and 31, 1974, p. 1104.

12. Unit train history, Interstate Commerce Commission *Ex Parte 307*, "Investigation into the Distribution and Manipulation of Rail Rolling Stock to Depress Prices on Certain Grain Shipments for Export," 357 ICC 819, July 18, 1977. For Cargill's early experience see "A Background Paper Setting Forth Cargill's Basic Position with Regard to the Issues in Ex Parte 307," CA 6W7F (quotation "pretty urgent buyer," p. 33); testimony of James V. Springrose in *Small Business Problems Involved in the Marketing of Grain*, Appendix 1, Subcommittee on Special Small Business Problems, op. cit., pp. 785–99. See also testimony of James R. Spicola, ibid., pp. 80–132.

13. Export statistics from *Ex Parte 307*, "Investigation into the Distribution and Manipulation of Rail Rolling Stock," op. cit., Appendix 2; covered hopper car equipment, ibid., Appendix 8.

14. General Accounting Office field visit to Houston port, testimony of Darrell E. Eminhizer in *Small Business Problems in the Marketing of Grain*, Vol. 2, part A, op. cit., p. 219; James Springrose testimony, ibid., p. 787.

15. GAO, "Alleged Discriminations and Concessions in the Allocation of Railcars to Grain Shippers," B-114824, December 30, 1974; quotation that "Interstate Commerce Commission should be doing something it had not done" in cover letter in report addressed to Rep. John Melcher.

16. Quotations on "small shipper" in House Report No. 93-1529, *Small Business Problems Involved in the Marketing of Grain and Other Commodities, Vol. 2: Transportation: A Report of the Subcommittee on Special Small Business Problems*, 93d Cong., 2nd sess., December 9, 1974, pp. 57, 86. Testimony of George M. Stafford, chairman, Interstate Commerce Commission, *Small Business Problems Involved in the Marketing of Grain*, Vol. 2, part B, July 25, 1974, pp. 917–1034.

17. "Grain exporters involved," *Journal of Commerce*, March 6, 1975; "gouging grain farmers," *Des Moines Register*, March 13, 1975; Freedom of Information Act proceedings, *Journal of Commerce*, May 16, 1975; "at least eight grain merchandising companies," *Washington Star*, July 21, 1975; see also *Washington Post*, July 22, 1975. James Springrose quotation is from his "Verified Statement before the Interstate Commerce Commission, *Ex Parte 307*, n.d. (circa May 12, 1976), p. 73, CA 5H2B.

18. "Allegations not demonstrated" in "Investigation into the Distribution and Manipulation of Rail Rolling Stock," *Ex Parte 307*, op. cit., p. 92; "resolved in Cargill's favor," ibid., p. 71. For details of Joice, Iowa, country elevator, see "Brief of Cargill, Incorporated, Respondent before the Interstate Commerce Commission," *Ex Parte 307*, September 30, 1976, pp. 72–75.

19. Quotations from final decision in *Ex Parte 307* (see note 12 for citation): "obvious result of the matured unit train system," p. 70; "resolved by us in Cargill's favor," p. 71; "carried out by the exporters themselves," p. 87; "allegations of abuses have not been demonstrated," p. 92; "consecutive-trip provisions should be conditioned," p. 97. See also *Milmine Grain Company v. Norfolk & Western Railway Company, Interstate Commerce Commission Reports*, 352 ICC 575, February 5, 1976.

7. *The "Grain Scandal" (pp. 267–93)*

1. Harvard Business School, "Cargill, Inc.—Managing Corporate Public Policy in a Changing External Environment," Intercollegiate Case Clearing House, 4-578-088, 1977. For alleged grain inspection and grading practices, see "Outline of Charges Made Against Grain Firms and Others Involved in Export Marketing Activities," Cargill internal memorandum, June 17, 1975, CA 5J5F.

2. A number of Company internal documents elaborate the chronology of the grain irregularities story; see "The Grain Scandal in Perspective," June 23, 1975, CA 5J8F; "The Grain Inspection Controversy," October 9, 1975, CA 3F7B; "Review of Grain Developments in the 1970's and Implications for the Future," circa June 1976, CA 3F7B; "Grain Investigation Chronology," February 3, 1978, CA 5E3B. For the August 1974, indictments, see U.S. Department of Agriculture and Department of Justice news releases, August 8, 1974. Revised cleanliness examinations for grain ships, *Journal of Commerce*, August 15, 1974. The January 1976 case involving inspectors at Cargill's Baton Rouge terminal is noted in Robbin Johnson to Bill Pearce, March 1, 1978, CA 5E3B.

3. "Grain Ships: Dirt, Bribes," and "Grain Inspection Fraud," *Des Moines Register*, May 6, 1975. Sen. Dick Clark (Iowa) speech, *Congressional Register*, May 12, 1975. See also W. R. Pearce to E. E. Kelm and others, June 23, 1975, CA 5J8F. The Senate hearings were entitled "Grain Inspection," Subcommittee on Foreign Agricultural Policy and the Subcommittee on Agricultural Production, Marketing and the Stabilization of Prices of the Committee on Agriculture and Forestry, 94th Cong., 1st sess., June 19, July 8, August 14 and 15, September 25 and 26, 1975, and 94th Cong., 2nd sess., February 20, March 11, 12, and 16, 1976.

4. Dan Morgan column in May 21, 1975, *Washington Post* was reprinted in *Congressional Record*, June 7, 1975. "Foreign Fuss About U.S. Grain Quality Involves More Than Inspection Problem," *Wall Street Journal*, June 20, 1975; "Two Major Grain Companies Reportedly Under Inquiry," *New York Times*, June 25, 1975; "Peavey, Cargill Say Grain Probe Not Directed at Them," *Minneapolis Star*, May 29, 1975.

5. "Foreign Buyer Complaint Files," memorandum from Garland West, August 28, 1975, CA 3E8B. See also Rodney L. Elam, USDA, to West, July 21, 1975, with attached listing of cases. For discussion of the "confidentiality" of the USDA examination in Italy, West to L. L. Free, Office of Investigation, USDA, September 8, 1975, ibid. Telex copy of letter from Italian Grain Association to Ambassador John A. Volpe, Cargill wire 062370623, May 16, 1975, CA 3I6B. On problem with Turkish contracts, see *Minneapolis Tribune*, May 23, 1975, *Wall Street Journal*, July 2, 1975; Cargill telex, Tradax to Minneapolis, 0953/0954, May 13, 1975, CA 3I6B. In late May 1975, Conti-

nental Grain Co. approached Cargill about the possibility of establishing a "Webb Pomerene" corporation for a joint endeavor in settling the Turkish claims of both ccmpanies; once again, Cargill declined this approach. See "Memo to File," John F. McGrory, May 22, 1975, CA 3I6B.

6. Walter B. Saunders, "Problems in Handling Grain for Overseas Sale," *Minneapolis Tribune*, July 13, 1975; editorial response, "Investigating the Grain Trade." Fred M. Seed letter to employees, dated June 16, 1975, CA 5J5F.

7. On initial sales to Russia by Cook and Cargill, *New York Times*, July 17, 1975; *Des Moines Register*, ibid. Sales by Canada, *Bloomington Pantagraph*, ibid. Continental Grain sale, *Fargo Forum*, July 22. "Sales won't raise prices," *Des Moines Register*, August 1. Additional public reaction, "Grain Deals with Russia Are Still Marked by Secrecy," *New York Times*, July 20; "rapacious unions," ibid., August 20; "George Meany's Demagoguery," *Baltimore Sun*, ibid. Meany meeting with Pres. Ford, ibid., August 27; *Washington Star*, ibid. Temporary injunction, *New York Times*, August 28. Final agreement between U.S. and U.S.S.R., Presidential Documents of Gerald R. Ford, 1975, Vol. 11, No. 43, October 20, 1975. See Dan Morgan account in his *Merchants of Grain*, op. cit., chap. 11. See also *Grain Sales to the Soviet Union*, hearings before the Permanent Subcommittee on Investigations of the Committee on Government Operations, United States Senate, 94th Cong., 1st sess., July 31 and August 1, 1975.

8. Statement of Company goals, Whitney MacMillan to "Fellow Employees," November 5, 1975, CA 5I7B.

9. "Cargill Affirmative Action Program—Summary of Major Commitments Undertaken," *Cargill News*, Public Relations Department, March 16, 1976, CA 5D5B; USDA press release of this date elaborates the 13 specific commitments. See also *Washington Post*, March 17, 1976; *Wall Street Journal* and *Minneapolis Tribune*, ibid. "Taken the initiative," *Feedstuffs*, March 22, 1976. Quotations on implementation from "Memo to the File," March 26, CA 3E8B. Problems of Houston terminal, D. J. Berkley to Task Force members, June 25, CA 5D5B. On its overhaul, Berkley to David R. Galliart, director, Grain Division, AMS, USDA, ibid.

10. For Bunge Corporation case, see *New York Times*, December 3 and 20, 1975; the Archer-Daniels-Midland Co. and the Garnac Grain Co. cases, ibid., March 5, 1976. Polish ship inspection at Cook Industries export terminal at Destrehan, La., *Des Moines Register*, January 7, 1976; *New York Times*, January 19. Substantial coverage of the Polish ship incident, including pictures, is in *Grain Inspection*, hearings before the Subcommittee on Foreign Agriculture Policy . . . , part 7, March 12, 1976; quotation from Edward W. Cook, p. 129. Nolo contendere pleas of Cook Industries and Mississippi River Grain Elevator, Inc., *Wall Street Journal*, May 7 and August 18, 1976; *Des Moines Register*, September 24, 1976. Continental Grain Co. case, *Des Moines Register*, May 5, 1976. "Not much deterrence," ibid., May 11, 1976.

11. Indictment at Cargill Baton Rouge terminal, *New York Times*, January 20, 1976; *Des Moines Register*, ibid., *Minneapolis Star*, January 21. Accusations against Cargill, *New York Times*, June 12; *Des Moines Register*, ibid. India suit filed, *New York Times*, May 4, 1976; "cargoes destined for . . . South Asia ports," *Wall Street Journal*, May 7, 1976. Trial of case on statute of limitations, *Government of India and Food Corporation of India v. Cargill, Inc.*, U.S. District Court S.D. New York, January 16, 1978, 569 F. 2d 737 (1978). Possible jury trial, *Journal of Commerce*, January 25, 1978. Settlement, files of Peter Gruenberger, Weil, Gotshal & Manges, New York. "Forced the Gandhi government," David Hansen to Bob Kohlmeyer, June 29, 1976, CA 6V2B.

12. "Investigators are concentrating," Bill Pearce to Cargill Grain Irregularities Task Force, November 24, 1975, CA, 5J8F; task force meeting, November 28, 1975, CA 5J5F. USDA, "Report of Investigation, Export Terminal Grain Overages, Cargill, Inc.," Region IV, Chicago, Ch-180-16, February 6, 1976. "U.S. Warned That Exporters of Grain Have Defrauded Foreign Customers Over the Last Five Years," *New York Times*, February 19, 1976.

13. "U.S. Agents Hint $45 Million in Excessive Grain Inventories of Three Companies," *New York Times*, May 2, 1976. Erwin E. Kelm letter "To All Employees," circa May 10, 1976, CA 3E8B, 5I5F. Gallinghouse quotation, *Wall Street Journal*, July 1, 1976. Pearce memoranda to the files on interchanges with Undersecretary of Agriculture John Knebel, July 14 and 20 and August 10, 1976; see also memorandum of Robbin Johnson, August 4. Pearce memorandum on meeting with Secretary Butz, August 30 (all memoranda in CA 3E8B). "Laying Overage to Rest," *Milling and Baking News*, August 17, 1976. C. M. Christensen article, "Gain in Weight of Grains and Grain Products Exposed to Relative Humidities of 80–90%," was written with H. H. Kaufmann, A. Hawk, and F. Wade, and published in *Miscellaneous Journal* 1632 (1976), University of

Minnesota Experiment Station; the reprint in *Milling and Baking News*, August 10, 1976. See also William R. Pearce to Hon. Earl L. Butz, September 1, 1976, and memorandum of August 18, "Evaluation of Overages Reported by the U.S. Department of Agriculture's Office of Investigation," CA 3E8B and 5I5F.

14. History of grain regulation, *Report on Irregularities in the Marketing of Grain: An Evaluation of the Inspection and Weighing of Grain*, prepared by the U.S. General Accounting Office for the Committee on Agriculture and Forestry, U.S. Senate and the Committee on Agriculture, U.S. House of Representatives, Joint Committee Print, 94th Cong. 2nd sess. February 17, 1976, p. 82. For the final legislation, passed in 1976 (U.S. Grain Standards Act of 1976), see Conference Report No. 94-1389, 94th Cong. 2nd sess., October 1, 1976. Specific provisions analyzed in *Minneapolis Tribune*, September 23, 1976; *Des Moines Register* September 25 and 26, 1976. For an excellent analysis of Cargill's positions, see Robbin S. Johnson to Hon. W. Henson Moore, U.S. House of Representatives, October 9, 1975, CA 5J8F; see also Company working paper, no title, October 9, 1975, CA 3F7B. Sen. Hubert Humphrey, "harvest the ground," *Minneapolis Tribune*, September 23, 1976. On kidnapping of the Borns, Dan Morgan, *Merchants of Grain*, op. cit., pp. 220–25. Cargill board concerns, minutes of July 6, 1973; draft letter to senior management on kidnapping, June 20, 1974, CA, 3F8F.

15. *Wall Street Journal*, November 7, 1975.

8. The Multinational Hearings (pp. 295–338)

1. James T. Halverson, "F.T.C. and the Food Industries—1974's Major Antitrust Emphasis," Eighth Annual Antitrust Institute of the Ohio State Bar Association, Columbus, Ohio, October 18, 1974, CA 6V2B. The merger provisions of Section 7 of the Clayton Act were tightened in 1950 with the passage of the Cellar-Kefauver Act; Section 2 of the Clayton Act, on price discrimination, was substantially amended in 1936 by the Robinson-Patman Act. See, particularly, W. Kip Viscusi, John M. Vernon, and Joseph E. Harrington, Jr., *Economics of Regulation and Antitrust* (Cambridge, Mass.: MIT Press, 1995), pp. 64–71.

2. Peter C. Ward, Assistant Director, Bureau of Competition, Federal Trade Commission, to Fred M. Seed, October 23, 1974, CA 6V2B.

3. Ward to Seed, op. cit., December 2, 1974.

4. See *Missouri Portland Cement Company v. Cargill Incorporated and the First Boston Corporation*, U.S. District Court, S.D. New York, April 15, 1974, 375 F. Supp. 249 (1974); ibid., U.S. Court of Appeals, Second Circuit, June 10, 1974, 498 F. 2nd 851 (1974). Cargill's original proposal for a cement project of "$20 to $40 million," Long Range Planning Committee, September 25–28, 1973; the alternative proposal for Amcord, Inc. (formerly American Cement Co.), F. Clayton Tonnemaker to E. E. Kelm and others, October 29, 1973, LRPC Annual Meeting minutes, October 29, 1973. For skirmishes with Missouri Portland, *Wall Street Journal*, January 9, 10, and 18, 1974; the circuit court decision is reported in detail, ibid., June 12, 1974. FTC's proposed complaint, *Wall Street Journal*, November 1, 1974; sale of Cargill's interest in MP, ibid., August 29, 1975. "1976 Budget Overview Prepared by the Federal Trade Commission Office of Policy Planning and Evaluation," Bureau of National Affairs ATRR No. 692, December 10, 1974. "Expending energy," *Wall Street Journal*, November 7, 1975.

5. *Des Moines Register* analysis of the FTC task force, May 10, 1976. See also Jerry W. Markham, *The History of Commodity Futures Trading and Its Regulation* (New York: Praeger, 1987), pp. 73–101.

6. The Subcommittee on Multinational Corporations of the U.S. Senate Committee on Foreign Relations conducted hearings over the period March 1973–September 1976 (93rd and 94th Congresses) and published 17 separate hearings proceedings under the title *Multinational Corporations and United States Foreign Policy*; the hearings on "international grain companies" was part 16, 94th Cong., second sess., June 18, 23, and 24, 1976. These hearings were widely covered by the public press; see particularly, the *New York Times* articles as follows: on Chile, June 22 and August 8, 1973 and September 16, 17, and 18, 1974; oil companies in Iran, March 19, 1975, in Libya, January 15, 1974, in Bolivia, May 17, 1975, in Italy, July 13, 17, 18, and 19, 1975; on the Arab boycott, February 27, 1975, on aircraft company sales, June 7, 9, and 10, 1975, February 5, 6, and 8, 1976.

7. "Memorandum to File," Robbin S. Johnson, July 24, 1975, CA 4E8B. Questions concerning relationship among FTC, GAO, and the Church subcommittee, ibid., November 21, 1975.

8. Additional questions, ibid., August 28, 1975; see also ibid., September 8 and 23. "Dragging our feet," Johnson to Gilmore, October 27, CA 3F7B.

9. The trip report of Richard Gilmore relating to his meetings in the Soviet Union in November 1975 became a published staff report of the Subcommittee on Multinational Corporations of the Senate Committee on Foreign Relations, *U.S.S.R. and Soviet Grain*, 94th Cong., 2nd sess., April 1976. For press coverage, see *Des Moines Register*, April 8, 1976. Senator Church's press release was also dated April 8, CA 4E8B.

10. Constraints imposed by Swiss law were noted once again in Jacques Werner to John McGrory, August 29, 1975, CA 4E8B; Article 271 of the Swiss Criminal Code is elaborated here. Response of the Swiss authorities is discussed ibid., November 24, 1975. Clearance for visit out of the country, Werner to H. Sontheim, January 21, 1976, ibid. Verbatim minutes of the meeting in Divonne-les-Bains, January 27, CA 5J7B. Concern about topics of this meeting, Pierre de Charmant to Sontheim, February 9, CA 4E8B.

11. "Grain Marketing Systems in Argentina, Australia, Canada and the European Community; Soybean Marketing System in Brazil," *Report of the Comptroller General of the United States*, May 28, 1976, CA 5J7B. Comment on Cargill, p. 76; discussion of international grain companies, pp. 84–85.

12. On initial hearings schedule of the Senate Subcommittee on Multinational Corporations, see "Memo to File," Robbin Johnson, June 16, 1976, CA 3E8F; Sen. Frank Church to Erwin Kelm, June 14, 1976, ibid. Subcommittee queries concerning Tradax organization, Ira Nordlicht to Robbin Johnson, May 28 and June 4, CA 5J7B; Johnson to Nordlicht, June 2 and June 14, ibid. For a comprehensive statement of the subcommittee's full set of questions, Robbin Johnson to Bill Pearce and John McGrory, June 11, 1976, ibid. Quotations on Pearce and Fahs's visit with Sen. Percy, Pearce memorandum to the file, June 10, CA 5J7B. "Executive session," June 14, 1976, CA 1X1X. "Shame and dishonor," Sen. Dick Clark in *Grain Inspection*, part 6, Subcommittee on Foreign Agricultural Policy and Subcommittee on Agricultural Production, Marketing and Stabilization of Prices, Committee on Agriculture and Forestry, U.S. Senate, 94th Cong., 2nd sess., March 11, 1976, p. 2.

13. Cargill's first knowledge of the Alan Trick memorandum came on June 15, in a conversation between Robbin Johnson and Ira Nordlicht, "Memo to file," Johnson, CA 4E8B; entitled "Hamburg Telex Operation Study," February 9, 1967, Trick memorandum reprinted in full in *Hearings before the Subcommittee on Multinational Corporations*, part 16, op. cit., pp. 184–98. For press reaction to the first two days' testimony, *Washington Post* and *New York Times*, June 19, 1976; *Journal of Commerce*, June 21; *Des Moines Register*, June 19 and 24; *Minneapolis Tribune*, June 23. Minneapolis television clip, KSTP, June 19, 6:00 P.M. news; Earl Butz radio quote, WINS, New York, June 20, CA 4E8B. "System the same," *Hearings*, op. cit., p. 25; "pyramid of power," ibid., p. 31; "exactly the same price," ibid., p. 61.

14. Exchanges about Trick memorandum, *Hearings*, op. cit., pp. 113–14; "if we don't, we won't," ibid., p. 131; "not a shred," ibid., p. 132. Testimony of Galesburg farmers (Sen. Percy), *Congressional Record—Senate*, June 25, 1976, S 10689. *Milling and Baking News*, July 13, 1976, CA 4E8P.

15. On the reorganization of Tradax Export, see Robbin Johnson to Ira Nordlicht, June 17, 1976, CA 3E8F. In Cargill's *Annual Report to Shareholders*, 1975–1976, this change is briefly reported, although the Swiss Credit Bank is not identified by name. See also *Resolutions of Executive Committee*, May 24 and June 18, 1976. The reasons for the changes are described by Bill Pearce in the subcommittee hearings, *Multinational Corporations and United States Foreign Policy*, op. cit., part 16, U.S. Senate, 94th Cong., 2nd sess. pp. 144–46; Swiss Credit Bank identified, p. 141. For analysis of Subpart F restrictions, see Pearce to Hubert F. Sontheim, July 9, 1975, CA 3I6B.

16. On DISC, see two letters from Robbin Johnson to Richard Gilmore, both dated June 22, 1976 (one with attachments), CA 5J7B. For concerns expressed in 1972 at the time of the Russian grain sales, see, especially, *New York Times*, September 24, 1972; *Washington Post*, September 28 and 30 (in the latter, an article and an editorial); there was extensive coverage in the second week of November (see CA 81-03).

17. *Feedstuffs*, June 28, 1976. "Tax costs . . . important," *Hearings*, op. cit., p. 101; "all of the income," ibid., 134; table of Cargill tax rates, ibid., 133; tax burden of major industrial companies, ibid., pp. 235–39; "you're paying a full share," ibid., p. 140. "Finance Committee keep in mind,"

Tradax Internacional S.A. and Subsidiaries, *Annual Report to Shareholders*, June 1, 1975–May 31, 1976, p. 45, CA 5M7B; "less likely with a foreign parent," *Hearings*, op. cit., pp. 152–53.

18. "Positioned to retain," *Cargill News* press release and attachment, "Cargill Earnings—a Perspective," June 23, 1976, CA 5I5F. M. D. McVay, "Cargill Investment Philosophy," May 23, 1977, CA 3I1B.

19. "Continental . . . sufficiently impressed," *Feedstuffs*, June 28, 1976, CA 5J7B. "Have you back," *Hearings*, op. cit., p. 162; "largely undecided," *Feedstuffs*, June 28, 1976, CA 5J7B; "the victory," ibid., "Inside Washington" column, CA 4E8B. *Milling and Baking News*, July 13, 1976, CA 5J7B; "embarassment over staff," *Journal of Commerce*, June 28, 1976, CA 5J7B; "offending the powerful grain dealers," *New Republic*, December 18, 1976, CA 5J7B; "defensive disclosure," Ralph Nader and William Taylor, *The Big Boys: Power and Position in American Business* (New York, Pantheon Books, 1986). EEC disclosure, *Journal of Commerce*, July 1, 1976, CA 4E8B; *Milling and Baking News*, June 29, 1976, CA 5J7B. Alan Trick response, telex, June 21, 1976, CA 5J7B.

20. "How to Avoid Antitrust," *Business Week*, January 27, 1975, CA 3I4B. See also "Cargill Antitrust Compliance Program" (draft), James D. Moe to John McGrory and others, August 30, 1976, CA 5E3B. "No further action is warranted," Carol M. Thomas to Whitney MacMillan, April 27, 1979, CA 5E3B. "Mound of paper," *The Progressive*, July 1976, p. 26. Richard E. Caves, "Organization, Scale and Performance in the Grain Trading Industry," Discussion Paper No. 546, April, 1977, Harvard Institute of Economic Research, CA 3E4F; the draft manuscript was entitled "Competition in the Grain Trading Industry," September 1976 (excerpt from Chapter 9, "Conclusions"). The "intellectual attraction" quotation from Caves to John McGrory, March 3, 1975, CA 5E3B; see also ibid. September 5, 1975, CA 3E4F. "House view," Caves to Linda L. Cutler, October 27, 1976, ibid.

21. Colloquial terms, Thomas H. Middleton, "Baksheesh, Cumshaw and All That Grease," *Saturday Review* 4 (July 9, 1977): pp. 20–21. For SEC report on individual cases, *Report of the Securities and Exchange Commission on Questionable and Illegal Corporate Payments and Practices, Submitted to the Committee on Banking, Housing and Urban Affairs*, U.S. Senate, 94th Cong., 2nd sess. (May 1976), Exhibit A; see also *Congressional Quarterly*, August 28, 1976. Ralph Nader visit to Senate hearings, U.S. Senate, Committee on Banking, Housing and Urban Affairs, *Foreign and Corporate Bribes, Hearings on S. 3133*, 94th Cong., 2nd sess., April 5, 1976; see also Frank P. Cihlar to James D. Moe, ibid., CA 5I7B. The Foreign Corrupt Practices Act of 1977, Public Law 95-213, December 19, 1977, amended U.S.C 15, 1934 Securities Exchange Act; for the legislative history of both acts, see George C. Greanias and Duane Windsor, *The Foreign Corrupt Practices Act: Anatomy of a Statute* (Lexington, Mass.: Lexington Books, 1982), chap. 5. For listing of "eleven questions," see "IRS Statement, April 7, 1976, to IRS Field Offices on Questions to Be Asked in Investigations of 'Corporate Slush Funds,' Supplement to IRS Manual on Such Funds, and Amendment to the Manual Supplement," Bureau of National Affairs Taxation and Finance 68, CA 5I7B; for Cargill announcement of their "unusual payments, *Minneapolis Tribune*, March 18, 1977; for *Minneapolis Star* disclosure of Spanish tax case, March 17, 1977. Explanation to employees, *Green Wave*, March 16, 1977. "Doesn't have to make a publicly available statement," *Wall Street Journal*, March 18, 1977. Cargill response to IRS, Charles E. Rice to Loren Westman, Case Manager, Large Case Audits, Internal Revenue Service. There are many press items on later developments in the case. Quotation in text on Spanish tax case, Ralph Nader and William Taylor, *The Big Boys*, op. cit., 331–32. For case itself, *U.S. v. Harold Bonnell and Charles Rice*, U.S. District Court, D. Minnesota, Fourth District, December 27, 1979, 483 F. Supp. 1070 (1979); 483 F. Supp. 1085 (1979). There are additional federal court cases in 1979 and 1981. "Voiced great concern," Heinz Hutter to Bill Pearce, August 19, 1980, CA 5E7F. Announcement to employees on final disposition, *Green Wave*, November 13, 1981; see also separate announcement to "Cargill Managers" from Whitney MacMillan, ibid.

22. "USDA Forecast of 1977 Soviet Grain Crop Unchanged," USDA, *Foreign Agriculture Circular*, September 9, 1977; Thomas R. Hughes to Dale E. Hathaway, September 15, 1977, CA 5D8B. See also Cargill draft memo, "USSR Review—9/22/77," CA, 6V3B. An early mention of Soviet intentions, *Journal of Commerce*, October 31, 1977, CA 6F3B. Chairman Brezhnev's announcement of 194 million ton prediction, *USDA News*, release 3156-77, November 2, CA 3E7F. Sen. Dole call for hearings, press release of November 5, CA 5D8B; Sen. McGovern press release, November 30, ibid. For press reaction, "Soviets Staging Re-run of 1972's 'Grain Drain'?" *Journal*

of Commerce, November 11, 1977; "Against the Grain," *New York Times*, November 10; "Soviet Graindoggle," *Christian Science Monitor*, November 17; "Soviet Grain Deal—Another 1972?" *New York Times*, November 21; "Russia Shops for Grain Again," *Business Week*, November 21; "It Looks Like Another 'Grain Robbery' for Russia," *U.S. News and World Report*, November 21; "Another Soviet Grain Sting," *Time magazine*, November 28. For Cong. Jim Leach comments, *Iowa City Press Citizen*, November 22; *Des Moines Register*, ibid. Cargill's required USDA report, "Report of Export Sales and Exports," was dated November 11, 1977. There were two separate Company reports entitled "Russian Sales Issues," one by Walter B. Saunders and the other anon., CA 6V3B. See also *Public Affairs Newsletter*, November 29, 1977. Russian crop year sales in 1977–1978 and 1978–1979 from *USDA News*, October 3, 1979.

23. For Cargill position prior to the farmers' strike on December 14, see Robbin Johnson to Bill Pearce and Heinz Hutter, November 9, 1977, CA 79-09. *Business Week* quotations from its article "The Uneven Squeeze on the U.S. Farmer," December 19. For Company public statement, M. D. McVay, "Statement for Cargill Managers," December 20; memorandum on "Farm Strike," n.d., circa January 1978, ibid. Secretary Bob Bergland position, news clips, January 10 and 24, 1978; Sen. George McGovern quotation, ibid., January 12. See also Greg Lauser, "Ty Thayer Conversation with Strike Leaders in Aberdeen, S.D.," January 18, ibid. For USDA analysis of effects on food prices, "Analysis of American Agricultural Movement Proposal," Issue Briefing Paper, USDA, March 3, 1978, CA 79-09. AAM position, *New York Times*, April 18, 1978. "Long, flag-waving statements," Garland West to Bob Fahs and Robbin Johnson, February 16, ibid. The *Cargill News* article on the strike was in its May–June 1978 issue.

9. The Cargill Culture—a Reprise (pp. 344–76)

1. "Contentious . . . creative goad," "The Two-Billion-Dollar Company that Lives by the Cent," *Fortune*, December 1965, p. 81; "radical ideas," Cargill MacMillan to John MacMillan, Jr., June 20, 1941, CA 40-03. "Just too fat," John MacMillan, Jr., Cargill Management Conference Series, March 27, 1953, CA Lake 14. "Climbing the ladder," Ralph Nader and William Taylor, *The Big Boys*, op. cit., p. 293.

2. "A Timely Statement from Ownership to Management," May 18, 1961, MS collection, James F. Cargill; Sumner B. Young to Hugh MacMillan, April 13, 1961, MS collection, Whitney MacMillan. Thomas Mann, *Verfall einer Familie* (*Buddenbrooks*), (Berlin: S. Fischer, 1901; English Translation, New York: Knopf, 1924) 1901.

3. Wayne G. Broehl, Jr., *John Deere's Company* (New York: Doubleday, 1982).

4. "No one . . . match," *Business Week*, April 16, 1979; "farmers . . . weren't aware," *Wall Street Journal*, November 7, 1975; "sun never sets," *New York Times*, September 25, 1972; "capital rich overnight," Robert L. Lumpkins to M. D. McVay, July 22, 1976, CA 4I1F; "unlimited patience," *Wall Street Journal*, May 7, 1982.

5. "International Organization," E. E. Kelm, August 22, 1966, CA 5K4B. "Organizing for Most Effective Operations—Some Opinions and Observations," M. D. McVay, August 18, 1972, CA 4C6F; Heinz Hutter to McVay, September 4, 1972, ibid. "Gone too far in matrixing," H. F. Hutter, July 2, 1982, ibid.

6. "Elements of Geneva Climate," Brewster B. Hanson, November 26, 1982, MS collection of author; "air of excitement," *Cargill News*, July–August 1984. "Shake the economic pillars," *Fortune*, August 1949. "Buccaneer spirit," *Minneapolis*, September, 1976; "worry . . . later," *Wall Street Journal*, November 7, 1975. "Risk they couldn't hedge against," *Corporate Report—Minnesota*, May 1983; "backbone of our credit," John Jr. to all division heads, September 28, 1951, CA; "word is our bond," *Corporate Report—Minnesota*, op. cit. "Proud to be a part," "Pete McVay, Cargill President, Retires after 44 Years," *Cargill News*, July–August 1984.

7. "Professors don't train managers," Heinz Hutter in *Minneapolis Star Tribune*, February 18, 1991; "Cargill MBA," ibid. "Can't keep pace," *Corporate Report—Minnesota*, op. cit. "BAH crew members have acquired," E. E. Kelm to R. J. Harrigan, May 25, 1949, CA 53-01.

8. "Competitive secrecy and speed," E. E. Kelm in *Business Week*, December 9, 1967. "Patents not available," Whitney MacMillan in *Chicago Tribune*, December 14, 1977; "keeping our competitors in the dark," "close second to used-car dealers," *Wall Street Journal*, November 5, 1975; "no reservoir," *International Directory of Company Histories* (Chicago: St. James Press, 1990), vol. 2, p. 616; "tremendous size of Cargill," Heinz Hutter to Whitney MacMillan, September 24,

1975, CA 4C6F. "Reticence caused problems," *Forbes*, September 18, 1978. "Baronial grounds," *Forbes*, September 18, 1978; "French chateau," *Business Week*, December 9, 1967; "pondering," *New York Times*, September 25, 1972; "set back," *Chicago Tribune*, December 14, 1977; "a little nervous," *Minneapolis Tribune*, January 5, 1967; "charmed," *Cargill News*, November–December 1979. "Preferred you were not here," Whitney MacMillan in *Forbes*, November 17, 1986.

9. Not idle flattery," E. E. Kelm in "Business Management Program," February 26, 1973; "Cargill man," *Corporate Report—Minnesota*, op. cit.; "stamped all over me," L. W. Johnson to E. J. Grimes, August 2, 1947, CA 47-04. "Same vitality still exists," John Cole in "Grain Division Program—Plans and Outlook for the Future," April 1964, CA 3E1F. "Spartan," M. D. McVay, "Capital Investment Philosophy," speech to CMD managers, May 23, 1977, CA 3E1B.

10. "Deceptive calm," *Business Week*, April 16, 1979; "newly formed," *Chicago Tribune*, November 14, 1977; "Dominated from the trading side," *Business Week*, op. cit.; "largest privately held," *Forbes*, September 18, 1978. Continental Grain–Cargill comparisons, *Minneapolis Tribune*, August 6, 1973. Corporate goals and individual division goals were promulgated October 1, 1973, CA 4C6F; the former were also printed in *Cargill News*, January–February 1975. A rewritten "Corporate Guidelines" was printed in the minutes of the board of directors meeting of July 25, 1977; included also was a separate paper on the "Cargill Incentive Program." For "Future Strategic Profile," July 16, 1979, CA 4C6F.

Illustrations

Index

Page numbers in **bold** refer to illustrations.

UNIVERSITY PRESS OF NEW ENGLAND publishes books under its own imprint and is the publisher for Brandeis University Press, Dartmouth College, Middlebury College Press, University of New Hampshire, Tufts University, and Wesleyan University Press

LIBRARY OF CONGRESS CATALOGING-IN-PUBLICATION DATA
Broehl, Wayne G.
Cargill: going global / Wayne G. Broehl, Jr.
    p.   cm.
Continues: Cargill.
"This book . . . carried the history of the firm through the years
1960–1978"—Ackn.
Includes bibliographical references and index.
ISBN 0–87451–854–7 (cl)
          1. Cargill, Inc.   2. Grain trade—United States.   3. Grain trade.
          I. Broehl, Wayne G. Cargill.   II. Title.
HD9039.C37B758   1998
380.1'4131'0973—dc21   97–35033